These safety symbols are used in laboratory and field investigations in this book to indicate possible hazards. Learn the meaning of each symbol and refer to this page often. *Remember to wash your hands thoroughly after completing lab procedures.*

PROTECTIVE EQUIPMENT

Do not begin any lab without the proper protection equipment.

GOGGLES 	Proper eye protection must be worn when performing or observing science activities that involve items or conditions as listed below.	**APRON** 	Wear an approved apron when using substances that could stain, wet, or destroy cloth.	**SOAP** 	Wash hands with soap and water before removing goggles and after all lab activities.	**GLOVES** 	Wear gloves when working with biological materials, chemicals, animals, or materials that can stain or irritate hands.

LABORATORY HAZARDS

Symbols	Potential Hazards	Precaution	Response
DISPOSAL	contamination of classroom or environment due to improper disposal of materials such as chemicals and live specimens	• DO NOT dispose of hazardous materials in the sink or trash can. • Dispose of wastes as directed by your teacher.	• If hazardous materials are disposed of improperly, notify your teacher immediately.
EXTREME TEMPERATURE	skin burns due to extremely hot or cold materials such as hot glass, liquids, or metals; liquid nitrogen; dry ice	• Use proper protective equipment, such as hot mitts and/or tongs, when handling objects with extreme temperatures.	• If injury occurs, notify your teacher immediately.
SHARP OBJECTS	punctures or cuts from sharp objects such as razor blades, pins, scalpels, and broken glass	• Handle glassware carefully to avoid breakage. • Walk with sharp objects pointed downward, away from you and others.	• If broken glass or injury occurs, notify your teacher immediately.
ELECTRICAL	electric shock or skin burn due to improper grounding, short circuits, liquid spills, or exposed wires	• Check condition of wires and apparatus for fraying or uninsulated wires, and broken or cracked equipment. • Use only GFCI-protected outlets	• DO NOT attempt to fix electrical problems. Notify your teacher immediately.
CHEMICAL	skin irritation or burns, breathing difficulty, and/or poisoning due to touching, swallowing, or inhalation of chemicals such as acids, bases, bleach, metal compounds, iodine, poinsettias, pollen, ammonia, acetone, nail polish remover, heated chemicals, mothballs, and any other chemicals labeled or known to be dangerous	• Wear proper protective equipment such as goggles, apron, and gloves when using chemicals. • Ensure proper room ventilation or use a fume hood when using materials that produce fumes. • NEVER smell fumes directly. • NEVER taste or eat any material in the laboratory.	• If contact occurs, immediately flush affected area with water and notify your teacher. • If a spill occurs, leave the area immediately and notify your teacher.
FLAMMABLE	unexpected fire due to liquids or gases that ignite easily such as rubbing alcohol	• Avoid open flames, sparks, or heat when flammable liquids are present.	• If a fire occurs, leave the area immediately and notify your teacher.
OPEN FLAME	burns or fire due to open flame from matches, Bunsen burners, or burning materials	• Tie back loose hair and clothing. • Keep flame away from all materials. • Follow teacher instructions when lighting and extinguishing flames. • Use proper protection, such as hot mitts or tongs, when handling hot objects.	• If a fire occurs, leave the area immediately and notify your teacher.
ANIMAL SAFETY	injury to or from laboratory animals	• Wear proper protective equipment such as gloves, apron, and goggles when working with animals. • Wash hands after handling animals.	• If injury occurs, notify your teacher immediately.
BIOLOGICAL	infection or adverse reaction due to contact with organisms such as bacteria, fungi, and biological materials such as blood, animal or plant materials	• Wear proper protective equipment such as gloves, goggles, and apron when working with biological materials. • Avoid skin contact with an organism or any part of the organism. • Wash hands after handling organisms.	• If contact occurs, wash the affected area and notify your teacher immediately.
FUME	breathing difficulties from inhalation of fumes from substances such as ammonia, acetone, nail polish remover, heated chemicals, and mothballs	• Wear goggles, apron, and gloves. • Ensure proper room ventilation or use a fume hood when using substances that produce fumes. • NEVER smell fumes directly.	• If a spill occurs, leave area and notify your teacher immediately.
IRRITANT	irritation of skin, mucous membranes, or respiratory tract due to materials such as acids, bases, bleach, pollen, mothballs, steel wool, and potassium permanganate	• Wear goggles, apron, and gloves. • Wear a dust mask to protect against fine particles.	• If skin contact occurs, immediately flush the affected area with water and notify your teacher.
RADIOACTIVE	excessive exposure from alpha, beta, and gamma particles	• Remove gloves and wash hands with soap and water before removing remainder of protective equipment.	• If cracks or holes are found in the container, notify your teacher immediately.

INTEGRATED iSCIENCE

GLENCOE

INDIANA

GRADE 6

McGraw Hill Education

COVER: Tom Reichner/Shutterstock

mheducation.com/prek-12

Send all inquiries to:
McGraw-Hill Education
8787 Orion Place
Columbus, OH 43240

ISBN: 978-0-07-898596-6
MHID: 0-07-898596-X

Printed in the United States of America.

2 3 4 5 6 7 QVS 21 20 19 18 17

Contents in Brief

Authors and Contributors

Authors

American Museum of Natural History
New York, NY

Michelle Anderson, MS
Lecturer
The Ohio State University
Columbus, OH

Juli Berwald, PhD
Science Writer
Austin, TX

John F. Bolzan, PhD
Science Writer
Columbus, OH

Rachel Clark, MS
Science Writer
Moscow, ID

Patricia Craig, MS
Science Writer
Bozeman, MT

Randall Frost, PhD
Science Writer
Pleasanton, CA

Lisa S. Gardiner, PhD
Science Writer
Denver, CO

Jennifer Gonya, PhD
The Ohio State University
Columbus, OH

Mary Ann Grobbel, MD
Science Writer
Grand Rapids, MI

Whitney Crispen Hagins, MA, MAT
Biology Teacher
Lexington High School
Lexington, MA

Carole Holmberg, BS
Planetarium Director
Calusa Nature Center and Planetarium, Inc.
Fort Myers, FL

Tina C. Hopper
Science Writer
Rockwall, TX

Jonathan D. W. Kahl, PhD
Professor of Atmospheric Science
University of Wisconsin-Milwaukee
Milwaukee, WI

Nanette Kalis
Science Writer
Athens, OH

S. Page Keeley, MEd
Maine Mathematics and Science Alliance
Augusta, ME

Cindy Klevickis, PhD
Professor of Integrated Science and Technology
James Madison University
Harrisonburg, VA

Kimberly Fekany Lee, PhD
Science Writer
La Grange, IL

Michael Manga, PhD
Professor
University of California, Berkeley
Berkeley, CA

Devi Ried Mathieu
Science Writer
Sebastopol, CA

Elizabeth A. Nagy-Shadman, PhD
Geology Professor
Pasadena City College
Pasadena, CA

William D. Rogers, DA
Professor of Biology
Ball State University
Muncie, IN

Donna L. Ross, PhD
Associate Professor
San Diego State University
San Diego, CA

Marion B. Sewer, PhD
Assistant Professor
School of Biology
Georgia Institute of Technology
Atlanta, GA

Julia Meyer Sheets, PhD
Lecturer
School of Earth Sciences
The Ohio State University
Columbus, OH

Michael J. Singer, PhD
Professor of Soil Science
Department of Land, Air and Water Resources
University of California
Davis, CA

Karen S. Sottosanti, MA
Science Writer
Pickerington, Ohio

Paul K. Strode, PhD
I.B. Biology Teacher
Fairview High School
Boulder, CO

Jan M. Vermilye, PhD
Research Geologist
Seismo-Tectonic Reservoir Monitoring (STRM)
Boulder, CO

Judith A. Yero, MA
Director
Teacher's Mind Resources
Hamilton, MT

Dinah Zike, MEd
Author, Consultant, Inventor of Foldables
Dinah Zike Academy; Dinah-Might Adventures, LP
San Antonio, TX

Margaret Zorn, MS
Science Writer
Yorktown, VA

Consulting Authors

Alton L. Biggs
Biggs Educational Consulting
Commerce, TX

Ralph M. Feather, Jr., PhD
Assistant Professor
Department of Educational Studies and Secondary Education
Bloomsburg University
Bloomsburg, PA

Douglas Fisher, PhD
Professor of Teacher Education
San Diego State University
San Diego, CA

Edward P. Ortleb
Science/Safety Consultant
St. Louis, MO

Series Consultants

Science

Solomon Bililign, PhD
Professor
Department of Physics
North Carolina Agricultural and Technical State University
Greensboro, NC

John Choinski
Professor
Department of Biology
University of Central Arkansas
Conway, AR

Anastasia Chopelas, PhD
Research Professor
Department of Earth and Space Sciences
UCLA
Los Angeles, CA

David T. Crowther, PhD
Professor of Science Education
University of Nevada, Reno
Reno, NV

A. John Gatz
Professor of Zoology
Ohio Wesleyan University
Delaware, OH

Sarah Gille, PhD
Professor
University of California San Diego
La Jolla, CA

David G. Haase, PhD
Professor of Physics
North Carolina State University
Raleigh, NC

Janet S. Herman, PhD
Professor
Department of Environmental Sciences
University of Virginia
Charlottesville, VA

David T. Ho, PhD
Associate Professor
Department of Oceanography
University of Hawaii
Honolulu, HI

Ruth Howes, PhD
Professor of Physics
Marquette University
Milwaukee, WI

Jose Miguel Hurtado, Jr., PhD
Associate Professor
Department of Geological Sciences
University of Texas at El Paso
El Paso, TX

Monika Kress, PhD
Assistant Professor
San Jose State University
San Jose, CA

Mark E. Lee, PhD
Associate Chair & Assistant Professor
Department of Biology
Spelman College
Atlanta, GA

Linda Lundgren
Science writer
Lakewood, CO

Keith O. Mann, PhD
Ohio Wesleyan University
Delaware, OH

Charles W. McLaughlin, PhD
Adjunct Professor of Chemistry
Montana State University
Bozeman, MT

Katharina Pahnke, PhD
Research Professor
Department of Geology and Geophysics
University of Hawaii
Honolulu, HI

Jesús Pando, PhD
Associate Professor
DePaul University
Chicago, IL

Hay-Oak Park, PhD
Associate Professor
Department of Molecular Genetics
Ohio State University
Columbus, OH

David A. Rubin, PhD
Associate Professor of Physiology
School of Biological Sciences
Illinois State University
Normal, IL

Toni D. Sauncy
Assistant Professor of Physics
Department of Physics
Angelo State University
San Angelo, TX

Series Consultants, continued

Malathi Srivatsan, PhD
Associate Professor of Neurobiology
College of Sciences and Mathematics
Arkansas State University
Jonesboro, AR

Cheryl Wistrom, PhD
Associate Professor of Chemistry
Saint Joseph's College
Rensselaer, IN

Reading

ReLeah Cossett Lent
Author/Educational Consultant
Blue Ridge, GA

Math

Vik Hovsepian
Professor of Mathematics
Rio Hondo College
Whittier, CA

Series Reviewers

Thad Boggs
Mandarin High School
Jacksonville, FL

Catherine Butcher
Webster Junior High School
Minden, LA

Erin Darichuk
West Frederick Middle School
Frederick, MD

Joanne Hedrick Davis
Murphy High School
Murphy, NC

Anthony J. DiSipio, Jr.
Octorara Middle School
Atglen, PA

Adrienne Elder
Tulsa Public Schools
Tulsa, OK

Carolyn Elliott
Iredell-Statesville Schools
Statesville, NC

Christine M. Jacobs
Ranger Middle School
Murphy, NC

Jason O. L. Johnson
Thurmont Middle School
Thurmont, MD

Felecia Joiner
Stony Point Ninth Grade Center
Round Rock, TX

Joseph L. Kowalski, MS
Lamar Academy
McAllen, TX

Brian McClain
Amos P. Godby High School
Tallahassee, FL

Von W. Mosser
Thurmont Middle School
Thurmont, MD

Ashlea Peterson
Heritage Intermediate Grade Center
Coweta, OK

Nicole Lenihan Rhoades
Walkersville Middle School
Walkersvillle, MD

Maria A. Rozenberg
Indian Ridge Middle School
Davie, FL

Barb Seymour
Westridge Middle School
Overland Park, KS

Ginger Shirley
Our Lady of Providence Junior-Senior High School
Clarksville, IN

Curtis Smith
Elmwood Middle School
Rogers, AR

Sheila Smith
Jackson Public School
Jackson, MS

Sabra Soileau
Moss Bluff Middle School
Lake Charles, LA

Tony Spoores
Switzerland County Middle School
Vevay, IN

Nancy A. Stearns
Switzerland County Middle School
Vevay, IN

Kari Vogel
Princeton Middle School
Princeton, MN

Alison Welch
Wm. D. Slider Middle School
El Paso, TX

Linda Workman
Parkway Northeast Middle School
Creve Coeur, MO

Indiana Reviewers

Each reviewer provided valuable feedback and suggestions regarding the effectiveness of the science instruction. We thank them for their feedback.

LaTheresa King
Secondary Curriculum Coordinator
Fort Wayne Community Schools

Deborah Watson
Secondary Curriculum Coordinator
East Allen County Schools

Rosie Easterday
Math Department Chair
DeKalb County Eastern

Ginger Shirley
Secondary Science
Education Specialist
New Albany High School

Jill Swango
Secondary Science
Education Specialist
Brownsburg East Middle School

Jane Buckingham
Secondary Science
Education Specialist
Secondary Administrator
Indianapolis Public Schools

Teacher Advisory Board

The Teacher Advisory Board gave the authors, editorial staff, and design team feedback on the content and design of the Student Edition. They provided valuable input in the development of *Glencoe Integrated iScience*.

Frances J. Baldridge
Department Chair
Ferguson Middle School
Beavercreek, OH

Jane E. M. Buckingham
Teacher
Crispus Attucks Medical Magnet
High School
Indianapolis, IN

Elizabeth Falls
Teacher
Blalack Middle School
Carrollton, TX

Nelson Farrier
Teacher
Hamlin Middle School
Springfield, OR

Michelle R. Foster
Department Chair
Wayland Union Middle School
Wayland, MI

Rebecca Goodell
Teacher
Reedy Creek Middle School
Cary, NC

Mary Gromko
Science Supervisor K–12
Colorado Springs District 11
Colorado Springs, CO

Randy Mousley
Department Chair
Dean Ray Stucky Middle School
Wichita, KS

David Rodriguez
Teacher
Swift Creek Middle School
Tallahassee, FL

Derek Shook
Teacher
Floyd Middle Magnet School
Montgomery, AL

Karen Stratton
Science Coordinator
Lexington School District One
Lexington, SC

Stephanie Wood
Science Curriculum Specialist, K–12
Granite School District
Salt Lake City, UT

Welcome to iSCIENCE

We are your partner in learning by meeting your diverse 21st century needs. Designed for today's tech-savvy middle school students, the McGraw-Hill Education Indiana *iScience* program offers hands-on investigations, rigorous science content, and engaging, real-world applications to make science fun, exciting, and stimulating.

Quick Start Guide
Indiana iScience | Student Center

Login information

1. Go to **connected.mcgraw-hill.com.**
2. Enter your registered Username and Password.
3. For **new users** click here to create a new account.
4. Get **ConnectED Help** for creating accounts, verifying master codes, and more.

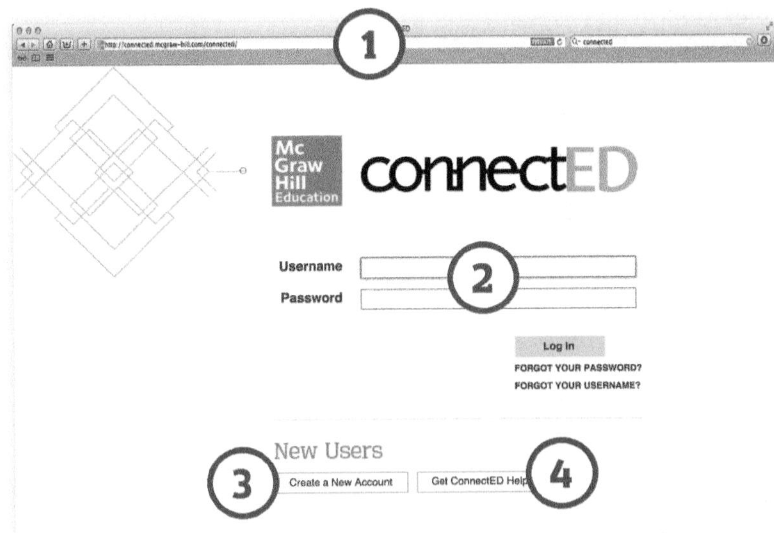

Your ConnectED Center

5. Scroll down to find the program from which you would like to work.

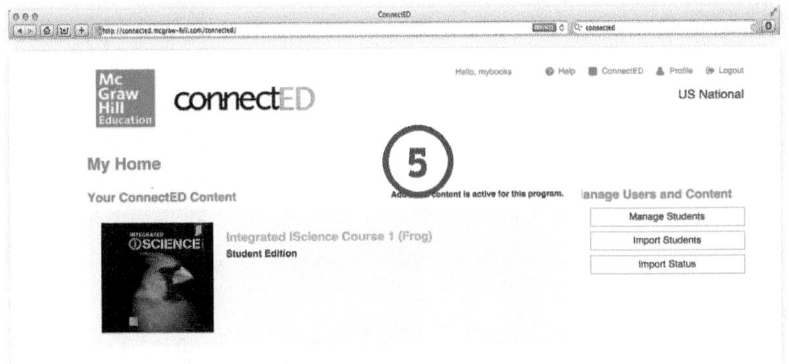

Quick Start Guide
Indiana iScience | Student Center

1. The Menu allows you to easily jump to anywhere you need to be.

2. Click the **program icon** at the top left to **return to the main page** from any screen.

3. **Select a Chapter and Lesson**
Use the drop down boxes to quickly jump to any lesson in any chapter.

4. Return to your **My Home** page for all your **ConnectED** content.

5. The **Help** icon will guide you to online help. It will also allow for a quick logout.

6. The **Search Bar** allows you to search content by topic or standard.

7. **Access the eBook**
Use the **Student Edition** to see content.

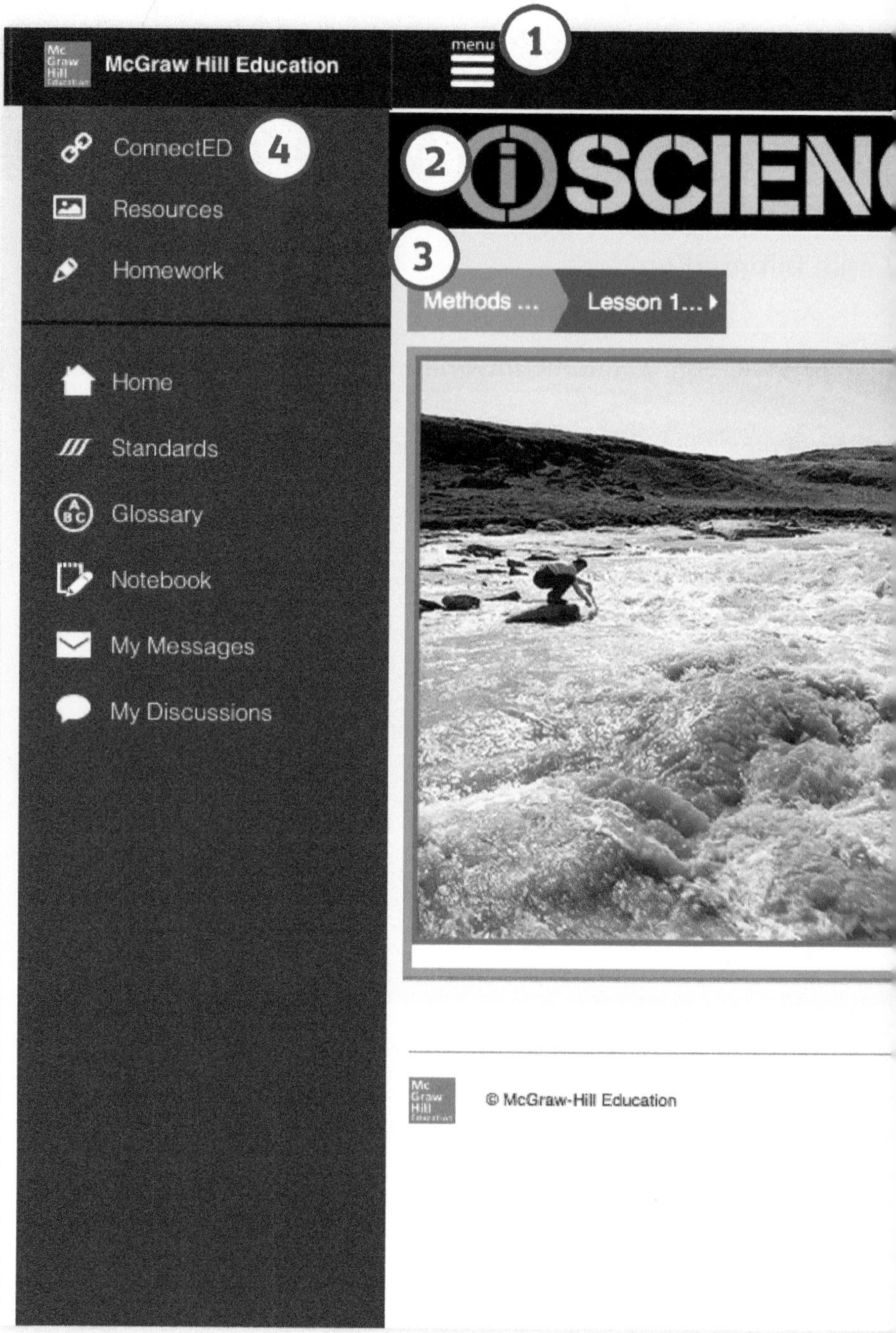

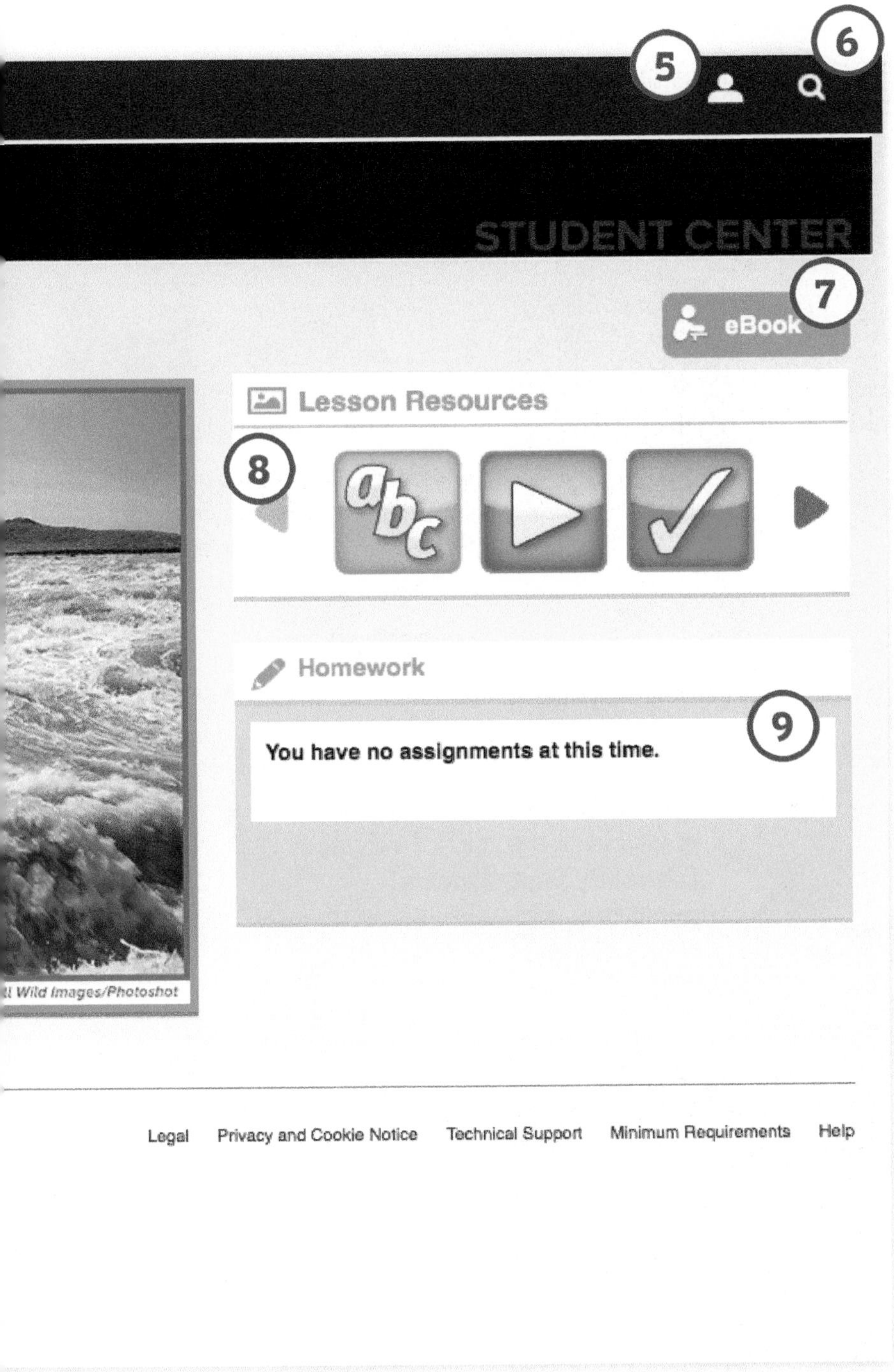

5 6

STUDENT CENTER

7 eBook

Lesson Resources

8

Homework

You have no assignments at this time.

9

...l Wild Images/Photoshot

Legal Privacy and Cookie Notice Technical Support Minimum Requirements Help

8 Quickly access helpful links to **multiple resources**, such as:

LearnSmart

Chapter Resources Files, Reading Essentials, Get Ready to Read, Quick Vocabulary

Animations, Videos, Interactive tables

Self-check quizzes, online and standardized test practice

Project-Based Learning activities

Lab manuals, safety videos, virtual labs & other tools

Vocabulary, Multilingual eGlossary, Vocab eGames, Vocab eFlashcards

Personal Tutors

Classroom Presentation Toolkit with Powerpoints

Dinah Zike's Foldables and more

eGames

Science Notebook

Check your **Homework** assignments here.

Treasure Hunt

Your science book has many features that will aid you in your learning. Some of these features are listed below. You can use the activity at the right to help you find these and other special features in the book.

- THE BIG IDEA can be found at the start of each chapter.
- The Reading Guide at the start of each lesson lists **Key Concepts,** vocabulary terms, and online supplements to the content.
- connectED icons direct you to online resources such as animations, personal tutors, math practices, and quizzes.
- Inquiry Labs and Skill Practices are in each chapter.
- Your FOLDABLES help organize your notes.

START
1 What four margin items can help you build your vocabulary?
2 On what page does the glossary begin? What glossary is online?
3 In which Student Resource at the back of your book can you find a listing of Laboratory Safety Symbols?
4 Suppose you want to find a list of all the Launch Labs, MiniLabs, Skill Practices, and Labs, where do you look?

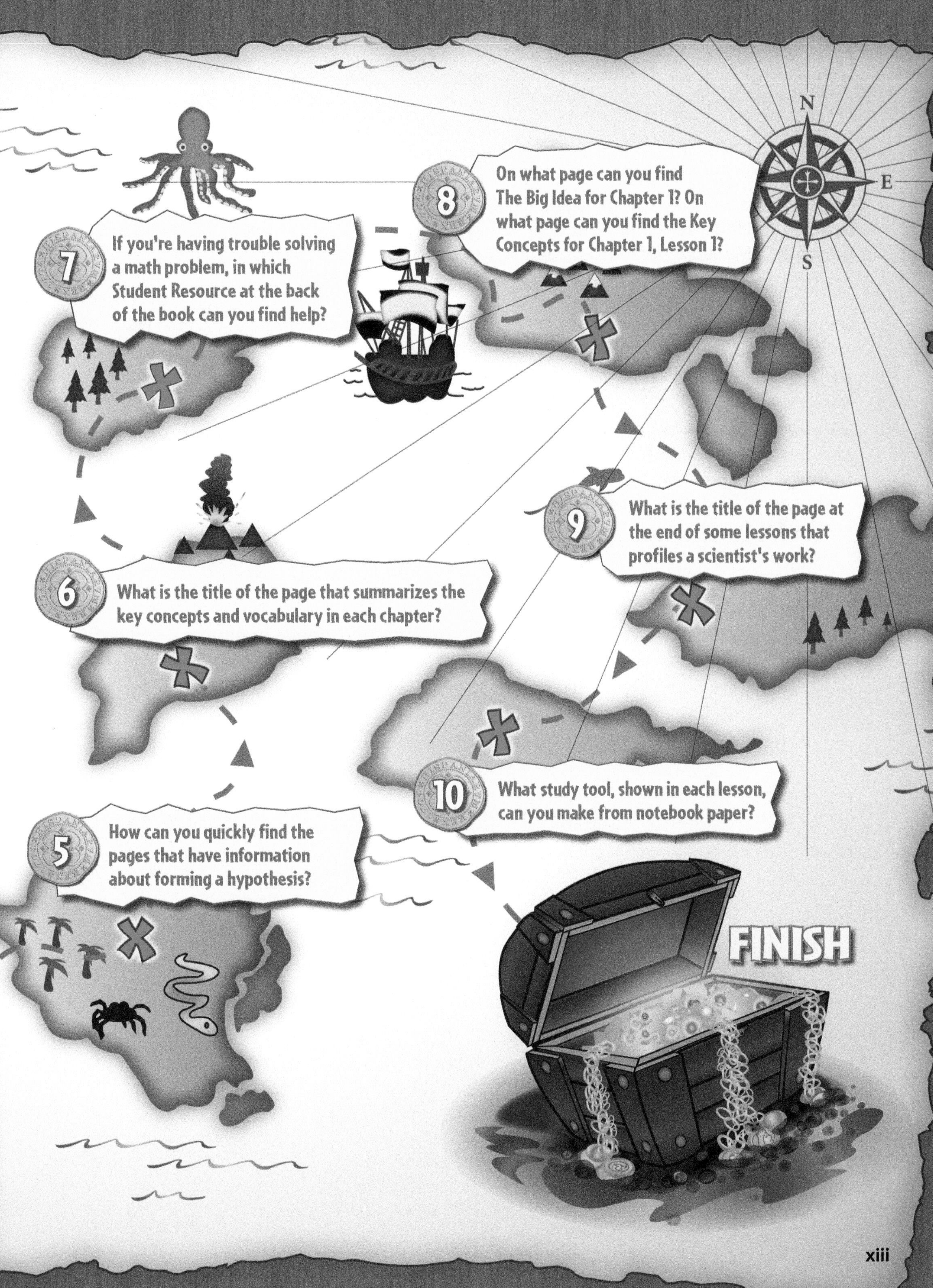
N
E
S
8
On what page can you find The Big Idea for Chapter 1? On what page can you find the Key Concepts for Chapter 1, Lesson 1?
7
If you're having trouble solving a math problem, in which Student Resource at the back of the book can you find help?
9
What is the title of the page at the end of some lessons that profiles a scientist's work?
6
What is the title of the page that summarizes the key concepts and vocabulary in each chapter?
10
What study tool, shown in each lesson, can you make from notebook paper?
5
How can you quickly find the pages that have information about forming a hypothesis?
FINISH

Table of Contents

Student Resources

 Launch Labs

MiniLabs

Skill Practice

Labs

TABLE OF CONTENTS

Features

HOW IT WORKS

GREEN SCIENCE

SCIENCE & SOCIETY

CAREERS in SCIENCE

Nature of Science

SEPS.1, SEPS.2, SEPS.3, SEPS.4, SEPS.5, SEPS.6, SEPS.8, 6-8.E.1, 6-8.E.2, 6-8.E.3, 6-8.E.4, 6-8.LST.4.2

Methods of Science

THE BIG IDEA

What processes do scientists use when they perform scientific investigations?

Inquiry Pink Water?

This scientist is using pink dye to measure the speed of glacier water in the country of Greenland. Scientists are testing the hypothesis that the speed of the glacier water is increasing because amounts of meltwater, caused by climate change, are increasing.

- What is a hypothesis?
- What other ways do scientists test hypotheses?
- What processes do scientists use when they perform scientific investigations?

Nature of SCIENCE

This chapter begins your study of the nature of science, but there is even more information about the nature of science in this book. Each unit begins by exploring an important topic that is fundamental to scientific study. As you read these topics, you will learn even more about the nature of science.

Lesson 1 Understanding Science

Reading Guide

Key Concepts

ESSENTIAL QUESTIONS

- What is scientific inquiry?
- How do scientific laws and scientific theories differ?
- What is the difference between a fact and an opinion?

Vocabulary

science p. NOS 4
observation p. NOS 6
inference p. NOS 6
hypothesis p. NOS 6
prediction p. NOS 6
technology p. NOS 8
scientific theory p. NOS 9
scientific law p. NOS 9
critical thinking p. NOS 10

Multilingual eGlossary

BrainPOP®
What's Science Got to do With It?

SEPS.1, SEPS.2, SEPS.3, SEPS.4, SEPS.5, SEPS.6, SEPS.8, 6-8.E.1, 6-8.E.2, 6-8.E.3, 6-8.E.4, 6-8. LST.4.2

PBL Go to the resource tab in ConnectED to find the PBL *Cracking Up.*

What is science?

Did you ever hear a bird sing and then look in nearby trees to find the singing bird? Have you ever noticed how the Moon changes from a thin crescent to a full moon each month? When you do these things, you are doing science. **Science** *is the investigation and exploration of natural events and of the new information that results from those investigations.*

For thousands of years, men and women of all countries and cultures have studied the natural world and recorded their observations. They have shared their knowledge and findings and have created a vast amount of scientific information. Scientific knowledge has been the result of a great deal of debate and confirmation within the science community.

People use science in their everyday lives and careers. For example, firefighters, as shown in Figure 1, wear clothing that has been developed and tested to withstand extreme temperatures and not catch fire. Parents use science when they set up an aquarium for their children's pet fish. Athletes use science when they use high-performance gear or wear high-performance clothing. Without thinking about it, you use science or the results of science in almost everything you do. Your clothing, food, hair products, electronic devices, athletic equipment, and almost everything else you use are results of science.

Figure 1 Firefighters' clothing, oxygen tanks, and equipment are all results of science.

Branches of Science

There are many different parts of the natural world. Because there is so much to study, scientists often focus their work in one branch of science or on one topic within that branch of science. There are three main branches of science–Earth science, life science, and **physical** science.

WORD ORIGIN

physical
from Latin *physica,* means "study of nature"

Earth Science

The study of Earth, including rocks, soils, oceans, and the atmosphere is Earth science. The Earth scientist to the right is collecting lava samples for research. Earth scientists might ask other questions such as

- How do different shorelines react to tsunamis?
- Why do planets orbit the Sun?
- What is the rate of climate change?

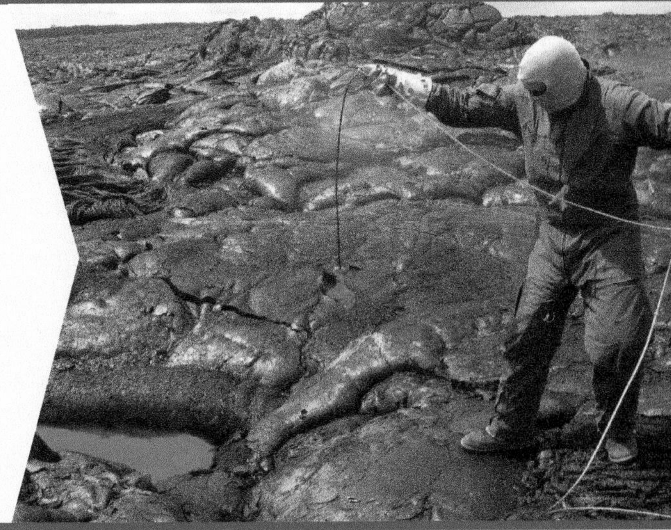

Life Science

The study of living things is life science, or biology. These biologists are attaching a radio collar to a tiger to help track its movements and learn more about its behavior. They are also weighing and measuring the tiger to gain information about this species. Biologists also ask questions such as

- Why do some trees lose their leaves in winter?
- How do birds know which direction they are going?
- How do mammals control their body temperature?

Physical Science

The study of matter and energy is physical science. It includes both physics and chemistry. This research chemist is preparing chemical solutions for analysis. Physicists and chemists ask other questions such as

- What chemical reactions must take place to launch a spaceship into space?
- Is it possible to travel faster than the speed of light?
- What makes up matter?

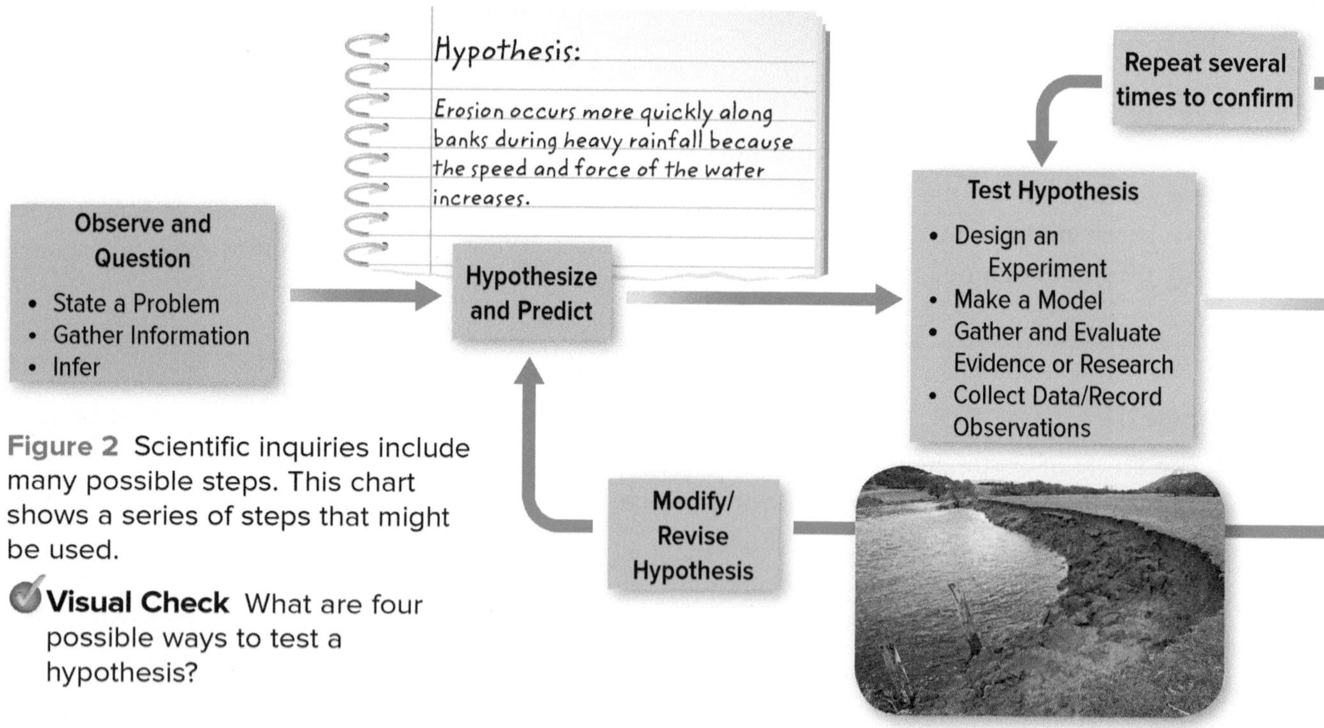

Figure 2 Scientific inquiries include many possible steps. This chart shows a series of steps that might be used.

Visual Check What are four possible ways to test a hypothesis?

Scientific Inquiry

When scientists conduct scientific investigations, they use scientific inquiry. Scientific inquiry is a process that uses a set of skills to answer questions or to test ideas about the natural world. There are many kinds of scientific investigations, and there are many ways to conduct them. The series of steps used in each investigation often varies. The flow chart in **Figure 2** shows an example of the skills used in scientific inquiry.

Key Concept Check What is scientific inquiry?

Ask Questions

One way to begin a scientific inquiry is to observe the natural world and ask questions. **Observation** *is the act of using one or more of your senses to gather information and taking note of what occurs.* Suppose you observe that the banks of a river have eroded more this year than in the previous year, and you want to know why. You also note that there was an increase in rainfall this year. After these observations, you make an inference based on these observations. *An* **inference** *is a logical explanation of an observation that is drawn from prior knowledge or experience.*

You infer that the increase in rainfall caused the increase in erosion. You decide to investigate further. You develop a hypothesis and a method to test it.

Hypothesize and Predict

A **hypothesis** *is a possible explanation for an observation that can be tested by scientific investigations.* A hypothesis states an observation and provides an explanation. For example, you might make the following hypothesis: More of the riverbank eroded this year because the amount, the speed, and the force of the river water increased.

When scientists state a hypothesis, they often use it to make predictions to help test their hypothesis. *A* **prediction** *is a statement of what will happen next in a sequence of events.* Scientists make predictions based on what information they think they will find when testing their hypothesis. For example, predictions for the hypothesis above could be: If rainfall increases, then the amount, the speed, and the force of river water will increase. If the amount, the speed, and the force of river water increase, then there will be more erosion.

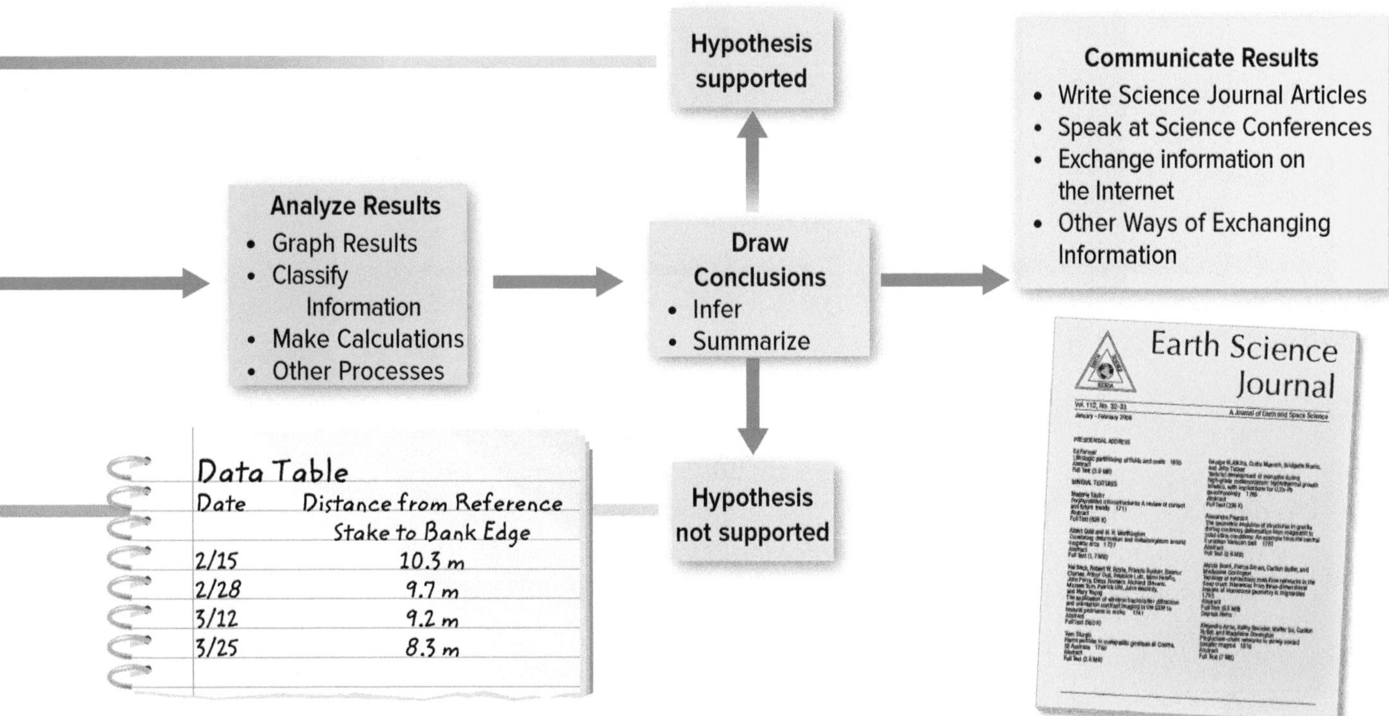

Test Hypothesis

When you test a hypothesis, you often test whether your predictions are true. If a prediction is confirmed, then it supports your hypothesis. If your prediction is not confirmed, you might need to modify your hypothesis and retest it.

There are several ways to test a hypothesis when performing a scientific investigation. Four possible ways are shown in Figure 2. For example, you might make a model of a riverbank in which you change the speed and the amount of water and record results and observations.

Analyze Results

After testing your hypothesis, you analyze your results using various methods, as shown in Figure 2. Often, it is hard to see trends or relationships in data while collecting it. Data should be sorted, graphed, or classified in some way. After analyzing the data, additional inferences can be made.

Draw Conclusions

Once you find the relationships among data and make several inferences, you can draw conclusions.

A conclusion is a summary of the information gained from testing a hypothesis. Scientists study the available information and draw conclusions based on that information.

Communicate Results

An important part of the scientific inquiry process is communicating results. Several ways to communicate results are listed in Figure 2. Scientists might share their information in other ways, too. Scientists communicate results of investigations to inform other scientists about their research and their conclusions. When a scientist uses that information to repeat another scientist's experiment, he or she is replicating the experiment to confirm results.

Further Scientific Inquiry

After finishing an experiment, a scientist must verify his or her results. If the hypothesis is supported, the scientist will repeat the experiment several times to make sure the conclusions are the same—this is called experimental repetition. If the hypothesis is not supported, any new information gained can be used to revise the hypothesis. Hypotheses can be revised and tested many times.

Results of Science

The results and conclusions from an investigation can lead to many outcomes, such as the answers to a question, more information on a specific topic, or support for a hypothesis. Other outcomes are described below.

Technology

During scientific inquiry, scientists often look for answers to questions such as, "How can the hearing impaired hear better?" After investigation, experimentation, and research, the conclusion might be the development of a new technology. **Technology** *is the practical use of scientific knowledge, especially for industrial or commercial use.* Technology, such as the cochlear implant, can help some deaf people hear.

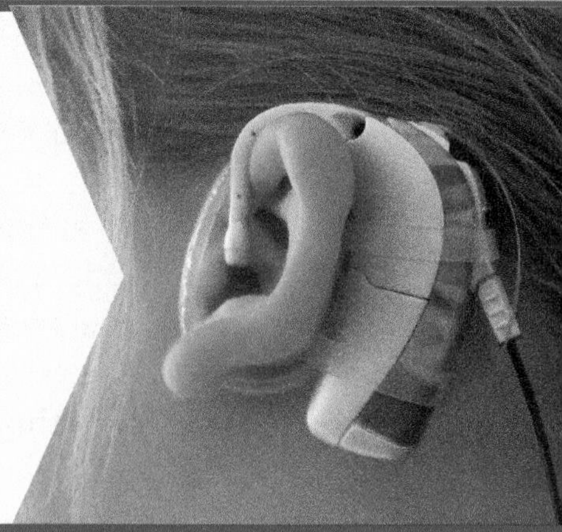

New Materials

Space travel has unique challenges. Astronauts must carry oxygen to breathe. They also must be protected against temperature and pressure extremes, as well as small, high-speed flying objects. Today's spacesuit, a result of research, testing, and design changes, consists of layers of material. The outer layer is made of a blend of materials. One material is waterproof and another material is heat and fire-resistant.

Possible Explanations

Scientists often perform investigations to find explanations as to why or how something happens. NASA's *Spitzer Space Telescope,* which has aided in our understanding of star formation, shows a cloud of gas and dust with newly formed stars.

 **Reading Check** What are some results of science?

Scientific Theory and Scientific Law

Another outcome of science is the development of scientific theories and laws. Recall that a hypothesis is a possible explanation about an observation that can be tested by scientific investigations. What happens when a hypothesis or a group of hypotheses has been tested many times and has been supported by the repeated scientific investigations? The hypothesis can become a scientific theory.

(t)Hannah Gal/Science Source; (c)john angerson/Alamy; (b)NASA/JPL-Caltech/Harvard-Smithsonian CfA

Scientific Theory

Often, the word *theory* is used in casual conversations to mean an untested idea or an opinion. However, scientists use *theory* differently. *A* **scientific theory** *is an explanation of observations or events that is based on knowledge gained from many observations and investigations.*

Scientists regularly question scientific theories and test them for validity. A scientific theory generally is accepted as true until it is disproved. An example of a scientific theory is the theory of plate tectonics. The theory of plate tectonics explains how Earth's crust moves and why earthquakes and volcanoes occur. Another example of a scientific theory is discussed in Figure 3.

▲ **Figure 3** Scientists once believed Earth was the center of the solar system. In the 16th century, Nicolaus Copernicus hypothesized that Earth and the other planets actually revolve around the Sun.

Scientific Law

A scientific law is different from a social law, which is an agreement among people concerning a behavior. *A* **scientific law** *is a rule that describes a pattern in nature.* Unlike a scientific theory that explains why an event occurs, a scientific law only states that an event will occur under certain circumstances. For example, Newton's law of gravitational force implies that if you drop an object, it will fall toward Earth. Newton's law does not explain why the object moves toward Earth when dropped, only that it will.

Key Concept Check How do scientific laws and theories differ?

New Information

Scientific information constantly changes as new information is discovered or as previous hypotheses are retested. New information can lead to changes in scientific theories, as explained in Figure 4. When new facts are revealed, a current scientific theory might be revised to include the new facts, or it might be disproved and rejected.

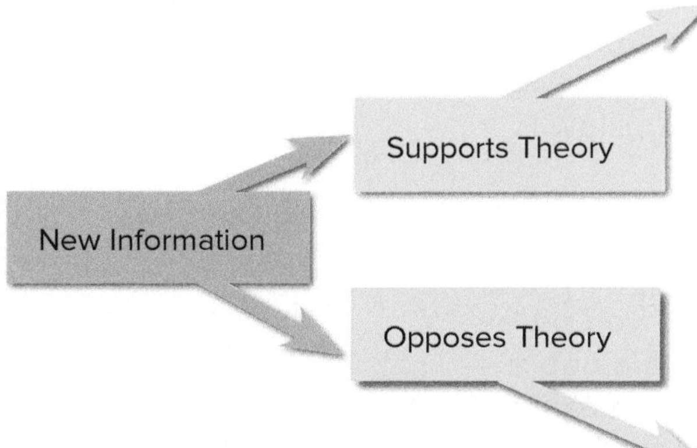

If new information supports a current scientific theory, then the theory is not changed. The information might be published in a scientific journal to show further support of the theory. The new information might also lead to advancements in technology or spark new questions that lead to new scientific investigations.

If new information opposes, or does not support a current scientific theory, the theory might be modified or rejected altogether. Often, new information will lead scientists to look at the original observations in a new way. This can lead to new investigations with new hypotheses. These investigations can lead to new theories.

▲ **Figure 4** New information can lead to changes in scientific theories.

FOLDABLES®

Make a six-tab book, and label it as shown. Use it to organize your notes about a scientific inquiry.

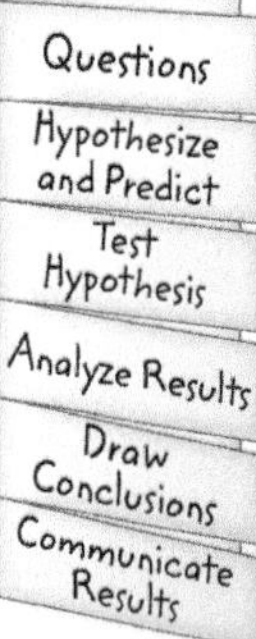

Evaluating Scientific Evidence

Did you ever read an advertisement, such as the one below, that made extraordinary claims? If so, you have practiced **critical thinking**—*comparing what you already know with the information you are given in order to decide whether you agree with it.* To determine whether information is true and scientific or pseudoscience (information incorrectly represented as scientific), you should be skeptical and identify facts and opinions. This helps you evaluate the strengths and weaknesses of information and make informed decisions. Critical thinking is important in all decision making—from everyday decisions to community, national, and international decisions.

 **Key Concept Check** How do a fact and an opinion differ?

Learn Algebra *While You Sleep!*

Have you struggled to learn algebra? Struggle no more.

Math-er-ific's new algebra pillow is scientifically proven to transfer math skills from the pillow to your brain while you sleep. This revolutionary scientific design improved the algebra test scores of laboratory mice by 150 percent.

Dr. Tom Equation says, "I have never seen students or mice learn algebra so easily. This pillow is truly amazing."

For only $19.95, those boring hours spent studying are a thing of the past. So act fast! If you order today, you can get the algebra pillow and the equally amazing geometry pillow for only $29.95. That is a $10 savings!

Skepticism

To be skeptical is to doubt the truthfulness or accuracy of something. Because of skepticism, science can be self-correcting. If someone publishes results or if an investigation gives results that don't seem accurate, a skeptical scientist usually will challenge the information and test the results for accuracy.

Identifying Facts

The prices of the pillows and the savings are facts. A fact is a measurement, observation, or statement that can be strictly defined. Many scientific facts can be evaluated for their validity through investigations.

Identifying Opinions

An opinion is a personal view, feeling, or claim about a topic. Opinions are neither true nor false.

Mixing Facts and Opinions

Sometimes people mix facts and opinions. You must read carefully to determine which information is fact and which is opinion.

Science cannot answer all questions.

Scientists recognize that some questions cannot be studied using scientific inquiry. Questions that deal with opinions, beliefs, values, and feelings cannot be answered through scientific investigation. For example, questions that cannot be answered through scientific investigation might include

- Are comedies the best kinds of movies?
- Is it ever okay to lie?
- Which food tastes best?

The answers to all of these questions are based on opinions, not facts.

Figure 5 Always use safe lab practices when doing scientific investigations.

Safety in Science

It is very important for anyone performing scientific investigations to use safe practices, such as the student shown in **Figure 5.** You should always follow your teacher's instructions. If you have questions about potential hazards, use of equipment, or the meaning of safety symbols, ask your teacher. Always wear protective clothing and equipment while performing scientific investigations. If you are using live animals in your investigations, provide appropriate care and ethical treatment to them. For more information on practicing safe and ethical science, consult the Science Safety Skill Handbook in the back of this book.

ACADEMIC VOCABULARY

potential
(adjective) possible, likely, or probable

Online Quiz
Virtual Lab

Lesson 1 Review

Use Vocabulary

1. The practical use of science, especially for industrial or commercial use, is ________.
2. **Distinguish** between a hypothesis and a prediction.
3. **Define** *observation* in your own words.

Understand Key Concepts

4. Which is NOT part of scientific inquiry?
   A. analyze results **C.** make a hypothesis
   B. falsify results D. make observations
5. **Explain** the difference between a scientific theory and a scientific law. Give an example of each.
6. **Write** an example of a fact and an example of an opinion.

Interpret Graphics

7. **Organize** Draw a graphic organizer similar to the one below. List four ways a scientist can communicate results.

Critical Thinking

8. **Identify** a real-world problem related to your home, your community, or your school that could be investigated scientifically.
9. **Design** a scientific investigation to test one possible solution to the problem you identified in the previous question.

Science & Engineering

The Design Process

Scientists & Engineers

Scientists investigate and explore natural events. Then they interpret data and share information learned from those investigations. How do engineers differ from scientists?

Engineers design, construct, and maintain the human-made world. Look around you and notice things that do not occur in nature. Schools, roads, airplanes, toys, microscopes, amusement parks, computer programs, and video games all result from engineering. Science involves the practice of scientific inquiry, but engineering involves the design process—a set of methods used to create a solution to a problem or need.

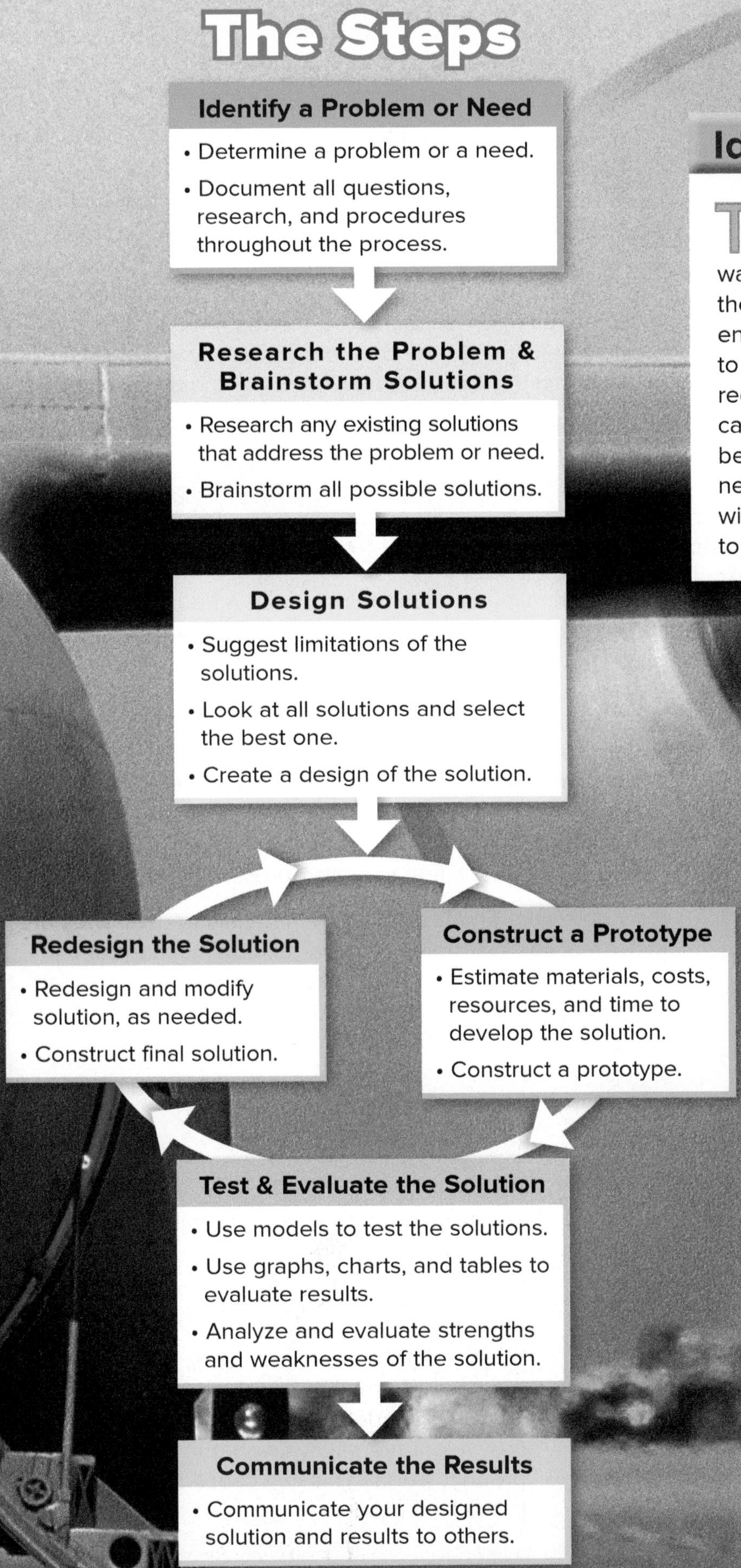

The Steps

Identify a Problem or Need

- Determine a problem or a need.
- Document all questions, research, and procedures throughout the process.

Research the Problem & Brainstorm Solutions

- Research any existing solutions that address the problem or need.
- Brainstorm all possible solutions.

Design Solutions

- Suggest limitations of the solutions.
- Look at all solutions and select the best one.
- Create a design of the solution.

Construct a Prototype

- Estimate materials, costs, resources, and time to develop the solution.
- Construct a prototype.

Redesign the Solution

- Redesign and modify solution, as needed.
- Construct final solution.

Test & Evaluate the Solution

- Use models to test the solutions.
- Use graphs, charts, and tables to evaluate results.
- Analyze and evaluate strengths and weaknesses of the solution.

Communicate the Results

- Communicate your designed solution and results to others.

Identify a Problem

Transporting goods by air has become an expensive way to move materials due to the high cost of fuel. A team of engineers has been assigned to come up with a way to reduce the costs of shipping cargo by air. The problem has been identified. What is the next step that these engineers will take in creating a solution to this problem?

Project-Based Learning Activity

Cracking Up Go online to design a solution to a problem involving the motion of two colliding objects.

Science & Engineering

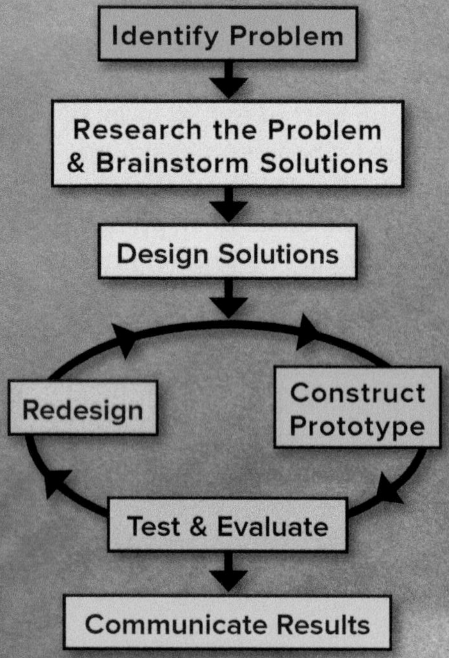

Identify Problem

Research the Problem & Brainstorm Solutions

Design Solutions

Redesign

Construct Prototype

Test & Evaluate

Communicate Results

Research the Problem & Brainstorm Solutions

After identifying the problem, the engineers' next step in the design process is to research what other people have done to solve this problem. Researching solutions that have been tried before is critical in determining if the problem statement is still accurate. If the original problem statement has a solution, the statement will need to be redefined. After the research is completed the team will brainstorm multiple solutions to the problem. Creativity is extremely important in the brainstorming phase of the design process.

Design Solutions

Once engineers have brainstormed a list of solutions, the best design solution should be selected. The design process can then progress. Before designing the solution, engineers must consider its constraints. Constraints are limitations put on the product from outside factors. These factors can include cost, ethical issues such as animal testing, environmental impacts, or attractiveness. Other constraints such as political and social issues or product safety can limit choices for product design. The materials required for the solution may also present some constraints.

How do engineers decide which materials to use? They are chosen based on chemical, physical, and mechanical properties as well as their interactions with other materials. It also might not make sense to use materials that are expensive, rare, or difficult to work with.

Construct a Prototype

A product prototype is the first example of the design. Prototypes are developed to test the design under real conditions. A prototype also can be called a model.

Models are used to think about processes that happen too slowly, too quickly, or on too small a scale to observe directly, as well as ones that are potentially dangerous or too large to otherwise study. Models that can be seen and touched are called physical models. Engineers also develop mathematical models and graphical models. In many instances multiple types of models are produced during the development of a product.

Limitations of Models

When scientists create models, they are using the best information they have at the time. However, models can be misleading because they might not always work the way a real product works. This can cause dissatisfaction in the final product.

Graphical Models

Some models are ideas or concepts that describe how someone thinks about something in the natural world. Graphical models are sketches or drawings. For example, Leonardo da Vinci, the inventor, was trained as an artist and made many graphical models of his designs.

One of his famous sketches was of the Helical Air Screw, drawn in 1480. This sketch, or graphical model, depicts an early form of what would become the helicopter. Modern helicopters look very different from da Vinci's, but the scientific principles behind helicopter flight remain the same since the time of da Vinci.

Mathematical Models

A mathematical model uses numerical data and equations to model an event or idea. They allow engineers to determine how changing one variable affects the product's design.

The image on the right is a computer simulation of the test conditions for one of NASA's experimental vehicles.

Mathematical variables can be adjusted in the simulation to change conditions and see the effects. The wing model was produced with a computer-aided design program (CAD). CAD programs can produce 2D and 3D models.

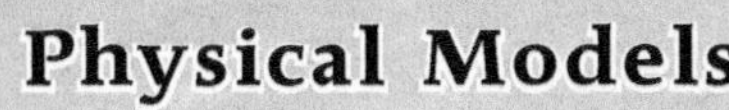

Physical Models

Physical models are those that you can see and touch. Models, such as NASA's experimental vehicle, show how parts relate to one another. Physical models are much easier to evaluate because their properties can be tested.

Science & Engineering

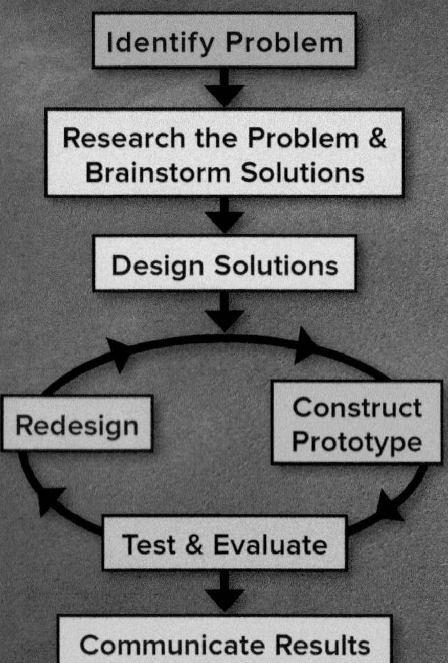

Test & Evaluate

At all stages of the design process, the design must be tested and reviewed. Testing and evaluating the solution allows the engineer to find and correct problems. Sometimes the design is changed. Ideas are always being changed. After evaluation and testing, one solution will be chosen as the best.

Redesign

After testing and evaluating is completed, the engineers could determine that the model needs to be redesigned. This can be due to information gained in the testing process, or finding out that the model did not behave in the expected manner. The model might be redesigned to better solve the current problem or to avoid developing a new one. After the model is redesigned, it is tested and evaluated again.

Communicate Results

After testing the aircraft model, engineers share the data with other engineers and scientists. The team might need to conduct more research, modify the prototype, and test again. Engineers may go through this process many times before they develop a model that meets their needs. The final design and prototype are then sent to manufacturing for production.

(bkgd)Design Pics/David Chapman, (inset)Steve Cole/Getty Images

It's Your Turn

Design a Zipline Ride

The engineers you just read about used the design process to solve a problem in airplane development. Using this same process, you can be an engineer and solve a very different kind of problem.

You are a guide for an adventure tour company that specializes in physically challenging activities in natural environments. You have been hired to design an exciting zipline ride near your town.

Identify the Problem

You know nothing about zipline rides or the requirements to construct a fast and safe zipline course. Consider the best location, platform design and construction, maximum angle of descent, length of ride, and materials required. Is it possible to zip too quickly or too slowly? Record your problem and questions with possible solutions in your Science Journal.

Research Existing Solutions

Begin answering your questions by researching existing ziplines, roller coasters, and other similar thrill rides. Note possible limitations to your solutions, such as cost, size, materials, location, time, or other restraints.

Design Solutions

Continue recording ideas for your zipline ride. Include possible locations for it in your environment, sites for launching and safe-landing platforms, length of zipline, materials and equipment needed for the zipline and rider, estimated costs, and time of development and construction.

Construct a Prototype

Draw several plans to answer your problems. Use simple materials to construct a scale model of your zipline. Check for accurate scale of dimensions and weight for each element to guarantee a fun, fast, and safe ride.

Test and Evaluate Solutions

Test your model many times to guarantee weight, speed, distance, and safe solutions. Use graphs, charts, and tables to evaluate the process and identify strengths and weaknesses in your solutions.

Redesign your Zipline and Communicate Your Results

Communicate your design process and solution to peers using your visual displays and model. Discuss and critique your working solution. Do further research and testing, if necessary. Redesign and modify your solution to meet design objectives. Finally, construct a model of your solution.

Graeme Pitman

Lesson 2

Measurement and Scientific Tools

Reading Guide

Key Concepts
ESSENTIAL QUESTIONS

- Why is it important for scientists to use the International System of Units?
- What causes measurement uncertainty?
- What are mean, median, mode, and range?

Vocabulary

description p. NOS 18
explanation p. NOS 18
International System of Units (SI) p. NOS 18
significant digits p. NOS 20

Multilingual eGlossary

SEPS.2, SEPS.5

Description and Explanation

The scientist in Figure 6 is observing a volcano. He describes in his journal that the flowing lava is bright red with a black crust, and it has a temperature of about 630°C. *A* **description** *is a spoken or written summary of observations.* There are two types of descriptions. When making a qualitative description, such as *bright red,* you use your senses (sight, sound, smell, touch, taste) to describe an observation. When making a quantitative description, such as *630°C,* you use numbers and measurements to describe an observation. Later, the scientist might explain his observations. *An* **explanation** *is an interpretation of observations.* Because the lava was bright red and about 630°C, the scientist might explain that these conditions indicate the lava is cooling and the volcano did not recently erupt.

The International System of Units

At one time, scientists in different parts of the world used different units of measurement. Imagine the confusion when a British scientist measured weight in pounds-force, a French scientist measured weight in Newtons, and a Japanese scientist measured weight in momme (MOM ee). Sharing scientific information was difficult, if not impossible.

In 1960, scientists adopted a new system of measurement to eliminate this confusion. *The* **International System of Units (SI)** *is the internationally accepted system for measurement.* SI uses standards of measurement, called base units, which are shown in Table 1 on the next page. A base unit is the most common unit used in the SI system for a given measurement.

Figure 6 Scientists use descriptions and explanations when observing natural events.

Table 1 SI Base Units		
Quantity Measured	**Unit**	**Symbol**
Length	meter	m
Mass	kilogram	kg
Time	second	s
Electric current	ampere	A
Temperature	Kelvin	K
Amount of substance	mole	mol
Intensity of light	candela	cd

Interactive Table

Table 1 You can use SI units to measure the physical properties of objects.

SI Unit Prefixes

In addition to base units, SI uses prefixes to identify the size of the unit, as shown in Table 2. Prefixes are used to indicate a fraction of ten or a multiple of ten. In other words, each unit is either ten times smaller than the next larger unit or ten times larger than the next smaller unit. For example, the prefix *deci-* means 10^{-1}, or 1/10. A decimeter is 1/10 of a meter. The prefix *kilo-* means 10^3, or 1,000. A kilometer is 1,000 m.

Converting Between SI Units

Because SI is based on ten, it is easy to convert from one SI unit to another. To convert SI units, you must multiply or divide by a factor of ten. You also can use proportions as shown below in the Math Skills activity.

Key Concept Check Why is it important for scientists to use the International System of Units (SI)?

Table 2 Prefixes are used in SI to indicate the size of the unit.

Table 2 Prefixes	
Prefix	**Meaning**
Mega- (M)	1,000,000 (10^6)
Kilo- (k)	1,000 (10^3)
Hecto- (h)	100 (10^2)
Deka- (da)	10 (10^1)
Deci- (d)	0.1 (10^{-1})
Centi- (c)	0.01 (10^{-2})
Milli- (m)	0.001 (10^{-3})
Micro- (μ)	0.000 001 (10^{-6})

Math Skills — Use Proportions

A book has a mass of 1.1 kg. Using a proportion, find the mass of the book in grams.

1. Use the table to determine the correct relationship between the units. One kg is 1,000 times greater than 1 g. So, there are 1,000 g in 1 kg.
2. Then set up a proportion.

$$\left(\frac{x}{1.1\ \text{kg}}\right) = \left(\frac{1{,}000\ \text{g}}{1\ \text{kg}}\right)$$

$$x = \left(\frac{(1{,}000\ \text{g})(1.1\ \cancel{\text{kg}})}{1\ \cancel{\text{kg}}}\right) = 1{,}100\ \text{g}$$

3. Check your units. The answer is 1,100 g.

Practice

1. Two towns are separated by 15,328 m. What is the distance in kilometers?
2. A dosage of medicine is 325 mg. What is the dosage in grams?

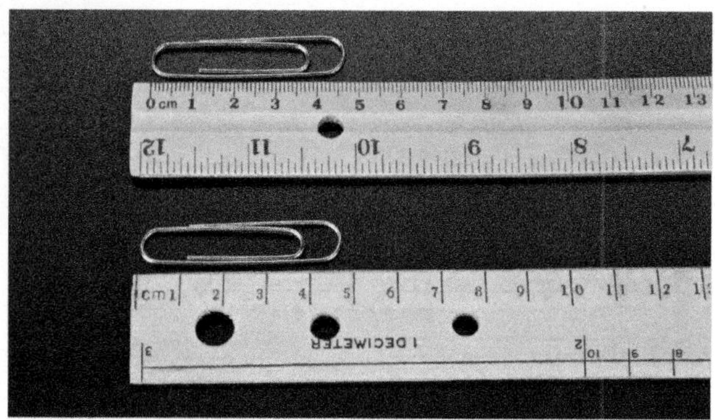

Figure 7 All measurements have some uncertainty.

Make a vertical two-tab book using the labels shown. Use it to organize your notes about SI conversions and rounding significant digits.

Personal Tutor

Table 3 Significant Digits Rules

1. All nonzero numbers are significant.
2. Zeros between significant digits are significant.
3. All final zeros to the right of the decimal point are significant.
4. Zeros used solely for spacing the decimal point are NOT significant. The zeros only indicate the position of the decimal point.

* The blue numbers in the examples are the significant digits.

Number	Significant Digits	Applied Rules
1.234	4	1
1.02	3	1, 2
0.023	2	1, 4
0.200	3	1, 3
1,002	4	1, 2
3.07	3	1, 2
0.001	1	1, 4
0.012	2	1, 4
50,600	3	1, 2, 4

Measurement and Uncertainty

Have you ever measured an object, such as a paper clip? The tools used to take measurements can limit the accuracy of the measurements. Look at the bottom ruler in Figure 7. Its measurements are divided into centimeters. The paper clip is between 4 cm and 5 cm. You might guess that it is 4.7 cm long. Now, look at the top ruler. Its measurements are divided into millimeters. You can say with more precision that the paper clip is about 4.75 cm long. This measurement is more precise than the first measurement.

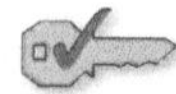

Key Concept Check What causes measurement uncertainty?

Significant Digits and Rounding

Because scientists duplicate each other's work, they must record numbers with the same degree of precision as the original data. Significant digits allow scientists to do this. **Significant digits** *are the number of digits in a measurement that you know with a certain degree of reliability.* Table 3 lists the rules for expressing and determining significant digits.

In order to achieve the same degree of precision as a previous measurement, it often is necessary to round a measurement to a certain number of significant digits. Suppose you have the number below, and you need to round it to four significant digits.

1,348.527 g

To round to four significant digits, you need to round the 8. If the digit to the right of the 8 is 0, 1, 2, 3, or 4, the digit being rounded (8) remains the same. If the digit to the right of the 8 is 5, 6, 7, 8, or 9, the digit being rounded (8) increases by one. The rounded number is 1,349 g.

What if you need to round 1,348.527 g to two significant digits? You would look at the number to the right of the 3 to determine how to round. 1,348.527 rounded to two significant digits would be 1,300 g. The 4 and 8 become zeros.

Matt Meadows

Mean, Median, Mode, and Range

A rain gauge measures the amount of rain that falls on a location over a period of time. A rain gauge can be used to collect data in scientific investigations, such as the data shown in Table 4a. Scientists often need to analyze their data to obtain information. Four values often used when analyzing numbers are median, mean, mode, and range.

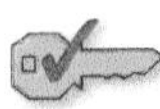 **Key Concept Check** What are mean, median, and mode?

Median

The median is the middle number in a data set when the data are arranged in numerical order. The rainfall data are listed in numerical order in Table 4b. If you have an even number of data items, add the two middle numbers together and divide by two to find the median.

$$\text{median} = \frac{8.18 \text{ cm} + 8.84 \text{ cm}}{2}$$

$$= 8.51 \text{ cm}$$

Table 4a Rainfall Data

Month	Rainfall
January	7.11 cm
February	11.89 cm
March	9.58 cm
April	8.18 cm
May	7.11 cm
June	1.47 cm
July	18.21 cm
August	8.84 cm

Mean

The mean, or average, of a data set is the sum of the numbers in a data set divided by the number of entries in the set. To find the mean, add the numbers in your data set and then divide the total by the number of items in your data set.

$$\text{mean} = \frac{\text{(sum of numbers)}}{\text{(number of items)}}$$

$$= \frac{72.39 \text{ cm}}{8 \text{ months}}$$

$$= \frac{9.05 \text{ cm}}{\text{month}}$$

Mode

The mode of a data set is the number or item that appears most often. The number in blue in Table 4b appears twice. All other numbers appear only once.

mode = 7.11 cm

Table 4b Rainfall Data (numerical order)

Rainfall
1.47 cm
7.11 cm
7.11 cm
8.18 cm
8.84 cm
9.58 cm
11.89 cm
18.21 cm

Range

The range is the difference between the greatest number and the least number in the data set.

$$\text{range} = 18.21 \text{ cm} - 1.47 \text{ cm}$$

$$= 16.74 \text{ cm}$$

Scientific Tools

As you engage in scientific inquiry, you will need tools to help you take quantitative measurements. Always follow appropriate safety procedures when using scientific tools. For more information about the proper use of these tools, see the Science Skill Handbook at the back of this book.

◄ Science Journal

Use a science journal to record observations, questions, hypotheses, data, and conclusions from your scientific investigations. A science journal is any notebook that you use to take notes or record information and data while you conduct a scientific investigation. Keep it organized so you can find information easily. Write down the date whenever you record new information in the journal. Make sure you are recording your data honestly and accurately.

Rulers and Metersticks ►

Use rulers and metersticks to measure lengths and distances. The SI unit of measurement for length is the meter (m). For small objects, such as pebbles or seeds, use a metric ruler with centimeter and millimeter markings. To measure larger objects, such as the length of your bedroom, use a meterstick. To measure long distances, such as the distance between cities, use an instrument that measur es in kilometers. Be careful when carrying rulers and metersticks, and never point them at anyone.

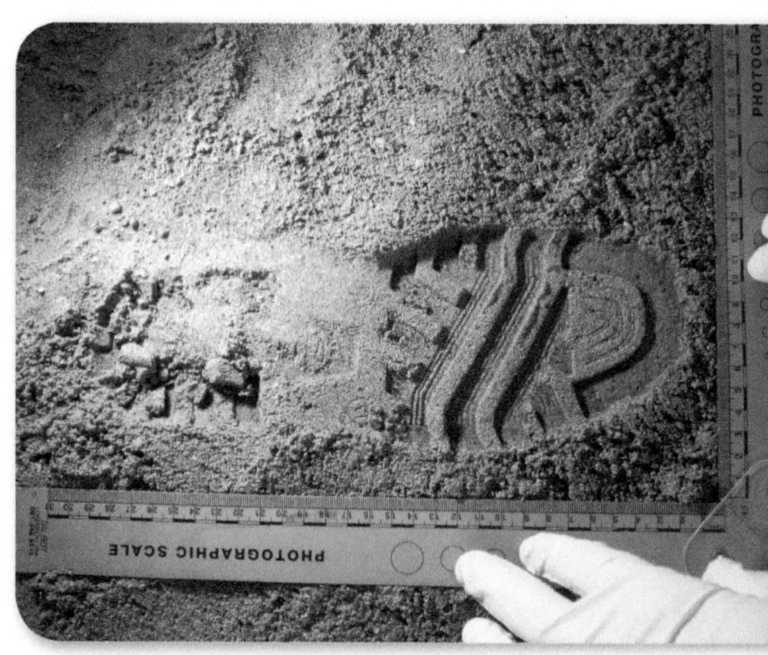

◄ Glassware

Use beakers to hold and pour liquids. The lines on a beaker do not provide accurate measurements. Use a graduated cylinder to measure the volume of a liquid. Volume is typically measured in liters (L) or milliliters (mL).

(t)Matt Meadows; (c)By Ian Miles-Flashpoint Pictures/Alamy; (b)Joseph Clark/Photodisc/Getty Images

Triple-Beam Balance ►

Use a triple-beam balance to measure the mass of an object. The mass of a small object is measured in grams. The mass of large object is usually measured in kilograms. Triple-beam balances are instruments that require some care when using. Follow your teacher's instructions so that you do not damage the instrument. Digital balances also might be used.

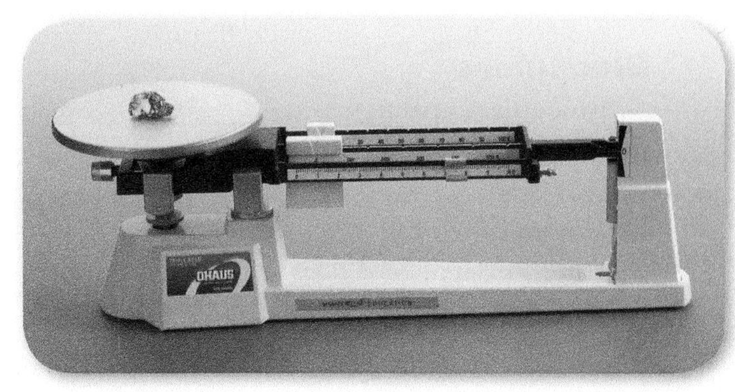

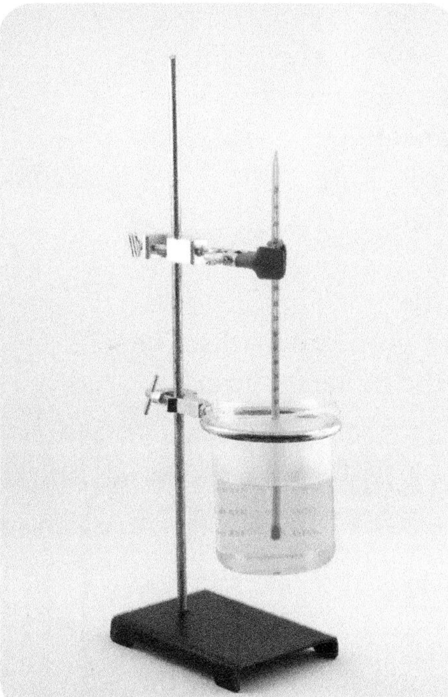

◄ Thermometer

Use a thermometer to measure the temperature of a substance. Kelvin is the SI unit for temperature, but you will use a thermometer to measure temperature in degrees Celsius (°C). To use a thermometer, place a room-temperature thermometer into the substance for which you want to measure temperature. Do not let the thermometer touch the bottom of the container that holds the substance or you will get an inaccurate reading. When you finish, remember to place your thermometer in a secure place. Do not lay it on a table, because it can roll off the table. Never use a thermometer as a stirring rod.

Computers and the Internet ►

Use a computer to collect, organize, and store information about a research topic or scientific investigation. Computers are useful tools to scientists for several reasons. Scientists use computers to record and analyze data, to research new information, and to quickly share their results with others worldwide over the Internet.

(t)Hutchings Photography/Digital Light Source; (cl)McGraw-Hill Education; (br)Steve Cole/Getty Images

Tools Used by Earth Scientists

Binoculars

Binoculars are instruments that enable people to view faraway objects more clearly. Earth scientists use them to view distant landforms, animals, or even incoming weather.

Compass

A compass is an instrument that shows magnetic north. Earth scientists use compasses to navigate when they are in the field and to determine the direction of distant landforms or other natural objects.

Wind Vane and Anemometer

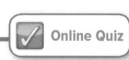

A wind vane is a device, often attached to the roofs of buildings, that rotates to show the direction of the wind. An anemometer, or wind-speed gauge, is used to measure the speed and the force of wind.

Streak Plate

A streak plate is a piece of hard, unglazed porcelain that helps you identify minerals. When you scrape a mineral along a streak plate, the mineral leaves behind powdery marks. The color of the mark is the mineral's streak.

Lesson 2 Review

Online Quiz

Use Vocabulary

1 **Distinguish** between description and explanation.

2 **Define** *significant digits* in your own words.

Understand Key Concepts 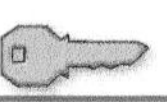

3 Which base unit is NOT part of the International System of Units?

A. ampere
B. meter
C. pound
D. second

4 **Give an example** of how scientific tools cause measurement uncertainty.

5 Differentiate among mean, median, mode, and range.

Interpret Graphics

6 **Change** Copy the graphic organizer below, and change the number shown to have the correct number of significant digits indicated.

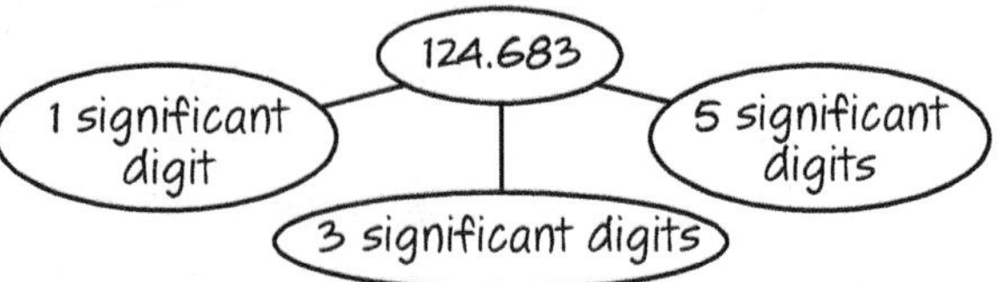

Critical Thinking

7 **Write** a short essay explaining why the United States should consider adopting SI as the measurement system used by supermarkets and other businesses.

Math Skills

8 **Convert** 52 m to kilometers. Explain how you got your answer.

Skill Practice **Collect and Analyze Data** **45 minutes**

Materials

250-mL beaker

large piece of newsprint

1-L containers

forceps

strainer

probe

Also needed: soil mixture, balance, plastic containers

Safety

What can you learn by collecting and analyzing data?

People who study ancient cultures often collect and analyze data from soil samples. Soil samples contain bits of pottery, bones, seeds, and other clues to how ancient people lived and what they ate. In this activity, you will separate and analyze a simulated soil sample from an ancient civilization.

Learn It

Data includes observations you can make with your senses and observations based on measurements of some kind. **Collecting and analyzing data** includes collecting, classifying, comparing and contrasting, and interpreting (looking for meaning in the data).

Try It

1. Read and complete a lab safety form.
2. Obtain a 200-mL sample of "soil."
3. Spread the newsprint over your workspace. Slowly pour the soil through a strainer over a plastic container. Shake the strainer gently so that all of the soil enters the container.
4. Pour the remaining portion of the soil sample onto the newsprint. Use a probe and forceps to separate objects. Classify different types of objects, and place them into the other plastic containers.
5. Copy the data tables from the board into your Science Journal.
6. Use the balance to measure and record the masses of each group of objects found in your soil sample. Write your group's data in the data table on the board.
7. When all teams have finished, use the class data from the board to find the mean, the median, the mode, and the range for each type of object.

Apply It

8. **Make Inferences** Assuming that the plastic objects represented animal bones, how many different types of animals were indicated by your analysis? Explain.
9. **Evaluate** Archaeologists often include information about the depth at which soil samples are taken. If you received a soil sample that kept the soil and other objects in their original layers, what more might you discover?
10. **Key Concept** Why didn't everyone in the class get the same data? What were some possible sources of uncertainty in your measurements?

Lesson 3 Case Study

Reading Guide

Key Concepts

ESSENTIAL QUESTIONS

- How are independent variables and dependent variables related?
- How is scientific inquiry used in a real-life scientific investigation?

Vocabulary

variable p. NOS 27

independent variable p. NOS 27

dependent variable p. NOS 27

Multilingual eGlossary

SEPS.3, SEPS.4, SEPS.6

The Iceman's Last Journey

The Tyrolean Alps border western Austria, northern Italy, and eastern Switzerland, as shown in **Figure 8.** They are popular with tourists, hikers, mountain climbers, and skiers. In 1991, two hikers discovered the remains of a man, also shown in **Figure 8,** in a melting glacier on the border between Austria and Italy. They thought the man had died in a hiking accident. They reported their discovery to the authorities.

Initially authorities thought the man was a music professor who disappeared in 1938. However, they soon learned that the music professor was buried in a nearby town. Artifacts near the frozen corpse indicated that the man died long before 1938. The artifacts, as shown in **Figure 9,** were unusual. The man, nicknamed the Iceman, was dressed in leggings, a loincloth, and a goatskin jacket. A bearskin cap lay nearby. He wore shoes made of red deerskin with thick bearskin soles. The shoes were stuffed with grass for insulation. In addition, investigators found a copper ax, a partially constructed longbow, a quiver containing 14 arrows, a wooden backpack frame, and a dagger at the site.

Figure 8 Excavators used jackhammers to free the man's body from the ice, which caused serious damage to his hip. Part of a longbow also was found nearby.

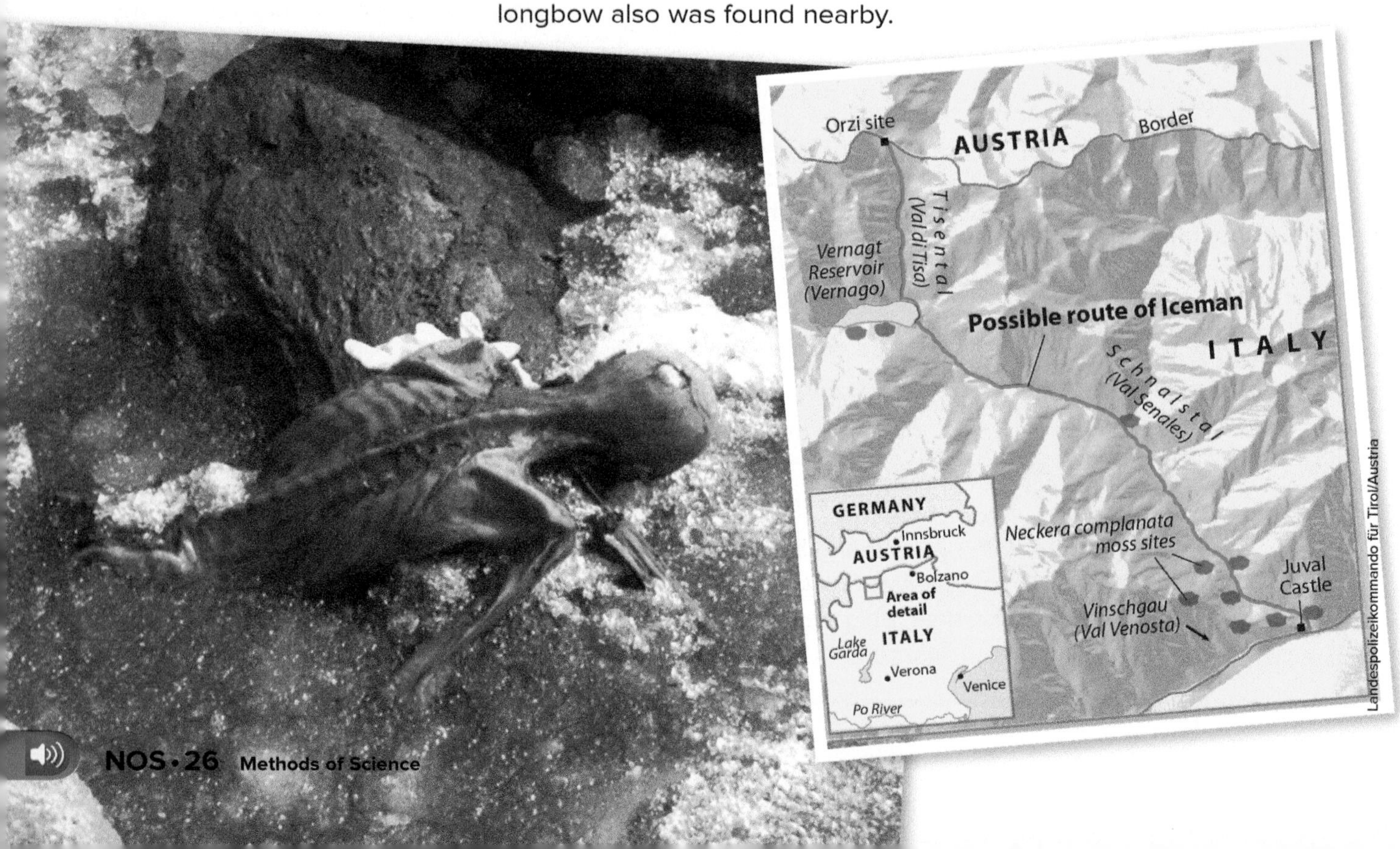

Landespolizeikommando für Tirol/Austria

A Controlled Experiment

The identity of the corpse was a mystery. Several people hypothesized about his identity, but controlled experiments were needed to unravel the mystery of who the Iceman was. Scientists and the public wanted to know the identity of the man, why he had died, and when he had died.

Identifying Variables and Constants

When scientists design a controlled experiment, they have to identify factors that might affect the outcome of an experiment. *A* **variable** *is any factor that can have more than one value.* In controlled experiments, there are two kinds of variables. *The* **independent variable** *is the factor that you want to test. It is changed by the investigator to observe how it affects a dependent variable. The* **dependent variable** *is the factor you observe or measure during an experiment.* When the independent variable is changed, it causes the dependent variable to change.

A controlled experiment has two groups—an experimental group and a control group. The experimental group is used to study how a change in the independent variable changes the dependent variable. The control group contains the same factors as the experimental group, but the independent variable is not changed. Without a control, it is difficult to know if your experimental observations result from the variable you are testing or from another factor.

Scientists used inquiry to investigate the mystery of the Iceman. As you read the rest of the story, notice how scientific inquiry was used throughout the investigation. The blue boxes in the margins point out examples of the scientific inquiry process. The notebooks in the margin identify what a scientist might have written in a journal.

Figure 9 These models show what the Iceman and the artifacts found with him might have looked like.

Scientific investigations often begin when someone asks a question about something observed in nature.

Observation: A corpse was found buried in ice in the Tyrolean Alps.
Hypothesis: The corpse found in the Tyrolean Alps is the body of a missing music professor because he disappeared in 1938, and had not been found.
Observation: Artifacts near the body suggested that the body was much older than the music professor would have been.
Revised Hypothesis: The corpse found was dead long before 1938 because the artifacts found near him appear to date before the 1930s.
Prediction: If the artifacts belong to the corpse, and date back before 1930, then the corpse is not the music professor.

An inference is a logical explanation of observations based on past experiences.

Inference: Based on its construction, the ax is at least 4,000 years old.
Prediction: If the ax is at least 4,000 years old, then the body found near it is also at least 4,000 years old.
Test Results: Radiocarbon dating showed the man to be 5,300 years old.

After many observations, revised hypotheses, and tests, conclusions often can be made.

Conclusion: The Iceman is about 5,300 years old. He was a seasonal visitor to the high mountains. He died in autumn. When winter came the Iceman's body became buried and frozen in the snow, which preserved his body.

An Early Conclusion

Konrad Spindler was a professor of archeology at the University of Innsbruck in Austria when the Iceman was discovered. Spindler estimated that the ax, shown in **Figure 10,** was at least 4,000 years old based on its construction. If the ax was that old, then the Iceman was also at least 4,000 years old. Later, radiocarbon dating showed that the Iceman actually lived about 5,300 years ago.

The Iceman's body was in a mountain glacier 3,210 m above sea level. What was this man doing so high in the snow- and ice-covered mountains? Was he hunting for food, shepherding his animals, or looking for metal ore?

Spindler noted that some of the wood used in the artifacts was from trees that grew at lower elevations. He concluded that the Iceman was probably a seasonal visitor to the high mountains.

Spindler also hypothesized that shortly before the Iceman's death, the Iceman had driven his herds from their summer high mountain pastures to the lowland valleys. However, the Iceman soon returned to the mountains where he died of exposure to the cold weather.

The Iceman's body was extremely well preserved. Spindler inferred that ice and snow covered the Iceman's body shortly after he died. Spindler concluded that the Iceman died in autumn and was quickly buried and frozen, which preserved his body and all his possessions.

Figure 10 This ax, bow and quiver, and dagger and sheath were found with the Iceman's body.

More Observations and Revised Hypotheses

When the Iceman's body was discovered, Klaus Oeggl was an assistant professor of botany at the University of Innsbruck. His area of study was plant life during prehistoric times in the Alps. He was invited to join the research team studying the Iceman.

Upon close examination of the Iceman and his belongings, Professor Oeggl found three plant materials–grass from the Iceman's shoe, as shown in **Figure 11,** a splinter of wood from his longbow, and a tiny fruit called a sloe berry.

Over the next year, Professor Oeggl examined bits of charcoal wrapped in maple leaves that had been found at the discovery site. Examination of the samples revealed the charcoal was from the wood of eight different types of trees. All but one of the trees grew only at lower elevations than where the Iceman's body was found. Like Spindler, Professor Oeggl suspected that the Iceman had been at a lower elevation shortly before he died. From Oeggl's observations, he formed a hypothesis and made some predictions.

Oeggl realized that he would need more data to support his hypothesis. He requested that he be allowed to examine the contents of the Iceman's digestive tract. If all went well, the study would show what the Iceman had swallowed just hours before his death.

Figure 11 Professor Oeggl examined the Iceman's belongings along with the leaves and grass that were stuck to his shoe.

South Tyrol Museum of Archaeology, Italy (www.iceman.it)

Scientific investigations often lead to new questions.

Observations: Plant matter near body to study—grass on shoe, splinter from longbow, sloe berry fruit, charcoal wrapped in maple leaves, wood in charcoal from 8 different trees—7 of 8 types of wood in charcoal grow at lower elevations
Hypothesis: The Iceman had recently been at lower elevations before he died because the plants identified near him grow only at lower elevations.
Prediction: If the identified plants are found in the digestive tract of the corpse, then the man actually was at lower elevations just before he died.
Question: What did the Iceman eat the day before he died?

Experiment to Test Hypothesis

The research teams provided Professor Oeggl with a tiny sample from the Iceman's digestive tract. He was determined to study it carefully to obtain as much information as possible. Oeggl carefully planned his scientific inquiry. He knew that he had to work quickly to avoid the decomposition of the sample and to reduce the chances of contaminating the samples.

His plan was to divide the material from the digestive tract into four samples. Each sample would undergo several chemical tests. Then, the samples would be examined under an electron microscope to see as many details as possible.

Professor Oeggl began by adding a saline solution to the first sample. This caused it to swell slightly, making it easier to identify particles using the microscope at a relatively low magnification. He saw particles of a wheat grain known as einkorn, which was a common type of wheat grown in the region during prehistoric times. He also found other edible plant material in the sample.

Oeggl noticed that the sample also contained pollen grains in the digestive tract of the Iceman, who is shown in **Figure 12**. To see the pollen grains more clearly, he used a chemical that separated unwanted substances from the pollen grains. He washed the sample a few times with alcohol. After each wash, he examined the sample under a microscope at a high magnification. The pollen grains became more visible. Many more microscopic pollen grains could now be seen. Professor Oeggl identified these pollen grains as those from a hop-hornbeam tree.

There is more than one way to test a hypothesis. Scientists might gather and evaluate evidence, collect data and record their observations, create a model, or design and perform an experiment. They also might perform a combination of these skills.

Test Plan:

- *Divide a sample of the Iceman's digestive tract into four sections.*
- *Examine the pieces under microscopes.*
- *Gather data from observations of the pieces and record observations.*

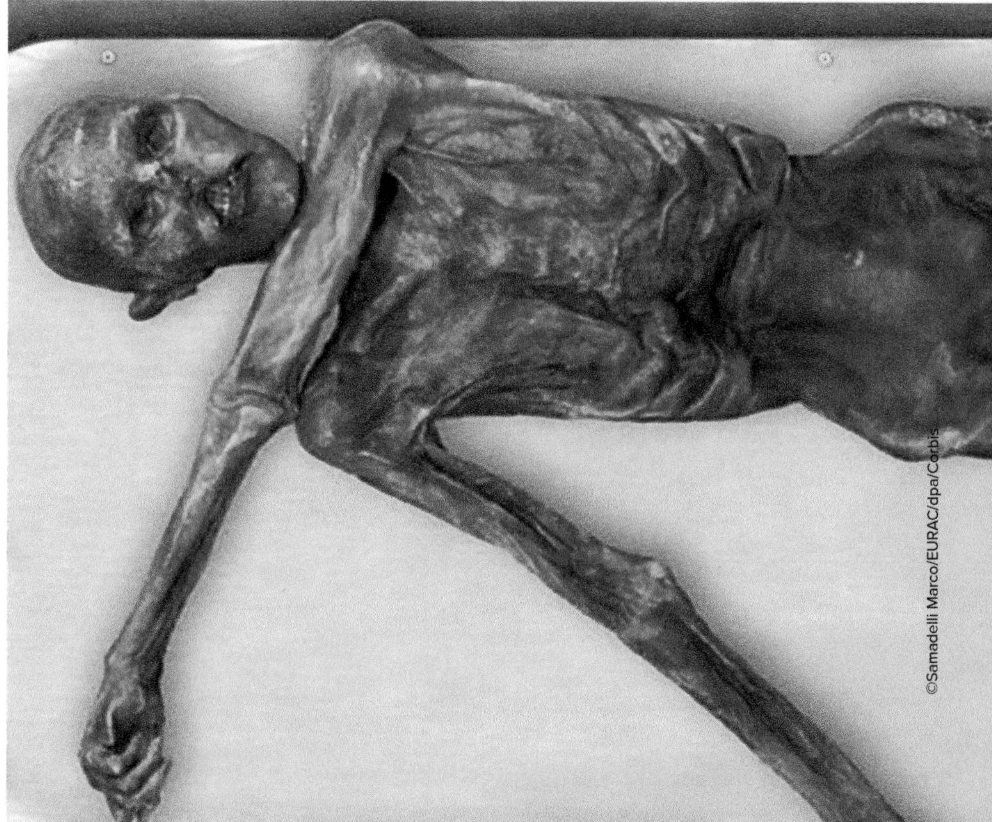

Figure 12 The Iceman, shown here, had pollen grains from hop hornbeam trees in his digestive tract.

Analyzing Results

Professor Oeggl observed that the hop-hornbeam pollen grains had not been digested. Therefore, the Iceman must have swallowed them within hours before his death. But, hop-hornbeam trees only grow in lower valleys. Oeggl was confused. How could pollen grains from trees at low elevations be ingested within a few hours of this man dying in high, snow-covered mountains? Perhaps the samples from the Iceman's digestive tract had been contaminated. Oeggl knew he needed to investigate further.

Further Experimentation

Oeggl realized that the most likely source of contamination would be Oeggl's own laboratory. He decided to test whether his lab equipment or saline solution contained hop-hornbeam pollen grains. To do this, he prepared two identical, sterile slides with saline solution. Then, on one slide, he placed a sample from the Iceman's digestive tract. The slide with the sample was the experimental group. The slide without the sample was the control group.

The independent variable, or the variable that Oeggl changed, was the presence of the sample on the slide. The dependent variable, or the variable Oeggl measured, was whether hop-hornbeam pollen grains showed up on the slides. Oeggl examined the slides carefully.

Analyzing Additional Results

The experiment showed that the control group (the slide without the digestive tract sample) contained no hop-hornbeam pollen grains. Therefore, the pollen grains had not come from his lab equipment or solutions. Each sample from the Iceman's digestive tract was closely re-examined. All of the samples contained the same hop-hornbeam pollen grains. The Iceman had indeed swallowed the hop-hornbeam pollen grains.

Error is unavoidable in scientific research. Scientists are careful to document procedures and any unanticipated factors or accidents. They also are careful to document possible sources of error in their measurements.

Procedure:
- *Sterilize laboratory equipment.*
- *Prepare saline slides.*
- *View saline slides under electron microscope. Results: no hop-hornbeam pollen grains*
- *Add digestive tract sample to one slide.*
- *View this slide under electron microscope. Result: hop-hornbeam pollen grains present*

Controlled experiments contain two types of variables.

Dependent Variables: amount of hop-hornbeam pollen grains found on slide
Independent Variable: digestive tract sample on slide

Without a control group, it is difficult to determine the origin of some observations.

Control Group: sterilized slide
Experimental Group: sterilized slide with digestive tract sample

An inference is a logical explanation of an observation that is drawn from prior knowledge or experience. Inferences can lead to predictions, hypotheses, or conclusions.

Observation: The Iceman's digestive tract contains pollen grains from the hop-hornbeam tree and other plants that bloom in spring.
Inference: Knowing the rate at which food and pollen decompose after swallowed, it can be inferred that the Iceman ate three times on the day that he died.
Prediction: The Iceman died in the spring within hours of digesting the hop-hornbeam pollen grains.

Mapping the Iceman's Journey

The hop-hornbeam pollen grains were helpful in determining the season the Iceman died. Because the pollen grains were whole, Professor Oeggl inferred that the Iceman swallowed the pollen grains during their blooming season. Therefore, the Iceman must have died between March and June.

After additional investigation, Professor Oeggl was ready to map the Iceman's final trek up the mountain. Because Oeggl knew the rate at which food travels through the digestive system, he inferred that the Iceman had eaten three times in the final day and a half of his life. From the digestive tract samples, Oeggl estimated where the Iceman was located when he ate.

First, the Iceman ingested pollen grains native to higher mountain regions. Then he swallowed hop-hornbeam pollen grains from the lower mountain regions several hours later. Last, the Iceman swallowed other pollen grains from trees of higher mountain areas again. Oeggl proposed the Iceman traveled from the southern region of the Italian Alps to the higher, northern region as shown in **Figure 13**, where he died suddenly. He did this all in a period of about 33 hours.

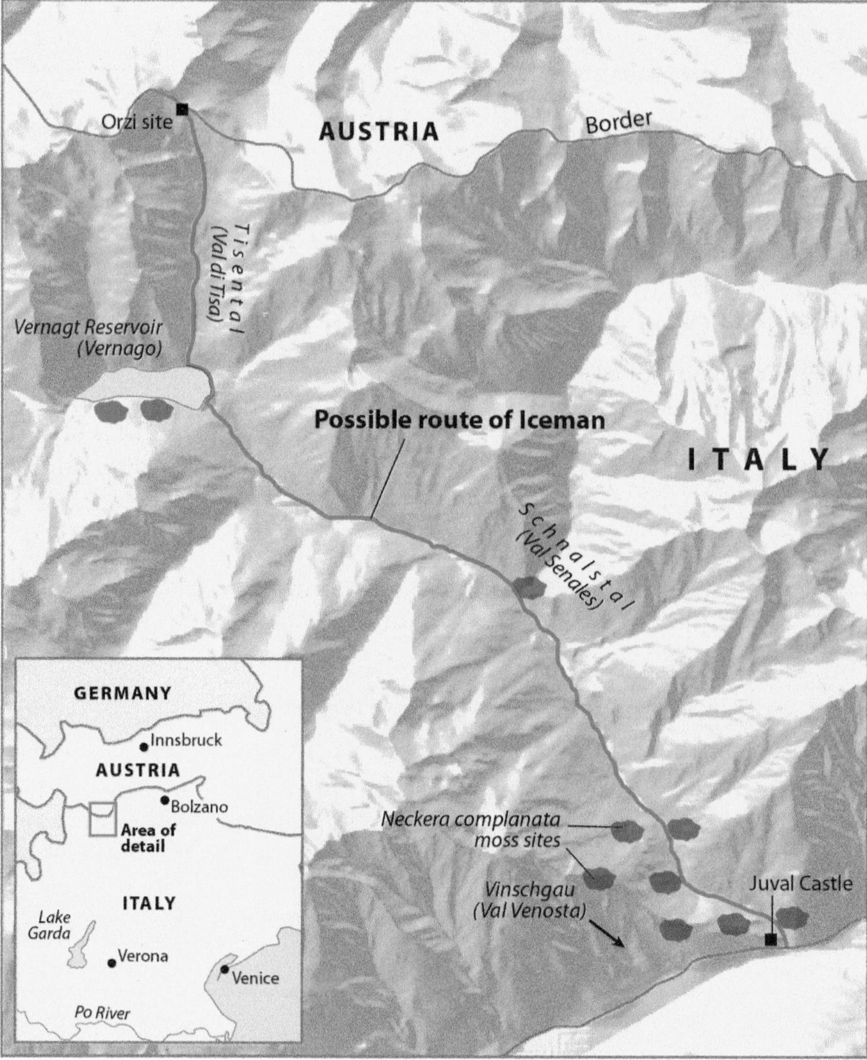

Figure 13 By examining the contents of the Iceman's digestive tract, Professor Oeggl was able to reconstruct the Iceman's last journey.

Conclusion

Researchers from around the world worked on different parts of the Iceman mystery and shared their results. Analysis of the Iceman's hair revealed his diet usually contained vegetables and meat. Examining the Iceman's one remaining fingernail, scientists determined that he had been sick three times within the last six months of his life. X-rays revealed an arrowhead under the Iceman's left shoulder. This suggested that he died from that serious injury rather than from exposure.

Finally, scientists concluded that the Iceman traveled from the high alpine region in spring to his native village in the lowland valleys. There, during a conflict, the Iceman sustained a fatal injury. He retreated back to the higher elevations, where he died. Scientists recognize their hypotheses can never be proved, only supported or not supported. However, with advances in technology, scientists are able to more thoroughly investigate mysteries of nature.

Scientific investigations may disprove early hypotheses or conclusions. However, new information can cause a hypothesis or conclusion to be revised many times.

Revised Conclusion:
In spring, the Iceman traveled from the high country to the valleys. After he was involved in a violent confrontation, he climbed the mountain into a region of permanent ice where he died of his wounds.

Lesson 3 Review

Online Quiz

Use Vocabulary

1. A factor that can have more than one value is a(n) ________.
2. **Differentiate** between independent and dependent variables.

Understand Key Concepts 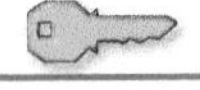

3. Which part of scientific inquiry was NOT used in this case study?
   A. Draw conclusions.
   B. Make observations.
   C. Hypothesize and predict.
   D. Make a computer model.
4. **Determine** which is the control group and which is the experimental group in the following scenario: Scientists are testing a new kind of aspirin to see whether it will relieve headaches. They give one group of volunteers the aspirin. They give another group of volunteers pills that look like aspirin but are actually sugar pills.

Interpret Graphics

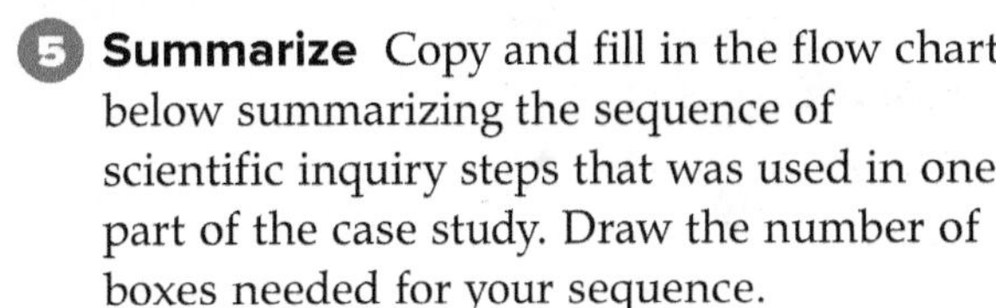

5. **Summarize** Copy and fill in the flow chart below summarizing the sequence of scientific inquiry steps that was used in one part of the case study. Draw the number of boxes needed for your sequence.

6. **Explain** What is the significance of the hop-hornbeam pollen found in the Iceman's digestive tract?

Critical Thinking

7. **Formulate** more questions about the Iceman. What would you want to know next?
8. **Evaluate** the hypotheses and conclusions made during the study of the Iceman. Do you see anything that might be an assumption? Are there holes in the research?

Lab

1-2 class periods

Materials

owl pellet

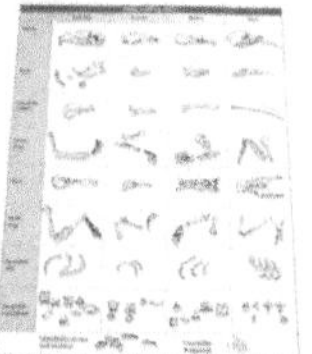

bone identification chart

probe

forceps

magnifying lens

Also needed: toothpicks, small brush, paper plate, ruler

Safety

Inferring from Indirect Evidence

In the case study about the Iceman, you learned how scientists used evidence found in or near the body to learn how the Iceman might have lived and what he ate. In this investigation, you will use similar indirect evidence to learn more about an owl.

An owl pellet is a ball of fur and feathers that contains bones, teeth, and other undigested parts of animals eaten by the owl. Owls and other birds, such as hawks and eagles, swallow their prey whole. Stomach acids digest the soft parts of the food. Skeletons and body coverings are not digested and form a ball. When the owl coughs up the ball, it might fall to the ground. Feathers, straw, or leaves often stick to the moist ball when it strikes the ground.

Ask a Question

What kinds of information can I learn about an owl by analyzing an owl pellet?

Make Observations

1. Read and complete a lab safety form.
2. Carefully measure the length, the width, and the mass of your pellet. Write the data in your Science Journal.
3. Gently examine the outside of the pellet using a magnifying lens. Do you see any sign of fur or feathers? What other substances can you identify? Record your observations.
4. Use a probe, toothpicks, and forceps to gently pull apart the pellet. Try to avoid breaking any of the tiny bones. Spread out the parts on a paper plate.
5. Copy the table into your Science Journal. Use the bone identification chart to identify each of the bones and other materials found in your pellet. Make a mark in the table for each part you identify.

2

Bone Identification Chart

Bone	Animal	Number
Skull		
Jaw		
Shoulder blade		
Forelimb		
Hind limb		
Hip/pelvis		
Rib		
Vertebrae		
Insect parts		

(t to b)Ken Karp/McGraw-Hill Education; (2-3)McGraw-Hill Education; (4-5, r)Hutchings Photography/Digital Light Source

Analyze and Conclude

6 **Assemble** the bones you find into a skeleton. You may need to locate pictures of rodents, shrews, moles, and birds.

7 **Discuss** with your teammates why parts of an animal skeleton might be missing.

8 **Write** a report that includes your data and conclusions about the owl's diet.

9 **Identify Cause and Effect** Is every bone you found in the pellet necessarily from the owl's prey? Why or why not?

10 **Analyze** What conclusions can you reach about the diet of the particular owl from which your pellet came? Can you extend this conclusion to the diets of all owls? Why or why not?

11 **The Big Idea** How did the scientific inquiry you used in the investigation compare to those used by the scientists studying the Iceman? In what ways were they the same? In what ways were they different?

Communicate Your Results

Compare your results with those of several other teams. Discuss any evidence to support that the owl pellets did or did not come from the same area.

Inquiry Extension

Put your data on the board. Use the class data to determine a mean, median, mode, and range for each type of bone.

Lab Tips

- When using your forceps, squeeze the sides very lightly so that you don't crush fragile bones.
- Use the brush to clean each bone. Try rotating the bones as you match them to the chart.
- Lay the bones on the matching box on the chart as you separate them. Then count them when you are finished.

4

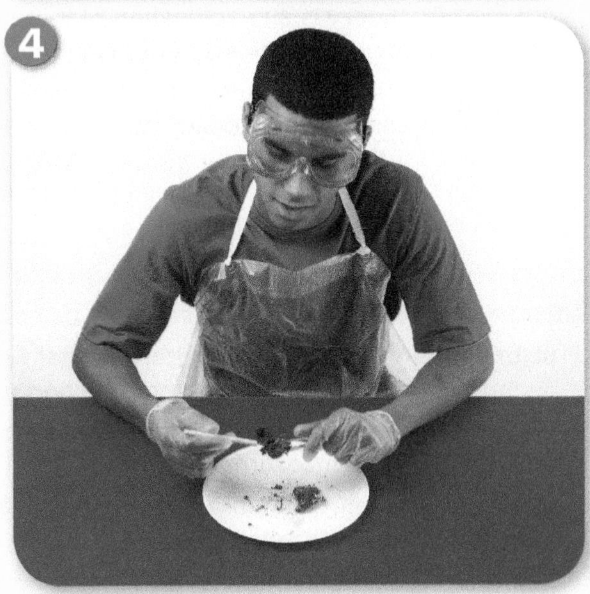

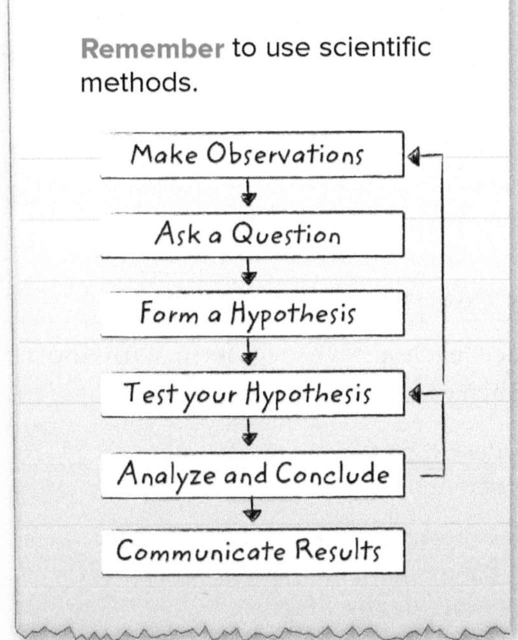

(l)U.S. Fish & Wildlife Service/John & Karen Hollingsworth; (r)Hutchings Photography/Digital Light Source

Chapter Study Guide and Review

Scientists use the process of scientific inquiry to perform scientific investigations.

Key Concepts Summary	Vocabulary
Lesson 1: Understanding Science • Scientific inquiry is a process that uses a set of skills to answer questions or to test ideas about the natural world. • A **scientific law** is a rule that describes a pattern in nature. A **scientific theory** is an explanation of things or events that is based on knowledge gained from many **observations** and investigations. • Facts are measurements, observations, and theories that can be evaluated for their validity through objective investigation. Opinions are personal views, feelings, or claims about a topic that cannot be proven true or false.	**science** p. NOS 4 **observation** p. NOS 6 **inference** p. NOS 6 **hypothesis** p. NOS 6 **prediction** p. NOS 6 **technology** p. NOS 8 **scientific theory** p. NOS 9 **scientific law** p. NOS 9 **critical thinking** p. NOS 10
Lesson 2: Measurement and Scientific Tools • Scientists worldwide use the **International System of Units (SI)** because their work is easier to confirm and repeat by their peers. • Measurement uncertainty occurs because no scientific tool can provide a perfect measurement. • Mean, median, mode, and range are statistical calculations that are used to evaluate sets of data.	**description** p. NOS 18 **explanation** p. NOS 18 **International System of Units (SI)** p. NOS 18 **significant digits** p. NOS 20
Lesson 3: Case Study: The Iceman's Last Journey • The **independent variable** is the factor a scientist changes to observe how it affects a **dependent variable.** A dependent variable is the factor a scientist measures or observes during an experiment. • Scientific inquiry was used throughout the investigation of the Iceman when hypotheses, predictions, tests, analysis, and conclusions were developed.	**variable** p. NOS 27 **independent variable** p. NOS 27 **dependent variable** p. NOS 21

Use Vocabulary

Replace each underlined term with the correct vocabulary word.

1. A description is an interpretation of observations.
2. The means are the numbers of digits in a measurement that you know with a certain degree of reliability.
3. The act of watching something and taking note of what occurs is a(n) inference.
4. A scientific theory is a rule that describes a pattern in nature.

Understand Key Concepts

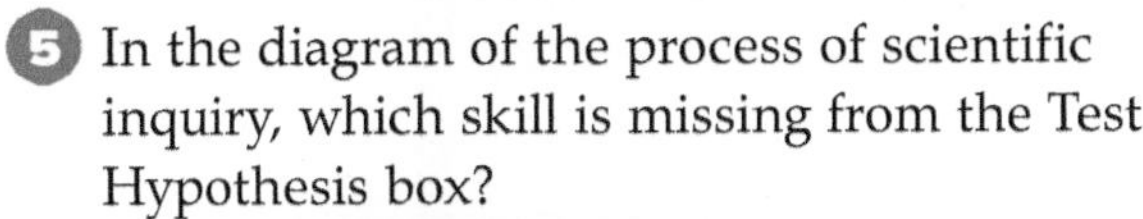

5 In the diagram of the process of scientific inquiry, which skill is missing from the Test Hypothesis box?

Test Hypothesis
- Design an Experiment
- Gather and Evaluate Evidence
- Collect Data/Record Observations

A. Analyze results.

B. Communicate results.

C. Make a model.

D. Make observations.

6 You have the following data set: 2, 3, 4, 4, 5, 7, and 8. Is 6 the mean, the median, the mode, or the range of the data set?

A. mean

B. median

C. mode

D. range

7 Which best describes an independent variable?

A. It is a factor that is not in every test.

B. It is a factor the investigator changes.

C. It is a factor you measure during a test.

D. It is a factor that stays the same in every test.

Critical Thinking

8 **Predict** what would happen if every scientist tried to use all the skills of scientific inquiry in the same order in every investigation.

9 **Assess** the role of measurement uncertainty in scientific investigations.

10 **Evaluate** the importance of having a control group in a scientific investigation.

Writing in Science

11 **Write** a five-sentence paragraph explaining why the International System of Units (SI) is an easier system to use than the English system of measurement. Be sure to include a topic sentence and a concluding sentence in your paragraph.

REVIEW THE BIG IDEA

12 What process do scientists use to perform scientific investigations? List and explain three of the skills involved.

13 Infer the purpose of the pink dye in the scientific investigation shown in the photo.

Ashley Cooper/Woodfall Wild Images/Photoshot

Math Skills

Math Practice

Use Numbers

14 Convert 162.5 hg to grams.

15 Convert 89.7 cm to millimeters.

Unit 1

Motion & Energy

1000 B.C. — 1600 — 1700

3500 B.C.
The oldest wheeled vehicle is depicted in Mesopotamia, near the Black Sea.

400 B.C.
The Greeks invent the stone-hurling catapult.

1698
English military engineer Thomas Savery invents the first crude steam engine while trying to solve the problem of pumping water out of coal mines.

1760–1850
The Industrial Revolution results in massive advances in technology and social structure in England.

1769
The first vehicle to move under its own power is designed by Nicholas Joseph Cugnot and constructed by M. Breszin. A second replica is built that weighs 3,629 kg and has a top speed of 3.2 km per hour.

1794
Eli Whitney receives a patent for the mechanical cotton gin.

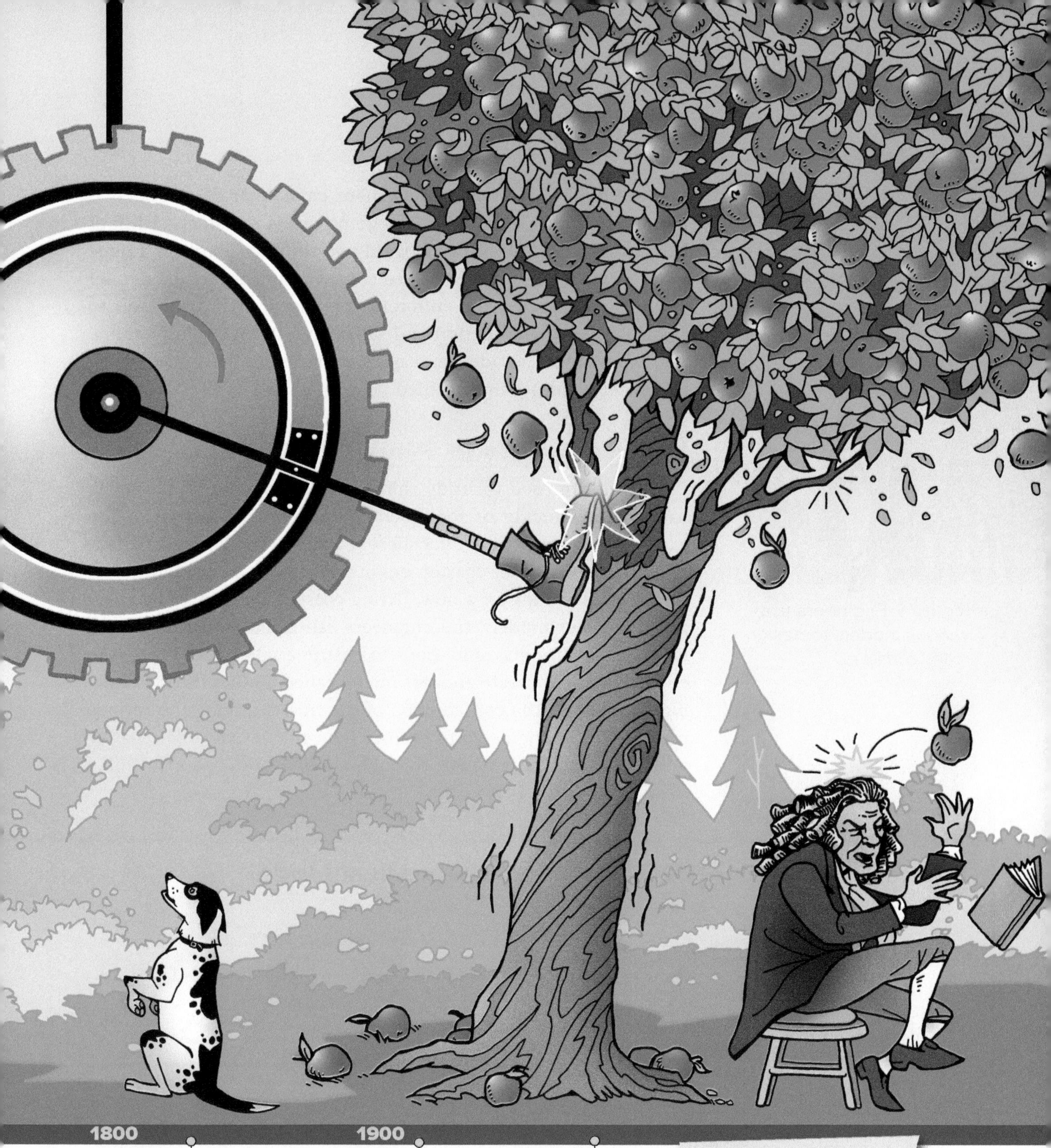

1800

1900

1817
Baron von Drais invents a machine to help him quickly wander the grounds of his estate. The machine is made of two wheels on a frame with a seat and a pair of pedals. This machine is the beginning design of the modern bicycle.

1903
Wilbur and Orville Wright build their airplane, called the Flyer, and take the first successful, powered, piloted flight.

1976
The first computer for home use is invented by college dropouts Steve Wozniak and Steve Jobs, who go on to found Apple Computer, Inc.

Visit ConnectED for this unit's STEM activity.

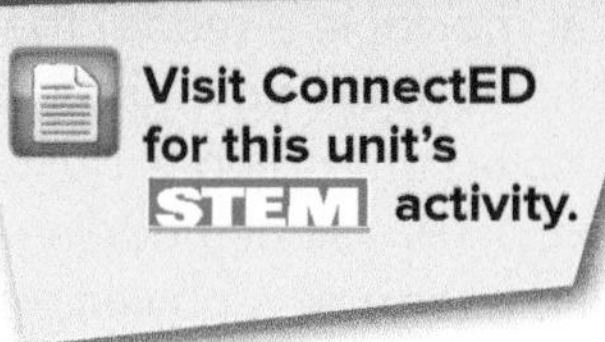

Unit 1

Nature of SCIENCE

Models

Figure 1 Engineers use various models to design roller coasters.

Have you ridden on an amusement park roller coaster such as the one in Figure 1? As you were going down the steepest hill or hanging upside down in a loop, did you think to yourself, "I hope I don't fly off this thing"? Before construction begins on a roller coaster, engineers build different models of the thrill ride to ensure proper construction and safety. A **model** is a representation of an object, an idea, or a system that is similar to the physical object or idea being studied.

Using Models in Physical Science

Models are used to study things that are too big or too small, happen too quickly or too slowly, or are too dangerous or too expensive to study directly. Different types of models serve different purposes. Roller-coaster engineers might build a physical model of their idea for a new, daring coaster. Using mathematical and computer models, the engineers can calculate the measurements of hills, angles, and loops to ensure a safe ride. Finally, the engineers might create another model called a blueprint, or drawing, that details the construction of the ride. Studying the various models allows engineers to predict how the actual roller coaster will behave when it travels through a loop or down a giant hill.

Types of Models

Physical Model

A physical model is a model that you can see and touch. It shows how parts relate to one another, how something is built, or how complex objects work. Physical models often are built to scale. A limitation of a physical model is that it might not reflect the physical behavior of the full-size object. For example, this model will not accurately show how wind will affect the ride.

Mathematical Model

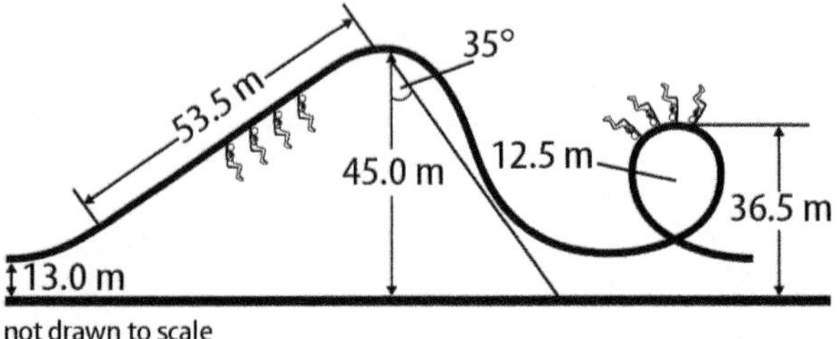

A mathematical model uses numerical data and equations to model an event or idea. Mathematical models often include input data, constants, and output data. When designing a thrill ride, engineers use mathematical models to calculate the heights, the angles of loops and turns, and the forces that affect the ride. One limitation of a mathematical model is that you cannot use it to model how different parts are assembled.

Making Models

An important factor in making a model is determining its purpose. You might need a model that physically represents an object. Or, you might need a model that includes only important elements of an object or a process. When you build a model, first determine the function of the model. What variables need to change? What materials should you use? What do you need to communicate to others? Figure 2 shows two models of a glucose molecule, each with a different purpose.

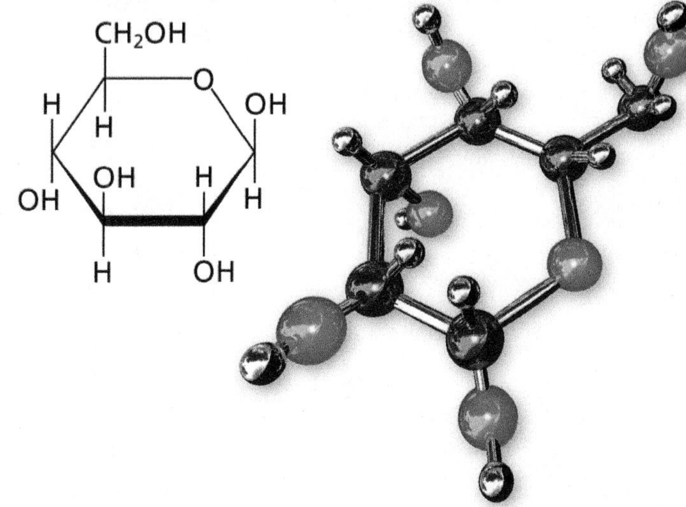

Figure 2 The model on the left is used to represent how the atoms in a glucose molecule bond together. The model on the right is a 3-D representation of the molecule, which shows how atoms might interact.

Limitations of Models

It is impossible to include all the details about an object or an idea into one model. All models have limitations. When using models to design a structure, an engineer must be aware of the information each model does and does not provide. For example, a blueprint of a roller coaster does not show the maximum weight that a car can support. However, a mathematical model would include this information. Scientists and engineers consider the purpose and the limitations of the model they use to ensure they draw accurate conclusions from models.

Computer Simulation

A computer simulation is a model that combines large amounts of data and mathematical models with computer graphic and animation programs. Simulations can contain thousands of complex mathematical models. When roller coaster engineers change variables in mathematical models, they use computer simulation to view the effects of the change.

MiniLab 30 minutes

Can you model a roller coaster?

You are an engineer with an awesome idea for a new roller coaster—the car on your roller coaster makes a jump and then lands back on the track. You model your idea to show it to managers at a theme park in hopes that you can build it.

1. Read and complete a lab safety form.
2. Create a blueprint of your roller coaster. Include a scale and measurements.
3. Follow your blueprint to build a scaled physical model of your roller coaster. Use **foam hose insulation, tape,** and other **craft supplies.**
4. Use a **marble** as a model for a roller-coaster car. Test your model. Record your observations in your Science Journal.

Analyze and Conclude

1. **Compare** your blueprint and physical model.
2. **Evaluate** After you test your physical model, list the design changes you would make to your blueprint.
3. **Identify** What are the limitations of each of your models?

Chapter 1

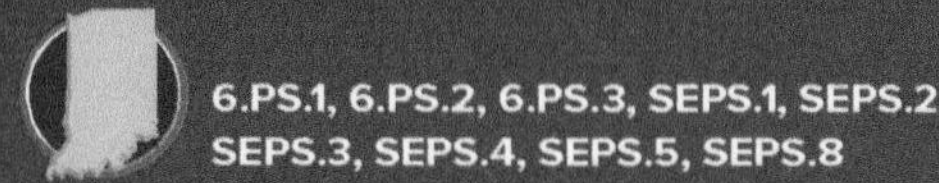

Describing Motion

What are some ways to describe motion?

How is their motion changing?

Have you ever seen a group of planes zoom through the sky at an air show? When one plane speeds up, all the planes speed up. When one plane turns, all the other planes turn in the same direction.

- What might happen if all the planes did not move in the same way?
- How could you describe the positions of the planes in the photo?
- What are some ways you could describe the motion of the planes?

Andrew Holt/Getty Images

Get Ready to Read

What do you think?

Before you read, decide if you agree or disagree with each of these statements. As you read this chapter, see if you change your mind about any of the statements.

1. Displacement is the distance an object moves along a path.
2. The description of an object's position depends on the reference point.
3. Constant speed is the same thing as average speed.
4. Velocity is another name for speed.
5. You can calculate average acceleration by dividing the change in velocity by the change in distance.
6. An object accelerates when either its speed or its direction changes.

McGraw Hill Education connectED

Your one-stop online resource

connectED.mcgraw-hill.com

LearnSmart®

Chapter Resources Files, Reading Essentials, Get Ready to Read, Quick Vocabulary

Animations, Videos, Interactive Tables

Self-checks, Quizzes, Tests

Project-Based Learning Activities

Lab Manuals, Safety Videos, Virtual Labs & Other Tools

Vocabulary, Multilingual eGlossary, Vocab eGames, Vocab eFlashcards

Personal Tutors

Lesson 1

Reading Guide

Key Concepts 

ESSENTIAL QUESTIONS

- How does the description of an object's position depend on a reference point?
- How can you describe the position of an object in two dimensions?
- What is the difference between distance and displacement?

Vocabulary

reference point p. 9

position p. 9

motion p. 13

displacement p. 13

 Multilingual eGlossary

6.PS.1, SEPS.5

Position and Motion

Inquiry Where are you?

A short time ago, people on this ship probably saw only open ocean. They knew where they were only by looking at the instruments on the ship. But the situation has changed. How can the lighthouse help the ship's crew guide the ship safely to shore?

Launch Lab

10 minutes

How do you get there from here?

How would you give instructions to a friend who was trying to walk from one place to another in your classroom?

1. Read and complete a lab safety form.
2. Place a sheet of **paper** labeled *North, East, South,* and *West* on the floor.
3. Walk from the paper to one of the three locations your teacher has labeled in the classroom. Have a partner record the number of steps and the directions of movement in his or her Science Journal.
4. Using these measurements, write instructions other students could follow to move from the paper to the location.
5. Repeat steps 3 and 4 for the other locations.

Think About This

1. How did your instructions to each location compare to those written by other groups?
2. **Key Concept** How did the description of your movement depend on the point at which you started?

Describing Position

How would you describe where you are right now? You might say you are sitting one meter to the left of your friend. Perhaps you would explain that you are at home, which is two houses north of your school. You might instead say that your house is ten blocks east of the center of town, or even 150 million kilometers from the Sun.

What do all these descriptions have in common? Each description states your location relative to a certain point. *A* **reference point** *is the starting point you choose to describe the location, or position, of an object.* The reference points in the first paragraph are your friend, your school, the center of town, and the Sun.

Each description of your location also includes your distance and direction from the reference point. Describing your location in this way defines your position. *A* **position** *is an object's distance and direction from a reference point.* A complete description of your position includes a distance, a direction, and a reference point.

Reading Check What are two ways you could describe your position right now?

SCIENCE USE V. COMMON USE

relative
Science Use compared (to)
Common Use a member of your family

Hutchings Photography/Digital Light Source

Describing Position 

Figure 1 The arrows indicate the distances and directions from different reference points.

Visual Check How do you know which reference point is farther from the table?

Using a Reference Point to Describe Position

Why do you need a reference point to describe position? Suppose you are planning a family picnic. You want your cousin to arrive at the park early to save your favorite picnic table. The park is shown in Figure 1. How would you describe the position of your favorite table to your cousin? First, choose a reference point that a person can easily find. In this park, the statue is a good choice. Next, describe the direction that the table is from the reference point–toward the slide. Finally, say how far the table is from the statue–about 10 m. You would tell your cousin that the position of the table is about 10 m from the statue, toward the slide.

FOLDABLES®

Fold a sheet of paper to make a half book. Use it to organize your notes about how position and motion are related.

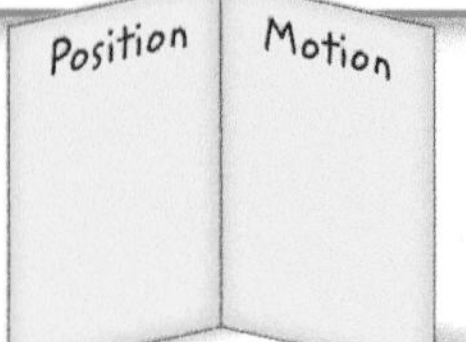

Reading Check How could you describe the position of a different table using the statue as a reference point?

Changing the Reference Point

The description of an object's position depends on the reference point. Suppose you choose the drinking fountain in Figure 1 as the reference point instead of the statue. You could say that the direction of the table is toward the dead tree. Now the distance is measured from the drinking fountain to the table. You could tell your cousin that the table is about 12 m from the drinking fountain, toward the dead tree. The description of the table's position changed because the reference point is different. Its actual position did not change at all.

 **Key Concept Check** How does the description of an object's position depend on a reference point?

Figure 2 If east is the reference direction, then the museum is in the positive direction from the bus stop. The library is in the negative direction.

The Reference Direction

When you describe an object's position, you compare its location to a reference direction. In Figure 1, the reference direction for the first reference point is toward the slide. Sometimes the words *positive* and *negative* are used to describe direction. The reference direction is the positive (+) direction. The opposite direction is the negative (−) direction. Suppose you specify east as the reference direction in Figure 2. You could say the museum's entrance is +80 m from the bus stop. The library's entrance is −40 m from the bus stop. To a friend, you would probably just say the museum is two buildings east of the bus stop and the library is the building west of the bus stop. Sometimes, however, using the words *positive* and *negative* to describe direction is useful for explaining changes in an object's position.

ACADEMIC VOCABULARY

specify
(verb) to indicate or identify

MiniLab

10 minutes

Why is a reference point useful? 

To find an object's position, you need to know its distance and direction from a reference point.

1. Read and complete a lab safety form.
2. Put a **sticky note** at the 50-cm mark of a **meterstick.** This is your reference point.
3. Place a **small object** at the 40-cm mark. It is 10 cm in the negative direction from the reference point.
4. Copy the table in your Science Journal. Continue moving the object and recording its distance, its reference direction, and its position to complete the table.

Position of Object

Distance (cm)	Reference Direction	Position (cm)
10 cm	negative	40 cm
40 cm	positive	
15 cm	positive	
	positive	75 cm
		30 cm

Analyze and Conclude

1. **Recognize Cause and Effect** How would the data in the table change if the positions were the same but the reference point was at the 40-cm mark?
2. **Key Concept** Why is a reference point useful in describing positions of an object?

Describing Position in Two Dimensions

Figure 3 You need two reference directions to describe the position of a building in the city.

Visual Check If the library is the reference point, how would you describe the position of your house in two dimensions?

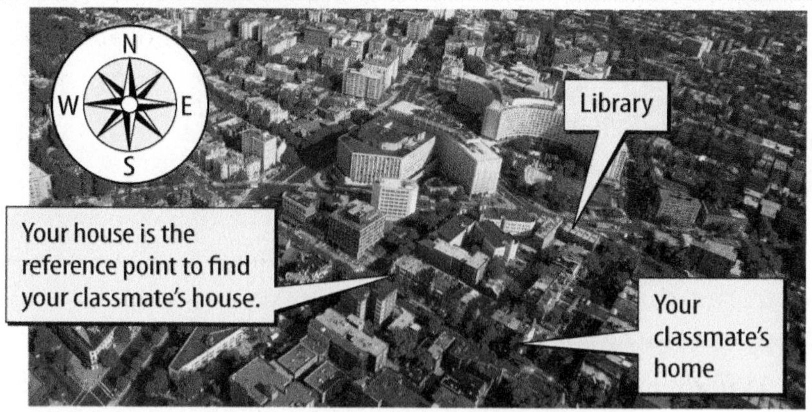

REVIEW VOCABULARY

dimension
distance or length measured in one direction

Describing Position in Two Dimensions

You were able to describe the position of the picnic table in the park in one dimension. Your cousin had to walk in only one direction to reach the table. But sometimes you need to describe an object's position using more than one reference direction. The city shown in Figure 3 is an example. To describe the position of a house in a city might require two reference directions. When you describe a position using two directions, you are using two dimensions.

Reference Directions in Two Dimensions

To describe a position on the map in Figure 3, you might choose north and east or south and west as reference directions. Sometimes north, south, east, and west are not the most useful reference directions. If you are playing checkers and want to describe the position of a certain checker, you might use "right" and "forward" as reference directions. If you are describing the position of a certain window on a skyscraper, you might choose "left" and "up" as reference directions.

Reading Check What are two other reference directions you might use to describe the position of a building in a city?

Locating a Position in Two Dimensions

Finding a position in two dimensions is similar to finding a position in one dimension. First, choose a reference point. To locate your classmate's home on the map in Figure 3, you could use your home as a reference point. Next, specify reference directions–north and east. Then, determine the distance along each reference direction. In the figure, your classmate's house is one block southeast of your house.

Key Concept Check How can you describe the position of an object in two dimensions?

Glowimages/Getty Images

Describing Changes in Position

Sometimes you need to describe how an object's position changes. You can tell that the boat in Figure 4 moved because its position changed relative, or compared, to the buoy. **Motion** *is the process of changing position.*

WORD ORIGIN

motion
from Latin *motere;* means "to move"

Motion Relative to a Reference Point

Is the man in the boat in Figure 4 in motion? Suppose the fishing pole is the reference point. Because the positions of the man and the pole do not change relative to each other, the man does not move relative to the pole. Now suppose the buoy is the reference point. Because the man's distance from the buoy changes, he is in motion relative to the buoy.

◀ **Figure 4** The man in the boat is not in motion compared to his fishing pole. He is in motion compared to the buoy.

Distance and Displacement

Suppose a baseball player runs the bases, as shown in Figure 5. Distance is the length of the path the player runs, as shown by the red arrows. **Displacement** *is the difference between the initial (first) position and the final position of an object.* It is shown in the figure by the blue arrows. Notice that distance and displacement are equal only if the motion is in one direction.

Key Concept Check What is the difference between distance and displacement?

Figure 5 Distance depends on the path taken. Displacement depends only on the initial and final positions. ▼

Distance and Displacement

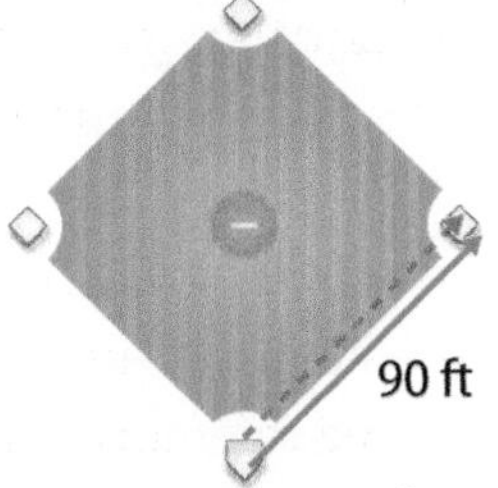

When a player runs to first base, the distance is 90 ft and the displacement is 90 ft toward first base.

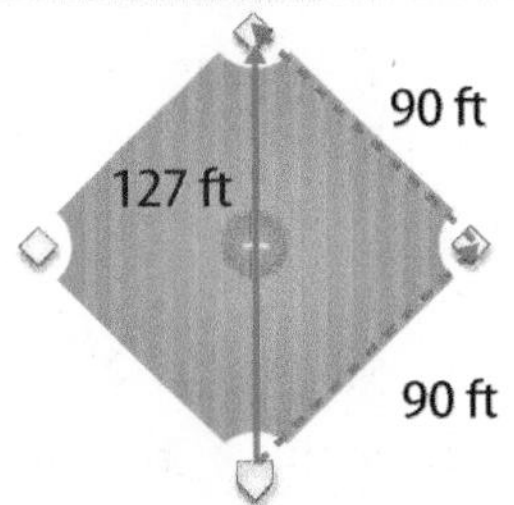

When a player runs to second base, the distance is 180 ft, but the displacement is 127 ft toward second base.

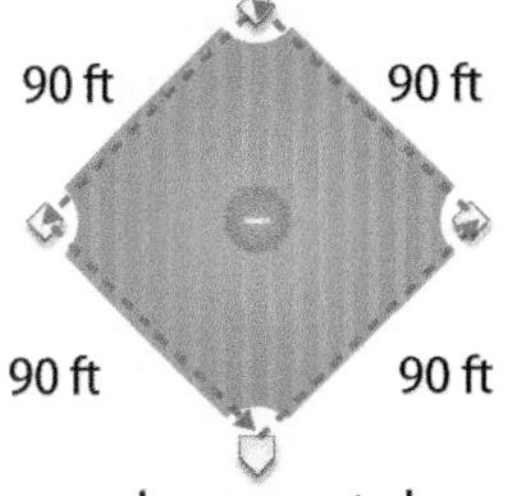

When a player runs to home base, the distance is 360 ft, but the displacement is 0 ft.

Lesson 1 Review

Visual Summary

A reference point, a reference direction, and distance are needed to describe the position of an object.

An object is in motion if its position changes relative to a reference point.

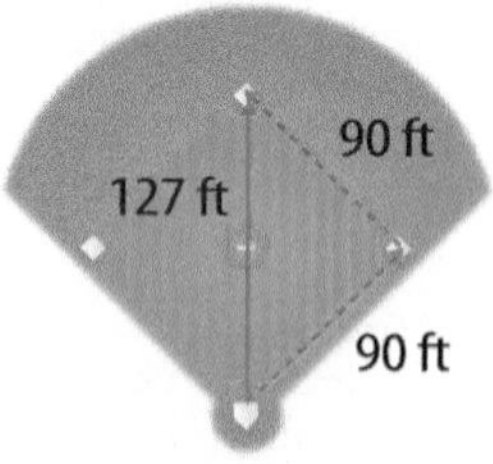

The distance an object moves and the object's displacement are not always the same.

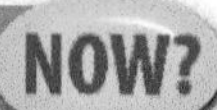

Use your lesson Foldable to review the lesson. Save your Foldable for the project at the end of the chapter.

What do you think NOW?

You first read the statements below at the beginning of the chapter.

1. Displacement is the distance an object moves along a path.
2. The description of an object's position depends on the reference point.

Did you change your mind about whether you agree or disagree with the statements? Rewrite any false statements to make them true.

Use Vocabulary

1. **Define** *motion* in your own words.
2. The difference between the initial position and the final position of an object is its ________.

Understand Key Concepts 

3. **Explain** why a description of position depends on a reference point.
4. To describe a position in more than one dimension, you must use more than one
   - **A.** displacement.
   - **B.** reference direction.
   - **C.** reference point.
   - **D.** type of motion.
5. **Apply** If you walk 2 km from your house to a store and then back home, what is your displacement?

Interpret Graphics

6. **Interpret** Using 12 as the reference point, how you can tell that the hands of the clock on the right have moved from their previous position, shown on the left?

7. **Summarize** Copy and fill in the graphic organizer below to identify the three things that must be included in the description of position.

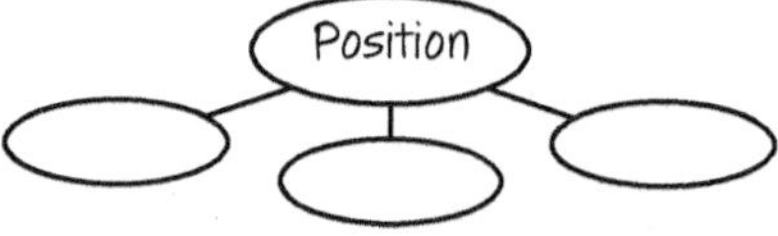

Critical Thinking

8. **Compare** Relative to some reference points, your nose is in motion when you run. Relative to others, it is not in motion. Give one example of each.

HOW IT WORKS

GPS to the Rescue!

How Technology Helps Bring Home Family Pets

You've seen the signs tacked to streetlights and telephone poles: *LOST! Golden retriever. Reward. Please Call!* Losing a pet can be heartbreaking. Fortunately, there's an alternative to posting fliers—a pet collar with a Global Positioning System (GPS) chip that helps locate the pet. Here is how GPS can help you track or locate your pet:

Cell phone tracking display ▶

Cell phone tower

GPS Collar

1 GPS is a network of at least 24 satellites in orbit around Earth. Each satellite circles Earth twice a day and sends information to ground receivers.

2 GPS satellites act as reference points. Ground-based GPS receivers compare the time a signal is transmitted by a satellite to the time it is received on Earth. The difference indicates the satellite's distance. Signals from as many as four satellites are used to pinpoint a user's exact position.

3 GPS uses computer technology to calculate location, speed, direction, and time. The same GPS technology used to locate or guide airplanes, cars, and campers can help find a lost pet anywhere on Earth!

4 A GPS pet collar works much the same as any other GPS receiver. Once it is activated, the collar can transmit a message to a Web site or to the owner's cell phone.

It's Your Turn

DESIGN GPS technology has revolutionized the way people track and locate almost everything. Can you think of a new application for GPS technology? Write an advertisement or a TV commercial for a new idea that puts GPS technology to work!

Lesson 2

Reading Guide

Key Concepts 

ESSENTIAL QUESTIONS

- What is speed?
- How can you use a distance-time graph to calculate average speed?
- What are ways velocity can change?

Vocabulary

speed p. 17
constant speed p. 18
instantaneous speed p. 18
average speed p. 19
velocity p. 23

Multilingual eGlossary

6.PS.1, 6.PS.2, SEPS.1, SEPS.2, SEPS.5

Speed and Velocity

How Fast?

When you hear the word *cheetah,* you might think of how fast a cheetah can run. As the fastest land animal on Earth, it can reach a speed of 30 m/s for a short period of time. Other than how fast it runs, how might you describe the motion of a cheetah?

Heinrich van den Berg/Getty Images

Launch Lab

10 minutes

How can motion change? 

Have you ever used a tube slide at a playground or at a water park? You can build a marble tube slide from foam tubes. You can then use the slide to observe how the motion of a marble changes as it rolls down the slide.

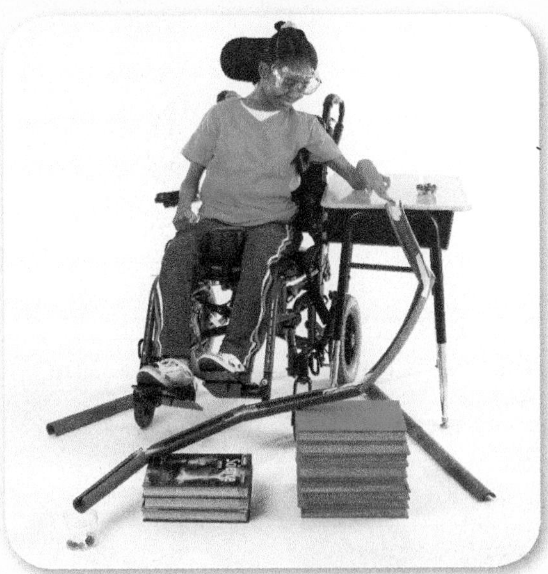

1. Read and complete a lab safety form.
2. Join **foam tubes** into a tube slide, using **masking tape** to connect the tubes. Use a desk and other objects to support the slide so that it changes direction and slopes toward the floor.
3. Drop a **marble** into the top of the slide. Observe the changes in its motion as it rolls through the tubes. Have the marble roll into a **container** at the bottom of the slide.

Think About This

1. In what ways did the motion of the marble change as it moved down the slide?
2. **Key Concept** At what parts of the tube slide did the marble move fastest? At what parts did it move slowest?

What is speed?

How fast do you walk when you are hungry and there is good food on the table? How fast do you move when you have a chore to do? Sometimes you move quickly, and sometimes you move slowly. One way you can describe how fast you move is to determine your speed. **Speed** *is a measure of the distance an object travels per unit of time.*

 **Key Concept Check** What is speed?

Units of Speed

You can calculate speed by dividing the distance traveled by the time it takes to go that distance. The units of speed are units of distance divided by units of time. The SI unit for speed is meters per second (m/s). Other units are shown in Table 1. What units of distance and time are used in each example?

Table 1 Typical Speeds

Airplane 245 m/s 882 km/h 548 mph	
Car on a Highway 27 m/s 97 km/h 60 mph	
Person Walking 1.3 m/s 4.7 km/h 2.9 mph	

Table 1 Different units of distance and time can be used to determine units of speed.

Constant and Changing Speed

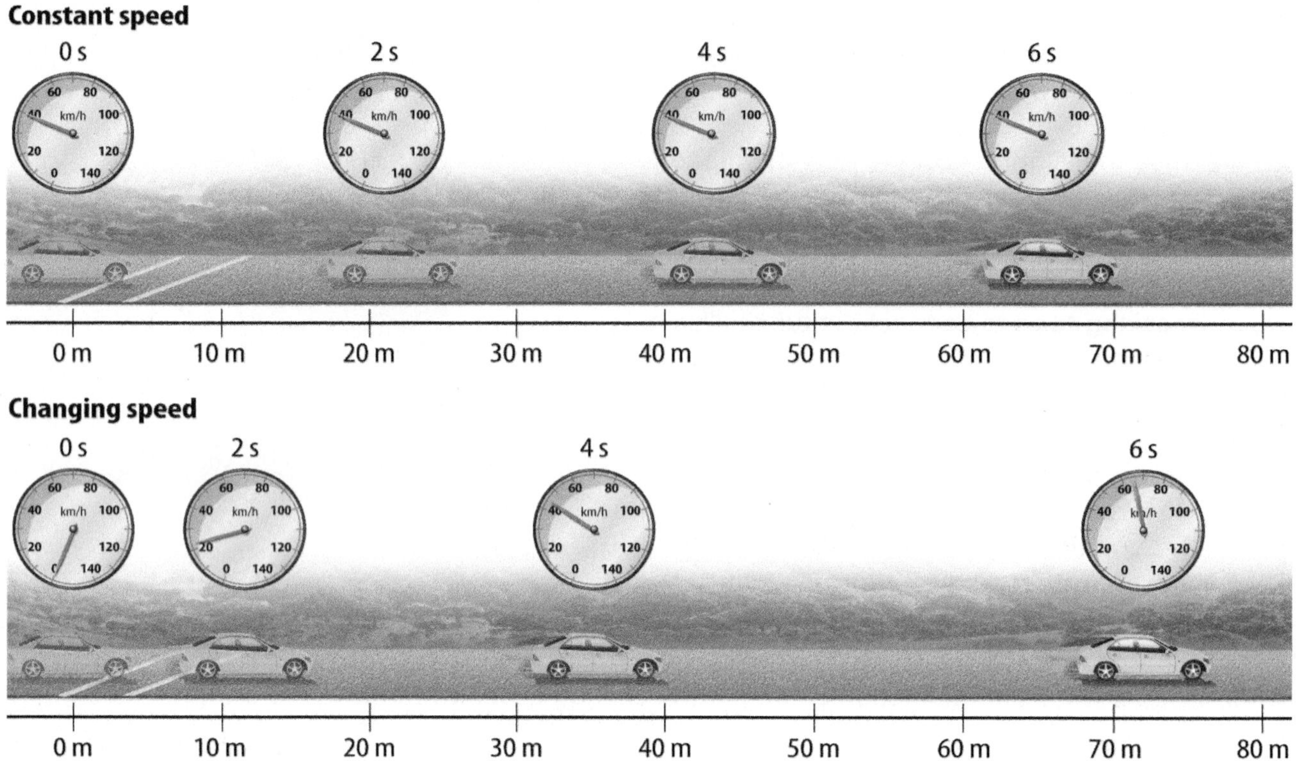

Figure 6 When the car moves with constant speed, it moves the same distance each period of time. When the car's speed changes, it moves a different distance each period of time.

Visual Check What is the bottom car's instantaneous speed at 6 s?

Constant Speed

What happens to your speed when you ride in a car? Sometimes you ride at a steady speed. If you move away from a stop sign, your speed increases. You slow down when you pull into a parking space.

Think about a time that a car's speed does not change. As the car at the top of Figure 6 travels along the road, the speedometer above each position shows that the car is moving at the same speed at each location and time. Each second, the car moves 11 m. Because it moves the same distance each second, its speed is not changing. **Constant speed** *is the rate of change of position in which the same distance is traveled each second.* The car is moving at a constant speed of 11 m/s.

Changing Speed

How is the motion of the car at the bottom of Figure 6 different from the motion of the car at the top? Between 0 s and 2 s, the car at the bottom travels about 10 m. Between 4 s and 6 s, however, the car travels more than 20 m. Because the car travels a different distance each second, its speed is changing.

If the speed of an object is not constant, you might want to know its speed at a certain moment. **Instantaneous speed** *is speed at a specific instant in time.* You can see a car's instantaneous speed on its speedometer.

Reading Check How would the distance the car travels each second change if it were slowing down?

Average Speed

Describing an object's speed is easy if the speed is constant. But how can you describe the speed of an object when it is speeding up or slowing down? One way is to calculate its average speed. **Average speed** *is the total distance traveled divided by the total time taken to travel that distance.* You can calculate average speed using the equation below.

Average Speed Equation

$$\text{average speed (in m/s)} = \frac{\text{total distance (in m)}}{\text{total time (in s)}}$$

$$\bar{v} = \frac{d}{t}$$

The symbol $\bar{v}$ represents the term "average velocity." You will read more about velocity, and how it relates to speed, later in this lesson. However, at this point, $\bar{v}$ is simply used as the symbol for "average speed." The SI unit for speed, meters per second (m/s), is used in the above equation. You could instead use other units of distance and time in the average speed equation, such as kilometers and hours.

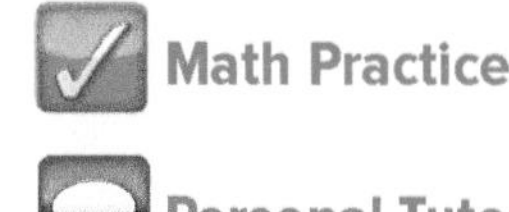

Personal Tutor

Math Skills — Average Speed Equation

Solve for Average Speed Melissa shot a model rocket 360 m into the air. It took the rocket 4 s to fly that far. What was the average speed of the rocket?

1. **This is what you know:** distance: $d = 360$ m; time: $t = 4$ s
2. **This is what you need to find:** average speed: $\bar{v}$
3. **Use this formula:** $\bar{v} = \frac{d}{t}$
4. **Substitute:** the values for *d* and *t* into the formula and divide. $\bar{v} = \frac{360 \text{ m}}{4 \text{ s}} = 90$ m/s

Answer: The average speed was 90 m/s.

Practice

1. It takes Ahmed 50 s on his bicycle to reach his friend's house 250 m away. What is his average speed?
2. A truck driver makes a trip that covers 2,380 km in 28 hours. What is the driver's average speed?

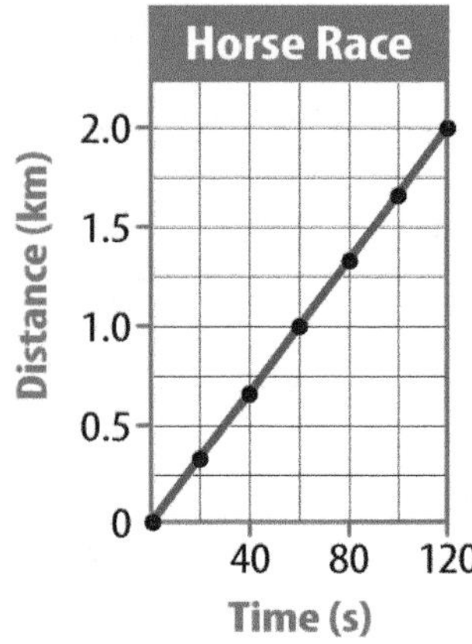

Figure 7 According to this distance-time graph, it took 2 min for the horse to run 2 km.

Visual Check How would this distance-time graph be different if the horse's speed changed over time?

Distance-Time Graphs

The Kentucky Derby is often described as the most exciting two minutes in sports. The thoroughbred horses in this race run for a distance of 2 km. The speeds of the horses change many times during a race, but Figure 7 describes what a horse's motion might be if its speed did not change. The graph shows the distance a horse might travel when distance measurements are made every 20 seconds. Follow the height of the line from the left side of the graph to the right side. You can see how the distance the horse ran changed over time.

Graphs like the one in Figure 7 can show how one measurement compares to another. When you study motion, two measurements frequently compared to each other are distance and time. The graphs that show these comparisons are called distance-time graphs. Notice that the change in the distance the horse ran around the track is the same each second on the graph. This means the horse was moving with a constant speed. Constant speed is shown as a straight line on a distance-time graph.

Reading Check How is constant speed shown on a distance-time graph?

MiniLab

15 minutes

How can you graph motion?

You can represent motion with a distance-time graph.

1. Read and complete a lab safety form.
2. Use **masking tape** to mark a starting point on the floor.
3. As you cross the starting point, start a **stopwatch.** Stop walking after 2 s. Measure the distance with a **meterstick.** Record the time and distance in your Science Journal.
4. Repeat step 3 by walking at about the same speed for 4 s and then for 6 s.
5. Use the graph in Figure 7 as an example to create a distance-time graph of your data. The line on the graph should be as close to the points as possible.

Analyze and Conclude

1. **Predict** Based on the graph, how far would you probably walk at the same speed in 8 s?
2. **Key Concept** Look back at the average speed equation. Explain how you could use your graph to find your average walking speed.

Comparing Speeds on a Distance-Time Graph

You can use distance-time graphs to compare the motion of two different objects. Figure 8 is a distance-time graph that compares the motion of two horses that ran the Kentucky Derby. The motion of horse A is shown by the blue line. The motion of horse B is shown by the orange line. Look at the far right side of the graph. When horse A reached the finish line, horse B was only 1.5 km from the starting point of the race.

Recall that average speed is distance traveled divided by time. Horse A traveled a greater distance than horse B in the same amount of time. Horse A had greater average speed. Compare how steep the lines are on the graph. The measure of steepness is the slope. The steeper the line, the greater the slope. The blue line is steeper than the orange line. Steeper lines on distance-time graphs indicate faster speeds.

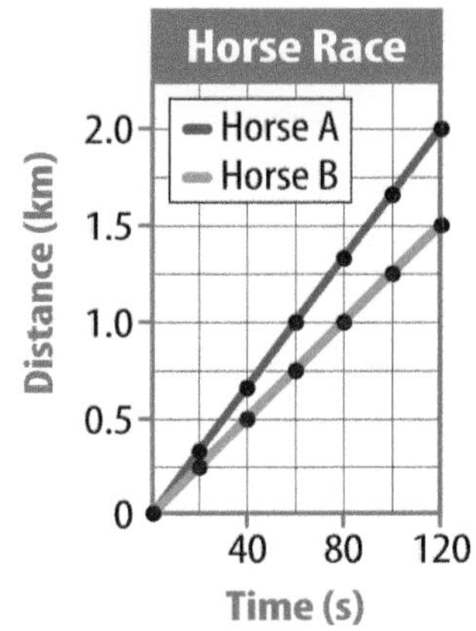

Figure 8 You can tell that horse A ran a faster race than horse B because the blue line is steeper than the orange line.

Using a Distance-Time Graph to Calculate Speed

You can use distance-time graphs to calculate the average speed of an object. The motion of a trail horse traveling at a constant speed is shown on the graph in Figure 9. The steps needed to calculate the average speed from a distance-time graph also are shown in the figure.

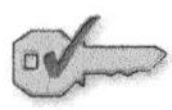

Key Concept Check How can you use a distance-time graph to calculate average speed?

Average Speed

Figure 9 The average speed of the horse from 60 s to 120 s can be calculated from this distance-time graph.

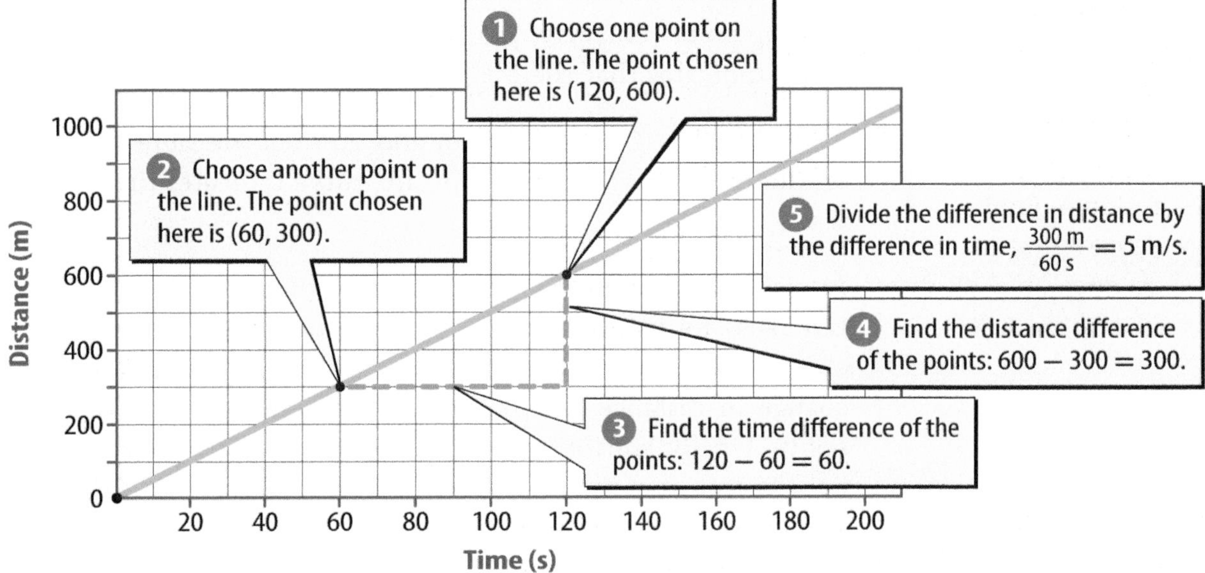

Visual Check How does the average speed of the horse from 60 s to 120 s compare to its average speed from 120 s to 180 s?

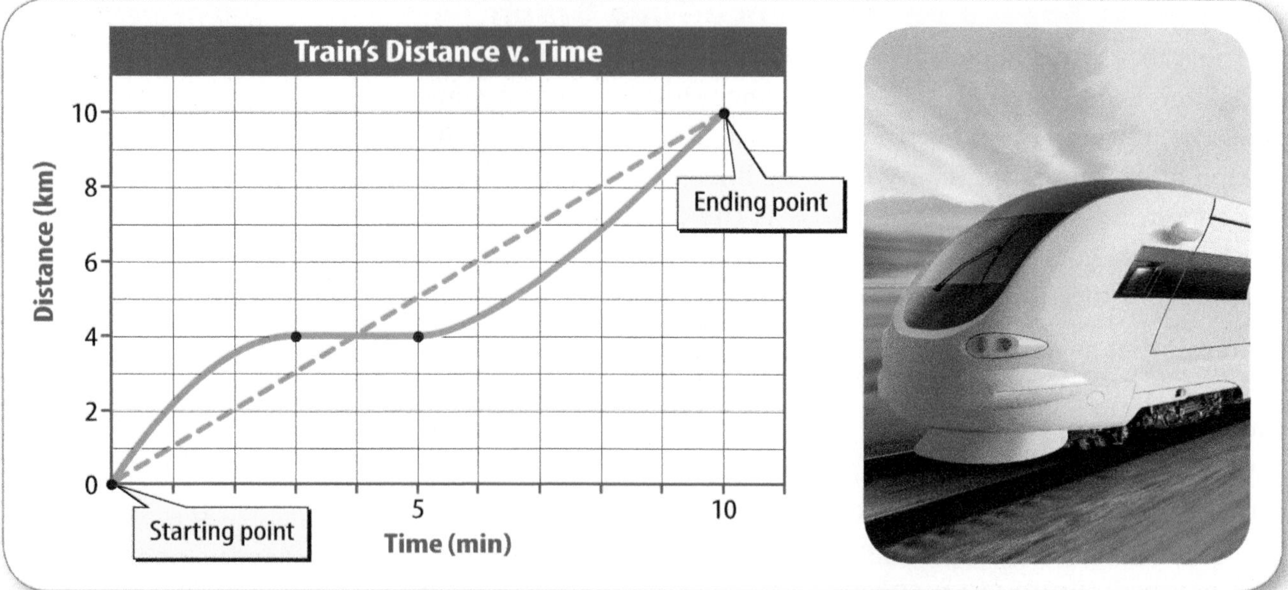

Animation

Figure 10 Even though the train's speed is not constant, you can calculate its average speed from a distance-time graph.

FOLDABLES®

Make a horizontal three-tab book and label it as shown. Use it to summarize how changes in speed are represented on a distance-time graph.

Distance-Time Graph and Changing Speed

So far, the distance-time graphs in this lesson have included straight lines. Distance-time graphs have straight lines only for objects that move at a constant speed. The graph in Figure 10 for the motion of a train is different. Because the speed of the train changes instead of being constant, its motion on a distance-time graph is a curved line.

Slowing Down Notice how the shape of the line in Figure 10 changes. Between 0 min and 3 min, its slope decreases. The downward curve indicates that the train slowed down.

Stopping What happened between 3 min and 5 min? The line during these times is horizontal. The train's distance from the starting point remains 4 km. A horizontal line on a distance-time graph indicates that there is no motion.

Speeding Up Between 5 min and 10 min, the slope of the line on the graph increases. The upward curve indicates that the train was speeding up.

Average Speed Even when the speed of an object changes, you can calculate its average speed from a distance-time graph. First, choose a starting point and an ending point. Next, determine the change in distance and the change in time between these two points. Finally, substitute these values into the average speed equation. The slope of the dashed line in Figure 10 represents the train's average speed between 0 minutes and 10 minutes.

Reading Check What is the average speed of the train for the trip shown in Figure 10?

Velocity

Often, describing just the speed of a moving object does not completely describe its motion. If you describe the motion of a bouncing ball, for example, you would also describe the direction of the ball's movement. Both speed and direction are part of motion. **Velocity** *is the speed and the direction of a moving object.*

Representing Velocity

In Lesson 1, an arrow represented the displacement of an object from a reference point. The velocity of an object also can be represented by an arrow, as shown in **Figure 11**. The length of the arrow indicates the speed. A greater speed is shown by a longer arrow. The arrow points in the direction of the object's motion.

In **Figure 11**, both students are walking at 1.5 m/s. Because the speeds are equal, both arrows are the same length. But the girl is walking to the left and the boy is walking to the right. The arrows point in different directions. The students have different velocities because each student has a different direction of motion.

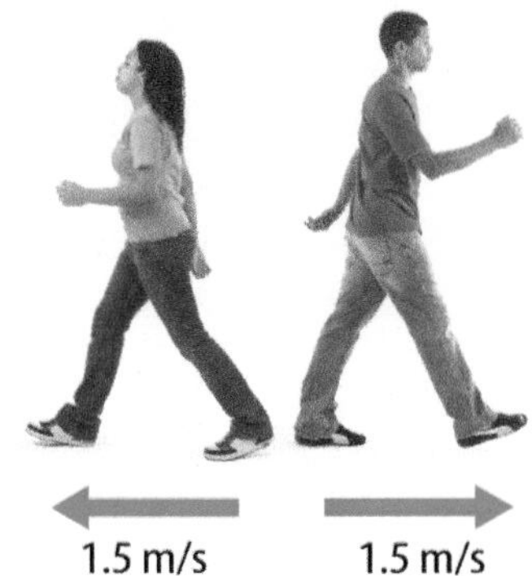

▲ **Figure 11** The students are walking with the same speed but different velocities.

WORD ORIGIN

velocity
from Latin *velocitas;* means "swiftness, speed"

Changes in Velocity

Look at the bouncing ball in **Figure 12**. Notice how from one position to the next, the arrows showing the velocity of the ball change direction and length. The changes in the arrows mean that the velocity is constantly changing. Velocity changes when the speed of an object changes, when the direction that the object moves changes, or when both the speed and the direction change. You will read about changes in velocity in Lesson 3.

 **Key Concept Check** How can velocity change?

Applying Practices

When and Where Go online to graphically describe an object's motion using time and position.

Figure 12 The velocity of the ball changes continually because both the speed and the direction of the ball change as the ball bounces. ▼

Changing Speed and Direction

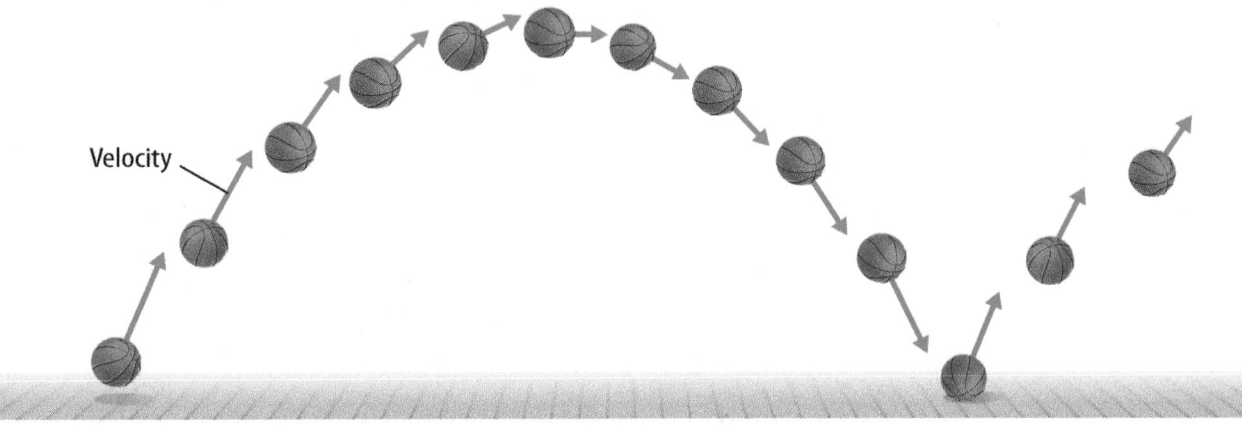

Hutchings Photography/Digital Light Source

Visual Check Are there two positions of the bouncing ball in which the velocity is the same? Explain.

Lesson 2 Review

Visual Summary

Speed is a measure of the distance an object travels per unit of time. You can describe an object's constant speed, instantaneous speed, or average speed.

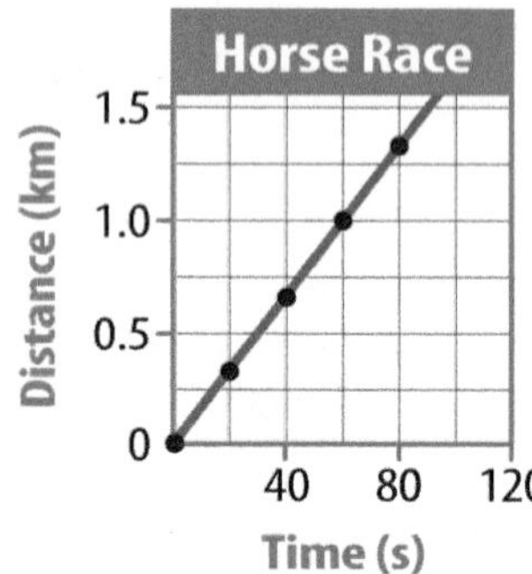

A distance-time graph shows the speed of an object.

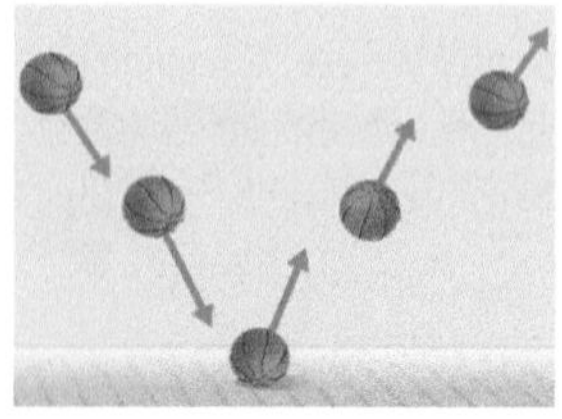

Velocity includes both the speed and the direction of motion.

FOLDABLES®

Use your lesson Foldable to review the lesson. Save your Foldable for the project at the end of the chapter.

What do you think NOW?

You first read the statements below at the beginning of the chapter.

3. Constant speed is the same thing as average speed.

4. Velocity is another name for speed.

Did you change your mind about whether you agree or disagree with the statements? Rewrite any false statements to make them true.

Use Vocabulary

1. **Distinguish** between speed and velocity.
2. **Define** *constant speed* in your own words.

Understand Key Concepts 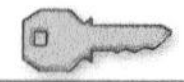

3. **Recall** How can you calculate average speed from a distance-time graph?
4. **Analyze** Describe three ways a bicyclist can change velocity.
5. Which choice is a unit of speed?

A. h/mi **C.** m^2/s
B. km/h **D.** $N \cdot m^2$

Interpret Graphics

6. **Organize Information** Copy and fill in the graphic organizer below to show possible steps for making a distance-time graph.

7. **Interpret** What does the shape of each line indicate about the object's speed?

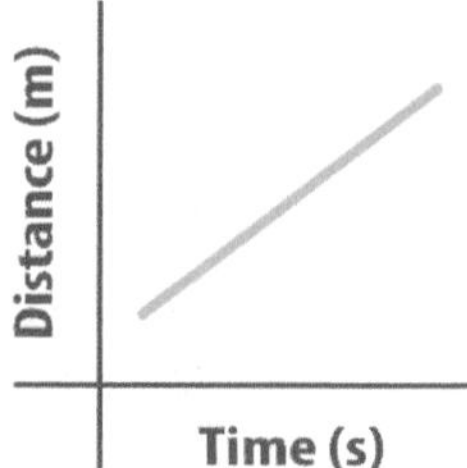

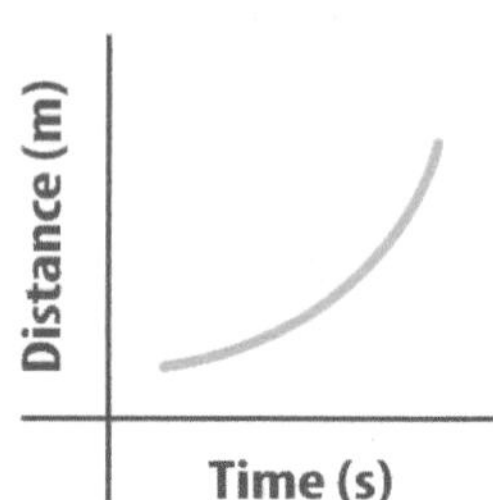

Critical Thinking

8. **Decide** Aaron leaves one city at noon. He has to be at another city 186 km away at 3:00 P.M. The speed limit the entire way is 65 km/h. Can he arrive at the second city on time? Explain.

Math Skills 

 Math Practice

9. A train traveled 350 km in 2.5 h. What was the average speed of the train?

What do you measure to calculate speed?

Materials

meterstick

stopwatch

wind-up toys (4)

calculator

graph paper

Safety

You turn on the television and see a news report. It shows trees that are bent almost to the ground because of a strong wind. Is it a hurricane or a tropical storm? The type of storm depends on the speed of the wind. A meteorologist must measure both distance and time before calculating the wind's speed.

Learn It

When you **measure,** you use a tool to find a quantity. To find the average speed of an object, you measure the distance it travels and the time it travels. You can then calculate speed using the average speed equation. In this lab, you use distance and time measurements to calculate speeds of moving toys.

Try It

1. Read and complete a lab safety form.
2. Copy the data table on this page into your Science Journal. Add more lines as you need them.
3. Choose appropriate starting and ending points on the floor. Use a meterstick to measure the distance between these points. Record this distance to the nearest centimeter.
4. Wind one toy. Measure in tenths of a second the time the toy takes to travel from start to finish. Record the time in the data table.
5. Repeat steps 3 and 4 for three more toys. Vary the distance from start to finish for each toy.

Apply It

6. **Calculate** the average speed of each toy. Record the speeds in your data table.
7. **Create** a bar graph of your data. Place the name of each toy on the *x*-axis and the average speed on the *y*-axis.
8. **Key Concept** Use the definition of *speed* to explain why the average speeds of the toys can be compared, even though the toys traveled different distances.

Toy Speeds

Toy	Distance (m)	Time (s)	Average Speed (m/s)

(b)Aaron Haupt, (others)Hutchings Photography/Digital Light Source

Lesson 3

Reading Guide

Key Concepts 
ESSENTIAL QUESTIONS

- What are three ways an object can accelerate?
- What does a speed-time graph indicate about an object's motion?

Vocabulary

acceleration p. 27

 Multilingual eGlossary

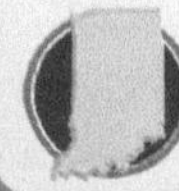 BrainPOP®

6.PS.1, 6.PS.3, SEPS.2, SEPS.3, SEPS.4, SEPS.5, SEPS.8

Acceleration

Inquiry Is velocity changing?

How does the velocity of this motorcycle racer change as he speeds along the track? As he enters a curve, he slows down, leans to the side, and changes direction. On a straightaway, he speeds up and moves in a straight line. How can the velocity of a moving object change?

Launch Lab

10 minutes

In what ways can velocity change?

As you walk, your motion changes in many ways. You probably slow down when the ground is uneven. You might speed up when you realize that you are late for dinner. You change direction many times. What would these changes in velocity look like on a distance-time graph?

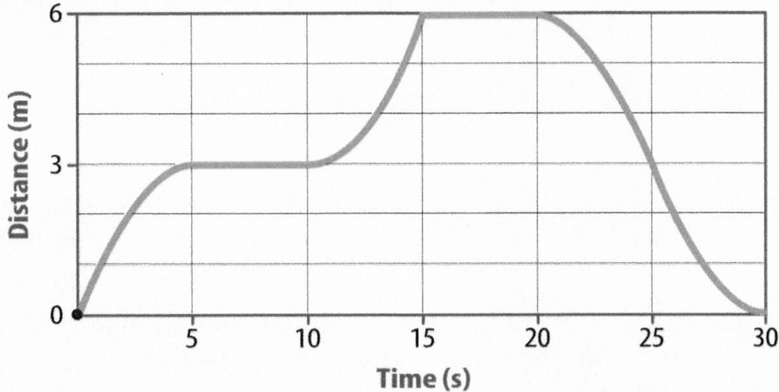

1. Read and complete a lab safety form.
2. Use a **meterstick** to measure a 6-m straight path along the floor. Place a mark with **masking tape** at 0 m, 3 m, and 6 m.
3. Look at the graph above. Decide what type of motion occurs during each 5-second period.
4. Try to walk along your path according to the motion shown on the graph. Have your partner time your walk with a **stopwatch.** Switch roles, and repeat this step.

Think About This

1. What does a horizontal line segment on a distance-time graph indicate?
2. **Key Concept** According to the graph, at what times do the following motions take place? **a.** You change direction. **b.** Your speed increases. **c.** Your speed decreases.

Acceleration—Changes in Velocity

Imagine riding in a car. The driver steps on the gas pedal, and the car moves faster. Moving faster means the car's velocity increases. The driver then takes her foot off the pedal, and the car's velocity decreases. Next the driver turns the steering wheel. The car's velocity changes because its direction changes. The car's velocity changes if either the speed or the direction of the car changes.

When a car's velocity changes, the car is accelerating. **Acceleration** *is a measure of the change in velocity during a period of time.* An object accelerates when its velocity changes as a result of increasing speed, decreasing speed, or changing direction.

You might have experienced a large acceleration if you have ever ridden a roller coaster. Think about all the changes in speed and direction you experience on a roller coaster ride. When you drop down a hill of a roller coaster, you reach a faster speed quickly. The roller coaster is accelerating because its speed is increasing. The roller coaster also accelerates any time it changes direction. It accelerates again when it slows down and stops at the end of the ride. Each time the velocity of the roller coaster changes, it accelerates.

Reading Check What is acceleration?

Ways an Object Can Accelerate

Figure 13 Acceleration occurs when an object speeds up, slows down, or changes its direction of motion.

Speeding Up

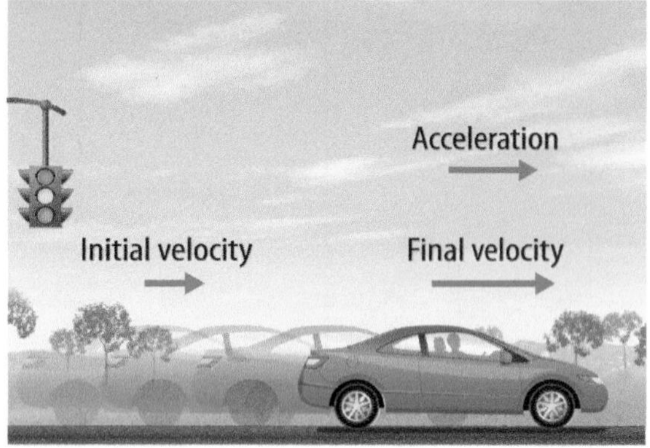

Slowing Down

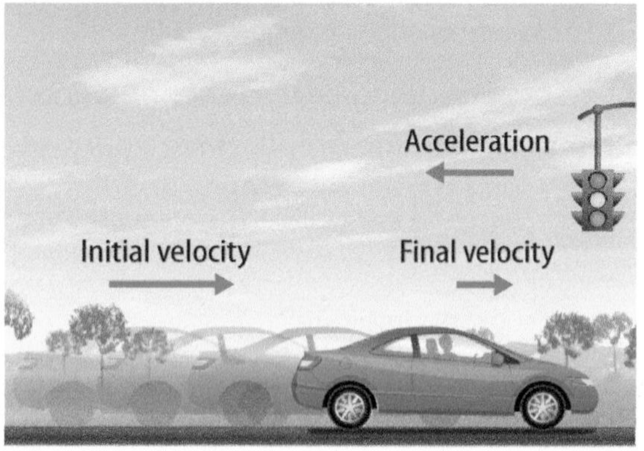

Changing Direction

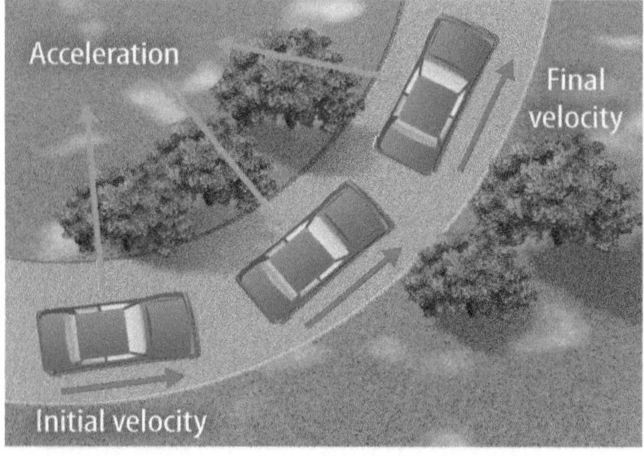

Visual Check If the car in the top picture moved faster, how would the acceleration arrow change?

Representing Acceleration

Like velocity, acceleration has a direction and can be represented by an arrow. Ways an object can accelerate are shown in **Figure 13.** The length of each blue acceleration arrow indicates the amount of acceleration. An acceleration arrow's direction depends on whether velocity increases or decreases.

Changing Speed

The car in the top picture of **Figure 13** is speeding up. At first it is moving slowly, so the arrow that represents its initial velocity is short. The car's speed increases, so the final velocity arrow is longer. As velocity increases, the car accelerates. Notice that the acceleration arrow points in the same direction as the velocity arrows.

The car in the middle picture of **Figure 13** is slowing down. At first it moves fast, so the arrow showing its velocity is long. After the car slows down, the arrow showing its final velocity is shorter. When velocity decreases, acceleration and velocity are in opposite directions. The arrow that represents acceleration is pointing in the direction opposite to the direction the car is moving.

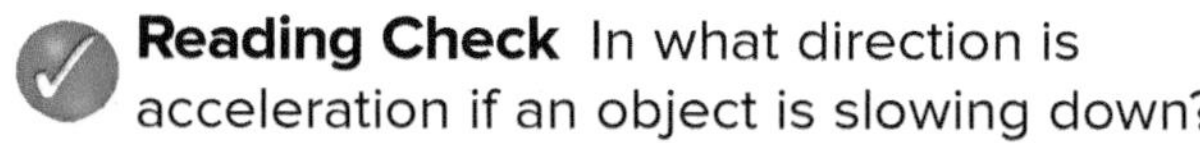

Reading Check In what direction is acceleration if an object is slowing down?

Changing Direction

The car in the bottom picture of **Figure 13** has a constant speed, so the velocity arrow is the same length at each point in the turn. But the car's velocity changes because its direction changes. Because velocity changes, the car is accelerating. Notice the direction of the blue acceleration arrows. It might surprise you that the car is accelerating toward the inside of the curve. Recall that acceleration is the change in velocity. If you compare one velocity arrow with the next, you can see that the change is always toward the inside of the curve.

Key Concept Check What are three ways an object can accelerate?

Calculating Acceleration

Acceleration is a change in velocity divided by the time interval during which the velocity changes. Recall that "velocity" is the speed of an object in a given direction. However, if an object moves along a straight line, you can calculate its acceleration without considering the object's direction. In this lesson, "velocity" refers to only an object's speed. Positive acceleration can be thought of as speeding up in the forward direction. Negative acceleration is slowing down in the forward direction as well as speeding up in the reverse direction.

FOLDABLES®

Make a horizontal two-tab Foldable and label it as shown. Use it to summarize information about the changes in velocity that can occur when an object is accelerating.

Changing speed | Changing direction

Acceleration

Acceleration Equation

acceleration (in m/s²) =

$$\frac{\textbf{final speed} \text{ (in m/s)} - \textbf{initial speed} \text{ (in m/s)}}{\textbf{total time} \text{ (in s)}}$$

$$a = \frac{v_f - v_i}{t}$$

Acceleration has SI units of meters per second per second (m/s/s). This can also be written as meters per second squared (m/s^2).

 Math Practice  Personal Tutor

Math Skills — Acceleration Equation

Solve for Acceleration A bicyclist started from rest along a straight path. After 2.0 s, his speed was 2.0 m/s. After 5.0 s, his speed was 8.0 m/s. What was his acceleration during the time 2.0 s to 5.0 s?

1. **This is what you know:** initial speed: $v_i = 2.0$ m/s; final speed: $v_f = 8.0$ m/s; total time: $t = 5.0\text{ s} - 2.0\text{ s} = 3.0\text{ s}$
2. **This is what you need to find:** acceleration: a
3. **Use this formula:** $a = \frac{v_f - v_i}{t}$
4. **Substitute:** the values for v_i, v_f, and t into the formula; subtract; then divide.

$$a = \frac{8.0/\text{ms} - 2.0\text{ m s}}{3.0\text{ s}} = \frac{6.0\text{ ms}}{3.0\text{ s}} = 2.0\text{ m/s}^2$$

Answer: The acceleration of the bicyclist was **2.0 m/s²**.

Practice

Aidan drops a rock from a cliff. After 4.0 s, the rock is moving at 39.2 m/s. What is the acceleration of the rock?

MiniLab

10 minutes

How is a change in speed related to acceleration?

What happens if the distance you walk each second increases? Follow these steps to demonstrate acceleration.

1. Read and complete a lab safety form.
2. Use **masking tape** to mark a course on the floor. Mark start, and place marks along a straight path at 10 cm, 40 cm, 90 cm, 160 cm, and 250 cm from the start.
3. Clap a steady beat. On the first beat, the person walking the course is at start. On the second beat, the walker should be at the 10-cm mark, and so on.

Analyze and Conclude

1. **Explain** what happened to your speed as you moved along the course.
2. **Key Concept** Suppose your speed at the final mark was 0.95 m/s. Calculate your average acceleration from start through the final segment of the course.

WORD ORIGIN

horizontal
from Greek *horizein,* means "limit, divide, separate"

vertical
from Latin *verticalis,* means "overhead"

Speed-Time Graphs

Recall that you can show an object's speed using a distance-time graph. You also can use a speed-time graph to show how speed changes over time. Just like a distance-time graph, a speed-time graph has time on the horizontal axis–the *x*-axis. But speed is on the vertical axis–the *y*-axis. The figures on the next few pages compare distance-time graphs and speed-time graphs for different types of motion.

Object at Rest

An object at rest is not moving, so its speed is always zero. As a result, the speed-time graph for an object at rest is a horizontal line at $y = 0$, as shown in **Figure 14.**

Figure 14 Both the distance-time graph and the speed-time graph are horizontal lines for an object at rest.

Distance vs. Time

The object's distance from the reference point does not change.

Speed vs. Time

The speed is zero and does not change.

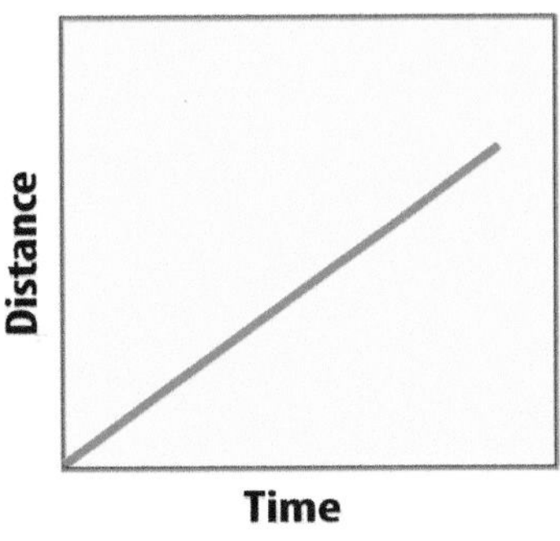

The distance increases at a steady rate over time.

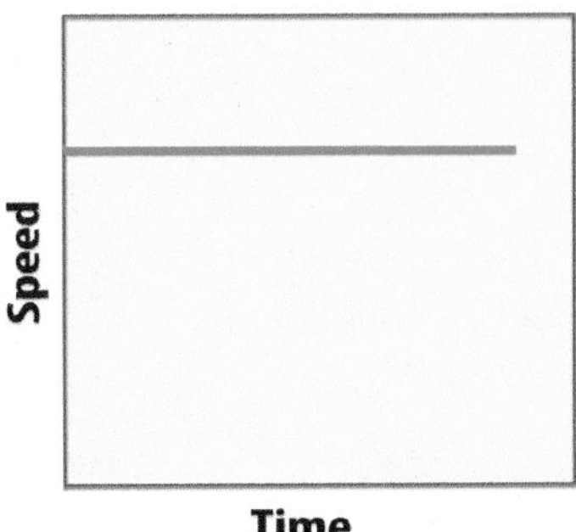

The object's speed does not change.

▲ **Figure 15** For an object moving at constant speed, the speed-time graph is a horizontal line.

Constant Speed

Think about a farm machine moving through a field at a constant speed. At every point in time, its speed is the same. If you plot its speed on a speed-time graph, the plotted line is horizontal, as shown in **Figure 15**. The speed of the object is represented by the distance the horizontal line is from the *x*-axis. If the line is farther from the *x*-axis, the object is moving at a faster speed.

Speeding Up

A plane speeds up as it moves down a runway and takes off. Suppose the speed of the plane increases at a steady rate. If you plot the speed of the plane on a speed-time graph, the line might look like the one in **Figure 16**. The line on the speed-time graph is closer to the *x*-axis at the beginning of the time period when the plane has a lower speed. It slants upward toward the right side of the graph as the speed increases.

Reading Check Why does the speed-time graph of an object that is speeding up slope upward from left to right?

Figure 16 The line on the speed-time graph for an object that is speeding up has an upward slope. ▼

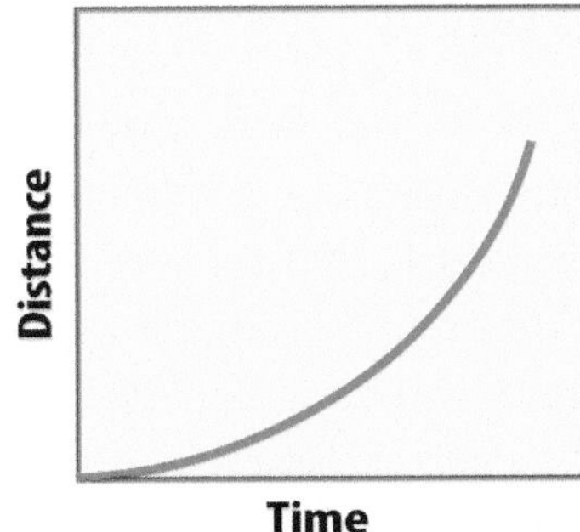

As the distance increases, the rate of increase gets larger over time.

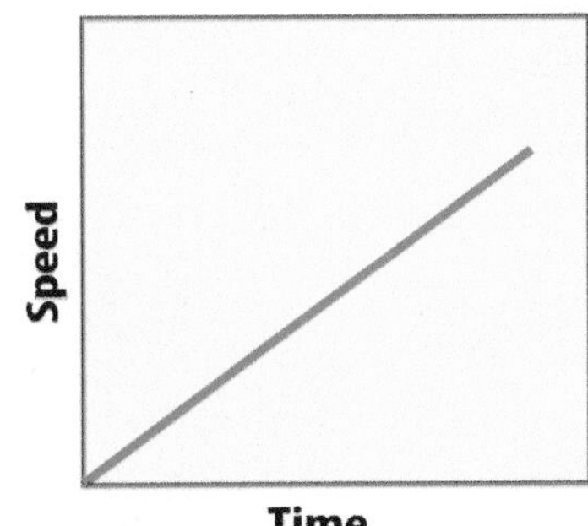

The speed of the object increases at a steady rate over time.

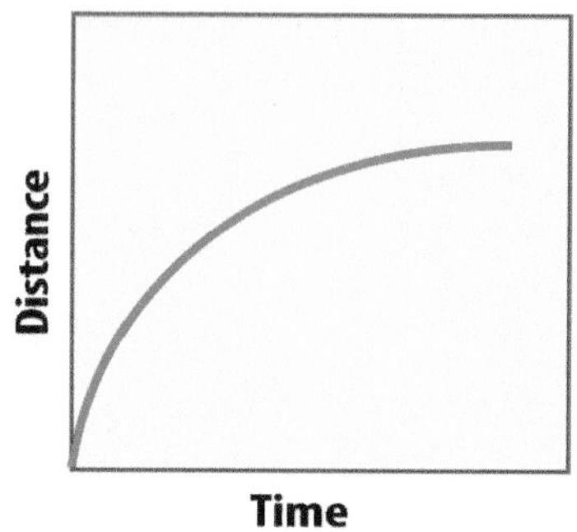

As the distance increases, the rate of increase gets smaller over time.

Speed

Time

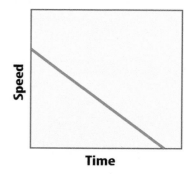

The speed of the object decreases at a steady rate over time.

▲ **Figure 17** The line on the speed-time graph for an object that is slowing down has a downward slope.

Slowing Down

The speed-time graph in **Figure 17** shows the motion of a space shuttle just after it lands. It slows down at a steady rate and then stops. Initially, the shuttle is moving at a high speed. The point representing this speed is far from the *x*-axis. As the shuttle's speed decreases, the points representing its speed are closer to the *x*-axis. The line on the speed-time graph slopes downward to the right. When the line touches the *x*-axis, the speed is zero and the shuttle is stopped.

Key Concept Check What does a speed-time graph show about the motion of an object?

Limits of Speed-Time Graphs

You have read that distance-time graphs show the speed of an object. However, they do not describe the direction in which an object is moving. In the same way, speed-time graphs show only the relationship between speed and time. A speed-time graph of the skier in **Figure 18** would show changes in his speed. It would not show what happens when the skier's velocity changes as the result of a change in his direction.

Figure 18 A speed-time graph of the motion of this skier would show changes in speed but not changes in direction. ▼

Summarizing Motion

Now that you know about motion, how might you describe a walk down the hallway at school? You can describe your position by your direction and distance from a reference point. You can compare your distance and your displacement and find your average speed. You know that you have an instantaneous speed and can tell when you walk at a constant speed. You can describe your velocity by your speed and your direction. You know you are accelerating if your velocity is changing.

Visual Check The skier slows down and speeds up along the curved path. Describe a speed-time graph of this motion.

Lesson 3 Review

Visual Summary

An object accelerates if it speeds up, slows down, or changes direction.

Acceleration in a straight line can be calculated by dividing the change in speed by the change in time.

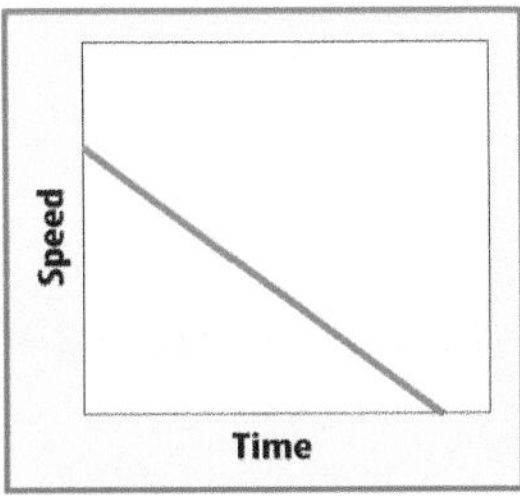

A speed-time graph shows how an object's speed changes over time.

FOLDABLES®

Use your lesson Foldable to review the lesson. Save your Foldable for the project aat the end of the chapter.

What do you think NOW?

You first read the statements below at the beginning of the chapter.

5. You can calculate acceleration by dividing the change in velocity by the change in distance.

6. An object accelerates when either its speed or its direction changes.

Did you change your mind about whether you agree or disagree with the statements? Rewrite any false statements to make them true.

Use Vocabulary

1. **Define** *acceleration* in your own words.
2. **Use the term** *acceleration* in a complete sentence.

Understand Key Concepts 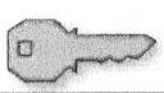

3. **Recall** how a roller coaster can accelerate, even when it is moving at a constant speed.
4. A speed-time graph is a horizontal line with a *y*-value of 4. Which describes the object's motion?
   A. at rest
   B. constant speed
   C. slowing down
   D. speeding up

Interpret Graphics

5. **Organize Information** Copy and fill in the graphic organizer below for the four types of speed-time graphs. For each, describe the motion of the object.

Critical Thinking

6. **Evaluate** A race car accelerates on a straight track from 0 to 100 km/h in 6 s. Another race car accelerates from 0 to 100 km/h in 5 s. Compare the velocities and accelerations of the cars during their races.

Math Skills

7. After 2.0 s, Isabela was riding her bicycle at 3.0 m/s on a straight path. After 5.0 s, she was moving at 5.4 m/s. What was her acceleration?
8. After 3.0 s, Mohammed was running at 1.2 m/s on a straight path. After 7.0 s, he was running at 2.0 m/s. What was his acceleration?

Lab

40 minutes

Materials

meltersticks (6)

stopwatches (6)

masking tape

tennis ball

Safety

Calculate Average Speed from a Graph

You probably do not walk the same speed uphill and downhill, or when you are just starting out and when you are tired. If you are walking and you measure and record the distance you walk every minute, the distances will vary. How might you use these measurements to calculate the average speed you walked? One way is to organize the data on a distance-time graph. In this activity, you will use such a graph to compare average speeds of a ball on a track using different heights of a ramp.

Ask a Question

How does the height of a ramp affect the speed of a ball along a track?

Make Observations

1. Read and complete a lab safety form.
2. Make a 3-m track. Place three metersticks end-to-end. Place three other metersticks end-to-end about 6 cm from the first set of metersticks. Use tape to hold the metersticks in place. Mark each half-meter with tape. Use books to make a ramp leading to the track.

3. A student should be at each half-meter mark with a stopwatch. Another student should be by the ramp to roll a ball along the track.
4. When the ball passes start, all group members should start their stopwatches. Each student should stop his or her stopwatch when the ball crosses the mark where the student is stationed.
5. Practice several times to get consistent rolls and times.

Hutchings Photography/Digital Light Source

Form a Hypothesis

6 Create a hypothesis about how the number of books used as a ramp affects the speed of the ball rolling along the track.

Test Your Hypothesis

7 Write a plan for varying the number of books and making distance and time measurements.

8 Create a data table in your Science Journal that matches your plan. A sample is shown to the right.

9 Use your plan to make the measurements. Record them in the data table.

10 Plot the data for each height of the ramp on a graph that shows the distance the ball traveled on the *x*-axis and time on the *y*-axis. For each ramp height, draw a straight line that goes through the most points.

11 Choose two points on each line. Calculate the average speed between these points by dividing the difference in the distances for the two points by the difference in the times.

Analyze and Conclude

12 **Compare** the average speeds for each ramp height. Use this comparison to decide whether your results support your hypothesis.

13 **The Big Idea** How was the distance-time graph useful for describing the motion of the ball?

Communicate Your Results

Prepare a poster that shows your graph and describes how it can be used to calculate average speed.

Inquiry Extension

Design and conduct an experiment comparing the average speed of different types of balls along the track.

8

Distance (m)	Time(s)		
	2 books	3 books	4 books
0.50			
1.00			
1.50			
2.00			
2.50			
3.00			

Lab Tips

- ☑ If the ball doesn't roll far enough, reduce the track length to 2 m.
- ☑ Practice using the stopwatches several times to gain experience in making accurate readings.

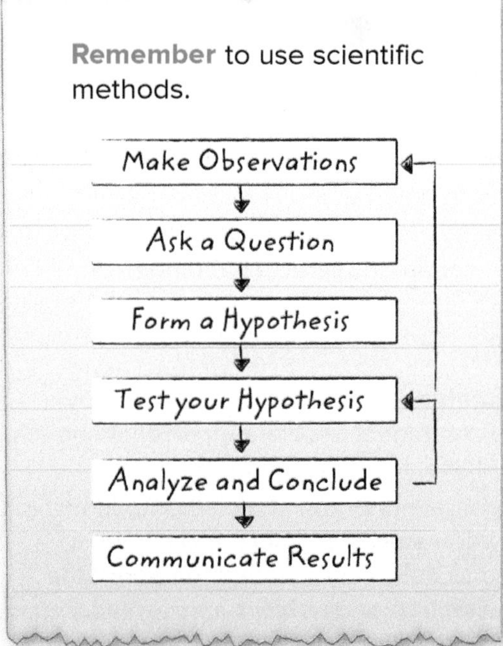

Chapter 1 Study Guide

The motion of an object can be described by the object's position, velocity, and acceleration.

Key Concepts Summary

Lesson 1: Position and Motion

- An object's **position** is its distance and direction from a **reference point.**
- The position of an object in two dimensions can be described by choosing a reference point and two reference directions, and then stating the distance along each reference direction.
- The distance an object moves is the actual length of its path. Its **displacement** is the difference between its initial position and its final position.

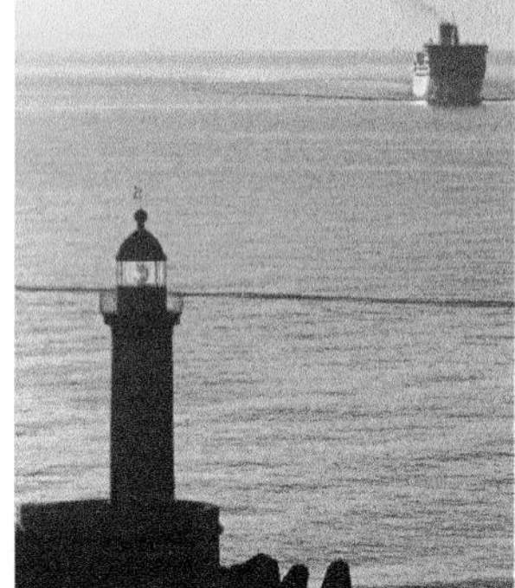

Vocabulary

reference point p. 9
position p. 9
motion p. 13
displacement p. 13

Lesson 2: Speed and Velocity

- **Speed** is the distance an object moves per unit of time.
- An object moving the same distance each second is moving at a **constant speed.** The speed of an object at a certain moment is its **instantaneous speed.**
- You can calculate an object's **average speed** from a distance-time graph by dividing the distance the object travels by the total time it takes to travel that distance.
- **Velocity** changes when speed, direction, or both speed and direction change.

Vocabulary

speed p. 17
constant speed p. 18
instantaneous speed p. 18
average speed p. 19
velocity p. 23

Lesson 3: Acceleration

- **Acceleration** is a change in velocity over time. An object accelerates when it speeds up, slows down, or changes direction.
- A speed-time graph shows the relationship between speed and time and can be used to determine information about the acceleration of an object.

Vocabulary

acceleration p. 27

Vocabulary eFlashcards
Vocabulary eGames
Personal Tutor

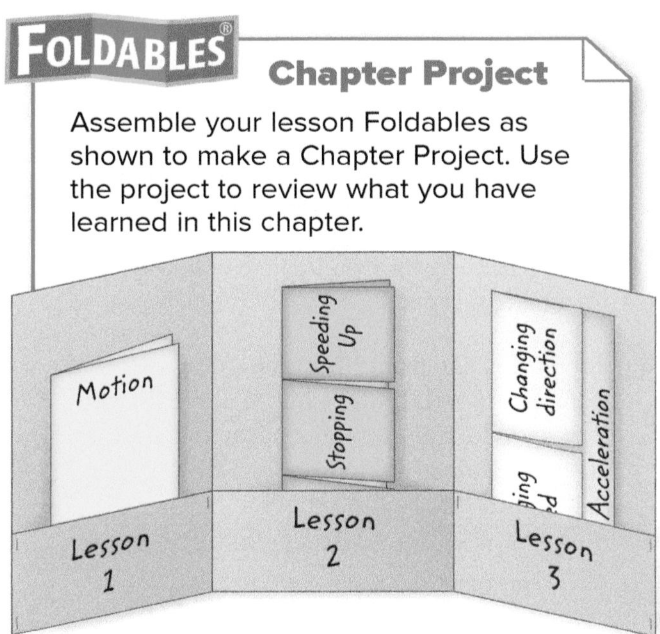

Assemble your lesson Foldables as shown to make a Chapter Project. Use the project to review what you have learned in this chapter.

Use Vocabulary

1. A pencil's ________ might be described as 3 cm to the left of the stapler.
2. An object that changes position is in ________.
3. If an object is traveling at a ________, it does not speed up or slow down.
4. An object's ________ includes both its speed and the direction it moves.
5. An object's change in velocity during a time interval, divided by the time interval during which the velocity changed, is its ________.
6. A truck driver stepped on the brakes to make a quick stop. The truck's ________ is in the opposite direction as its velocity.

Interactive Concept Map

Link Vocabulary and Key Concepts

Copy this concept map, and then use vocabulary terms from the previous page to complete the concept map.

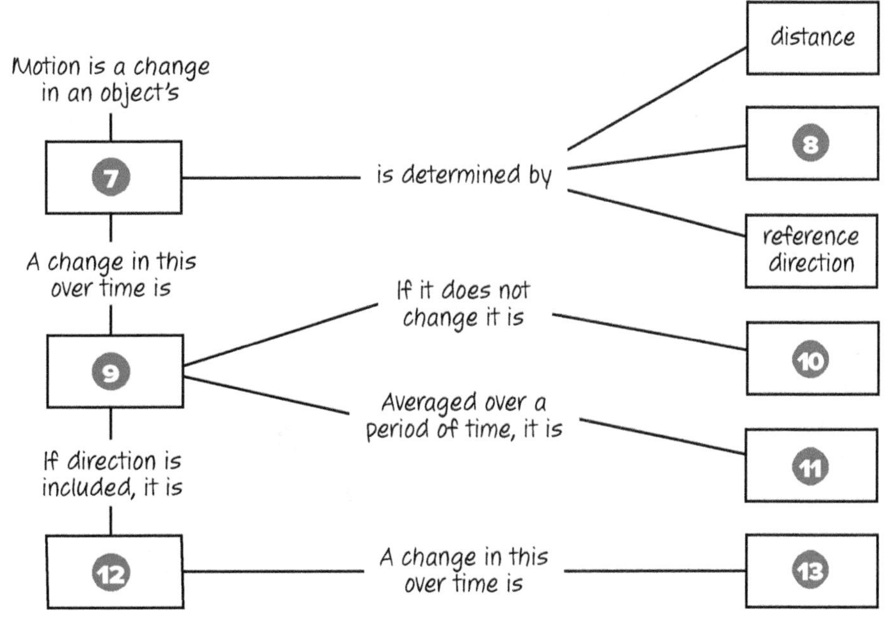

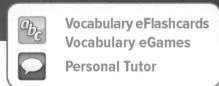

Chapter 1 Review

Understand Key Concepts 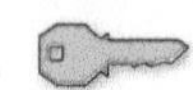

1. An airplane rolls down the runway. Compared to which reference point is the airplane in motion?
   A. the cargo the plane carries
   B. the control tower
   C. the pilot flying the plane
   D. the plane's wing

2. Which describes motion in two dimensions?
   A. a car driving through a city
   B. a rock dropping off a cliff
   C. a sprinter on a 100-m track
   D. a train on a straight track

3. Which line represents the greatest average speed during the 30-s time period?

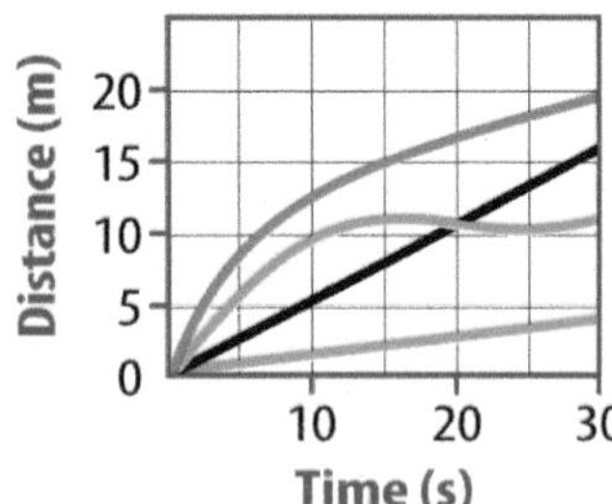

   A. the blue line
   B. the black line
   C. the green line
   D. the orange line

4. Which describes the greatest displacement?
   A. walking 3 m east, then 3 m north, then 3 m west
   B. walking 3 m east, then 3 m south, then 3 m east
   C. walking 3 m north, then 3 m south, then 3 m north
   D. walking 3 m north, then 3 m west, then 3 m south

5. Which has the greatest average speed?
   A. a boat sailing 80 km in 2 hours
   B. a car driving 90 km in 3 hours
   C. a train traveling 120 km in 3 hours
   D. a truck moving 50 km in 1 hour

6. Which describes motion in which the person or object is accelerating?
   A. A bird flies straight from a tree to the ground without changing speed.
   B. A dog walks at a constant speed along a straight sidewalk.
   C. A girl runs along a straight path the same distance each second.
   D. A truck moves around a curve without changing speed.

7. Richard walks from his home to his school at a constant speed. It takes him 4 min to travel 100 m. Which of the lines in the following distance-time graph could show Richard's motion on the way to school?

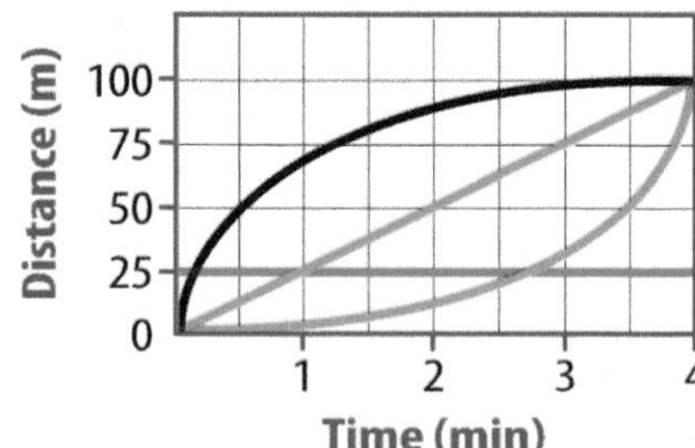

   A. the black line
   B. the blue line
   C. the green line
   D. the orange line

8. Which is a unit of acceleration?
   A. kg/m
   B. kg•m/s^2
   C. m/s
   D. m/s^2

9. Which have the same velocity?
   A. a boy walking east at 2 km/h and a man walking east at 4 km/h
   B. a car standing still and a truck driving in a circle at 4 km/h
   C. a dog walking west at 3 km/h and a cat walking west at 3 km/h
   D. a girl walking west at 3 km/h and a boy walking south at 3 km/h

Critical Thinking

10 **Describe** A ruler is on the table with the higher numbers to the right. An ant crawls along the ruler from 6 cm to 2 cm in 2 seconds. Distinguish among the ant's position, distance, displacement, speed, and velocity.

11 **Describe** a theme-park ride that has constant speed but changing velocity.

12 **Construct** a distance-time graph that shows the following motion: A person leaves a starting point at a constant speed of 4 m/s and walks for 4 s. The person then stops for 2 s. The person then continues walking at a constant speed of 2 m/s for 4 s.

13 **Calculate** A truck driver travels 55 km in 1 hour. He then drives a speed of 35 km/h for 2 hours. Next, he drives 175 km in 3 hours. What was his average speed?

14 **Interpret** Keisha measured the distance her friend Morgan ran on a straight track every 2 s. Her measurements are recorded in the table below. What was Morgan's average speed? What was her acceleration for the entire trip?

Time (s)	Distance (m)
0	0
2	2
4	6
6	8
8	14
10	20

Writing in Science

15 **Write** A friend tells you he is 30 m from the fountain in the middle of the city. Write a short paragraph explaining why you cannot identify your friend's position from this description.

REVIEW THE BIG IDEA

16 Nora rides a bicycle for 5 min on a curvy road at a constant speed of 10 m/s. Describe Nora's ride in terms of position, velocity, and acceleration. Compare the distance she rides and her displacement.

17 What are some ways to describe the motion of the jets in the photograph below?

Math Skills

Solve One-Step Equations

18 A model train moves 18.3 m in 122 s. What is the train's average speed?

19 A car travels 45 km in an hour. In each of the next two hours, it travels 78 km. What is the average speed of the car?

20 The speed of a car traveling on a straight road increases from 63 m/s to 75 m/s in 4.2 s. What is the car's acceleration?

21 A girl starts from rest and reaches a walking speed of 1.4 m/s in 3.0 s. She walks at this speed for 6.0 s. The girl then slows down and comes to a stop during a 10.0-s period. What was the girl's acceleration during each of the three time periods?

Standardized Test Practice

Record your answers on the answer sheet provided by your teacher or on a sheet of paper.

Multiple Choice

1 Radar tells an air traffic controller that a jet is slowing as it nears the airport. Which might represent the jet's speed?

A 700 h

B 700 h/km

C 700 km

D 700 km/h

Use the diagram below to answer question 2.

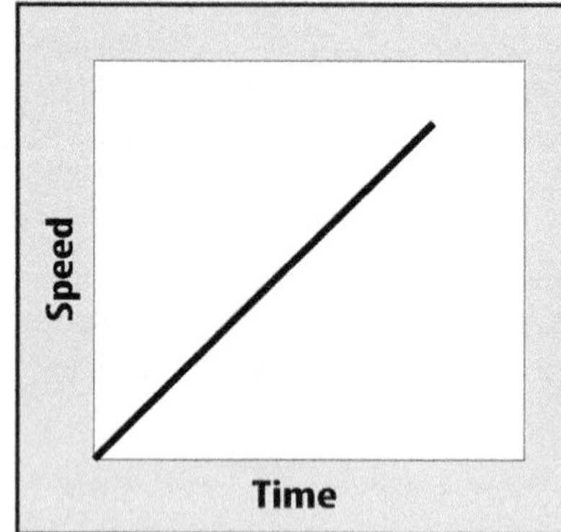

2 What does the graph above illustrate?

A average speed

B constant speed

C decreasing speed

D increasing speed

3 Why is a car accelerating when it is circling at a constant speed?

A It is changing its destination.

B It is changing its direction.

C It is changing its distance.

D It is changing its total mass.

4 Which is defined as the process of changing position?

A displacement

B distance

C motion

D relativity

5 Each diagram below shows two sliding boxes. Which boxes have the same velocity?

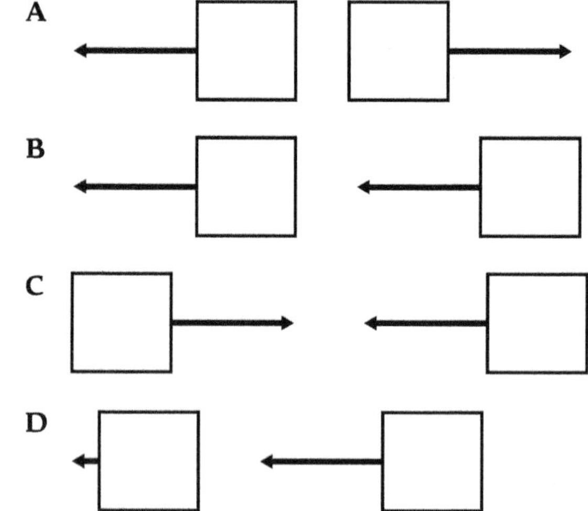

6 In the phrase "two miles southeast of the mall," what is the mall?

A a dimension

B a final destination

C a position

D a reference point

7 The initial speed of a dropped ball is 0 m/s. After 2 seconds, the ball travels at a speed of 20 m/s. What is the acceleration of the ball?

A 5 m/s^2

B 10 m/s^2

C 20 m/s^2

D 40 m/s^2

8 Which could be described by the expression "100 m/s northwest"?

A acceleration

B distance

C speed

D velocity

Use the diagram below to answer question 9.

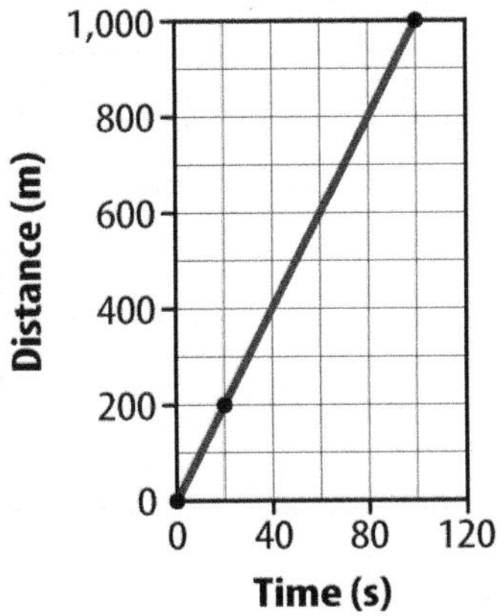

9 In the above graph, what is the average speed of the moving object between 20 and 60 seconds?

A 5 m/s

B 10 m/s

C 20 m/s

D 40 m/s

10 A car travels 250 km and stops twice along the way. The entire trip takes 5 hours. What is the average speed of the car?

A 25 km/h

B 40 km/h

C 50 km/h

D 250 km/h

Constructed Response

Use the diagram below to answer questions 11 and 12.

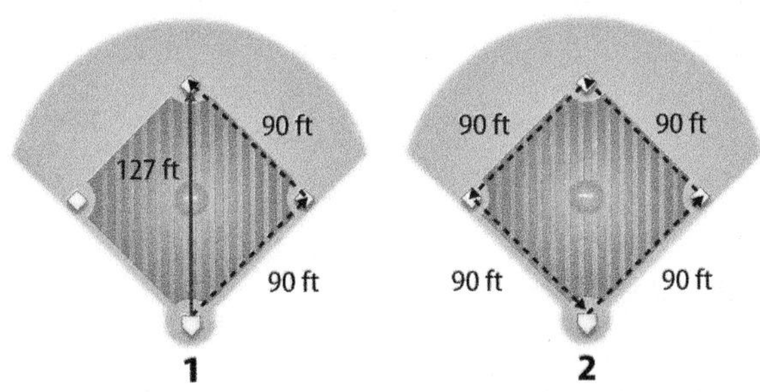

11 The dashed lines show the paths two players run on baseball diamonds. What distance does the player travel on diamond 1? How does it compare to the distance the player runs on diamond 2?

12 Calculate the displacement of the runners on diamonds 1 and 2. Explain your answers.

Use the diagram below to answer question 13.

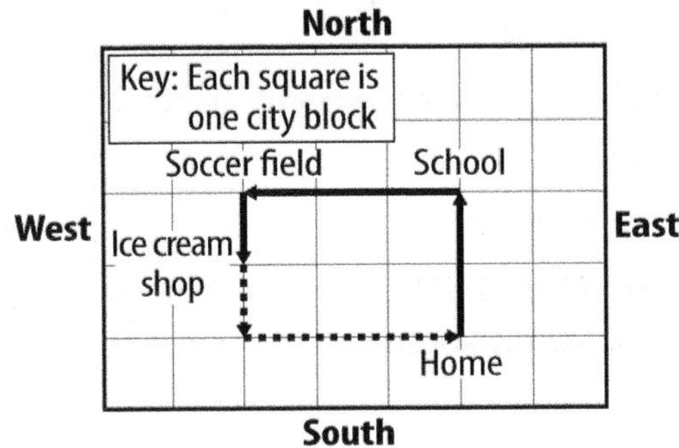

13 A student walks from home to school, on to a soccer field, then to an ice cream shop, and finally home. Use grid distances and directions to describe each leg of his trip. What is the distance between the student's home and the ice cream shop?

NEED EXTRA HELP?													
If You Missed Question...	1	2	3	4	5	6	7	8	9	10	11	12	13
Go to Lesson...	2	3	3	1	2	1	3	2	2	2	1	1	1

Chapter 2

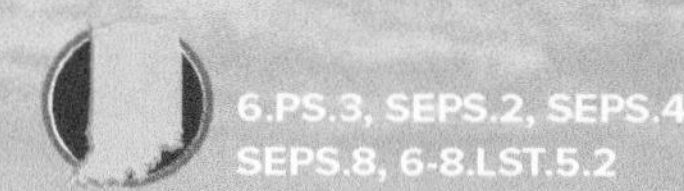

Energy and Energy Transformations

What is energy, and what are energy transformations?

Which objects have energy?

If your answer is everything in the photo, you are right. All objects contain energy. Some objects contain more energy than other objects. The Sun contains so much energy that it is considered an energy resource.

- From where do you think the energy that powers the cars comes?
- Do you think the energy in the Sun and the energy in the green plants are related?
- What do the terms *energy* and *energy transformations* mean to you?

Get Ready to Read

What do you think?

Before you read, decide if you agree or disagree with each of these statements. As you read this chapter, see if you change your mind about any of the statements.

1. A fast-moving baseball has more kinetic energy than a slow-moving baseball.
2. A large truck and a small car moving at the same speed have the same kinetic energy.
3. A book sitting on a shelf has no energy.
4. Energy can change from one form to another.
5. Energy is destroyed when you apply the brakes on a moving bicycle or a moving car.
6. The Sun releases radiant energy.

Your one-stop online resource
connectED.mcgraw-hill.com

LearnSmart®

Chapter Resources Files, Reading Essentials, Get Ready to Read, Quick Vocabulary

Animations, Videos, Interactive Tables

Self-checks, Quizzes, Tests

Project-Based Learning Activities

Lab Manuals, Safety Videos, Virtual Labs & Other Tools

Vocabulary, Multilingual eGlossary, Vocab eGames, Vocab eFlashcards

Personal Tutors

Lesson 1

Reading Guide

Key Concepts

ESSENTIAL QUESTIONS

- What is energy?
- What are potential and kinetic energy?
- How is energy related to work?
- What are the different forms of energy?

Vocabulary

energy p. 45
kinetic energy p. 46
potential energy p. 46
work p. 48
mechanical energy p. 49
sound energy p. 49
thermal energy p. 49
electric energy p. 49
radiant energy p. 49
nuclear energy p. 49

Multilingual eGlossary

BrainPOP®

6.PS.3

Forms of Energy

Inquiry Why is this cat glowing?

A camera that detects temperature made this image. Dark colors represent cooler temperatures, and light colors represent warmer temperatures. Temperatures are cooler where the cat's body emits less radiant energy and warmer where the cat's body emits more radiant energy.

Launch Lab

20 minutes

Can you change matter?

You observe many things changing. Birds change their positions when they fly. Bubbles form in boiling water. The filament in a lightbulb glows when you turn on a light. How can you cause a change in matter?

1. Read and complete the lab safety form.
2. Half-fill a **foam cup** with **sand.** Place the bulb of a **thermometer** about halfway into the sand. *Do not stir*. Record the temperature in your Science Journal.
3. Remove the thermometer and place a **lid** on the cup. Hold down the lid and shake the cup vigorously for 10 min.
4. Remove the lid. Measure and record the temperature of the sand.

Think About This

1. What change did you observe in the sand?
2. How could you change your results?
3. **Key Concept** What do you think caused the change you observed in the sand?

What is energy?

It might be exciting to watch a fireworks display, such as the one shown in Figure 1. Over and over, you hear the crack of explosions and see bursts of colors in the night sky. Fireworks release energy when they explode. **Energy** is the ability to cause change. The energy in the fireworks causes the changes you see as bursting flashes of light and hear as loud booms.

Energy also causes other changes. The plant in Figure 1 uses the energy from the Sun and makes food that it uses for growth and other processes. Energy can cause changes in the motions and positions of objects, such as the nail in Figure 1. Can you think of other ways energy might cause changes?

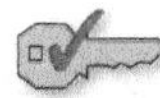 **Key Concept Check** What is energy?

WORD ORIGIN

energy
from Greek *energeia,* means "activity"

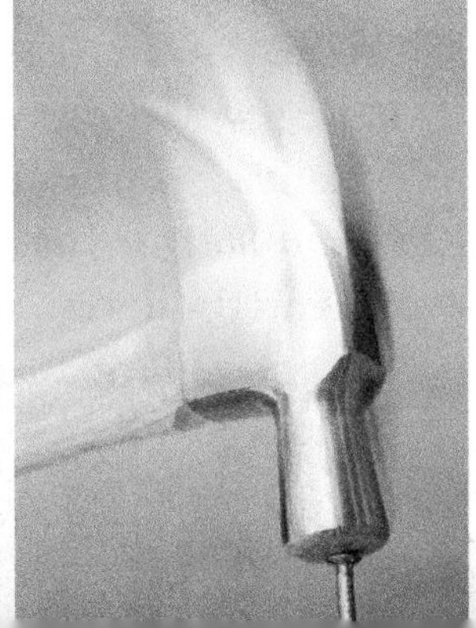

Figure 1 The explosion of fireworks, the growth of a plant, and the motion of a hammer all involve energy.

Figure 2 The kinetic energy (KE) of an object depends on its speed and its mass. The vertical bars show the kinetic energy of each vehicle.

Kinetic Energy—Energy of Motion

Have you ever been to a bowling alley? When you rolled the ball and it hit the pins, a change occurred–the pins fell over. This change occurred because the ball had a form of energy called kinetic (kuh NEH tik) energy. **Kinetic energy** *is energy due to motion.* All moving objects have kinetic energy.

Kinetic Energy and Speed

An object's kinetic energy depends on its speed. The faster an object moves, the more kinetic energy it has. For example, the blue car has more kinetic energy than the green car in Figure 2 because the blue car is moving faster.

Kinetic Energy and Mass

A moving object's kinetic energy also depends on its mass. If two objects move at the same speed, the object with more mass has more kinetic energy. For example, the truck and the green car in Figure 2 are moving at the same speed, but the truck has more kinetic energy because it has more mass.

 **Key Concept Check** What is kinetic energy?

FOLDABLES®

Make a 18-cm fold along the long edge of a sheet of paper to make a two-pocket book. Label it as shown. Organize information about the forms of energy on quarter sheets of paper, and put them in the pockets.

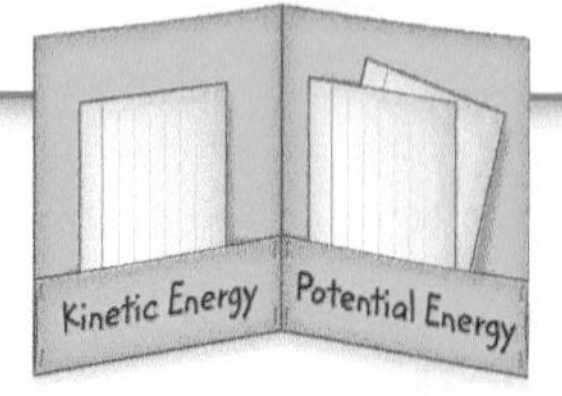

Potential Energy—Stored Energy

Energy can be present even if objects are not moving. If you hold a ball in your hand and then let it go, the gravitational interaction between the ball and Earth causes a change to occur. Before you dropped the ball, it had a form of energy called potential (puh TEN chul) energy. **Potential energy** *is stored energy due to the interactions between objects or particles.* Gravitational potential energy, elastic potential energy, and chemical potential energy are all forms of potential energy.

Gravitational Potential Energy

Even when you are just holding a book, gravitational potential energy is stored between the book and Earth. The girl shown in Figure 3 increases the gravitational potential energy between her backpack and Earth by lifting the backpack higher from the ground.

The gravitational potential energy stored between an object and Earth depends on the object's weight and height. Dropping a bowling ball from a height of 1 m causes a greater change than dropping a tennis ball from 1 m. Similarly, dropping a bowling ball from 3 m causes a greater change than dropping the same bowling ball from only 1 m.

Reading Check What factors determine the gravitational potential energy stored between an object and Earth?

Elastic Potential Energy

When you stretch a rubber band, as in Figure 3, another form of potential energy, called elastic (ih LAS tik) potential energy, is being stored in the rubber band. Elastic potential energy is energy stored in objects that are compressed or stretched, such as springs and rubber bands. When you release the end of a stretched rubber band, the stored elastic potential energy is transformed into kinetic energy. This transformation is obvious when it flies across the room.

Chemical Potential Energy

Food, gasoline, and other substances are made of atoms joined together by chemical bonds. Chemical potential energy is energy stored in the chemical bonds between atoms, as shown in Figure 3. Chemical potential energy is released when chemical reactions occur. Your body uses the chemical potential energy in foods for all its activities. People also use the chemical potential energy in gasoline to power cars and buses.

Key Concept Check In what way are all forms of potential energy the same?

Potential Energy

Figure 3 There are different forms of potential energy.

Gravitational Potential Energy
Gravitational potential energy increases when the girl lifts her backpack.

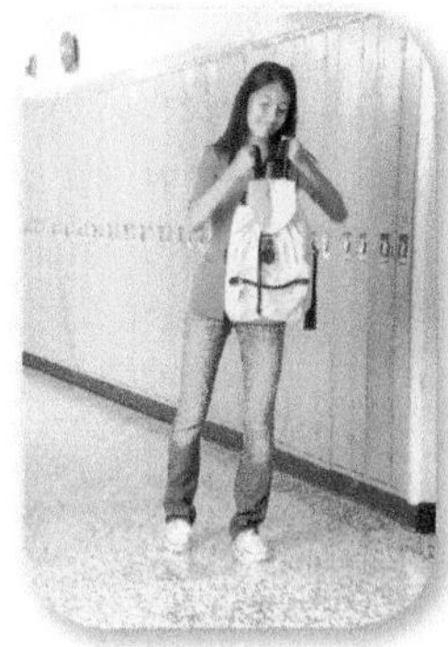

Elastic Potential Energy
The rubber band's elastic potential energy increases when it is stretched.

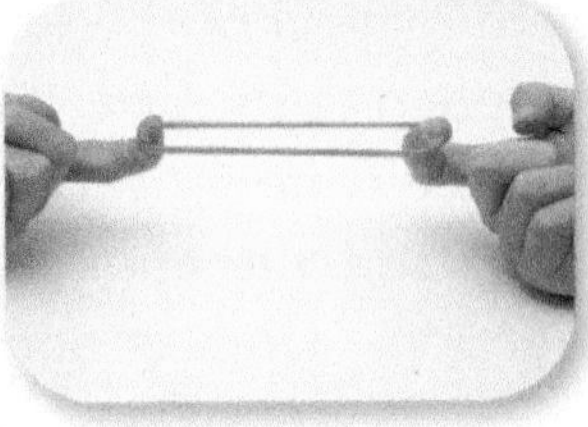

Chemical Potential Energy
Foods and other substances, including glucose, have chemical potential energy stored in the bonds between atoms.

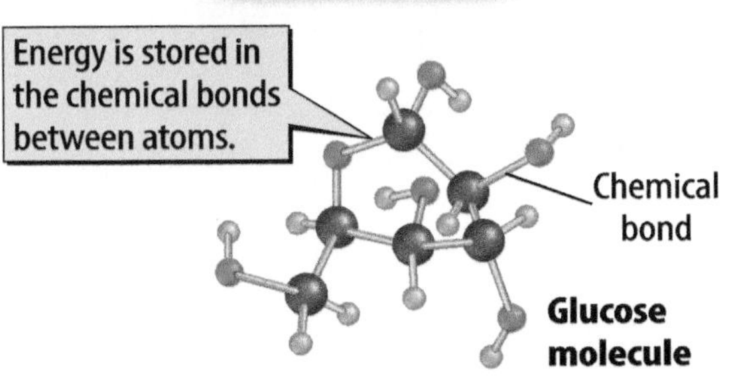

Figure 4 The girl does work on the box as she lifts it and increases its gravitational potential energy. The colored bars show the work that the girl does (W) and the box's potential energy (PE).

Energy and Work

You can transfer energy by doing work. **Work** *is the transfer of energy that occurs when a force makes an object move in the direction of the force while the force is acting on the object.* For example, as the girl lifts the box onto the shelf in Figure 4, she transfers energy from herself to the box. She does work only while the box moves in the direction of the force and while the force is applied to the box. If the box stops moving, the force is no longer applied, or the box movement and the applied force are in different directions, work is not done on the box.

 **Key Concept Check** How is energy related to work?

An object that has energy also can do work. For example, when a bowling ball collides with a bowling pin, the bowling ball does work on the pin. Some of the ball's kinetic energy is transferred to the bowling pin. Because of this connection between energy and work, energy is sometimes described as the ability to do work.

Other Forms of Energy

Some other forms of energy are shown in Table 1. All energy can be measured in joules (J). A softball dropped from a height of about 0.5 m has about 1 J of kinetic energy just before it hits the floor.

MiniLab

20 minutes

Can a moving object do work? 

Is work done when a moving object hits another object?

1. Read and complete a lab safety form.
2. **Tape** one end of a **30-cm grooved ruler** to the edge of a stack of **books** about 8 cm high. Put the lower end of the ruler in a **paper cup** lying on its side.
3. Place a **marble** in the groove at the top end of the ruler and release it.
4. Record your observations in your Science Journal.

Analyze and Conclude

1. **Compare** the kinetic energy of the marble just before and after it hit the cup.
2.  **Key Concept** Is work being done on the cup? Explain your answer.

Table 1 Forms of Energy

Mechanical Energy *The sum of potential energy and kinetic energy in a system of objects is* **mechanical energy.** For example, the mechanical energy of a basketball increases when a player shoots the basketball. Both the kinetic energy and gravitational potential energy of the ball increases in the player-ball-ground system.	
Sound Energy When you pluck a guitar string, the string vibrates and produces sound. *The energy that sound carries is* **sound energy.** Vibrating objects emit sound energy. However, sound energy cannot travel through a vacuum, such as the space between Earth and the Sun.	
Thermal Energy All objects and materials are made of particles that have energy. **Thermal energy** *is the sum of kinetic energy and potential energy of the particles that make up an object.* Mechanical energy is due to large-scale motions and interactions in a system and thermal energy is due to atomic-scale motions and interactions of particles. Thermal energy moves from warmer objects, such as burning logs, to cooler objects, such as air.	
Electric Energy An electrical fan uses another form of energy–electric energy. When you turn on a fan, there is an electric current through the fan's motor. **Electric energy** *is the energy an electric current carries.* Electrical appliances, such as fans and dishwashers, change electric energy into other forms of energy.	
Radiant Energy—Light Energy The Sun gives off energy that travels to Earth as electromagnetic waves. Unlike sound waves, electromagnetic waves can travel through a vacuum. Light waves, microwaves, and radio waves are all electromagnetic waves. *The energy that electromagnetic waves carry is* **radiant energy.** Radiant energy sometimes is called light energy.	
Nuclear Energy At the center of every atom is a nucleus. **Nuclear energy** *is energy that is stored and released in the nucleus of an atom.* In the Sun, nuclear energy is released when nuclei join together. In a nuclear power plant, nuclear energy is released when the nuclei of uranium atoms are split apart.	

 **Key Concept Check** Describe three forms of energy.

Lesson 1 Review

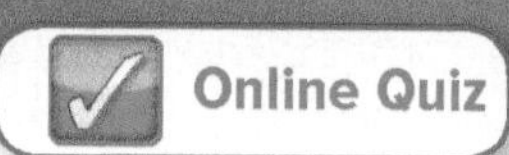

Visual Summary

Energy is the ability to cause change.

The gravitational potential energy between an object and Earth increases when you lift the object.

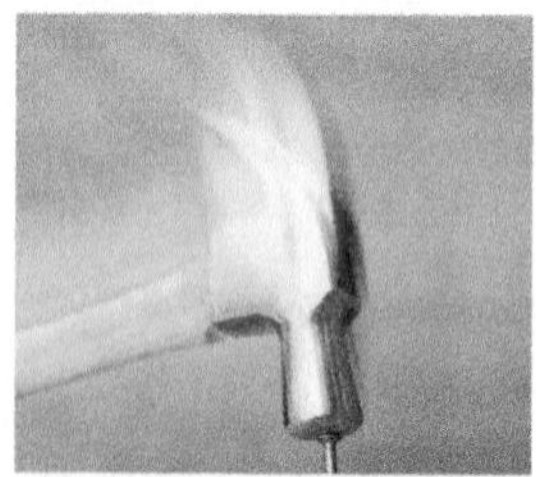

You do work on an object when you apply a force to that object over a distance.

FOLDABLES®

Use your lesson Foldable to review the lesson. Save your Foldable for the project at the end of the chapter.

What do you think NOW?

You first read the statements below at the beginning of the chapter.

1. A fast-moving baseball has more kinetic energy than a slow-moving baseball.
2. A large truck and a small car moving at the same speed have the same kinetic energy.
3. A book sitting on a shelf has no energy.

Did you change your mind about whether you agree or disagree with the statements? Rewrite any false statements to make them true.

Use Vocabulary

1. **Distinguish** between kinetic energy and potential energy.

Understand Key Concepts 

2. **Write** a definition of work.
3. Which type of energy increases when you compress a spring?
   - **A.** elastic potential energy
   - **B.** kinetic energy
   - **C.** radiant energy
   - **D.** sound energy
4. **Infer** How could you increase the gravitational potential energy between yourself and Earth?
5. **Infer** how a bicycle's kinetic energy changes when that bicycle slows down.
6. **Compare and contrast** radiant energy and sound energy.

Interpret Graphics

7. **Identify** Copy and fill in the graphic organizer below to identify three types of potential energy.

8. **Describe** where chemical potential energy is stored in the molecule shown below.

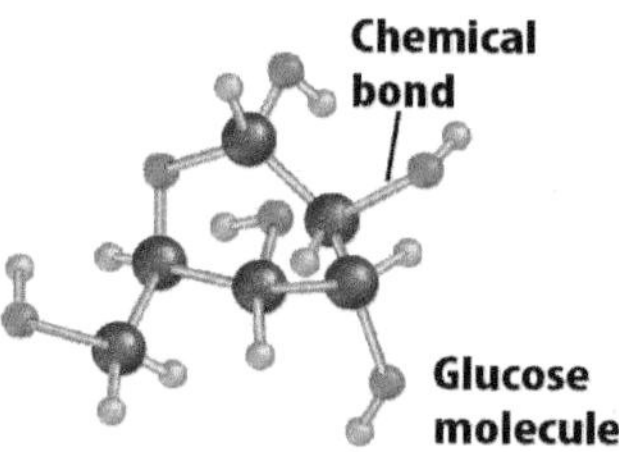

Critical Thinking

9. **Analyze** Will pushing on a car always change the car's mechanical energy? What must happen for the car's kinetic energy to increase?

Skill Practice **Analyze Results** 45 minutes

Can you identify potential and kinetic energy?

Materials

string

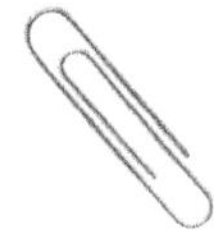
paper clip

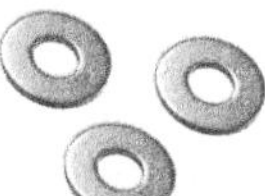
three large washers

meterstick

tape

small box

ruler

Safety

Have you ever watched the pendulum move in a grandfather clock? The pendulum has energy because it causes change as it moves back and forth. What kind of energy does a moving pendulum have? Can it do work on an object? In this lab, you will analyze the movement and energy of a pendulum.

Learn It

Before you can draw valid conclusions from any scientific experiment, you must **analyze the results** of that experiment. This means you must look for patterns in the results.

Try It

1. Read and complete a lab safety form.
2. Use the photo below as a guide to make a pendulum. Hang one washer on a paper clip. Place a box so it will block the swinging pendulum. Mark the position of the box with tape.
3. Pull the pendulum back until the bottom of the washer is 15 cm from the floor. Release the pendulum. Measure and record the distance the box moves in your Science Journal. Repeat two more times.
4. Repeat step 3 using pendulum heights of 30 cm and 45 cm.
5. Repeat steps 3 and 4 with two washers, then with three washers.

Apply It

6. Does the pendulum have potential energy? Explain.
7. Does it have kinetic energy? How do you know?
8. How does the gravitational potential energy depend on the pendulum's weight and height?
9. How does the distance the box travels depend on the initial gravitational potential energy?
10. Does the pendulum do work on the box? Explain your answer.
11. **Key Concept** Determine when the pendulum had maximum potential energy and maximum kinetic energy. Explain your reasoning.

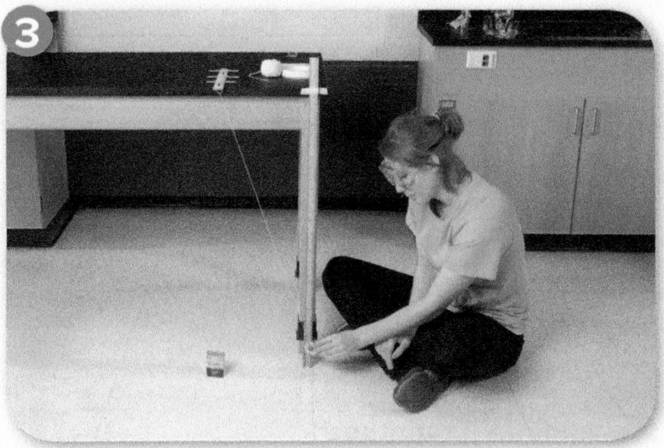

Lesson 2

Reading Guide

Key Concepts 

ESSENTIAL QUESTIONS

- What is the law of conservation of energy?
- How does friction affect energy transformations?
- How are different types of energy used?

Vocabulary

law of conservation of energy p. 54

friction p. 55

 Multilingual eGlossary

6.PS.3, SEPS.2, SEPS.4, SEPS.8, 6-8.LST.5.2

 Go to the resource tab in ConnectED to find the PBL *Tearin' It Up!*

Energy Transformations

Inquiry What's that sound?

Blocks of ice breaking off the front of this glacier can be bigger than a car. Imagine the loud rumble they make as they crash into the sea. But after the ice falls into the sea, it will melt gradually. All of these processes involve energy transformations—energy changing from one form to another.

sorincolac/Getty Images

Launch Lab

15 minutes

Is energy lost when it changes form?

Energy can have different forms. What happens when energy changes from one form to another?

1. Read and complete a lab safety form.
2. Three students should sit in a circle. One student has 30 **buttons,** one has 30 **pennies,** and one has 30 **paper clips.**
3. Each student should exchange 10 items with the student to the right and 10 items with the student to the left.
4. Repeat step 3.

Think About This

1. If the buttons, the pennies, and the paper clips represent different forms of energy, what represents changes from one form of energy to another?
2. **Key Concept** If each button, penny, and paper clip represents one unit of energy, does the total amount of energy increase, decrease, or stay the same? Explain your answer.

Changes Between Forms of Energy

It is the weekend and you are ready to make some popcorn in the microwave and watch a movie. Energy changes form when you make popcorn and watch TV. As shown in Figure 5, a microwave changes electric energy into radiant energy. Radiant energy changes into thermal energy in the popcorn kernels.

The changes from electric energy to radiant energy to thermal energy are called energy transformations. As you watch the movie, energy transformations also occur in the television. A television transforms electric energy into sound energy and radiant energy.

SCIENCE USE V. COMMON USE

radiant

Science Use energy transmitted by electromagnetic waves

Common Use bright and shining; glowing

Figure 5 Energy changes from one form to another when you use a microwave oven to make popcorn.

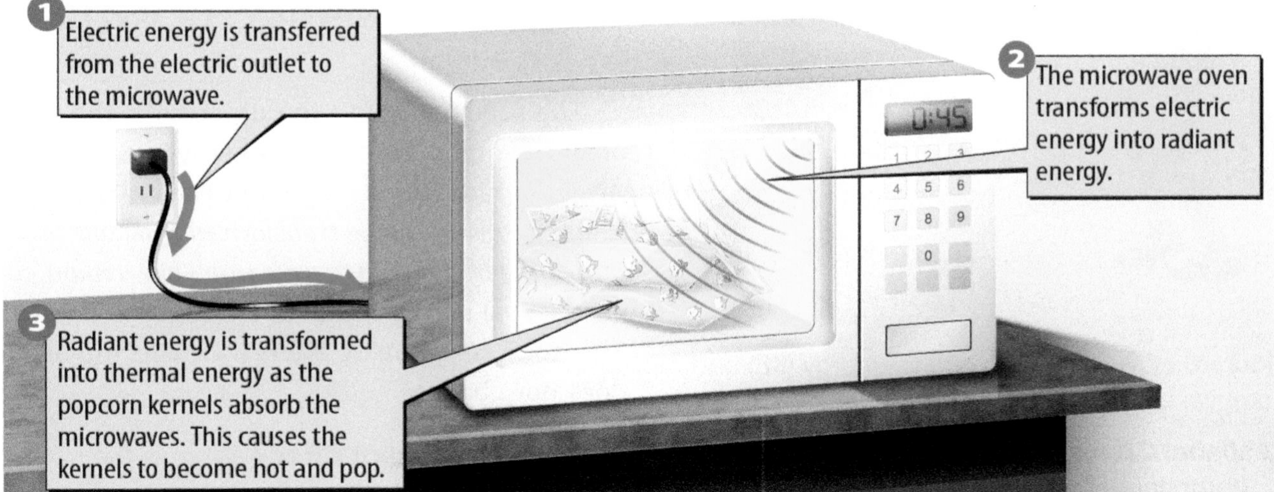

1 Electric energy is transferred from the electric outlet to the microwave.
2 The microwave oven transforms electric energy into radiant energy.
0:45
1 2 3
4 5 6
7 8 9
0
3 Radiant energy is transformed into thermal energy as the popcorn kernels absorb the microwaves. This causes the kernels to become hot and pop.

Conservation of Energy

Animation

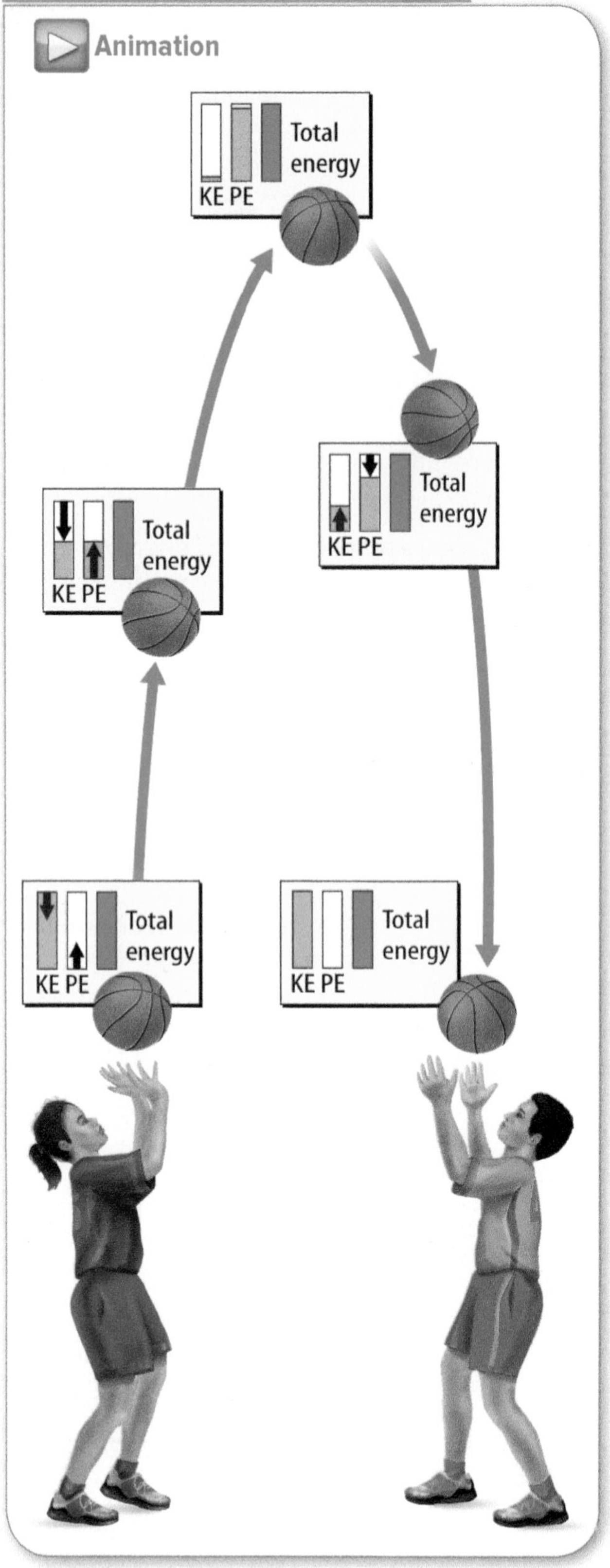

Figure 6 The ball's kinetic energy (KE) and potential energy (PE) change as it moves.

Visual Check When is the gravitational potential energy the greatest?

Changes Between Kinetic and Potential Energy

Energy transformations also occur when you toss a ball upward, as shown in Figure 6. The ball slows down as it moves upward and then speeds up as it moves downward. The ball's speed and height change as energy changes from one form to another.

Kinetic Energy to Potential Energy

The ball is moving fastest and has the most kinetic energy as it leaves your hand, as shown in Figure 6. As the ball moves upward, its speed and kinetic energy decrease. However, the potential energy is increasing because the ball's height is increasing. Kinetic energy is changing into potential energy. At the ball's highest point, the gravitational potential energy is at its greatest, and the ball's kinetic energy is at its lowest.

Potential Energy to Kinetic Energy

As the ball moves downward, its potential energy decreases. At the same time, the ball's speed increases. Therefore, the ball's kinetic energy increases. Potential energy is transformed into kinetic energy. When the ball reaches the other player's hand, its kinetic energy is at the maximum value again.

Reading Check Why does the potential energy decrease as the ball falls?

The Law of Conservation of Energy

The total energy in the universe is the sum of all the different forms of energy everywhere. *According to the* **law of conservation of energy,** *energy can be transformed from one form into another or transferred from one region to another, but energy cannot be created or destroyed.* The total amount of energy in the universe does not change.

Key Concept Check What is the law of conservation of energy?

Friction and the Law of Conservation of Energy

Sometimes it may seem as if the law of conservation of energy is not accurate. Imagine riding a bicycle, as in Figure 7. The moving bicycle has mechanical energy. What happens to this mechanical energy when you apply the brakes and the bicycle stops?

When you apply the brakes, the bicycle's mechanical energy is not destroyed. Instead the bicycle's mechanical energy is transformed to thermal energy, as shown in Figure 7. The total amount of energy never changes. The additional thermal energy causes the brakes, the wheels, and the air around the bicycle to become slightly warmer.

Friction between the bicycle's brake pads and the moving wheels transforms mechanical energy into thermal energy. **Friction** *is a force that resists the sliding of two surfaces that are touching.*

Key Concept Check How does friction affect energy transformations?

There is always some friction between any two surfaces that are rubbing against each other. As a result, some mechanical energy always is transformed into thermal energy when two surfaces rub against each other.

It is easier to pedal a bicycle if there is less friction between the bicycle's parts. With less friction, less of the bicycle's mechanical energy is transformed into thermal energy. One way to reduce friction is to apply a lubricant, such as oil, grease, or graphite, to surfaces that rub against each other.

FOLDABLES®

Cut three sheets of paper in half. Use the six half sheets to make a side-tab book with five tabs and a cover. Use your book to organize your notes on energy transformations.

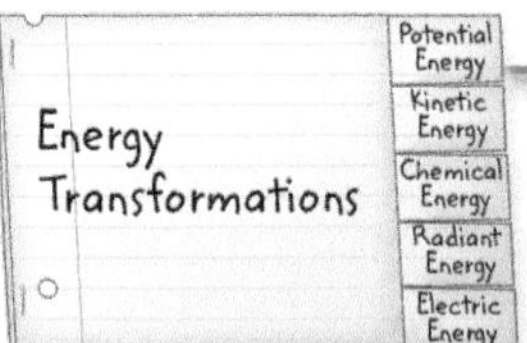

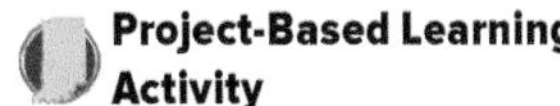

WORD ORIGIN

friction
from Latin *fricare,* means "to rub"

Project-Based Learning Activity

Tearin' It Up! Go online to describe how potential and kinetic energy can be transferred between forms when snowboarding.

Friction and Thermal Energy

Personal Tutor

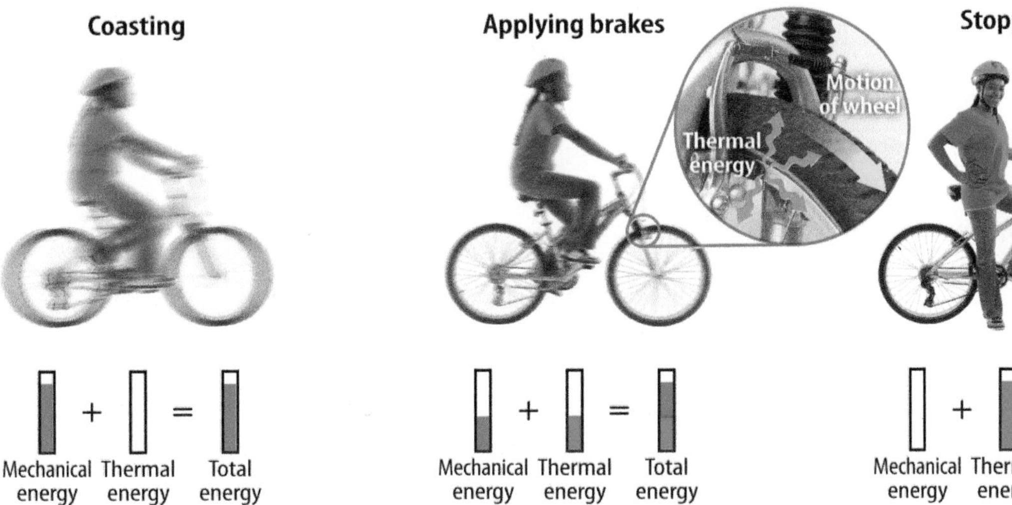

Figure 7 When the girl applies the brakes, friction between the bicycle's brake pads and its wheels transforms mechanical energy into thermal energy. As mechanical energy changes into thermal energy, the bicycle slows down. The total amount of energy does not change.

Math Skills

Solve a One-Step Equation

Electric energy often is measured in units called kilowatt-hours (kWh). To calculate the electric energy used by an appliance in kWh, use this equation:

$$\text{kWh} = \left(\frac{\text{watts}}{1{,}000}\right) \times \text{hours}$$

Appliances typically have a power rating measured in watts (W).

Practice

A hair dryer is rated at 1,200 W. If you use the dryer for 0.25 h, how much electric energy do you use?

 Math Practice

 Personal Tutor

Using Energy

Every day you use different forms of energy to do different things. You might use the radiant energy from a lamp to light a room, or you might use the chemical energy stored in your body to run a race. When you use energy, you usually change it from one form into another. For example, the lamp changes electric energy into radiant energy and thermal energy.

Using Thermal Energy

All forms of energy can be transformed into thermal energy. People often use thermal energy to cook food or provide warmth. A gas stove transforms the chemical energy stored in natural gas into the thermal energy that cooks food. An electric space heater transforms the electric energy from a power plant into the thermal energy that warms a room. In a jet engine, burning fuel releases thermal energy that the engine transforms into mechanical energy.

Using Chemical Energy

During photosynthesis, a plant transforms the Sun's radiant energy into chemical energy that it stores in chemical compounds. Some of these compounds become food for other living things. Your body transforms the chemical energy from your food into the kinetic energy necessary for movement. Your body also transforms chemical energy into the thermal energy necessary to keep you warm.

Using Radiant Energy

The cell phone in Figure 8 sends and receives radiant energy using microwaves. When you are listening to someone on a cell phone, that cell phone is transforming radiant energy into electric energy and then into sound energy. When you are speaking into a cell phone, it is transforming sound energy into electric energy and then into radiant energy.

Sound waves carry energy into the cell phone.
The cell phone converts the energy carried by sound waves into radiant energy that is carried away by microwaves.

Figure 8 A cell phone changes sound energy into radiant energy when you speak.

Using Electric Energy

Many of the devices you might use every day, such as handheld video games, MP3 players, and hair dryers, use electric energy. Some devices, such as hair dryers, use electric energy from electric power plants. Other appliances, such as handheld video games, transform the chemical energy stored in batteries into electric energy.

 **Key Concept Check** How are different types of energy used?

Waste Energy

When energy changes form, some thermal energy is always released. For example, a lightbulb converts some electric energy into radiant energy. However, the lightbulb also transforms some electric energy into thermal energy. This is what makes the lightbulb hot. Some of this thermal energy moves into the air and cannot be used.

Scientists often refer to thermal energy that cannot be used as waste energy. Whenever energy is used, some energy is transformed into useful energy and some is transformed into waste energy. For example, we use the chemical energy in gasoline to make cars, such as those in Figure 9, move. However, most of that chemical energy ends up as waste energy—thermal energy that moves into the air.

 **Reading Check** What is waste energy?

 **MiniLab** **20 minutes**

How does energy change form?

When an object falls, energy changes form. How can you compare energies for falling objects?

1. Read and complete a lab safety form.
2. Place a piece of **clay** about 10 cm wide and 3 cm thick on a **small paper plate.**
3. Drop a **marble** onto the clay from a height of about 20 cm, and measure the depth of the depression caused by the marble. Record the measurement in your Science Journal.
4. Repeat step 3 with a heavier marble.

Analyze and Conclude

1. **Infer** Which marble had more kinetic energy just before it hit the clay? Explain your answer.
2. **Key Concept** For which marble was the potential energy greater just before the marble fell? Explain your answer using the law of conservation of energy.

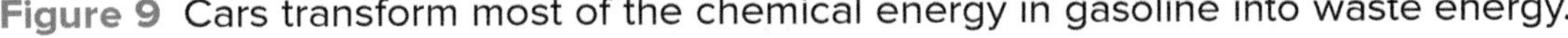

Figure 9 Cars transform most of the chemical energy in gasoline into waste energy.

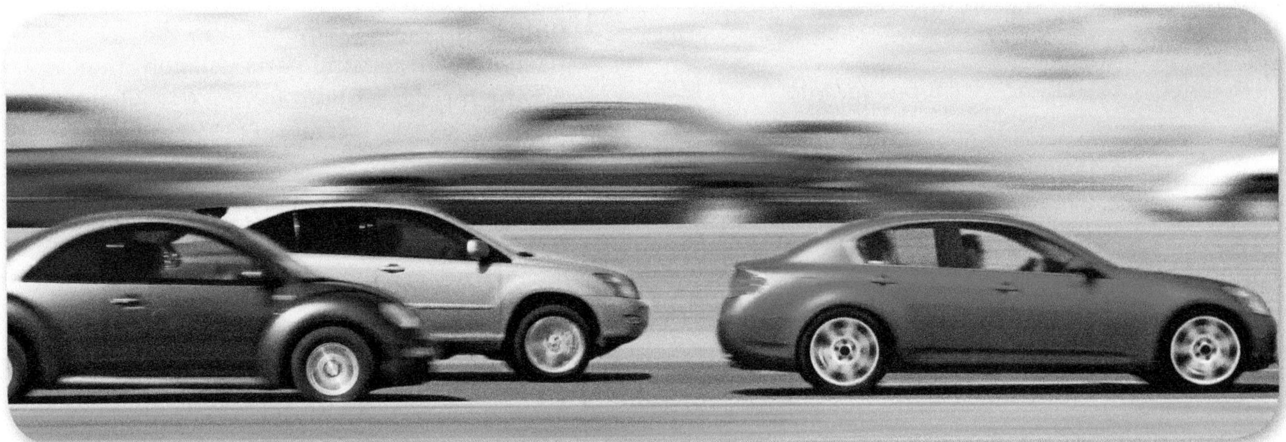

Lesson 2 Review

Visual Summary

Energy can change form, but according to the law of conservation of energy, energy can never be created or destroyed.

Friction transforms mechanical energy into thermal energy.

Different forms of energy, such as sound and radiant energy, are used when someone talks on a cell phone.

FOLDABLES®

Use your lesson Foldable to review the lesson. Save your Foldable for the project at the end of the chapter.

What do you think NOW?

You first read the statements below at the beginning of the chapter.

4. Energy can change from one form to another.

5. Energy is destroyed when you apply the brakes on a moving bicycle or a moving car.

6. The Sun releases radiant energy.

Did you change your mind about whether you agree or disagree with the statements? Rewrite any false statements to make them true.

Use Vocabulary

1. **Use the term** *friction* in a complete sentence.

Understand Key Concepts

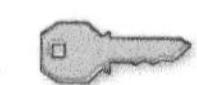

2. **Explain** the law of conservation of energy in your own words.
3. **Describe** the energy transformations that occur when a piece of wood burns.
4. **Identify** the energy transformation that takes place when you apply the brakes on a bicycle.
5. Which energy transformation occurs in a toaster?
   A. chemical to electric
   B. electric to thermal
   C. kinetic to chemical
   D. thermal to potential

Interpret Graphics

6. **Organize Information** Copy and fill in the graphic organizer below to show how kinetic and potential energy change when a ball is thrown straight up and then falls down.

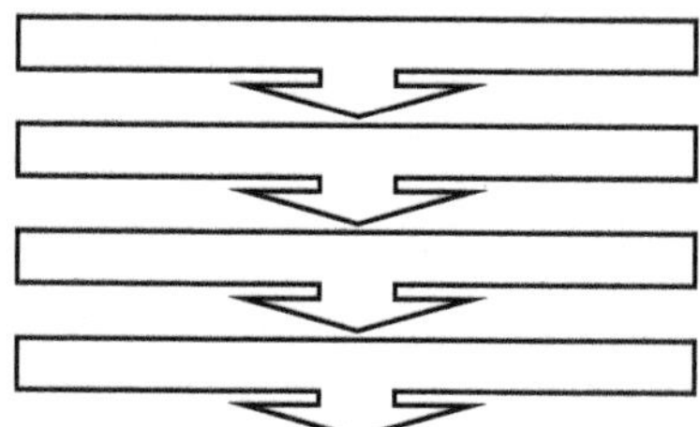

Critical Thinking

7. **Judge** An advertisement states that a machine with moving parts will continue moving forever without having to add any energy. Can this be correct? Explain.

Math Skills

8. **Calculate** If you use a 1,000-W microwave for 0.15 h, how much electric energy do you use?

Fossil Fuels and Rising CO_2

Investigate the link between energy use and carbon dioxide in the atmosphere.

You use energy every day—when you ride in a car or on a bus, turn on a television or a radio, and even when you send an e-mail.

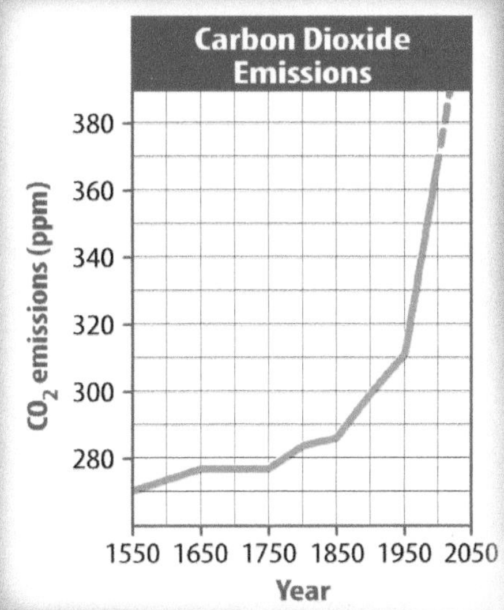

Much of the energy that produces electricity, heats and cools buildings, and powers engines, comes from burning fossil fuels—coal, oil, and natural gas. When fossil fuels burn, the carbon in them combines with oxygen in the atmosphere and forms carbon dioxide gas (CO_2). Carbon dioxide is a greenhouse gas. Greenhouse gases absorb energy. This causes the atmosphere and Earth's surface to become warmer. Greenhouse gases make Earth warm enough to support life. Without greenhouse gases, Earth's surface would be frozen.

However, over the past 150 years, the amount of CO_2 in the atmosphere has increased faster than at any time in the past 800,000 years. Most of this increase is the result of burning fossil fuels. More carbon dioxide in the atmosphere might cause average global temperatures to increase. As temperatures increase, weather patterns worldwide could change. More storms and heavier rainfall could occur in some areas, while other regions could become drier. Increased temperatures could also cause more of the polar ice sheets to melt and raise sea levels. Higher sea levels would cause more flooding in coastal areas.

Developing other energy sources such as geothermal, solar, nuclear, wind, and hydroelectric power would reduce the use of fossil fuels and slow the increase in atmospheric CO_2.

It's Your Turn

MAKE A LIST How can CO_2 emissions be reduced? Work with a partner. List five ways people in your home, school, or community could reduce their energy consumption. Combine your list with your classmates' lists to make a master list.

300 Years OF CARBON DIOXIDE

- **1712**
  A new invention, the steam engine, is powered by burning coal that heats water to produce steam.
- **Early 1800s**
  Coal-fired steam engines, able to pull heavy trains and power steamboats, transform transportation.
- **1882**
  Companies make and sell electricity from coal for everyday use. Electricity is used to power the first lightbulbs, which give off 20 times the light of a candle.
- **1908**
  The first mass-produced automobiles are made available. By 1915, Ford is selling 500,000 cars a year. Gasoline becomes the fuel of choice for car engines.
- **Late 1900s**
  Electrical appliances transform the way we live, work, and communicate. Most electricity is generated by coal-burning power plants.
- **2007**
  There are more than 800 million cars and light trucks on the world's roads.

 Lab

45 minutes

Pinwheel Power

Moving air, or wind, is an energy source. In some places, wind turbines transform the kinetic energy of wind into electric energy. This electric energy can be used to do work by making an object move. In this lab, you will construct a pinwheel turbine and observe how changes in wind speed affect the rate at which your wind turbine does work.

Materials

round pencil with unused eraser

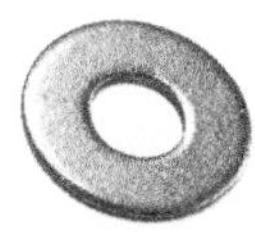

metal washers

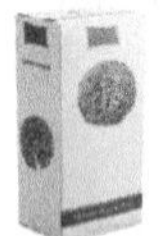

cardboard container

sand or small rocks

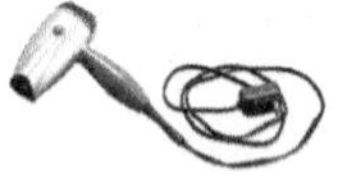

three-speed hair dryer

stopwatch

Also needed: manila folder, metric ruler, scissors, hole punch, thread, pushpin

Safety

Ask a Question

How does wind speed affect the rate at which a wind turbine does work?

Make Observations

1. Read and complete a lab safety form.
2. Construct a pinwheel from a manila folder using the diagram below.
3. Use a plastic pushpin to carefully attach the pinwheel to the eraser of a pencil.
4. Use a hole punch to make holes on opposite sides of the top of a container. Use your ruler to make sure the holes are exactly opposite each other. Weigh down the container with sand or small rocks.
5. Put the pencil through the holes, and make sure the pinwheel spins freely. Blow against the blades of the pinwheel with varying amounts of force to observe how the pinwheel moves. Record your observations in your Science Journal.
6. Measure and cut 100 cm of thread. Tie two washers to one end of the thread. Tape the other end of the thread to the pencil.

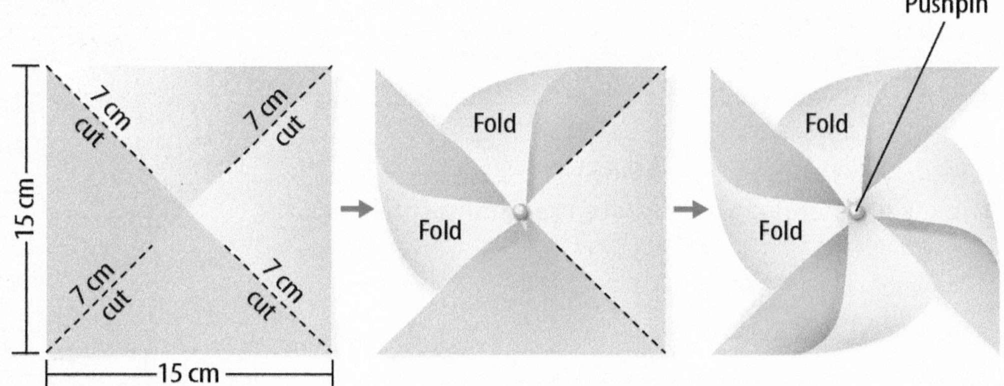

Form a Hypothesis

7. Use your observations from step 5 to form a hypothesis about how wind speed will affect the rate at which the wind turbine does work.

Test Your Hypothesis

8. Work with two other students to test your hypothesis. One person will use the hair dryer to model a slow wind speed. Another person will stop the pencil's movement after 5 seconds on the stopwatch. The third person will measure the length of thread remaining between the pencil and the top of the washers. Then someone will unwind the thread and the group will repeat this procedure four more times with the dryer on low. Record all data in your Science Journal.
9. Repeat step 8 with the dryer on medium.
10. Repeat step 8 with the dryer on high.

Analyze and Conclude

11. **Interpret Data** Did your hypothesis agree with your data and observations? Explain.
12. **Sequence** Describe how energy was transformed from one form into another in this lab.
13. **Draw Conclusions** What factors might have affected the rate at which your pinwheel turbine did work?
14. **The Big Idea** Explain how wind is used as an energy resource.

Communicate Your Results

Use your data and observations to write a paragraph explaining how wind speed affects the rate at which a wind turbine can do work.

8

Inquiry

Extension

Research the designs of real wind turbines. Create a model of an actual wind turbine. Write a short explanation of its advantages and disadvantages compared to other wind turbines.

Lab TIPS

☑ You measure the rate at which the wind turbine does work by measuring how fast the turbine lifts the metal washers.

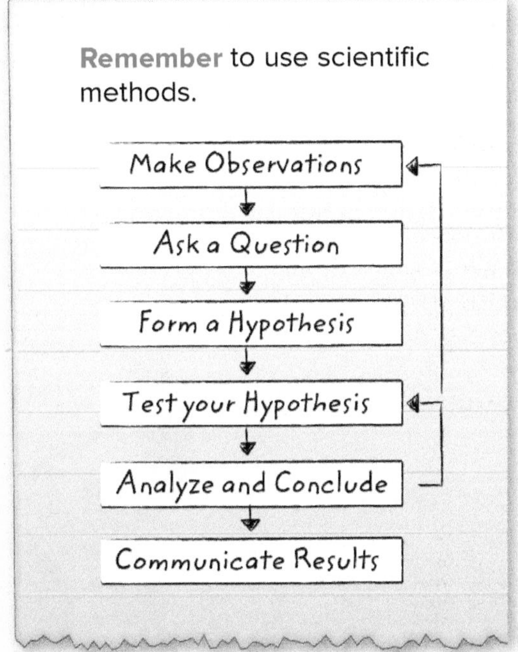
Remember to use scientific methods.
Make Observations
Ask a Question
Form a Hypothesis
Test your Hypothesis
Analyze and Conclude
Communicate Results

Chapter 2 Study Guide

Energy is the ability to cause change. Energy transformations occur when one form of energy changes into another form of energy.

Key Concepts Summary

Lesson 1: Forms of Energy

- **Energy** is the ability to cause change.
- **Kinetic energy** is the energy an object has because of its motion. **Potential energy** is stored energy.
- **Work** is the transfer of energy that occurs when a force makes an object move in the direction of the force while the force is acting on the object.
- Different forms of energy include **thermal energy** and **radiant energy.**

Vocabulary

energy p. 45
kinetic energy p. 46
potential energy p. 46
work p. 48
mechanical energy p. 49
sound energy p. 49
thermal energy p. 49
electric energy p. 49
radiant energy p. 49
nuclear energy p. 49

Lesson 2: Energy Transformations

- According to the **law of conservation of energy,** energy can be transformed from one form into another or transferred from one region to another, but energy cannot be created or destroyed.
- **Friction** transforms mechanical energy into thermal energy.
- Different types of energy are used in many ways including providing energy to move your body, to light a room, and to make and to receive cell phone calls.

Vocabulary

law of conservation of energy p. 54
friction p. 55

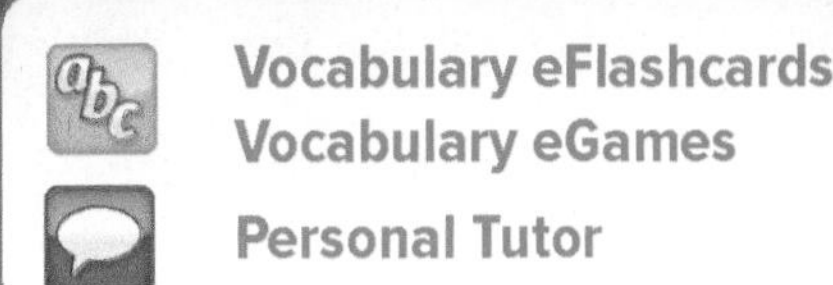

FOLDABLES® Chapter Project

Assemble your Lesson Foldables as shown to make a Chapter Project. Use the project to review what you have learned in this chapter.

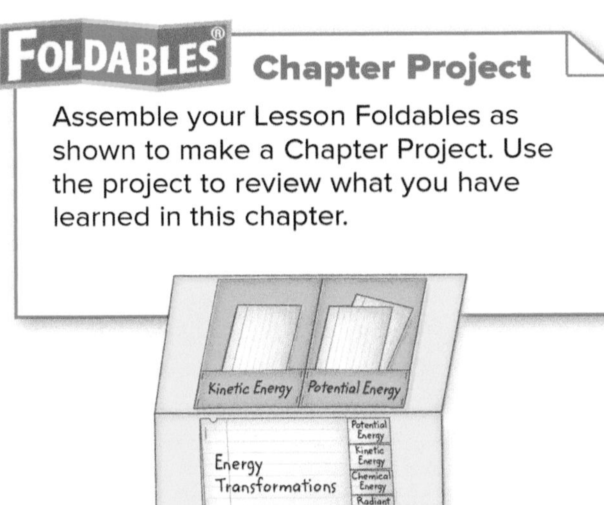

Use Vocabulary

Each of the following sentences is false. Make the sentence true by replacing the italicized word with a vocabulary term.

1. *Thermal energy* is the form of energy carried by an electric current.
2. The *chemical potential energy* of an object depends on its mass and its speed.
3. *Friction* is the transfer of energy that occurs when a force is applied over a distance.
4. A lubricant, such as oil, grease, or graphite, reduces *radiant energy* between rubbing objects.
5. *Radiant energy* is energy that is stored in the nucleus of an atom.

Link Vocabulary and Key Concepts

Copy this concept map, and then use vocabulary terms from the previous page to complete the concept map.

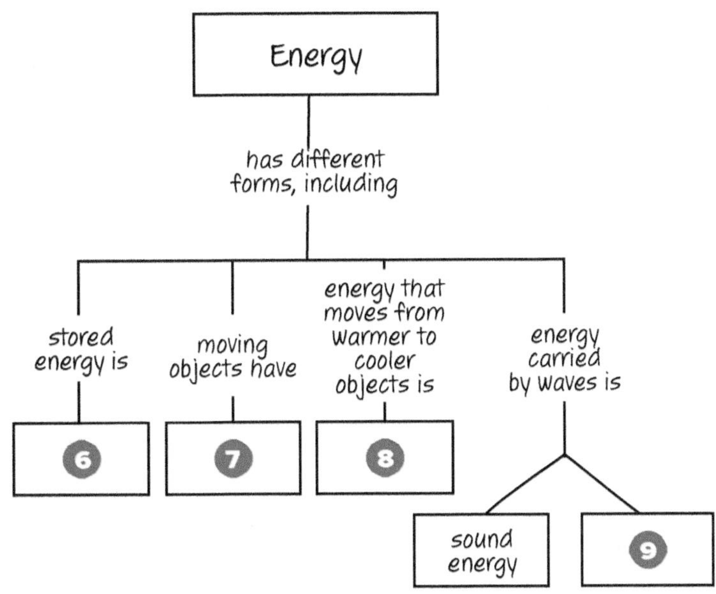

Chapter 2 Review

Understand Key Concepts 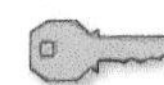

1. What factors determine an object's kinetic energy?
   A. its height and its mass
   B. its mass and its speed
   C. its size and its weight
   D. its speed and its height

2. The gravitational potential energy stored between an object and Earth depends on
   A. the object's height and weight.
   B. the object's mass and speed.
   C. the object's size and weight.
   D. the object's speed and height.

3. When a ball is thrown upward, where does it have the least kinetic energy?
   A. at its highest point
   B. at its lowest point when it is moving downward
   C. at its lowest point when it is moving upward
   D. midway between its highest point and its lowest point

4. Which type of energy is released when the string in the photo below is plucked?

   A. electric energy
   B. nuclear energy
   C. radiant energy
   D. sound energy

5. According to the law of conservation of energy, which is always true?
   A. Energy can never be created or destroyed.
   B. Energy is always converted to friction in moving objects.
   C. The universe is always gaining energy in many different forms.
   D. Work is done when a force is exerted on an object.

6. Which energy transformation is occurring in the food below?

   A. chemical energy to mechanical energy
   B. electric energy to radiant energy
   C. nuclear energy to thermal energy
   D. radiant energy to thermal energy

7. In which situation would the gravitational potential energy between you and Earth be greatest?
   A. You are running down a hill.
   B. You are running up a hill.
   C. You stand at the bottom of a hill.
   D. You stand at the top of a hill.

8. When you speak into a cell phone which energy conversion occurs?
   A. chemical energy to radiant energy
   B. mechanical energy to chemical energy
   C. sound energy to radiant energy
   D. thermal energy to sound energy

9. Which type of energy is released when a firecracker explodes?
   A. chemical potential energy
   B. elastic potential energy
   C. electric energy
   D. nuclear energy

10. Inside the engine of a gasoline-powered car, chemical energy is converted primarily to which kind of energy?
   A. kinetic
   B. potential
   C. sound
   D. waste

Andrew Lambert Photography/Science Source

Critical Thinking

11. **Determine** if work is done on the nail shown below if a person pulls the handle to the left and the handle moves. Explain.

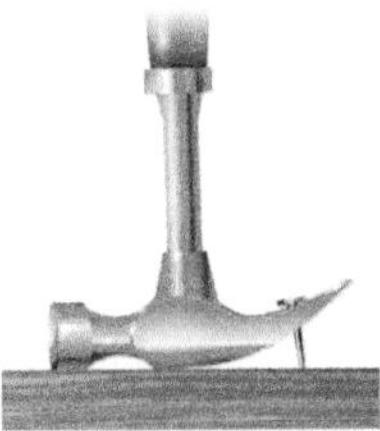

12. **Contrast** the energy transformations that occur in a electrical toaster oven and in an electrical fan.

13. **Infer** A red box and a blue box are on the same shelf. There is more gravitational potential energy between the red box and Earth than between the blue box and Earth. Which box weighs more? Explain your answer.

14. **Infer** Juanita moves a round box and a square box from a lower shelf to a higher shelf. The gravitational potential energy for the round box increases by 50 J. The gravitational potential energy for the square box increases by 100 J. On which box did Juanita do more work? Explain your reasoning.

15. **Explain** why a skateboard coasting on a flat surface slows down and comes to a stop.

16. **Describe** how energy is conserved when a basketball is thrown straight up into the air and falls back into your hands.

17. **Decide** Harold stretches a rubber band and lets it go. The rubber band flies across the room. Harold says this demonstrates the transformation of kinetic energy to elastic potential energy. Is Harold correct? Explain.

Writing in Science

18. **Write** a short essay explaining the energy transformations that occur in an incandescent lightbulb.

REVIEW THE BIG IDEA

19. Write an explanation of energy and energy transformations for a fourth grader who has never heard of these terms.

20. Identify five energy transformations occurring in the photo below.

Math Skills

Math Practice

Solve One-Step Equations

21. An electrical water heater is rated at 5,500 W and operates for 106 h per month. How much electric energy in kWh does the water heater use each month?

22. A family uses 1,303 kWh of electric energy in a month. If the power company charges $0.08 cents per kilowatt hour, what is the total electric energy bill for the month?

Standardized Test Practice

Record your answers on the answer sheet provided by your teacher or on a sheet of paper.

Multiple Choice

1 Which is true when a player throws a basketball toward a hoop?

A Kinetic energy is constant.

B Potential energy is constant.

C Work is done on the player.

D Work is done on the ball.

Use the diagram below to answer questions 2 and 3.

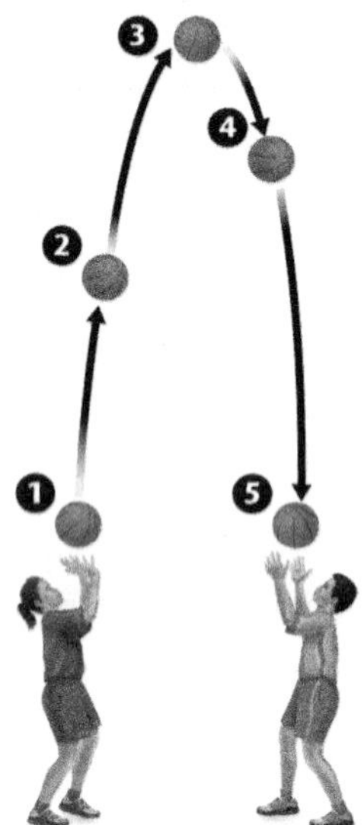

2 At which points is the kinetic energy of the basketball greatest?

A 1 and 5

B 2 and 3

C 2 and 4

D 3 and 4

3 At which point is the gravitational potential energy at its maximum?

A 1

B 2

C 3

D 4

Use the table below to answer question 4.

Vehicle	Mass	Speed
Car 1	1,200 kg	20 m/s
Car 2	1,500 kg	20 m/s
Truck 1	4,800 kg	20 m/s
Truck 2	6,000 kg	20 m/s

4 Which vehicle has the most kinetic energy?

A car 1

B car 2

C truck 1

D truck 2

5 When you compress a spring, which type of energy increases?

A kinetic

B nuclear

C potential

D radiant

6 Sound energy cannot travel through

A a vacuum.

B a wooden table.

C polluted air.

D pond water.

7 A bicyclist uses brakes to slow from 3 m/s to a stop. What stops the bike?

A friction

B gravity

C kinetic energy

D thermal energy

Use the diagram below to answer question 8.

8 The work being done in the diagram above transfers energy to

A the box.

B the floor.

C the girl.

D the shelf.

9 Which is true of energy?

A It cannot be created or destroyed.

B It cannot change form.

C Most forms cannot be conserved.

D Most forms cannot be traced to a source.

10 Which energy transformation occurs when you light a gas burner?

A chemical to thermal

B electric to chemical

C nuclear to chemical

D radiant to thermal

Constructed Response

Use the table below to answer questions 11 and 12.

Form of Energy	Definition

11 Copy the table above, and list six forms of energy. Briefly define each form.

12 Provide real-life examples of each of the listed forms of energy.

Use the diagram below to answer question 13.

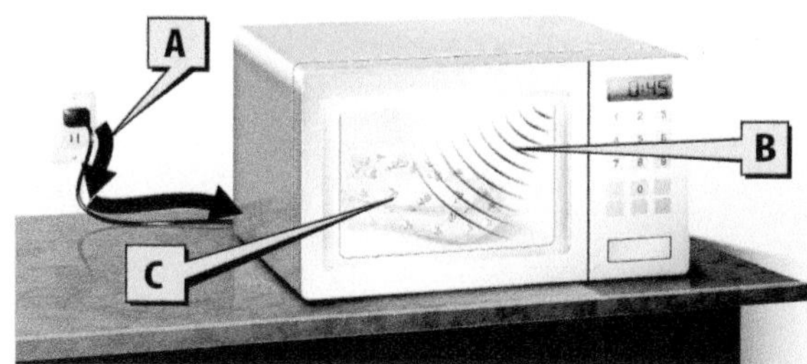

13 Describe the energy transformations that occur at locations A, B, and C.

NEED EXTRA HELP?													
If You Missed Question...	1	2	3	4	5	6	7	8	9	10	11	12	13
Go to Lesson...	1	2	2	1	1	1	2	1	2	2	1	2	2

1600 — 1700 — 1800

1660
Robert Hooke publishes the wave theory of light, comparing light's movement to that of waves in water.

1705
Francis Hauksbee experiments with a clock in a vacuum and proves that sound cannot travel without air.

1820
Danish physicist Hans Christian Ørsted publishes his discovery that an electric current passing through a wire produces a magnetic field.

1878
Thomas Edison develops a system to provide electricity to homes and businesses using locally generated and distributed direct current (DC) electricity.

1882
Thomas Edison develops and builds the first electricity-generating plant in New York City, which provides 110 V of direct current to 59 customers in lower Manhattan.

I don't know why I wear these shades, I NEVER get the spotlight!

1900

2000

1883
The first standardized incandescent electric lighting system using overhead wires begins service in Roselle, New Jersey.

1890s
Physicist Nikola Tesla introduces alternating current (AC) by inventing the alternating current generator, allowing electricity to be transmitted at higher voltages over longer distances.

1947
Chuck Yeager becomes the first pilot to travel faster than the speed of sound.

Visit ConnectED for this unit's
STEM activity.

Graphs

Have you ever felt a shock from static electricity? The electric energy that you feel is similar to the electric energy you see as a flash of lightning, such as in Figure 1, only millions of times smaller. Scientists are still investigating what causes lightning and where it will occur. They use graphs to learn about the risk of lightning in different places and at different times. A **graph** is a type of chart that shows relationships between variables. Graphs organize and summarize data in a visual way. Three of the most common graphs are circle graphs, bar graphs, and line graphs.

Types of Graphs

Line Graphs

A line graph is used when you want to analyze how a change in one variable affects another variable. This line graph shows how the average number of lightning flashes changes over time in Illinois. Time is plotted on the *x*-axis. The average numbers of lightning flashes are plotted on the *y*-axis. Each dot, called a data point, indicates the average number of flashes recorded during that hour. A line connects the data points so a trend can be analyzed.

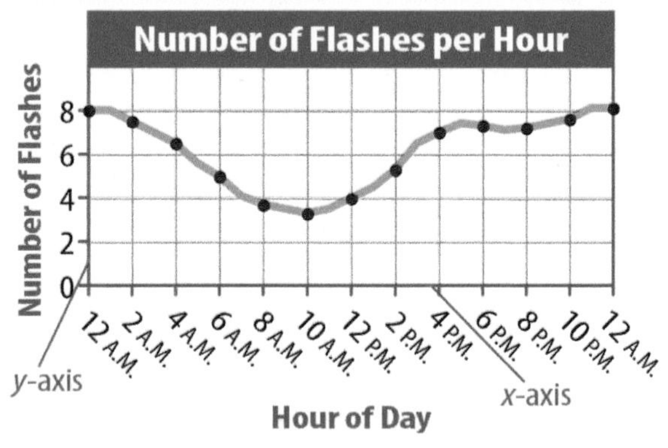

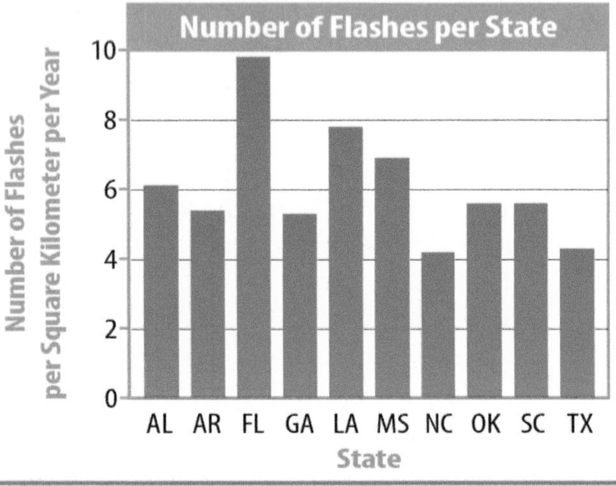

Bar Graphs

When you want to compare amounts in different categories, you use a bar graph. The horizontal axis often contains categories instead of numbers. This bar graph shows the average number of lightning flashes that occur in different states. On average, about 9.8 lightning flashes strike each square kilometer of land in Florida every year. Florida has more lightning flashes per square kilometer than all other states shown on the graph.

Circle Graphs

If you want to show how the parts of something relate to the whole, use a circle graph. This circle graph shows the average percentage of lightning flashes each U.S. region receives in a year. The graph shows that the mountain region of the United States receives about 14 percent of all lightning flashes that strike the country each year. From the graph, you can also determine that the southeast receives the most lightning in a given year.

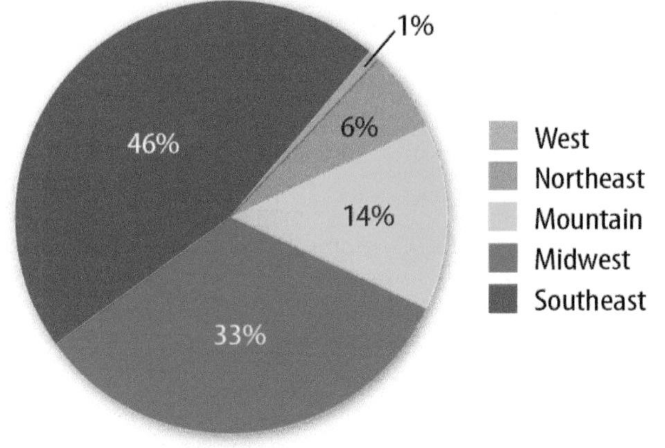

Line Graphs and Trends

Suppose you are planning a picnic in an area that experiences quite a bit of lightning. When would be the safest time to go? First, you gather data about the average number of lightning flashes per hour. Next, you plot the data on a line graph and analyze trends. Trends are patterns in data that help you find relationships among the data and make predictions.

Follow the orange line on the line graph from 12 A.M. to 10 A.M. in **Figure 2.** Notice that the line slopes downward, indicated by the green arrow. A downward slope means that as measurements on the *x*-axis increase, measurements on the *y*-axis decrease. So, as time passes from 12 A.M. to 10 A.M., the number of lightning flashes decreases.

If you follow the orange line on the line graph from 12 P.M. to 5 P.M., you will notice that the line slopes upward. This is indicated by the blue arrow. An upward slope means that as the measurements on the *x*-axis increase, the measurements on the *y*-axis also increase. So, as time passes from 12 P.M. to 5 P.M., the number of lightning flashes increases.

The line graph shows you that between about 8 A.M. and 12 P.M., you would have the least risk of lightning during your picnic.

▲ **Figure 1** Scientists study lightning to get a better understanding of what causes it and to predict when it will occur.

Figure 2 The slope of a line in a line graph shows the relationship between the variables on the *x*-axis and the variables on the *y*-axis. ▼

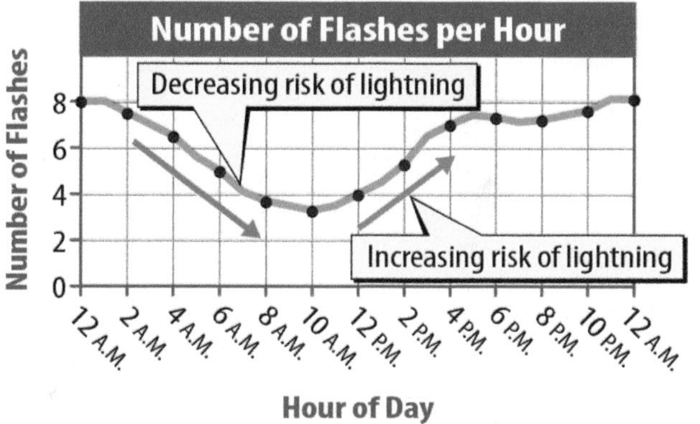

MiniLab — 25 minutes

When does lightning strike?

Meteorologists in New Mexico collected data on the number of lightning flashes throughout the day. How can you use a line graph to plan the safest day trip?

1. Make a line graph of the data in the table.
2. Find the trends that show when the risk for lightning is increasing and when it is decreasing.

Hour	# of Flashes
12:00 A.M.	2
3:00 A.M.	2
6:00 A.M.	2
9:00 A.M.	2
12:00 P.M.	5
3:00 P.M.	21
6:00 P.M.	36
9:00 P.M.	22
12:00 A.M.	2

Analyze and Conclude

Decide How could you use your graph to plan a day trip in New Mexico with the least risk of lightning?

Chapter 3

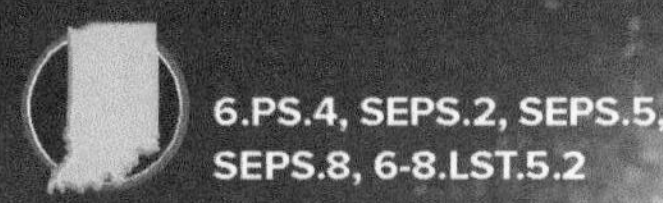

Waves

THE BIG IDEA How do waves travel through matter?

Inquiry What causes waves?

Waves are actually energy moving through matter. Think about the amount of energy this wave must be carrying.

- What do you think caused this giant wave?
- Do you think this is the only large wave in the area?
- How do you think this wave moves through water?

Kaz Mori/Getty Images

Get Ready to Read

What do you think?

Before you read, decide if you agree or disagree with each of these statements. As you read this chapter, see if you change your mind about any of the statements.

1. Waves carry matter as they travel from one place to another.
2. Sound waves can travel where there is no matter.
3. Waves that carry more energy cause particles in a material to move a greater distance.
4. Sound waves travel fastest in gases, such as those in the air.
5. When light waves strike a mirror, they change direction.
6. Light waves travel at the same speed in all materials.

Your one-stop online resource
connectED.mcgraw-hill.com

LearnSmart®

Chapter Resources Files, Reading Essentials, Get Ready to Read, Quick Vocabulary

Animations, Videos, Interactive Tables

Self-checks, Quizzes, Tests

Project-Based Learning Activities

Lab Manuals, Safety Videos, Virtual Labs & Other Tools

Vocabulary, Multilingual eGlossary, Vocab eGames, Vocab eFlashcards

Personal Tutors

Reading Guide

Key Concepts

ESSENTIAL QUESTIONS

- What is a wave?
- How do different types of waves make particles of matter move?
- Can waves travel through empty space?

Vocabulary

wave p. 75
mechanical wave p. 77
medium p. 77
transverse wave p. 77
crest p. 77
trough p. 77
longitudinal wave p. 78
compression p. 78
rarefaction p. 78
electromagnetic wave p. 81

Multilingual eGlossary

What are waves?

Inquiry Why Circles?

Have you ever seen raindrops falling on a smooth pool of water? If so, you probably saw a pattern of circles forming. What are these circles? The circles are small waves that spread out from where the raindrops hit the water.

Deco/Alamy

Launch Lab

20 minutes

How can you make waves? 

Oceans, lakes, and ponds aren't the only places you can find waves. Can you create waves in a cup of water?

1. Read and complete a lab safety form.
2. Add **water** to a **clear plastic cup** until it is about two-thirds full. Place the cup on a **paper towel.**
3. Explore ways of producing water waves by touching the cup. Do not move the cup.
4. Now explore ways of producing water waves without touching the cup. Do not move the cup.

Think About This

1. How did the water's surface change when you produced water waves in the cup?
2. **Key Concept** What did the different ways of producing water waves have in common?

What are waves?

Imagine a warm summer day. You are floating on a raft in the middle of a calm pool. Suddenly, a friend does a cannonball dive into the pool. You probably know what happens next–you are no longer resting peacefully on your raft. Your friend's dive causes you to start bobbing up and down on the water. You might notice that after you stop moving up and down, you haven't moved forward or backward in the pool.

Review Vocabulary
energy
the ability to cause change

Why did your friend's dive make you move up and down? Your friend created waves by jumping into the pool. *A* **wave** *is a disturbance that transfers energy from one place to another without transferring matter.* You moved up and down because these waves transferred energy.

 **Key Concept Check** What is a wave?

A Source of Energy

The photo on the previous page shows the waves produced when raindrops fall into a pond. The impact of the raindrops on the water is the source of energy for these water waves. Waves transfer energy away from the source of the energy. Figure 1 shows how light waves spread out in all directions away from a flame. The burning wick is the energy source for these light waves.

Figure 1 All waves, such as light waves, spread out from the energy source that produces the waves.

Hutchings Photography/Digital Light Source

Figure 2 Water waves transfer energy across the pool, but not matter. As a result, the raft does not move along with the waves. Instead, the raft returns to its initial position.

The raft is at rest in its initial position.

A wave begins to lift the raft upward when it reaches the raft.

The wave transfers energy to the raft as it lifts it upward.

The wave passes the raft and continues to move across the pool.

The raft returns to its initial position after the wave passes.

Visual Check Describe what happens to the raft when the waves transfer energy to it.

Energy Transfer

Think about the waves created by a cannonball dive. When the diver hits the water, the diver's energy transfers to the water. Recall that energy is the ability to cause change. The energy transferred to the water produces waves. The waves transfer energy from the place where the diver hits the water to the place where your raft is floating. Figure 2 shows that the energy transferred by a wave lifts your raft when the wave reaches it.

Reading Check What do waves transfer from place to place?

The waves created in the pool caused you to move up and then down on your raft. As Figure 2 shows, however, after the waves passed, you were in the same place in the pool. The waves didn't carry you along after they reached you. Waves transfer energy, but they leave matter in the same place after they pass. Because the water under your raft was not carried along with the waves, you remained in the same place in the pool.

How Waves Transfer Energy

Why wouldn't a water wave carry a raft along with it? How do waves transfer energy without transferring matter? Think about the diver hitting the water. Like all materials, water is made of tiny particles. When the diver hit the water, the impact of the diver exerted a force on water particles. The force of the impact transferred energy to the water by pushing and pulling on water particles. These particles then pushed and pulled on neighboring water particles, transferring energy outward from the point of impact. In this way, the energy of the falling diver is transferred to the water. This energy then travels through the water, from particle to particle, as a wave.

Mechanical Waves

A water wave is an example of a mechanical wave. *A wave that can travel only through matter is a* **mechanical wave.** Mechanical waves can travel through solids, liquids, and gases. They cannot travel through a vacuum. *A material in which a wave travels is called a* **medium.** Two types of mechanical waves are transverse waves and longitudinal waves.

Transverse Waves

You can make a wave on a rope by shaking the end of the rope up and down, as shown in Figure 3. A wave on a rope is a transverse wave. *A* **transverse wave** *is a wave in which the disturbance is perpendicular to the direction the wave travels.* Figure 3 shows that the particles in the rope move up and down while the wave travels horizontally. The up-and-down movement of the rope particles is at right angles to the direction of wave movement.

Key Concept Check How do particles move in a transverse wave?

The dotted line in Figure 3 shows the position of the rope before you start shaking it. This position is called the rest position. The transverse wave on the rope has high points and low points. *The highest points on a transverse wave are* **crests.** *The lowest points on a transverse wave are* **troughs.**

Animation

MiniLab **15 minutes**

How do waves travel through matter?

When a wave travels through matter, energy transfers from particle to particle. How do particles move in different types of waves?

1. Read and complete a lab safety form.
2. Tie a piece of **yarn** around a **rope.** Stretch the rope on the floor between you and a partner. Make a transverse wave by moving the rope side to side on the floor. Observe how the yarn moves.
3. Tie a piece of yarn around one coil near the middle of a **metal spring toy.** Stretch the toy between you and a partner on the floor. Sharply push one end of the spring toy forward. Observe how the yarn moves.

Analyze and Conclude

1. **Compare and contrast** the motion of the yarn on the rope and the motion of the yarn on the spring.
2. **Key Concept** Write a statement about the motion of the particles of a medium as a wave passes.

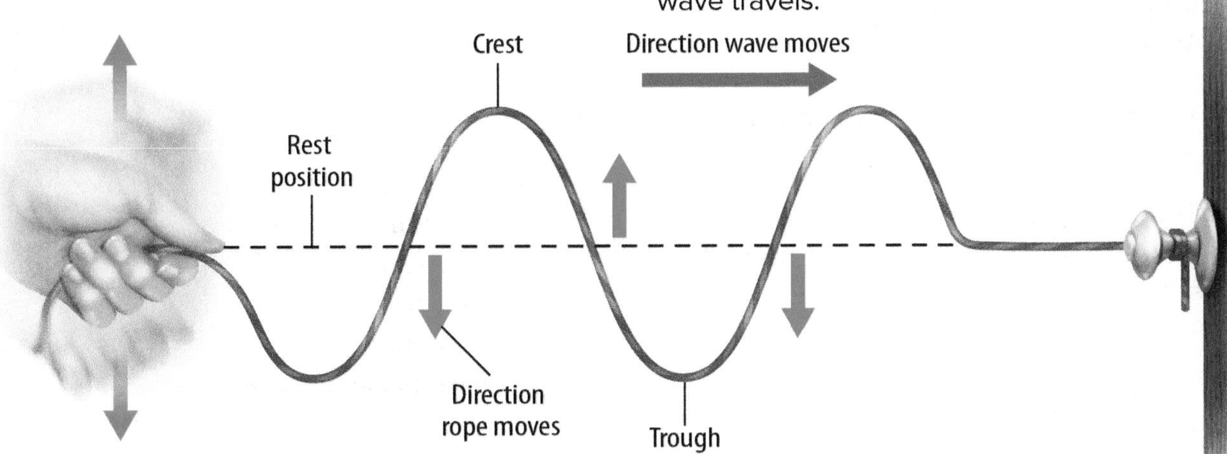

Figure 3 In a transverse wave, particles move at right angles to the direction the wave travels.

Longitudinal Waves

Animation

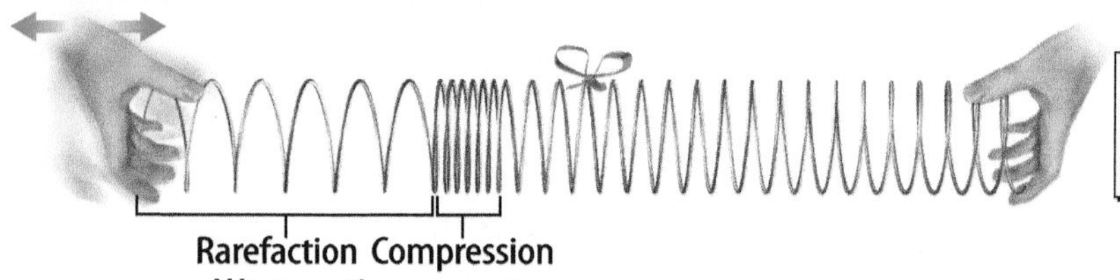

Rarefaction Compression
Wave motion
A back-and-forth movement of the hand on the left produces a longitudinal wave that travels to the right.

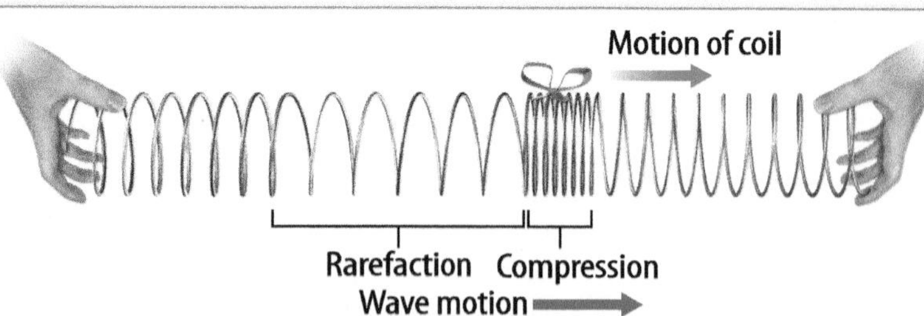

Motion of coil
Rarefaction Compression
Wave motion
The wave makes the coil with the yarn move to the right as the compression of the wave reaches that coil.

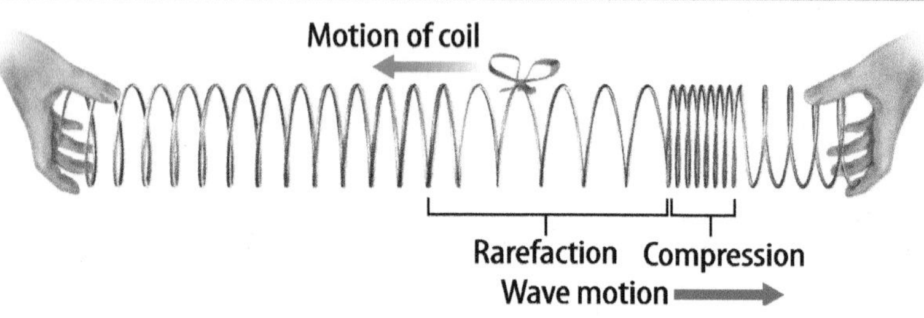

Motion of coil
Rarefaction Compression
Wave motion
The wave makes the coil with the yarn move to the left as the rarefaction of the wave reaches that coil.

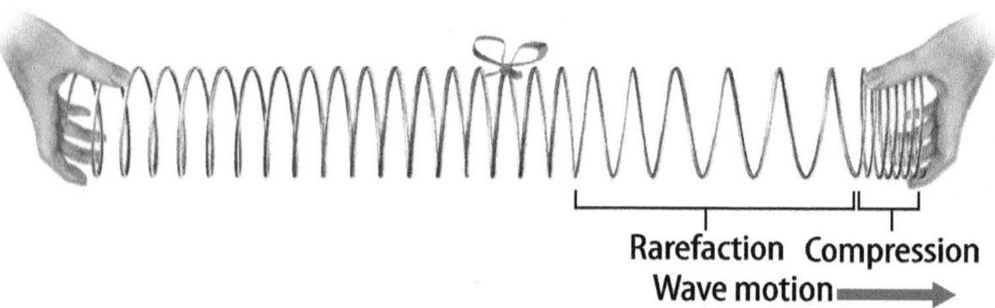

Rarefaction Compression
Wave motion
The coil with the yarn returns to its original position after the wave passes.

Figure 4 A longitudinal wave travels along the spring when the hand moves back and forth. The coils of the spring move back and forth along the same direction that the wave travels.

Longitudinal Waves

Another type of mechanical wave is a longitudinal (lahn juh TEWD nul) wave. *A* **longitudinal wave** *makes the particles in a medium move parallel to the direction that the wave travels.* A longitudinal wave traveling along a spring is shown in Figure 4. As the wave passes, the coils of the spring move closer together, then farther apart, and then return to their original positions. The coils move back and forth parallel to the direction that the wave moves.

Before a wave is produced in the spring, the coils are the same distance apart. This is the rest position of the spring. Figure 4 shows that the wave produces regions in the spring where the coils are closer together than they are in the rest position and regions where they are farther apart. *The regions of a longitudinal wave where the particles in the medium are closest together are* **compressions.** *The regions of a longitudinal wave where the particles are farthest apart are* **rarefactions.**

Key Concept Check How do particles move in a longitudinal wave?

Vibrations and Mechanical Waves

If you hit a large drum with a drumstick, the surface of the drum vibrates, or moves up and down. A vibration is a back-and-forth or an up-and-down movement of an object. Vibrating objects, such as a drum or a guitar string, are the sources of energy that produce mechanical waves.

Reading Check What produces mechanical waves?

One Wave per Vibration Suppose you move the end of a rope down, up, and back down to its original position. Then you make a transverse wave with a crest and a trough, as shown in the top of Figure 5. The up-and-down movement of your hand is one vibration. One vibration of your hand produces a transverse wave with one crest and one trough.

Similarly, a single back-and-forth movement of the end of a spring produces a longitudinal wave with one compression and one rarefaction. In both cases, the vibration of your hand is the source of energy that produces the transverse or longitudinal wave.

Vibrations Stop—Waves Go Now imagine that you move the end of the rope up and down several times. The motion of your hand transfers energy to the rope and produces several crests and troughs, as the bottom of Figure 5 shows. As long as your hand keeps moving up and down, energy transfers to the rope and produces waves.

When your hand stops moving, waves no longer are produced. However, as shown in both parts of Figure 5, waves produced by the earlier movements of your hand continue to travel along the rope. This is true for any vibrating object. Waves can keep moving even after the object stops vibrating.

Reading Check If your hand makes four vibrations, how many waves are created?

Figure 5 Vibrations produce waves that keep traveling even when the vibrations stop.

Vibrations and Waves

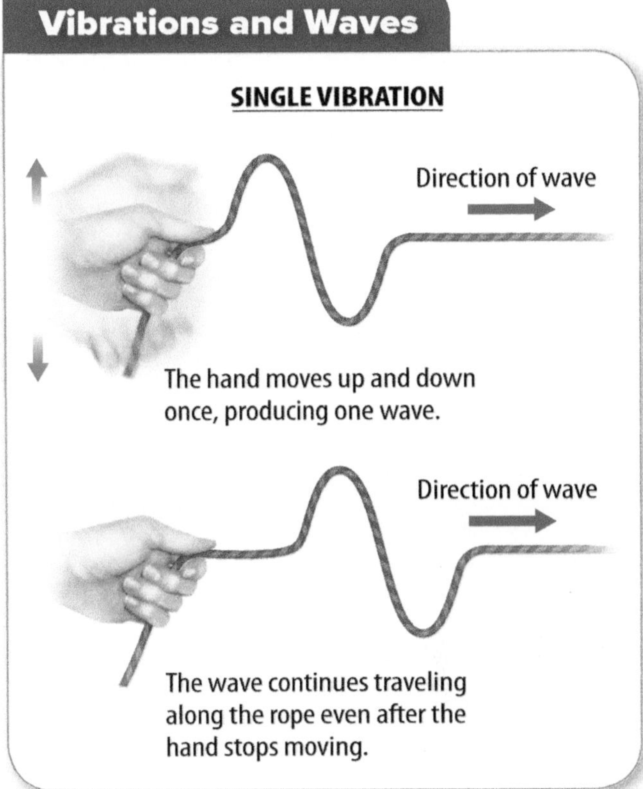

SINGLE VIBRATION
Direction of wave
The hand moves up and down once, producing one wave.
Direction of wave
The wave continues traveling along the rope even after the hand stops moving.

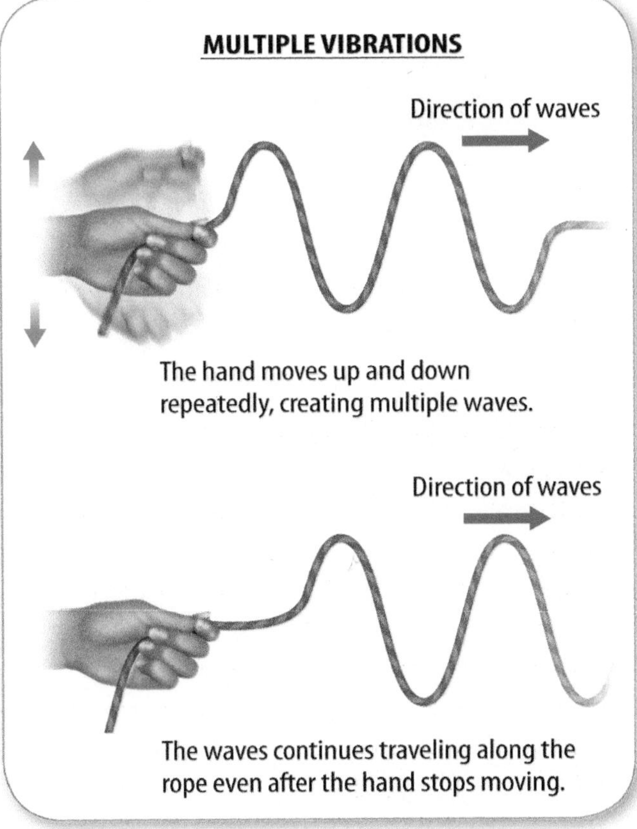

MULTIPLE VIBRATIONS
Direction of waves
The hand moves up and down repeatedly, creating multiple waves.
Direction of waves
The waves continues traveling along the rope even after the hand stops moving.

Types of Mechanical Waves

All mechanical waves travel only in matter. Sound waves, water waves, and waves produced by earthquakes are mechanical waves that travel in different mediums. Table 1 shows examples of these mechanical waves.

Visual Check What are the mediums for each of the mechanical waves in Table 1?

Table 1 Types of Mechanical Waves

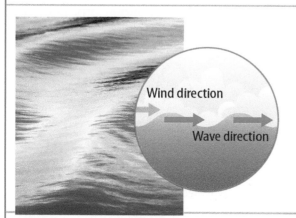

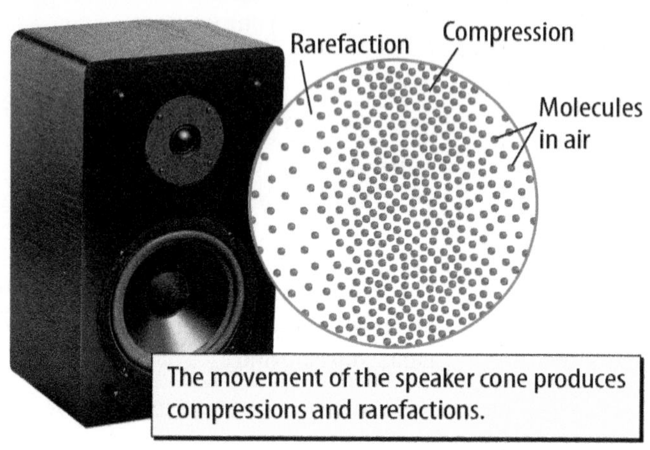 The movement of the speaker cone produces compressions and rarefactions.	**Sound Waves** • Sound waves are longitudinal waves that travel in solids, liquids, and gases. • A sound wave is made of a series of compressions and rarefactions. • A paper cone inside the speaker vibrates in and out, producing sound waves. • The speaker makes a compression when the speaker cone pushes air molecules together as it moves outward. • The speaker makes a rarefaction when the speaker cone moves inward and the air molecules spread out.
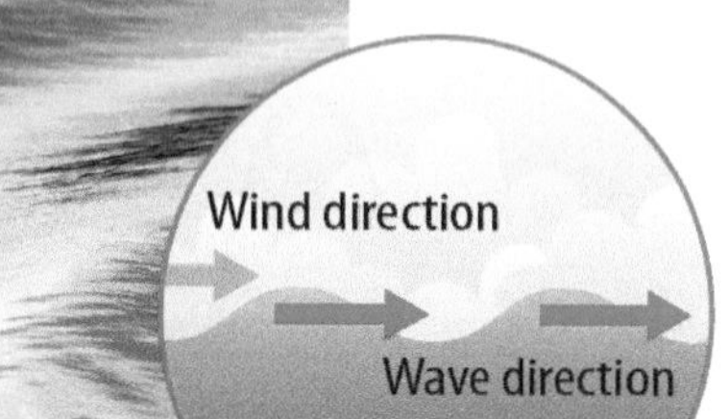	**Water Waves** • Water waves are a combination of transverse waves and longitudinal waves. • Wind produces most waves in oceans and lakes by pushing on the surface of the water.
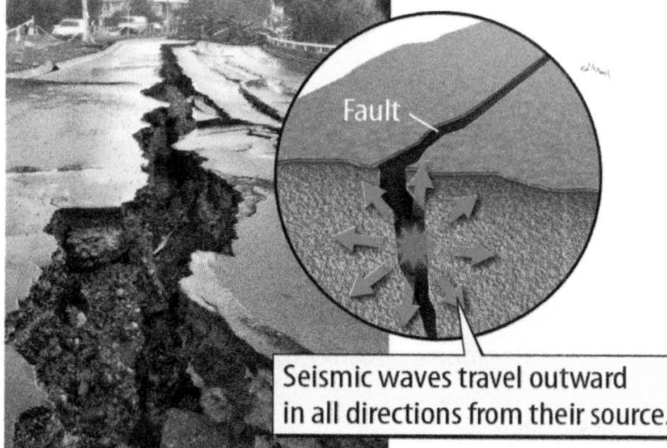 Seismic waves travel outward in all directions from their source.	**Seismic Waves** • Waves in Earth's crust, called seismic (SIZE mihk) waves, cause earthquakes. • Seismic waves are mechanical waves that travel within Earth and on Earth's surface. • There are both longitudinal and transverse seismic waves. • In some places, parts of Earth's upper layers can move along a crack called a fault. The movement of Earth's upper layers along a fault produces seismic waves.

Electromagnetic Waves

The Sun gives off light that travels through space to Earth. Like sound waves and water waves, light is also a type of wave. However, light is not a mechanical wave. A mechanical wave cannot travel through the space between the Sun and Earth. Light is an electromagnetic wave. *An* **electromagnetic wave** *is a wave that can travel through empty space and through matter.*

Key Concept Check Identify a type of wave that can travel through a vacuum.

WORD ORIGIN

electromagnetic
from Greek *elektron,* means "amber" and *magnes,* means "lodestone"

Types of Electromagnetic Waves

In addition to light waves, other types of electromagnetic waves include radio waves, microwaves, infrared waves, and ultraviolet waves. Cell phones use microwaves that carry sounds from one phone to another. When you stand by a fire, infrared waves striking your skin cause the warmth you feel. Ultraviolet waves from the Sun cause sunburns.

FOLDABLES®

Make a two-tab book and label it as shown. Use your book to organize information about mechanical and electromagnetic waves.

Mechanical Waves | Electromagnetic Waves

Electromagnetic Waves and Objects

Every object, including you, gives off electromagnetic waves. The type of electromagnetic waves that an object gives off depends mainly on the temperature of the object. For example, you give off mostly infrared waves. Other objects near human body temperature also give off mostly infrared waves. Hotter objects, such as a piece of glowing metal, give off visible light waves as well as infrared waves. Some animals, such as the copperhead in Figure 6, have specialized detectors for perceiving the infrared waves given off by their prey.

Electromagnetic Waves from the Sun

Like all waves, electromagnetic waves carry energy. Scientists often call this radiant energy. Infrared and visible light waves carry about 92 percent of the radiant energy that reaches Earth from the Sun. Ultraviolet waves carry about 7 percent of the Sun's energy.

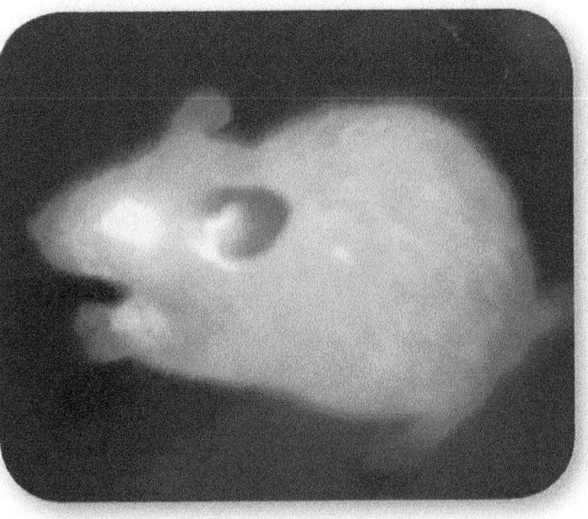

Figure 6 Some snakes have special organs on their heads that allow them to detect infrared waves from prey, such as mice. The right photo shows the infrared waves that a mouse gives off.

Lesson 1 Review

Visual Summary

Waves, such as those from a burning candle, the Sun, or a loudspeaker, transfer energy away from the source of the wave.

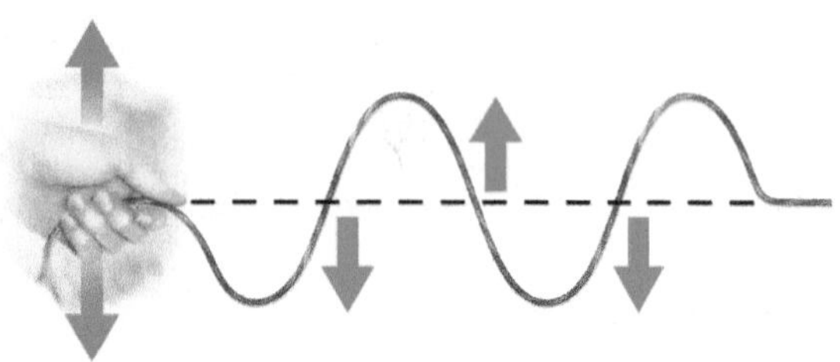

A transverse wave makes particles in a medium move perpendicular to the direction of the wave.

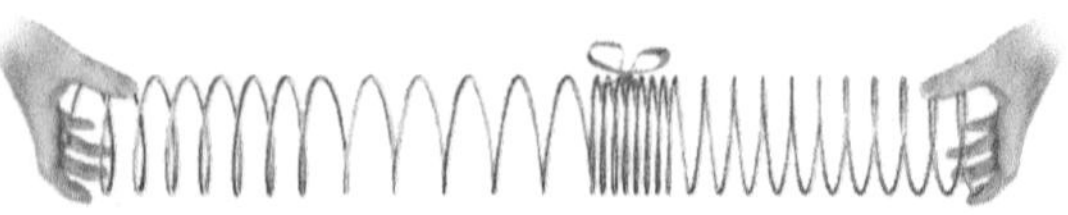

A longitudinal wave makes the particles in a medium move in a direction that is parallel to the direction the wave travels.

FOLDABLES®

Use your lesson Foldable to review the lesson. Save your Foldable for the project at the end of the chapter.

What do you think 

You first read the statements below at the beginning of the chapter.

1. Waves carry matter as they travel from one place to another.

2. Sound waves can travel where there is no matter.

Did you change your mind about whether you agree or disagree with the statements? Rewrite any false statements to make them true.

Use Vocabulary

1. **Define** *wave* in your own words.
2. **Distinguish** between a *transverse wave* and a *longitudinal wave.*

Understand Key Concepts 

3. What causes a wave?
   A. a crest
   B. a rarefaction
   C. a rope
   D. a vibration
4. **Differentiate** How are sound waves and water waves similar? How are they different?

Interpret Graphics

5. **Describe** what happens to the wave shown below when the hand stops vibrating.

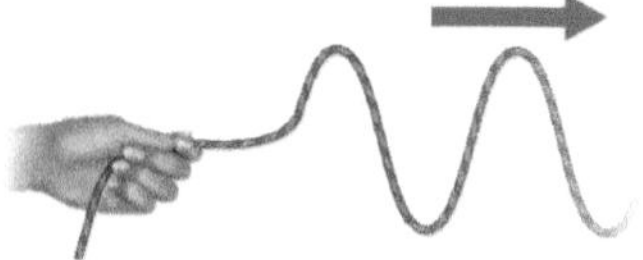

6. **Compare and Contrast** Copy and fill in the graphic organizer below to compare and contrast mechanical waves and electromagnetic waves.

Similarities	Differences

Critical Thinking

7. **Analyze** A scientist wants to analyze signals from outer space that tell her about the age of the universe. Her lab is equipped with advanced sensors that detect sound waves, radio waves, and seismic waves. Which of these sensors will provide the best information? Explain your reasoning.
8. **Predict** You are floating motionless on a rubber raft in the middle of a pool. A friend forms a wave by slapping the water every second. Will the wave carry you to the edge of the pool? Explain your answer.

Making a Computer Tsunami

CAREERS in SCIENCE

Meet Vasily Titov, a scientist working to predict the next big wave.

On the morning of December 26, 2004, a magnitude 9.3 earthquake in the Indian Ocean caused an enormous tsunami. On the other side of the world, a scientist in Seattle, Washington, sprang into action. Vasily Titov worked through the night to develop the first-ever computer model of the tsunami.

Titov is a mathematician for the National Oceanic and Atmospheric Administration (NOAA). His computer model solves equations that describe how tsunamis are produced and how they move. The model includes data about an earthquake's energy, the shape of the ocean floor, and the ocean's depth. When there is an earthquake on the ocean floor, Titov's model predicts the properties of the resulting tsunami.

A tsunami moves about as fast as a jet airplane. By the time Titov's computer model was ready, the 2004 Indian Ocean tsunami had already hit the coast and killed more than 280,000 people. But Titov hopes this new tool will help communities prepare for future tsunamis.

AMERICAN MUSEUM OF NATURAL HISTORY

Now Titov is applying his computer model to the Pacific Northwest. His model shows how tsunamis could affect the coastlines of Washington, Oregon, and northern California. Emergency managers can use these results to predict when tsunami waves will reach different parts of the coast. Warnings could be issued to communities just minutes after an earthquake triggers a tsunami.

What's a tsunami?

Wind causes most ordinary water waves, but tsunamis are not ordinary waves. Underwater earthquakes usually cause these giant, destructive waves. As a tectonic plate moves upward, it raises the water above it. As this water falls back down, it forms a massive wave that spreads in all directions.

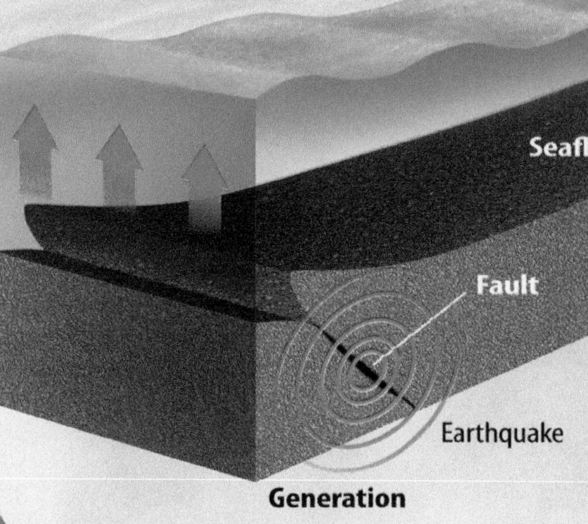

1 In deep water, tsunamis usually travel faster than 250 m/s, but they are only a few centimeters high. Most ships in deep water cannot even detect a passing tsunami.

2 As the wave approaches shore, much of its kinetic energy is transformed into gravitational potential energy. The water piles up, forming enormous walls of water that flood coastal areas.

It's Your Turn

WRITE Suppose you were a witness to the 2004 tsunami. Write a diary entry recording your experience. What was your first hint that something was wrong? What was happening around you? What did you see and hear?

Lesson 2

Reading Guide

Key Concepts
ESSENTIAL QUESTIONS

- What are properties of waves?
- How are the frequency and the wavelength of a wave related?
- What affects wave speed?

Vocabulary

amplitude p. 85
wavelength p. 87
frequency p. 88

Multilingual eGlossary

BrainPOP® Science Video

SEPS.2, SEPS.5

Wave Properties

Inquiry Why So Big?

Have you ever watched a surfer on a huge wave? If so, you might have wondered why some waves are huge and why others are small. The size of a water wave depends on the energy it carries.

Launch Lab

20 minutes

Which sounds have more energy?

Some sounds are loud and others are soft. What is the difference between loud and soft sounds?

1. Read and complete a lab safety form.
2. Place a **bowl of water** over a sheet of **white paper.**
3. Strike a **tuning fork** gently on your hand so it makes a soft sound and then quickly place its prongs in the bowl of water. Remove the tuning fork.
4. Strike the tuning fork sharply on your hand so it makes a loud sound and then quickly place its prongs in the bowl of water.

Think About This

1. **Contrast** the waves made by the tuning fork in steps 3 and 4 in your Science Journal.
2. In which step did the tuning fork transfer more energy to the water? Explain your answer.
3. **Key Concept** How are the loudness of the sounds and the vibrations of the tuning fork related?

Amplitude and Energy

Imagine you are floating on a raft in a pool and someone gently splashes the water near you, creating waves. You might barely feel these waves lift you up and down as they pass. If someone dives off the diving board, this makes waves that bounce you up and down. What's the difference between these waves?

Initially, the surface of the water you are floating on is nearly flat. This is the rest position for the water. The dive produced waves with higher crests and deeper troughs than those of the waves produced by gently splashing the water. This means that the dive caused water to move a greater distance from its rest position, producing a wave with a greater amplitude. *The* **amplitude** *of a wave is the maximum distance that the wave moves from its rest position.*

For any wave, the larger the amplitude, the more energy the wave carries. The wave produced by the diver hitting the water caused a greater change than the wave produced by the gentle splash. The first wave had more energy.

Reading Check What is the amplitude of a wave? How are the amplitude of a wave and energy related?

WORD ORIGIN

amplitude
from Latin *amplitudinem,* means "width"

FOLDABLES®

Make a layered book from two half sheets of paper. Label it as shown. Use your book to organize your notes about the properties of waves.

Properties of Waves
Amplitude
Wavelength
Frequency

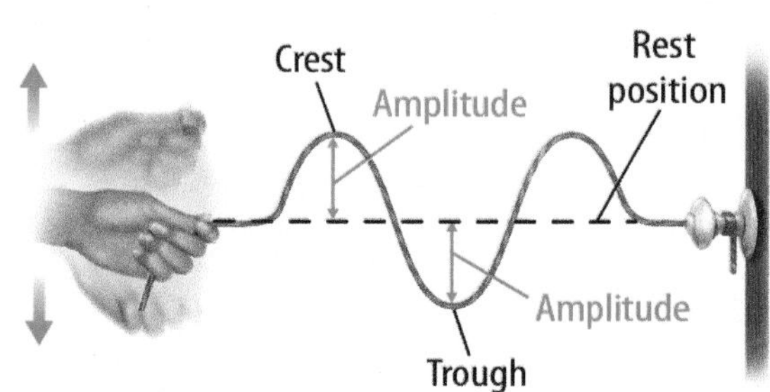

This wave has a smaller amplitude and carries less energy.

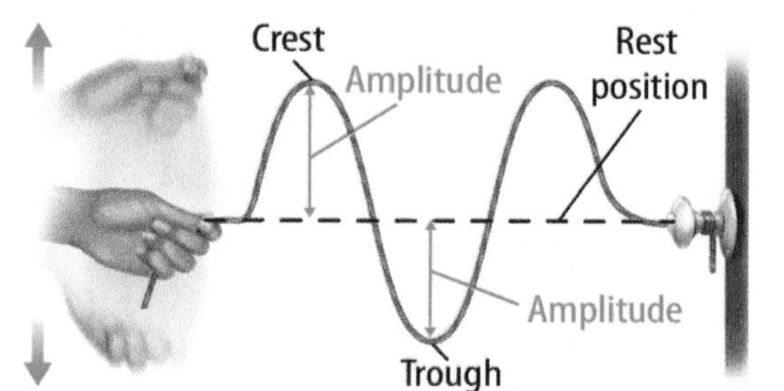

This wave has a greater amplitude and carries more energy.

▲ **Figure 7** The amplitude of a transverse wave is the distance from the resting position to a crest or a trough.

Amplitude and Energy of Transverse Waves

You produce a transverse wave on a rope when you move the rope up and down. For a transverse wave, the greatest distance a particle moves from the rest position is to the top of a crest or to the bottom of a trough. This distance is the amplitude of a transverse wave, as shown in **Figure 7**. The energy carried by a transverse wave increases as the amplitude of the wave increases as shown in **Figure 8**.

Amplitude and Energy of Longitudinal Waves

The amplitude of a longitudinal wave depends on the distance between particles in the compressions and rarefactions. When the amplitude of a longitudinal wave increases, the particles in the medium get closer together in the compressions and farther apart in the rarefactions, as shown in **Figure 9** on the next page. In a longitudinal wave, you transfer more energy when you push and pull the end of the spring a greater distance. Just as for transverse waves, the energy carried by a longitudinal wave increases as its amplitude increases.

Reading Check When comparing two longitudinal waves that are traveling through the same medium, how can you tell which has the greater amount of energy?

Figure 8 The wave with the larger amplitude carries more energy and makes the ball bounce higher. ▼

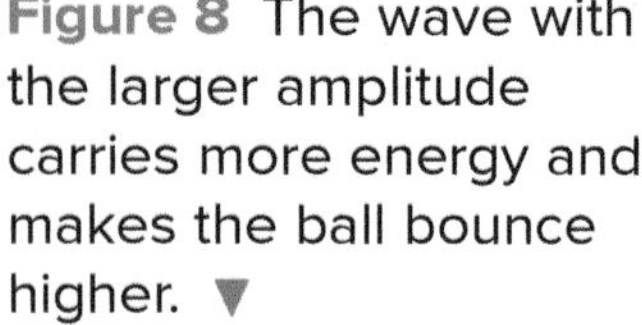

Visual Check What is the source of energy for these waves?

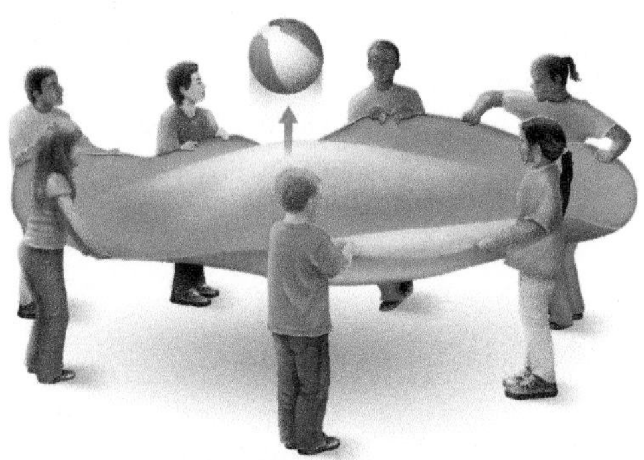

Lower Amplitude Wave
The parachute transfers less energy to the ball.

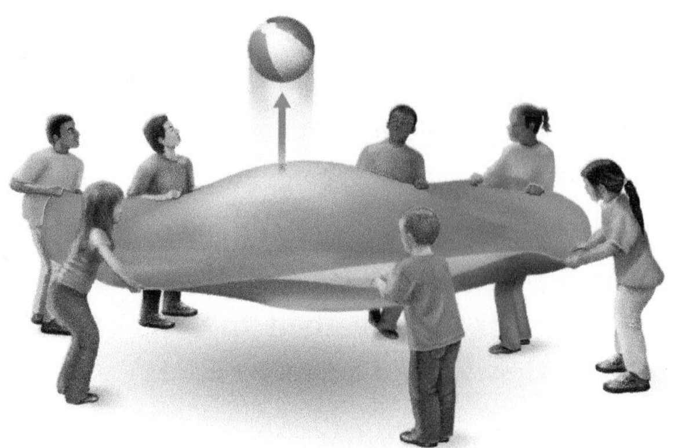

Higher Amplitude Wave
The parachute transfers more energy to the ball.

Lower-Amplitude Wave

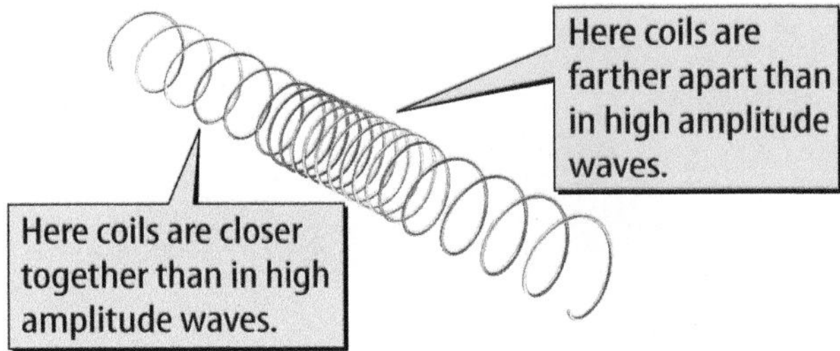

Here coils are farther apart than in high amplitude waves.
Here coils are closer together than in high amplitude waves.

Higher-Amplitude Wave

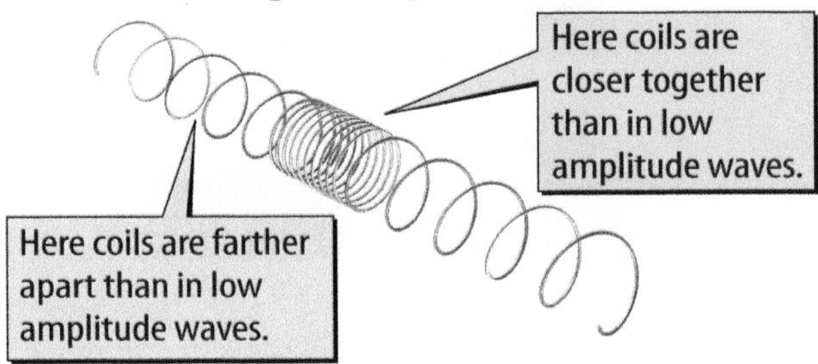

Here coils are closer together than in low amplitude waves.
Here coils are farther apart than in low amplitude waves.

 Animation

▲ **Figure 9** Amplitude depends on the spacings in the compressions and rarefactions.

Wavelength

The **wavelength** *of a wave is the distance from one point on a wave to the same point on the next wave.* The wavelengths of a transverse wave and a longitudinal wave are shown in **Figure 10**. To measure the wavelength of a transverse wave, you can measure the distance from one crest to the next crest or from one trough to the next trough. To measure the wavelength of a longitudinal wave, you can measure the distance from one compression to the next compression or from one rarefaction to the next rarefaction. Wavelength is measured in units of distance, such as meters.

MiniLab — 20 minutes

How are wavelength and frequency related?

Waves traveling in a material can have different frequencies and wavelengths. Is there a relationship between the wavelength and frequency of a wave?

1. Read and complete a lab safety form.
2. With a partner, stretch a **piece of rope,** approximately 2–3 m long, across a lab table or the floor. Move your hand side to side while your partner holds the other end of the rope in place. Observe the wavelength.
3. Move your hand side to side faster. Observe the wavelength.

Analyze and Conclude

1. **Explain** When was the frequency of the wave higher? Lower?
2. **Key Concept** How are wavelength and frequency related?

Figure 10 Wavelength is the distance from one point on a wave to the nearest point just like it. ▼

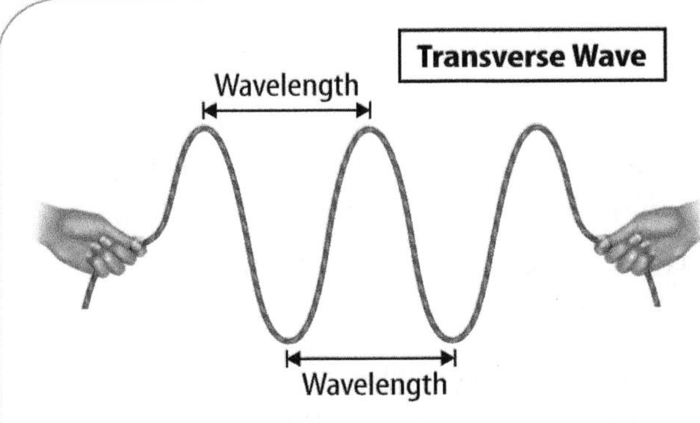

Wavelength is the distance from one crest to the next crest or from one trough to the next trough.

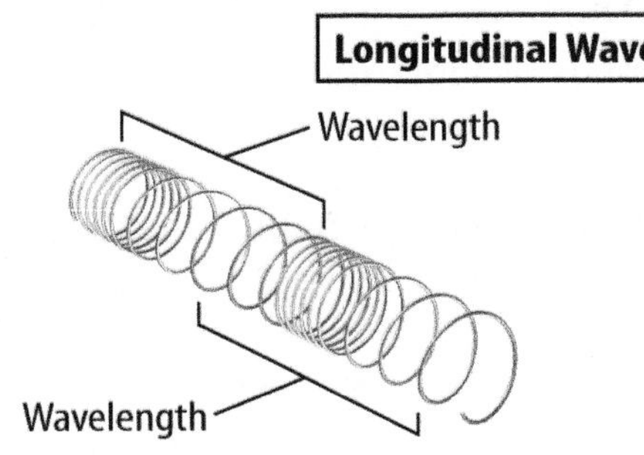

Wavelength is the distance from one compression to the next compression or from one rarefaction to the next rarefaction.

Frequency and Wavelength

Wave direction →

0:00

0:01

0:02

0:03

0:04

- Longer wavelength
- Lower frequency
- One complete wave passes in four seconds.

- Shorter wavelength
- Higher frequency
- Two complete waves pass in four seconds.

Figure 11 Frequency is the number of wavelengths that pass a point each second. When the frequency increases, the wavelength decreases.

Frequency

Waves have another property called frequency. *The* **frequency** *of a wave is the number of wavelengths that pass by a point each second.* Frequency is related to how rapidly the object or material producing the wave vibrates. Each vibration of the object produces one wavelength. The frequency of a wave is the same as the number of vibrations the vibrating object makes each second.

Key Concept Check What are three properties of waves?

The Unit for Frequency

The SI unit for frequency is hertz (Hz). A wave with a frequency of 2 Hz means that two wavelengths pass a point each second. The unit Hz is the same unit as 1/s.

Wavelength and Frequency

Figure 11 shows how frequency and wavelength are related. The wavelength of the waves in the left column is longer than that of the wave in the right column. To calculate the frequency of waves, divide the number of wavelengths by the time. For the wave on the left, the frequency is 1 wavelength divided by 4 s, which is 0.25 Hz. The wave on the right has a frequency of 2 wavelengths divided by 4 s, which is 0.5 Hz. The wave on the right has a shorter wavelength and a higher frequency. As the frequency of a wave increases, the wavelength decreases.

Key Concept Check How does the wavelength change if the frequency of a wave decreases? What if the frequency increases?

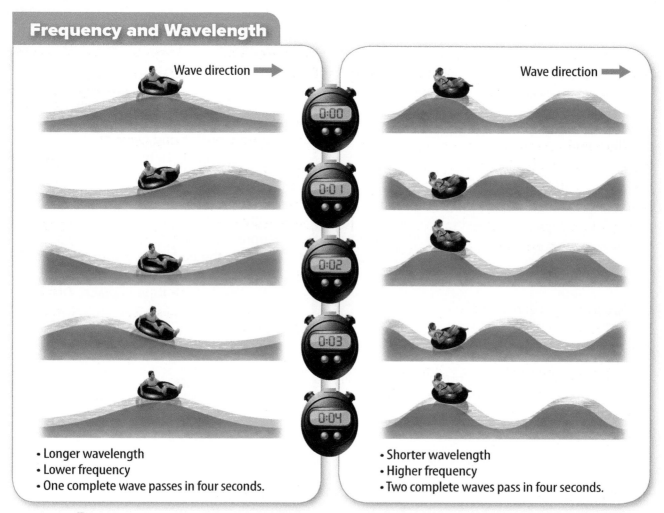

Wave Speed

Different types of waves travel at different speeds. For example, light waves from a lightning flash travel almost 1 million times faster than the sound waves you hear as thunder.

Wave Speed Through Different Materials

The same type of waves travel at different speeds in different materials. Mechanical waves, such as sound waves, usually travel fastest in solids and slowest in gases, as shown in Table 2. Mechanical waves also usually travel faster as the temperature of the medium increases. Unlike mechanical waves, electromagnetic waves move fastest in empty space and slowest in solids.

Key Concept Check What does wave speed depend on?

Calculating Wave Speed

You can calculate the speed of a wave by multiplying its wavelength and its frequency together, as shown below. The symbol for wavelength is λ, which is the Greek letter *lambda*.

Wave Speed Equation

wave speed (in m/s) = frequency (in Hz) × wavelength (in m)

$$s = f\lambda$$

When you multiply wavelength and frequency, the result has units of m × Hz. This equals m/s–the unit for speed.

Table 2 Speed of Sound Waves in Different Materials

Material	Wave Speed (m/s)
Gases (0°C)	
Oxygen	316
Dry air	331
Liquids (25°C)	
Ethanol	1,207
Water	1,500
Solids	
Ice	3,850
Aluminum	6,420

Math Skills Use a Simple Equation

Solve for Wave Speed A mosquito beating its wings produces sound waves with a frequency of 700 Hz and a wavelength of 0.5 m. How fast are the sound waves traveling?

1. **This is what you know:** frequency: $f = 700$ Hz; wavelength: $\lambda = 0.5$ m
2. **This is what you need to find:** wave speed: s
3. **Use this formula:** $s = f\lambda$
4. **Substitute:** the values for f and λ into the formula and multiply: $s = 700 \text{ Hz} \times 0.5 \text{ m} = 350 \text{ Hz} \times \text{m}$
5. **Convert units:** $(\text{Hz}) \times (\text{m}) = (1/\text{s}) \times (\text{m}) = \text{m/s}$

Answer: The wave speed is 350 m/s.

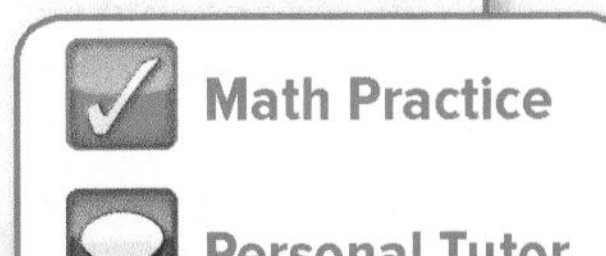

Practice

What is the speed of a wave that has a frequency of 8,500 Hz and a wavelength of 1.5 m?

Lesson 2 Review

Visual Summary

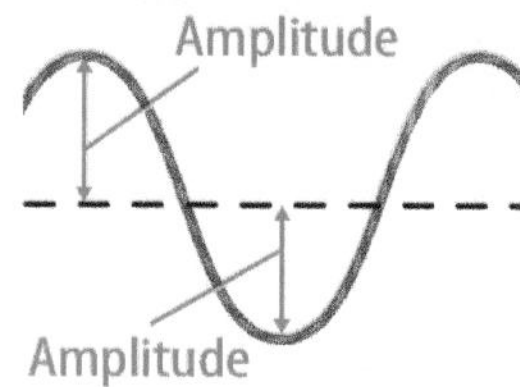

The amplitude of a transverse wave is the maximum distance that the wave moves from its rest position.

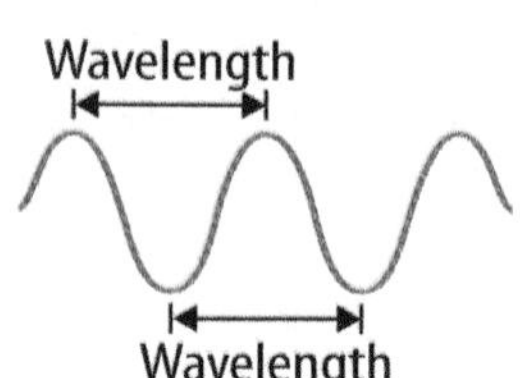

The wavelength of a transverse wave is the distance from one point on a wave to the same point on the next wave, such as from crest to crest or from trough to trough.

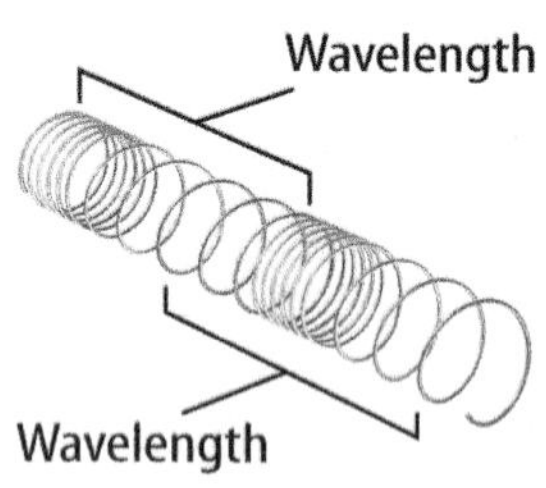

The wavelength of a longitudinal wave is the distance from one point on a wave to the nearest point just like it, such as from compression to compression or from rarefaction to rarefaction.

FOLDABLES®

Use your lesson Foldable to review the lesson. Save your Foldable for the project at the end of the chapter.

What do you think NOW?

You first read the statements below at the beginning of the chapter.

3. Waves that carry more energy cause particles in a material to move a greater distance.

4. Sound waves travel fastest in gases, such as those in the air.

Did you change your mind about whether you agree or disagree with the statements? Rewrite any false statements to make them true.

Use Vocabulary

1 For a transverse wave, the ________ depends on the distance from the rest position to a crest or a trough.

2 The unit for the ________ of a wave is the Hz, which means "per second."

Understand Key Concepts 

3 **Compare** Which wave would have the greatest wave speed, a wave from a vibrating piano string in an auditorium or a sound wave created by a boat anchor striking an underwater rock? Explain.

4 In which medium would an electromagnetic wave travel the fastest?

A. air
B. granite
C. vacuum
D. water

Interpret Graphics

5 **Determine** which wave carries the greater amount of energy. Explain.

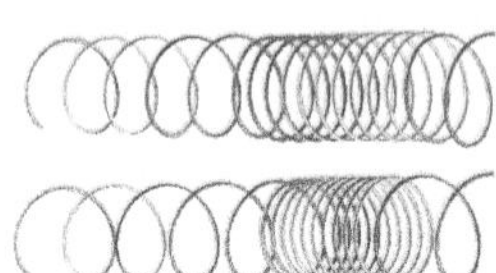

6 **Determine Cause and Effect** Copy and fill in the graphic organizer below.

Critical Thinking

7 **Infer** A loudspeaker produces sound waves that change in wavelength from 1.0 m to 1.5 m. If the wave speed is constant, how did the vibration of the loudspeaker change? Explain.

Math Skills  Math Practice

8 **Use a Simple Equation** A water wave has a frequency of 10 Hz and a wavelength of 150 m. What is the wave speed?

Skill Practice **Model**

25 minutes

How are the properties of waves related?

Materials

meter tapes (2)

masking tape

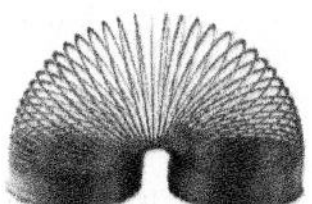

coiled spring toy

stopwatch or clock with second hand

Safety

All waves have amplitude, wavelength, and frequency. The properties of a wave are related and also determine the amount of energy the wave carries.

Learn It

Scientists create **models** to study many objects and concepts that are difficult to observe directly. You used a coiled spring toy in previous labs to model a longitudinal wave. In this lab, you will use the same toy to model transverse waves.

Try It

1. Read and complete a lab safety form.
2. With a partner, use masking tape to secure the meter tapes to the floor, creating *x*- and *y*-axes.
3. With your partner, stretch the spring toy across the tape representing the *x*-axis. Generate a transverse wave by moving the toy back and forth on the floor. Try to be as steady and even as possible to generate consistent waves.
4. Using the tape on the *y*-axis, measure and record the amplitude of the wave in your Science Journal.
5. Using the tape representing the *x*-axis, measure the wavelength of the wave. Record your measurement.
6. Using a stopwatch, count and record the number of crests or troughs that cross the *y*-axis in 10 seconds.
7. Repeat steps 3–6 for waves with different properties by moving the toy faster and slower.

Apply It

8. Calculate the frequency of each wave generated.
9. Which wave transferred the most energy? Explain.
10. **Key Concept** What happened to the frequency and wavelength of the waves when you moved the spring toy faster and slower? How are frequency and wavelength related?

6

(t to b)Ken Cavanagh/McGraw-Hill Education, (2, 4, br)Hutchings Photography/Digital Light Source, (3)Comstock Images/Alamy

Lesson 3

Reading Guide

Key Concepts
ESSENTIAL QUESTIONS

- How do waves interact with matter?
- What are reflection, refraction, and diffraction?
- What is interference?

Vocabulary

absorption p. 94
transmission p. 94
reflection p. 94
law of reflection p. 95
refraction p. 96
diffraction p. 96
interference p. 97

Multilingual eGlossary

Science Video

6.PS.4, SEPS.2, SEPS.5, SEPS.8, 6-8.LST.5.2

Go to the resource tab in ConnectED to find the PBL *Cookin' with the Sun.*

Wave Interactions

Inquiry Can waves change?

Have you ever watched two waves bump into each other? If so, you might have noticed that the shapes of the waves changed. How do the shapes of waves change when they interact?

Gustoimages/Science Source

Launch Lab

20 minutes

What happens in wave collisions?

You might have seen ripples on a water surface spreading out from different points. As the water waves reach each other, they collide. Do waves change after they collide?

1. Read and complete a lab safety form.
2. Stretch a **metal coiled spring toy** about 30–40 cm between you and a partner.
3. Make a wave by grabbing about five coils at one end and then releasing them. Record your observations in your Science Journal.
4. Make waves at both ends of the spring with your partner. Make waves that appear much different from each other so you can distinguish them easily. Then release them at the same time. Observe and record how each wave moves before, during, and after the collision.

Think About This

1. **Describe** how the two waves moved after the coils were released.
2. **Key Concept** How were the two waves affected by their collision?

Interaction of Waves with Matter

Have you seen photos, like the one shown in Figure 12, of objects in space taken with the *Hubble Space Telescope*? The *Hubble* orbits Earth collecting light waves before they enter Earth's atmosphere. Photos taken with the *Hubble* are clearer than photos taken with telescopes on Earth's surface. This is because light waves strike the telescope before they interact with matter in Earth's atmosphere.

Waves interact with matter in several ways. Waves can be reflected by matter or they can change direction when they travel from one material to another. In addition, as waves pass through matter, some of the energy they carry can be transferred to matter. For example, the energy from sound waves can be transferred to soft surfaces, such as the padded walls in movie theaters. Waves also interact with each other. When two different waves overlap, a new wave forms. The new wave has different properties from either original wave.

Figure 12 This *Hubble Space Telescope* photo shows a giant cloud of dust and gas called NGC 3603. Many stars are forming in this cloud.

(t)Hutchings Photography/Digital Light Source, (b)NASA, ESA, and the Hubble Heritage (STScI/AURA)-ESA/Hubble Collaboration

Waves Interact With Matter

The chrome looks shiny because it reflects most of the light waves that strike it.
The glass absorbs only a small amount of the energy carried by light waves. As a result, light waves pass through the glass.
Black paint absorbs almost all the energy carried by light waves.

Figure 13 Waves can be absorbed, transmitted, or reflected by matter.

Visual Check Do tires usually absorb, transmit, or reflect light waves? Explain your answer.

Absorption

When you shout, you create sound waves. As these waves travel in air, some of their energy transfers to particles in the air. As a result, the energy the waves carry decreases as they travel through matter. **Absorption** *is the transfer of energy by a wave to the medium through which it travels.* The amount of energy absorbed depends on the type of wave and the material in which it moves.

Reading Check Give one reason why the energy carried by sound waves decreases as those sound waves travel through air.

Absorption also occurs for electromagnetic waves. All materials absorb electromagnetic waves, although some materials absorb more electromagnetic waves than others. Darker materials, such as tinted glass, absorb more visible light waves than lighter materials, such as glass that is not tinted.

Absorption occurs at the surface of the car in Figure 13. The car's black paint absorbs much of the energy carried by light waves.

Transmission

Why can you see through a sheet of clear plastic wrap but not through a sheet of black construction paper? When visible light waves reach the paper, almost all their energy is absorbed. As a result, no light waves pass through the paper. However, light waves pass through the plastic wrap because the plastic absorbs only a small amount of the wave's energy. **Transmission** *is the passage of light through an object,* such as the windows in Figure 13.

Reflection

When waves reach the surface of materials, they can also be reflected. **Reflection** *is the bouncing of a wave off a surface.* Reflection causes the chrome on the car in Figure 13 to appear silver instead of black. An object that reflects all visible light appears white, while an object that reflects no visible light appears black.

Key Concept Check What are three ways that waves interact with matter?

All types of waves, including sound waves, light waves, and water waves, can reflect when they hit a surface. Light waves reflect when they reach a mirror. Sound waves reflect when they reach a wall. Reflection causes waves to change direction. When you drop a basketball at an angle, it bounces up at the same angle but in the opposite direction. When waves reflect from a surface, they change direction like a basketball bouncing off a surface.

The Law of Reflection

The direction of a wave that hits a surface and the reflected wave are related. As shown in Figure 14, an imaginary line, perpendicular to a surface, is called a normal. The angle between the direction of the incoming wave and the normal is the angle of incidence. The angle between the direction of the reflected wave and the normal is the angle of reflection. According to the **law of reflection,** *when a wave is reflected from a surface, the angle of reflection is equal to the angle of incidence.*

Reading Check What is the law of reflection?

Reflection of Waves

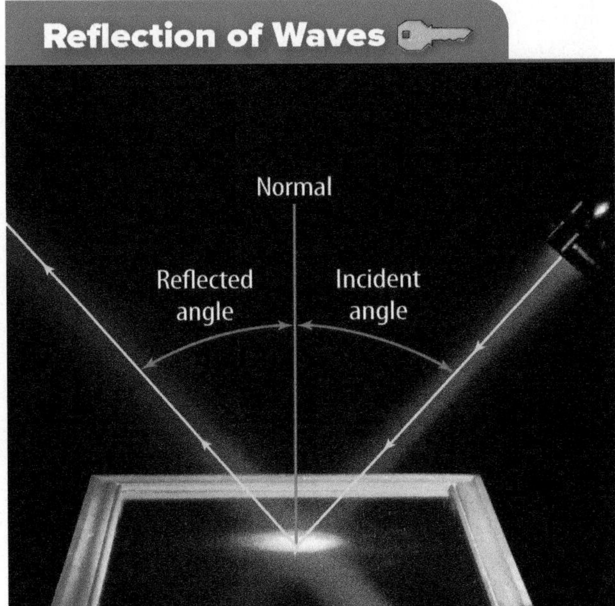

Figure 14 All waves obey the law of reflection. According to the law of reflection, the incident angle equals the reflected angle.

SCIENCE USE V. COMMON USE

normal
Science Use perpendicular to or forming a right angle with a line or plane

Common Use conforming to a standard or common

MiniLab

20 minutes

How can reflection be used?

Light waves, like all waves, obey the law of reflection. By using mirrors, you can see around corners.

1. Read and complete a lab safety form.
2. Place a **small object** on a table and stand a **book** vertically about 30 cm in front of the object.
3. Position a **mirror** vertically so an observer on the opposite side of the book from the object can see the object. Use **modeling clay** to prop up the mirror.
4. Use **string** to represent the path light waves travel from the observer to the mirror and then to the object. Draw the outlined path in your Science Journal.
5. Repeat steps 3–4 with two mirrors.

Analyze and Conclude

Key Concept How could three mirrors be used to see the object behind the book?

Refraction of Waves

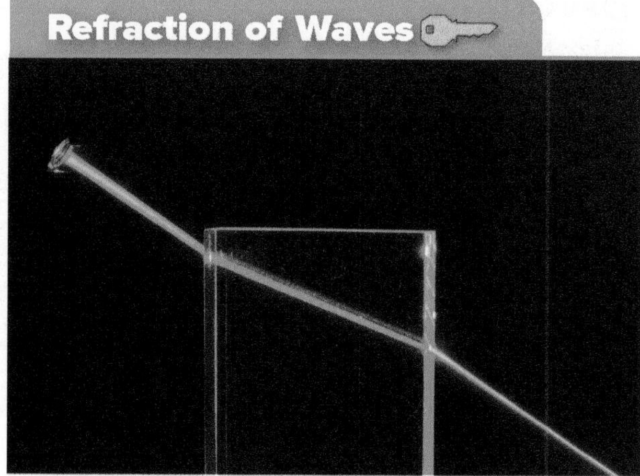

▲ Figure 15 Refraction occurs when a wave changes speed. The beam of light changes direction because light waves slow down as they move from air into acrylic.

Personal Tutor

WORD ORIGIN

refraction
from Latin *refractus,* means "to break up"

Project-Based Learning Activity

Cookin' with the Sun Go online to design a solar cooker to investigate how waves are reflected, absorbed, and transmitted.

Refraction

Sometimes waves change direction even if they are not reflected from a surface. The light beam in Figure 15 changes direction as it travels from air into acrylic and it changes again when the light beam travels from acrylic into air. When light waves slow down or speed up, they change direction. **Refraction** *is the change in direction of a wave that occurs as the wave changes speed when moving from one medium to another.* The greater the change in speed, the more the wave changes direction.

Diffraction

Waves can also change direction as they travel by objects. Have you ever been walking down a hallway and heard people talking in a room before you got to the open door of the room? You heard some of the sound waves because they changed direction and spread out as they traveled through the doorway.

What is diffraction?

The change in direction of a wave when it travels by the edge of an object or through an opening is called **diffraction.** Examples of diffraction are shown in Figure 16. Diffraction causes the water waves to travel around the edges of the object and to spread out after they travel through the opening. More diffraction occurs as the size of the object or opening becomes similar in size to the wavelength of the wave.

Figure 16 Waves diffract as they pass by an object or pass through an opening. ▼

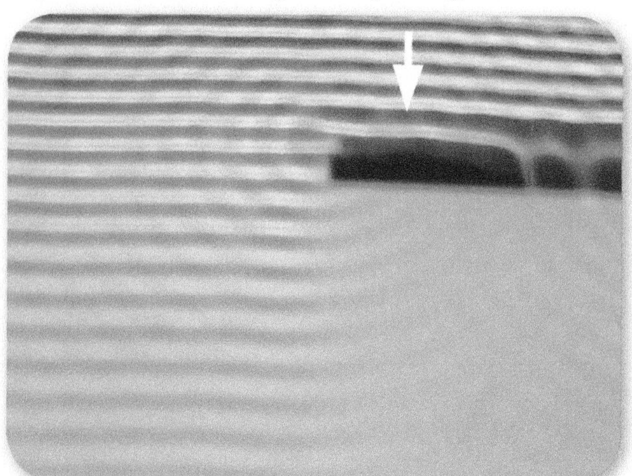

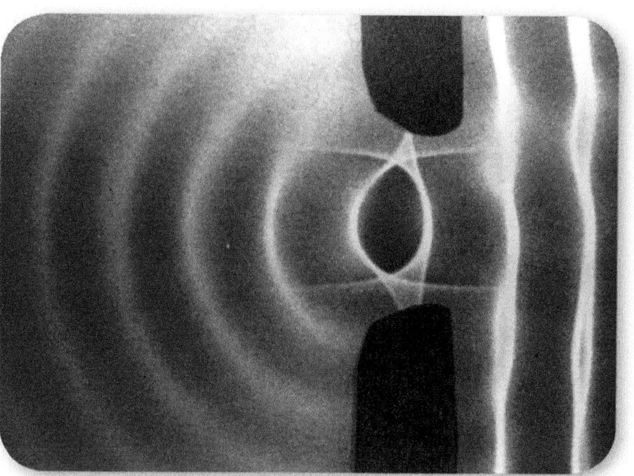

Diffraction of Sound Waves and Light Waves

The wavelengths of sound waves are similar in size to many common objects. Because of this size similarity, you often hear sound from sources that you can't see. For example, the wavelengths of sound waves are roughly the same size as the width of the doorway. Therefore, sound waves spread out as they travel through the doorway. The wavelengths of light waves are more than a million times smaller than the width of a doorway. As a result, light waves do not spread out as they travel through the doorway. Because the wavelengths of light waves are so much smaller than sound waves, you can't see into the room until you reach the doorway. However, you can hear the sounds much sooner.

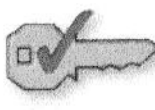

Key Concept Check Compare and contrast reflection, refraction, and diffraction.

FOLDABLES®

Make a tri-fold book and label the columns as shown. Use your book to record information about how waves interact with matter.

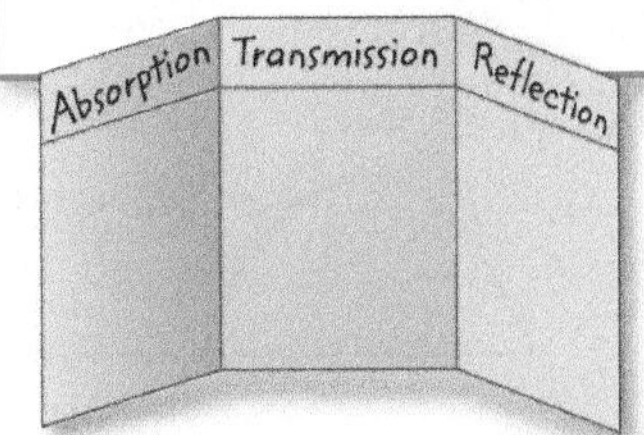

Interference

Waves not only interact with matter. They also interact with each other. Suppose you throw two pebbles into a pond. Waves spread out from the impact of each pebble and move toward each other. When the waves meet, they overlap for a while as they travel through each other. **Interference** *occurs when waves that overlap combine, forming a new wave,* as shown in Figure 17. However, after the waves travel through each other, they keep moving without having been changed.

Wave Interference

Two waves approach each other from opposite directions.

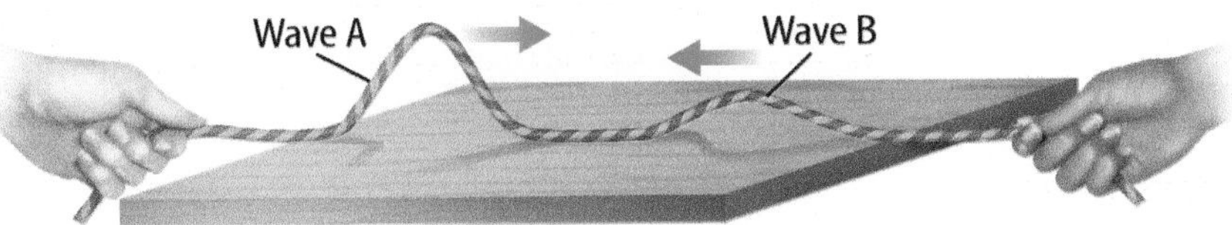

The waves interfere with each other and form a large amplitude wave.

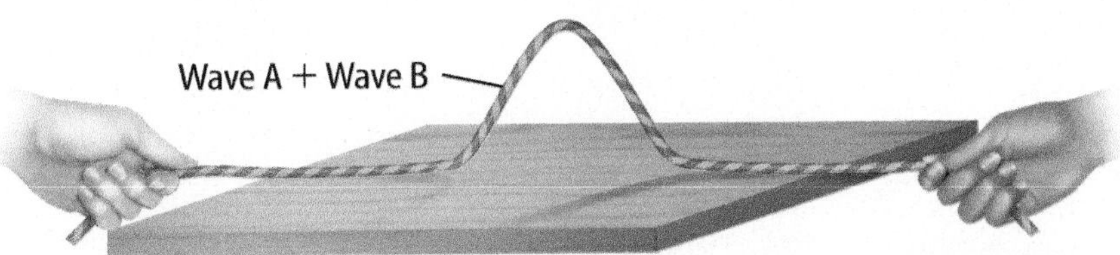

The waves keep traveling in opposite directions after they move through each other.

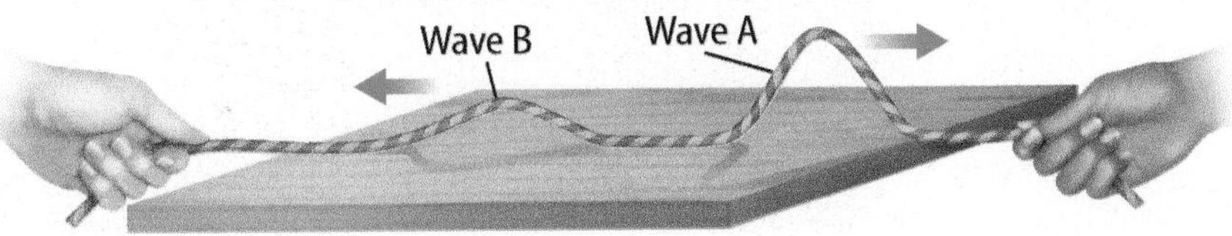

Figure 17 When waves interfere with each other, they create a new wave that has a different amplitude than either original wave.

Visual Check Which wave has the larger amplitude?

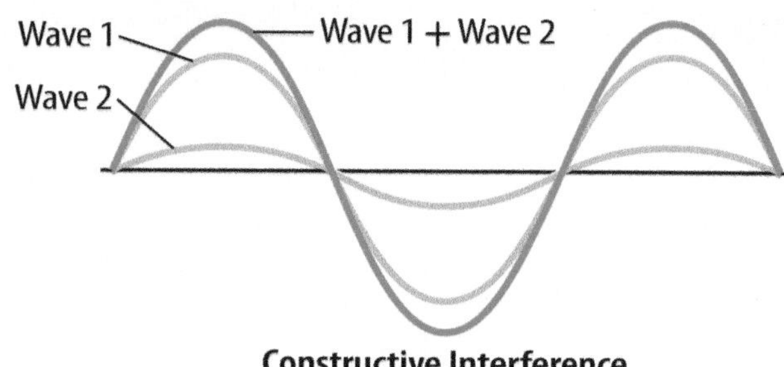

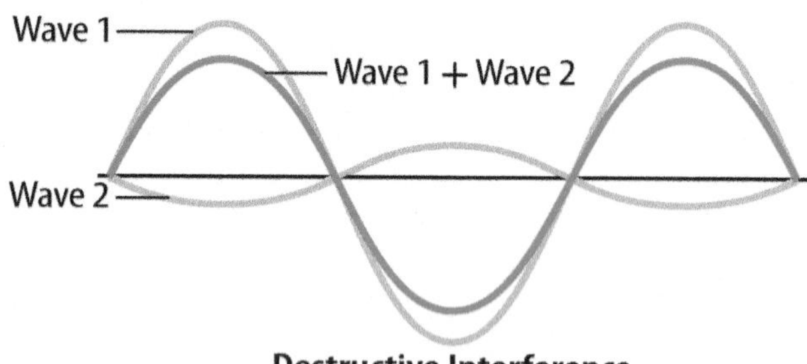

▲ **Figure 18** When constructive interference occurs, the new wave has a greater amplitude than either original wave. When destructive interference occurs, the new wave has a smaller amplitude than the sum of the amplitudes of the original waves.

ACADEMIC VOCABULARY

constructive
(adjective) pertaining to building or putting parts together to make a whole

Constructive and Destructive Interference

As waves travel through each other, sometimes the crests of both waves overlap, as shown in the top image of **Figure 18**. A new wave forms with greater amplitude than either of the original waves. This type of interference is called **constructive** interference. It occurs when crests overlap with crests and troughs overlap with troughs.

Destructive interference occurs when a crest of one wave overlaps the trough of another wave. The new wave that forms has a smaller amplitude than the sum of the amplitudes of the original waves, as shown in the bottom image of **Figure 18**. If the two waves have the same amplitude, they cancel each other when their crests and troughs overlap.

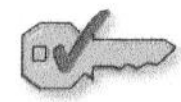 **Key Concept Check** Describe two types of wave interference.

Standing Waves

Suppose you shake one end of a rope that has the other end attached to a wall. You create a wave that travels away from you and then reflects off the wall. As the wave you create and the reflected wave interact, interference occurs. For some values of the wavelength, the wave that forms from the combined waves seems to stand still. This wave is called a standing wave. An example is shown in **Figure 19**.

Figure 19 A standing wave can occur when two waves with the same wavelength travel in opposite directions and overlap. The wave that forms seems to be standing still. ▼

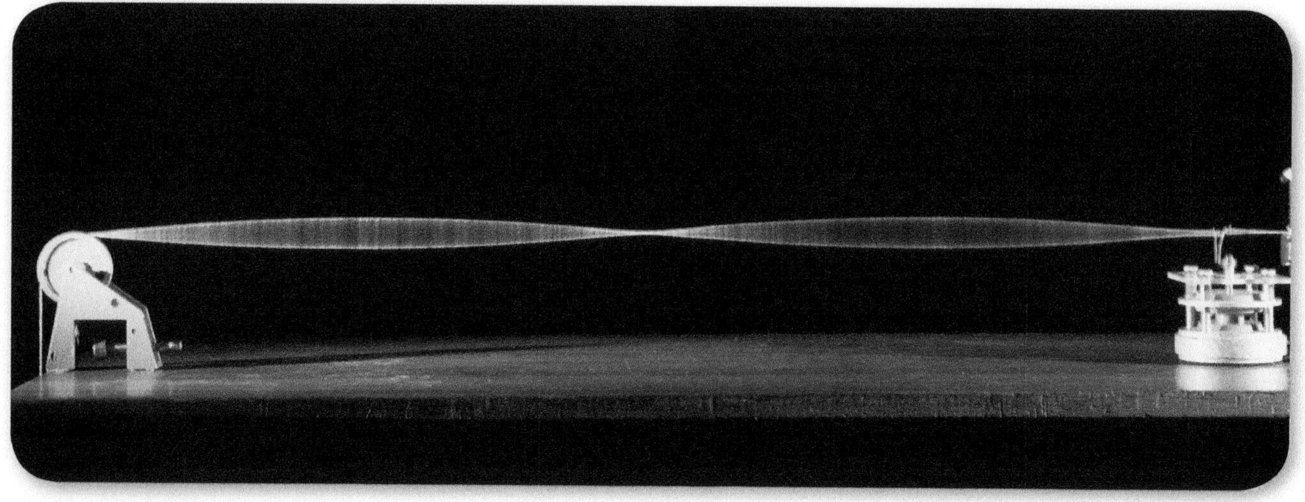

Andrew Lambert/Science Source

Lesson 3 Review

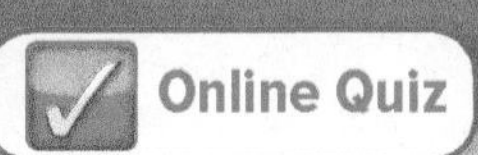

Visual Summary

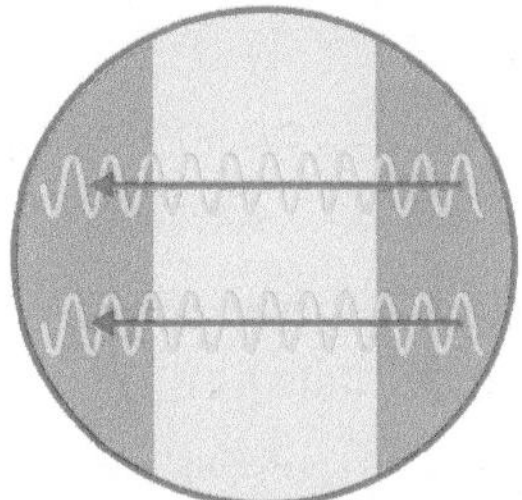

Transmission occurs when waves travel through a material.

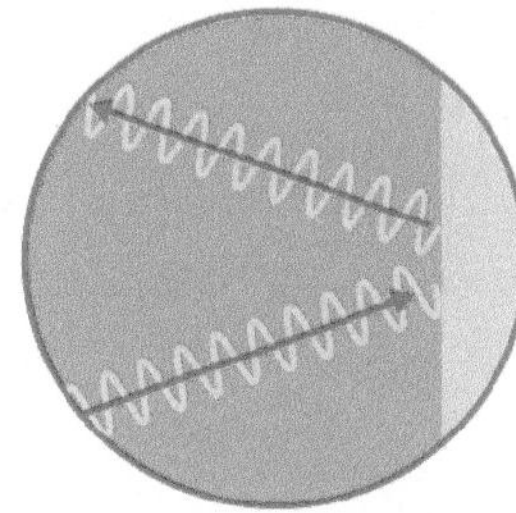

Reflection occurs when waves bounce off the surface of a material.

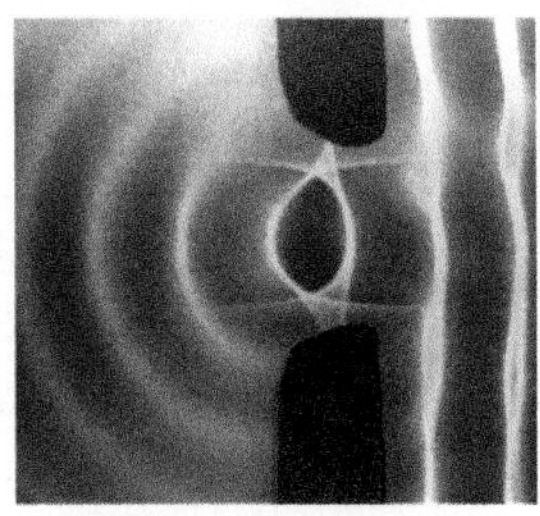

The change in direction of a wave when it travels through an opening is diffraction.

FOLDABLES®

Use your lesson Foldable to review the lesson. Save your Foldable for the project at the end of the chapter.

What do you think NOW?

You first read the statements below at the beginning of the chapter.

5. When light waves strike a mirror, they change direction.

6. Light waves travel at the same speed in all materials.

Did you change your mind about whether you agree or disagree with the statements? Rewrite any false statements to make them true.

Use Vocabulary

1. **Explain** the *law of reflection.*
2. **Distinguish** between *refraction* and *diffraction.*

Understand Key Concepts

3. **Contrast** the behavior of a water wave that travels by a stone barrier to a sound wave that travels through a door.
4. Which will NOT occur when a light ray interacts with a smooth pane of glass?
   - **A.** absorption
   - **B.** diffraction
   - **C.** reflection
   - **D.** transmission

Interpret Graphics

5. **Describe** what is occurring in the figure below.

Wave 1
Wave 2
Wave 1 + Wave 2

6. **Organize** Copy and fill in the graphic organizer below. In each oval, list something that can happen to a wave when it interacts with matter.

Critical Thinking

7. **Construct** Biologists know that chlorophyll, the pigment responsible for photosynthesis in plants, absorbs red light. Design a machine that you could use to test for the presence of chlorophyll.
8. **Recommend** An architect wants to design a conference room that reduces noise coming from outside the room. Suggest some design features that should be considered in this project.

55 minutes

Measuring Wave Speed

When you make a wave on a spring toy, the frequency is how many wavelengths pass a point per second. Wavelength is the distance between one point on the wave and the nearest point just like it. If you can measure the frequency and wavelength of a wave, you can determine the wave speed.

Materials

meter tapes (2)

masking tape

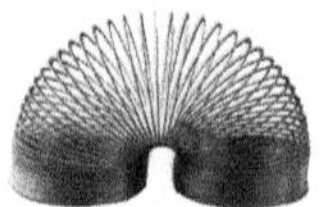

coiled spring toy

twine, 0.25 m

stopwatch or clock with second hand

Safety

Ask a Question

How can you determine the speed of a wave?

Make Observations

1. Read and complete a lab safety form.
2. Lay the meter tapes on the floor perpendicular to each other to make an *x*- and *y*-axis. Fasten them in place with masking tape.
3. Tie a piece of twine around the last coil of the spring toy.
4. With a partner, stretch the spring toy along the *x*-axis. One person should hold one end at the *y*-axis. The other person should hold the twine at the end of the outstretched spring.
5. One student creates a transverse wave by moving his or her hand up and down along the *y*-axis at a constant rate. When the wave is consistent, another student times a 10-second period while the third person counts the number of vibrations in 10 seconds. Record the number of vibrations in your Science Journal in a data table like the one shown below.
6. As the student continues making the wave, another student should estimate the wavelength along the *x*-axis using the meter tape.
7. Calculate the frequency of the wave. Then calculate the wave speed using the equation, wave speed = frequency × wavelength.
8. Repeat steps 5 through 7 using a different frequency.

Trial	Number of Vibrations in 10 s	Frequency (Hz)	Wavelength (cm)	Wave Speed (cm/s)
1				
2				

(t to b)Ken Cavanagh/McGraw-Hill Education, (2, 4-5)Hutchings Photography/Digital Light Source, (3)Comstock Images/Alamy

Form a Hypothesis

9. Form a hypothesis about the relationship between frequency and wavelength.

Test Your Hypothesis

10. Choose a frequency that you did not use during **Make Observations.** Predict the wavelength for a wave with this frequency.
11. Practice making a wave on the toy spring with your chosen frequency. Repeat steps 4–7 for this wave. Did your prediction results support your hypothesis? If not, revise your hypothesis and repeat steps 4–7.

Analyze and Conclude

12. **Conclude** How did your prediction of wavelength compare to your measurement?
13. **Think Critically** What measurements were the most difficult to make accurately? Suggest ways to improve on the method.
14. THE BIG IDEA **The Big Idea** How did the wavelength, frequency, and wave speed change for the different waves that you created?

Communicate Your Results

Write a report explaining the steps you took in this lab. Include a table of the measurements you made. Be sure to describe sources of error in your measurements and ways that you might improve the accuracy of your experiment.

Inquiry Extension

Try measuring the wave speed of other waves. Try stretching your spring toy to different lengths or try measuring the wave speed of longitudinal waves. You also might try working with ropes of different thicknesses, different spring toys, or even water in a wave tank.

Lab Tips

- ☑ Keep the amplitude constant by moving the same distance on the *y*-axis in each vibration.
- ☑ Twenty vibrations in 10 s make a wave with a frequency of 2 Hz.

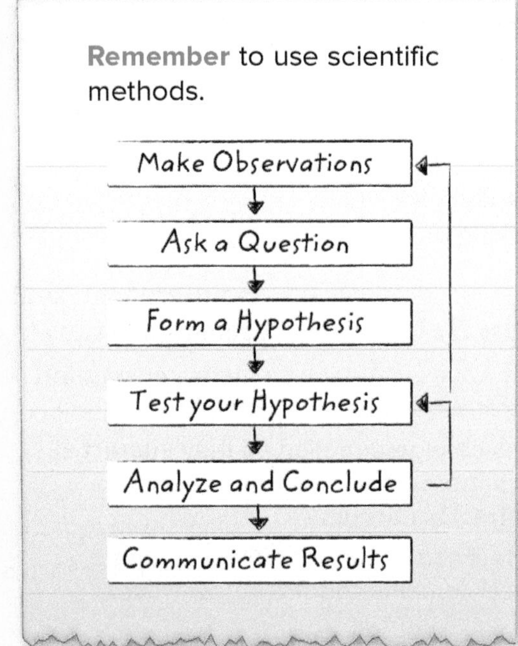
Remember to use scientific methods.
Make Observations
Ask a Question
Form a Hypothesis
Test your Hypothesis
Analyze and Conclude
Communicate Results

Chapter 3 Study Guide

Waves transfer energy but not matter as they travel.

Key Concepts Summary 

Lesson 1: What are waves?

- Vibrations cause **waves.**
- **Transverse waves** make particles in a **medium** move at right angles to the direction that the wave travels. **Longitudinal waves** make particles in a medium move parallel to the direction that the wave travels.
- **Mechanical waves** cannot move through empty space, but **electromagnetic waves** can.

Direction wave moves

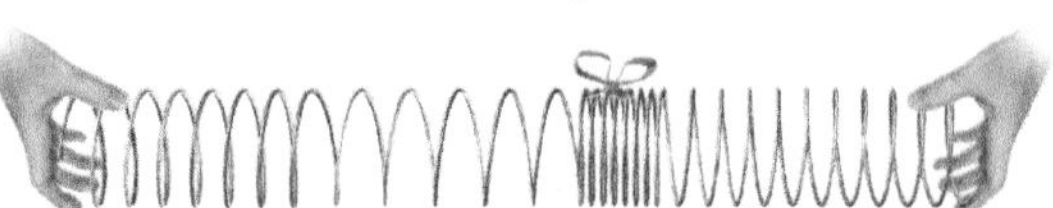

Lesson 2: Wave Properties

- All waves have the properties of **amplitude, wavelength,** and **frequency.**
- Increasing the frequency of a wave decreases the wavelength, and decreasing the frequency increases the wavelength.
- The speed of a wave depends on the type of material in which it is moving and the temperature of the material.

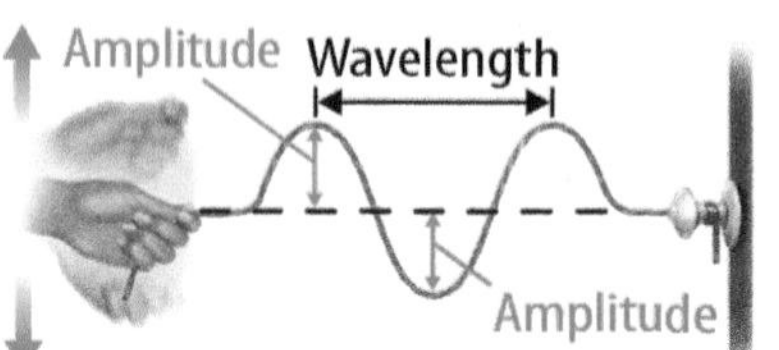

Lesson 3: Wave Interactions

- When waves interact with matter, **absorption** and **transmission** can occur.
- Waves change direction as they interact with matter when **reflection, refraction,** or **diffraction** occurs.
- **Interference** occurs when waves that overlap combine to form a new wave.

GIPhotoStock/Science Source

Vocabulary

Lesson 1

wave p. 75
mechanical wave p. 77
medium p. 77
transverse wave p. 77
crest p. 77
trough p. 77
longitudinal wave p. 78
compression p. 78
rarefaction p. 78
electromagnetic wave p. 81

Lesson 2

amplitude p. 85
wavelength p. 87
frequency p. 88

Lesson 3

absorption p. 94
transmission p. 94
reflection p. 94
law of reflection p. 95
refraction p. 96
diffraction p. 96
interference p. 97

Vocabulary eFlashcards
Vocabulary eGames

Personal Tutor

FOLDABLES® Chapter Project

Assemble your lesson Foldables as shown to make a Chapter Project. Use the project to review what you have learned in this chapter.

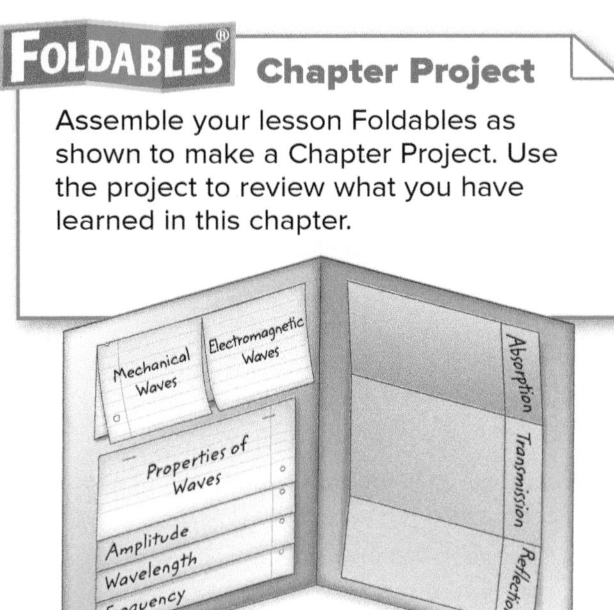

Use Vocabulary

1. A material though which a wave travels is a(n) ________.
2. A(n) ________ is a region where matter is more closely spaced in a longitudinal wave.
3. The Sun gives off energy that travels through space in the form of ________.
4. The product of ________ and wavelength is the speed of the wave.
5. ________ is a property of waves that is measured in hertz.
6. The highest point on a transverse wave is a(n) ________.
7. ________ is when two waves pass through each other and keep going.

Link Vocabulary and Key Concepts

Interactive Concept Map

Copy this concept map, and then use vocabulary terms from the previous page to complete the concept map.

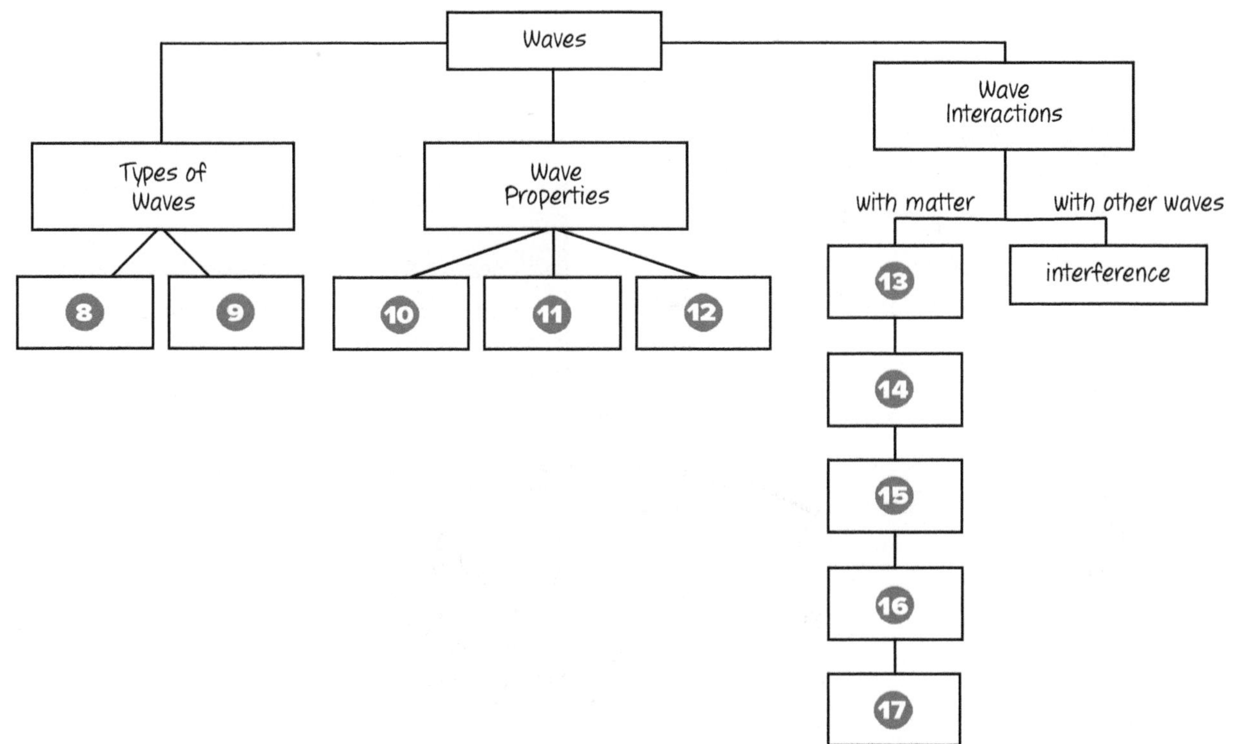

Chapter 3 Review

Understand Key Concepts 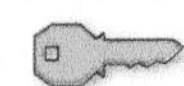

1. What is transferred by a radio wave?
   A. air
   B. energy
   C. matter
   D. space

2. In a longitudinal wave, where are the particles most spread out?
   A. compression
   B. crest
   C. rarefaction
   D. trough

3. Which would produce mechanical waves?
   A. burning a candle
   B. hitting a wall with a hammer
   C. turning on a flashlight
   D. tying a rope to a doorknob

4. Which is an electromagnetic wave?
   A. a flag waving in the wind
   B. a vibrating guitar string
   C. the changes in the air that result from blowing a horn
   D. the waves that heat a cup of water in a microwave oven

5. Identify the crest of the wave in the illustration below.

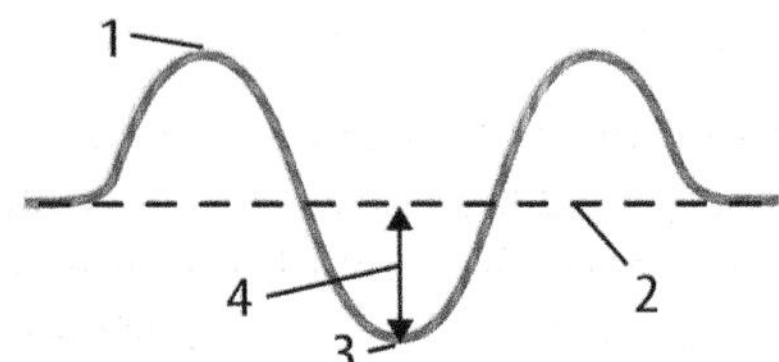

   A. 1
   B. 2
   C. 3
   D. 4

6. If the energy carried by a wave increases, which other wave property also increases?
   A. amplitude
   B. medium
   C. wavelength
   D. wave speed

7. In which medium is the speed of a sound wave the greatest?
   A. air in your classroom
   B. iron railroad track
   C. pool of water
   D. vacuum in space

8. A vibration that produces a wave takes 0.5 seconds to complete. What is the frequency of the wave?
   A. 0.25 Hz
   B. 0.5 Hz
   C. 2 Hz
   D. 4 Hz

9. What does the amount of refraction of a wave depend on?
   A. change in wave speed
   B. location of the normal line
   C. size of the object
   D. size of the opening between objects

10. Two waves travel through each other, and a crest forms with an amplitude smaller than either original wave. What has happened?
    A. constructive interference
    B. destructive interference
    C. reflection
    D. refraction

11. According to the table below, which material is probably a solid?

The Speed of Light in Different Materials

Material	Speed (km/s)
1	300,000
2	298,600
3	225,000
4	125,000

    A. material 1
    B. material 2
    C. material 3
    D. material 4

Critical Thinking

12 **Assess** A student sets up a line of dominoes so that each is standing vertically next to another. He then pushes the first one and each falls down in succession. How does this demonstration represent a wave? How is it different?

13 **Infer** In the figure below, suppose wave 1 and wave 2 have the same amplitude. Describe the wave that forms when destructive interference occurs.

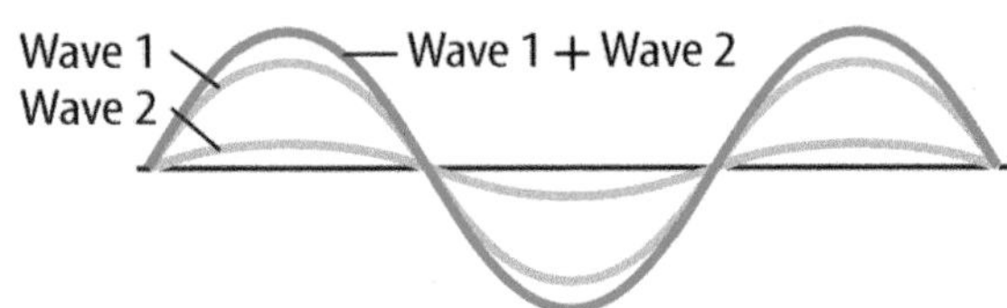

14 **Compare** A category 5 hurricane has more energy than a category 3 hurricane. Which hurricane will create water waves with greater amplitude? Why?

15 **Infer** At a baseball game when you are far from the batter, you might see the batter hit the ball before you hear the sound of the bat hitting the ball. Explain why this happens.

16 **Evaluate** Geologists measure the amplitude of seismic waves using the Richter scale. If an earthquake of 7.3 has a greater amplitude than an earthquake of 4.4, which one carries more energy? Explain your answer.

17 **Recommend** Some medicines lose their potency when exposed to ultraviolet light. Recommend the type of container in which these medicines should be stored.

18 **Explain** why the noise level rises in a room full of many talking people.

Writing in Science

19 **Write** a short essay explaining how an earthquake below the ocean floor can affect the seas near the earthquake area.

REVIEW THE BIG IDEA

20 What are waves and how do they travel? Describe the movement of particles from their resting positions for transverse and longitudinal waves.

21 The photo below shows waves in the ocean. Describe the waves using vocabulary terms from the chapter.

Math Skills

Use Numbers

22 A hummingbird can flap its wings 200 times per second. If the hummingbird produces waves that travel at 340 m/s by flapping its wings, what is the wavelength of these waves?

23 A student did an experiment in which she collected the data shown in the table. What can you conclude about the wave speed and rope diameter in this experiment? What can you conclude about frequency and wavelength?

Wave Speed and Diameter			
Trial	Rope Diameter (cm)	Frequency (Hz)	Wavelength (m)
1	2.0	2.0	8.0
2	2.0	8.0	2.0
3	4.0	2.0	10.0
4	4.0	4.0	5.0

Standardized Test Practice

Record your answers on the answer sheet provided by your teacher or on a sheet of paper.

Multiple Choice

1 Through which medium would sound waves move most slowly?

A air

B aluminum

C glass

D water

Use the diagram below to answer question 2.

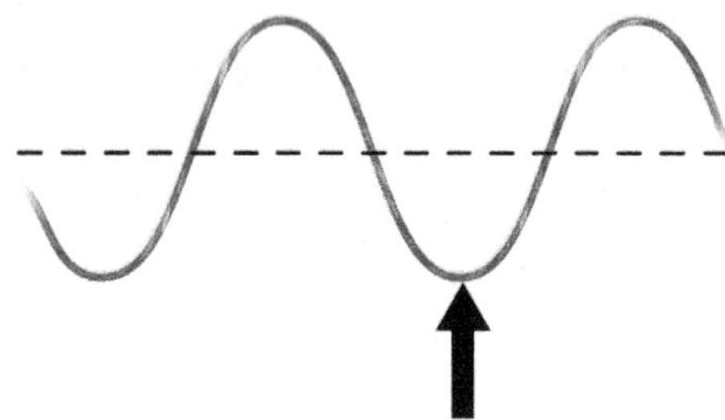

2 The diagram illustrates a mechanical wave. To which does the arrow point?

A compression

B crest

C rarefaction

D trough

3 Which is an electromagnetic wave?

A light

B seismic

C sound

D water

4 Which statement about waves is false?

A Waves transfer matter.

B Waves can change direction.

C Waves can interact with each other.

D Waves can transfer energy to matter.

Use the diagram below to answer question 5.

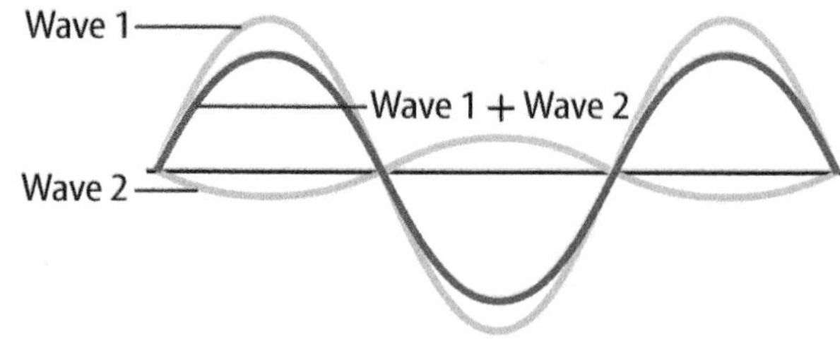

5 Which does the figure illustrate?

A constructive interference

B destructive interference

C diffraction

D reflection

6 In what region of a longitudinal wave are particles closest together?

A compression

B crest

C rarefaction

D trough

7 What happens to most of the light waves that strike a transparent pane of glass?

A absorption

B diffraction

C reflection

D transmission

8 Which wave can travel in both empty space and matter?

A radio

B seismic

C sound

D water

Use the figure below to answer question 9.

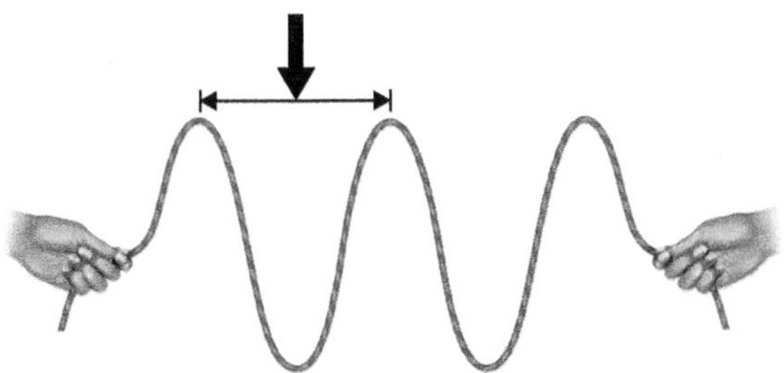

9 To which does the arrow point in the transverse wave diagram?

A amplitude

B crest

C frequency

D wavelength

10 Which is an example of diffraction?

A a flashlight beam hitting a mirror

B a shout crossing a crowded room

C a sunbeam striking a window

D a water wave bending around a rock

11 Which property of waves helps explain why a human shout cannot be heard a mile away?

A absorption

B diffraction

C reflection

D transmission

Constructed Response

Use the table below to answer questions 12 and 13.

	Wave A	Wave B
Number of Wavelengths that pass a point	5	8
Time for wavelengths to pass a point(s)	10	10

12 Which wave has a higher frequency? Why? How does wavelength change as frequency increases?

13 Write and solve an equation to find the speed of wave B if its wavelength is 2 m.

14 Two ocean waves approach a floating beach ball at different times. The second wave has more energy than the first wave. Which wave will have the higher amplitude? Explain your reasoning.

15 Explain why and how the waves from a passing speedboat rock a rowboat. Was the rowboat moved from its original location? Why or why not? Include the definition of a wave in your explanation.

NEED EXTRA HELP?															
If You Missed Question...	1	2	3	4	5	6	7	8	9	10	11	12	13	14	15
Go to Lesson...	2	1	1	1	3	1	3	1	2	3	3	2	2	2	1

6.PS.4, SEPS.1, SEPS.2, SEPS.4, SEPS.6, SEPS.8, 6-8.LST.5.2, 6-8.LST.7.1

Sound and Light

THE BIG IDEA

How do sound and light waves travel and interact with matter?

Inquiry Why is this reflection weird?

The mirror's curved surface forms unusual images. You can see these images because of reflected light waves.

- How are light waves reflected from a surface?
- How does the shape of a shiny surface affect the image you see?
- How do your eyes see the reflection?

Get Ready to Read

What do you think?

Before you read, decide if you agree or disagree with each of these statements. As you read this chapter, see if you change your mind about any of the statements.

1. Vibrating objects make sound waves.
2. Human ears are sensitive to more sound frequencies than any other animal's ears.
3. Unlike sound waves, light waves can travel through a vacuum.
4. Light waves always travel at the same speed.
5. All mirrors form images that appear identical to the object itself.
6. Lenses always magnify objects.

Lesson 1

Reading Guide

Key Concepts

ESSENTIAL QUESTIONS

- How are sound waves produced?
- Why does the speed of sound waves vary in different materials?
- How do your ears enable you to hear sounds?

Vocabulary

sound wave p. 111

pitch p. 115

echo p. 117

Multilingual eGlossary

Science Video

6.PS.4, SEPS.8, 6-8.LST.7.1

Why are its ears so big?

The ears of this brown long-eared bat are nearly as long as its body. This bat finds its next meal by listening for the faint sounds that come from spiders and insects. How do large ears help a long-eared bat hear these sounds?

Grzegorz Gust/Alamy

Launch Lab

15 minutes

How is sound produced?

When an object vibrates, it produces sound. How does the sound produced depend on how the object vibrates?

1. Read and complete a lab safety form.
2. Place a **ruler** on a table so it extends over the table edge. Hold the ruler firmly on the table with one hand.
3. With the other hand, lightly bend the protruding end of the ruler down and then release it. Observe the ruler's motion and note the sound it produces.
4. Move the ruler back 2 cm so there is less of it extending over the edge of the table. Repeat step 3.

Think About This

1. How did the vibration rate and the sound change as the length of the ruler over the side of the table decreased?
2. **Key Concept** Were the sound and the ruler's vibration rate related? Explain.

What is sound?

Have you ever walked down a busy city street and noticed all the sounds? You might hear many sounds every day, such as the music from an MP3 player, as shown in Figure 1. All sounds have one thing in common. The sounds travel from one place to another as sound waves. *A* **sound wave** *is a longitudinal wave that can travel only through matter.*

Sound waves can travel only through matter–solids, liquids, and gases. The sounds you might hear now are traveling through air–a mixture of solids and gases. You might have dived underwater and heard someone call to you. Then the sound waves traveled through a liquid. Sound waves travel through a solid when you knock on a door. As you will read, vibrating objects produce sound waves.

All sounds might have something else in common, too. Vibrating objects produce sound waves. For example, when you knock on a door, you produce sound waves by making the door vibrate. How do vibrating objects make sound waves?

Review Vocabulary

longitudinal wave
a wave in which particles in a material move along the same direction that the wave travels

Figure 1 Headphones produce sound waves that travel into the listener's ears.

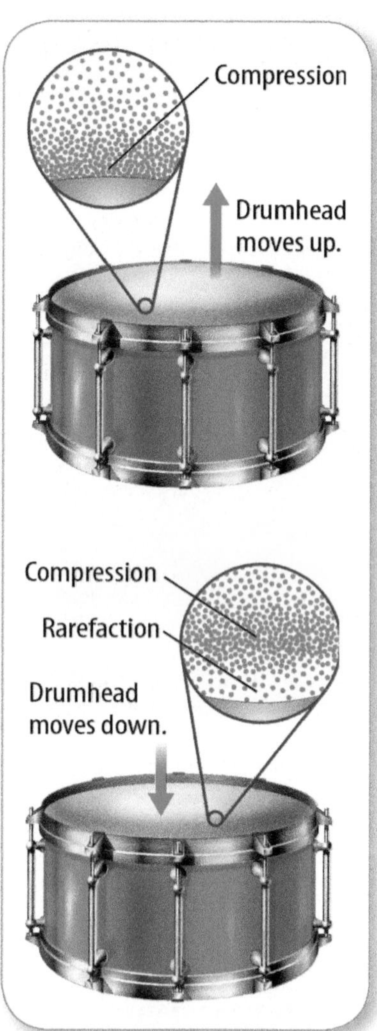

▲ Figure 2 Vibrations of the drumhead produce sound waves.

Vibrations and Sound

Objects such as doors or drums vibrate when you hit them. For example, when you hit a drum, the drumhead moves up and down, or vibrates, as shown in Figure 2. These vibrations produce sound waves by moving molecules in air.

Compressions and Rarefactions

As the drumhead moves up, it pushes the molecules in the air above it closer together. The region where molecules are closer together is a compression, as shown in Figure 2. When the drumhead moves down, it produces a rarefaction. This is a region where molecules are farther apart. As the drumhead vibrates down and up, it produces a series of rarefactions and compressions that travels away from the drumhead. This series of rarefactions and compressions is a sound wave.

The vibrating drumhead causes molecules in the air to move closer together and then farther apart. The molecules in air move back and forth in the same direction that the sound wave travels. As a result, a sound wave is a longitudinal wave.

Key Concept Check How do vibrating objects produce sound waves?

Wavelength and Frequency

A sound wave can be described by its wavelength and frequency. Wavelength is the distance between a point on a wave and the nearest point just like it, as shown in Figure 3. A sound wave's frequency is the number of wavelengths that pass a given point in one second. Recall that the SI unit of frequency is hertz (Hz). The faster an object vibrates, the higher the frequency of the sound wave produced.

Figure 3 Wavelength is the distance between one compression and the next compression or the distance between a rarefaction and the next rarefaction. ▼

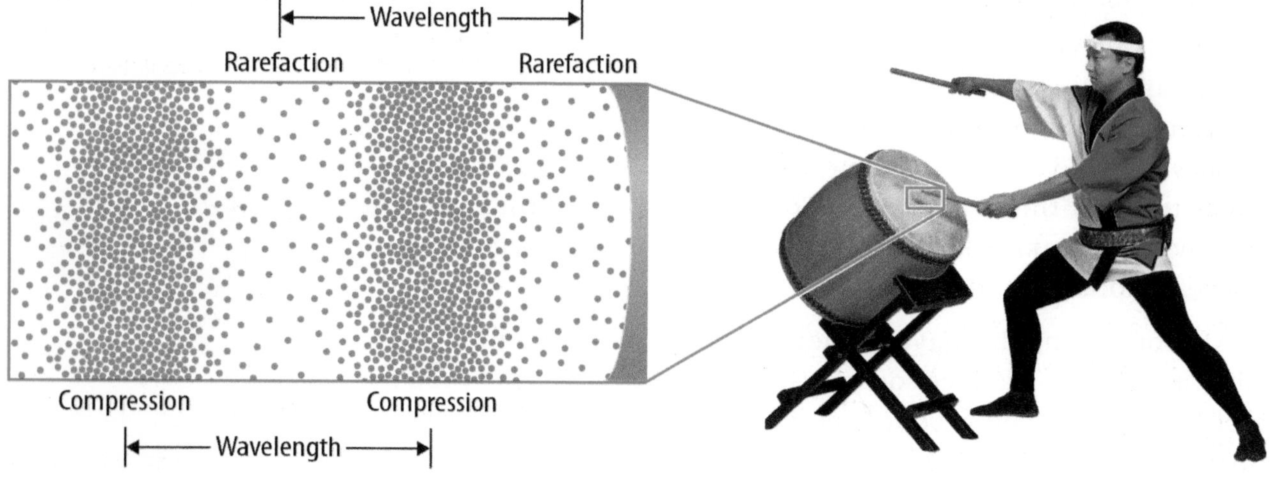

Table 1 The Speed of Sound Waves in Different Materials

Gases (0°C)		Liquids (25°C)		Solids	
Material	**Speed (m/s)**	**Material**	**Speed (m/s)**	**Material**	**Speed (m/s)**
Carbon dioxide	259	Ethanol	1,207	Brick	3,480
Dry Air	331	Mercury	1,450	Ice	3,850
Water vapor	405	Water	1,500	Aluminum	6,420
Helium	965	Glycerine	1,904	Diamond	17,500

Table 1 Sound waves travel at different speeds in different materials. Sound waves usually travel fastest in solids and slowest in gases.

Interactive Table

Speeds of Sound Waves

Sound waves traveling through air cause the sounds you might hear every day. Like all types of waves, the speed of a sound wave depends on the material in which it travels.

Sound in Gases, Liquids, and Solids

Table 1 lists the speeds of sound waves in different materials. A sound wave's speed increases when the material's density increases. Solids and liquids are usually more dense than gases.

In addition, a sound wave's speed increases when the strengths of the forces between the particles–atoms or molecules–in the material increase. These forces are usually strongest in solids and weakest in gases. Overall, sound waves usually travel faster in solids than in liquids or gases.

Key Concept Check Why is the speed of sound waves faster in solids than in liquids or gases?

Temperature and Sound Waves

The temperature of a material also affects the speed of a sound wave. The speed of a sound wave in a material increases as the temperature of the material increases. For example, the speed of a sound wave in dry air increases from 331 m/s to 343 m/s as the air temperature increases from 0°C to 20°C. A sound wave in air travels faster on a warm, summer day than on a cold, winter day.

MiniLab 20 minutes

Can you model a sound wave?

A wave on a coiled spring toy is similar to a sound wave.

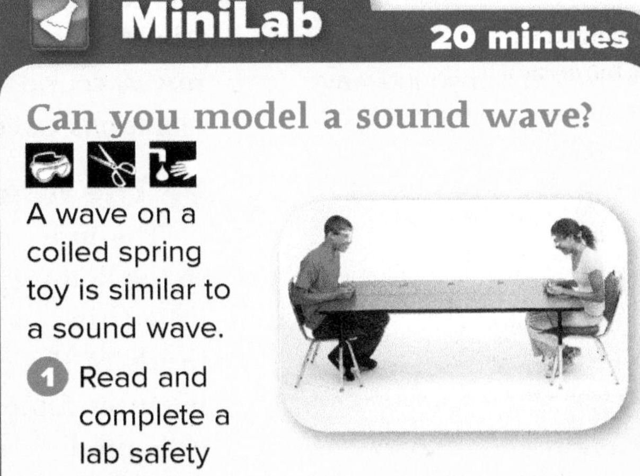

1. Read and complete a lab safety form.
2. Set a long **coiled spring toy** on a flat surface. Tie three small pieces of **yarn** on three different coils, dividing the spring into four equal sections. Stretch the spring about 2 m between you and a partner.
3. Squeeze together about one-fourth of the coils and hold the end of the spring with the other hand. While holding the end of the spring tightly, release the group of coils. Observe the wave.

Analyze and Conclude

1. **Draw** three sketches of the spring in your Science Journal, showing how the wave traveled through the spring. Label the compressions and rarefactions.
2. **Key Concept** Explain how the wave on the spring is similar to a sound wave.

Math Skills 

Use a Simple Equation

Speed (s) is equal to the distance (d) something travels divided by the time (t) it takes to cover that distance:

$$s = \frac{d}{t}$$

You can use this equation to calculate the speed of sound waves. For example, if a sound wave travels a distance of 662 meters in 2 seconds in air, its speed is:

$$s = \frac{d}{t} = \frac{662 \text{ m}}{2 \text{ s}} = 331 \text{ m/s}$$

Practice

How fast is a sound wave traveling if it travels 5,000 m in 5 s?

 Math Practice

 Personal Tutor

The Human Ear

When you think about your ears, you probably only think about the structure on each side of your head. However, there is more to your ears than those structures. The human ear has three parts–the outer ear, the middle ear, and the inner ear, as shown in Figure 4.

1 The Outer Ear

The outer ear collects sound waves. The structure on each side of your head is part of the outer ear. The ear canal is also part of the outer ear, as shown in Figure 4. The visible part of the outer ear funnels sound waves into the ear canal. The ear canal channels sound waves into the middle ear.

2 The Middle Ear

The middle ear amplifies sound waves. As shown in Figure 4, the middle ear includes the eardrum and three tiny bones. The eardrum is a thin membrane that stretches across the ear canal. The three tiny bones are called the hammer, the anvil, and the stirrup. A sound wave hitting the eardrum causes it to vibrate. The vibrations travel to the three bones, which amplify the sound.

3 The Inner Ear

The inner ear converts vibrations to nerve signals that travel to the brain. The inner ear consists of a small, fluid-filled chamber called the cochlea (KOH klee uh). Tiny hairlike cells line the inside of the cochlea. As a sound wave travels into the cochlea, it causes some hair cells to vibrate. The movements of these hair cells produce nerve signals that travel to the brain.

 **Key Concept Check** What is the function of each of the three parts of the ear?

Structure of the Ear 

Figure 4 The human ear has three parts. The outer ear collects sound waves, the middle ear amplifies these waves, and the inner ear converts them to nerve signals.

Visual Check Which parts of the ear are considered the middle ear?

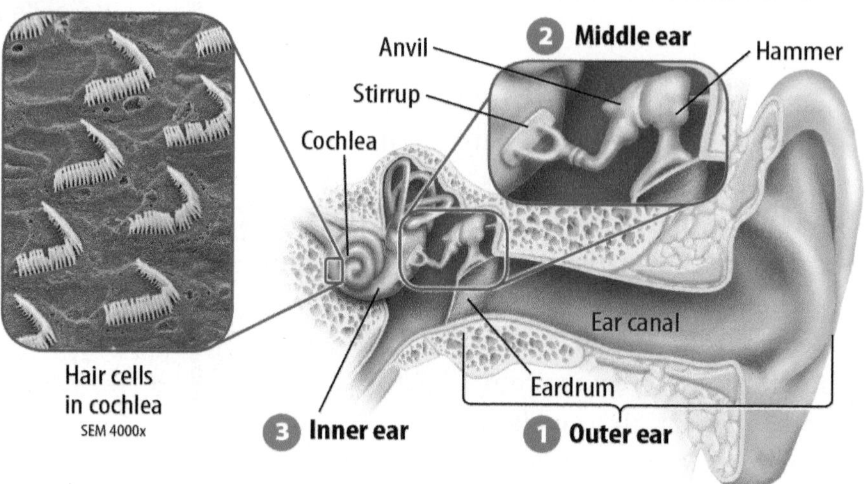

SPL/Science Source

Frequencies and the Human Ear

As you can see in Table 2, humans hear sounds with frequencies between about 20 and 20,000 Hz. Some mammals can hear sounds with frequencies greater than 100,000 Hz.

Sound and Pitch

Have you ever played a guitar? A guitar has strings with different thicknesses. If you pluck a thick string, you hear a low note. If you pluck a thin string, you hear a higher note. The sound a thick string makes has a lower pitch than the sound a thin string makes. *The* **pitch** *of a sound is the perception of how high or low a sound seems.* A sound wave with a higher frequency has a higher pitch. A sound wave with a lower frequency has a lower pitch.

Reading Check How does the pitch of a sound wave depend on the frequency of the sound wave?

You can produce sounds of different pitches by using your vocal cords. The vocal cords, shown in Figure 5, are two membranes in your neck above your windpipe, or trachea (TRAY kee uh). When you speak, you force air from your lungs through the space between the vocal cords. This causes the vocal cords to vibrate, creating sound waves you and other people hear as your voice.

Muscles connected to your vocal cords enable you to change the pitch of your voice. When these muscles contract, they pull on your vocal cords. This stretches the vocal cords and they become longer and thinner. The pitch of your voice is then higher, just as a thinner guitar string has a higher pitch than a thicker guitar string. When these muscles relax, the vocal cords become shorter and thicker and the pitch of your voice becomes lower.

Table 2 Frequencies Different Mammals Can Hear

Creature	Frequency Range (Hz)
Human	20–20,000
Dog	67–45,000
Cat	45–64,000
Bat	2,000–110,000
Beluga whale	1,000–123,000
Porpoise	75–150,000

▲ **Table 2** Different mammals can hear sound waves over different ranges of frequencies.

Make a two-tab concept map book. Label it as shown. Use it to organize information about pitch and loudness.

The Ear
Pitch | Loudness

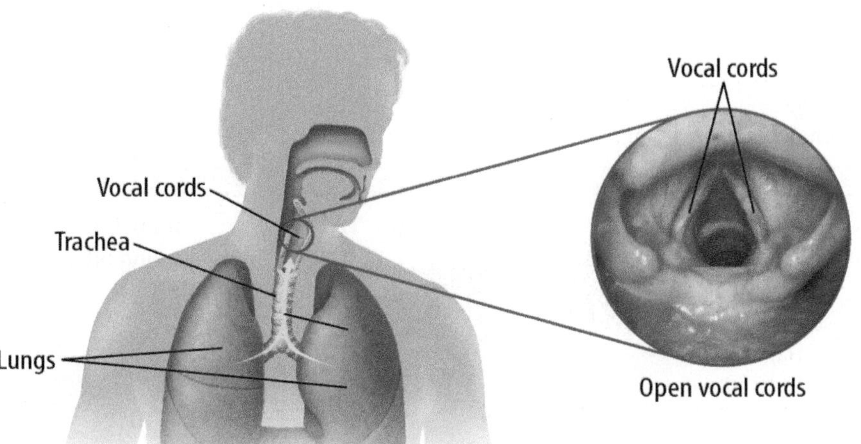

◄ **Figure 5** The vocal cords vibrate by opening and closing when air is forced through them. These vibrations produce the sounds of the human voice.

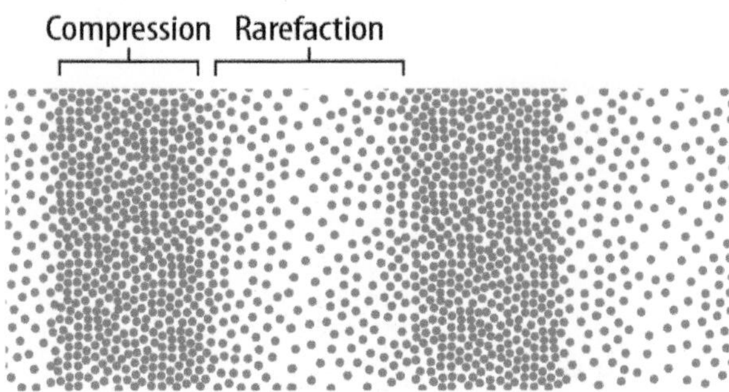

Low amplitude sound wave

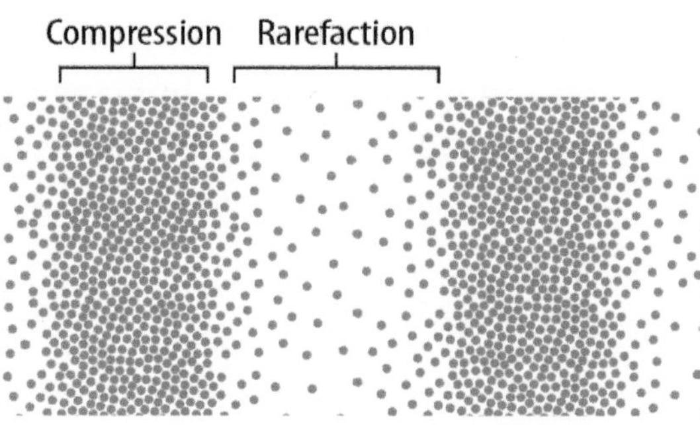

High amplitude sound wave

▲ **Figure 6** The amplitude of a sound wave depends on how close together or far apart the particles are in the compressions and rarefactions.

Visual Check How do distances between particles differ in high- and low-amplitude sound waves?

Sound and Loudness

Why is a shout louder than a whisper? Loudness is the human sensation of how much energy a sound wave carries. Sound waves produced by shouting carry more energy than sound waves produced by whispering. As a result, a shout sounds louder than a whisper.

Amplitude and Energy

The amplitude of a wave depends on the amount of energy that the wave carries. The more energy a wave has, the greater the amplitude. Figure 6 shows the difference between a high-amplitude sound wave and a low-amplitude sound wave. High-amplitude sound waves have particles that are closer together in the compressions and farther apart in the rarefactions.

The Decibel Scale

The decibel scale, shown in Figure 7, is one way to compare the loudness of sounds. On this scale, the softest sound a person can hear is about 0 decibels (dB), and a jet plane taking off is at about 150 dB. Normal conversation is at about 50 dB. A sound wave that is 10 dB higher than another sound wave carries 10 times more energy. However, people hear the higher-energy sound wave as being only twice as loud.

Figure 7 The loudness of sounds can be compared on the decibel scale. ▼

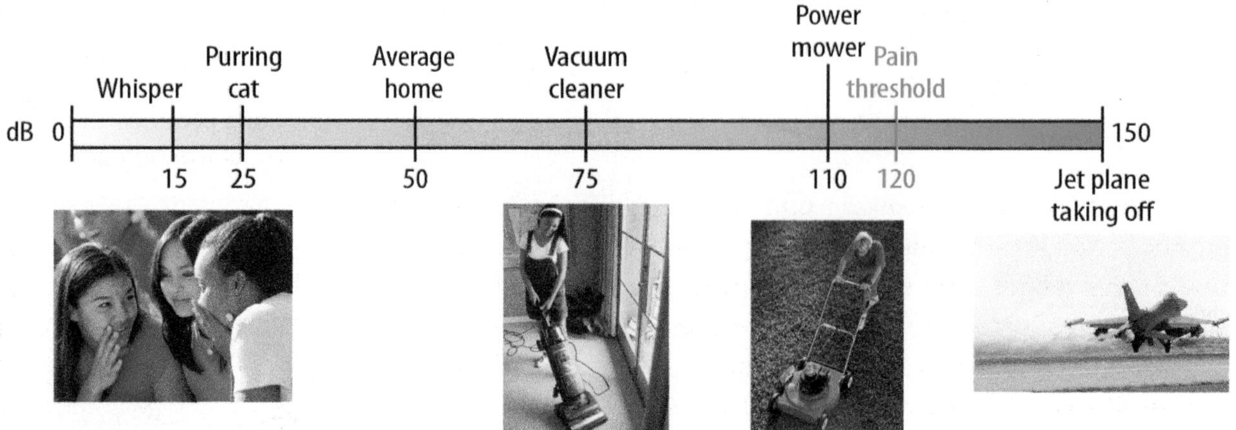

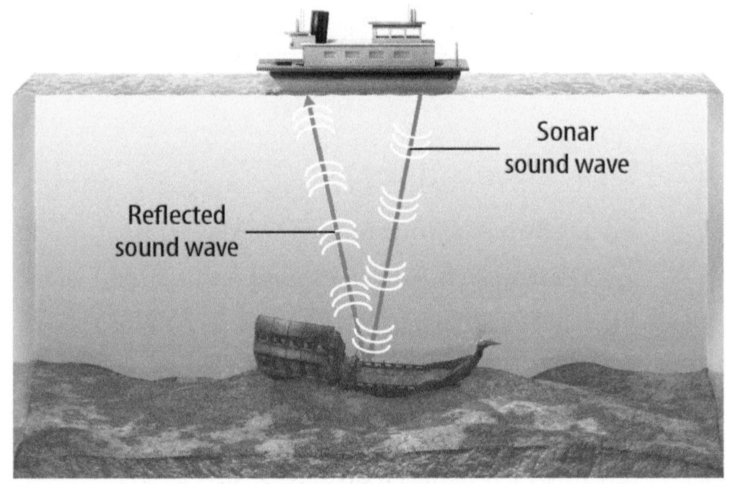

A Sonar System

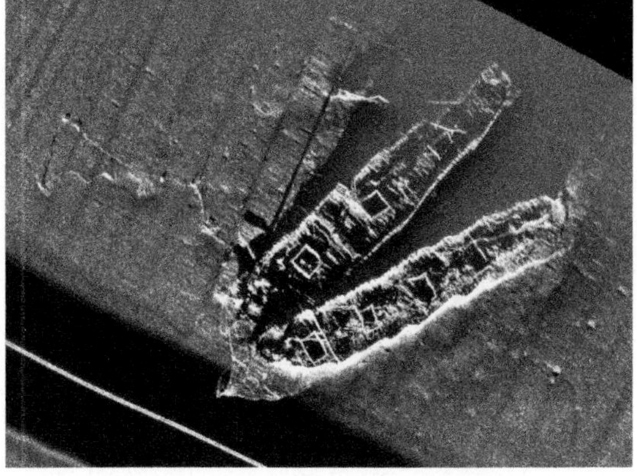
Image Made by Sonar System

▲ **Figure 8** A sonar system locates underwater objects by sending out sound waves and detecting the reflected sound waves. The photo on the right is a sonar image of two sunken ships.

Using Sound Waves

Have you ever yelled in a cave or a big, empty room? You might have heard the echo of your voice. *An* **echo** *is a reflected sound wave.* You may be able to hear echoes in a gymnasium or a cafeteria. You probably can't tell how far away a wall is by hearing an echo. However, sonar systems and some animals use reflected sound waves to determine how far away objects are.

Sonar and Echolocation

Sonar systems use reflected sound waves to locate objects under water, as shown in Figure 8. The sonar system emits a sound wave that reflects off an underwater object. The distance to the object can be calculated from the time difference between when the sound leaves the ship and when the sound returns to the ship. Sonar is used to map the ocean floor and to detect submarines, schools of fish, and other objects under water.

WORD ORIGIN
echo
from Greek *ekhe,* means "sound"

 **Reading Check** How do sonar systems use sound waves?

Some animals use a method called echolocation to navigate and hunt. Echolocation is a type of sonar. Bats and dolphins, for example, emit high-pitched sounds and interpret the echoes reflected from objects. Echolocation enables bats and dolphins to locate prey and detect objects.

Ultrasound

Ultrasound scanners, like the one shown in Figure 9, convert high-frequency sound waves to images of internal body parts. The sound waves reflect from structures within the body. The scanner analyzes the reflected waves and produces images, called sonograms, of the body structures. These images can be used to help diagnose disease or other medical conditions.

Figure 9 Ultrasound scanners produce images that doctors can use to diagnose diseases. ▼

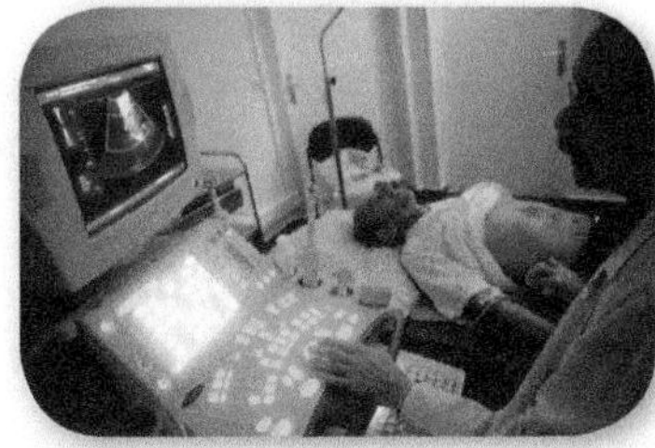

Lesson 1 Review

Visual Summary

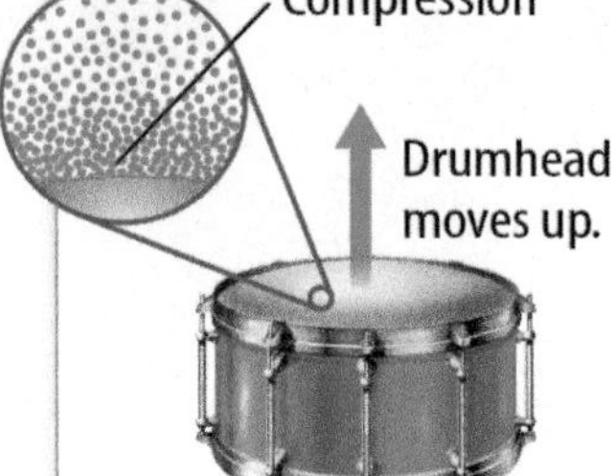

A sound wave is a longitudinal wave that can travel only through matter.

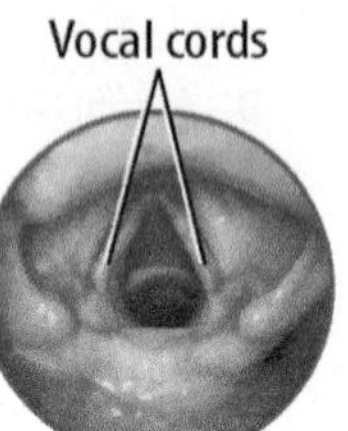

The pitch is how high or low the frequency of a sound wave is. You create different pitches using your vocal cords.

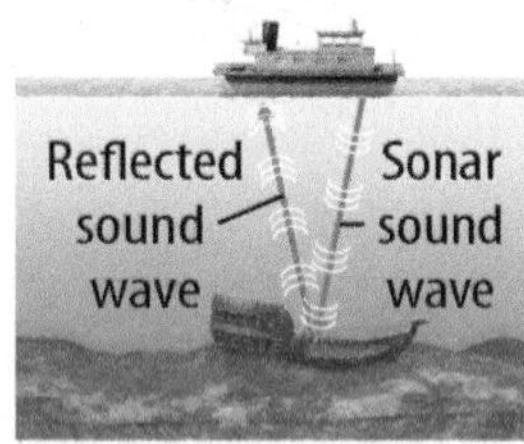

An echo is a reflected sound wave. Ships use sonar to find underwater objects.

FOLDABLES®

Use your lesson Foldable to review the lesson. Save your Foldable for the project at the end of the chapter.

What do you think NOW?

You first read the statements below at the beginning of the chapter.

1. Vibrating objects make sound waves.
2. Human ears are sensitive to more sound frequencies than any other animal's ears.

Did you change your mind about whether you agree or disagree with the statements? Rewrite any false statements to make them true.

Use Vocabulary

1. **Define** *echo* in your own words.
2. **Distinguish** between sound and a sound wave.
3. **Use the word** *pitch* in a sentence.

Understand Key Concepts

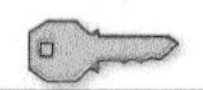

4. In which material do sound waves travel fastest?
   - **A.** aluminum
   - **B.** carbon dioxide
   - **C.** ethanol
   - **D.** water
5. **Predict** Would a barking dog produce sound waves that travel faster during the day or at night? Explain your answer.

Interpret Graphics

6. **Describe** The image below shows part of a sound wave. Describe how this image would change if the wavelength of the sound wave decreased.

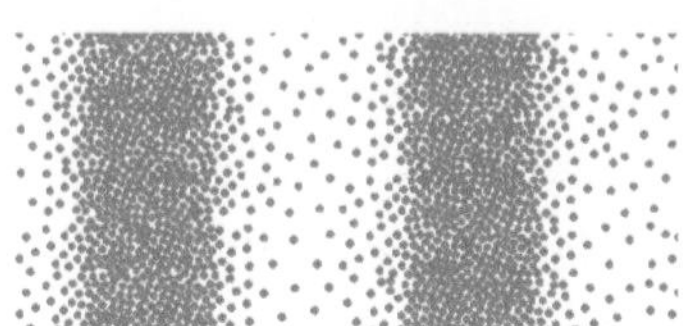

7. **Sequence** Copy and fill in a graphic organizer like the one below that shows the path a sound wave travels from the air until it is interpreted by the brain.

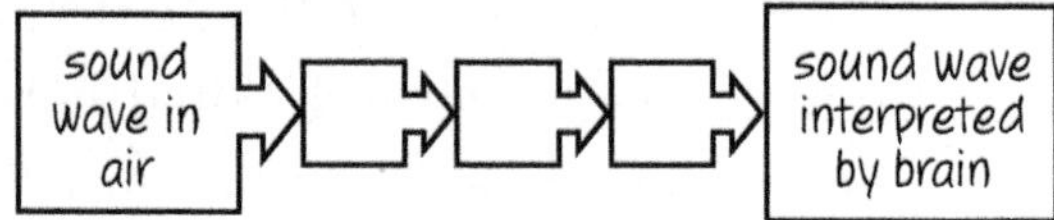

Critical Thinking

8. **Infer** A string vibrates with a frequency of 10 Hz. Why can't a person hear the sound waves produced by the vibrating string, no matter how large the amplitude of the waves?

Math Skills

Math Practice

9. If a sound wave travels 1,620 m in 3 s, what is its speed?

HOW IT WORKS

How do ultrasound machines work?

Using Ultrasound to Safely Monitor a Human Fetus

Ultrasound waves are sound waves with frequencies so high that humans cannot hear them. An ultrasound machine has a hand-held device, called a transducer, that emits and receives ultrasound waves. This enables medical professionals to see inside a human body.

1 A technician passes the transducer over the patient's skin, transmitting ultrasound waves into the patient's body.

2 When the ultrasound waves strike different surfaces, some of those waves reflect back to the transducer.

3 The transducer detects the reflected ultrasound waves and converts them into electronic signals.

4 A computer receives the signals from the transducer and produces an image.

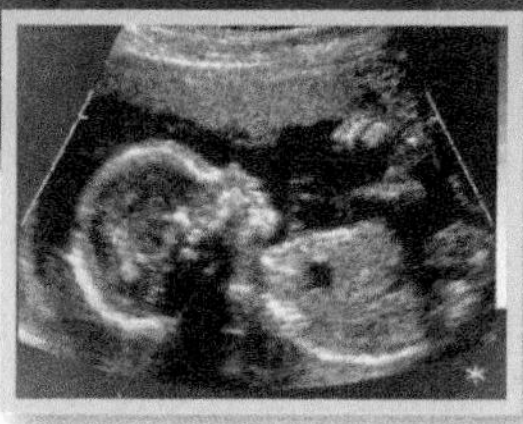

It's Your Turn

RESEARCH other ways that medical professionals use ultrasound machines.

UHB Trust/Getty Images

Lesson 2

Light

Reading Guide

Key Concepts
ESSENTIAL QUESTIONS

- How are light waves different from sound waves?
- How do waves in the electromagnetic spectrum differ?
- What happens to light waves when they interact with matter?

Vocabulary

light source p. 123
light ray p. 123
transparent p. 124
translucent p. 124
opaque p. 124

Multilingual eGlossary

BrainPOP® Science Video
What's Science Got to do With It?

6.PS.4, SEPS.2

Go to the resource tab in ConnectED to find the PBL *Build a Better Room.*

Inquiry Are both men real?

No, the man on the right is a hologram. A hologram is a type of image that seems to be three-dimensional. Light from a laser is reflected from the person and is used to create the life-like image. What are light waves and how do they interact with matter?

Launch Lab

15 minutes

What happens when light waves pass through water?  

Do light waves always travel in a straight line? What happens to light waves when they travel through water?

1. Read and complete a lab safety form.
2. Add **distilled water** to a **500-mL beaker** until it is two-thirds full.
3. Use **scissors** to cut a thin slit in a sheet of **paper. Tape** the paper over the lens of a **flashlight.**
4. Turn on the flashlight and tilt it slightly downward so the light beam is visible on the tabletop. Place the water-filled beaker in the light beam. Record your observations in your Science Journal.

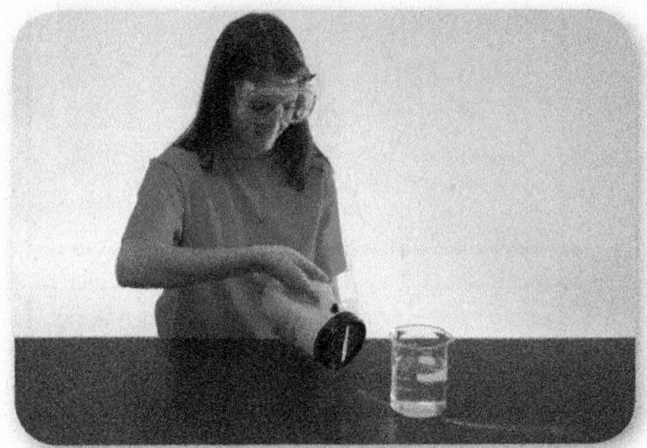

Think About This

Key Concept Compare the direction of the light beam before it entered the water to after it left the water.

What is light?

As you read these words, you are probably looking at a page in a book. You might also see the desk on which the book is resting as well as the light from a lamp. What do your eyes detect when you see something?

Your eyes sense light waves. You see books and desks when light waves reflect off these objects and enter your eyes. Some objects, like a candle flame and a lightbulb that is lit, also emit light waves. You see a candle flame or a glowing lightbulb because the light waves they emit enter your eyes.

Light—An Electromagnetic Wave

Light is a type of wave called an electromagnetic wave. Like sound waves, electromagnetic waves can travel through matter. But they can also travel through a vacuum, where no matter is present. For example, light can travel through the space between Earth and the Sun.

Light travels through a vacuum at a speed of about 300,000 km/s. However, light waves slow down when they travel through matter. The speed of light in some different materials is listed in Table 3. Light waves travel much faster than sound waves. For example, in air the speed of light is about 900,000 times faster than the speed of sound.

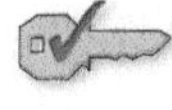 **Key Concept Check** How are light waves different from sound waves?

Table 3 Light waves travel fastest in empty space. When light waves travel in matter, they move fastest in gases and slowest in solids.

Table 3 Speed of Light Waves in Some Materials

Material	Wave Speed (km/s)
Vacuum	300,000
Air	299,920
Water	225,100
Glass	193,000

Hutchings Photography/Digital Light Source

The Electromagnetic Spectrum

Personal Tutor

Radios and TVs use radio waves. Radio waves have wavelengths greater than about 0.3 m.
Cell phones use microwaves. Microwaves have wavelengths between 0.3 m and 0.001 m.

Wavelength (billionths of a meter)
Light waves have wavelengths between about 700 nm and 400 nm.
Infrared waves have wavelengths between about 0.001 m and 700 nm.
Ultraviolet waves have wavelengths between 400 nm and 10 nm and can cause sunburn.
X-rays have wavelengths between 10 nm and 0.01 nm.

Figure 10 Electromagnetic waves are classified according to their wavelength or frequency. Visible light waves are part of the electromagnetic spectrum.

Visual Check Which type of electromagnetic waves have the longest wavelengths?

The Electromagnetic Spectrum

Besides visible light waves, there are other types of electromagnetic waves, such as X-rays and radio waves. Scientists classify electromagnetic waves into groups based on their wavelengths, as shown in Figure 10. The entire range of electromagnetic waves is called the electromagnetic spectrum.

Key Concept Check How are waves in the electromagnetic spectrum different?

Light waves are only a small part of the electromagnetic spectrum. The wavelengths of light waves are so short they are usually measured in nanometers (nm). One nanometer equals one-billionth of a meter. The wavelengths of light waves are from about 700 nm to about 400 nm. This is about one-hundredth the width of a human hair. You see different colors when different wavelengths of light waves enter your eyes.

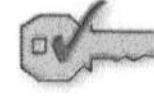

Microwaves
Infrared

Ultraviolet

Gamma rays
Increasing frequency
Increasing wavelength

600
500

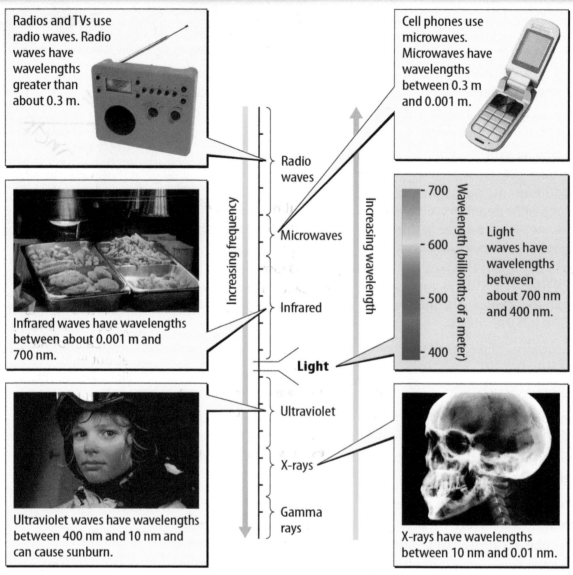

Light-Emitting Objects

Think about walking into a dark room and turning on a light. The lightbulb produces light waves that travel away from the bulb in all directions, as shown in Figure 11. *A* **light source** *is something that emits light.* In order to emit light, the lightbulb transforms electric energy into light energy. Other examples of light sources are the Sun and burning candles. The Sun transforms nuclear energy into light energy. Burning candles transform chemical energy into light energy. Light sources convert other forms of energy into light energy.

▲ Figure 11 Light travels in all directions away from its source.

Light Rays

As you just read, light waves spread out in all directions from a light source. You also can think of light in terms of light rays. *A* **light ray** *is a narrow beam of light that travels in a straight line.* The arrows in Figure 11 represent some of the light rays moving away from the light source. Unless light rays come in contact with a surface or pass through a different material, they travel in straight lines.

Reading Check What is a light ray?

Light Reflection

Suppose you are in a dark room. Do you see anything? Now you turn on a light. What do you see now? Light sources emit light. But other objects, like books, reflect light. In order to see an object that is not a light source, light waves must reflect from an object and enter your eyes.

Seeing Objects

When you see a light source, light rays travel directly from the light source into your eye. Light rays also reflect off objects, as shown in Figure 12. Light rays reflect from an object in many directions. Some of the light rays that reflect from an object enter your eye, enabling you to see the object.

FOLDABLES®

Make a layered book from two sheets of paper. Use it to summarize information about light and how light waves interact with matter.

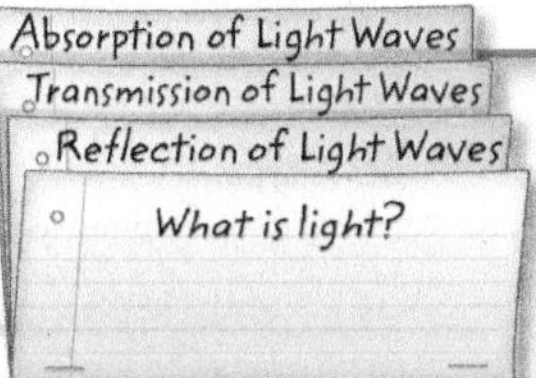

Project-Based Learning Activity

Build a Better Room Go online to investigate how sound, light, and other energy waves are reflected, absorbed, and transmitted.

◄ Figure 12 Some light waves from a light source reach the page and reflect off it. The girl sees the page when some of the reflected light enters her eyes.

Figure 13 The window pane, the frosted glass, and the curtains interact with light waves differently.

Transparent

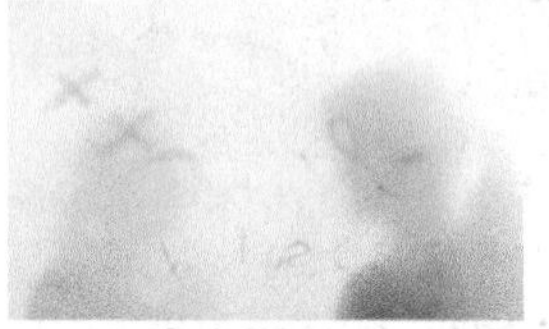

Translucent

Opaque

WORD ORIGIN

opaque
from Latin *opacus*, means "shady, dark"

The Interaction of Light and Matter

Like all waves, when light waves interact with matter they can be transmitted, absorbed, or reflected.

- Reflection occurs when light waves come in contact with the surface of a material and bounce off.
- Transmission occurs when light waves travel through a material.
- Absorption occurs when interactions with a material convert light energy into other forms such as thermal energy.

In many materials, reflection, transmission, and absorption occur at the same time. For example, the tinted glass of an office building reflects some light, transmits some light, and absorbs some light.

Key Concept Check What can happen to light waves when they interact with matter?

Depending on how they interact with light, materials can be classified as transparent, translucent, or opaque, as shown in Figure 13. *A material is* **transparent** *if it allows almost all light that strikes it to pass through and forms a clear image. A material is* **translucent** *if it allows most of the light that strikes it to pass but forms a blurry image. A material is* **opaque** *if light does not pass through it.* An opaque material, such as light-blocking cloth curtains, does not transmit light.

The Reflection of Light Waves

Figure 14 shows what happens when a surface reflects light waves. All waves, including light waves, obey the law of reflection. According to the law of reflection, the angle of incidence always equals the angle of reflection. In Figure 14, the line perpendicular to a surface is called the normal. The angle between the normal and the incoming light ray is the angle of incidence. The angle between the reflected light ray and the normal is the angle of reflection.

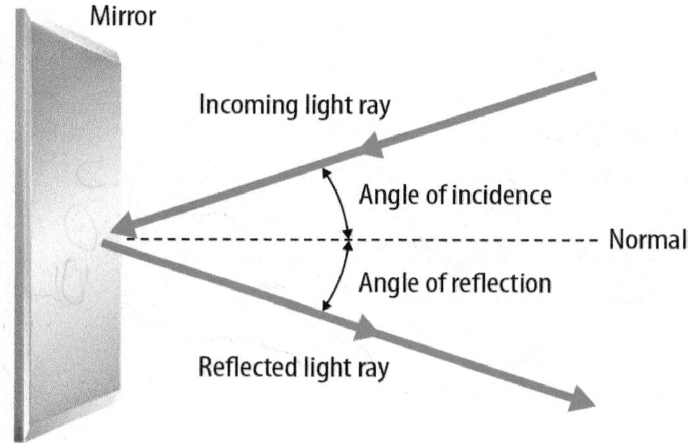

Figure 14 When a surface reflects a light ray, the angle of incidence equals the angle of reflection.

Visual Check How will the angle of reflection change if the angle of incidence increases?

Figure 15 Particles of dust floating in the air scatter light rays in a sunbeam. When light rays strike these particles, light rays reflect in many different directions. ▼

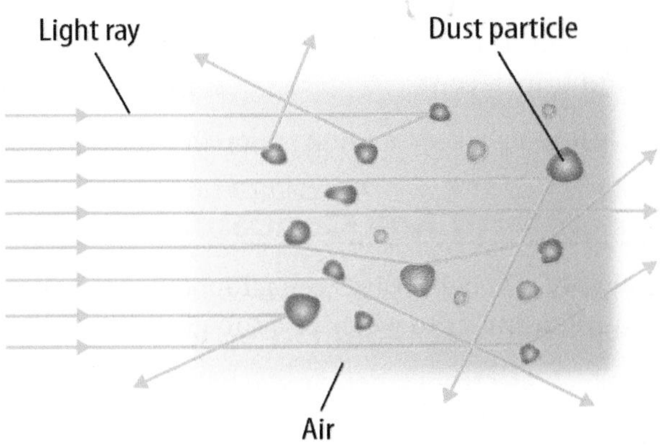

Scattering

When a beam of sunlight shines through a window, you might notice tiny particles of dust. You see the dust particles because they reflect light waves. As Figure 15 shows, dust particles reflect light waves in many different directions because they have different shapes. This is an example of scattering. Scattering occurs when light waves traveling in one direction are made to travel in many directions. The dust particles scatter the light waves in the sunbeam.

The Refraction of Light Waves

Like all types of waves, light waves can change direction when they travel from one material to another. The light beam in Figure 16 changes direction as it goes from the air into the acrylic and from the acrylic into the air. A wave that changes direction as it travels from one material into another is refracting.

Recall that light waves travel at different speeds in different materials. Refraction occurs when a wave changes speed. The greater the change in speed, the more the light wave refracts or changes direction.

Reading Check When does refraction occur?

MiniLab 15 minutes

Can you see a light beam in water?

Scattering by water droplets in air enables you to see a car's headlight beams on a foggy day or night. What could enable you to see a light beam traveling in water?

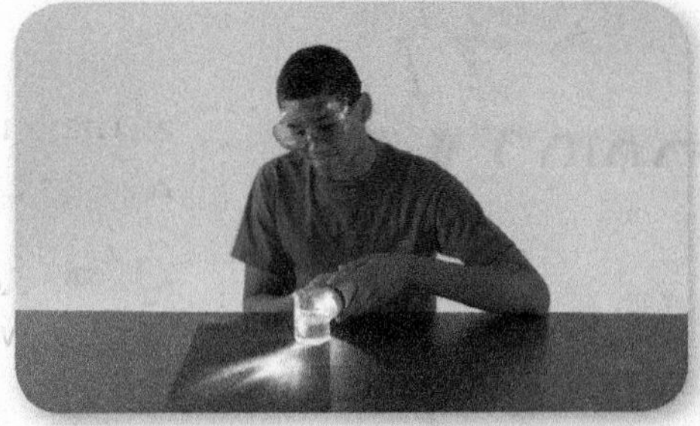

1. Read and complete a lab safety form.
2. Add **distilled water** to a **clear glass jar** until it is two-thirds full.
3. Shine the light from a **flashlight** through the water and record your observations in your Science Journal.
4. Add a few drops of **milk** to the water and swirl the jar to mix the milk and water. Repeat step 3.

Analyze and Conclude

1. **Compare** the appearance of the light beams in steps 3 and 4.
2. **Key Concept** Hypothesize how the milk enabled the light beam to be visible in the milk-water mixture.

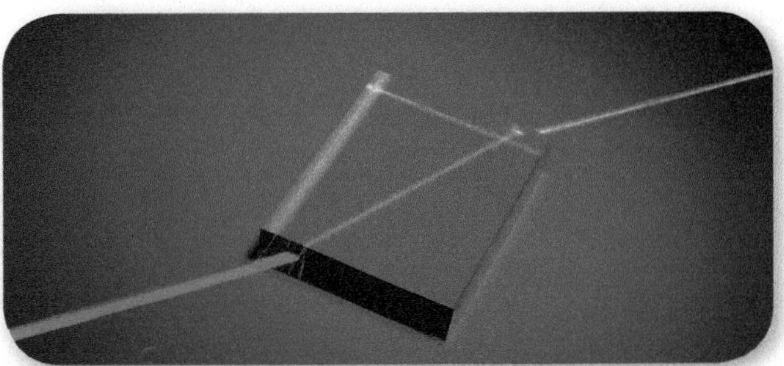

▲ Figure 16 The red beam of light slows down as it enters the acrylic block. It speeds up as it leaves the block and enters the air.

Lesson 2 Review

Visual Summary

An object is seen when light waves emitted by the object or reflected by the object enter the eye.

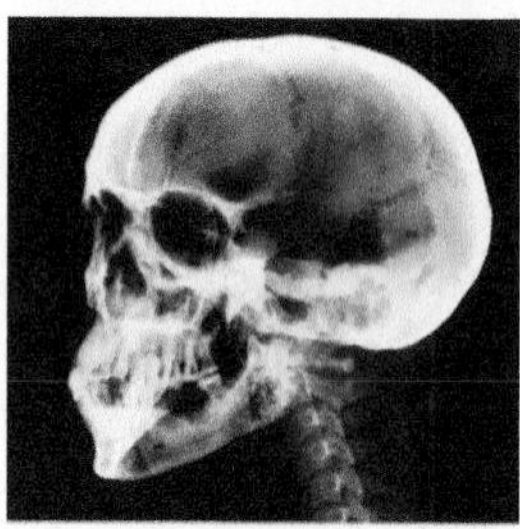

The electromagnetic spectrum includes electromagnetic waves of different wavelengths, such as X-rays.

When light waves interact with matter, they can be absorbed, reflected, or transmitted.

FOLDABLES®

Use your lesson Foldable to review the lesson. Save your Foldable for the project at the end of the chapter.

What do you think 

You first read the statements below at the beginning of the chapter.

3. Unlike sound waves, light waves can travel through a vacuum.

4. Light waves always travel at the same speed.

Did you change your mind about whether you agree or disagree with the statements? Rewrite any false statements to make them true.

Use Vocabulary

1. **Explain** the difference between transparent and translucent.
2. **Define** *light source* using your own words.

Understand Key Concepts 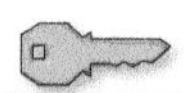

3. **Apply** Do light waves refract more when they travel from air to water or air to glass?
4. Which electromagnetic wave has the shortest wavelength?

   A. gamma
   B. infrared
   C. radio
   D. ultraviolet

Interpret Graphics

5. **Evaluate** If a light wave has an angle of incidence of 30° as shown below, what is its angle of reflection?

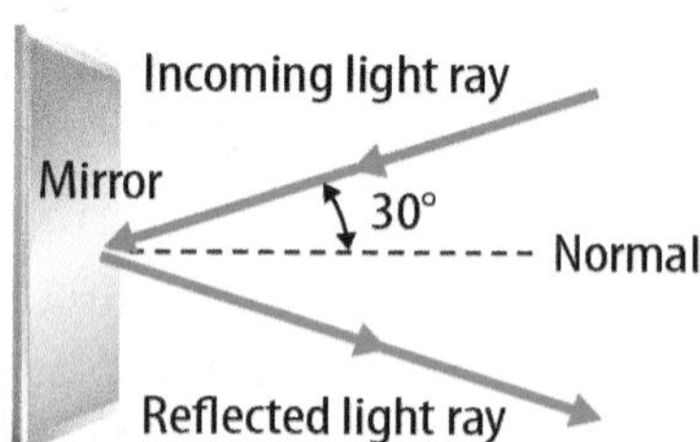

6. **Organize Information** Copy and fill in the table below.

Interaction	Description
Absorption	
	Light wave bounces off a surface.
Transmission	

Critical Thinking

7. **Describe** how the speed of light waves changes when they travel from air into a water-filled aquarium and back into air.
8. **Draw** You turn on a light in a dark room and see a chair. Sketch the path that the light waves traveled that enabled you to see the chair.

 Skill Practice **Model** 30 minutes

How are light rays reflected from a plane mirror?

Scientists use **models** to describe how the laws of science might work in real-life applications. How does the law of reflection look in a real-life application?

Materials

flashlight

protractor

metric ruler

scissors

tape

small plane mirror, at least 10 cm on a side

modeling clay

Also needed: white, unlined paper; black construction paper

Safety

Learn It

In science, **models** are used to demonstrate ideas and concepts that often are difficult to grasp. A model that you can see and manipulate with your hands helps you understand a difficult concept and observe how the natural process works.

Try It

1. Read and complete a lab safety form.
2. With the scissors, cut a narrow slit in the construction paper and tape it over the flashlight lens.
3. Place the mirror at one end of the unlined paper. Push the mirror into lumps of clay so it stands vertically, and tilt the mirror so it leans slightly toward the table.
4. Mark the center of the mirror on the unlined paper. Then draw a line on the paper perpendicular to the mirror from the mark. Label this line *N* for normal.
5. Draw lines on the paper from the center mark at angles 30°, 45°, and 60° to line *N*.
6. Turn on the flashlight and place it so the beam is along the 45° line. This is the angle of incidence. Have a partner draw a short line tracing the reflected light beam and mark the line *45*.
7. Repeat step 6 for the 30°, 60°, and *N* lines.
8. Remove the paper from the setup. Measure and record in your Science Journal the angles that the reflected beams made with *N*. These are the angles of reflection.

Apply It

9. **Key Concept** Infer from your results the relationship between the angle of incidence and the angle of reflection.

Lesson 3

Reading Guide

Key Concepts
ESSENTIAL QUESTIONS

- What is the difference between regular and diffuse reflection?
- What types of images are formed by mirrors and lenses?
- How does the human eye enable a person to see?

Vocabulary

mirror p. 130
lens p. 131
cornea p. 132
iris p. 133
pupil p. 133
retina p. 134

Multilingual eGlossary

BrainPOP®

6.PS.4, SEPS.1, SEPS.2, SEPS.4, SEPS.6, SEPS.8, 6-8.LST.5.2

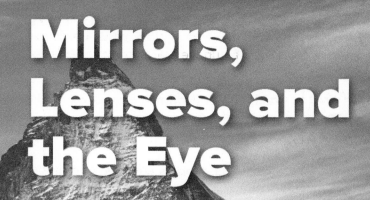

Mirrors, Lenses, and the Eye

Are there two mountains?

Have you ever seen an image on the surface of a lake? If so, you have observed light waves reflecting from a mirrorlike surface. Are all reflected images the same? How does the shape of a mirror's surface affect the image that you see?

altrendo nature/Getty Images

Launch Lab

15 minutes

Are there different types of reflections?

Some surfaces are like mirrors. Other surfaces do not form reflected images you can see. What is the difference between a surface that forms a sharp reflected image and one that does not?

1. Read and complete a lab safety form.
2. Place a **black bowl** on a **paper towel.** Look straight down at the bottom of the bowl. Record your observations in your Science Journal.
3. Carefully add about 3 cm of water to the bowl. Look at the bottom of the bowl. Record your observations.
4. Tap the side of the bowl gently and look again. Record your observations.

Think About This

1. Compare your observations in steps 2, 3, and 4.
2. **Key Concept** What do you think caused the differences in the images you observed?

Why are some surfaces mirrors?

When you look at a smooth pond, you can see a sharp image of yourself reflected off the water surface. When you look at a lake on a windy day, you do not see a sharp image. Why are these images different? A smooth surface reflects light rays traveling in the same direction at the same angle. This is called regular reflection, as shown in Figure 17. Because the light rays travel the same way relative to each other before and after reflection, the reflected light rays form a sharp image.

When a surface is not smooth, light rays still follow the law of reflection. However, light rays traveling in the same direction hit the rough surface at different angles. The reflected light rays travel in many different directions, as shown in Figure 17. This is called diffuse reflection. You do not see a clear image when diffuse reflection occurs.

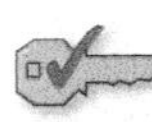

Key Concept Check Contrast regular and diffuse reflection.

Types of Reflection

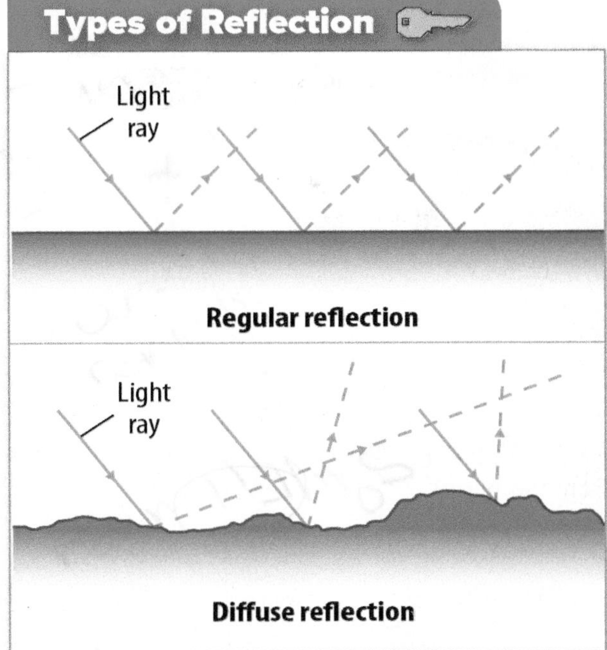

Figure 17 Light waves always obey the law of reflection, whether the surface is smooth or rough. Regular reflection occurs from a smooth surface and forms a sharp image. Diffuse reflection occurs from a rough surface and doesn't form a clear image.

Table 4 Images and Mirrors

Concave Mirror

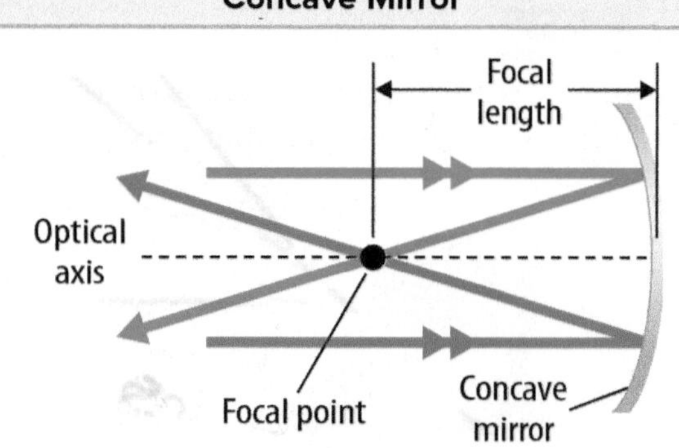

The focal length is the distance from the center of the mirror to the focal point.

The image in a concave mirror is upside down when an object is more than one focal length from the mirror.

Focal point
Object
Image

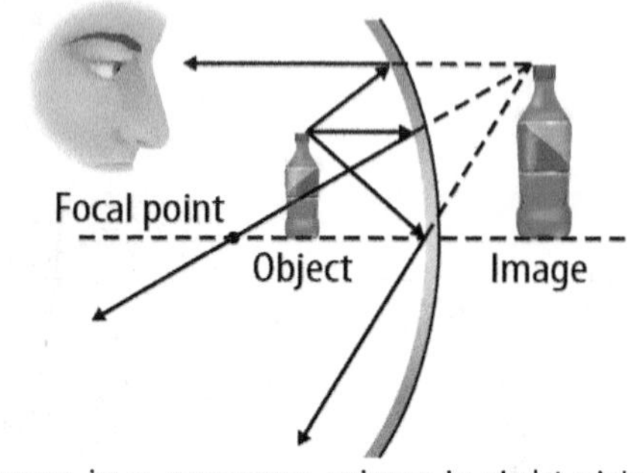

The image in a concave mirror is right-side up when an object is less than one focal length from the mirror.

Convex Mirror

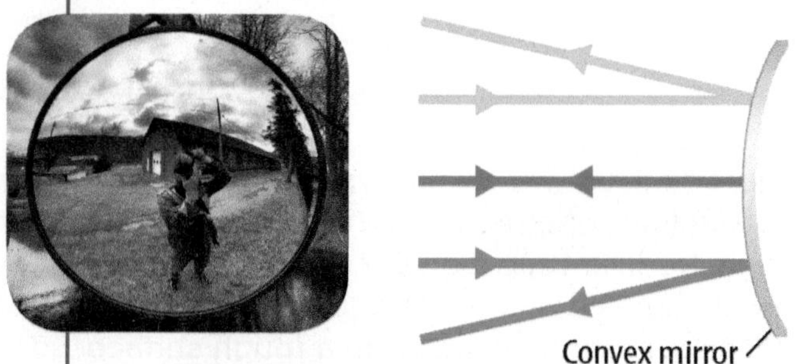

The image in a convex mirror is always right-side up and smaller than the object.

Types of Mirrors

When you look at a wall mirror, the image you see is about the same size that you are and right-side up. *A* **mirror** *is any reflecting surface that forms an image by regular reflection.* The image formed by a mirror depends on the shape of the mirror's surface.

Plane Mirrors

A plane mirror is a mirror that has a flat reflecting surface. The image formed by the mirror looks like a photograph of the object except that the image is reversed left to right. The size of the image in the mirror depends on how far the object is from the mirror. The image gets smaller as the object gets farther from the mirror.

Concave Mirrors

Reflecting surfaces that are curved inward are concave mirrors, as shown in Table 4. Light rays that are parallel to a line called the optical axis, which is shown in Table 4, are reflected through one point–the focal point. The distance from the mirror to the focal point is called the focal length.

The type of image formed depends on where the object is, as shown in Table 4. If an object is more than one focal length from a concave mirror, the image will be upside down. If the object is closer than one focal length, the image will be right-side up. If an object is placed exactly at the focal point, no image forms.

Convex Mirrors

A convex mirror has a reflecting surface that is curved outward, as shown in Table 4. The image is always right-side up and smaller than the object. Store security mirrors and passenger-side car mirrors are usually convex mirrors.

Key Concept Check How do the images formed by plane mirrors, concave mirrors, and convex mirrors depend on the distance of an object from the mirror?

Types of Lenses

Have you ever used a magnifying lens or binoculars? Or you might wear glasses that help you see more clearly. All of these items use lenses to change the way an image of an object forms. *A* **lens** *is a transparent object with at least one curved side that causes light to change direction.* The more curved the sides of a lens, the more the light changes direction as it passes through the lens.

Convex Lenses

A convex lens is curved outward on at least one side so it is thicker in the middle than at its edges. Just like a concave mirror, a convex lens has a focal point and a focal length, as shown in Table 5. The more curved the lens is, the shorter the focal length.

The image formed by a convex lens depends on where the object is just like it does for a concave mirror. When an object is farther than one focal length from a convex lens, the image is upside down, as shown to the right.

When an object is less than one focal length from a convex lens, the image is larger and right side up. For example, the dollar bill in Table 5 is less than one focal length from the lens. As a result, the image of the dollar bill is larger than the actual dollar bill and is right-side up. Both a magnifying lens and a camera lens are convex lenses.

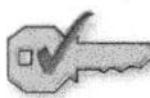

Key Concept Check How does the image formed by a convex lens depend on the distance of the object from the lens?

Concave Lenses

A concave lens is curved inward on at least one side and thicker at its edges. The image formed by a concave lens is upright and smaller than the object, as shown in Table 5. Concave lenses are usually used in combinations with other lenses in instruments such as telescopes and microscopes.

Table 5 Images and Lenses

Convex Lens

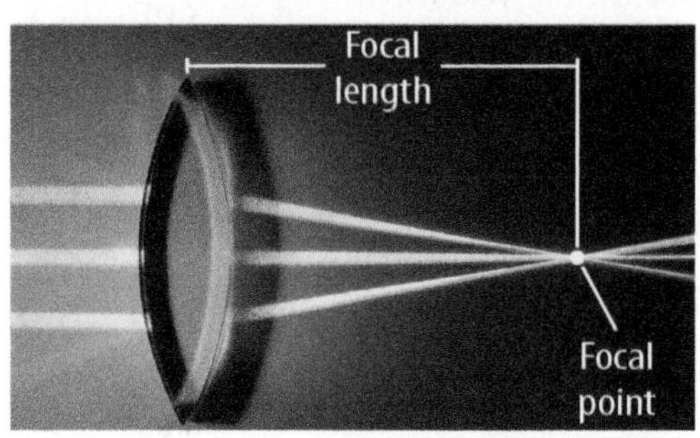

A convex lens is thicker in its middle than its edges. The focal length is the distance from the center of the lens to the focal point.

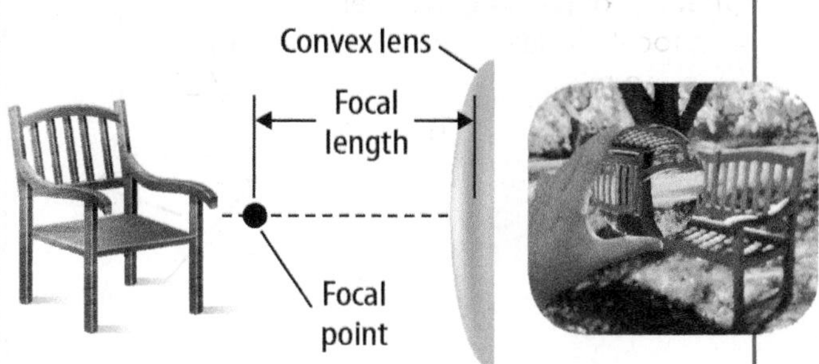

The image formed by a convex lens is upside down when an object is more than one focal length from the lens.

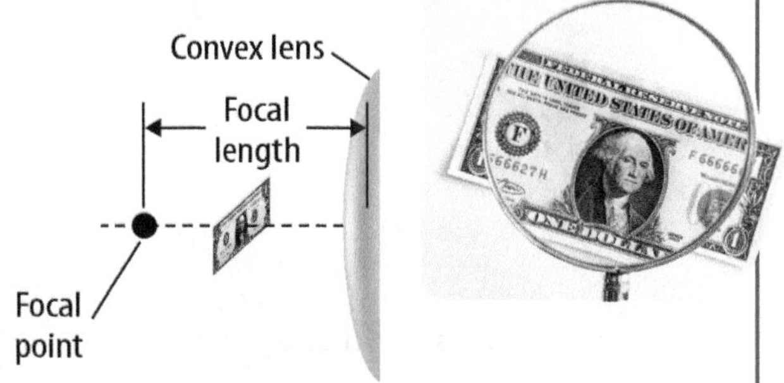

The image formed by a convex lens is right-side up when an object is less than one focal length from the lens.

Concave Lens

A concave lens is thinner in its middle than its edge. The image formed by a concave lens is always right-side up and smaller than the object.

(l to r, t to b) Don Farrall/Photographer's Choice/Getty Images, Derrick Alderman/Alamy, Dennis Hallinan/Alamy, Don Farrall/Photographer's Choice/Getty Images, Jerome Wexler/Science Source

FOLDABLES®
Make a half book from a sheet of paper. Use it to identify the parts of the eye and their function.
Iris
Retina
Cornea
Pupil
Lens
The Human Eye and Vision

Light and the Human Eye

Microscopes, binoculars, and telescopes are instruments that contain lenses that form images of objects. Human eyes also contain lenses, as well as other parts, that can enable a person to see.

The structure of a human eye is shown in Figure 18. To see an object, light waves from an object travel through two convex lenses in the eye. The first of these lenses is called the cornea, and the second is simply called the lens. These lenses form an image of the object on a thin layer of tissue at the back of the eye. Special cells in this layer convert the image into electrical signals. Nerves carry these signals to the brain.

Reading Check What is the function of the lenses in the eye?

ACADEMIC VOCABULARY

convert
(verb) to change from one form into another

Cornea

Light waves first travel through the cornea (KOR nee uh), as shown in Figure 18. *The* **cornea** *is a convex lens made of transparent tissue located on the outside of the eye.* Most of the change in direction of light rays occurs at the cornea. Some vision problems are corrected by changing the cornea's shape.

The Structure of the Human Eye

Figure 18 The eye is made of a number of parts that have different functions.

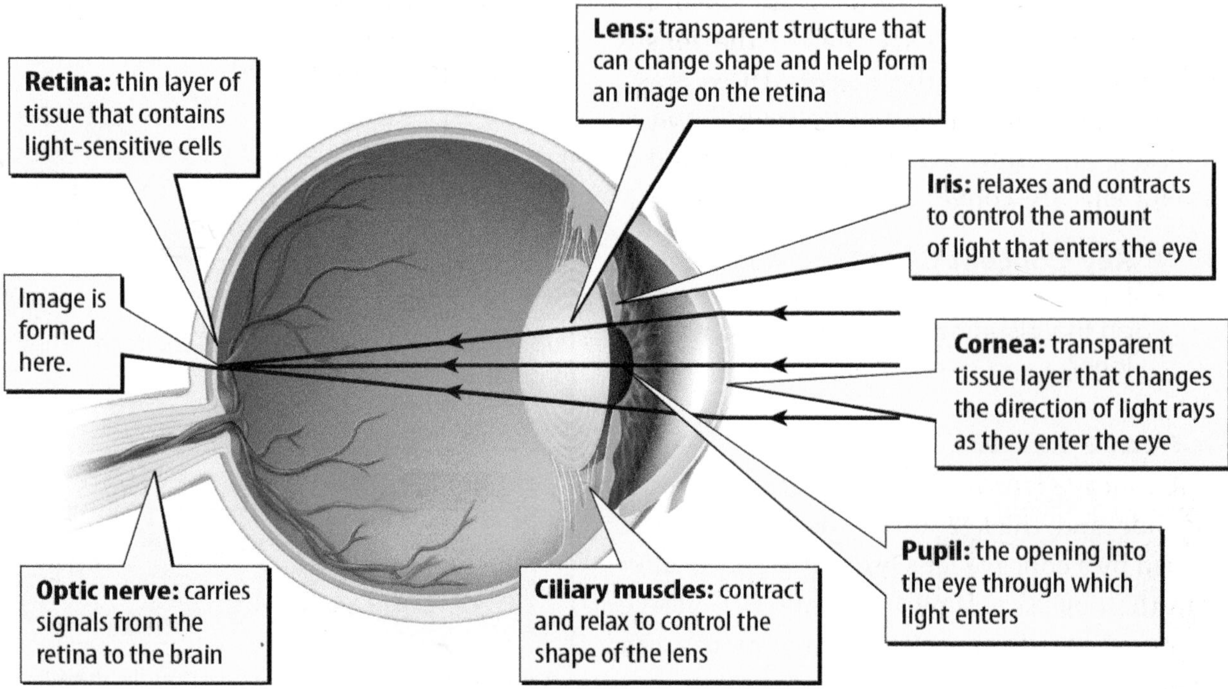
Retina: thin layer of tissue that contains light-sensitive cells
Lens: transparent structure that can change shape and help form an image on the retina
Iris: relaxes and contracts to control the amount of light that enters the eye
Image is formed here.
Cornea: transparent tissue layer that changes the direction of light rays as they enter the eye
Optic nerve: carries signals from the retina to the brain
Ciliary muscles: contract and relax to control the shape of the lens
Pupil: the opening into the eye through which light enters

Visual Check On which part of the eye is an image formed?

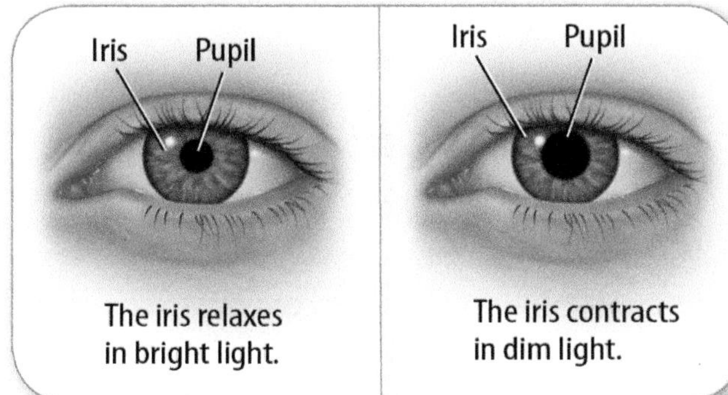

▲ **Figure 19** The iris controls the amount of light that enters the eye.

Iris and Pupil

The **iris** *is the colored part of the eye. The* **pupil** *is an opening into the interior of the eye at the center of the iris.* When the iris changes size, the amount of light that enters the eye changes. As shown in **Figure 19,** in bright light, the iris relaxes and the pupil becomes smaller. Then less light enters the eye. In dim light, the iris contracts and the pupil becomes larger. Then more light enters the eye.

Lens

Behind the iris is the lens, as shown in **Figure 18.** It is made of flexible, transparent tissue. The lens enables the eye to form a sharp image of nearby and distant objects. The muscles surrounding the lens change the lens's shape. To focus on nearby objects, these muscles relax and the lens becomes more curved, as shown in **Figure 20.** To focus on distant objects, these muscles pull on the lens and make it flatter.

MiniLab — 20 minutes

How does the size of an image change?

The size of the image divided by the size of the object is called the magnification. How do the magnification and the image size change as an object gets farther from a convex lens?

Data Table

Distance of Object from Lens (cm)	Magnification
20.0	3.00
30.0	1.00
45.0	0.50
75.0	0.25

1. Using **graph paper,** plot the data in the data table. Plot the distance of the object from the lens on the *x*-axis and the magnification on the *y*-axis.
2. Draw a smooth curve through the points.

Analyze and Conclude

1. **Estimate** from your graph how far the object is from the lens if the magnification is 2.00.
2. **Key Concept** If the object is 60 cm from the lens, would you move the lens closer or farther from the object to make it look larger? Explain your answer.

Figure 20 The lens in the eye changes shape, enabling the formation of sharp images of objects that are either nearby or far away. ▼

Animation

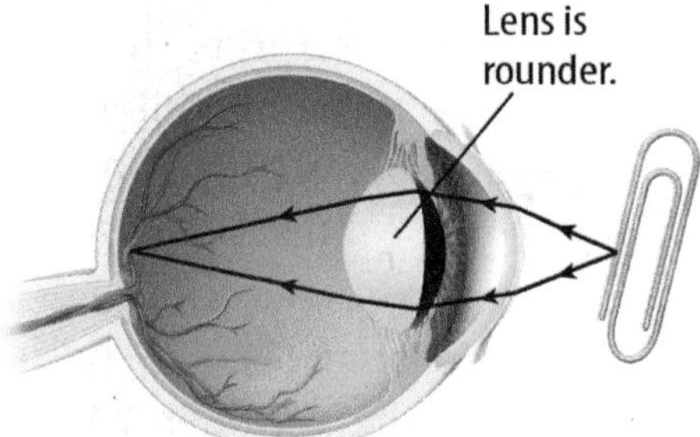

Lens becomes rounder and a sharp image forms of a nearby object.

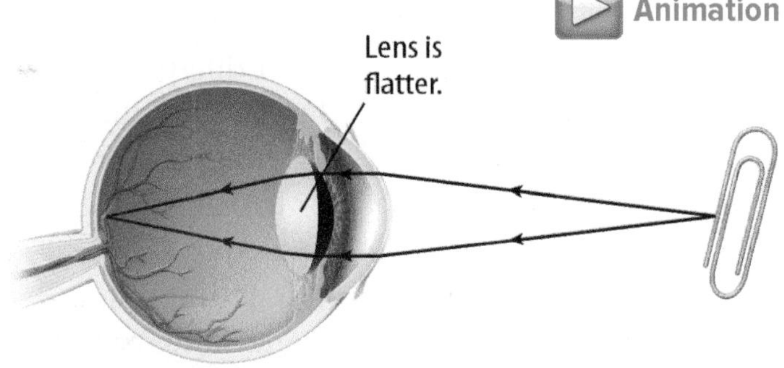

Lens becomes flatter and a sharp image forms of a distant object.

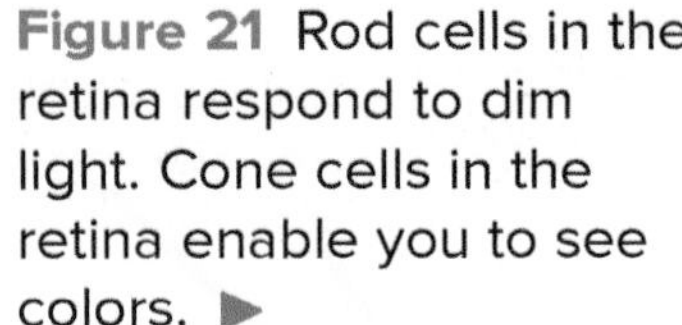

Figure 21 Rod cells in the retina respond to dim light. Cone cells in the retina enable you to see colors. ▶

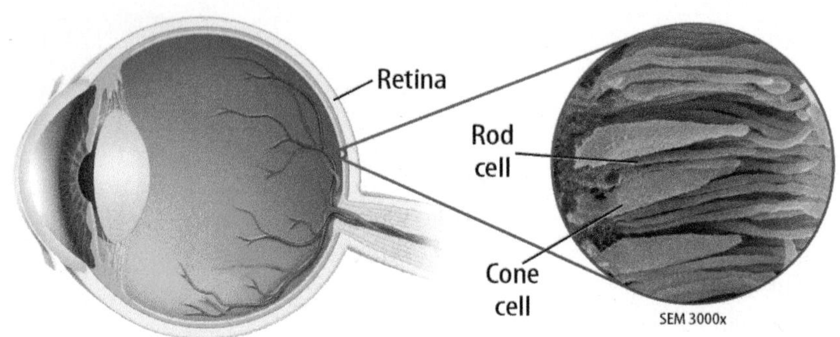

Retina

Word Origin

retina
from Latin *rete,* means "net"

The **retina** *is a layer of special light-sensitive cells in the back of the eye,* as shown in **Figure 21.** After light travels through the lens, an image forms on your retina. There, chemical reactions produce nerve signals that the optic nerve sends to your brain. There are two types of light-sensitive cells in your retina–rod cells and cone cells.

Key Concept Check Identify the parts of the eye that form a sharp image of an object and the parts that convert an image into electrical signals.

Rod Cells There are more than 100 million rod cells in a human retina. Rod cells are sensitive to low-light levels. They enable people to see objects in dim light. However, the signals rod cells send to your brain do not enable you to see colors.

Cone Cells A retina contains over 6 million cone cells. Cone cells enable a person to see colors. However, cone cells need brighter light than rod cells to function. In very dim light, only rod cells function. That is why objects seem to have no color in very dim light.

How do cone cells enable you to see colors? The responses of cone cells to light waves with different wavelengths enable you to see different colors.

The retina has three types of cone cells. Each type of cone cell responds to a different range of wavelengths. This means that different wavelengths of light cause each type of cone cell to send different signals to the brain. Your brain interprets the different combinations of signals from the three types of cone cells as different colors. However, in some people not all three types of cone cells function properly. These people cannot detect certain colors. This condition is commonly known as color blindness but is more appropriately called color deficiency. People with some kinds of color deficiency cannot see the number 74 in **Figure 22.**

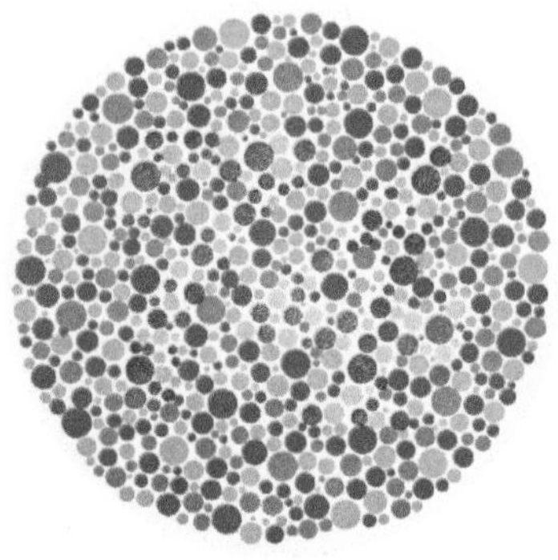

▲ **Figure 22** An image like this is used to test for color deficiency.

The Colors of Objects

The objects you see around you are different colors. A banana is mostly yellow, but a rose might be red. Why is a banana a different color from a rose? Bananas and roses do not give off, or emit, light. Instead, they reflect light. The colors of an object depend on the wavelengths of the light waves it reflects.

Reflection of Light and Color

When light waves of different wavelengths interact with an object, the object absorbs some light waves and reflects others. The wavelengths of light waves absorbed and reflected depend on the materials from which the object is made.

For example, Figure 23 shows that the rose is red because the petals of the rose reflect light waves with certain wavelengths. When these light waves enter your eye, they cause the cone cells in your retina to send certain nerve signals to your brain. These signals cause you to see the rose as red.

A banana reflects different wavelengths of light than a rose. These different wavelengths cause cone cells in the retina to send different signals to your brain. These signals cause you to see the banana as yellow instead of red.

You might think that light waves have colors. Color, however, is a sensation produced by your brain when light waves enter your eyes. Light waves have no color as they travel from an object to your eyes.

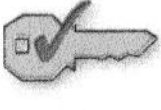

Key Concept Check Why do you experience the sensation of color?

The Color of Objects that Emit Light

Some objects such as the Sun, lightbulbs, and neon lights emit light. The color of an object that emits light depends on the wavelengths of the light waves it emits. For example, a red neon light emits light waves with wavelengths that you see as red.

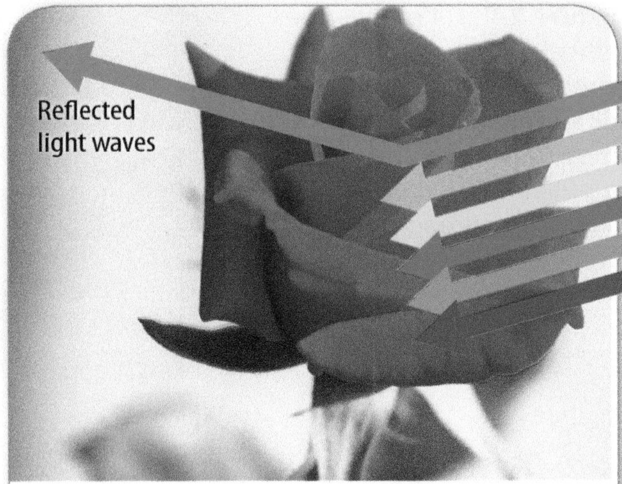

The rose reflects light waves with wavelengths that you see as red. It absorbs all other wavelengths of light.

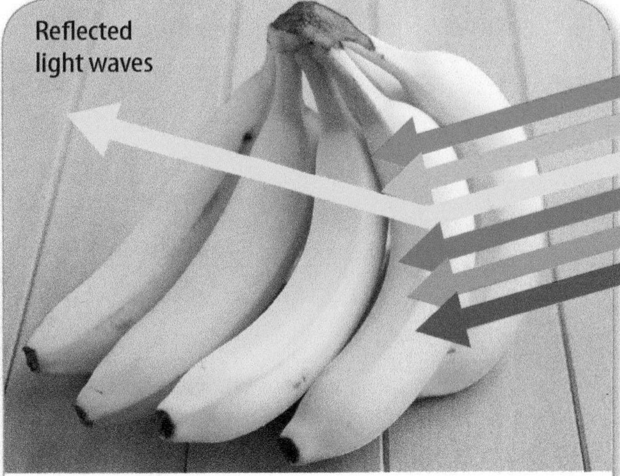

The banana reflects light waves with wavelengths that you see as yellow. It absorbs all other wavelengths of light.

 Animation

Figure 23 The color of an object depends on the wavelengths of the light waves the object reflects.

Figure 24 Different wavelengths of light change direction by different amounts when they move into and out of a prism. This causes the waves to spread out. ►

White Light—A Combination of Light Waves

You might have noticed at a concert that the colors of objects on stage depend on the colors of the spotlights. A shirt that appears blue when a white spotlight shines on it might appear black when a red spotlight shines on it. That same shirt will appear blue when a blue spotlight shines on it. How is light that is white different from light that is red or blue?

Light that you see as white is actually a combination of light waves of many different wavelengths. Figure 24 shows what happens when white light travels through a prism. Light waves with different wavelengths spread out after passing through the prism and form a color spectrum.

Changing Colors

Figure 25 shows why the color of a blue shirt appears different when different spotlights shine on it. The shirt reflects only those wavelengths that are seen as blue. It absorbs all other wavelengths of light. When white light or blue light hits the shirt, it reflects the wavelengths you see as blue. However, when red light strikes the shirt, almost no light is reflected. This causes the shirt to appear black. An object appears black when it absorbs almost all light waves that strike it.

Figure 25 The appearance of an object changes under different colors of light. ▼

When white light strikes the shirt, only the wavelengths that you see as blue are reflected. The shirt appears blue under white light.

When blue light strikes the shirt, the blue light is reflected. This makes the shirt appear blue under blue light.

When red light strikes the shirt, the light is absorbed and no light is reflected. This makes the shirt appear black under red light.

Lesson 3 Review

Online Quiz
Virtual Lab

Visual Summary

A mirror is a surface that causes a regular reflection. The shape of the reflecting surface and the position of the object determine what the image looks like.

A lens is a transparent object with at least one curved side that causes light waves to change direction. The shape of the lens and the position of the object determine how the image appears.

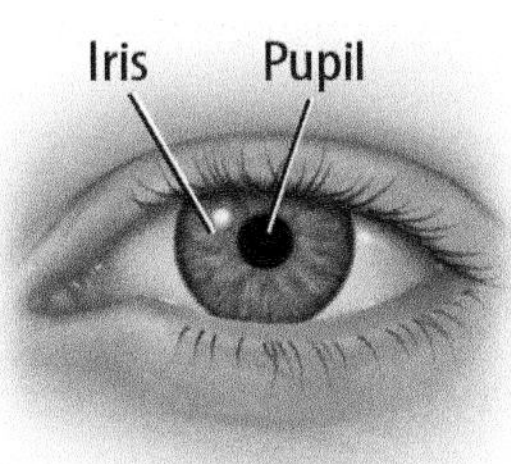

The eye has different parts with different functions. The iris is the colored part of your eye. The iris opens and closes, controlling the amount of light that enters the eye.

FOLDABLES

Use your lesson Foldable to review the lesson. Save your Foldable for the project at the end of the chapter.

What do you think NOW?

You first read the statements below at the beginning of the chapter.

5. All mirrors form images that appear identical to the object itself.

6. Lenses always magnify objects.

Did you change your mind about whether you agree or disagree with the statements? Rewrite any false statements to make them true.

Use Vocabulary

1 The layer of tissue in the eye that contains cells sensitive to light is the ________.

2 **Define** *cornea* in your own words.

3 **Distinguish** between a lens and a mirror.

Understand Key Concepts 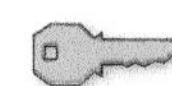

4 **Draw** a picture of two light rays that reflect off a smooth surface.

5 **Compare** the function of the cornea and the lens of the eye.

6 Which statement describes the image formed by a convex mirror?

A. It will be caused by refraction.
B. It will be smaller than the object.
C. It will be upside down.
D. It will produce a beam of light.

Interpret Graphics

7 **Describe** what is occurring in the figure below.

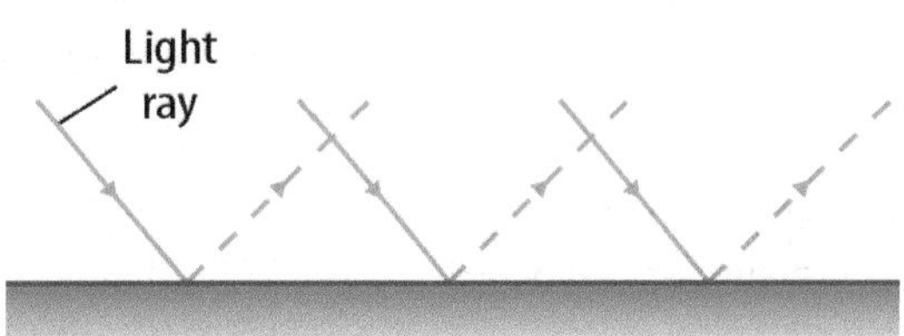

8 **Sequence** Copy and fill in the graphic organizer below to trace the path of light through the different parts of the human eye.

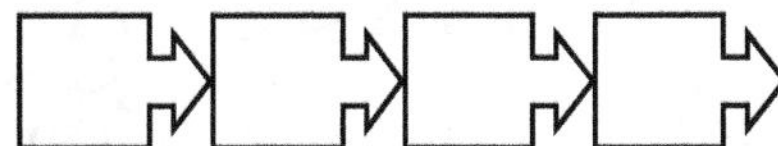

Critical Thinking

9 **Infer** A person cannot see well in dim light. What part of his or her eye is damaged?

(t) David LoSchiavo/Getty Images, (c) Dennis Hallinan/Alamy

The Images Formed by a Lens

Materials

convex lens

modeling clay

meterstick

flashlight

masking tape

20-cm square piece of white posterboard

Safety

The type of image formed by a convex lens is related to the distance of the object from the lens—the object distance. The distance from the lens to the image is called the image distance.

Ask a Question

How do the images formed by a convex lens depend on the distance of an object from the lens?

Make Observations

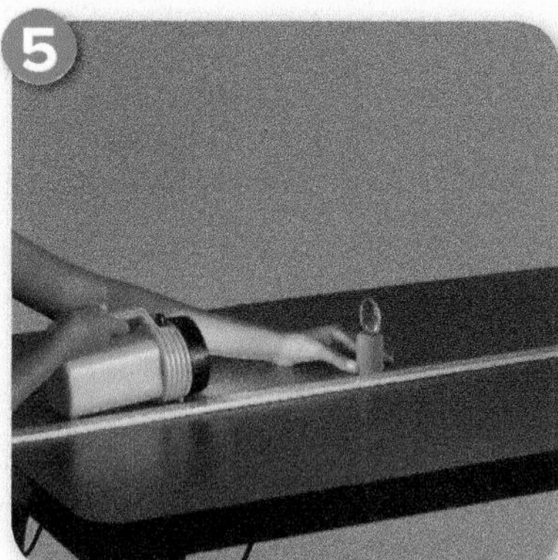

1. Read and complete a lab safety form.
2. Make a data table like the one shown below in your Science Journal to record your collected data.
3. Use the modeling clay to make the lens stand upright on the lab table.
4. Using masking tape, form the letter F on the surface of the flashlight lens. Turn on the flashlight and place it 0.25 m from the lens.
5. Position the flashlight so the flashlight beam is shining through the lens. Record the distance from the flashlight to the lens in the object distance column in your data table.
6. Hold the posterboard upright on the other side of the lens, and move it back and forth until a sharp image of the letter F is obtained.
7. Measure the distance of the card from the lens using a meterstick. Record this distance in the image distance column in your data table.
8. In the third column of your data table, record whether the image is upright or inverted, and smaller or larger.
9. Repeat steps 5 through 8 for object distances of 0.50 m, 1.5 m, and 2.0 m and record your data in your data table.

Convex Lens Data		
Object Distance (m)	Image Distance (m)	Image Type
0.25		
0.50		
1.5		
2.0		

Form a Hypothesis

10 Use your data to form a hypothesis about the type of image that would be formed if the object were far from the lens.

Test Your Hypothesis

11 Place the object far from the lens. Then repeat steps 6 through 8 to test your hypothesis.

Analyze and Conclude

12 **Make and Use Graphs** Plot your data with the object distance on the *x*-axis and the image distance on the *y*-axis. Using your graph, determine the image distance of an object that is placed at 1.25 m.

13 **The Big Idea** Obtain the focal length of the lens from your teacher. Mark the focal length of the lens on your graph with a dotted line. Explain how focal length, object distance, and image distance are related.

Lab Tips

☑ Be sure the flashlight's position does not change when the cardboard is being moved.

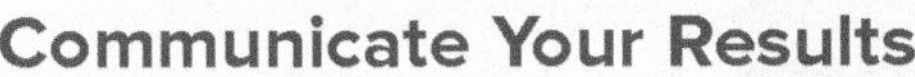

Communicate Your Results

Write a report explaining the steps you took in this lab. Include information on your initial observations, your hypothesis, information on how you tested your hypothesis, and your final conclusions.

Inquiry Extension

Use your graph to predict the image distance of an object that is placed at an object distance of 0.1 m. If possible, test your prediction.

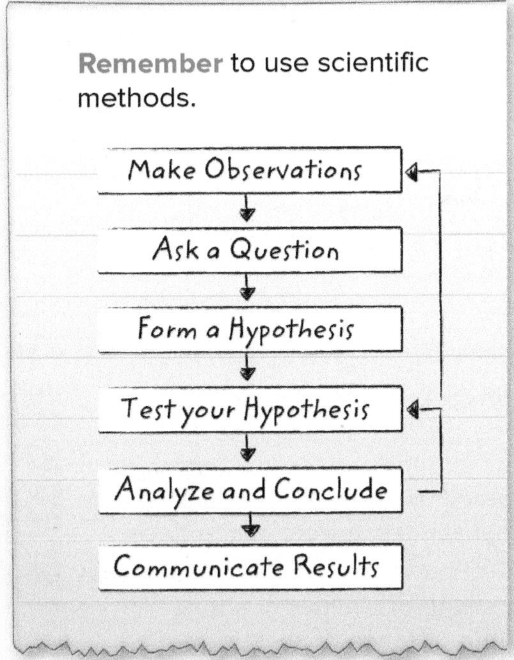

Hutchings Photography/Digital Light Source

Chapter 4 Study Guide

Sound waves must travel through matter, while light waves can also travel in a vacuum. Waves interact with matter through absorption, transmission, and reflection.

Key Concepts Summary

Lesson 1: Sound

- Vibrating objects produce **sound waves.**
- Sound waves travel at different speeds in different materials. Sound waves usually travel fastest in solids and slowest in gases.
- The outer ear collects sound waves. The middle ear amplifies sound waves. The inner ear converts sound waves to nerve signals.

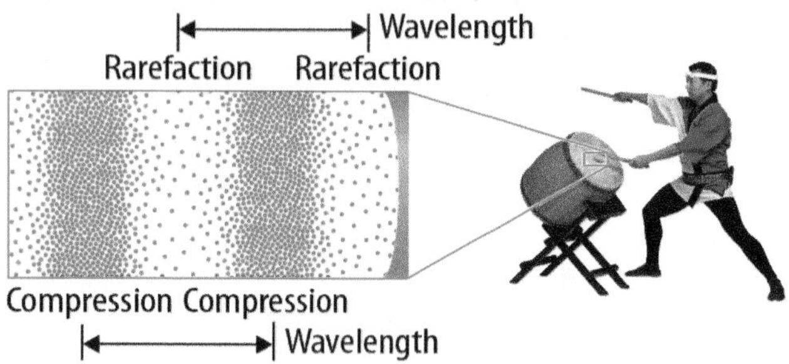

Vocabulary

sound wave p. 111
pitch p. 115
echo p. 117

Lesson 2: Light

- Light waves are electromagnetic waves that can travel in matter and through a vacuum.
- Electromagnetic waves have different wavelengths and frequencies.
- When light waves interact with matter, they are reflected, transmitted, or absorbed.

light source p. 123
light ray p. 123
transparent p. 124
translucent p. 124
opaque p. 124

Lesson 3: Mirrors, Lenses, and the Eye

- When regular reflection occurs from a surface, a clear image forms and the surface is a **mirror.** When diffuse reflection occurs from a surface, a clear image does not form.
- The shape of a mirror or a **lens** and the distance of an object from the mirror or lens determine how the image appears.
- When light rays enter the eye through the **cornea** and pass through the **pupil,** an image forms on the **retina.** Rod and cone cells convert the image to nerve signals that travel to the brain.

mirror p. 130
lens p. 131
cornea p. 132
iris p. 133
pupil p. 133
retina p. 134

Study Guide

Vocabulary eFlashcards
Vocabulary eGames

Personal Tutor

FOLDABLES® **Chapter Project**

Assemble your lesson Foldables as shown to make a Chapter Project. Use the project to review what you have learned in this chapter.

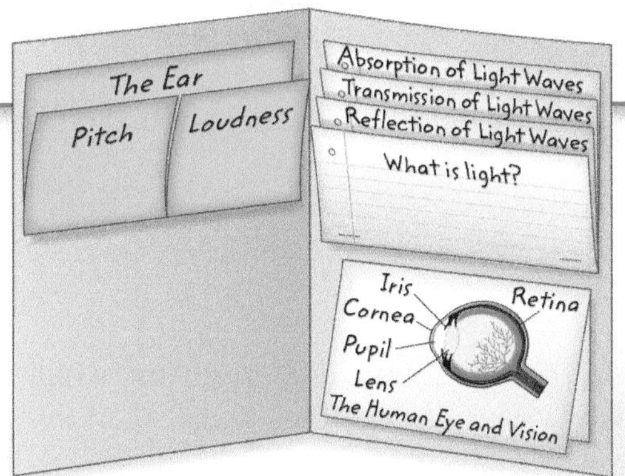

Use Vocabulary

1. A vibrating object produces ________.
2. A sonar system detects the ________ of a sound wave.
3. A(n) ________ travels in a straight path until it is refracted, reflected, or absorbed.
4. A window is a(n) ________ object because you can see objects clearly through it.
5. The Sun is a(n) ________ ________ because it emits light waves.
6. The ________ of the eye controls how much light enters it.
7. A(n) ________ is a surface that produces a regular reflection.

Link Vocabulary and Key Concepts

Interactive Concept Map

Copy this concept map, and then use vocabulary terms from the previous page to complete the concept map.

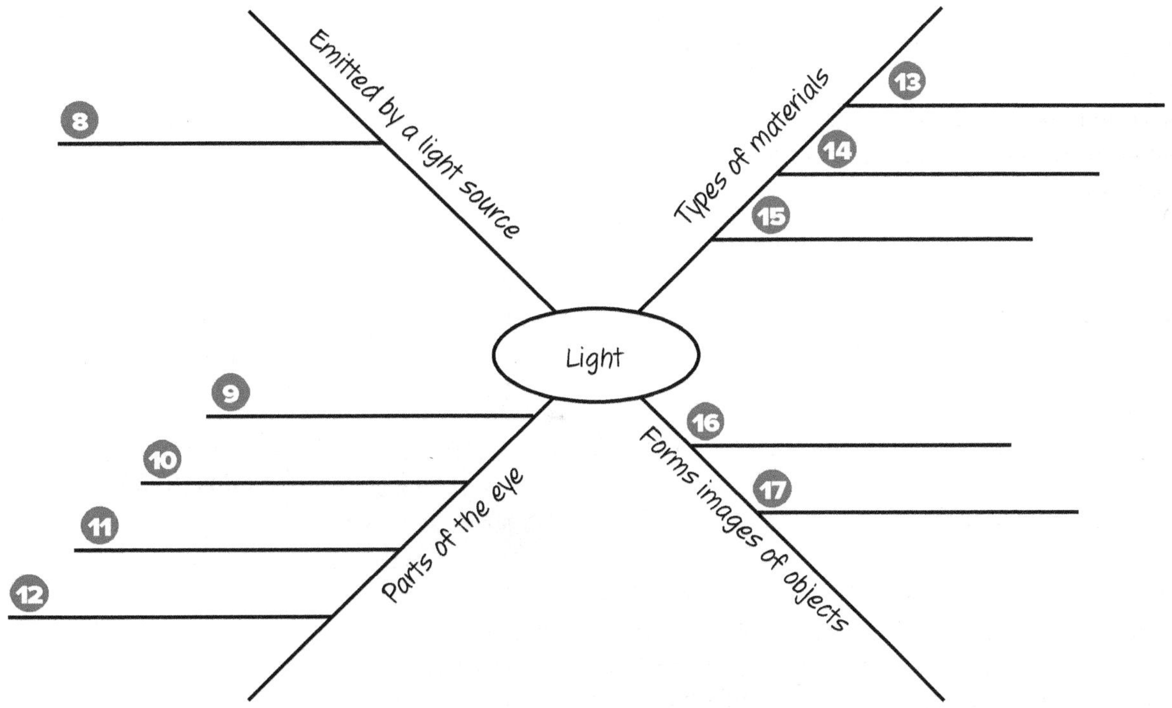

Chapter 4 Review

Understand Key Concepts 

1. Which part of the ear acts as the amplifier?
   A. cochlea
   B. nerves
   C. inner ear
   D. middle ear

2. Identify the part of the ear that serves as the sound-wave collector.

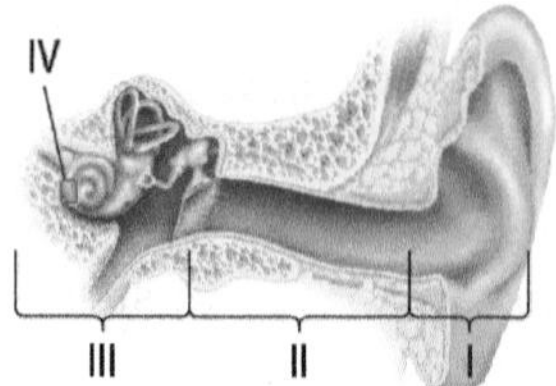

   A. I
   B. II
   C. III
   D. IV

3. Which produces sound that has the highest pitch?
   A. a tuba
   B. emergency siren
   C. lion's roar
   D. thunder

4. The speed of light is slowest in which medium?
   A. cold air
   B. outer space
   C. pond water
   D. window glass

5. A shirt appears red under white light. What color would it appear under blue light?
   A. black
   B. blue
   C. red
   D. white

6. Which enables a person to see color?
   A. cone cells
   B. cornea
   C. iris
   D. rod cells

7. The loudness of a sound wave depends on which of these?
   A. amplitude
   B. frequency
   C. pitch
   D. wavelength

8. What is the function of the cornea?
   A. changes the direction of light waves that enter the eye
   B. controls the amount of light that enters the eye
   C. controls the shape of the lens
   D. enables eye to focus on near and distant objects

9. On the electromagnetic spectrum, which waves have wavelengths longer than the wavelengths of visible light?
   A. gamma rays
   B. radio waves
   C. ultraviolet waves
   D. X-rays

10. What type of image will form in the mirror shown below?

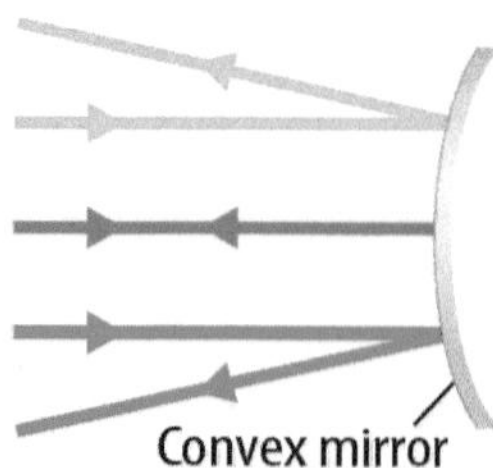

   A. Image is larger and right-side up.
   B. Image is larger and upside down.
   C. Image is smaller and right-side up.
   D. Image is smaller and upside down.

11. A reflected light ray makes an angle of 60° to the normal. At what angle did the light ray strike the surface?
   A. 30° to the normal
   B. 60° to the normal
   C. parallel to the normal
   D. perpendicular to the normal

Critical Thinking

12 **Compare** an echo to light that hits a mirror.

13 **Summarize** Listen to the sounds around you. Choose one sound and describe its path from its source to the point where the nerve signal is sent to your brain.

14 **Judge** Frosted glass is made of glass with a scratched surface. Decide whether frosted glass is opaque, translucent, or transparent and explain your reasoning.

15 **Infer** On a hot summer day, black pavement feels much hotter than light-gray concrete. Explain why this is so.

16 **Evaluate** Stores are often equipped with mirrors like the one shown below. What type of mirror is this and why is it useful?

17 **Compare** When you enter a room filled with many hard surfaces and start talking, your voice echoes all around you. How is this similar to what happens when light rays scatter?

18 **Infer** A film camera forms an upside-down image of a tree on the film. What is the location of the tree relative to the focal length of the lens?

Writing in Science

19 **Write** a 500–700-word essay about an object such as a telescope, a microscope, or a periscope that uses mirrors or lenses to create an image. Describe how and why the mirrors and lenses are used in the object.

REVIEW THE BIG IDEA

20 What are three possible results when light waves strike matter?

21 In many movies, you can both see and hear explosions that happen in outer space. Explain how this is inaccurate.

22 The photo below shows a Chicago sculpture named "Cloud Gate." What happens to light waves when they strike the surface of the sculpture? What type of surface is this?

Math Skills

Math Practice

Use Equations

23 What is the speed of a sound wave if it travels 2,500 m in 2 s?

24 A sound wave travels through air at 331 m/s. How far would it travel at 0°C in 5 s?

25 A sound wave travels through water at 1,500 m/s. How far would it travel in 5 s?

Standardized Test Practice

Record your answers on the answer sheet provided by your teacher or on a sheet of paper.

Multiple Choice

1 Which statement about sound waves is false?

A They are longitudinal waves.

B They consist of compressions and rarefactions.

C They travel in empty space.

D They result from the vibrations of objects.

Use the diagram below to answer question 2.

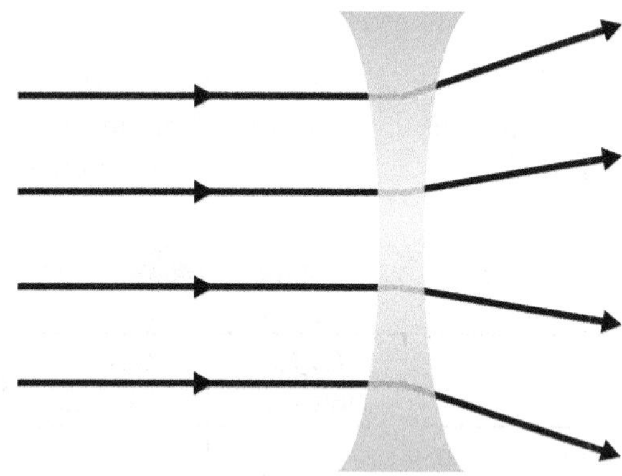

2 Which describes the image formed by the lens shown above?

A right-side up, larger than the object

B right-side up, smaller than the object

C upside down, larger than the object

D upside down, smaller than the object

3 A shirt that appears red under red light will also appear red under which color light?

A blue

B green

C yellow

D white

Use the table below to answer question 4.

Wave Type	Wavelength
Radio waves	More than 0.001 m
Microwaves	0.3 m to 0.001 m
Visible light	700 nm to 400 nm
Ultraviolet light	400 nm to 10 nm
X-rays	10 nm to 0.01 nm

4 Which electromagnetic waves can have wavelengths of 500 nm?

A microwaves

B ultraviolet light

C visible light

D X-rays

5 When does the refraction of light waves occur?

A when they bounce off a reflecting surface

B when they are absorbed

C when they move far from their source

D when they pass from one material to another and change speed

6 On which property of the particles in a material does the speed of sound depend?

A the dimensions of the particles

B the forces between the particles

C the shape of the particles

D the number of particles

7 Which property of sound waves does the decibel scale compare?

A frequency

B volume

C pitch

D speed

Use the diagram below to answer question 8.

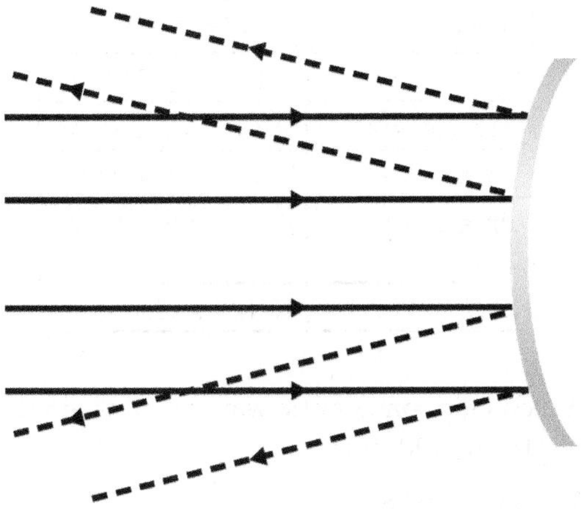

8 Which describes the image formed by the mirror shown above?

A larger than the object, right-side up

B larger than the object, upside down

C smaller than the object, right-side up

D smaller than the object, upside down

9 Which surface produces a diffuse reflection of light?

A a bathroom mirror

B the surface of a calm lake

C the hood of a newly waxed car

D a white painted wall

10 Which illustrates how the ear responds to sound waves?

A amplify → collect → transmit

B collect → amplify → convert

C convert → transmit → collect

D transmit → convert → amplify

Constructed Response

Use the table below to answer question 11.

Part of the Eye	Function
Cornea	
Iris	
Pupil	
Lens	
Retina	

11 Complete the table above. Which parts of the eye form a sharp image inside the eye? Explain how a person is able to see colors.

Use the table below to answer question 12.

	Light Waves	Sound Waves
Type of wave		
Material in which wave moves slowest		
Speed in air		
Human structure that detects these waves		

12 Complete the table above to compare and contrast light and sound waves.

13 When you turn on a lamp, you are able to see everything in a room. Explain why you see the lamp. Then, explain why you see other objects in the room.

NEED EXTRA HELP?													
If You Missed Question...	1	2	3	4	5	6	7	8	9	10	11	12	13
Go to Lesson...	1	3	3	2	2	1	1	3	3	1	3	1, 2	2

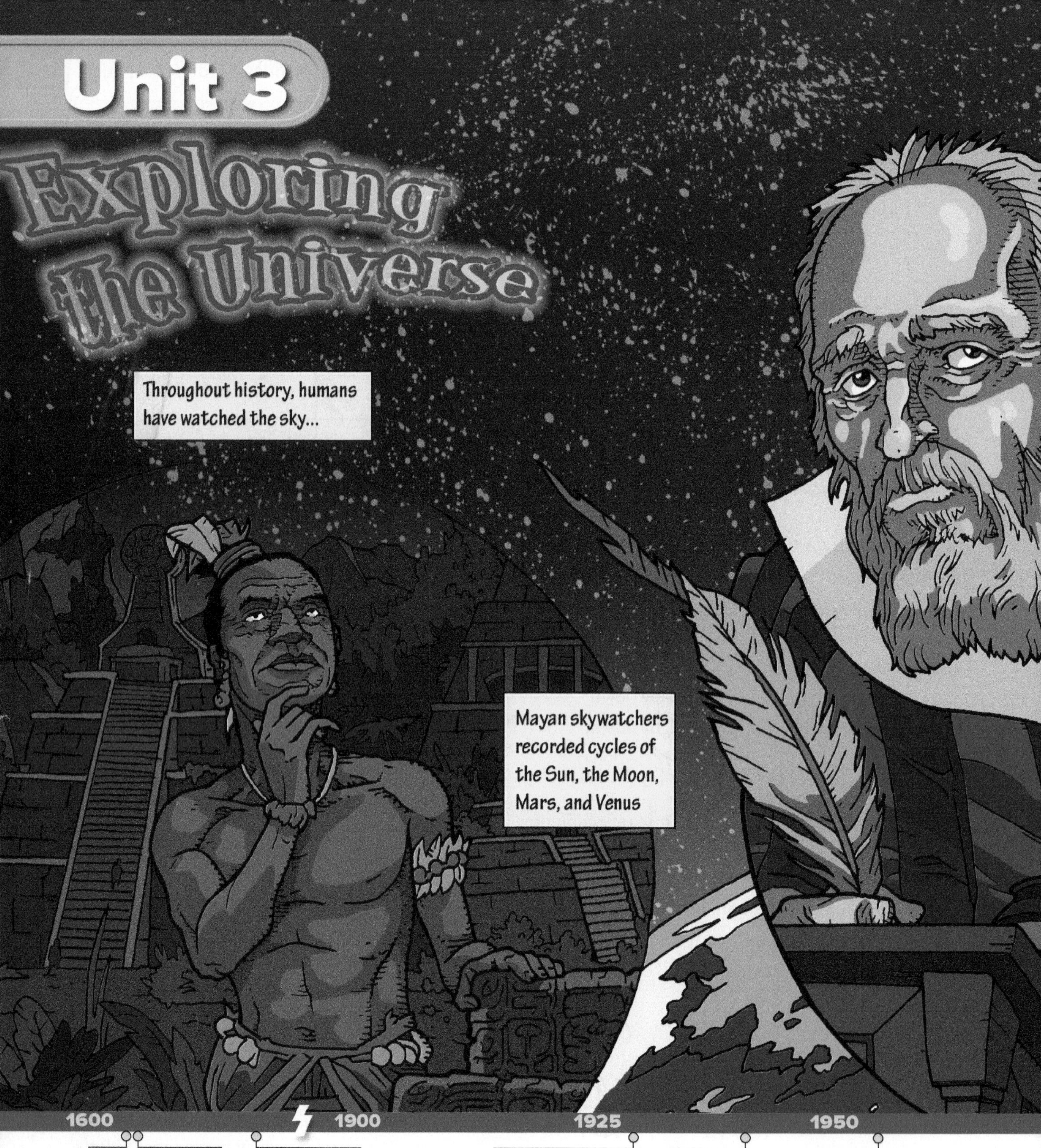

Unit 3
Exploring the Universe
Throughout history, humans have watched the sky...
Mayan skywatchers recorded cycles of the Sun, the Moon, Mars, and Venus

1600 · 1900 · 1925 · 1950

1608
A Dutch scientist named Hans Lippershey invents the first telescope. Galileo improves on the design soon after.

1610
Galileo observes the moons of Jupiter, Saturn's rings, individual stars in the Milky Way, and the phases of Venus via telescope.

1687
Sir Isaac Newton publishes a book outlining the law of universal gravitation and laws for the motions of the planets.

1926
Robert H. Goddard launches the first liquid-fueled rocket. Its flight lasts less than 3 seconds, but sets the stage for the U.S. rocket program.

1942
The German VS-2 rocket is the first human-made object to achieve suborbital spaceflight.

1957
The *Sputnik 1* spacecraft is the first artificial satellite to successfully orbit around Earth.

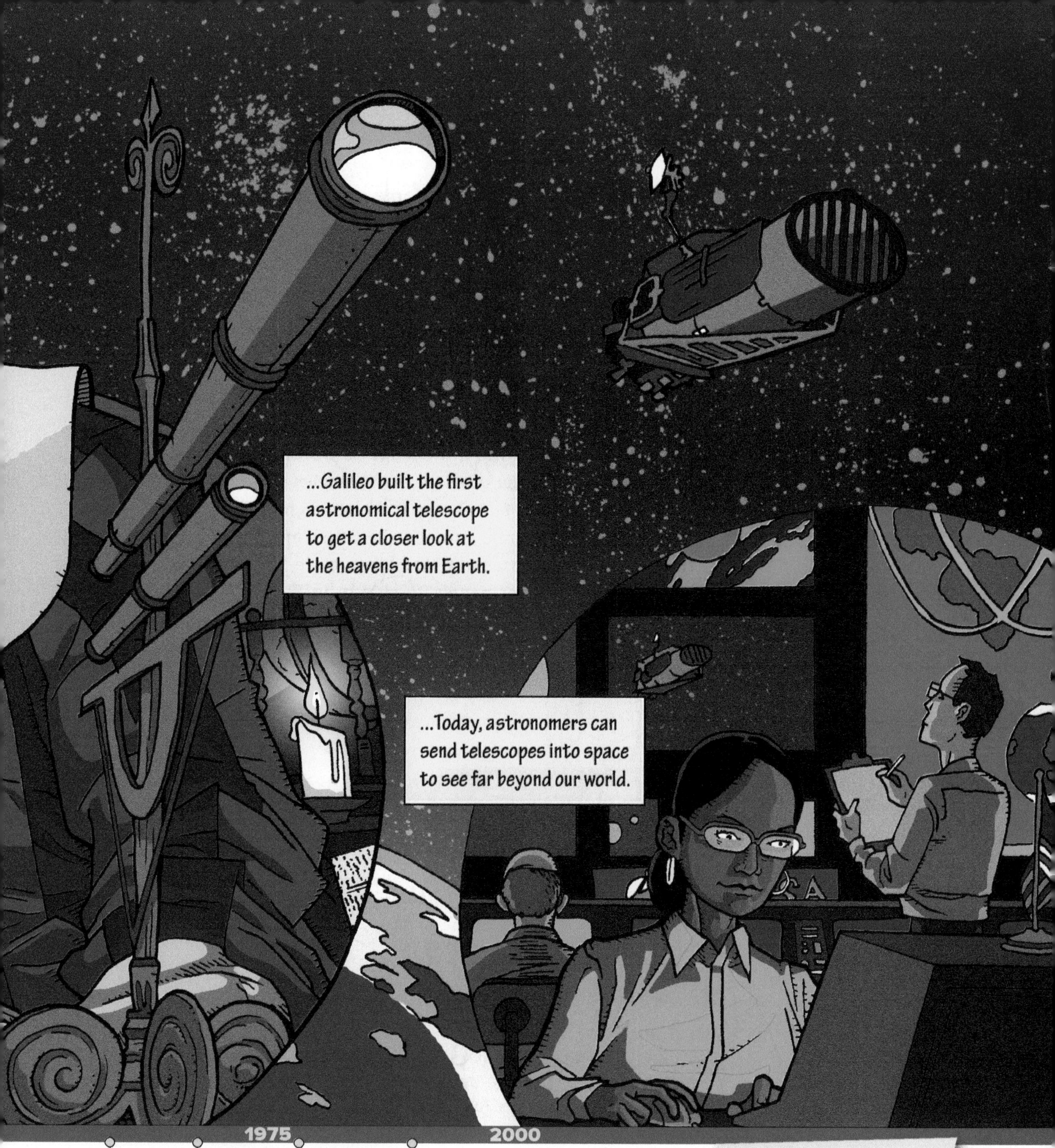

...Galileo built the first astronomical telescope to get a closer look at the heavens from Earth.
...Today, astronomers can send telescopes into space to see far beyond our world.

1975

2000

1961
Yuri Gagarin becomes the first human to enter space and the first to orbit Earth.

1969
Neil Armstrong is the first person to walk on the Moon, followed by Edwin "Buzz" Aldrin.

1977
Voyager 2 spacecraft is launched to explore the outer planets of the solar system, including Jupiter, Saturn, Uranus, and Neptune.

1990
The *Hubble Space Telescope* is carried into orbit by a space shuttle. This mission is the first for NASA's Great Observatories Program and is the largest, most versatile, and well-known of the space telescopes.

Visit ConnectED for this unit's STEM activity.

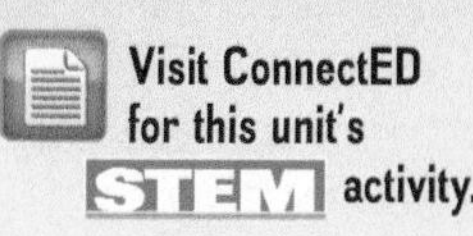

Unit 3

Nature of SCIENCE

Technology

Figure 1 Lightweight, flexible solar cells developed for spacecraft help to conserve Earth's resources.

It may sound strange, but some of the greatest benefits of the space program are benefits to life here on Earth. Devices ranging from hand-held computers to electric socks rely on technologies first developed for space exploration. **Technology** is the practical application of science to commerce or industry. Space technologies have increased our understanding of Earth and our ability to locate and conserve resources.

Problems, such as how best to explore the solar system and outer space, often send scientists on searches for new knowledge. Engineers use scientific knowledge to develop new technologies for space. Then, some of those technologies are modified to solve problems on Earth. For example, lightweight solar panels on the outside of a spacecraft convert the Sun's energy into electricity that powers the spacecraft for long space voyages. Similar but smaller, flexible solar panels, as shown in Figure 1 are now available for consumers to purchase. They can be used to power small electronics when traveling. Figure 2 shows how other technologies from space help conserve natural resources.

This image was taken by the *Terra* satellite and shows fires burning in California. The image helps firefighters see the size and the location of the fires. It also helps scientists study the effect of fires on Earth's atmosphere. ▼

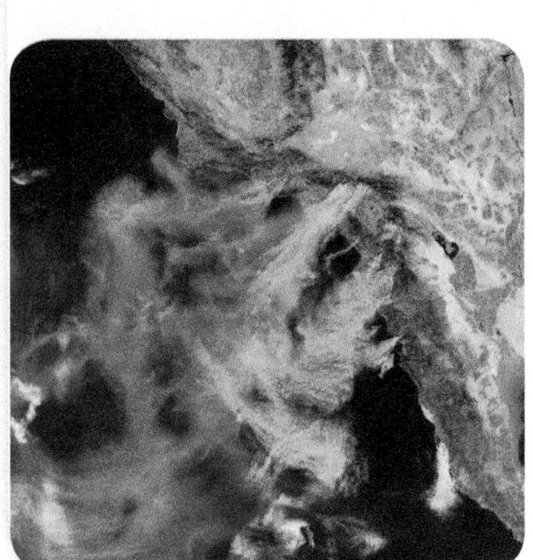

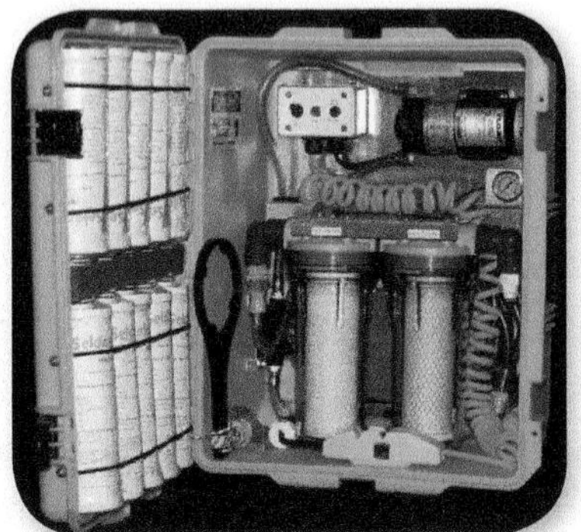

Some portable water purification kits use technologies developed to provide safe, clean drinking water for astronauts. This kit can provide clean, safe drinking water for an entire village in a remote area or supply drinking water after a natural disaster.

Engineers developed glass spheres about the size of a grain of flour to insulate super-cold spacecraft fuel lines. Similar microspheres act as insulators when mixed with paints. This technology can help reduce the energy needed to heat and cool buildings. ▼

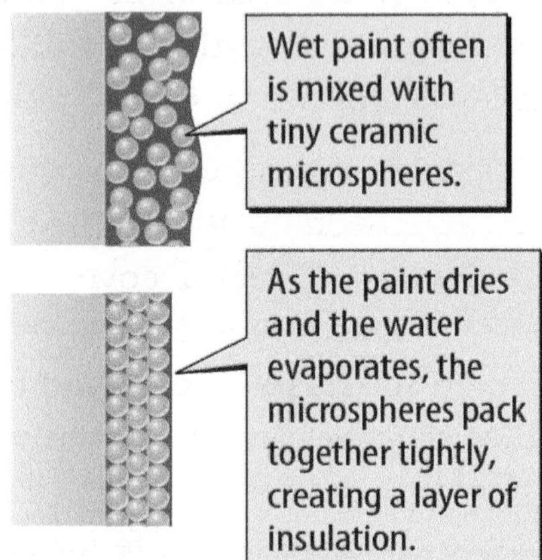

Wet paint often is mixed with tiny ceramic microspheres.
As the paint dries and the water evaporates, the microspheres pack together tightly, creating a layer of insulation.

Figure 2 Some technologies developed as part of the space program have greatly benefited life on Earth.

Figure 3 The satellite image on the left is similar to what you would see with your eyes from space. A satellite sensor that detects other wavelengths of light produced the colored satellite image on the right. It shows the locations of nearly a dozen different minerals.

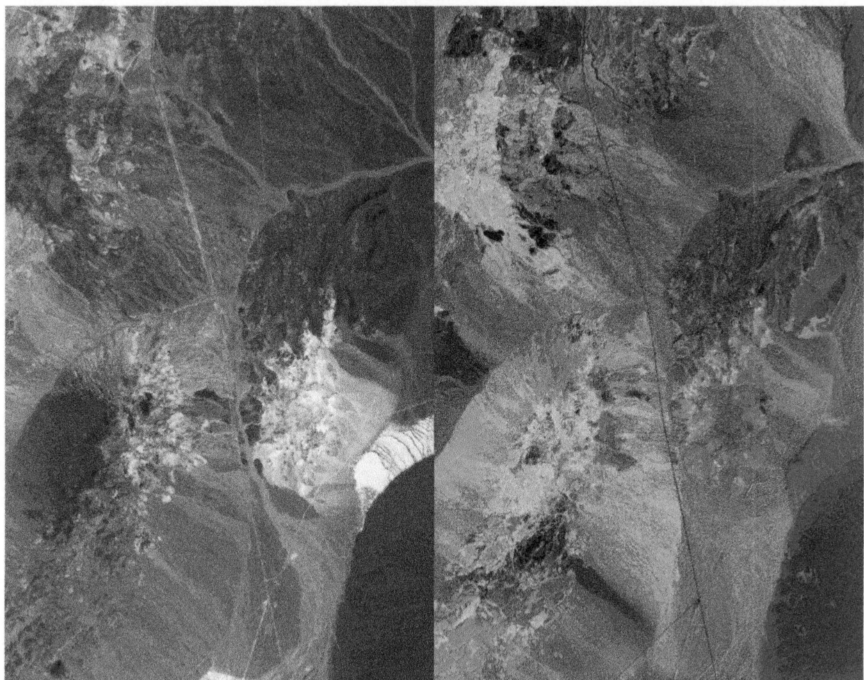

How would you use space technology?

Many uses for space technology haven't been discovered yet. Can you develop one?

1. Identify a problem locating, protecting, or preserving resources that could be solved using space technology.
2. Prepare a short oral presentation explaining your technology.

Analyze and Conclude

1. **Describe** How is your technology used in space?
2. **Explain** How do you use technology to solve a problem on Earth?

Solving Problems and Improving Abilities

Science and technology depend on each other. For example, images from space greatly improve our understanding of Earth. Figure 3 above shows a satellite image of a Nevada mine. The satellite is equipped with sensors that detect visible light, much like your eyes do. The image on the right shows a satellite image of the same site taken with a sensor that detects wavelengths of light your eyes cannot see. This image provides information about the types of minerals in the mine. Each color in the image on the right shows the location of a different mineral, reducing the time it takes geologists to locate mineral deposits.

Scientists use other kinds of satellite sensors for different purposes. Engineers have modified space technology to produce satellite images of cloud cover over Earth's surface, as shown in Figure 4. Images like this one improve global weather forecasting and help scientists understand changes in Earth's atmosphere. Of course, science can answer only some of society's questions, and technology cannot solve all problems. But together, they can improve the quality of life for all.

Figure 4 This satellite image shows cloud cover over the south-west region of the United States.

(t)USGS, (b)NOAA

Chapter 5

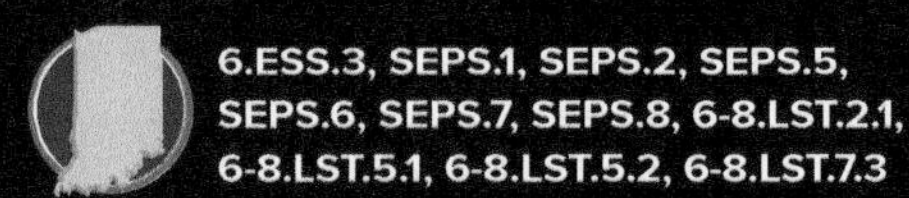

Exploring Space

THE BIG IDEA How do humans observe and explore space?

Inquiry Can satellites see into space?

Yes, they can! The satellite shown here is a telescope. It collects light from distant objects in space. But, most satellites you might be familiar with point toward Earth. They provide navigation assistance, monitor weather, and bounce communication signals to and from Earth.

- Why would scientists want to put a telescope in space?
- In what other ways do scientists observe and explore space?
- What are goals of some current and future space missions?

Stocktrek/age fotostock

Get Ready to Read

What do you think?

Before you read, decide if you agree or disagree with each of these statements. As you read this chapter, see if you change your mind about any of the statements.

1. Astronomers put telescopes in space to be closer to the stars.
2. Telescopes can work only using visible light.
3. Humans have walked on the Moon.
4. Some orthodontic braces were developed using space technology.
5. Humans have landed on Mars.
6. Scientists have detected water on other bodies in the solar system.

Your one-stop online resource
connectED.mcgraw-hill.com

LearnSmart®

Chapter Resources Files, Reading Essentials, Get Ready to Read, Quick Vocabulary

Animations, Videos, Interactive Tables

Self-checks, Quizzes, Tests

Project-Based Learning Activities

Lab Manuals, Safety Videos, Virtual Labs & Other Tools

Vocabulary, Multilingual eGlossary, Vocab eGames, Vocab eFlashcards

Personal Tutors

Lesson 1

Reading Guide

Key Concepts

ESSENTIAL QUESTIONS

- How do scientists use the electromagnetic spectrum to study the universe?
- What types of telescopes and technology are used to explore space?

Vocabulary

electromagnetic spectrum p. 154

refracting telescope p. 156

reflecting telescope p. 156

radio telescope p. 157

Multilingual eGlossary

Science Video

SEPS.2, SEPS.6

Observing the Universe

How can you see this?

This is an expanding halo of dust in space, illuminated by the light from the star in the center. This photo was taken with a telescope. How do you think telescopes obtain such clear images?

NASA and The Hubble Heritage Team (AURA/STScI)

Launch Lab

15 minutes

Do you see what I see?

Your eyes have lenses. Eyeglasses, cameras, telescopes, and many other tools involving light also have lenses. Lenses are transparent materials that refract light, or cause light to change direction. Lenses can cause light rays to form images as they come together or move apart.

1. Read and complete a lab safety form.
2. Place each of the **lenses** on the words of this sentence.
3. Slowly move each lens up and down over the words to observe if or how the words change. Record your observations in your Science Journal.
4. Hold each lens at arm's length and focus on an object a few meters away. Observe how the object looks through each lens. Make simple drawings to illustrate what you observe.

Think About This

1. What happened to the words as you moved the lenses toward and away from the sentence?
2. What did the distant object look like through each lens?
3. **Key Concept** How do you think lenses are used in telescopes to explore space?

Observing the Sky

If you look up at the sky on a clear night, you might be able to see the Moon, planets, and stars. These objects have not changed much since people first turned their gaze skyward. People in the past spent a lot of time observing the sky. They told stories about the stars, and they used stars to tell time. Most people thought Earth was the center of the universe.

Astronomers today know that Earth is part of a system of eight planets revolving around the Sun. The Sun, in turn, is part of a larger system called the Milky Way galaxy that contains billions of other stars. And the Milky Way is one of billions of other galaxies in the universe. As small as Earth might seem in the universe, it could be unique. Scientists have not found life anywhere else.

One advantage astronomers have over people in the past is the **telescope.** Telescopes enable astronomers to observe many more stars than they could with their eyes alone. Telescopes gather and focus light from objects in space. The photo on the opposite page was taken with a telescope that orbits Earth. Astronomers use many kinds of telescopes to study the energy emitted by stars and other objects in space.

Word Origin

telescope
from Greek *tele,* means "far"; and Greek *skopos,* means "seeing"

Reading Check What is the purpose of telescopes?

FOLDABLES®

Use seven quarter-sheets of paper to make a tabbed diagram illustrating the electromagnetic spectrum. In the middle section of a large shutterfold project, tape or glue the left edges of the tabs so they overlap to illustrate the varying sizes of the waves from longest to shortest.

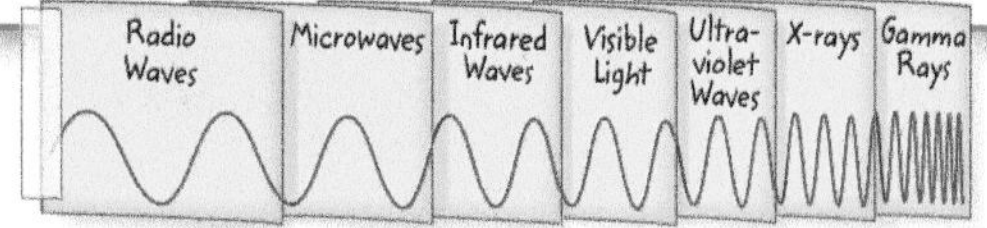

Figure 1 Objects emit radiation in continuous wavelengths. Most wavelengths are not visible to the human eye.

Visual Check Approximately how long are the wavelengths of microwaves?

Relative size	Wavelength	Uses	Name
	10^{-6} nm		
	10^{-4} nm		Gamma rays
	10^{-2} nm		
	1 nm		X-rays
	10 nm		Ultraviolet waves
	1 µm		Visible light
	100 µm		Infrared waves
	1 mm		Microwaves
	1 m		
	100 m		Radio waves
	1 km		
	100 km		

Increasing wavelength

Ada 17 KILOMETERS

Long wavelength, low energy	Short wavelength, high energy

Electromagnetic Waves

Stars emit energy that radiates into space as electromagnetic (ih lek troh mag NEH tik) waves. Electromagnetic waves are different from mechanical waves, such as sound waves. Sound waves can transfer energy through solids, liquids, or gases. Electromagnetic waves can transfer energy through matter or through a vacuum, such as space. The energy they carry is called radiant energy.

The Electromagnetic Spectrum

The entire range of radiant energy carried by electromagnetic waves is the **electromagnetic spectrum.** As shown in Figure 1, waves of the electromagnetic spectrum are continuous. They range from gamma rays with short wavelengths at one end to radio waves with long wavelengths at the other end. Radio waves can be thousands of kilometers in length. Gamma rays, which are used in fighting cancer cells, can be smaller in length than the size of an atom.

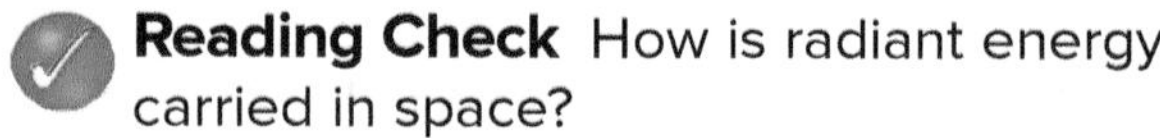
Reading Check How is radiant energy carried in space?

Humans observe only a small part of the electromagnetic spectrum–visible light. Visible light includes all the colors you see. You cannot see the other parts of the electromagnetic spectrum, but you can use them. When you talk on a cellular phone, you use microwaves. When you change the TV channel with a remote-control device or view an object with thermal imaging, you use infrared waves.

Radiant Energy and Stars

Most stars emit energy in all wavelengths. But how much of each wavelength they emit depends on their temperatures. Hot stars emit mostly shorter waves with higher energy, such as X-rays, gamma rays, and ultraviolet waves. Cool stars emit mostly longer waves with lower energy, such as infrared waves and radio waves. The Sun has a medium temperature range. It emits much of its energy as visible light.

MiniLab

15 minutes

What is white light?

Sunlight and the light from an ordinary lightbulb are both examples of visible light. You might think that white light is all white. Is it?

1. Read and complete a lab safety form.
2. Darken the room, and shine a **flashlight** through a **prism** on a flat surface. Adjust the positions of the prism and the flashlight until you observe the entire visible light spectrum.
3. In your Science Journal, use **colored pencils** to draw what you see.

Analyze and Conclude

1. **Define** What is white light?
2. **Compare and Contrast** Which component of white light has the longest wavelength? Which has the shortest wavelength? Explain your answers.
3. **Key Concept** How does visible light fit into the electromagnetic spectrum?

Why You See Planets and Moons

Planets and moons are much cooler than even the coolest stars. They do not make their own energy and, therefore, do not emit light. However, you can see the Moon and the planets because they reflect light from the Sun.

Light from the Past

All electromagnetic waves, from radio waves to gamma rays, travel through space at a constant speed of 300,000 km/s. This is called the speed of light. The speed of light might seem incredibly fast, but the universe is very large. Even moving at the speed of light, it can take millions or billions of years for some light waves to reach Earth because of the large distances in space.

Because it takes time for light to travel, you see planets and stars as they were when their light started its journey to Earth. It takes very little time for light to travel within the solar system. Reflected light from the Moon reaches Earth in about 1 second. Light from the Sun reaches Earth in about 8 minutes. It reaches Jupiter in about 40 minutes.

Light from stars is much older. Some stars are so far away that it can take millions or billions of years for their radiant energy to reach Earth. Therefore, by studying energy from stars, astronomers can learn what the universe was like millions or billions of years ago.

Reading Check How is looking at stars like looking at the past?

Math Skills

Scientific Notation

Scientists use scientific notation to work with large numbers. Express the speed of light in scientific notation using the following process.

1. Move the decimal point until only one nonzero digit remains on the left.

   300,000 → 3.00000

2. Use the number of places the decimal point moved (5) as a power of ten.

   300,000 km/s = 3.0×10^5 km/s

Practice

The Sun is 150,000,000 km from Earth. Express this distance in scientific notation.

Math Practice

Personal Tutor

Hutchings Photography/Digital Light Source

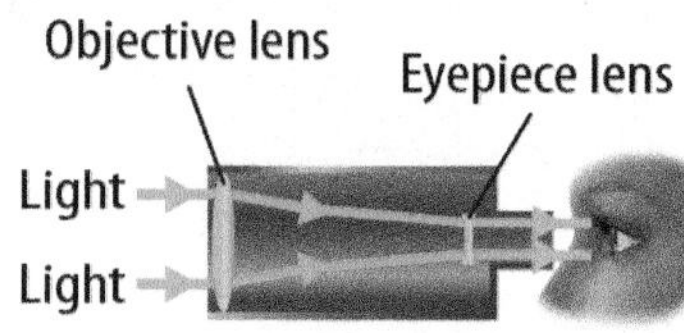

▲ **Figure 2** Optical telescopes collect visible light in two different ways.

Earth-Based Telescopes

Telescopes are designed to collect a certain type of electromagnetic wave. Some telescopes detect visible light, and others detect radio waves and microwaves.

Optical Telescopes

There are two kinds of optical telescopes–refracting telescopes and reflecting telescopes, illustrated in **Figure 2.**

Refracting Telescopes Have you ever used a magnifying lens? You might have noticed that the lens was curved and thick in the middle. This is a convex lens. *A telescope that uses a convex lens to concentrate light from a distant object is a* **refracting telescope.** As shown at the top of **Figure 2,** the objective lens in a refracting telescope is the lens closest to the object being viewed. The light goes through the objective lens and refracts, forming a small, bright image. The eyepiece is a second lens that magnifies the image.

Key Concept Check Which electromagnetic waves do refracting telescopes collect?

Reflecting Telescopes Most large telescopes use curved mirrors instead of curved lenses. *A telescope that uses a curved mirror to concentrate light from a distant object is a* **reflecting telescope.** As shown at the bottom of **Figure 2,** light is reflected from a primary mirror to a secondary mirror. The secondary mirror is tilted to allow the viewer to see the image. Generally, larger primary mirrors produce clearer images than smaller mirrors. However, there is a limit to mirror size. The largest reflecting telescopes, such as the Keck Telescopes on Hawaii's Mauna Kea, shown in **Figure 3,** have many small mirrors linked together. These small mirrors act as one large primary mirror.

Figure 3 Each 10-m primary mirror in the twin Keck Telescopes consists of 36 small mirrors. ▼

Radio Telescope

Radio image

▲ Figure 4 Radio telescopes are often built in large arrays. Computers convert radio data into images.

Radio Telescopes

Unlike a telescope that collects visible light waves, a **radio telescope** *collects radio waves and some microwaves using an antenna that looks like a TV satellite dish.* Because these waves have long wavelengths and carry little energy, radio antennae must be large to collect them. Radio telescopes are often built together and used as if they were one telescope. The telescopes shown in Figure 4 are part of the Very Large Array in New Mexico. The 27 instruments in this array act as a single telescope with a 36-km diameter.

Reading Check Why are radio telescopes built together in large arrays?

Distortion and Interference

Moisture in Earth's atmosphere can absorb and distort radio waves. Therefore, most radio telescopes are located in remote deserts, which have dry environments. Remote deserts also tend to be far from radio stations, which emit radio waves that interfere with radio waves from space.

Water vapor and other gases in Earth's atmosphere also distort visible light. Stars seem to twinkle because gases in the atmosphere move, refracting the light. This causes the location of a star's image to change slightly. At high elevations, the atmosphere is thin and produces less distortion than it does at low elevations. That is why most optical telescopes are built on mountains. New technology called adaptive optics lessens the effects of atmospheric distortion even more, as shown in Figure 5.

Figure 5 Adaptive optics sharpens images by reducing atmospheric distortion. ▼

Before Adaptive Optics

After Adaptive Optics

Wavelengths from Space

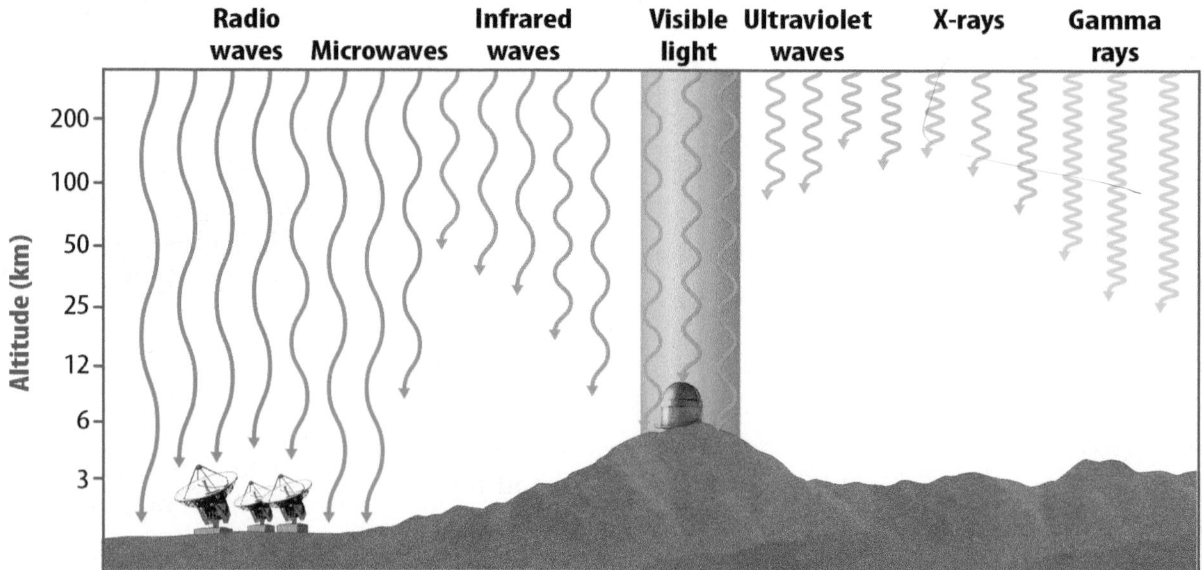

▲ **Figure 6** Most electromagnetic waves do not penetrate Earth's atmosphere. Even though the atmosphere blocks most UV rays, some still reach Earth's surface.

Visual Check About how far above Earth's surface do gamma waves reach?

Figure 7 The *Hubble Space Telescope* is controlled by astronomers on Earth. ▼

Space Telescopes

Why would astronomers want to put a telescope in space? The reason is Earth's atmosphere. Earth's atmosphere absorbs some types of electromagnetic radiation. As shown in Figure 6, visible light, radio waves, and some microwaves reach Earth's surface. But other types of electromagnetic waves do not. Telescopes on Earth can collect only the electromagnetic waves that are not absorbed by Earth's atmosphere. Telescopes in space can collect energy at all wavelengths, including those that Earth's atmosphere would absorb, such as most infrared light, most ultraviolet light, and X-rays.

Key Concept Check Why do astronomers put some telescopes in space?

Optical Space Telescopes

Optical telescopes collect visible light on Earth's surface, but optical telescopes work better in space. The reason, again, is Earth's atmosphere. As you read earlier, gases in the atmosphere can absorb some wavelengths. In space, there are no atmospheric gases. The sky is darker, and there is no weather.

The first optical space telescope was launched in 1990. The *Hubble Space Telescope*, shown in Figure 7, is a reflecting telescope that orbits Earth. Its primary mirror is 2.4 m in diameter. At first the *Hubble* images were blurred because of a flaw in the mirror. In 1993, astronauts repaired the telescope. Since then, *Hubble* has routinely sent to Earth spectacular images of far-distant objects. The photo at the beginning of this lesson was taken with the *Hubble* telescope.

Using Other Wavelengths

The *Hubble Space Telescope* is the only space telescope that collects visible light. Dozens of other space telescopes, operated by many different countries, gather ultraviolet, X-ray, gamma ray, and infrared light. Each type of telescope can point at the same region of sky and produce a different image. The image of the star Cassiopeia A (ka see uh PEE uh • AY) in Figure 8 was made with a combination of optical, X-ray, and infrared data. The colors represent different kinds of material left over from the star's explosion many years ago.

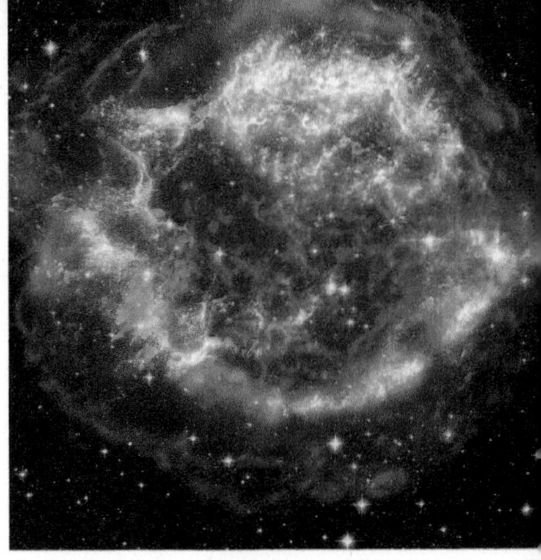

▲ Figure 8 Each color in this image of Cassiopeia A is derived from a different wavelength—yellow: visible; pink/red: infrared; green and blue: X-ray.

Spitzer Space Telescope Young stars and planets hidden by dust and gas cannot be viewed in visible light. However, infrared wavelengths can penetrate the dust and reveal what is beyond it. Infrared can also be used to observe objects too old and too cold to emit visible light. In 2003, the *Spitzer Space Telescope* was launched to collect infrared waves, as it orbits the Sun.

 **Reading Check** Which type of radiant energy does the *Spitzer Space Telescope* collect?

James Webb Space Telescope A larger space telescope, scheduled for launch in 2018, is also designed to collect infrared radiation as it orbits the Sun. The *James Webb Space Telescope,* illustrated in Figure 9, will have a mirror with an area 50 times larger than *Spitzer*'s mirror and seven times larger than *Hubble*'s mirror. Astronomers plan to use the telescope to detect galaxies that formed early in the history of the universe.

Figure 9 The advanced technology of the *James Webb Space Telescope* will help astronomers study the origin of the universe. ▼

James Webb Space Telescope

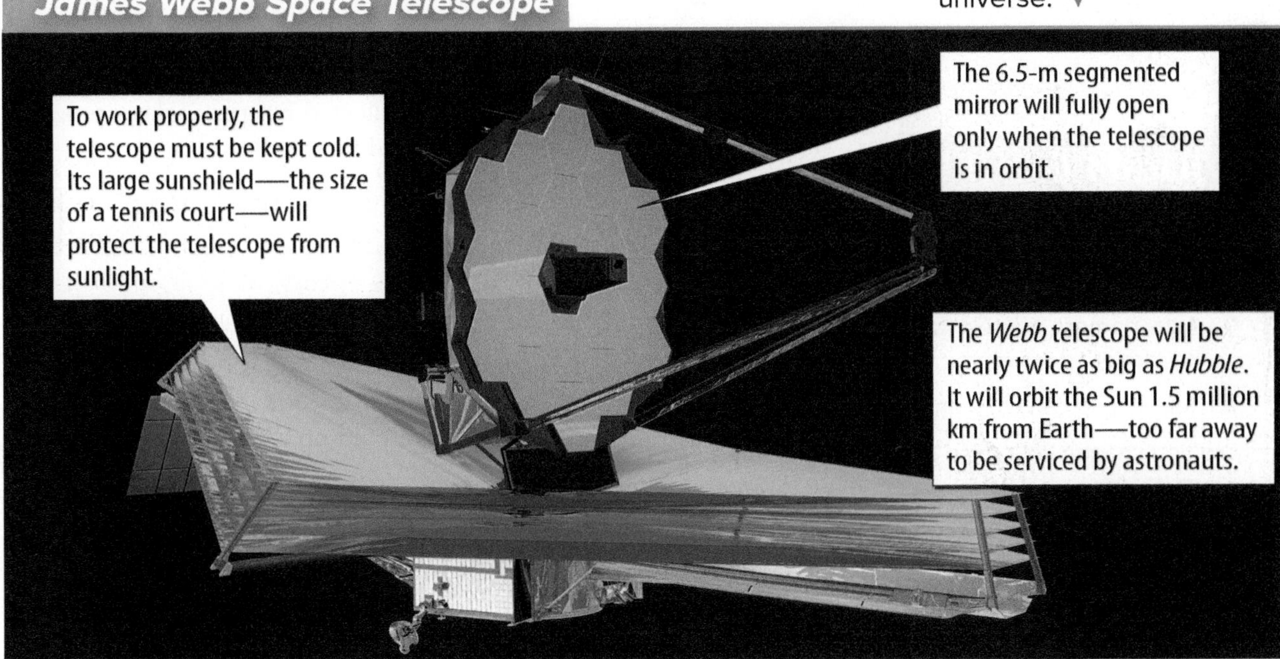

To work properly, the telescope must be kept cold. Its large sunshield—the size of a tennis court—will protect the telescope from sunlight.
The 6.5-m segmented mirror will fully open only when the telescope is in orbit.
The *Webb* telescope will be nearly twice as big as *Hubble*. It will orbit the Sun 1.5 million km from Earth—too far away to be serviced by astronauts.

(t)NASA/JPL-Caltech/STScI/CXC/SAO; (b)NASA/GSFC

Lesson 1 Review

Visual Summary

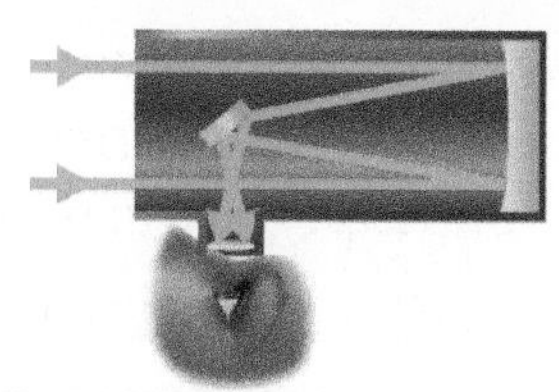

Reflecting telescopes use mirrors to concentrate light.

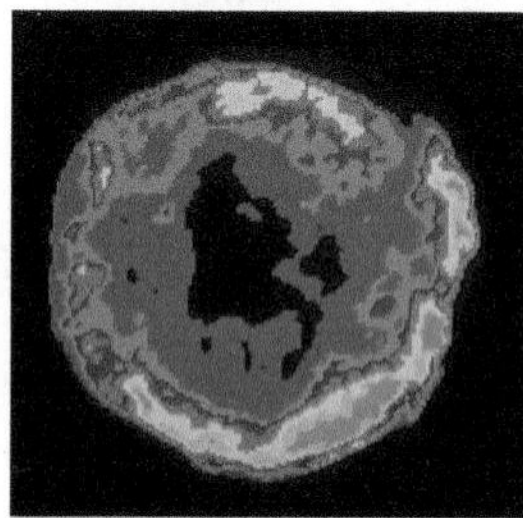

Earth-based telescopes can collect energy in the visible, radio, and microwave parts of the electromagnetic spectrum.

Space-based telescopes can collect wavelengths of energy that cannot penetrate Earth's atmosphere.

FOLDABLES®

Use your lesson Foldable to review the lesson. Save your Foldable for the project at the end of the chapter.

What do you think NOW?

You first read the statements below at the beginning of the chapter.

1. Astronomers put telescopes in space to be closer to the stars.
2. Telescopes can work only using visible light.

Did you change your mind about whether you agree or disagree with the statements? Rewrite any false statements to make them true.

Use Vocabulary

1. **Distinguish** between a reflecting telescope and a refracting telescope.
2. **Use the term** *electromagnetic spectrum* in a sentence.
3. **Define** *radio telescope* in your own words.

Understand Key Concepts

4. Which emits visible light?
   - **A.** moon
   - **B.** planet
   - **C.** satellite
   - **D.** star
5. **Draw** a sketch that shows the difference in wavelength of a radio wave and a visible light wave. Which transfers more energy?
6. **Contrast** the *Hubble Space Telescope* and the *James Webb Space Telescope.*

Interpret Graphics

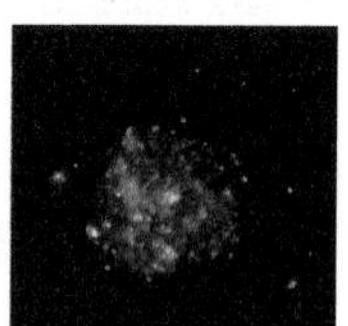

7. **Explain** The three images above represent the same area of sky. Explain why each looks different.
8. **Organize Information** Copy and fill in the graphic organizer below, listing the wavelengths collected by space telescopes, from the longest to the shortest.

Critical Thinking

9. **Suggest** a reason—besides the lessening of atmospheric distortion—why optical telescopes are built on remote mountains.

Math Skills

10. Light travels 9,460,000,000,000 km in 1 year. Express this number in scientific notation.

Skill Practice **Follow a Procedure** 30 minutes

How can you construct a simple telescope?

Have you ever looked at the night sky and wondered what you were looking at? Stars and planets look much the same. How can you distinguish them? In this lab, you will construct a simple telescope you can use to observe and distinguish distant objects.

Materials

lenses

cardboard tubes

silicon putty

wax pencil

rubber bands

masking tape

Safety

Learn It

In many science experiments, you must **follow a procedure** in order to know what materials to use and how to use them. In this activity, you will follow a procedure to construct a simple telescope.

Try It

1. Read and complete a lab safety form.
2. Move both lenses up and down over the print on this page to determine which lens has a shorter focal length. Use a marker to put a small dot on its edge. This will be your eyepiece lens.
3. Make a silicon putty rope 2–3 mm in diameter and about 15 cm long. Wrap the rope around the edge of one of the open ends of the smaller cardboard tube. Remove any extra putty.

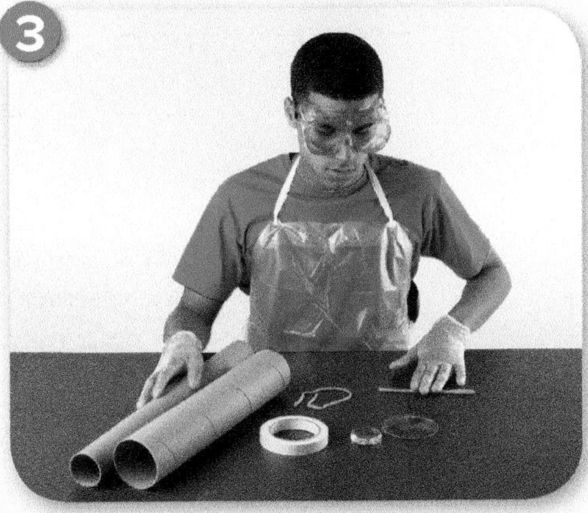

4. Gently push the eyepiece lens onto the ring of putty. Wrap a piece of masking tape around the edge of the lens to secure it firmly.
5. Repeat steps 4 and 5 using the larger tube and the objective lens.
6. Place the smaller tube into the larger tube so that the eyepiece lens, in the smaller tube, extends outside the larger tube.
7. Use your telescope to view distant objects. Move the smaller tube in and out to focus your instrument. If possible, view the night sky with your telescope. ⚠ *Do not use your telescope or any other instrument to directly view the Sun.*
8. Record your observations in your Science Journal.

Apply It

9. **Identify** What type of telescope did you construct?
10. **Key Concept** How does your telescope collect light?

(t to b, 6, br)Hutchings Photography/Digital Light Source; (2-5)McGraw-Hill Education

Lesson 2

Reading Guide

Key Concepts

ESSENTIAL QUESTIONS

- How are rockets and artificial satellites used?
- Why do scientists send both crewed and uncrewed missions into space?
- What are some ways that people use space technology to improve life on Earth?

Vocabulary

rocket p. 163
satellite p. 164
space probe p. 165
lunar p. 165
Project Apollo p. 166
space shuttle p. 166

Multilingual eGlossary

Science Video

SEPS.7, 6-8.LST.2.1, 6-8.LST.7.3

Early History of Space Exploration

Inquiry Where is it headed?

Have you ever witnessed a rocket launch? Rockets produce gigantic clouds of smoke, long plumes of exhaust, and thundering noise. How are rockets used to explore space? What do they carry?

Stockbyte/Alamy

Launch Lab

10 minutes

How do rockets work?

Space exploration would be impossible without rockets. Become a rocket scientist for a few minutes, and find out what sends rockets into space.

1. Read and complete a lab safety form.
2. Use **scissors** to carefully cut a 5-m piece of **string.**
3. Insert the string into a **drinking straw.** Tie each end of the string to a stationary object. Make sure the string is taut. Slide the drinking straw to one end of the string.
4. Blow up a **balloon.** Do not tie it. Instead, twist the neck and clamp it with a **clothespin** or a **paper clip. Tape** the balloon to the straw.
5. Remove the clothespin or paperclip to launch your rocket. Observe how the rocket moves. Record your observations in your Science Journal.

Think About This

1. Describe how your rocket moved along the string.
2. How might you get your rocket to go farther or faster?
3.  **Key Concept** How do you think rockets are used in space exploration?

Rockets

Think about listening to a recording of your favorite music. Now think about how different it is to experience the same music at a live performance. This is like the difference between exploring space from a distance, with a telescope, and actually going there.

A big problem in launching an object into space is overcoming the force of Earth's gravity. This is accomplished with rockets. *A* **rocket** *is a vehicle designed to propel itself by ejecting exhaust gas from one end.* Fuel burned inside the rocket builds up pressure. The force from the exhaust thrusts the rocket forward, as shown in Figure 10. Rocket engines do not draw in oxygen from the surrounding air to burn their fuel, as jet engines do. They carry their oxygen with them. As a result, rockets can operate in space where there is very little oxygen.

 **Key Concept Check** How are rockets used in space exploration?

Scientists launch rockets from Florida's Cape Canaveral Air Force Station or the Kennedy Space Center nearby. However, space missions are managed by scientists at several different research stations around the country.

Figure 10 Exhaust gases ejected from the end of a rocket push the rocket forward.

WORD ORIGIN

satellite
from Latin *satellitem*, means "attendant" or "bodyguard"

FOLDABLES®

Make a vertical two-tab book. Record what you learn about crewed and uncrewed space missions under the tabs.

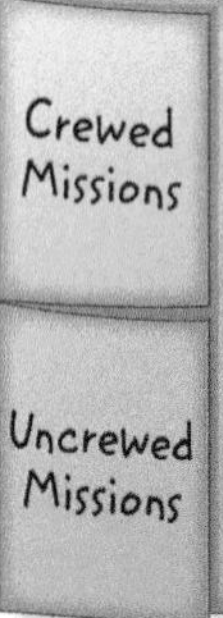

Artificial Satellites

Any small object that orbits a larger object is a **satellite.** The Moon is a natural satellite of Earth. Artificial satellites are made by people and launched by rockets. They orbit Earth or other bodies in space, transmitting radio signals back to Earth.

The First Satellites—*Sputnik* and *Explorer*

The first artificial, Earth-orbiting satellite was *Sputnik 1.* Many people think this satellite, launched in 1957 by the former Soviet Union, represents the beginning of the space age. In 1958, the United States launched its first Earth-orbiting satellite, *Explorer I.* Today, thousands of satellites orbit Earth.

How Satellites Are Used

The earliest satellites were developed by the military for navigation and to gather information. Today, Earth-orbiting satellites are also used to transmit television and telephone signals and to monitor weather and climate. An array of satellites called the Global Positioning System (GPS) is used for navigation in cars, boats, airplanes, and even for hiking.

Key Concept Check How are Earth-orbiting satellites used?

Early Exploration of the Solar System

In 1958, the U.S. Congress established the National Aeronautics and Space Administration (NASA). NASA oversees all U.S. space missions, including space telescopes. Some early steps in U.S. space exploration are shown in **Figure 11.**

Figure 11 Space exploration began with the first rocket launch in 1926.

Visual Check How many years after the first rocket was the first U.S. satellite launched into space?

Early Space Exploration

◄ **1926 First rocket:** Robert Goddard's liquid-fueled rocket rose 12 m into the air.

◄ **1962 First planetary probe:** *Mariner 2* traveled to Venus and collected data for 3 months. The spacecraft now orbits the Sun.

1958 First U.S. satellite: In the same year NASA was founded, *Explorer 1* was launched. It orbited Earth 58,000 times before burning up in Earth's atmosphere in 1970. ►

1972 First probe to outer solar system: After flying past Jupiter, *Pioneer 10* is still traveling onward, someday to exit the solar system. ►

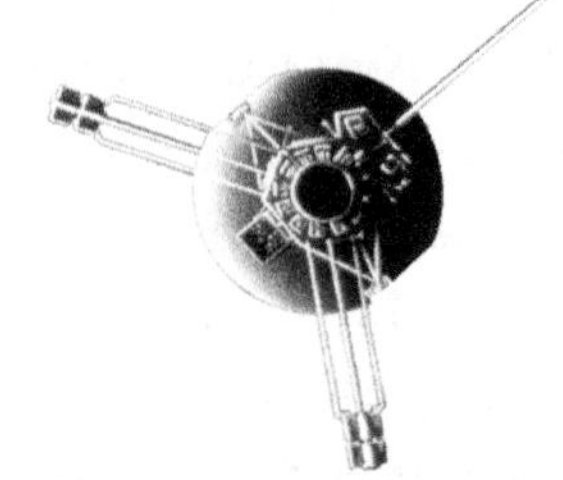

Space Probes

Figure 12 Scientists use space probes to explore the planets and some moons in the solar system.

Visual Check Which type of probe might use a parachute?

Orbiter

Once orbiters reach their destinations, they use rockets to slow down enough to be captured in a planet's orbit. How long they orbit depends on their fuel supply. The orbiter probe here, *Pioneer,* orbited Venus.

Lander

Landers touch down on surfaces. Sometimes they release rovers. Landers use rockets and parachutes to slow their descent. The lander probe here, *Phoenix,* analyzed the Martian surface for evidence of water.

Flyby

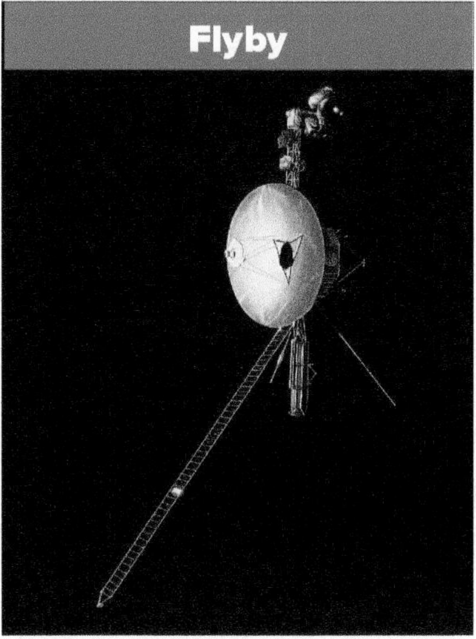

Flybys do not orbit or land. When its mission is complete, a flyby continues through space, eventually leaving the solar system. *Voyager 1,* here, explored Jupiter and Saturn and has entered interstellar space.

Space Probes

Some spacecraft have human crews, but most do not. *A* **space probe** *is an uncrewed spacecraft sent from Earth to explore objects in space.* Space probes are robots that work automatically or by remote control. They take pictures and gather data. Probes are cheaper to build than crewed spacecraft, and they can make trips that would be too long or too dangerous for humans. Space probes are not designed to return to Earth. The data they gather are relayed to Earth via radio waves. Figure 12 shows three major types of space probes.

SCIENCE USE V. COMMON USE

probe

Science Use an uncrewed spacecraft

Common Use question or examine closely

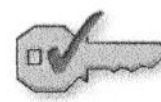

Key Concept Check Why do scientists send uncrewed missions to space?

Lunar and Planetary Probes

The first probes to the Moon were sent by the United States and the former Soviet Union in 1959. Probes to the Moon are called lunar probes. *The term* **lunar** *refers to anything related to the Moon.* The first spacecraft to gather information from another planet was the flyby *Mariner 2,* sent to Venus in 1962. Since then, space probes have been sent to all the planets.

Human Spaceflight

Sending humans into space was a major goal of the early space program. However, scientists worried about how radiation from the Sun and weightlessness in space might affect people's health. Because of this, they first sent dogs, monkeys, and chimpanzees. In 1961, the first human–an astronaut from the former Soviet Union–was launched into Earth's orbit. Shortly thereafter, the first American astronaut orbited Earth. Some highlights of the early U.S. human spaceflight program are shown in Figure 13.

The Apollo Program

In 1961, U.S. President John F. Kennedy challenged the American people to place a person on the Moon by the end of the decade. The result was **Project Apollo**–*a series of space missions designed to send people to the Moon.* In 1969, Neil Armstrong and Buzz Aldrin, Apollo 11 astronauts, were the first people to walk on the Moon.

Reading Check What was the goal of Project Apollo?

Space Transportation Systems

Early spacecraft and the rockets used to launch them were used only once. **Space shuttles** *are reusable spacecraft that transport people and materials to and from space.* Space shuttles return to Earth and land much like airplanes. NASA's fleet of space shuttles began operating in 1981. As the shuttles aged, NASA began developing a new transportation system, *Orion,* to replace them.

The *International Space Station*

The United States has its own space program. But it also cooperates with the space programs of other countries. In 1998, it joined 15 other nations to begin building the *International Space Station.* Occupied since 2000, this Earth-orbiting satellite is a research laboratory where astronauts from many countries work and live.

Research conducted aboard the *International Space Station* includes studying fungus, plant growth, and how human body systems react to low gravity conditions.

U.S. Human Spaceflight

Figure 13 Forty years after human spaceflight began, people were living and working in space.

Animation

▲ Apollo moon walk

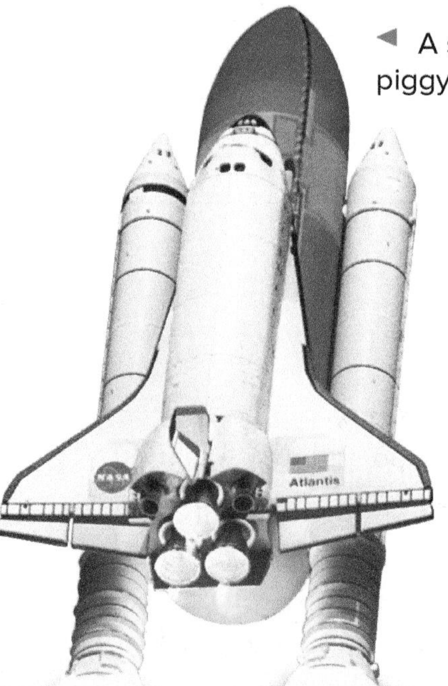

◄ A space shuttle piggybacked on rockets

International Space Station orbiting Earth ▼

(l, r)NASA; (c)Stocktrek/age fotostock

MiniLab

15 minutes

How does lack of friction in space affect simple tasks? 

Because objects are nearly weightless in space, there is little friction. What do you think might happen if an astronaut applied too much force when trying to move an object?

1. Read and complete a lab safety form.
2. Use **putty** to attach a **small thread spool** over the hole of a **CD.**
3. Inflate a **large, round balloon.** Twist the neck to keep the air inside. Stretch the neck of the balloon over the spool without releasing the air.
4. Place the CD on a smooth surface. Release the twist, and gently flick the CD with your finger. Describe your observations in your Science Journal.

Analyze and Conclude

1. **Infer** Why did the balloon craft move so easily?
2. **Draw Conclusions** How hard would it be to move a large object on the *International Space Station?*
3. 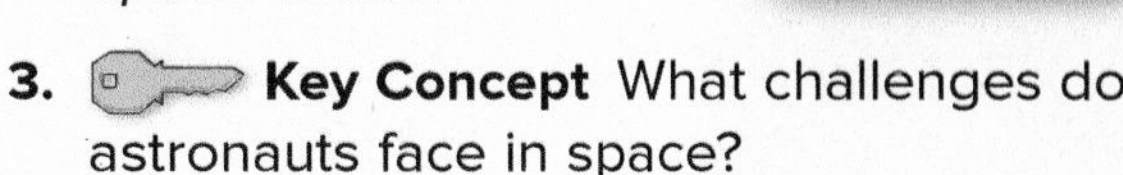 **Key Concept** What challenges do astronauts face in space?

Space Technology

The space program requires materials that can withstand the extreme temperatures and pressures of space. Many of these materials have been applied to everyday life on Earth.

New Materials

Space materials must protect people from extreme conditions. They also must be flexible and strong. Materials developed for spacesuits are now used to make racing suits for swimmers, lightweight firefighting gear, running shoes, and other sports clothing.

Safety and Health

NASA developed a strong, fibrous material to make parachute cords for spacecraft that land on planets and moons. This material, five times stronger than steel, is used to make radial tires for automobiles.

Medical Applications

Artificial limbs, infrared ear thermometers, and robotic surgery all have roots in the space program. So do the orthodontic braces shown in Figure 14. These braces contain ceramic material originally developed to strengthen the heat resistance of space shuttles.

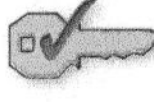 **Key Concept Check** What are some ways that space exploration has improved life on Earth?

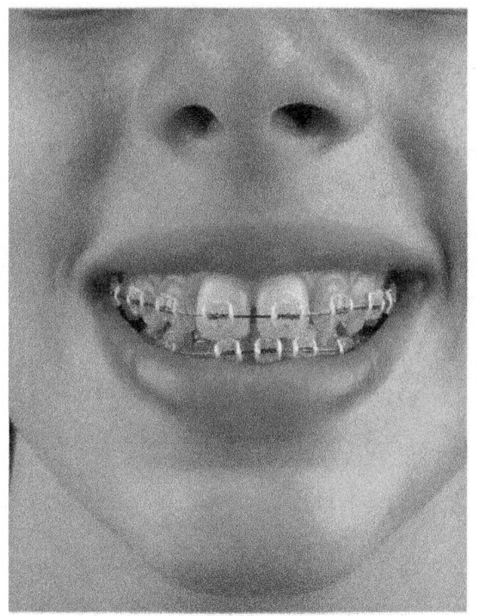

Figure 14 These braces contain a hard, strong ceramic originally developed for spacecraft.

Lesson 2 Review

Visual Summary

Exhaust from burned fuel accelerates a rocket.

Some space probes can land on the surface of a planet or a moon.

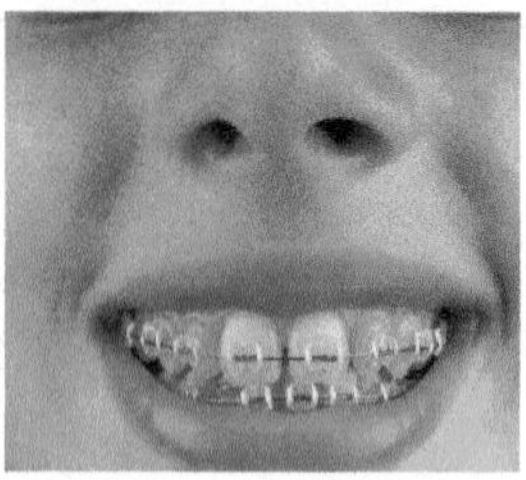

Technologies developed for the space program have been applied to everyday life on Earth.

FOLDABLES®

Use your lesson Foldable to review the lesson. Save your Foldable for the project at the end of the chapter.

What do you think NOW?

You first read the statements below at the beginning of the chapter.

3. Humans have walked on the Moon.

4. Some orthodontic braces were developed using space technology.

Did you change your mind about whether you agree or disagree with the statements? Rewrite any false statements to make them true.

Use Vocabulary

1. **Define** *rocket* in your own words.
2. **Use the term** *satellite* in a sentence.
3. The mission that sent people to the Moon was ________.

Understand Key Concepts 

4. What are rockets used for?
   - **A.** carrying people
   - **B.** launching satellites
   - **C.** observing planets
   - **D.** transmitting signals
5. **Explain** why *Sputnik 1* is considered the beginning of the space age.
6. **Compare and contrast** crewed and uncrewed space missions.

Interpret Graphics

7. **Infer** How is the balloon above like a rocket?
8. **Organize Information** Copy and fill in the graphic organizer below and use it to place the following in the correct order: *first human in space, invention of rockets, first human on the Moon, first artificial satellite.*

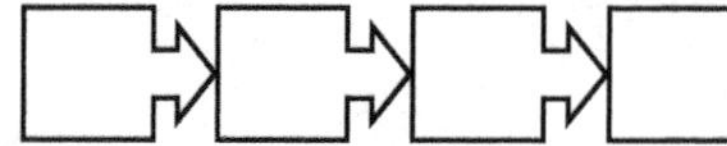

Critical Thinking

9. **Predict** how your life would be different if all artificial satellites stopped working.
10. **Evaluate** the benefits and drawbacks of international cooperation in space exploration.

(tl)Stocktrek/age fotostock; (cl)NASA/JPL; (r)Hutchings Photography/Digital Light Source; (bl)Alex Bartel/Science Source

Going Up

Could a space elevator make space travel easier?

If you wanted to travel into space, the first thing you would have to do is overcome the force of Earth's gravity. So far, the only way to do that has been to use rockets. Rockets are expensive, however. Many are used only once, and they require a lot of fuel. It takes a lot of resources to build and power a rocket. But what if you could take an elevator into space instead?

Space elevators were once science fiction, but scientists are now taking the possibility seriously. With the lightweight but strong materials under development today, experts say it could take only 10 years to build a space elevator. The image here shows how it might work.

It generally costs more than $100 million to place a 2,000-kg spacecraft into orbit using a rocket. Some people estimate that a space elevator could place the same craft into orbit for less than $120,000. A human passenger with luggage, together totaling 150 kg, might be able to ride the elevator to space for less than $1,500.

Counterweight: The spaceward end of the cable would attach to a captured asteroid or an artificial satellite. The asteroid or satellite would stabilize the cable and act as a counterweight.

Cable: Made of super-strong but thin materials, the cable would be the first part of the elevator to be built. A rocket-launched spacecraft would carry reels of cable into orbit. From there the cable would be unwound until one end reached Earth's surface.

Anchor Station: The cable's Earthward end would be attached here. A movable platform would allow operators to move the cable away from space debris in Earth's orbit that could collide with it. The platform would be movable because it would float on the ocean.

Climber: The "elevator car" would carry human passengers and objects into space. It could be powered by Earth-based laser beams, which would activate solar-cell "ears" on the outside of the car.

It's Your Turn

DEBATE Form an opinion about the space elevator and debate with a classmate. Could a space elevator become a reality in the near future? Would a space elevator benefit ordinary people? Should the space elevator be used for space tourism?

Lesson 3

Reading Guide

Key Concepts
ESSENTIAL QUESTIONS

- What are goals for future space exploration?
- What conditions are required for the existence of life on Earth?
- How can exploring space help scientists learn about Earth?

Vocabulary

extraterrestrial life p. 175
astrobiology p. 175

Multilingual eGlossary

Science Video
What's Science Got to do With It?

6.ESS.3, SEPS.1, SEPS.2, SEPS.5, SEPS.6, SEPS.7, SEPS.8, 6-8.LST.5.1, 6-8.LST.5.2

Recent and Future Space Missions

Inquiry Blue Moon?

No, this is Mars! It is a false-color photo of an area on Mars where a future space probe might land. Of all the planets in the solar system, Mars is most like Earth. Recent missions to Mars have found evidence of water on its surface. Could this planet support life?

NASA/JPL/University of Arizona

Launch Lab

10 minutes

How is gravity used to send spacecraft farther in space?  

Spacecraft use fuel to get to where they are going. But fuel is expensive and adds mass to the craft. Some spacecraft travel to far-distant regions with the help of gravity from the planets they pass by. This is a technique called gravity assist. You can model gravity assist using a simple table tennis ball.

1. Read and complete a lab safety form.
2. Set a **turntable** in motion.
3. Gently throw a **table tennis ball** so that it just skims the top of the spinning surface. You might have to practice before you're able to get the ball to glide over the surface.
4. In your Science Journal, describe or draw a picture of what you observed.

Think About This

1. Use your observations to describe how this activity is similar to gravity assist.
2. **Key Concept** How do you think gravity assist helps scientists learn about the solar system?

Missions to the Sun and the Moon

Scientists at NASA and other space agencies around the world have cooperatively developed goals for future space exploration. One goal is to expand human space travel within the solar system. Two steps leading to this goal are sending probes to the Sun and sending probes to the Moon.

 **Key Concept Check** What is a goal of space exploration?

Solar Probes

The Sun emits high-energy radiation and charged particles. Storms on the Sun can eject powerful jets of gas and charged particles into space, as shown in Figure 15. The Sun's high-energy radiation and charged particles can harm astronauts and damage spacecraft. To better understand these hazards, scientists study data collected by solar probes that orbit the Sun. The solar probe *Ulysses,* launched in 1990, orbited the Sun and gathered data for 19 years. *Solar Probe Plus,* a new solar probe set to launch in 2018, will gather data on solar winds and coronal heating, among other data.

Figure 15 Storms on the Sun send charged particles far into space.

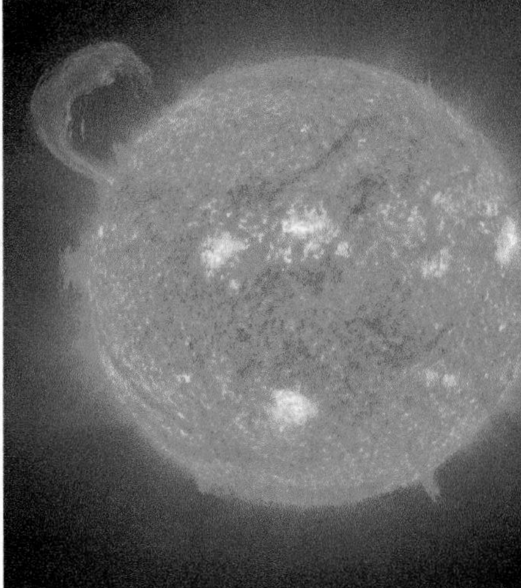

Lunar Probes

NASA and other space agencies also plan to send several probes to the Moon. The *Lunar Reconnaissance Orbiter,* launched in 2009, collects data that will help scientists select the best location for a future lunar outpost.

(t)Hutchings Photography/Digital Light Source; (b)SOHO (NASA & ESA)

FOLDABLES®

Use a sheet of copy paper to make a vertical three-tab Foldable. Draw a Venn diagram on the front tabs and use it to compare and contrast space missions to the inner and outer planets.

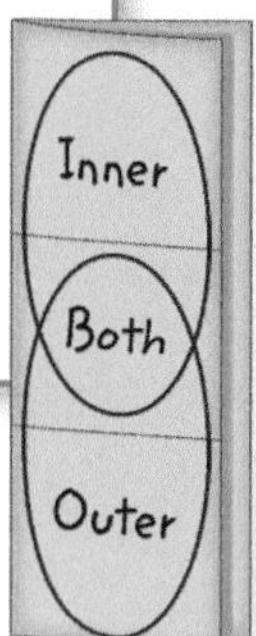

Missions to the Inner Planets

The inner planets are the four rocky planets closest to the Sun–Mercury, Venus, Earth, and Mars. Scientists have sent many probes to the inner planets, and more are planned. These probes help scientists learn how the inner planets formed, what geologic forces are active on them, and whether any of them could support life. Some recent and current missions to the inner planets are described in **Figure 16.**

Reading Check What do scientists want to learn about the inner planets?

Planetary Missions

Figure 16 Studying the solar system remains a major goal of space exploration.

◄ ***Messenger*** The first probe to visit Mercury—the planet closest to the Sun—since *Mariner 10* flew by the planet in 1975 is *Messenger.* After a 2004 launch and two passes of Venus, *Messenger* flew past Mercury several times before entering its orbit in 2011. *Messenger* studied Mercury's geology and chemistry. It sent images and data back to Earth for one Earth year. On its first pass by Mercury, in 2008, *Messenger* returned over 1,000 images in many wavelengths. The mission came to an end in 2015 when Messenger crashed into Mercury's surface.

Mars Reconnaissance Orbiter. Since the first flyby reached Mars in 1964, many probes, rovers, and orbiters have been sent to the red planet. Recently, the *Mars Reconnaissance Orbiter* (MRO) indicated that water flows periodically on the Martian surface. Researchers noticed mysterious, dark streaks on the slopes of craters that seemed to flow downward during warm seasons, and recede during cooler seasons. These streaks were confirmed to be liquid water. This mission continues to send back valuable information about Mars. ►

Missions to the Outer Planets and Beyond

The outer planets are the four large planets farthest from the Sun–Jupiter, Saturn, Uranus, and Neptune. Pluto was once considered an outer planet, but it is now included with other small, icy **dwarf planets** observed orbiting the Sun outside the orbit of Neptune. Missions to outer planets are long and difficult because the planets are so far from Earth. Some missions to the outer planets and beyond are described in **Figure 16** below. The next major mission to the outer planets will be an international mission to Jupiter and its four largest moons.

REVIEW VOCABULARY

dwarf planet
a round body that orbits the Sun but is not massive enough to clear away other objects in its orbit

 **Reading Check** Why are missions to the outer planets difficult?

Visual Check Which planet has been explored by rovers?

◄ ***Cassini*** The first orbiter sent to Saturn, *Cassini,* was launched in 1997 as part of an international effort involving 19 countries. *Cassini* traveled for 7 years before entering Saturn's orbit in 2004. When it arrived, it sent a smaller probe to the surface of Saturn's largest moon, Titan, as shown at left. This event was the first landing on a moon in the outer solar system. *Cassini's* accomplishments include the discovery of geysers on Saturn's moon Enceladus, a greater understanding of Saturn's active ring system, and the discovery of massive hurricanes at the planet's poles. Data collected from *Cassini's* mission help scientists understand how planets, like Saturn, form and evolve.

New Horizons After a 9 year journey from Earth, the *New Horizons* spacecraft arrived at Pluto in 2015. It became the first spacecraft to explore the dwarf planet up close. Data collected from this mission included mapping the geology of Pluto and its moon—Charon, investigating the planets surface compositions and temperatures, and examining its atmosphere. *New Horizons* is projected to leave the solar system in 2029. ►

Figure 17 This structure, at the Johnson Space Center, could serve as housing for up to four astronauts. It has been evaluated to ensure safety for humans living on other planetary bodies.

Future Space Missions

Human space travel remains a goal of NASA and other space agencies around the world. Human exploration missions greatly expand our scientific understanding of our solar system and the origins of life.

A New Era of Spaceflight

Future missions to space, including the goal of astronauts working and living on Mars, are dependent upon how humans will get there. The *Orion* spacecraft is a human space flight system that is capable of missions to a variety of interplanetary destinations. The purpose of *Orion* is to safely take astronauts to places in deep space that have never been explored by humans.

Once a destination has proven suitable for human exploration, astronauts will need secure housing. The structure in **Figure 17** is one of those options.

ACADEMIC VOCABULARY
option
(noun) something that can be chosen

Studying and Visiting Mars

A visit to Mars will probably not occur for several more decades. In preparation, NASA has sent orbiters, landers, and rovers to explore sites and resources that could potentially support life on Mars. The *MAVEN* spacecraft, for example, studied the atmosphere of Mars and how it has evolved over time. The *Mars Reconnaissance Orbiter* (MRO) was sent to search for evidence of water on the planet. The *Curiosity* rover analyzed rock and soil samples to evaluate the planet's past climate and geology, and also investigate if its environment was once able to support life. The data collected from each mission makes a human exploration mission more obtainable.

MiniLab

20 minutes

What conditions are required for life on Earth?

Billions of organisms live on Earth. What are the requirements for life?

1. Observe a **terrarium.** In your Science Journal, make a sketch of this environment and label every component as either living or nonliving.
2. Observe an **aquarium.** Again, make a sketch of this environment and label every component as living or nonliving.

Analyze and Conclude

1. **Compare and Contrast** Describe what the organisms in both environments need to survive.
2. **Draw Conclusions** Do all living things have the same needs? Support your answer using examples from your observations.
3. **Key Concept** What conditions are required for life on Earth? How would knowing these requirements help scientists look for life in space?

The Search for Life

No one knows if life exists beyond Earth, but people have thought about the possibility for a long time. It even has a name. *Life that originates outside Earth is* **extraterrestrial** (ek struh tuh RES tree ul) **life.**

Conditions Needed for Life

Astrobiology *is the study of life in the universe, including life on Earth and the possibility of extraterrestrial life.* Investigating the conditions for life on Earth helps scientists predict where they might find life elsewhere in the solar system. Astrobiology also can help scientists locate environments in space where humans and other Earth life might be able to survive.

Life exists in a wide range of environments on Earth. Life-forms survive on dark ocean floors, deep in solid rocks, and in scorching water, such as the hot spring shown in Figure 18. No matter how extreme their environments, all known life-forms on Earth need liquid water, organic molecules, and some source of energy to survive. Scientists assume that if life exists elsewhere in space it would have the same requirements.

Key Concept Check What is required for life on Earth?

Water in the Solar System

As scientists explore our solar system, they continue to find water in unexpected places. For example, a lunar space probe found water in a crater on the Moon. Enough frozen water was found in a single crater to fill 1,500 Olympic swimming pools. Evidence from other space probes suggests that liquid water, water vapor, or ice exists on many planets and moons in the solar system.

Some of the moons in the outer solar system, such as Jupiter's moon Europa, shown in Figure 19, might also have large amounts of liquid water beneath their surfaces.

▲ **Figure 18** Bacteria live in the boiling water of this hot spring in Yellowstone National Park.

WORD ORIGIN

astrobiology
from Greek *astron,* means "star"; Greek *bios,* means "life"; and Greek *logia,* means "study"

Figure 19 The dark patches in the inset photo might represent areas where water from an underground ocean has seeped to Europa's surface. ▼

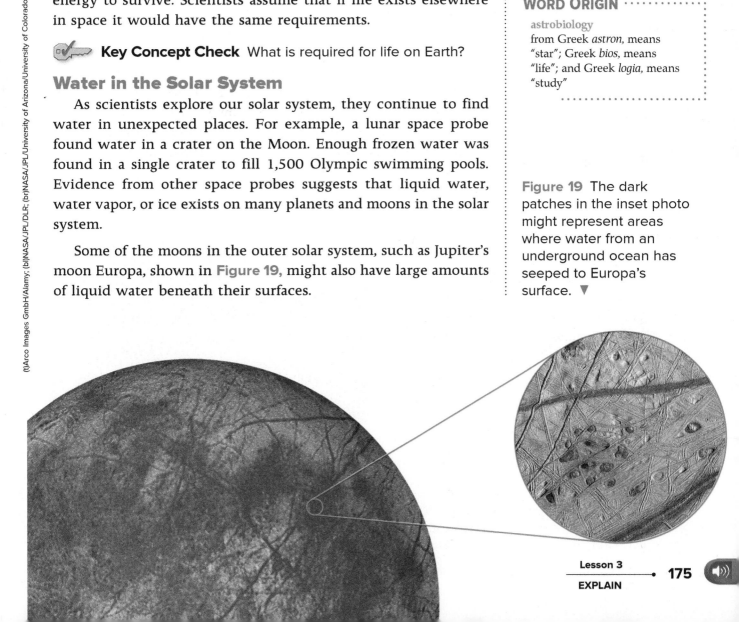

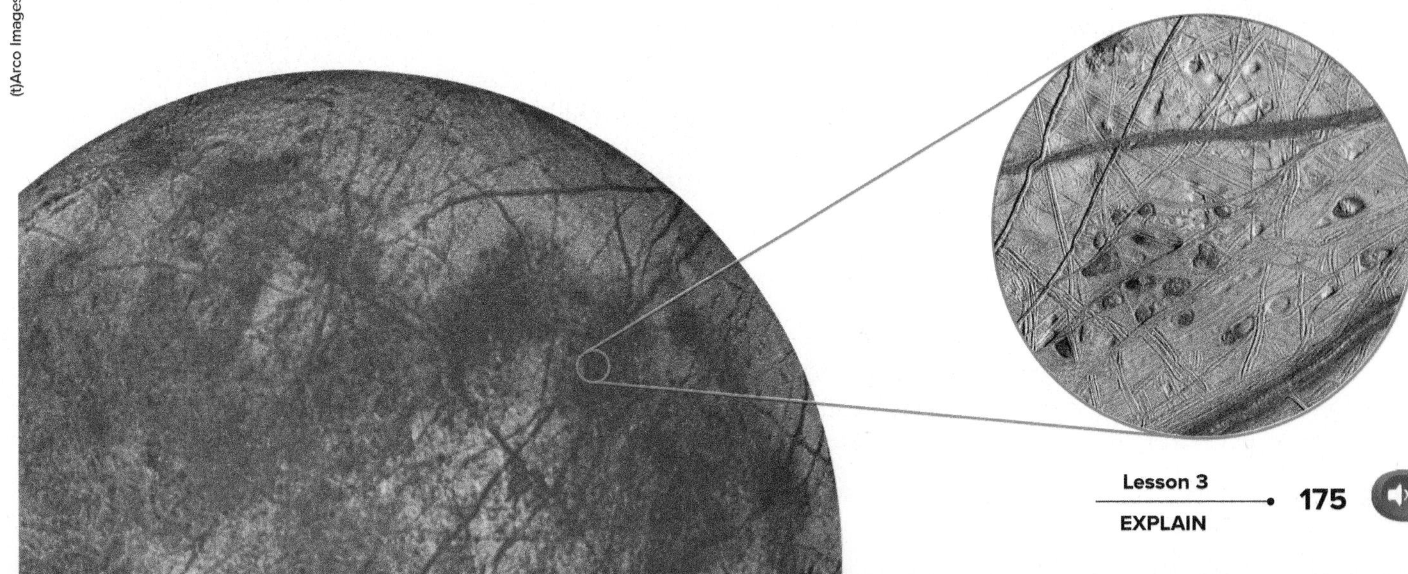

▲ Figure 20 The Kepler telescope, shown here, is currently orbiting the Sun, searching a single area of sky for Earthlike planets.

Understanding Earth by Exploring Space

Space provides frontiers for the human spirit of exploration and discovery. The exploration of space also provides insight into planet Earth. Information gathered in space helps scientists understand how the Sun and other bodies in the solar system influence Earth, how Earth formed, and how Earth supports life. Looking for Earthlike planets outside the solar system helps scientists learn if Earth is unique in the universe.

Searching for Other Planets

Astronomers have detected thousands of planets outside the solar system. Most of these planets are much bigger than Earth and probably could not support liquid water–or life. To search for Earthlike planets, NASA launched the *Kepler* telescope in 2009. The *Kepler* telescope, shown in Figure 20, focuses on a single area of sky containing about 100,000 stars. However, though it might detect Earthlike planets orbiting other stars, *Kepler* will not be able to detect life on any planet.

Understanding Our Home Planet

Not all of NASA's missions are to other planets, to other moons, or to look at stars and galaxies. NASA and space agencies around the world also launch and maintain Earth observing satellites. Satellites that orbit Earth provide large-scale images of Earth's surface. These images help scientists understand Earth's climate and weather. Figure 21 is a satellite image showing changes in ocean temperature associated with Hurricane Katrina, one of the deadliest storms in U.S. history.

Key Concept Check How can exploring space help scientists learn about Earth?

Figure 21  Earth-orbiting satellites collect data in many wavelengths. This satellite image of Hurricane Katrina was made with a microwave sensor. ▶

Visual Check Which part of the United States did Hurricane Katrina affect?

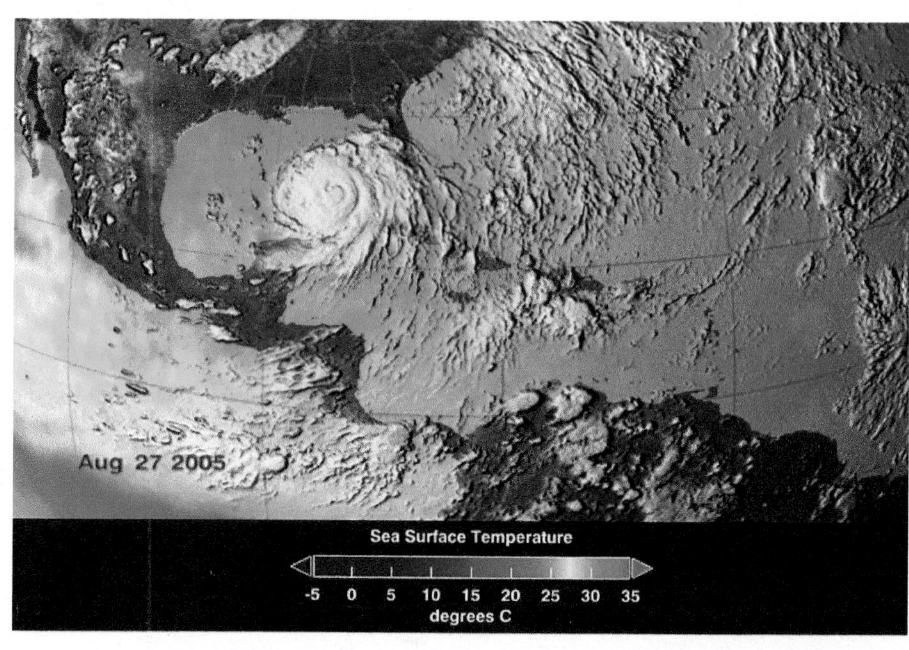

Lesson 3 Review

Visual Summary

The *New Horizons* spacecraft was the first to explore Pluto.

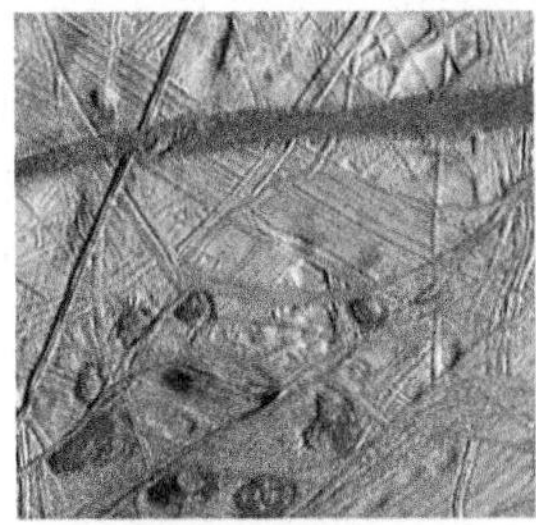

Scientists think liquid water might exist on or below the surfaces of some moons.

Earth-orbiting satellites help scientists understand weather and climate patterns on Earth.

FOLDABLES®

Use your lesson Foldable to review the lesson. Save your Foldable for the project at the end of the chapter.

What do you think NOW?

You first read the statements below at the beginning of the chapter.

5. Humans have landed on Mars.

6. Scientists have detected water on other bodies in the solar system.

Did you change your mind about whether you agree or disagree with the statements? Rewrite any false statements to make them true.

Use Vocabulary

1. **Use the term** *extraterrestrial life* in a sentence.
2. The study of life in the universe is ________.

Understand Key Concepts

3. *Cassini* sent a probe to which moon?
   - **A.** Europa
   - **B.** Titan
   - **C.** Rhea
   - **D.** Enceladus
4. **Explain** why bodies that have liquid water are the best candidates for supporting life.
5. **Assess** the benefits of an inflatable structure over a concrete structure on the Moon.
6. **Identify** some phenomena on Earth best viewed by artificial satellites.

Interpret Graphics

7. **Assess** The figure above represents a possible design for a new solar probe that would orbit close to the Sun. What purpose might the part labeled *A* serve?
8. **Organize Information** Copy and fill in the graphic organizer below to list requirements for life on Earth.

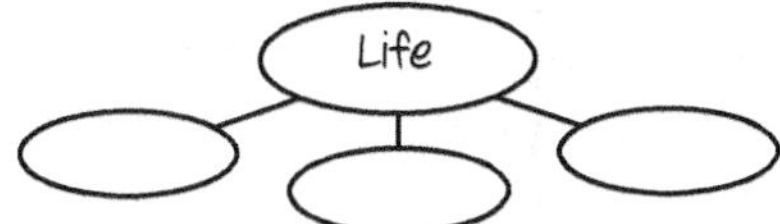

Critical Thinking

9. **Predict** some of the challenges people might face living in a lunar outpost.
10. **Debate** whether scientists should look first for life on Mars or on Europa.

(tl)NASA/Johns Hopkins University Applied Physics Laboratory/Southwest Research Institute (NASA/JHUAPL/SwRI); (c)NASA/JPL/University of Arizona/University of Colorado; (b)NASA/Goddard Space Flight Center Scientific Visualization Studio; (r)NASA/Johns Hopkins University Applied Physics Laboratory

Design and Construct a Moon Habitat

No one has visited the Moon since 1972. NASA plans to send astronauts to Mars and beyond. You might be one of the lucky ones who will be sent to find a suitable location for an outpost. To get a head start, your task is to design and build a model of a habitat where people can live and work for months at a time. You can use any materials provided or other materials approved by your teacher. Before you begin, think about some of the things people will need in order to survive on other planets.

Materials

newspaper

creative building materials

masking tape

cup varieties

office supplies

craft supplies

scissors

Safety

Question

Think about what humans need on a daily basis. How can you design a habitat that would meet people's needs in a place very unlike Earth?

Procedure

1. Read and complete a lab safety form.
2. Think about construction. Consider the function each material might represent in a moon habitat. The materials will have to be transported from Earth before any construction can begin.
3. Draw plans for your habitat. Be sure to include an airlock, a small room that separates an outer door from an inner door. Label the materials you will use and what each represents.
4. Copy the data table below into your Science Journal. Complete the table by listing each material you plan to use, its purpose or function, and why you chose it.

Materials for a Moon Habitat

Material	Function	Why I Chose the Material

(t to b, 3, r)Hutchings Photography/Digital Light Source; (2, 4-6)McGraw-Hill Education; (7)Jacques Cornell/McGraw-Hill Education

Lab Tips

- ☑ Before you begin, make a list of conditions on other planets, such as Mars, that are much different from those on Earth.
- ☑ If you can think of any materials not listed that you would like to use, ask your teacher's permission to use them.

5. Build your habitat. When you are finished, check to see that your habitat satisfies the conditions in your original question. If not, revise your habitat or make a note in your Science Journal about how you would improve it.

6. In addition to meeting people's needs in space, the habitat should be easy to construct in the harsh environments of space. Remember that the materials should be easy to transport from Earth.
7. Some things might not go as planned as you construct your model, or you might get new ideas as you proceed with building. As you go along, you can adapt your structure to improve the final product. Record any changes you make to your design or materials in your Science Journal.

Analyze and Conclude

8. **Explain** in detail why you chose the materials and the design that you did.
9. **Evaluate** Which materials or designs did not work as expected? Explain.
10. **Compare and Contrast** What differences between the Martian environment and Earth's environment did you consider in your design?
11. THE BIG IDEA **The Big Idea** What requirements must be met for humans to live, work, and be healthy on other planets?

Communicate Your Results

Imagine that your design is part of a NASA competition to find the best habitat. Write and give a 2–3 minute presentation convincing NASA to use your model for its habitat.

Compare your habitat to the habitats of at least three other groups. Discuss how you might combine your ideas to build a bigger and better habitat.

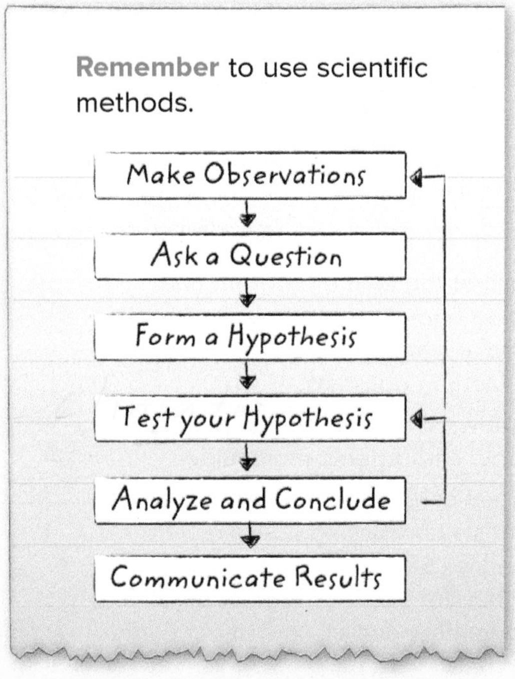

Hutchings Photography/Digital Light Source

Chapter 5 Study Guide

Humans observe the universe with Earth-based and space-based telescopes. They explore the solar system with crewed and uncrewed space probes.

Key Concepts Summary 

Lesson 1: Observing the Universe

- Scientists use different parts of the **electromagnetic spectrum** to study stars and other objects in space and to learn what the universe was like many millions of years ago.
- Telescopes in space can collect radiant energy that Earth's atmosphere would absorb or refract.

Vocabulary

electromagnetic spectrum p. 154
refracting telescope p. 156
reflecting telescope p. 156
radio telescope p. 157

Lesson 2: Early History of Space Exploration

- **Rockets** are used to overcome the force of Earth's gravity when sending **satellites, space probes,** and other spacecraft into space.
- Uncrewed missions can make trips that are too long or too dangerous for humans.
- Materials and technologies from the space program have been applied to everyday life.

Vocabulary

rocket p. 163
satellite p. 164
space probe p. 165
lunar p. 165
Project Apollo p. 166
space shuttle p. 166

Lesson 3: Recent and Future Space Missions

- A goal of the space program is to expand human space travel within the solar system and develop lunar and Martian outposts.
- All known life-forms need liquid water, energy, and organic molecules.
- Information gathered in space helps scientists understand how the Sun influences Earth, how Earth formed, whether life exists outside of Earth, and how weather and climate affect Earth.

Vocabulary

extraterrestrial life p. 175
astrobiology p. 175

(t) NASA, (c) ©Stocktrek/age fotostock, (b) McGraw-Hill Education

Personal Tutor
Vocabulary eGames
Vocabulary eFlashcards

FOLDABLES® Chapter Project

Assemble your lesson Foldables as shown to make a Chapter Project. Use the project to review what you have learned in this chapter.

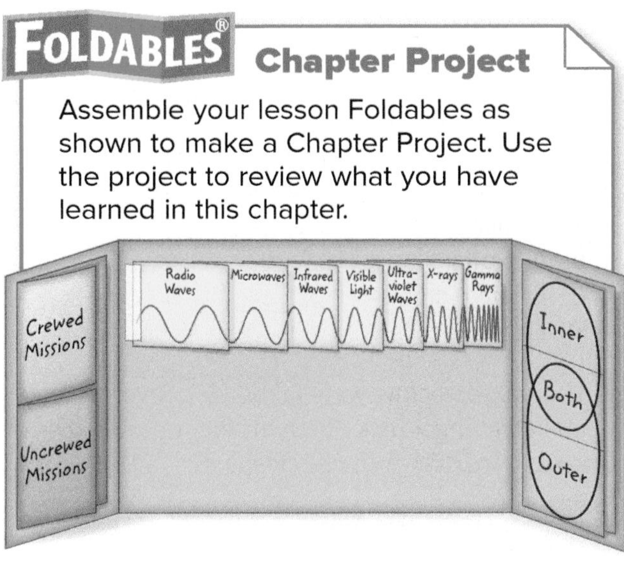

Use Vocabulary

1. All radiation is classified by wavelength in the ________.
2. Two types of telescopes that collect visible light are ________ and ________.
3. The space mission that sent the first humans to the Moon was ________.
4. An example of a human space transportation system is a(n) ________.
5. An uncrewed spacecraft is a(n) ________.
6. The discipline that investigates life in the universe is ________.
7. The best place to find ________ is on solar system bodies containing water.

Interactive Concept Map

Link Vocabulary and Key Concepts

Copy this concept map, and then use vocabulary terms from the previous page to complete the concept map.

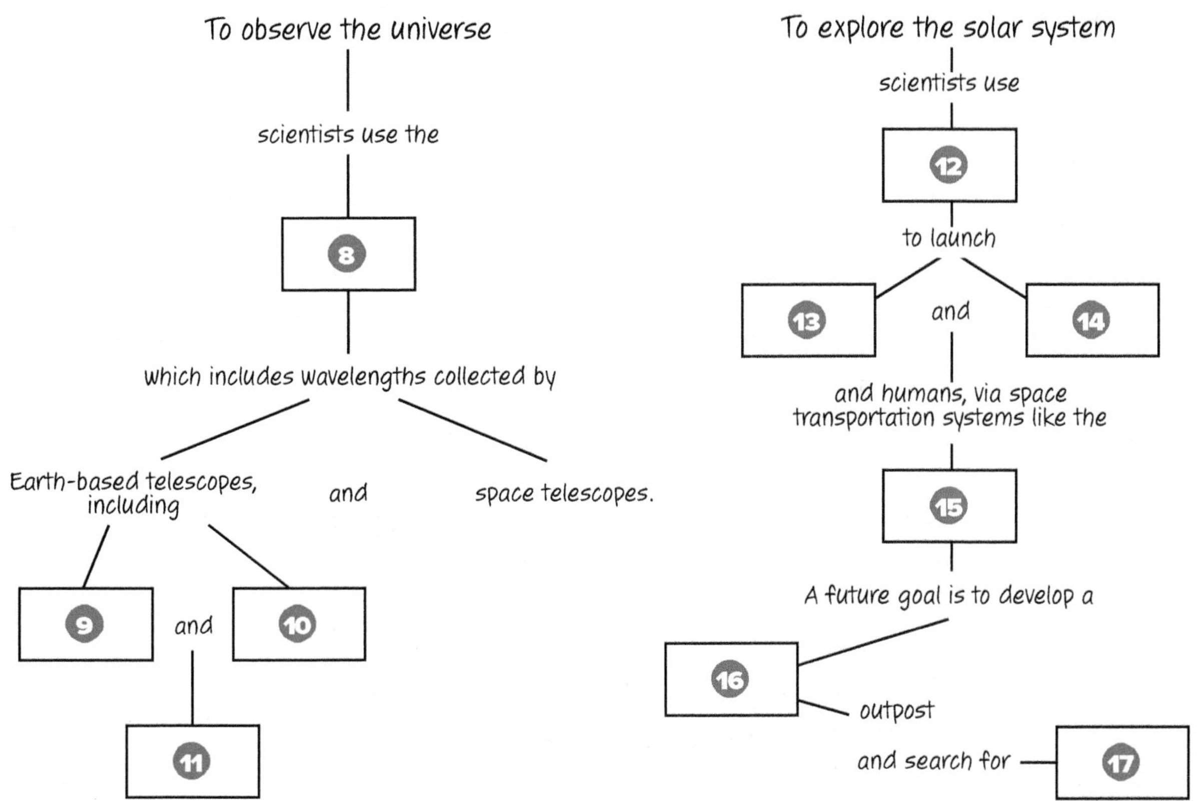

Chapter 5 Review

Understand Key Concepts 

1. Which type of telescope is shown in the figure below?

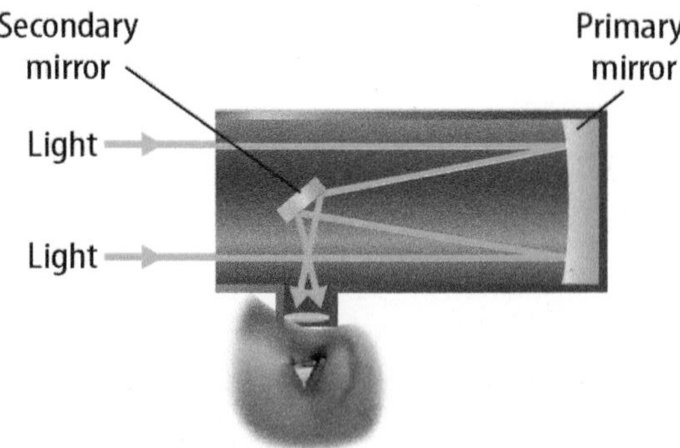

A. infrared telescope
B. radio telescope
C. reflecting telescope
D. refracting telescope

2. In which wavelength would you expect the hottest stars to emit most of their energy?

A. gamma rays
B. microwaves
C. radio waves
D. visible light

3. Which best describes *Hubble?*

A. infrared telescope
B. radio telescope
C. refracting telescope
D. space telescope

4. What is special about the *Kepler* mission?

A. *Kepler* can detect objects at all wavelengths.
B. *Kepler* has found the most distant objects in the universe.
C. *Kepler* is dedicated to finding Earthlike planets.
D. *Kepler* is the first telescope to orbit the Sun.

5. Where is the *International Space Station?*

A. on Mars
B. on the Moon
C. orbiting Earth
D. orbiting the Sun

6. Which mission sent people to the Moon?

A. Apollo
B. Explorer
C. Galileo
D. Pioneer

7. The images below were taken by a rover as it moved along a rocky body in the inner solar system in 2004. Which body is it?

A. Europa
B. Mars
C. Titan
D. Venus

8. Which is NOT a satellite?

A. a flyby
B. a moon
C. an orbiter
D. space telescope

NASA/JPL/Cornell

Critical Thinking

9. **Contrast** waves in the electromagnetic spectrum with water waves in the ocean.

10. **Differentiate** If you wanted to study new stars forming inside a huge dust cloud, which wavelength might you use? Explain.

11. **Deduce** Why do Earth-based optical telescopes work best at night, while radio telescopes work all day and all night long?

12. **Analyze** Why it is more challenging to send space probes to the outer solar system than to the inner solar system?

13. **Create** a list of requirements that must be satisfied before humans can live on the Moon.

14. **Choose** a body in the solar system that you think would be a good place to look for life. Explain.

15. **Interpret Graphics** Copy the diagram of electromagnetic waves below, and label the relative positions of ultraviolet waves, X-rays, visible light, infrared waves, microwaves, gamma rays, and radio waves.

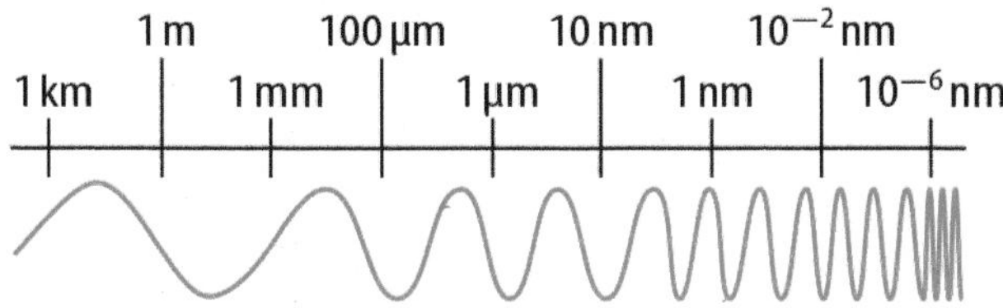

Writing in Science

16. **Write** a paragraph comparing colonizing North America and colonizing the Moon. Include a main idea, supporting details, and a concluding sentence.

REVIEW THE BIG IDEA

17. In what different ways do humans observe and explore space?

18. The photo below shows the *Hubble Space Telescope* orbiting Earth. What are advantages of space-based telescopes? What are disadvantages?

Math Skills

Math Practice

Use Scientific Notation

19. The distance from Saturn to the Sun averages 1,430,000,000 km. Express this distance in scientific notation.

20. The nearest star outside our solar system is Proxima Centauri, which is about 39,900,000,000,000 km from Earth. What is this distance in scientific notation?

21. The *Hubble Space Telescope* has taken pictures of an object that is 1,400,000,000,000,000,000,000 km away from Earth. Express this number in scientific notation.

Stocktrek/age fotostock

Standardized Test Practice

Record your answers on the answer sheet provided by your teacher or on a sheet of paper.

Multiple Choice

1 Which is NOT a good place to build a radio telescope?

A a location near a radio station

B a location that is remote

C a location with a large cleared area

D a location with dry air

2 Which has the power to overcome the force of Earth's gravity to be launched into space?

A a probe

B a rocket

C a satellite

D a telescope

Use the figure below to answer question 3.

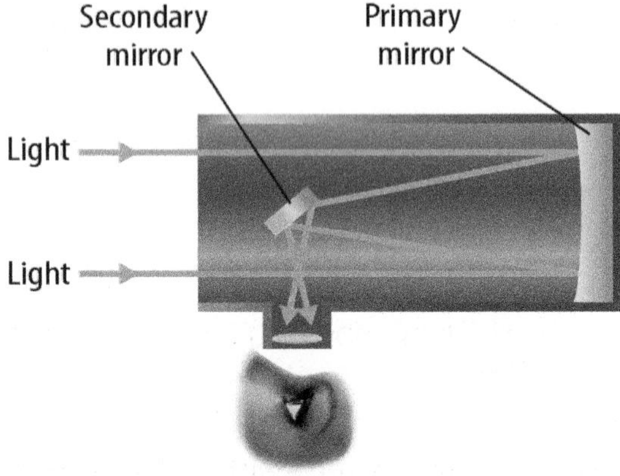

3 Which could increase the light-gathering power of the telescope in the figure?

A adaptive optics

B a larger eyepiece

C multiple small mirrors

D thicker lenses

4 Which lists the minimum resources needed for life-forms to survive on Earth?

A liquid water, an energy source, and sunshine

B liquid water, sunshine, and organic molecules

C organic molecules, an energy source, and liquid water

D organic molecules, an energy source, and sunshine

Use the table below to answer questions 5 and 6.

Planet	Average Distance from Sun (in millions of kilometers)
Earth	150
Mars	228
Saturn	1,434

5 It takes about 8.3 min for light to travel from the Sun to Earth. It takes about 40 min for light to travel from the Sun to Jupiter. How long would you expect it to take light to travel from the Sun to Saturn?

A 8.5 min

B 1.3 h

C 13.5 h

D 26.3 h

6 Which shows the distance between Saturn and the Sun expressed in scientific notation?

A 1.434×10^6 km

B 1.434×10^8 km

C 1.434×10^9 km

D 14.34×10^7 km

7 What is the advantage of using gravity assist for a mission to Saturn?

A The spacecraft can be made of a nonmagnetic material.

B The spacecraft can travel at the speed of light.

C The spacecraft needs less fuel.

D The spacecraft needs more weight.

8 Which was the first satellite to orbit Earth?

A *Apollo 1*

B *Explorer 1*

C *Mariner 1*

D *Sputnik 1*

Use the figure below to answer question 9.

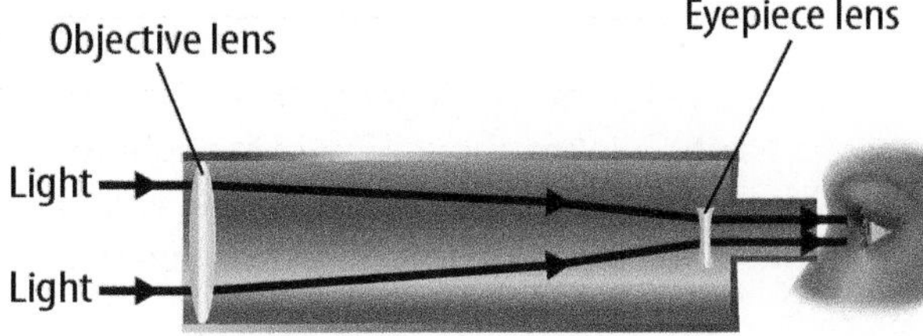

9 Which is true of the telescope above?

A The eyepiece and the objective lens are concave lenses.

B Light is bent as it goes through the objective lens.

C Light is reflected from the eyepiece lens to the objective lens.

D The eyepiece lens can be made of many smaller lenses.

Constructed Response

Use the figure below to answer questions 10 and 11.

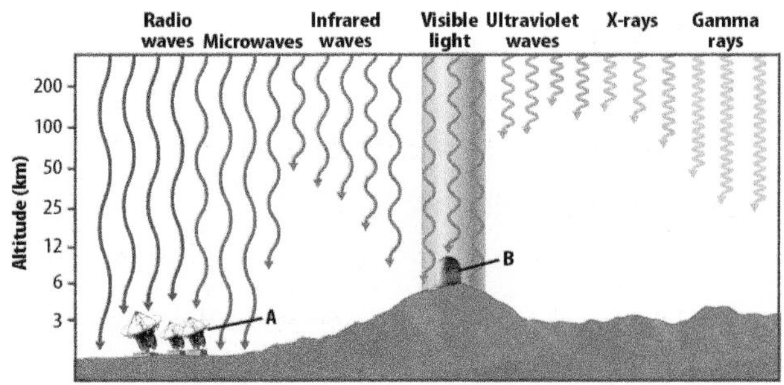

10 Identify the types of telescopes labeled *A* and *B* in the figure. Briefly explain what radiant energy each gathers and how each telescope works.

11 Use the information in the figure to explain why X-ray images can be obtained only using telescopes located above Earth's atmosphere.

12 How does studying radiant energy help scientists learn about the universe?

13 How might the properties of materials developed for use in space be useful on Earth? Give examples.

14 How does information gathered in space help scientists learn about Earth?

15 How does the *Kepler telescope* differ from other telescopes in space?

NEED EXTRA HELP?															
If You Missed Question...	1	2	3	4	5	6	7	8	9	10	11	12	13	14	15
Go to Lesson...	1	2	1	3	1	1	3	2	1	1	1	1	2	3	3

Chapter 6

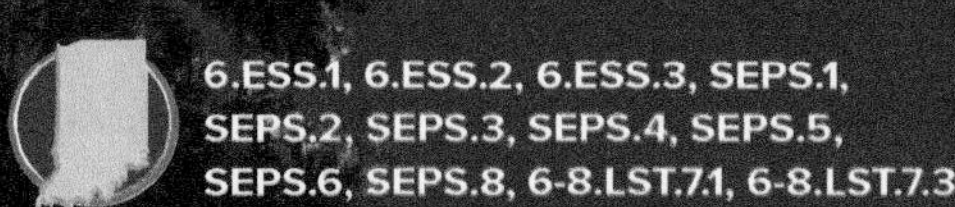

The Sun-Earth-Moon System

What natural phenomena do the motions of Earth and the Moon produce?

Sun Bites?

Look at this time-lapse photograph. The "bites" out of the Sun occurred during a solar eclipse. The Sun's appearance changed in a regular, predictable way as the Moon's shadow passed over a part of Earth.

- How does the Moon's movement change the Sun's appearance?
- What predictable changes does Earth's movement cause?
- What other natural phenomena do the motions of Earth and the Moon cause?

Get Ready to Read

What do you think?

Before you read, decide if you agree or disagree with each of these statements. As you read this chapter, see if you change your mind about any of the statements.

1. Earth's movement around the Sun causes sunrises and sunsets.
2. Earth has seasons because its distance from the Sun changes throughout the year.
3. The Moon was once a planet that orbited the Sun between Earth and Mars.
4. Earth's shadow causes the changing appearance of the Moon.
5. A solar eclipse happens when Earth moves between the Moon and the Sun.
6. The gravitational pull of the Moon and the Sun on Earth's oceans causes tides.

Your one-stop online resource
connectED.mcgraw-hill.com

LearnSmart®

Chapter Resources Files, Reading Essentials, Get Ready to Read, Quick Vocabulary

Animations, Videos, Interactive Tables

Self-checks, Quizzes, Tests

Project-Based Learning Activities

Lab Manuals, Safety Videos, Virtual Labs & Other Tools

Vocabulary, Multilingual eGlossary, Vocab eGames, Vocab eFlashcards

Personal Tutors

Lesson 1

Reading Guide

Key Concepts 

ESSENTIAL QUESTIONS

- How does Earth move?
- Why is Earth warmer at the equator and colder at the poles?
- Why do the seasons change as Earth moves around the Sun?

Vocabulary

orbit p. 190
revolution p. 190
rotation p. 191
rotation axis p. 191
solstice p. 195
equinox p. 195

Multilingual eGlossary

6.ESS.1, SEPS.1, SEPS.2, SEPS.3, SEPS.4, SEPS.5, SEPS.8

PBL Go to the resource tab in ConnectED to find the PBL *Gravity Glue*.

Earth's Motion

NASA Human Spaceflight Collection

Inquiry Floating in Space?

From the *International Space Station,* Earth might look like it is just floating, but it is actually traveling around the Sun at more than 100,000 km/h. What phenomena does Earth's motion cause?

Launch Lab

15 minutes

Does Earth's shape affect temperatures on Earth's surface?

Temperatures near Earth's poles are colder than temperatures near the equator. What causes these temperature differences?

1. Read and complete a lab safety form.
2. Inflate a **spherical balloon** and tie the balloon closed.
3. Using a **marker,** draw a line around the balloon to represent Earth's equator.
4. Using a **ruler**, place a lit **flashlight** about 8 cm from the balloon so the flashlight beam strikes the equator straight on.
5. Using the marker, trace around the light projected onto the balloon.
6. Have someone raise the flashlight vertically 5–8 cm without changing the direction that the flashlight is pointing. Do not change the position of the balloon. Trace around the light projected onto the balloon again.

Think About This

1. Compare and contrast the shapes you drew on the balloon.
2. At which location on thae balloon is the light more spread out? Explain your answer.
3. **Key Concept** Use your model to explain why Earth is warmer near the equator and colder near the poles.

Earth and the Sun

If you look outside at the ground, trees, and buildings, it does not seem like Earth is moving. Yet Earth is always in motion, spinning in space and traveling around the Sun. As Earth spins, day changes to night and back to day again. The seasons change as Earth travels around the Sun. Summer changes to winter because Earth's motion changes how energy from the Sun spreads out over Earth's surface.

The Sun

The nearest star to Earth is the Sun, which is shown in Figure 1. The Sun is approximately 150 million km from Earth. Compared to Earth, the Sun is enormous. The Sun's diameter is more than 100 times greater than Earth's diameter. The Sun's mass is more than 300,000 times greater than Earth's mass.

Deep inside the Sun, nuclei of atoms combine, releasing huge amounts of energy. This process is called nuclear fusion. The Sun releases so much energy from nuclear fusion that the temperature at its core is more than 15,000,000°C. Even at the Sun's surface, the temperature is about 5,500°C. A small part of the Sun's energy reaches Earth as light and thermal energy.

Figure 1 The Sun is a giant ball of hot gases that emits light and energy.

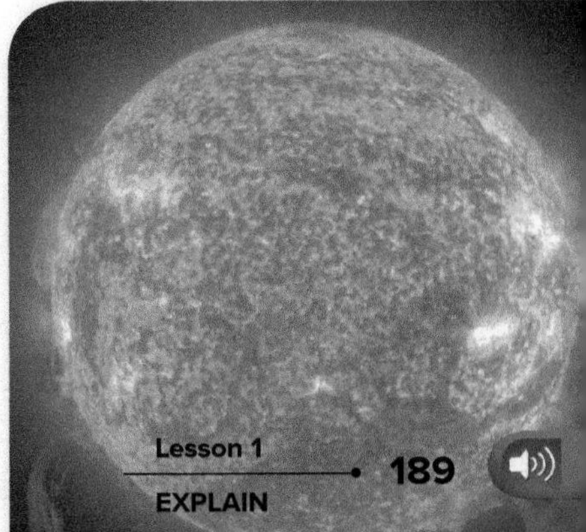

MiniLab 10 minutes

What keeps Earth in orbit?

Why does Earth move around the Sun and not fly off into space?

1. Read and complete a lab safety form.
2. Tie a piece of **strong thread** securely to a **plastic, slotted golf ball.**
3. Swing the ball in a horizontal circle above your head.

Analyze and Conclude

1. **Predict** what would happen if you let go of the thread.
2. **Key Concept** Which part of the experiment represents the force of gravity between Earth and the Sun?

Earth's Orbit

As shown in Figure 2, Earth moves around the Sun in a nearly circular path. *The path an object follows as it moves around another object is an* **orbit.** *The motion of one object around another object is called* **revolution.** Earth makes one complete revolution around the Sun every 365.24 days.

The Sun's Gravitational Pull

Why does Earth orbit the Sun? The answer is the law of universal gravitation. This law states that the pull of gravity between two objects depends on the masses of the objects and the distance between them. The more mass either object has, or the closer together they are, the stronger the gravitational pull.

The Sun's effect on Earth's motion is illustrated in Figure 2. Earth's motion around the Sun is like the motion of an object twirled on a string. The string pulls on the object and makes it move in a circle. If the string breaks, the object flies off in a straight line. In the same way, the pull of the Sun's gravity keeps Earth revolving around the Sun in a nearly circular orbit. If the gravity between Earth and the Sun were to somehow stop, Earth would fly off into space in a straight line.

Key Concept Check What produces Earth's revolution around the Sun?

Figure 2 Earth moves in a nearly circular orbit. The pull of the Sun's gravity on Earth causes Earth to revolve around the Sun.

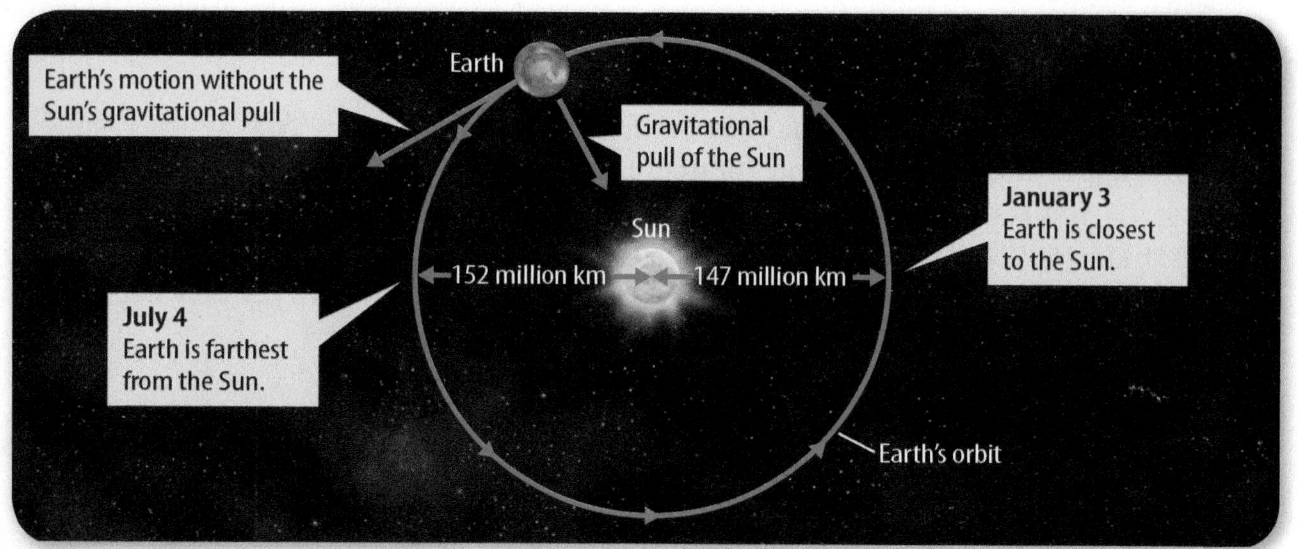

Earth's Rotation Axis

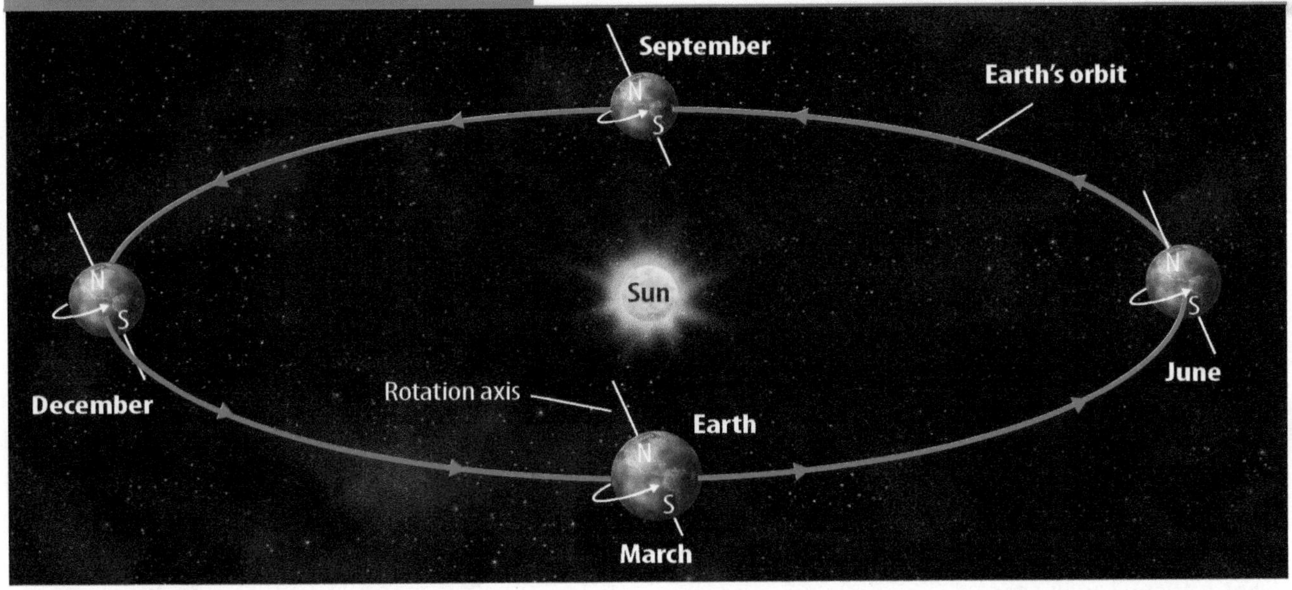

Figure 3 This diagram shows Earth's orbit, which is nearly circular, from an angle. Earth spins on its rotation axis as it revolves around the Sun. Earth's rotation axis always points in the same direction.

Visual Check Between which months is the north end of Earth's rotation axis away from the Sun?

Earth's Rotation

As Earth revolves around the Sun, it spins. *A spinning motion is called* **rotation.** Some spinning objects rotate on a rod or axle. Earth rotates on an imaginary line through its center. *The line on which an object rotates is the* **rotation axis.**

Suppose you could look down on Earth's North Pole and watch Earth rotate. You would see that Earth rotates on its rotation axis in a counterclockwise direction, from west to east. One complete rotation of Earth takes about 24 hours. This rotation helps produce Earth's cycle of day and night. It is daytime on the half of Earth facing toward the Sun and nighttime on the half of Earth facing away from the Sun.

The Sun's Apparent Motion Each day the Sun appears to move from east to west across the sky. It seems as if the Sun is moving around Earth. However, it is Earth's rotation that causes the Sun's apparent motion.

Earth rotates from west to east. As a result, the Sun appears to move from east to west across the sky. The stars and the Moon also seem to move from east to west across the sky due to Earth's west to east rotation.

To better understand this, imagine riding on a merry-go-round. As you and the ride move, people on the ground appear to be moving in the opposite direction. In the same way, as Earth rotates from west to east, the Sun appears to move from east to west.

Reading Check What causes the Sun's apparent motion across the sky?

The Tilt of Earth's Rotation Axis As shown in Figure 3, Earth's rotation axis is tilted. The tilt of Earth's rotation axis is always in the same direction by the same amount. This means that during half of Earth's orbit, the north end of the rotation axis is toward the Sun. During the other half of Earth's orbit, the north end of the rotation axis is away from the Sun.

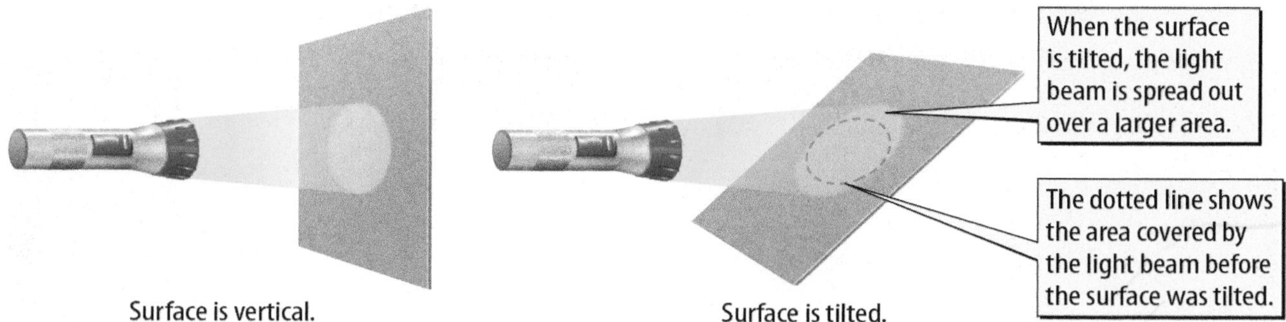

When the surface is tilted, the light beam is spread out over a larger area.
The dotted line shows the area covered by the light beam before the surface was tilted.
Surface is vertical.
Surface is tilted.

Figure 4 The light energy on a surface becomes more spread out as the surface becomes more tilted relative to the light beam.

Visual Check Is the light energy more spread out on the vertical or tilted surface?

Temperature and Latitude

As Earth orbits the Sun, only one half of Earth faces the Sun at a time. A beam of sunlight carries energy. The more sunlight that reaches a part of Earth's surface, the warmer that part becomes. Because Earth's surface is curved, different parts of Earth's surface receive different amounts of the Sun's energy.

Energy Received by a Tilted Surface

Suppose you shine a beam of light on a flat card, as shown in Figure 4. As you tilt the card relative to the direction of the light beam, light becomes more spread out on the card's surface. As a result, the energy that the light beam carries also spreads out more over the card's surface. An area on the surface within the light beam receives less energy when the surface is more tilted relative to the light beam.

The Tilt of Earth's Curved Surface

Instead of being flat like a card, Earth's surface is curved. Relative to the direction of a beam of sunlight, Earth's surface becomes more tilted as you move away from the equator. As shown in Figure 5, the energy in a beam of sunlight tends to become more spread out the farther you travel from the equator. This means that regions near the poles receive less energy than regions near the equator. This makes Earth colder at the poles and warmer at the equator.

Academic Vocabulary
equator
(noun) the imaginary line that divides Earth into its northern and southern hemispheres

Key Concept Check Why is Earth warmer at the equator and colder at the poles?

Animation

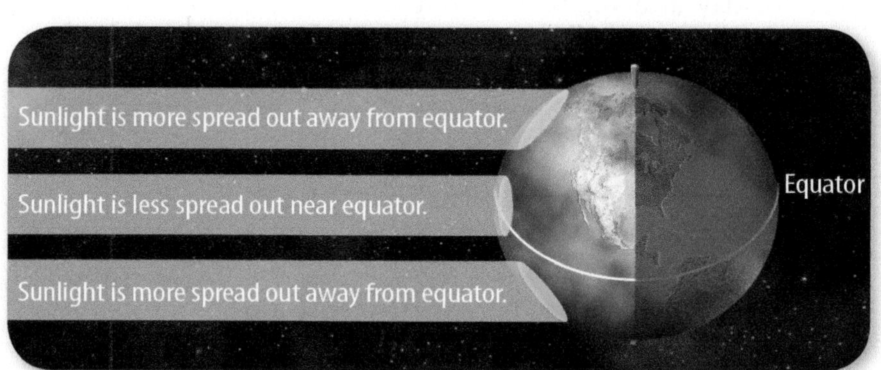

Sunlight is more spread out away from equator.
Sunlight is less spread out near equator.
Sunlight is more spread out away from equator.
Equator

Figure 5 Energy from the Sun becomes more spread out as you move away from the equator.

North end of rotation axis is away from the Sun.

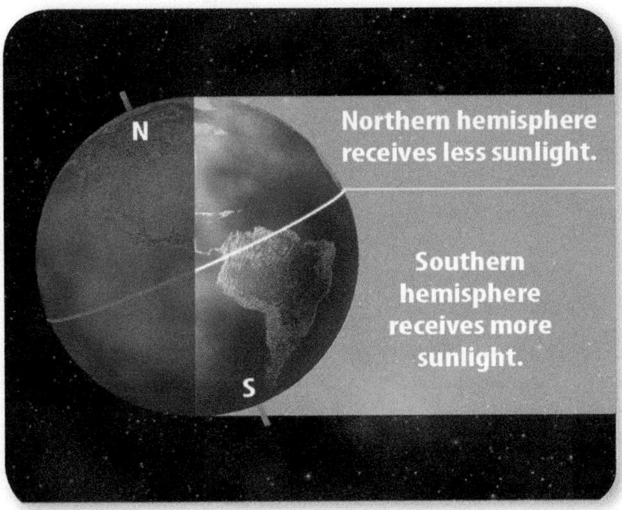
N
Northern hemisphere receives less sunlight.
Southern hemisphere receives more sunlight.
S

North end of rotation axis is toward the Sun.

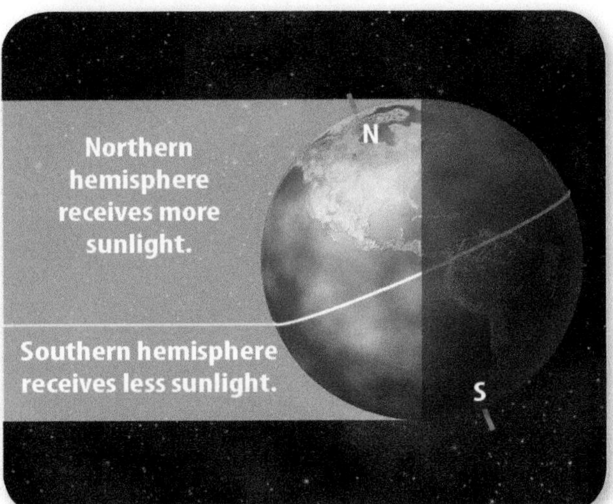
Northern hemisphere receives more sunlight.
N
Southern hemisphere receives less sunlight.
S

Figure 6 The northern hemisphere receives more sunlight in June, and the southern hemisphere receives more sunlight in December.

Seasons

You might think that summer happens when Earth is closest to the Sun, and winter happens when Earth is farthest from the Sun. However, seasonal changes do not depend on Earth's distance from the Sun. In fact, Earth is closest to the Sun in January! Instead, it is the tilt of Earth's rotation axis, combined with Earth's motion around the Sun, that causes the seasons to change.

Spring and Summer in the Northern Hemisphere

During one half of Earth's orbit, the north end of the rotation axis is toward the Sun. Then, the northern hemisphere receives more energy from the Sun than the southern hemisphere, as shown in **Figure 6**. Temperatures increase in the northern hemisphere and decrease in the southern hemisphere. Daylight hours last longer in the northern hemisphere, and nights last longer in the southern hemisphere. This is when spring and summer happen in the northern hemisphere, and fall and winter happen in the southern hemisphere.

Fall and Winter in the Northern Hemisphere

During the other half of Earth's orbit, the north end of the rotation axis is away from the Sun. Then, the northern hemisphere receives less solar energy than the southern hemisphere, as shown in **Figure 6**. Temperatures decrease in the northern hemisphere and increase in the southern hemisphere. This is when fall and winter happen in the northern hemisphere, and spring and summer happen in the southern hemisphere.

 **Key Concept Check** How does the tilt of Earth's rotation axis affect Earth's weather?

Math Skills 

Convert Units

During January, Earth is 147,000,000 km from the Sun, how far is Earth from the Sun in miles? To calculate the distance in miles, multiply the distance in km by the conversion factor

$$147{,}000{,}000 \text{ km} \times \frac{0.62 \text{ miles}}{1 \text{ km}}$$

$$= 91{,}100{,}000 \text{ miles}$$

Practice

During June, Earth is 152,000,000 km from the Sun, how far is Earth from the Sun in miles?

 Math Practice

 Personal Tutor

Earth's Seasonal Cycle

Personal Tutor

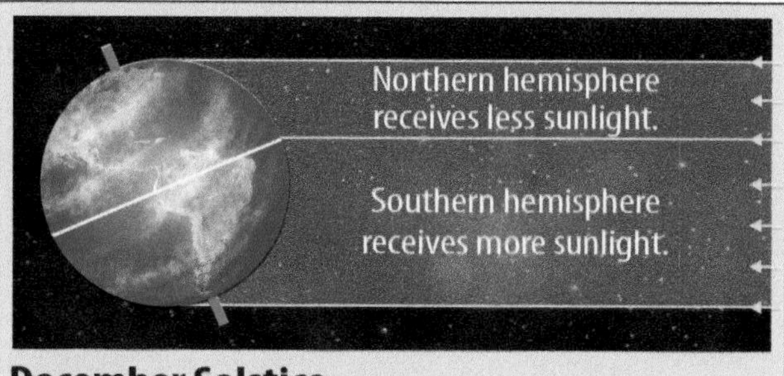

December Solstice
The December solstice is on December 21 or 22.
On this day
- the north end of Earth's rotation axis is away from the Sun;
- days in the northern hemisphere are shortest and nights are longest; winter begins;
- days in the southern hemisphere are longest and nights are shortest; summer begins.

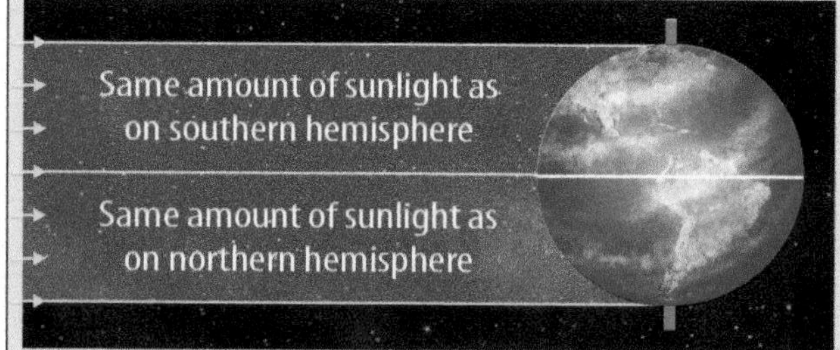

September Equinox
The September equinox is on September 22 or 23.
On this day
- the north end of Earth's rotation axis leans along Earth's orbit;
- there are about 12 hours of daylight and 12 hours of darkness everywhere on Earth;
- autumn begins in the northern hemisphere;
- spring begins in the southern hemisphere.

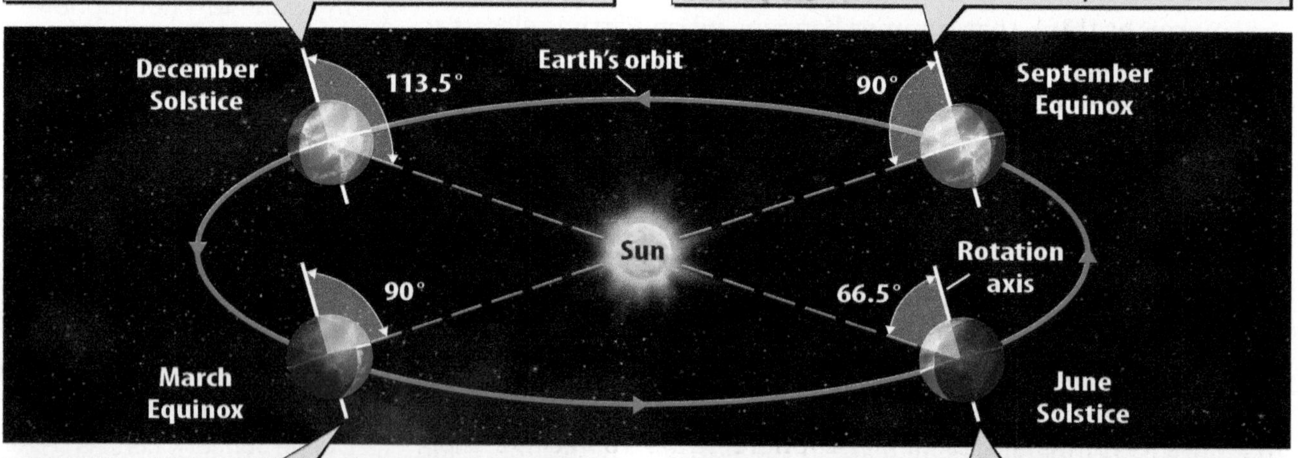

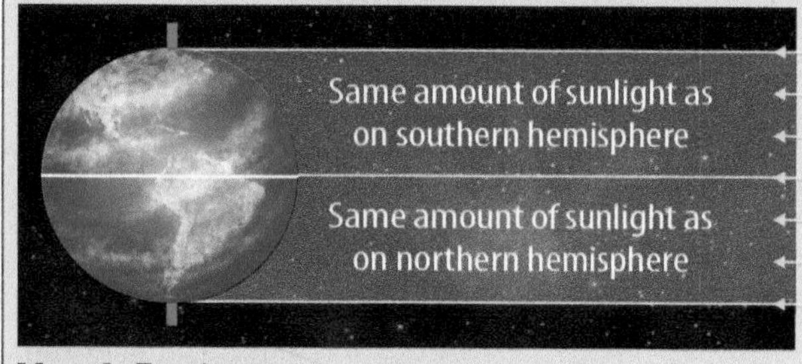

March Equinox
The March equinox is on March 20 or 21.
On this day
- the north end of Earth's rotation axis leans along Earth's orbit;
- there are about 12 hours of daylight and 12 hours of darkness everywhere on Earth;
- spring begins in the northern hemisphere;
- autumn begins in the southern hemisphere.

June Solstice
The June solstice is on June 20 or 21.
On this day
- the north end of Earth's rotation axis is toward the Sun;
- days in the northern hemisphere are longest and nights are shortest; summer begins;
- days in the southern hemisphere are shortest and nights are longest; winter begins.

Figure 7 The seasons change as Earth moves around the Sun. Earth's motion around the Sun causes Earth's tilted rotation axis to be leaning toward the Sun and away from the Sun.

Solstices, Equinoxes, and the Seasonal Cycle

Figure 7 shows that as Earth travels around the Sun, its rotation axis always points in the same direction in space. However, the amount that Earth's rotation axis is toward or away from the Sun changes. This causes the seasons to change in a yearly cycle.

There are four days each year when the direction of Earth's rotation axis is special relative to the Sun. *A* **solstice** *is a day when Earth's rotation axis is the most toward or away from the Sun. An* **equinox** *is a day when Earth's rotation axis is leaning along Earth's orbit, neither toward nor away from the Sun.*

March Equinox to June Solstice When the north end of the rotation axis gradually points more and more toward the Sun, the northern hemisphere gradually receives more solar energy. This is spring in the northern hemisphere.

June Solstice to September Equinox The north end of the rotation axis continues to point toward the Sun but does so less and less. The northern hemisphere starts to receive less solar energy. This is summer in the northern hemisphere.

September Equinox to December Solstice The north end of the rotation axis now points more and more away from the Sun. The northern hemisphere receives less and less solar energy. This is fall in the northern hemisphere.

December Solstice to March Equinox The north end of the rotation axis continues to point away from the Sun but does so less and less. The northern hemisphere starts to receive more solar energy. This is winter in the northern hemisphere.

Changes in the Sun's Apparent Path Across the Sky

Figure 8 shows how the Sun's apparent path through the sky changes from season to season in the northern hemisphere. The Sun's apparent path through the sky in the northern hemisphere is lowest on the December solstice and highest on the June solstice.

FOLDABLES®

Make a bound book with four full pages. Label the pages with the names of the solstices and equinoxes. Use each page to organize information about each season.

WORD ORIGIN

equinox
from Latin *equinoxium,* means "equality of night and day"

Figure 8 As the seasons change, the path of the Sun across the sky changes. In the northern hemisphere, the Sun's path is lowest on the December solstice and highest on the June solstice.

Visual Check When is the Sun highest in the sky in the northern hemisphere?

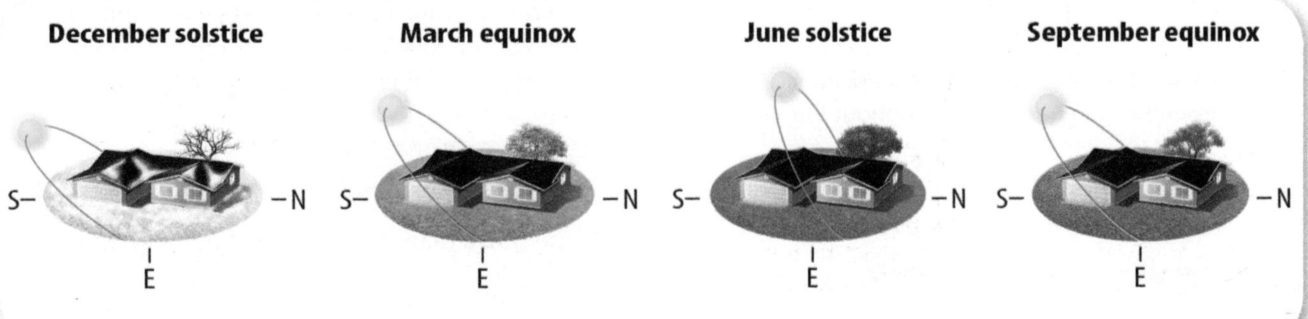

Lesson 1 Review

Visual Summary

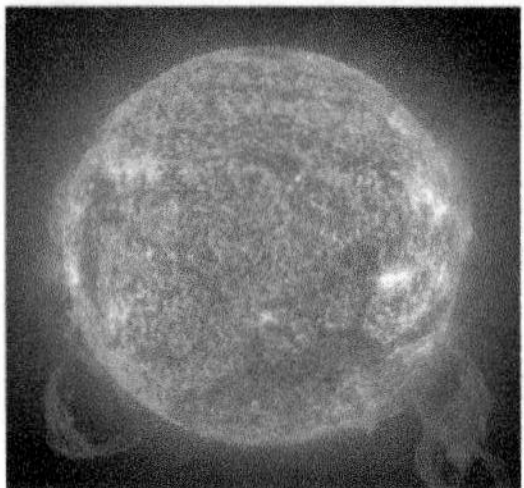

The gravitational pull of the Sun causes Earth to revolve around the Sun in a near-circular orbit.

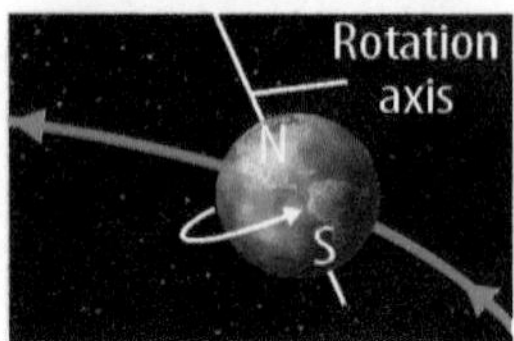

Earth's rotation axis is tilted and always points in the same direction in space.

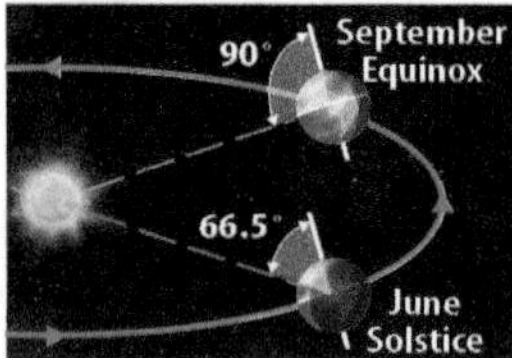

Equinoxes and solstices are days when the direction of Earth's rotation axis relative to the Sun is special.

FOLDABLES®

Use your lesson Foldable to review the lesson. Save your Foldable for the project at the end of the chapter.

What do you think NOW?

You first read the statements below at the beginning of the chapter.

1. Earth's movement around the Sun causes sunrises and sunsets.
2. Earth has seasons because its distance from the Sun changes throughout the year.

Did you change your mind about whether you agree or disagree with the statements? Rewrite any false statements to make them true.

Use Vocabulary

1. **Distinguish** between Earth's rotation and Earth's revolution.
2. The path Earth follows around the Sun is Earth's ________.
3. When a(n) ________ occurs, the northern hemisphere and the southern hemisphere receive the same amount of sunlight.

Understand Key Concepts 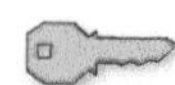

4. What is caused by the tilt of Earth's rotational axis?
   A. Earth's orbit
   B. Earth's seasons
   C. Earth's revolution
   D. Earth's rotation
5. **Contrast** the amount of sunlight received by an area near the equator and a same-sized area near the South Pole.
6. **Contrast** the Sun's gravitational pull on Earth when Earth is closest to the Sun and when Earth is farthest from the Sun.

Interpret Graphics

7. **Summarize** Copy and fill in the table below for the seasons in the northern hemisphere.

Season	Starts on Solstice or Equinox?	How Rotation Axis Leans
Summer		
Fall		
Winter		
Spring		

Critical Thinking

8. **Defend** The December solstice is often called the winter solstice. Do you think this is an appropriate label? Defend your answer.

Math Skills

 Math Practice

9. The Sun's diameter is about 1,390,000 km. What is the Sun's diameter in miles?

SOHO (ESA & NASA)

Skill Practice Draw Conclusions

25 minutes

How does Earth's tilted rotation axis affect the seasons?

The seasons change as Earth revolves around the Sun. How does Earth's tilted rotation axis change how sunlight spreads out over different parts of Earth's surface?

Materials

large foam ball

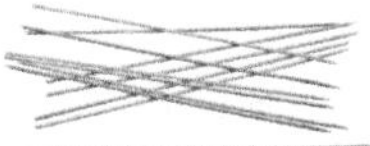

wooden skewer

foam cup

masking tape

flashlight

marker

Safety

Learn It

Using a flashlight as the Sun and a foam ball as Earth, you can model how solar energy spreads out over Earth's surface at different times during the year. This will help you **draw conclusions** about Earth's seasons.

Try It

1. Read and complete a lab safety form.
2. Insert a wooden skewer through the center of a foam ball. Draw a line on the ball to represent Earth's equator. Insert one end of the skewer into an upside-down foam cup so the skewer tilts.
3. Prop a flashlight on a stack of books about 0.5 m from the ball. Turn on the flashlight and position the ball so the skewer points toward the flashlight, representing the June solstice.
4. In your Science Journal, draw how the ball's surface is tilted relative to the light beam.

2

3

5. Under your diagram, state whether the northern (upper) or southern (lower) hemisphere receives more light energy.
6. With the skewer always pointing in the same direction, move the ball around the flashlight. Turn the flashlight to keep the light on the ball. At the three positions corresponding to the equinoxes and other solstice, make drawings like those in step 4 and statements like those in step 5.

Apply It

7. How did the tilt of the surfaces change relative to the light beam as the ball circled the flashlight?
8. How did the amount of light energy on each hemisphere change as the ball moved around the flashlight?
9. **Key Concept** Draw conclusions about how Earth's tilt affects the seasons.

Lesson 2

Reading Guide

Key Concepts 

ESSENTIAL QUESTIONS

- How does the Moon move around Earth?
- Why does the Moon's appearance change?

Vocabulary

maria p. 200

phase p. 202

waxing phase p. 202

waning phase p. 202

 Multilingual eGlossary

6.ESS.1, 6.ESS.2, 6.ESS.3, SEPS.2, 6-8.LST.7.3

Earth's Moon

Inquiry Two Planets?

The smaller body is Earth's Moon, not a planet. Just as Earth moves around the Sun, the Moon moves around Earth. The Moon's motion around Earth causes what kinds of changes to occur?

Launch Lab

15 minutes

Why does the Moon appear to change shape?

The Sun is always shining on Earth and the Moon. However, the Moon's shape seems to change from night to night and day to day. What could cause the Moon's appearance to change?

1. Read and complete a lab safety form.
2. Place a **ball** on a level surface.
3. Position a **flashlight** so that the light beam shines fully on one side of the ball. Stand behind the flashlight.
4. Make a drawing of the ball's appearance in your Science Journal.
5. Stand behind the ball, facing the flashlight, and repeat step 4.
6. Stand to the left of the ball and repeat step 4.

Think About This

1. What caused the ball's appearance to change?
2. **Key Concept** What do you think produces the Moon's changing appearance in the sky?

Seeing the Moon

Imagine what people thousands of years ago thought when they looked up at the Moon. They might have wondered why the Moon shines and why it seems to change shape. They probably would have been surprised to learn that the Moon does not emit light at all. Unlike the Sun, the Moon is a solid object that does not emit its own light. You only see the Moon because light from the Sun reflects off the Moon and into your eyes. Some facts about the Moon, such as its mass, size, and distance from Earth, are shown in Table 1.

Table 1 Moon Data

Mass	Diameter	Average distance from Earth	Time for one rotation	Time for one revolution
1.2% of Earth's mass	27% of Earth's diameter	384,000 km	27.3 days	27.3 days

FOLDABLES®

Use two sheets of paper to make a bound book. Use it to organize information about the lunar cycle. Each page of your book should represent one week of the lunar cycle.

Figure 9 The Moon probably formed when a large object collided with Earth 4.5 billion years ago. Material ejected from the collision eventually clumped together and became the Moon.

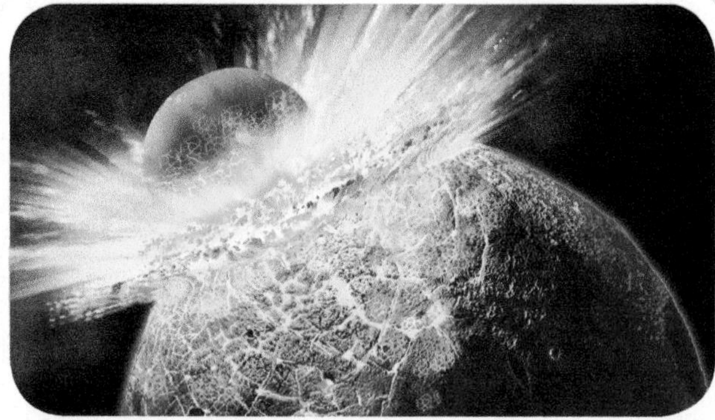

An object the size of Mars crashes into the semi-molten Earth about 4.5 billion years ago.

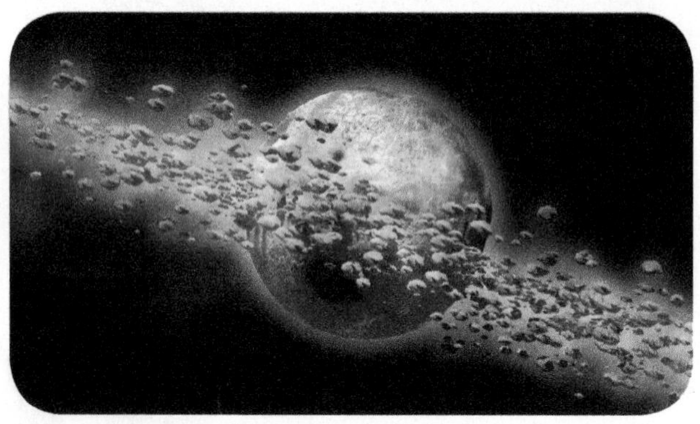

The impact ejects vaporized rock into space. As the rock cools, it forms a ring of particles around Earth.

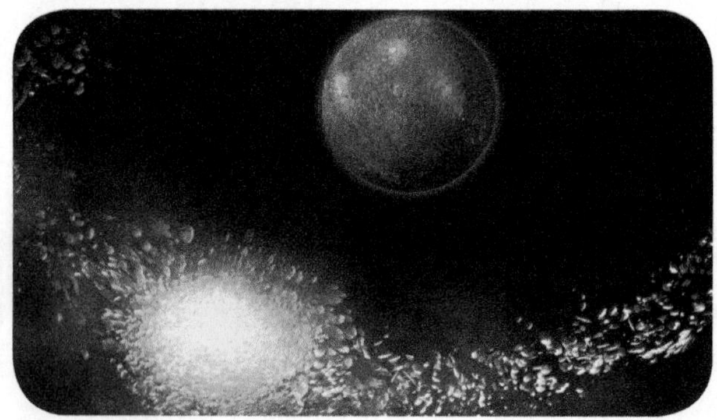

The particles gradually clump together and form the Moon.

The Moon's Formation

The most widely accepted idea for the Moon's formation is the giant impact hypothesis, shown in Figure 9. According to this hypothesis, shortly after Earth formed about 4.6 billion years ago, an object about the size of the planet Mars collided with Earth. The impact ejected vaporized rock that formed a ring around Earth. Eventually, the material in the ring cooled, clumped together, and formed the Moon.

The Moon's Surface

The surface of the Moon was shaped early in its history. Examples of common features on the Moon's surface are shown in Figure 10.

Craters The Moon's craters were formed when objects from space crashed into the Moon. Light-colored streaks called rays extend outward from some craters.

Most of the impacts that formed the Moon's craters occurred more than 3.5 billion years ago, long before dinosaurs lived on Earth. Earth was also heavily bombarded by objects from space during this time. However, on Earth, wind, liquid water, and plate tectonics erased the craters. The Moon has no atmosphere, liquid water, or plate tectonics, so craters formed billions of years ago on the Moon have hardly changed.

Maria *The large, dark, flat areas on the Moon are called* **maria** (MAR ee uh). The maria formed after most impacts on the Moon's surface had stopped. Maria formed when lava flowed up through the Moon's crust and solidified. The lava covered many of the Moon's craters and other features. When this lava solidified, it was dark and flat.

Reading Check How were maria produced?

Highlands The light-colored highlands are too high for the lava that formed the maria to reach. The highlands are older than the maria and are covered with craters.

WORD ORIGIN

maria
from Latin *mare*, means "sea"

The Moon's Surface Features

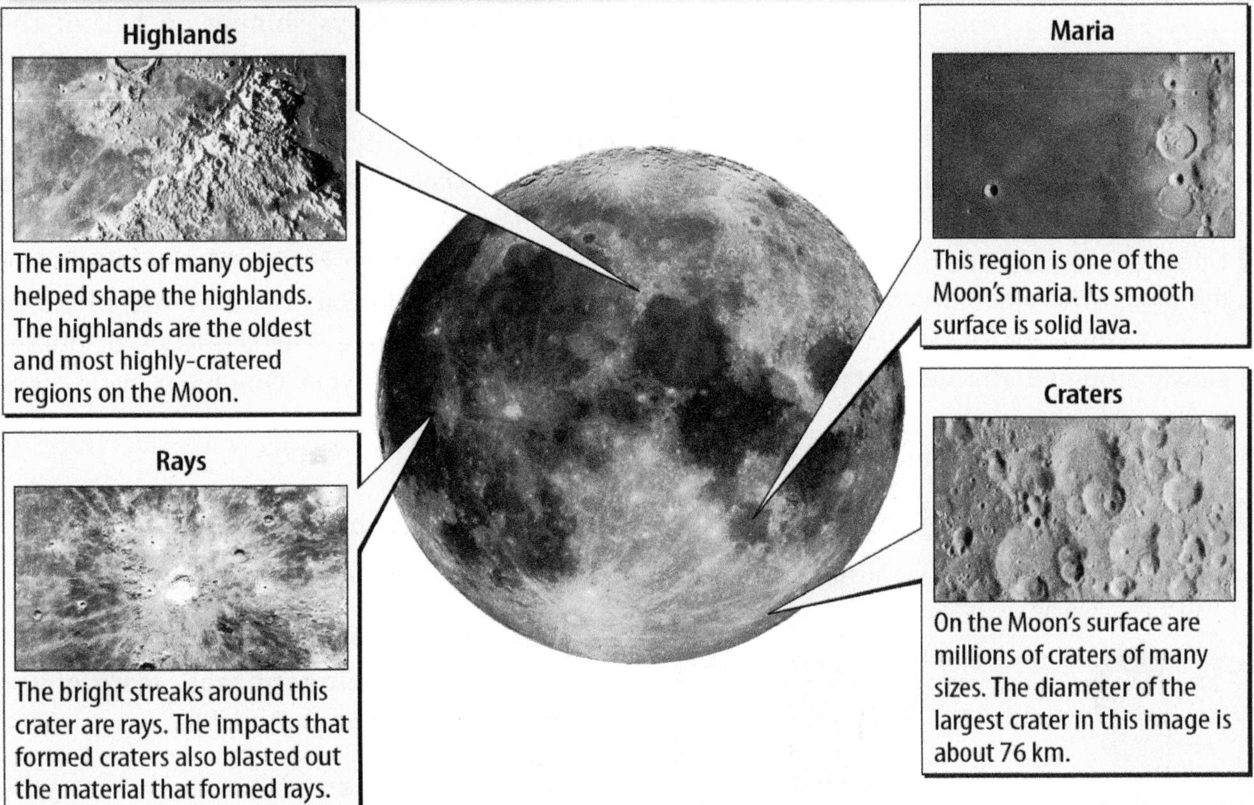

Highlands
The impacts of many objects helped shape the highlands. The highlands are the oldest and most highly-cratered regions on the Moon.
Rays
The bright streaks around this crater are rays. The impacts that formed craters also blasted out the material that formed rays.
Maria
This region is one of the Moon's maria. Its smooth surface is solid lava.
Craters
On the Moon's surface are millions of craters of many sizes. The diameter of the largest crater in this image is about 76 km.

▲ **Figure 10** The Moon's surface features include craters, rays, maria, and highlands.

The Moon's Motion

While Earth is revolving around the Sun, the Moon is revolving around Earth. The gravitational pull of Earth on the Moon causes the Moon to move in an orbit around Earth. The Moon makes one revolution around Earth every 27.3 days.

 **Key Concept Check** What produces the Moon's revolution around Earth?

The Moon also rotates as it revolves around Earth. One complete rotation of the Moon also takes 27.3 days. This means the Moon makes one rotation in the same amount of time that it makes one revolution around Earth. **Figure 11** shows that, because the Moon makes one rotation for each revolution of Earth, the same side of the Moon always faces Earth. This side of the Moon is called the near side. The side of the Moon that cannot be seen from Earth is called the far side of the Moon.

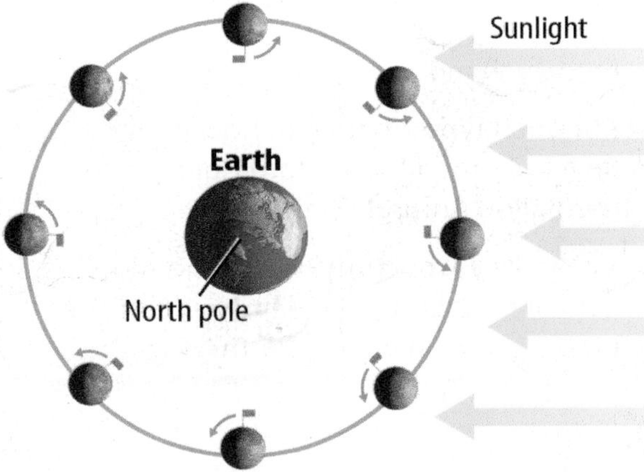

▲ **Figure 11** The Moon rotates once on its axis and revolves around Earth in the same amount of time. As a result, the same side of the Moon always faces Earth.

MiniLab 10 minutes

How can the Moon be rotating if the same side of the Moon is always facing Earth?

The Moon revolves around Earth. Does the Moon also rotate as it revolves around Earth?

1. Choose a partner. One person represents the Moon. The other represents Earth.
2. While Earth is still, the Moon moves slowly around Earth, always facing the same wall.
3. Next, the Moon moves around Earth always facing Earth.

Analyze and Conclude

1. For which motion was the Moon rotating?
2. For each type of motion, how many times did the Moon rotate during one revolution around Earth?
3. **Key Concept** How is the Moon actually rotating if the same side of the Moon is always facing Earth?

SCIENCE USE V. COMMON USE

phase

Science Use how the Moon or a planet is lit as seen from Earth

Common Use a part of something or a stage of development

Phases of the Moon

The Sun is always shining on half of the Moon, just as the Sun is always shining on half of Earth. However, as the Moon moves around Earth, usually only part of the Moon's near side is lit. *The portion of the Moon or a planet reflecting light as seen from Earth is called a* **phase.** As shown in Figure 12, the motion of the Moon around Earth causes the phase of the Moon to change. The sequence of phases is called the lunar cycle. One lunar cycle takes 29.5 days or slightly more than four weeks to complete.

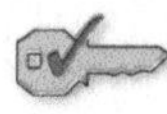

Key Concept Check What produces the phases of the Moon?

Waxing Phases

During the **waxing phases,** *more of the Moon's near side is lit each night.*

Week 1—First Quarter As the lunar cycle begins, a sliver of light can be seen on the Moon's western edge. Gradually the lit part becomes larger. By the end of the first week, the Moon is at its first quarter phase. In this phase, the Moon's entire western half is lit.

Week 2—Full Moon During the second week, more and more of the near side becomes lit. When the Moon's near side is completely lit, it is at the full moon phase.

Waning Phases

During the **waning phases,** *less of the Moon's near side is lit each night.* As seen from Earth, the lit part is now on the Moon's eastern side.

Week 3—Third Quarter During this week, the lit part of the Moon becomes smaller until only the eastern half of the Moon is lit. This is the third quarter phase.

Week 4—New Moon During this week, less and less of the near side is lit. When the Moon's near side is completely dark, it is at the new moon phase.

The Lunar Cycle

Animation

Figure 12 As the Moon revolves around Earth, the part of the Moon's near side that is lit changes. The figure below shows how the Moon looks at different places in its orbit.

Full moon

Waning gibbous

Waxing gibbous

Moon's orbit

You don't see the shadowed part.

You see the sunlit part.

Third quarter

First quarter

Earth

The new moon phase is not visible from Earth.

Waning crescent

Waxing crescent

Sunlight

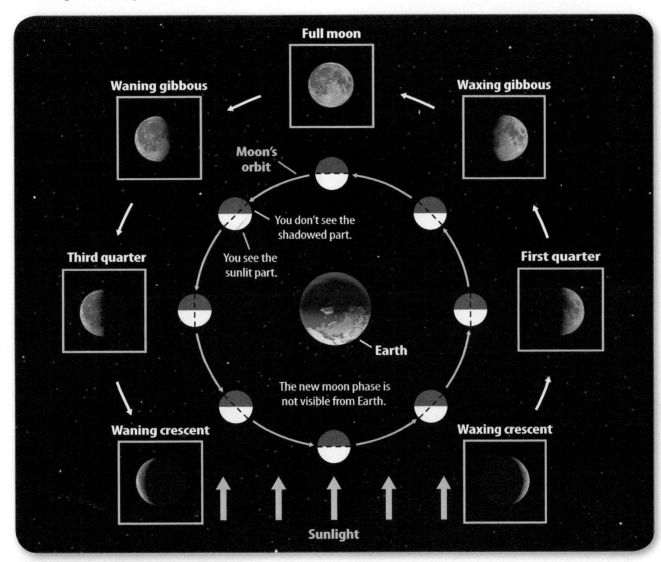

The Moon at Midnight

The Moon's motion around Earth causes the Moon to rise, on average, about 50 minutes later each day. The figure below shows how the Moon looks at midnight during three phases of the lunar cycle.

First quarter | **Full moon** | **Third quarter**

At midnight, the first quarter moon is setting. It rises during the day at about noon.

The full moon is highest in the sky at about midnight. It rises at sunset and sets at sunrise.

The third quarter moon rises at about midnight, about six hours later than the full moon rises.

Eckhard Slawik/Science Source

Lesson 2 Review

Visual Summary

According to the giant impact hypothesis, a large object collided with Earth about 4.5 billion years ago to form the Moon.

Features like maria, craters, and highlands formed on the Moon's surface early in its history.

The Moon's phases change in a regular pattern during the Moon's lunar cycle.

Use your lesson Foldable to review the lesson. Save your Foldable for the project at the end of the chapter.

What do you think NOW?

You first read the statements below at the beginning of the chapter.

3. The Moon was once a planet that orbited the Sun between Earth and Mars.

4. Earth's shadow causes the changing appearance of the Moon.

Did you change your mind about whether you agree or disagree with the statements? Rewrite any false statements to make them true.

Use Vocabulary

1. The lit part of the Moon as viewed from Earth is a(n) ________.
2. For the first half of the lunar cycle, the lit part of the Moon's near side is ________.
3. For the second half of the lunar cycle, the lit part of the Moon's near side is ________.

Understand Key Concepts

4. Which phase occurs when the Moon is between the Sun and Earth?
   A. first quarter **C.** new moon
   B. full moon **D.** third quarter
5. **Reason** Why does the Moon have phases?

Interpret Graphics

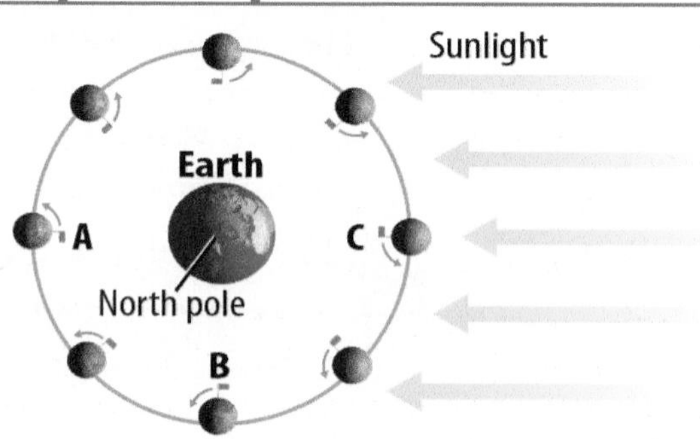

6. **Draw** how the Moon looks from Earth when it is at positions A, B, and C in the diagram above.
7. **Organize Information** Copy and fill in the table below with details about the lunar surface.

Crater	
Ray	
Maria	
Highland	

Critical Thinking

8. **Reflect** Imagine the Moon rotates twice in the same amount of time the Moon orbits Earth once. Would you be able to see the Moon's far side from Earth?

(t)Lunar and Planetary Institute; (b)Eckhard Slawik/Science Source

SCIENCE & SOCIETY

Return to the Moon

Exploring Earth's Moon is a step toward exploring other planets and building outposts in space.

The United States undertook a series of human spaceflight missions from 1961–1975 called the Apollo program. The goal of the program was to land humans on the Moon and bring them safely back to Earth. Six of the missions reached this goal. The Apollo program was a huge success, but it was just the beginning.

NASA began another space program that had a goal to return astronauts to the Moon to live and work. However, before that could happen, scientists needed to know more about conditions on the Moon and what materials are available there.

Collecting data was the first step. In 2009, NASA launched the *Lunar Reconnaissance Orbiter (LRO)* spacecraft. The *LRO* spent a year orbiting the Moon's two poles. It collected detailed data that scientists can use to make maps of the Moon's features and resources, such as deep craters that formed on the Moon when comets and asteroids slammed into it billions of years ago. Some scientists predicted that these deep craters contain frozen water.

One of the instruments launched with the *LRO* was the *Lunar Crater Observation and Sensing Satellite (LCROSS). LCROSS* observations confirmed the scientists' predictions that water exists on the Moon. A rocket launched from *LCROSS* impacted the Cabeus crater near the Moon's south pole. The material that was ejected after the rocket's impact included water.

NASA's goal of returning astronauts to the Moon was delayed, and their missions now focus on exploring Mars instead. But the discoveries made on the Moon will help scientists develop future missions that could take humans farther into the solar system.

NASA

Apollo SPACE PROGRAM

The Apollo Space Program included 17 missions. Here are some milestones:

January 27 1967

Apollo 1 Fire killed all three astronauts on board during a launch simulation for the first piloted flight to the Moon.

December 21–27 1968

Apollo 8 First manned spacecraft orbits the Moon.

July 16–24 1969

Apollo 11 First humans, Neil Armstrong and Buzz Aldrin, walk on the Moon.

July 1971

Apollo 15 Astronauts drive the first rover on the Moon.

December 7–19 1972

Apollo 17 The first phase of human exploration of the Moon ended with this last lunar landing mission.

It's Your Turn

BRAINSTORM As a group, brainstorm the different occupations that would be needed to successfully operate a base on the Moon or another planet. Discuss the tasks that a person would perform in each occupation.

Lesson 3

Reading Guide

Key Concepts

ESSENTIAL QUESTIONS

- What is a solar eclipse?
- What is a lunar eclipse?
- How do the Moon and the Sun affect Earth's oceans?

Vocabulary

umbra p. 207

penumbra p. 207

solar eclipse p. 208

lunar eclipse p. 210

tide p. 211

Multilingual eGlossary

BrainPOP®
Science Video

6.ESS.1, 6.ESS.2, SEPS.1, SEPS.2, SEPS.3, , SEPS.4, SEPS.5, SEPS.6, SEPS.8, 6-8.LST.7.1, 6-8.LST.7.3

Go to the resource tab in ConnectED to find the PBL *Patterns in the Sky.*

Eclipses and Tides

Inquiry What is this dark spot?

A NASA satellite took this photo as it orbited around Earth. An eclipse caused the shadow that you see. Do you know what kind of eclipse?

Jacques Descloitres, MODIS Rapid Response Team at NASA GSFC

Launch Lab

10 minutes

How do shadows change?

You can see a shadow when an object blocks a light source. What happens to an object's shadow when the object moves?

1. Read and complete a lab safety form.
2. Select an **object** provided by your teacher.
3. Shine a **flashlight** on the object, projecting its shadow on the wall.
4. While holding the flashlight in the same position, move the object closer to the wall—away from the light. Then, move the object toward the light. Record your observations in your Science Journal.

Think About This

1. Compare and contrast the shadows created in each situation. Did the shadows have dark parts and light parts? Did these parts change?
2. **Key Concept** Imagine you look at the flashlight from behind your object, looking from the darkest and lightest parts of the object's shadow. How much of the flashlight could you see from each location?

Shadows—the Umbra and the Penumbra

A shadow results when one object blocks the light that another object emits or reflects. When a tree blocks light from the Sun, it casts a shadow. If you want to stand in the shadow of a tree, the tree must be in a line between you and the Sun.

If you go outside on a sunny day and look carefully at a shadow on the ground, you might notice that the edges of the shadow are not as dark as the rest of the shadow. Light from the Sun and other wide sources casts shadows with two distinct parts, as shown in Figure 13. *The* **umbra** *is the central, darker part of a shadow where light is totally blocked. The* **penumbra** *is the lighter part of a shadow where light is partially blocked.* If you stood within an object's penumbra, you would be able to see only part of the light source. If you stood within an object's umbra, you would not see the light source at all.

Word Origin

penumbra
from Latin *paene,* means "almost"; and *umbra,* means "shade, shadow"

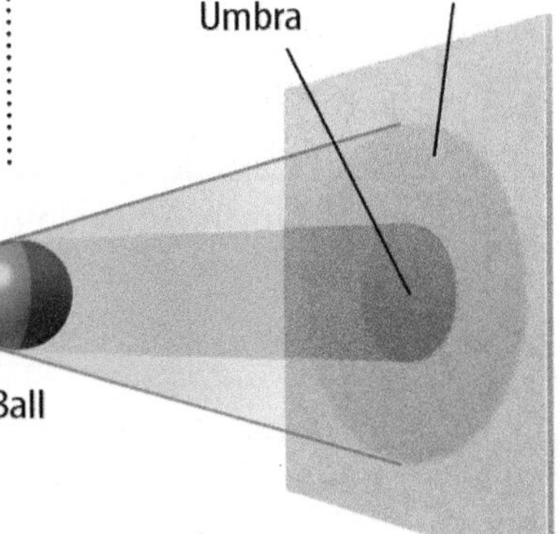

Figure 13 The shadow that a wide light source produces has two parts—the umbra and the penumbra. The light source cannot be seen from within the umbra. The light source can be partially seen from within the penumbra.

MiniLab 10 minutes

What does the Moon's shadow look like?

Like every shadow cast by a wide light source, the Moon's shadow has two parts.

1. Read and complete a lab safety form.
2. Working with a partner, use a **pencil** to connect two **foam balls**. One ball should be one-fourth the size of the other.
3. While one person holds the foam balls, the other should stand 1 m away and shine a **light** on the balls. The foam balls and light should be in a direct line, with the smallest foam ball closest to the light.
4. Sketch and describe your observations in your Science Journal.

Analyze and Conclude

1. **Key Concept** Explain the relationship between the two types of shadows and solar eclipses.

Solar Eclipses

As the Sun shines on the Moon, the Moon casts a shadow that extends out into space. Sometimes the Moon passes between Earth and the Sun. This can only happen during the new moon phase. When Earth, the Moon, and the Sun are lined up, the Moon casts a shadow on Earth's surface, as shown in Figure 14. You can see the Moon's shadow in the photo at the beginning of this lesson. *When the Moon's shadow appears on Earth's surface, a* ***solar eclipse*** *is occurring.*

Key Concept Check Why does a solar eclipse occur only during a new moon?

As Earth rotates, the Moon's shadow moves along Earth's surface, as shown in Figure 14. The type of eclipse you see depends on whether you are in the path of the umbra or the penumbra. If you are outside the umbra and penumbra, you cannot see a solar eclipse at all.

Total Solar Eclipses

You can only see a total solar eclipse from within the Moon's umbra. During a total solar eclipse, the Moon appears to cover the Sun completely, as shown in Figure 15 on the next page. Then, the sky becomes dark enough that you can see stars. A total solar eclipse lasts no longer than about 7 minutes.

Solar Eclipse

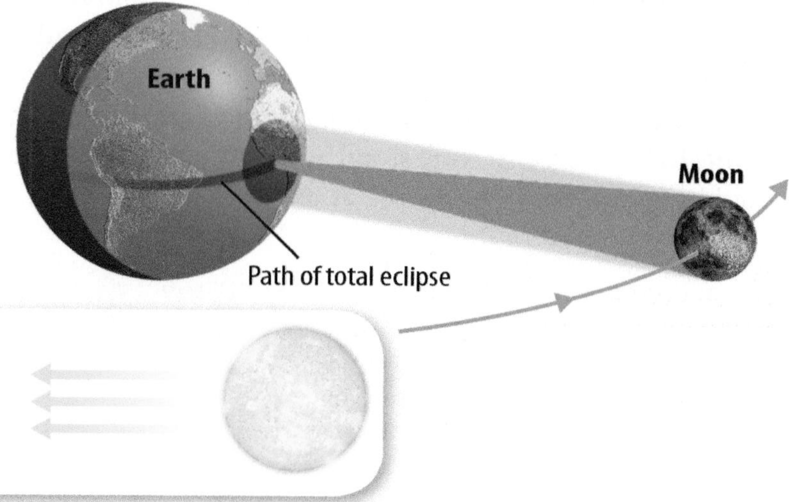

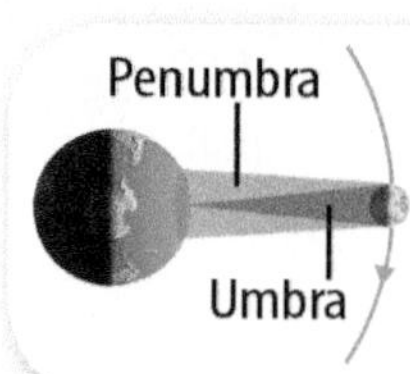

Figure 14 A solar eclipse occurs only when the Moon moves directly between Earth and the Sun. The Moon's shadow moves across Earth's surface.

Visual Check Why would a person in North America not see the solar eclipse shown here?

Hutchings Photography/Digital Light Source

The Sun's Changing Appearance During a Total Solar Eclipse

The Motion of the Moon in the Sky During a Total Solar Eclipse

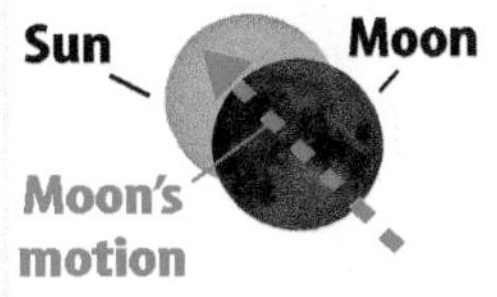
Sun
Moon
Moon's motion

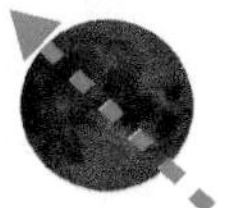
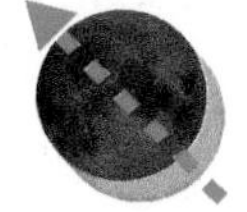

Figure 15 This sequence shows an example of how the Sun's appearance can change during a total solar eclipse.

Partial Solar Eclipses

You can only see a total solar eclipse from within the Moon's umbra, but you can see a partial solar eclipse from within the Moon's much larger penumbra. The stages of a partial solar eclipse are similar to the stages of a total solar eclipse, except that the Moon never completely covers the Sun.

Why don't solar eclipses occur every month?

Solar eclipses only can occur during a new moon, when Earth and the Sun are on opposite sides of the Moon. However, solar eclipses do not occur during every new moon phase. Figure 16 shows why. The Moon's orbit is tilted slightly compared to Earth's orbit. As a result, during most new moons, Earth is either above or below the Moon's shadow. However, every so often the Moon is in a line between the Sun and Earth. Then the Moon's shadow passes over Earth and a solar eclipse occurs.

Animation

Figure 16 A solar eclipse occurs only when the Moon crosses Earth's orbit and is in a direct line between Earth and the Sun.

The Moon's Tilted Orbit

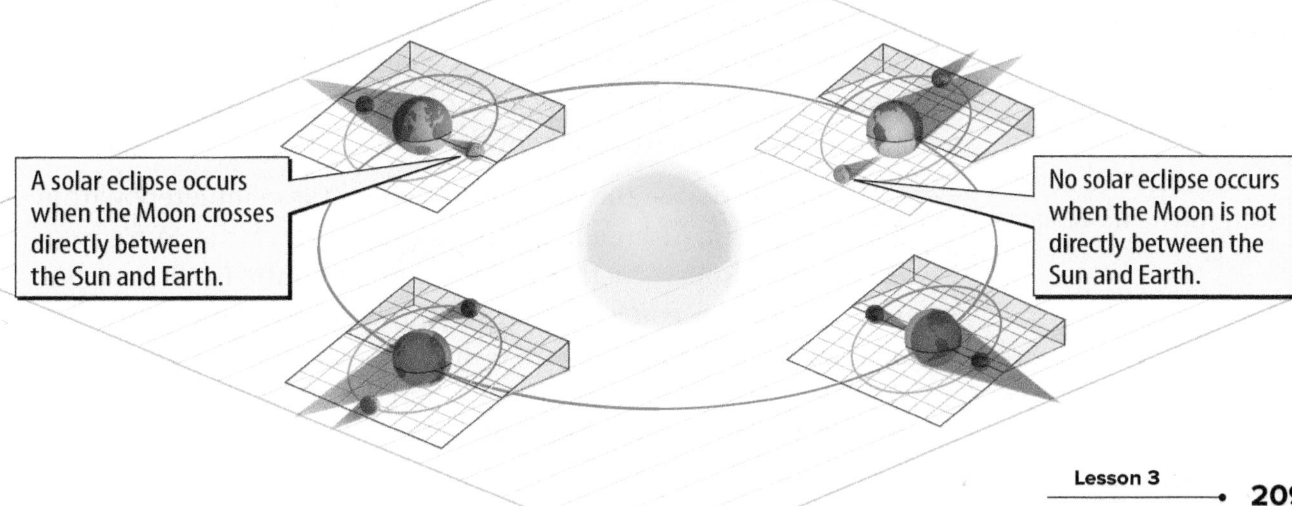
A solar eclipse occurs when the Moon crosses directly between the Sun and Earth.
No solar eclipse occurs when the Moon is not directly between the Sun and Earth.

Lunar Eclipse

Figure 17 A lunar eclipse occurs when the Moon moves through Earth's shadow.

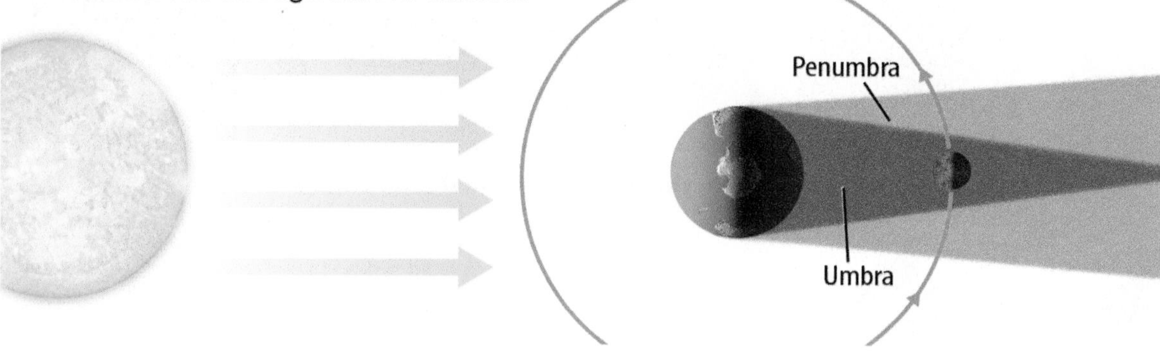

Visual Check Why would more people be able to see a lunar eclipse than a solar eclipse?

Lunar Eclipses

Just like the Moon, Earth casts a shadow into space. As the Moon revolves around Earth, it sometimes moves into Earth's shadow, as shown in Figure 17. *A* **lunar eclipse** *occurs when the Moon moves into Earth's shadow.* Then Earth is in a line between the Sun and the Moon. This means that a lunar eclipse can occur only during the full moon phase.

Like the Moon's shadow, Earth's shadow has an umbra and a penumbra. Different types of lunar eclipses occur depending on which part of Earth's shadow the Moon moves through. Unlike solar eclipses, you can see any lunar eclipse from any location on the side of Earth facing the Moon.

Key Concept Check When can a lunar eclipse occur?

FOLDABLES®

Make a two-tab book from a sheet of notebook paper. Label the tabs *Solar Eclipse* and *Lunar Eclipse*. Use it to organize your notes on eclipses.

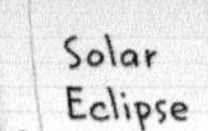

Total Lunar Eclipses

When the entire Moon moves through Earth's umbra, a total lunar eclipse occurs. Figure 18 on the next page shows how the Moon's appearance changes during a total lunar eclipse. The Moon's appearance changes as it gradually moves into Earth's penumbra, then into Earth's umbra, back into Earth's penumbra, and then out of Earth's shadow entirely.

You can still see the Moon even when it is completely within Earth's umbra. Although Earth blocks most of the Sun's rays, Earth's atmosphere deflects some sunlight into Earth's umbra. This is also why you can often see the unlit portion of the Moon on a clear night. Astronomers often call this Earthshine. This reflected light has a reddish color and gives the Moon a reddish tint during a total lunar eclipse.

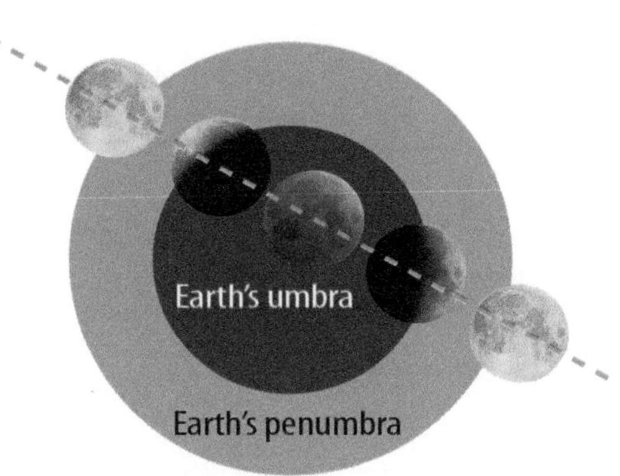

Figure 18 During a total lunar eclipse, the entire Moon passes through Earth's umbra. The Moon gradually darkens until a dark shadow covers it completely.

Visual Check How would a total lunar eclipse look different from a total solar eclipse?

Partial Lunar Eclipses

When only part of the Moon passes through Earth's umbra, a partial lunar eclipse occurs. The stages of a partial lunar eclipse are similar to those of a total lunar eclipse, shown in Figure 18, except the Moon is never completely covered by Earth's umbra. The part of the Moon in Earth's penumbra appears only slightly darker, while the part of the Moon in Earth's umbra appears much darker.

Why don't lunar eclipses occur every month?

Lunar eclipses can only occur during a full moon phase, when the Moon and the Sun are on opposite sides of Earth. However, lunar eclipses do not occur during every full moon because of the tilt of the Moon's orbit with respect to Earth's orbit. During most full moons, the Moon is slightly above or slightly below Earth's penumbra.

Tides

The positions of the Moon and the Sun also affect Earth's oceans. If you have spent time near an ocean, you might have seen how the ocean's height, or sea level, rises and falls twice each day. *A* **tide** is *the daily rise and fall of sea level.* Examples of tides are shown in Figure 19. It is primarily the Moon's gravity that causes Earth's oceans to rise and fall twice each day.

Figure 19 In the Bay of Fundy, high tides can be more than 10 m higher than low tides.

Robert Estall photo agency/Alamy

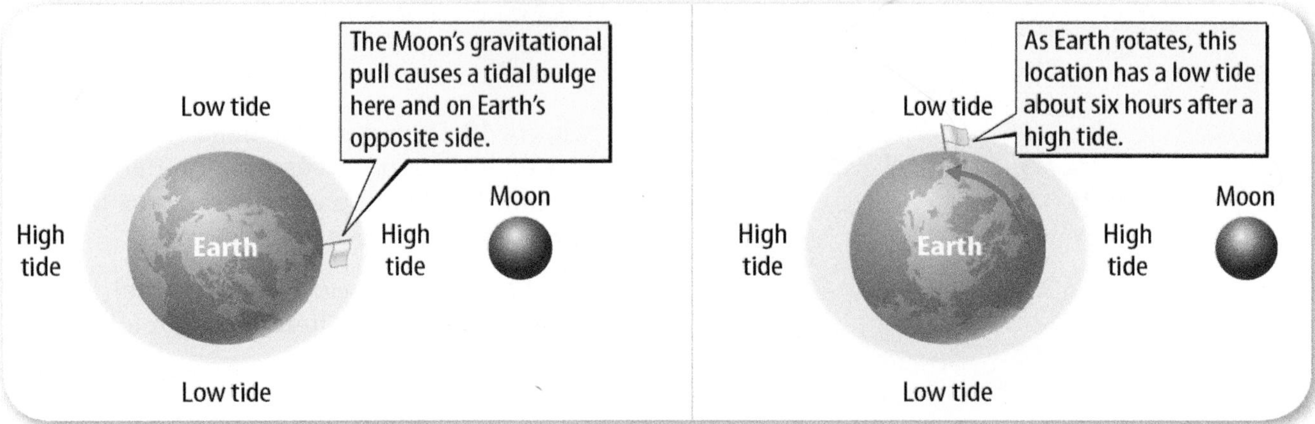

Figure 20 In this view down on Earth's North Pole, the flag moves into a tidal bulge as Earth rotates. A coastal area has a high tide about once every 12 hours.

The Moon's Effect on Earth's Tides

The difference in the strength of the Moon's gravity on opposite sides of Earth causes Earth's tides. The Moon's gravity is slightly stronger on the side of Earth closer to the Moon and slightly weaker on the side of Earth opposite the Moon. These differences cause tidal bulges in the oceans on opposite sides of Earth, shown in **Figure 20.** High tides occur at the tidal bulges, and low tides occur between them.

The Sun's Effect on Earth's Tides

Because the Sun is so far away from Earth, its effect on tides is about half that of the Moon. **Figure 21** shows how the positions of the Sun and the Moon affect Earth's tides.

Spring Tides During the full moon and new moon phases, spring tides occur. This is when the Sun's and the Moon's gravitational effects combine and produce higher high tides and lower low tides.

Neap Tides A week after a spring tide, a neap tide occurs. Then the Sun, Earth, and the Moon form a right angle. When this happens, the Sun's effect on tides reduces the Moon's effect. High tides are lower and low tides are higher at neap tides.

Key Concept Check Why is the Sun's effect on tides less than the Moon's effect?

Figure 21 A spring tide occurs when the Sun, Earth, and the Moon are in a line. A neap tide occurs when the Sun and the Moon form a right angle with Earth.

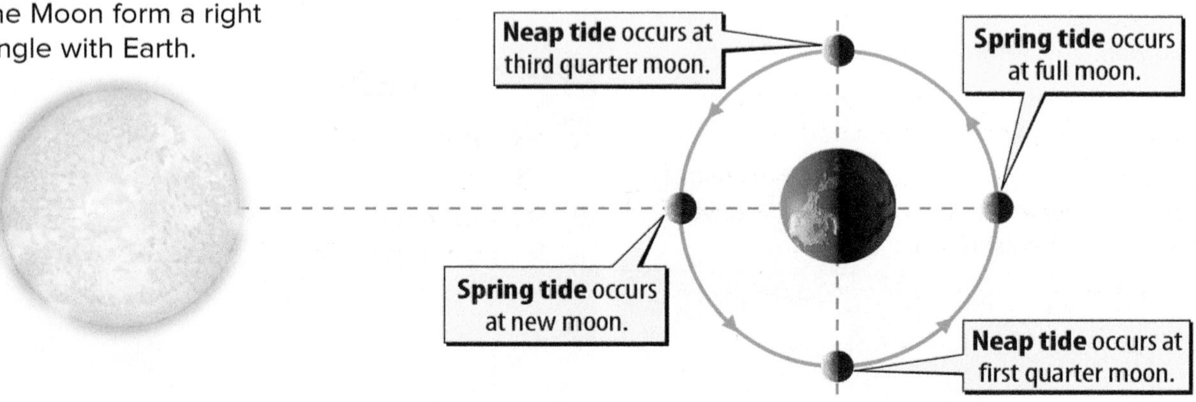

Lesson 3 Review

Visual Summary

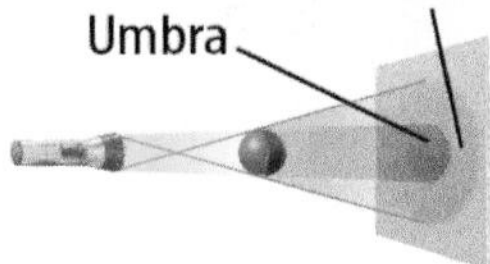

Shadows from a wide light source have two distinct parts.

The Moon's shadow produces solar eclipses. Earth's shadow produces lunar eclipses.

The positions of the Moon and the Sun in relation to Earth cause gravitational differences that produce tides.

FOLDABLES®

Use your lesson Foldable to review the lesson. Save your Foldable for the project at the end of the chapter.

What do you think NOW?

You first read the statements below at the beginning of the chapter.

5. A solar eclipse happens when Earth moves between the Moon and the Sun.

6. The gravitational pull of the Moon and the Sun on Earth's oceans causes tides.

Did you change your mind about whether you agree or disagree with the statements? Rewrite any false statements to make them true.

Use Vocabulary

1. **Distinguish** between an umbra and a penumbra.
2. **Use the term** *tide* in a sentence.
3. The Moon turns a reddish color during a total ________ eclipse.

Understand Key Concepts

4. **Summarize** the effect of the Sun on Earth's tides.
5. **Illustrate** the positions of the Sun, Earth, and the Moon during a solar eclipse and during a lunar eclipse.
6. **Contrast** a total lunar eclipse with a partial lunar eclipse.
7. Which could occur during a total solar eclipse?
   - **A.** first quarter moon
   - **B.** full moon
   - **C.** neap tide
   - **D.** spring tide

Interpret Graphics

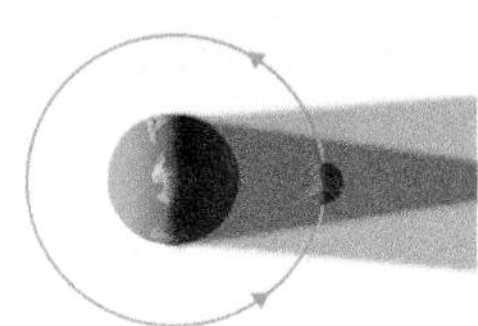

8. **Conclude** What type of eclipse does the figure above illustrate?
9. **Categorize Information** Copy and fill in the graphic organizer below to identify two bodies that affect Earth's tides.

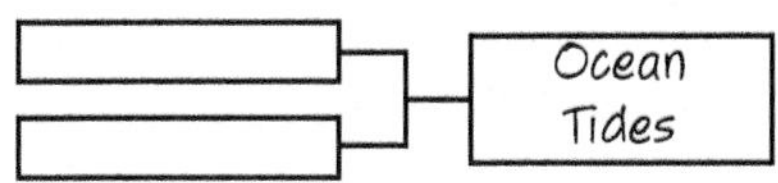

Critical Thinking

10. **Compose** a short story about a person long ago viewing a total solar eclipse.
11. **Research** ways to view a solar eclipse safely. Summarize your findings here.

Lab 35 minutes

Phases of the Moon

Materials

foam ball

pencil

lamp

stool

Safety

The Moon appears slightly different every night of its 29.5-day lunar cycle. The Moon's appearance changes as Earth and the Moon move. Depending on where the Moon is in relation to Earth and the Sun, observers on Earth see only part of the light the Moon reflects from the Sun.

Question

How do the positions of the Sun, the Moon, and Earth cause the phases of the Moon?

Procedure

1. Read and complete a lab safety form.
2. Hold a foam ball that represents the Moon. Make a handle for the ball by inserting a pencil about two inches into the foam ball. Your partner will represent an observer on Earth. Have your partner sit on a stool and record observations during the activity.
3. Place a lamp on a desk or other flat surface. Remove the shade from the lamp. The lamp represents the Sun.
4. Turn on the lamp and darken the lights in the room. ⚠ *Do not touch the bulb or look directly at it after the lamp is turned on.*
5. Position the Earth observer's stool about 1 m from the Sun. Position the Moon 0.5–1 m from the observer so that the Sun, Earth, and the Moon are in a line. The student holding the Moon holds the Moon so it is completely illuminated on one half. The observer records the phase and what the phase looks like in a data table.
6. Move the Moon clockwise about one-eighth of the way around its "orbit" of Earth. The observer swivels on the stool to face the Moon and records the phase.
7. Continue the Moon's orbit until the Earth observer has recorded all the Moon's phases.

Hutchings Photography/Digital Light Source

8. Return to your positions as the Moon and Earth observer. Choose a part in the Moon's orbit that you did not model. Predict what the Moon would look like in that position, and check if your prediction is correct.

Analyze and Conclude

9. **Explain** Use your observations to explain how the positions of the Sun, the Moon, and Earth produce the different phases of the Moon.
10. THE BIG IDEA **The Big Idea** Why is half of the Moon always lit? Why do you usually see only part of the Moon's lit half?
11. **Draw Conclusions** Based on your observations, why is the Moon not visible from Earth during the new moon phase?
12. **Summarize** Which parts of your model were waxing phases? Which parts were waning phases?
13. **Think Critically** During which phases of the Moon can eclipses occur? Explain.

Communicate Your Results

Create a poster of the results from your lab. Illustrate various positions of the Sun, the Moon, and Earth and draw the phase of the Moon for each. Include a statement of your hypothesis on the poster.

Inquiry Extension

The Moon is not the only object in the sky that has phases when viewed from Earth. The planets Venus and Mercury also have phases. Research the phases of these planets and create a calendar that shows when the various phases of Venus and Mercury occur.

Lab Tips

- ☑ Make sure the observer's head does not cast a shadow on the Moon.
- ☑ The student holding the Moon should hold the pencil so that he or she always stands on the unlit side of the Moon.

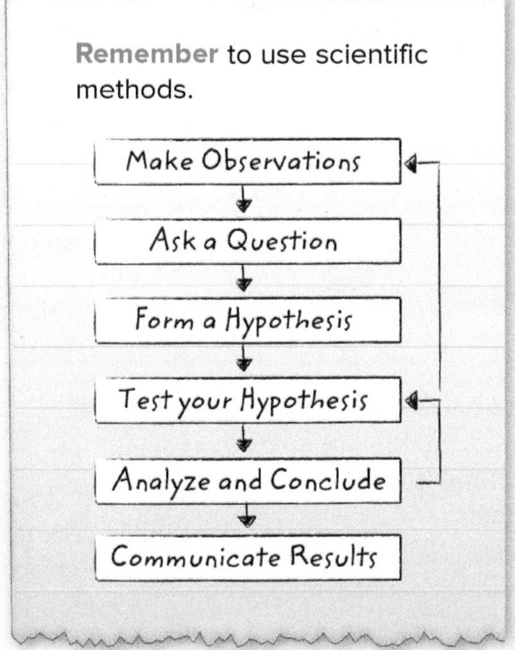
Remember to use scientific methods.
Make Observations
Ask a Question
Form a Hypothesis
Test your Hypothesis
Analyze and Conclude
Communicate Results

(t)NASA; (c)m-gucci/Getty Images; (b)Brian E. Kushner/Getty Images

Chapter 6 Study Guide

Earth's motion around the Sun causes seasons. The Moon's motion around Earth causes phases of the Moon. Earth and the Moon's motions together cause eclipses and ocean tides.

Key Concepts Summary

Lesson 1: Earth's Motion

- The gravitational pull of the Sun on Earth causes Earth to revolve around the Sun in a nearly circular **orbit.**
- Areas on Earth's curved surface become more tilted with respect to the direction of sunlight the farther you travel from the equator. This causes sunlight to spread out closer to the poles, making Earth colder at the poles and warmer at the equator.

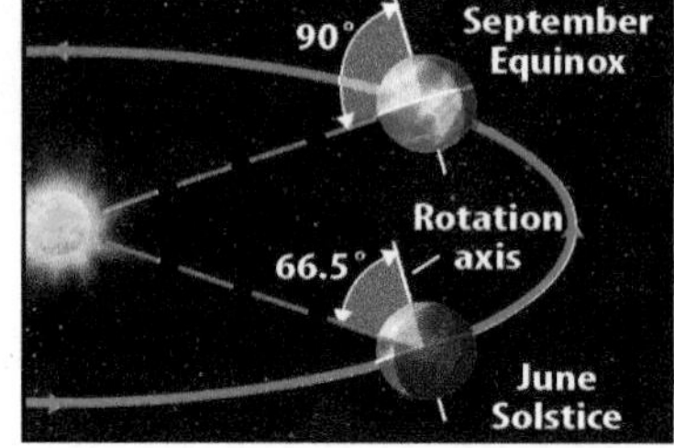

- As Earth revolves around the Sun, the tilt of Earth's **rotation axis** produces changes in how sunlight spreads out over Earth's surface. These changes in the concentration of sunlight cause the seasons.

Vocabulary

orbit p. 190
revolution p. 190
rotation p. 191
rotation axis p. 191
solstice p. 195
equinox p. 195

Lesson 2: Earth's Moon

- The gravitational pull of Earth on the Moon makes the Moon revolve around Earth. The Moon rotates once as it makes one complete orbit around Earth.
- The lit part of the Moon that you can see from Earth—the Moon's **phase**—changes during the lunar cycle as the Moon revolves around Earth.

Vocabulary

maria p. 200
phase p. 202
waxing phase p. 202
waning phase p. 202

Lesson 3: Eclipses and Tides

- When the Moon's shadow appears on Earth's surface, a **solar eclipse** occurs.
- When the Moon moves into Earth's shadow, a **lunar eclipse** occurs.
- The gravitational pull of the Moon and the Sun on Earth produces **tides,** the rise and fall of sea level that occurs twice each day.

Vocabulary

umbra p. 207
penumbra p. 207
solar eclipse p. 208
lunar eclipse p. 210
tide p. 211

Eckhard Slawik/Science Source

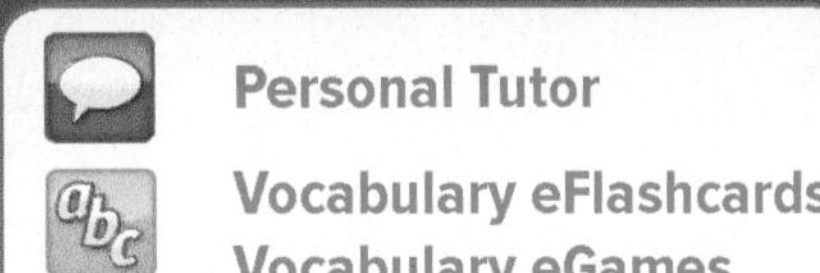

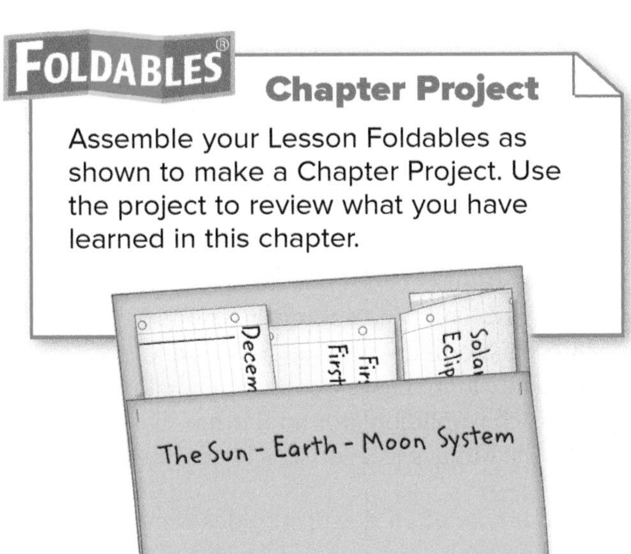

FOLDABLES
Chapter Project
The Sun - Earth - Moon System

Assemble your Lesson Foldables as shown to make a Chapter Project. Use the project to review what you have learned in this chapter.

Use Vocabulary

Distinguish between the terms in the each of the following pairs.

1. revolution, orbit
2. rotation, rotation axis
3. solstice, equinox
4. waxing phases, waning phases
5. umbra, penumbra
6. solar eclipse, lunar eclipse
7. tide, phase

Link Vocabulary and Key Concepts

Copy this concept map, and then use vocabulary terms from the previous page to complete the concept map.

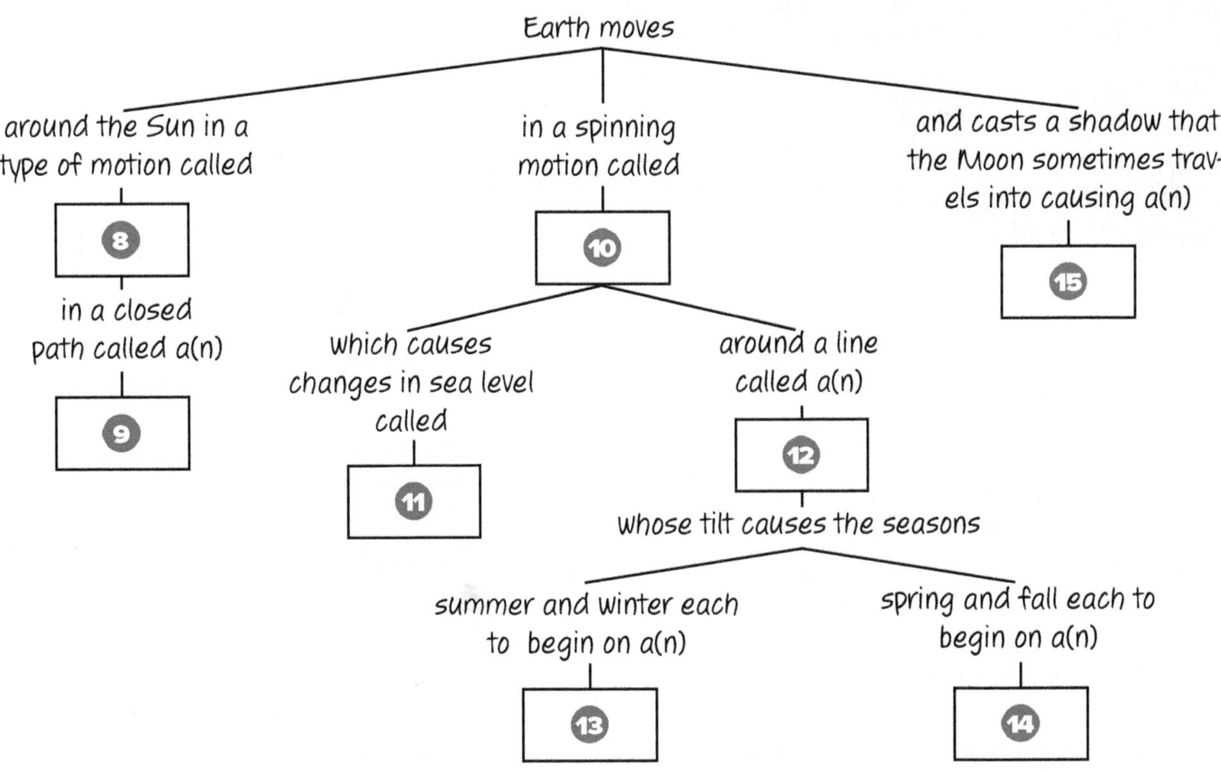

Chapter 6 Review

Understand Key Concepts

1 Which property of the Sun most affects the strength of gravitational attraction between the Sun and Earth?

A. mass
B. radius
C. shape
D. temperature

2 Which would be different if Earth rotated from east to west but at the same rate?

A. the amount of energy striking Earth
B. the days on which solstices occur
C. the direction of the Sun's apparent motion across the sky
D. the number of hours in a day

3 In the image below, the northern hemisphere is leaning toward the Sun. What season is it experiencing?

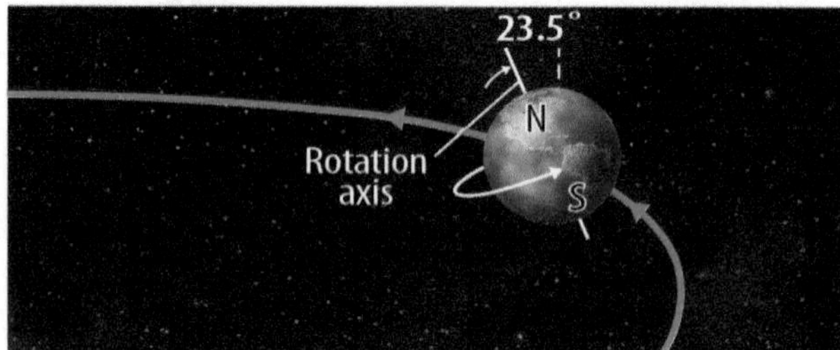

A. fall
B. spring
C. summer
D. winter

4 Which best explains why Earth is colder at the poles than at the equator?

A. Earth is farther from the Sun at the poles than at the equator.
B. Earth's orbit is not a perfect circle.
C. Earth's rotation axis is tilted.
D. Earth's surface is more tilted at the poles than at the equator.

5 How are the revolutions of the Moon and Earth alike?

A. Both are produced by gravity.
B. Both are revolutions around the Sun.
C. Both orbits are the same size.
D. Both take the same amount of time.

6 Which moon phase occurs about one week after a new moon?

A. another new moon
B. first quarter moon
C. full moon
D. third quarter moon

7 Why is the same side of the Moon always visible from Earth?

A. The Moon does not revolve around Earth.
B. The Moon does not rotate.
C. The Moon makes exactly one rotation for each revolution around Earth.
D. The Moon's rotation axis is not tilted.

8 About how often do spring tides occur?

A. once each month
B. once each year
C. twice each month
D. twice each year

9 If a coastal area has a high tide at 7:00 A.M., at about what time will the next low tide occur?

A. 11:00 A.M.
B. 1:00 P.M.
C. 3:00 P.M.
D. 7:00 P.M.

10 Which type of eclipse would a person standing at point X in the diagram below see?

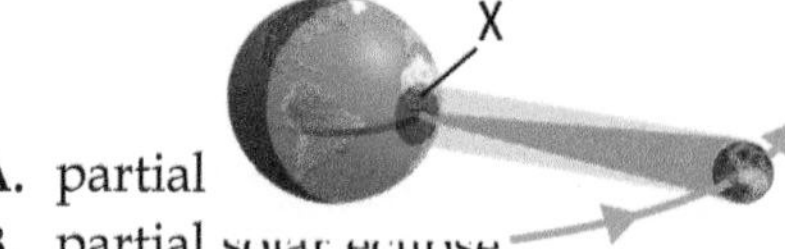

A. partial
B. partial solar eclipse
C. total lunar eclipse
D. total solar eclipse

Critical Thinking

11 **Outline** the ways Earth moves and how each affects Earth.

12 **Create** a poster that illustrates and describes the relationship between Earth's tilt and the seasons.

13 **Contrast** Why can you see phases of the Moon but not phases of the Sun?

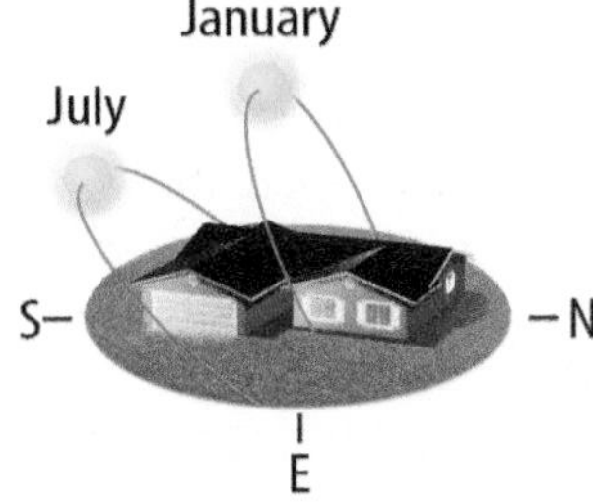

14 **Interpret Graphics** The figure above shows the Sun's position in the sky at noon in January and July. Is the house located in the northern hemisphere or the southern hemisphere? Explain.

15 **Illustrate** Make a diagram of the Moon's orbit and phases. Include labels and explanations with your drawing.

16 **Differentiate** between a total solar eclipse and a partial solar eclipse.

17 **Generalize** the reason that solar and lunar eclipses do not occur every month.

18 **Role Play** Write and present a play with several classmates that explains the causes and types of tides.

Writing in Science

19 **Survey** a group of at least ten people to determine how many know the cause of Earth's seasons. Write a summary of your results, including a main idea, supporting details, and a concluding sentence.

REVIEW THE BIG IDEA

20 At the South Pole, the Sun does not appear in the sky for six months out of the year. When does this happen? What is happening at the North Pole during these months? Explain why Earth's poles receive so little solar energy.

21 A solar eclipse, shown in the time-lapse photo below, is one phenomenon that the motions of Earth and the Moon produce. What other phenomena do the motions of Earth and the Moon produce?

Math Skills

Math Practice

Convert Units

22 When the Moon is 384,000 km from Earth, how far is the Moon from Earth in miles?

23 If you travel 205 mi on a train from Washington D.C. to New York City, how many kilometers do you travel on the train?

24 The nearest star other than the Sun is about 40 trillion km away. About how many miles away is the nearest star other than the Sun?

Standardized Test Practice

Record your answers on the answer sheet provided by your teacher or on a sheet of paper.

Multiple Choice

1 Which is the movement of one object around another object in space?

- **A** axis
- **B** orbit
- **C** revolution
- **D** rotation

Use the diagram below to answer question 2.

Time 1

Time 2

2 What happens between times *1* and *2* in the diagram above?

- **A** Days grow shorter and shorter.
- **B** The season changes from fall to winter.
- **C** The region begins to point away from the Sun.
- **D** The region gradually receives more solar energy.

3 How many times larger is the Sun's diameter than Earth's diameter?

- **A** about 10 times larger
- **B** about 100 times larger
- **C** about 1,000 times larger
- **D** about 10,000 times larger

4 Which diagram illustrates the Moon's third quarter phase?

A

B

C

D

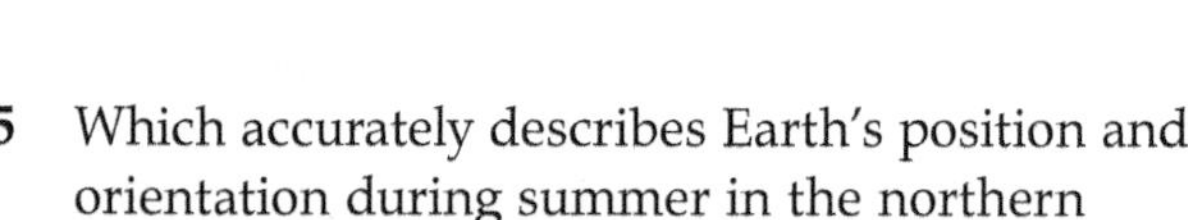

5 Which accurately describes Earth's position and orientation during summer in the northern hemisphere?

- **A** Earth is at its closest point to the Sun.
- **B** Earth's hemispheres receive equal amounts of solar energy.
- **C** The north end of Earth's rotational axis leans toward the Sun.
- **D** The Sun emits a greater amount of light and heat energy.

6 Which are large, dark lunar areas formed by cooled lava?

- **A** craters
- **B** highlands
- **C** maria
- **D** rays

7 During one lunar cycle, the Moon

- **A** completes its east-to-west path across the sky exactly once.
- **B** completes its entire sequence of phases.
- **C** progresses only from the new moon phase to the full moon phase.
- **D** revolves around Earth twice.

Use the diagram below to answer question 8.

8 What does the flag in the diagram above represent?

A high tide

B low tide

C neap tide

D spring tide

9 During which lunar phase might a solar eclipse occur?

A first quarter moon

B full moon

C new moon

D third quarter moon

10 Which does the entire Moon pass through during a partial lunar eclipse?

A Earth's penumbra

B Earth's umbra

C the Moon's penumbra

D the Moon's umbra

Constructed Response

Use the diagram below to answer questions 11 and 12.

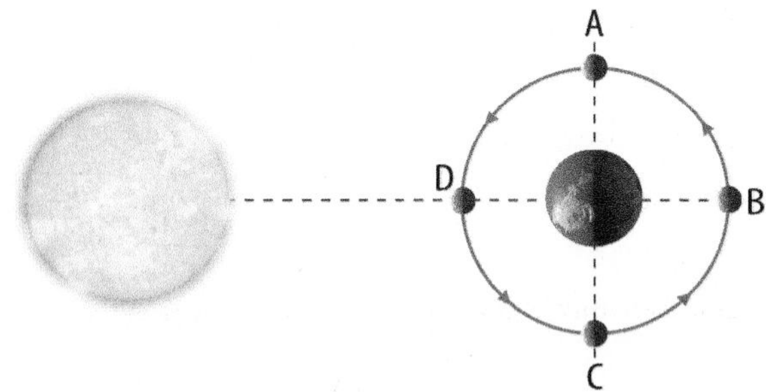

11 Where are neap tides indicated in the above diagram? What causes neap tides? What happens during a neap tide?

12 Where are spring tides indicated in the above diagram? What causes spring tides? What happens during a spring tide?

13 How would Earth's climate be different if its rotational axis were not tilted?

14 Why can we see only one side of the Moon from Earth? What is the name given to this side of the Moon?

15 What is a lunar phase? How do waxing and waning phases differ?

16 Why don't solar eclipses occur monthly?

NEED EXTRA HELP?																
If You Missed Question...	1	2	3	4	5	6	7	8	9	10	11	12	13	14	15	16
Go to Lesson...	1	1	1	2	1	2	2	3	3	3	3	3	1	2	2	3

Chapter 7

6.ESS.1, 6.ESS.3, SEPS.1, SEPS.2, SEPS.3, SEPS.4, SEPS.5, SEPS.7, SEPS.8, 6-8.LST.1.1, 6-8.LST.1.2, 6-8.LST.2.2, 6-8.LST.3.2, 6-8.LST.3.3, 6-8.LST.7.1, 6-8.LST.7.3

The Solar System

What kinds of objects are in the solar system?

One, Two, or Three Planets?

This photo, taken by the *Cassini* spacecraft, shows part of Saturn's rings and two of its moons. Saturn is a planet that orbits the Sun. The moons, tiny Epimetheus and much larger Titan, orbit Saturn. Besides planets and moons, many other objects are in the solar system.

- How would you describe a planet such as Saturn?
- How do astronomers classify the objects they discover?
- What types of objects do you think make up the solar system?

Get Ready to Read

What do you think?

Before you read, decide if you agree or disagree with each of these statements. As you read this chapter, see if you change your mind about any of the statements.

1. Astronomers measure distances between space objects using astronomical units.
2. Gravitational force keeps planets in orbit around the Sun.
3. Earth is the only inner planet that has a moon.
4. Venus is the hottest planet in the solar system.
5. The outer planets also are called the gas giants.
6. The atmospheres of Saturn and Jupiter are mainly water vapor.
7. Asteroids and comets are mainly rock and ice.
8. A meteoroid is a meteor that strikes Earth.

Mc Graw Hill Education connectED

Your one-stop online resource
connectED.mcgraw-hill.com

LearnSmart®

Chapter Resources Files, Reading Essentials, Get Ready to Read, Quick Vocabulary

Animations, Videos, Interactive Tables

Self-checks, Quizzes, Tests

Project-Based Learning Activities

Lab Manuals, Safety Videos, Virtual Labs & Other Tools

Vocabulary, Multilingual eGlossary, Vocab eGames, Vocab eFlashcards

Personal Tutors

Lesson 1

Reading Guide

Key Concepts 

ESSENTIAL QUESTIONS

- How are the inner planets different from the outer planets?
- What is an astronomical unit and why is it used?
- What is the shape of a planet's orbit?

Vocabulary

asteroid p. 227

comet p. 227

astronomical unit p. 228

period of revolution p. 228

period of rotation p. 228

 Multilingual eGlossary

 Science Video

 6.ESS.1, 6.ESS.3, SEPS.2, SEPS.5, SEPS.8, 6-8.LST.2.2, 6-8.LST.3.3, 6-8.LST.7.1

The Structure of the Solar System

Inquiry Are these stars?

If you were to gaze up at the sky on a moonless night away from city lights, you might observe a sky similar to the one shown in this photo. A few thousand stars are easily visible even though they are extremely far away. What other types of objects can be seen in the night sky?

Launch Lab

10 minutes

How do you know which distance unit to use?

You can use different units to measure distance. For example, millimeters might be used to measure the length of a bolt, and kilometers might be used to measure the distance between cities. In this lab, you will investigate why some units are easier to use than others for certain measurements.

1. Read and complete a lab safety form.
2. Use a **centimeter ruler** to measure the length of a **pencil** and the thickness of this **book.** Record the distances in your Science Journal.
3. Use the centimeter ruler to measure the width of your classroom. Then measure the width of the room using a **meterstick.** Record the distances in your Science Journal.

Think About This

1. Why are meters easier to use than centimeters for measuring the classroom?
2.  **Key Concept** Why do you think astronomers might need a unit larger than a kilometer to measure distances in the solar system?

What is the solar system?

Have you ever made a wish on a star? If so, you might have wished on a planet instead of a star. Sometimes, as shown in Figure 1, the first starlike object you see at night is not a star at all. It's Venus, the planet closest to Earth.

It's hard to tell the difference between planets and stars in the night sky because they all appear as tiny lights. Thousands of years ago, observers noticed that a few of these tiny lights moved, but others did not. The ancient Greeks called these objects planets, which means "wanderers." Astronomers now know that the planets do not wander about the sky; the planets move around the Sun. The Sun and the group of objects that move around it make up the solar system.

When you look at the night sky, a few of the tiny lights that you can see are part of our solar system. Almost all of the other specks of light are stars. They are much farther away than any objects in our solar system. Astronomers have discovered that some of those stars also have planets moving around them.

Reading Check What object do the planets in the solar system move around?

Figure 1 When looking at the night sky, you will likely see stars and planets. In the photo below, the planet Venus is the bright object seen above the Moon.

(t)Hutchings Photography/Digital Light Source; (b)Diego Barucco/Alamy

Objects in the Solar System

Ancient observers looking at the night sky saw many stars but only five planets–Mercury, Venus, Mars, Jupiter, and Saturn. The invention of the telescope in the 1600s led to the discovery of additional planets and many other space objects.

The Sun

The largest object in the solar system is the Sun, a **star.** Its diameter is about 1.4 million km–ten times the diameter of the largest planet, Jupiter. The Sun is made mostly of hydrogen gas. Its mass makes up about 99 percent of the entire solar system's mass.

SCIENCE USE V. COMMON USE

star

Science Use an object in space made of gases in which nuclear fusion reactions occur that emit energy

Common Use a shape that usually has five or six points around a common center

Inside the Sun, a process called nuclear fusion produces an enormous amount of energy. The Sun emits some of this energy as light. The light from the Sun shines on all of the planets every day. The Sun also applies gravitational forces to objects in the solar system. Gravitational forces cause the planets and other objects to move around, or **orbit,** the Sun.

REVIEW VOCABULARY

orbit

(noun) the path an object follows as it moves around another object

(verb) to move around another object

Objects That Orbit the Sun

Different types of objects orbit the Sun. These objects include planets, dwarf planets, asteroids, and comets. Unlike the Sun, these objects don't emit light but only reflect the Sun's light.

Planets Astronomers classify some objects that orbit the Sun as planets, as shown in **Figure 2.** An object is a planet only if it orbits the Sun and has a nearly spherical shape. Also, the mass of a planet must be much larger than the total mass of all other objects whose orbits are close by. The solar system has eight objects classified as planets.

Reading Check What is a planet?

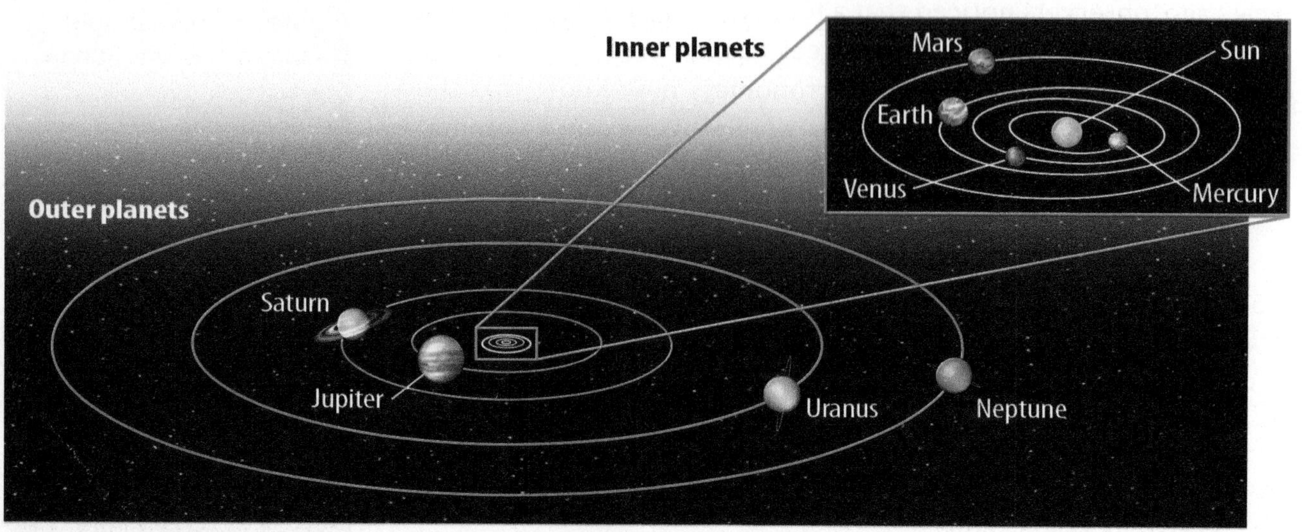

Figure 2 The orbits of the inner and outer planets are shown to scale. The Sun and the planets are not to scale. The outer planets are much larger than the inner planets.

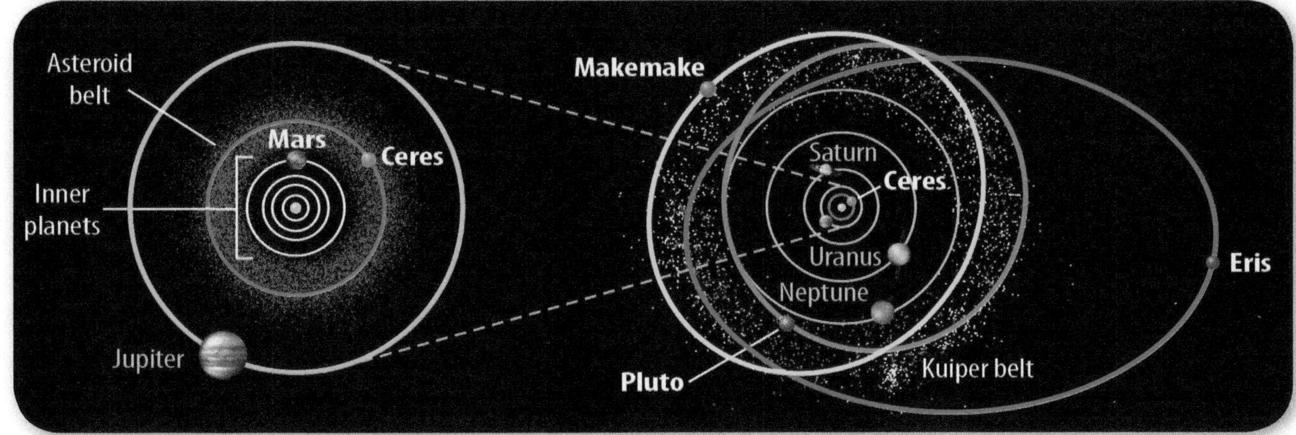

▲ **Figure 3** Ceres, a dwarf planet, orbits the Sun as planets do. The orbit of Ceres is in the asteroid belt between Mars and Jupiter.

Visual Check Which dwarf planet is farthest from the Sun?

Inner Planets and Outer Planets As shown in **Figure 2,** the four planets closest to the Sun are the inner planets. The inner planets are Mercury, Venus, Earth, and Mars. These planets are made mainly of solid rocky materials. The four planets farthest from the Sun are the outer planets. The outer planets are Jupiter, Saturn, Uranus (YOOR uh nus), and Neptune. These planets are made mainly of ice and gases such as hydrogen and helium. The outer planets are much larger than Earth and are sometimes called gas giants.

Key Concept Check Describe how the inner planets differ from the outer planets.

Dwarf Planets Scientists classify some objects in the solar system as dwarf planets. A dwarf planet is a spherical object that orbits the Sun. It is not a moon of another planet and is in a region of the solar system where there are many objects orbiting near it. But, unlike a planet, a dwarf planet does not have more mass than objects in nearby orbits. **Figure 3** shows the locations of the dwarf planets Ceres (SIHR eez), Eris (IHR is), Pluto, and Makemake (MAH kay MAH kay). Dwarf planets are made of rock and ice and are much smaller than Earth.

WORD ORIGIN

asteroid
from Greek *asteroeides,* means "resembling a star"

Asteroids *Millions of small, rocky objects called* **asteroids** *orbit the Sun in the asteroid belt between the orbits of Mars and Jupiter.* The asteroid belt is shown in **Figure 3.** Asteroids range in size from less than a meter to several hundred kilometers in length. Unlike planets and dwarf planets, asteroids, such as the one shown in **Figure 4,** usually are not spherical.

Figure 4 The asteroid Gaspra orbits the Sun in the asteroid belt. Its odd shape is about 19 km long and 11 km wide. ▼

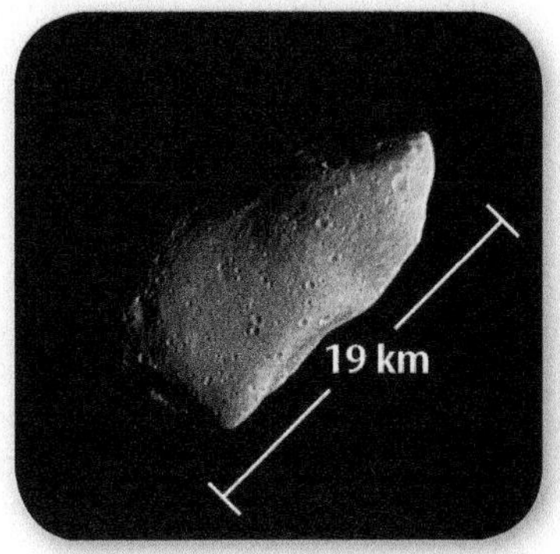

Comets You might have seen a picture of a comet with a long, glowing tail. *A* **comet** *is made of gas, dust, and ice and moves around the Sun in an oval-shaped orbit.* Comets come from the outer parts of the solar system. Most comets have never been seen. It is estimated that there might be 100 billion comets orbiting the Sun. You will read more about comets, asteroids, and dwarf planets in Lesson 4.

The Astronomical Unit

On Earth, distances are often measured in meters (m) or kilometers (km). Objects in the solar system, however, are so far apart that astronomers use a larger distance unit. *An* **astronomical unit** *(AU) is the average distance from Earth to the Sun–about 150 million km.* Table 1 lists each planet's average distance from the Sun in km and AU.

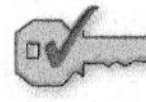 **Key Concept Check** Define what an astronomical unit is and explain why it is used.

Table 1 Because the distances of the planets from the Sun are so large, it is easier to express these distances using astronomical units rather than kilometers.

Table 1 Average Distance of the Planets from the Sun

Planet	Average Distance (km)	Average Distance (AU)
Mercury	57,910,000	0.39
Venus	108,210,000	0.72
Earth	149,600,000	1.00
Mars	227,920,000	1.52
Jupiter	778,570,000	5.20
Saturn	1,433,530,000	9.58
Uranus	2,872,460,000	19.20
Neptune	4,495,060,000	30.05

The Motion of the Planets

Have you ever swung a ball on the end of a string in a circle over your head? In some ways, the motion of a planet around the Sun is like the motion of that ball. As shown in Figure 5 on the next page, the Sun's gravitational force pulls each planet toward the Sun. This force is similar to the pull of the string that keeps the ball moving in a circle. The Sun's gravitational force pulls on each planet and keeps it moving along a curved path around the Sun.

 **Reading Check** What causes planets to orbit the Sun?

Make a tri-fold book from a sheet of paper and label it as shown. Use it to summarize information about the types of objects that make up the solar system.

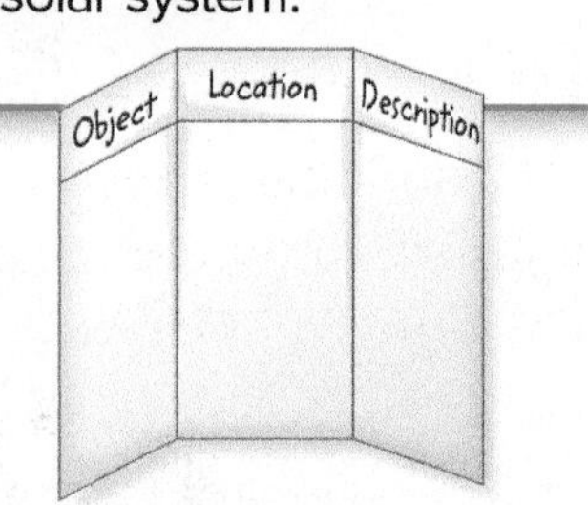

Revolution and Rotation

Objects in the solar system move in two ways. They orbit, or revolve, around the Sun. *The time it takes an object to travel once around the Sun is its* **period of revolution.** Earth's period of revolution is one year. The objects also spin, or rotate, as they orbit the Sun. *The time it takes an object to complete one rotation is its* **period of rotation.** Earth has a period of rotation of one day.

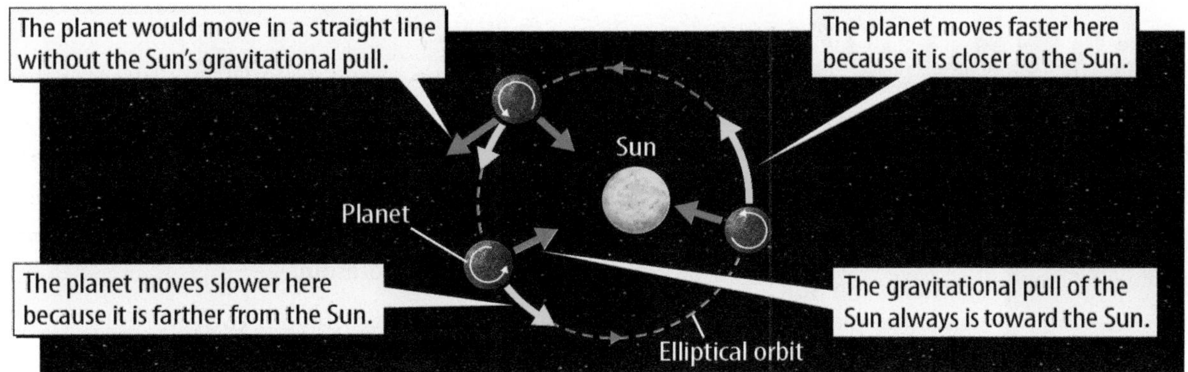

Planetary Orbits and Speeds

Earth was once thought to be the center of our solar system. In this geocentric model, the Sun, the Moon, and the planets revolved in circular orbits around a stationary Earth. In the early 1500s, Nicholas Copernicus proposed that Earth and other planets revolve in circular orbits around a stationary Sun, a heliocentric model.

In the 1600s, Johannes Kepler discovered that planets' orbits are ellipses, not circles. An ellipse contains two fixed points, called foci (singular, focus). Foci are equal distance from the ellipse's center and determine its shape. As shown in **Figure 5,** the Sun is at one focus. As a planet revolves, the distance between the planet and the Sun changes. Kepler also discovered that a planet's speed increases as it gets nearer to the Sun.

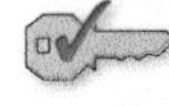 **Key Concept Check** Describe the shape of a planet's orbit.

Personal Tutor

Figure 5  Planets and other objects in the solar system revolve around the Sun because of its gravitational pull on them.

MiniLab

20 minutes

How can you model an elliptical orbit?

In this lab you will explore how the locations of foci affect the shape of an ellipse.

1. Read and complete a lab safety form.
2. Place a sheet of **paper** on a **corkboard.** Insert two **push pins** 8 cm apart in the center of the paper.
3. Use **scissors** to cut a 24-cm piece of **string.** Tie the ends of the string together.
4. Place the loop of string around the pins. Use a pencil to draw an ellipse as shown.
5. Measure the maximum width and length of the ellipse. Record the data in your Science Journal.
6. Move one of the push pins so that the pins are 5 cm apart. Repeat steps 4 and 5.

Analysis

1. **Compare and contrast** the two ellipses.
2.  **Key Concept** How are the shapes of the ellipses you drew similar to the orbits of the inner and outer planets?

Lesson 1 Review

Visual Summary

The solar system contains the Sun, the inner planets, the outer planets, the dwarf planets, asteroids, and comets.

An astronomical unit (AU) is a unit of distance equal to about 150 million km.

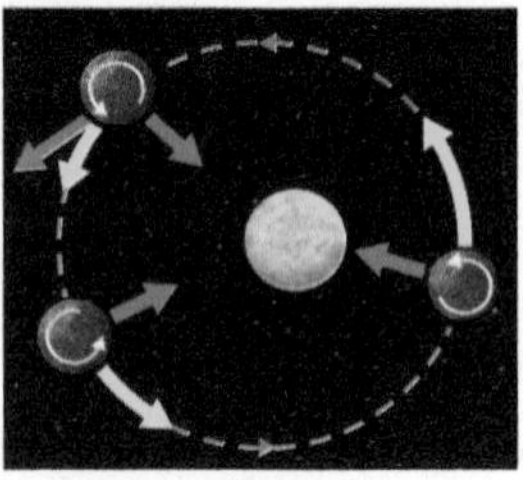

The speeds of the planets change as they move around the Sun in elliptical orbits.

FOLDABLES®

Use your lesson Foldable to review the lesson. Save your Foldable for the project at the end of the chapter.

What do you think NOW?

You first read the statements below at the beginning of the chapter.

1. Astronomers measure distances between space objects using astronomical units.
2. Gravitational force keeps planets in orbit around the Sun.

Did you change your mind about whether you agree or disagree with the statements? Rewrite any false statements to make them true.

Use Vocabulary

1. **Compare and contrast** a period of revolution and a period of rotation.
2. **Define** *dwarf planet* in your own words.
3. **Distinguish** between an asteroid and a comet.

Understand Key Concepts 

4. **Summarize** how and why planets orbit the Sun and how and why a planet's speed changes in orbit.
5. **Infer** why an astronomical unit is not used to measure distances on Earth.
6. Which distinguishes a dwarf planet from a planet?
   - **A.** mass
   - **B.** the object it revolves around
   - **C.** shape
   - **D.** type of orbit

Interpret Graphics

7. **Explain** what each arrow in the diagram represents.

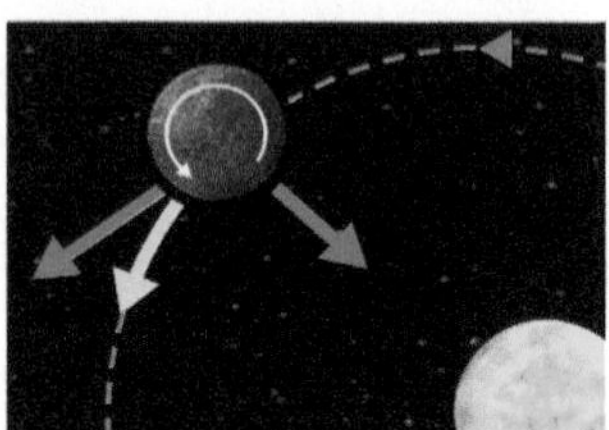

8. **Take Notes** Copy the table below. List information about each object or group of objects in the solar system mentioned in the lesson. Add additional lines as needed.

Object	Description
Sun	
Planets	

Critical Thinking

9. **Evaluate** How would the speed of a planet be different if its orbit were a circle instead of an ellipse?

Meteors are pieces of a comet or an asteroid that heat up as they fall through Earth's atmosphere. Meteors that strike Earth are called meteorites. ▶

CAREERS in SCIENCE

History from Space

Meteorites give a peek back in time.

About 4.6 billion years ago, Earth and the other planets did not exist. In fact, there was no solar system. Instead, a large disk of gas and dust, known as the solar nebula, swirled around a forming Sun, as shown in the top picture to the right. How did the planets and other objects in the solar system form?

Denton Ebel is looking for the answer. He is a geologist at the American Museum of Natural History in New York City. Ebel explores the hypothesis that over millions of years, tiny particles in the solar nebula clumped together and formed the asteroids, comets, and planets that make up our solar system.

▲ **Denton Ebel holds a meteorite that broke off the Vesta asteroid.**

The solar nebula contained tiny particles called chondrules (KON drewls). They formed when the hot gas of the nebula condensed and solidified. Chondrules and other tiny particles collided and then accreted (uh KREET ed) or clumped together. This process eventually formed asteroids, comets, and planets. Some of the asteroids and comets have not changed much in over 4 billion years. Chondrite meteorites are pieces of asteroids that fell to Earth. The chondrules within the meteorites are the oldest solid material in our solar system.

For Ebel, chondrite meteorites contain information about the formation of the solar system. Did the materials in the meteorite form throughout the solar system and then accrete? Or did asteroids and comets form and accrete near the Sun, drift outward to where they are today, and then grow larger by accreting ice and dust? Ebel's research is helping to solve the mystery of how our solar system formed.

Accretion Hypothesis

According to the accretion hypothesis, the solar system formed in stages.

First there was a solar nebula. The Sun formed when gravity caused the nebula to collapse.

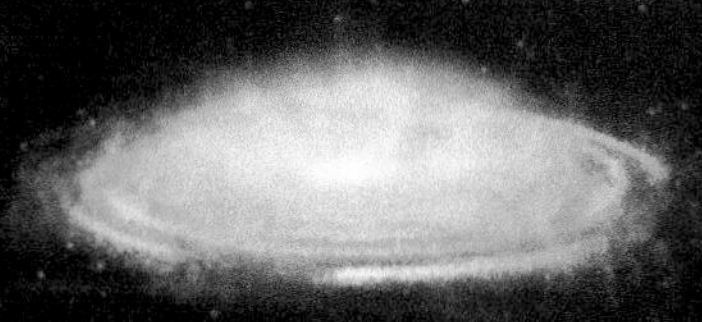

The rocky inner planets formed from accreted particles.

The gaseous outer planets formed as gas, ice, and dust condensed and accreted.

TIME LINE Work in groups. Learn more about the history of Earth from its formation until life began to appear. Create a time line showing major events. Present your time line to the class.

(t)Josef Muellek/Getty Images; (cl)American Museum of Natural History; (bkgd)NASA and H. Richer (University of British Columbia)

Lesson 2

The Inner Planets

Reading Guide

Key Concepts 

ESSENTIAL QUESTIONS

- How are the inner planets similar?
- Why is Venus hotter than Mercury?
- What kind of atmospheres do the inner planets have?

Vocabulary

terrestrial planet p. 331

greenhouse effect p. 333

 Multilingual eGlossary

 What's Science Got to do With It?

6.ESS.3, SEPS.2, SEPS.4, SEPS.5, 6-8.LST.1.1, 6-8.LST.2.2, 6-8.LST.3.3

Where is this?

This spectacular landscape is the surface of Mars, one of the inner planets. Other inner planets have similar rocky surfaces. It might surprise you to learn that there are planets in the solar system that have no solid surface on which to stand.

ESA/DLR/FU Berlin (G. Neukum);

Launch Lab

20 minutes

What affects the temperature on the inner planets?

Mercury and Venus are closer to the Sun than Earth. What determines the temperature on these planets? Let's find out.

1. Read and complete a lab safety form.
2. Insert a **thermometer** into a **clear 2-L plastic bottle.** Wrap **modeling clay** around the lid to hold the thermometer in the center of the bottle. Form an airtight seal with the clay.
3. Rest the bottle against the side of a **shoe box** in direct sunlight. Lay a second **thermometer** on top of the box next to the bottle so that the bulbs are at about the same height. The thermometer bulb should not touch the box. Secure the thermometer in place using **tape.**

4. Read the thermometers and record the temperatures in your Science Journal.
5. Wait 15 minutes and then read and record the temperature on each thermometer.

Think About This

1. How did the temperature of the two thermometers compare?
2. **Key Concept** What do you think caused the difference in temperature?

Planets Made of Rock

Imagine that you are walking outside. How would you describe the ground? You might say it is dusty or grassy. If you live near a lake or an ocean, you might say the ground is sandy or wet. But beneath the ground or lake or ocean is a layer of solid rock.

The inner planets–Mercury, Venus, Earth, and Mars–are also called terrestrial planets. **Terrestrial planets** are the planets closest to the Sun, are made of rock and metal, and have solid outer layers. Like Earth, the other inner planets also are made of rock and metallic materials and have a solid outer layer. However, as shown in Figure 6, the inner planets have different sizes, atmospheres, and surfaces.

WORD ORIGIN

terrestrial
from Latin *terrestris,* means "earthly"

Figure 6 The inner planets are roughly similar in size. Earth is about two and half times larger than Mercury. All inner planets have a solid outer layer.

INNER PLANETS

Visual Check Which is the smallest inner planet?

(t)Hutchings Photography/Digital Light Source; (b)NASA/Johns Hopkins University Applied Physics Laboratory/Carnegie Institution of Washington; (bcl)NASA, (bcr)NASA GSFC image by Robert Simmon and Reto Stöckli; (br)NASA/JPL/Malin Space Science Systems

Figure 7 The *Messenger* space probe collected data on Mercury's surface, geologic history, and polar regions. The exploration mission lasted from 2004 to 2015.

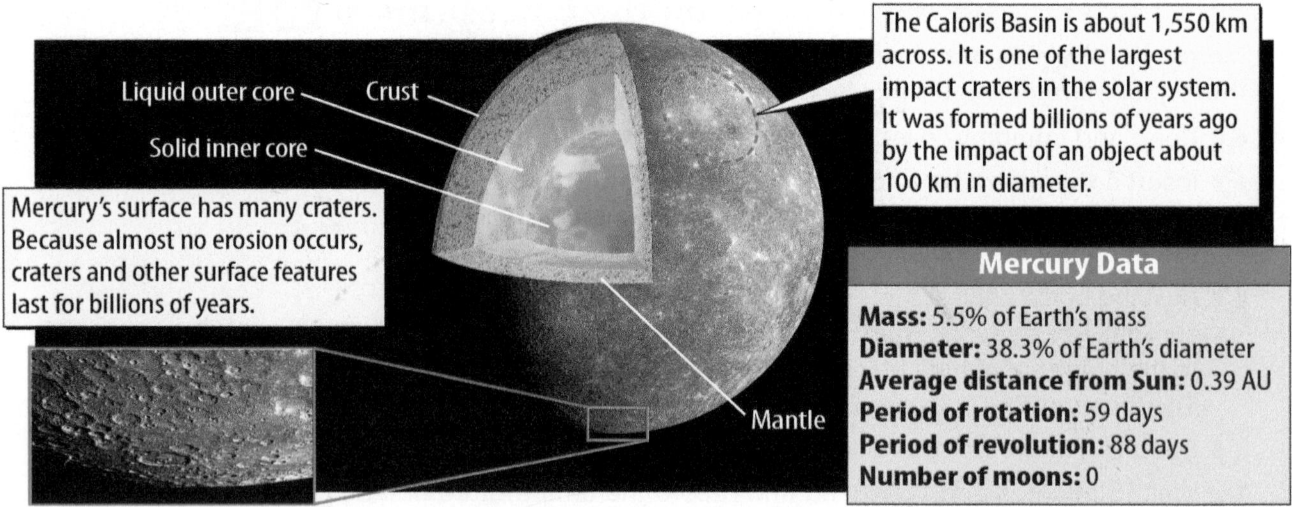

Liquid outer core
Crust
Solid inner core
Mantle
The Caloris Basin is about 1,550 km across. It is one of the largest impact craters in the solar system. It was formed billions of years ago by the impact of an object about 100 km in diameter.
Mercury's surface has many craters. Because almost no erosion occurs, craters and other surface features last for billions of years.

Mercury Data

Mass: 5.5% of Earth's mass
Diameter: 38.3% of Earth's diameter
Average distance from Sun: 0.39 AU
Period of rotation: 59 days
Period of revolution: 88 days
Number of moons: 0

Mercury

The smallest planet and the planet closest to the Sun is Mercury, shown in Figure 7. Mercury has no atmosphere. A planet has an atmosphere when its gravity is strong enough to hold gases close to its surface. The strength of a planet's gravity depends on the planet's mass. Because Mercury's mass is so small, its gravity is not strong enough to hold onto an atmosphere. Without an atmosphere there is no wind that moves energy from place to place across the planet's surface. This results in temperatures as high as 450°C on the side of Mercury facing the Sun and as cold as −170°C on the side facing away from the Sun.

Make a four-door book. Label each door with the name of an inner planet. Use the book to organize your notes on the inner planets.

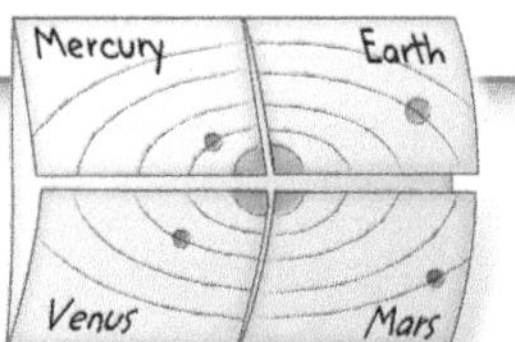

Mercury's Surface

Impact craters, depressions formed by collisions with objects from space, cover the surface of Mercury. There are smooth plains of solidified lava from long-ago eruptions. There are also high cliffs that might have formed when the planet cooled quickly, causing the surface to wrinkle and crack. Without an atmosphere, almost no erosion occurs on Mercury's surface. As a result, features that formed billions of years ago have changed very little.

Mercury's Structure

The structures of the inner planets are similar. Like all inner planets, Mercury has a core made of iron and nickel. Surrounding the core is a layer called the mantle. The mantle is mainly made of silicon and oxygen. The crust is a thin, rocky layer above the mantle. Mercury's large core might have been formed by a collision with a large object during Mercury's formation.

Key Concept Check How are the inner planets similar?

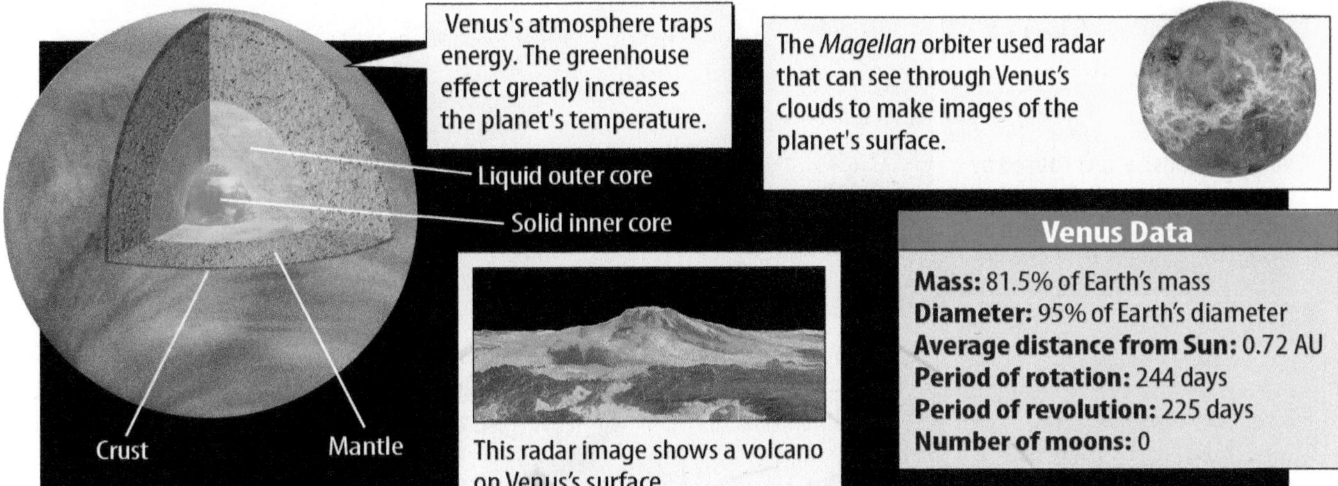
Venus's atmosphere traps energy. The greenhouse effect greatly increases the planet's temperature.
The *Magellan* orbiter used radar that can see through Venus's clouds to make images of the planet's surface.
Liquid outer core
Solid inner core
Crust
Mantle
This radar image shows a volcano on Venus's surface.
Venus Data
Mass: 81.5% of Earth's mass
Diameter: 95% of Earth's diameter
Average distance from Sun: 0.72 AU
Period of rotation: 244 days
Period of revolution: 225 days
Number of moons: 0

Figure 8 Because a thick layer of clouds covers Venus, its surface has not been seen. Between 1990 and 1994, the *Magellan* space probe mapped the surface using radar.

Venus

The second planet from the Sun is Venus, as shown in Figure 8. Venus is about the same size as Earth. It rotates so slowly that its period of rotation is longer than its period of revolution. This means that a day on Venus is longer than a year. Unlike most planets, Venus rotates from east to west. Several space probes have flown by or landed on Venus.

Venus's Atmosphere

The atmosphere of Venus is about 97 percent carbon dioxide. It is so dense that the atmospheric pressure on Venus is about 90 times greater than on Earth. Even though Venus has almost no water in its atmosphere or on its surface, a thick layer of clouds covers the planet. Unlike the clouds of water vapor on Earth, the clouds on Venus are made of acid.

The Greenhouse Effect on Venus

With an average temperature of about 460°C, Venus is the hottest planet in the solar system. The high temperatures are caused by the greenhouse effect. *The* **greenhouse effect** *occurs when a planet's atmosphere traps solar energy and causes the surface temperature to increase.* Carbon dioxide in Venus's atmosphere traps some of the solar energy that is absorbed and then emitted by the planet. This heats up the planet. Without the greenhouse effect, Venus would be almost 450°C cooler.

 **Key Concept Check** Why is Venus hotter than Mercury?

Venus's Structure and Surface

Venus's internal structure, as shown in Figure 8, is similar to Earth's. Radar images show that more than 80 percent of Venus's surface is covered by solidified lava. Much of this lava might have been produced by volcanic eruptions that occurred about half a billion years ago.

(l)NASA; (c)NASA/JPL; (r)NASA Jet Propulsion Laboratory (NASA-JPL)

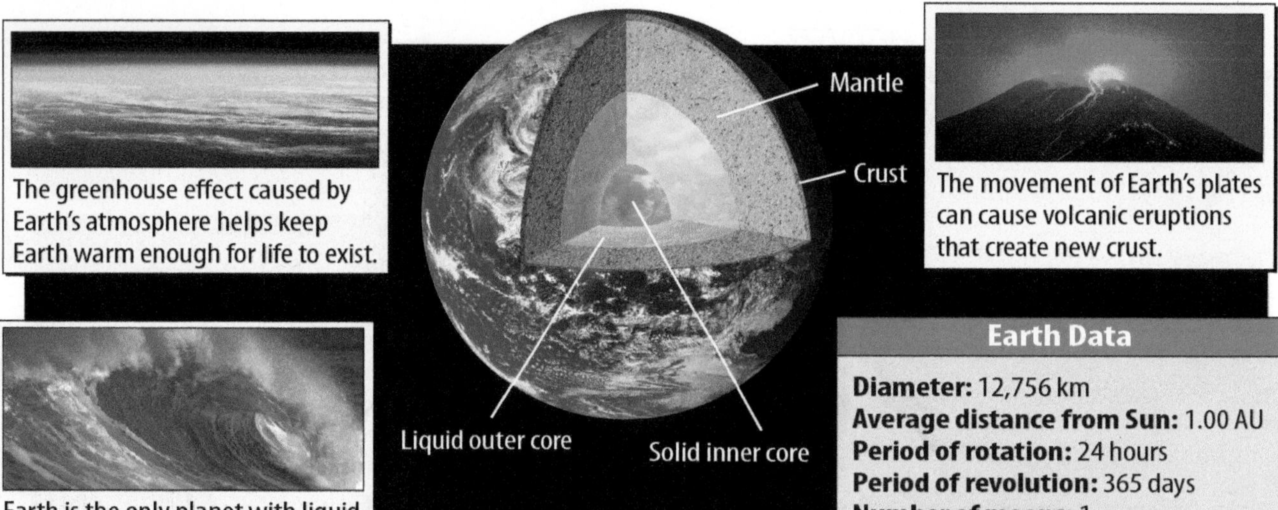

The greenhouse effect caused by Earth's atmosphere helps keep Earth warm enough for life to exist.
Mantle
Crust
The movement of Earth's plates can cause volcanic eruptions that create new crust.
Earth is the only planet with liquid water on its surface.
Liquid outer core
Solid inner core
Earth Data
Diameter: 12,756 km
Average distance from Sun: 1.00 AU
Period of rotation: 24 hours
Period of revolution: 365 days
Number of moons: 1

Figure 9 Earth has more water in its atmosphere and on its surface than the other inner planets. Earth's surface is younger than the surfaces of the other inner planets because new crust is constantly forming.

MiniLab

20 minutes

How can you model the inner planets?

In this lab, you will use modeling clay to make scale models of the inner planets.

Planet	Actual Diameter (km)	Model Diameter (cm)
Mercury	4,886	
Venus	12,118	
Earth	12,756	8.0
Mars	6,786	

1. Use the data above for Earth to calculate in your Science Journal each model's diameter for the other three planets.
2. Use **modeling clay** to make a ball that represents the diameter of each planet. Check the diameter with a **centimeter ruler**.

Analyze Your Results

1. **Explain** how you converted actual diameters (km) to model diameters (cm).
2. **Key Concept** How do the inner planets compare? Which planets have approximately the same diameter?

Earth

Earth, shown in **Figure 9**, is the third planet from the Sun. Unlike Mercury and Venus, Earth has a moon.

Earth's Atmosphere

A mixture of gases and a small amount of water vapor make up most of Earth's atmosphere. They produce a greenhouse effect that increases Earth's average surface temperature. This effect and Earth's distance from the Sun warm Earth enough for large bodies of liquid water to exist. Earth's atmosphere also absorbs much of the Sun's radiation and protects the surface below. Earth's protective atmosphere, the presence of liquid water, and the planet's moderate temperature range support a variety of life.

Earth's Structure

As shown in **Figure 9**, Earth has a solid inner core surrounded by a liquid outer core. The mantle surrounds the liquid outer core. Above the mantle is Earth's crust. It is broken into large pieces, called plates, that constantly slide past, away from, or into each other. The crust is made mostly of oxygen and silicon and is constantly created and destroyed.

Reading Check Why is there life on Earth?

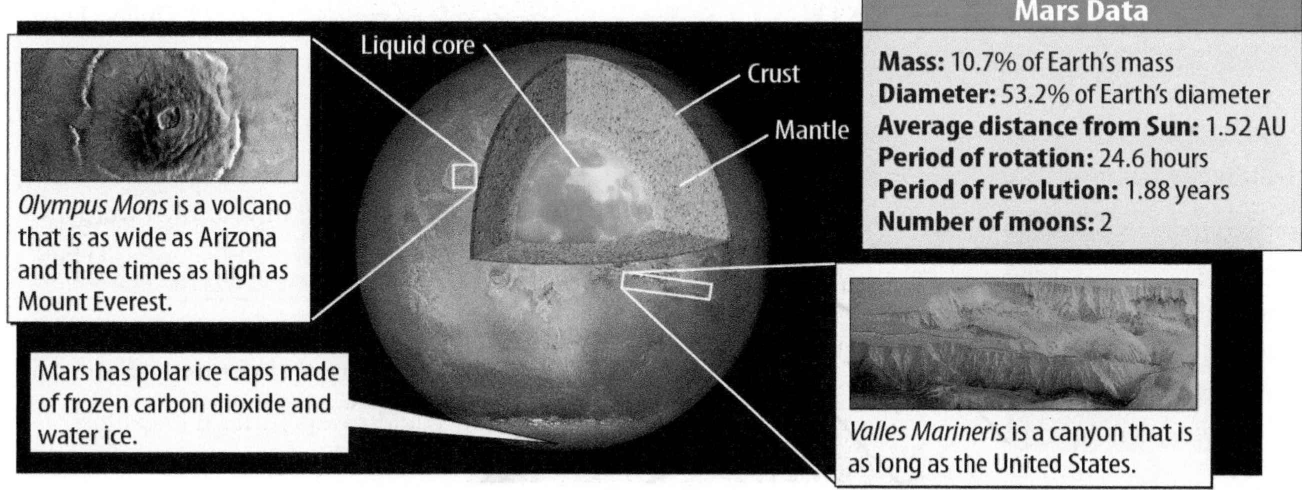

Liquid core
Crust
Mantle
Olympus Mons is a volcano that is as wide as Arizona and three times as high as Mount Everest.
Mars has polar ice caps made of frozen carbon dioxide and water ice.
Valles Marineris is a canyon that is as long as the United States.
Mars Data
Mass: 10.7% of Earth's mass
Diameter: 53.2% of Earth's diameter
Average distance from Sun: 1.52 AU
Period of rotation: 24.6 hours
Period of revolution: 1.88 years
Number of moons: 2

▲ **Figure 10** Mars is a small, rocky planet with deep canyons and tall mountains.

Mars

The fourth planet from the Sun is Mars, shown in Figure 10. Mars is about half the size of Earth. It has two very small and irregularly shaped moons. These moons might be asteroids that were captured by Mars's gravity.

Many space probes have visited Mars. Images of Mars show features that might have been made by water, such as the gullies in Figure 11. Recent findings from NASA's *Mars Reconnaissance Orbiters* (MRO) indicated that water flows periodically on the Martian surface.

Mars's Atmosphere

The atmosphere of Mars is about 95 percent carbon dioxide. It is thin and much less dense than Earth's atmosphere. Temperatures range from about −125°C at the poles to about 20°C at the equator during a martian summer. Winds on Mars sometimes produce great dust storms that last for months.

Mars's Surface

The reddish color of Mars is because its soil contains iron oxide, a compound in rust. Some of Mars's major surface features are shown in Figure 10. The enormous canyon Valles Marineris is about 4,000 km long. The Martian volcano Olympus Mons is the largest known mountain in the solar system. Mars also has polar ice caps made of frozen carbon dioxide and ice.

The southern hemisphere of Mars is covered with craters. The northern hemisphere is smoother and appears to be covered by lava flows. Some scientists have proposed that the lava flows were caused by the impact of an object about 2,000 km in diameter.

Key Concept Check Describe the atmosphere of each inner planet.

Figure 11 Gullies such as these might have been formed by the flow of liquid water on Mars billions of years ago. ▼

(t)NASA/JPL; (tc)NASA/JPL/Malin Space Science Systems; (tr)ESA/DLR/FU Berlin (G. Neukum); (b)NASA/JPL/University of Arizona

Lesson 2 Review

Visual Summary

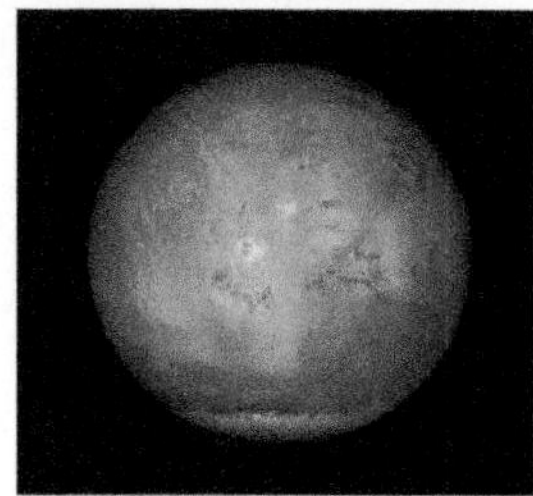

The terrestrial planets include Mercury, Venus, Earth, and Mars.

The inner planets all are made of rocks and minerals, but they have different characteristics. Earth is the only planet with liquid water.

The greenhouse effect greatly increases the surface temperature of Venus.

Use your lesson Foldable to review the lesson. Save your Foldable for the project at the end of the chapter.

What do you think NOW?

You first read the statements below at the beginning of the chapter.

3. Earth is the only inner planet that has a moon.

4. Venus is the hottest planet in the solar system.

Did you change your mind about whether you agree or disagree with the statements? Rewrite any false statements to make them true.

Use Vocabulary

1. **Define** *greenhouse effect* in your own words.

Understand Key Concepts

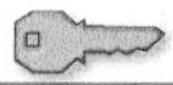

2. **Explain** why Venus is hotter than Mercury, even though Mercury is closer to the Sun.
3. **Infer** Why could rovers be used to explore Mars but not Venus?
4. Which of the inner planets has the greatest mass?

   A. Mercury
   B. Venus
   C. Earth
   D. Mars

5. **Relate** Describe the relationship between an inner planet's distance from the Sun and its period of revolution.

Interpret Graphics

6. **Infer** Which planet shown below is most likely able to support life now or was able to in the past? Explain your reasoning.

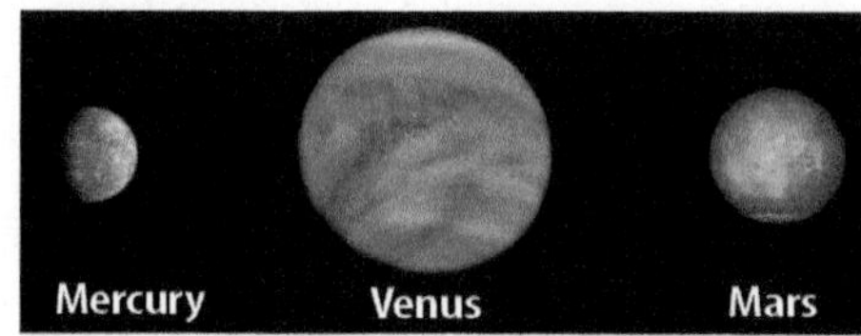

7. **Compare and Contrast** Copy and fill in the table below to compare and contrast properties of Venus and Earth.

Planet	Similarities	Differences
Venus		
Earth		

Critical Thinking

8. **Imagine** How might the temperatures on Mercury be different if it had the same mass as Earth? Explain.
9. **Judge** Do you think the inner planets should be explored or should the money be spent on other things? Justify your opinion.

(tl, br)NASA/JPL/Malin Space Science Systems; (cl)©Comstock/JupiterImages; (bl, bcr)NASA; (bcl)NASA/Johns Hopkins University Applied Physics Laboratory/Carnegie Institution of Washington

What can we learn about planets by graphing their characteristics?

Scientists collect and analyze data, and draw conclusions based on data. They are particularly interested in finding trends and relationships in data. One commonly used method of finding relationships is by graphing data. Graphing allows different types of data be to seen in relation to one another.

Learn It

Scientists know that some properties of the planets are related. **Graphing data** makes the relationships easy to identify. The graphs can show mathematical relationships such as direct and inverse relationships. Often, however, the graphs show that there is no relationship in the data.

Try It

1. You will plot two graphs that explore the relationships in data. The first graph compares a planet's distance from the Sun and its orbital period. The second graph compares a planet's distance from the Sun and its radius. Make a prediction about how these two sets of data are related, if at all. The data is shown in the table below.

Planet	Average Distance From the Sun (AU)	Orbital Period (yr)	Planet Radius (km)
Mercury	0.39	0.24	2440
Venus	0.72	0.62	6051
Earth	1.00	1.0	6378
Mars	1.52	1.9	3397
Jupiter	5.20	11.9	71,492
Saturn	9.58	29.4	60,268
Uranus	19.2	84.0	25,559
Neptune	30.1	164.0	24,764

2. Use the data in the table to plot a line graph showing orbital period versus average distance from the Sun. On the *x*-axis, plot the planet's distance from the Sun. On the *y*-axis, plot the planet's orbital period. Make sure the range of each axis is suitable for the data to be plotted, and clearly label each planet's data point.

3. Use the data in the table to plot a line graph showing planet radius versus average distance from the Sun. On the *y*-axis, plot the planet's radius. Make sure the range of each axis is suitable for the data to be plotted, and clearly label each planet's data point.

Apply It

4. Examine the *Orbital Period v. Distance from the Sun* graph. Does the graph show a relationship? If so, describe the relationship between a planet's distance from the Sun and its orbital period in your Science Journal.

5. Examine the *Planet Radius v. Distance from the Sun* graph. Does the graph show a relationship? If so, describe the relationship between a planet's distance from the Sun and its radius.

6. **Key Concept** Identify one or two characteristics the inner planets share that you learned from your graphs.

Lesson 3

Reading Guide

Key Concepts 

ESSENTIAL QUESTIONS

- How are the outer planets similar?
- What are the outer planets made of?

Vocabulary

Galilean moons p. 243

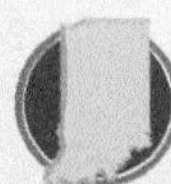 Multilingual eGlossary

SEPS.2, SEPS.5, SEPS.8, 6-8.LST.1.1, 6-8.LST.2.2, 6-8.LST.7.1, 6-8.LST.7.3

The Outer Planets

Inquiry What's below?

Clouds often prevent airplane pilots from seeing the ground below. Similarly, clouds block the view of Jupiter's surface. What do you think is below Jupiter's colorful cloud layer? The answer might surprise you—Jupiter is not at all like Earth.

NASA/JPL

Launch Lab

15 minutes

How do we see distant objects in the solar system?

Some of the outer planets were discovered hundreds of years ago. Why weren't all planets discovered?

1. Read and complete a lab safety form.
2. Use a **meterstick, masking tape,** and the **data table** to mark and label the position of each object on the tape on the floor along a straight line.
3. Shine a **flashlight** from "the Sun" horizontally along the tape.
4. Have a partner hold a page of this **book** in the flashlight beam at each planet location. Record your observations in your Science Journal.

Object	Distance from Sun (cm)
Sun	0
Jupiter	39
Saturn	71
Uranus	143
Neptune	295

Think About This

1. What happens to the image of the page as you move away from the flashlight?
2. **Key Concept** Why do you think it is more difficult to observe the outer planets than the inner planets?

The Gas Giants

Have you ever seen water drops on the outside of a glass of ice? They form because water vapor in the air changes to a liquid on the cold glass. Gases also change to liquids at high pressures. These properties of gases affect the outer planets.

The outer planets, shown in **Figure 12,** are called the gas giants because they are primarily made of hydrogen and helium. These elements are usually gases on Earth.

The outer planets have strong gravitational forces due to their large masses. The strong gravity creates tremendous atmospheric pressure that changes gases to liquids. Thus, the outer planets mainly have liquid interiors. In general, the outer planets have a thick gas and liquid layer covering a small, solid core.

Key Concept Check How are the outer planets similar?

Figure 12 The outer planets are primarily made of gases and liquids.

Visual Check Which outer planet is the largest?

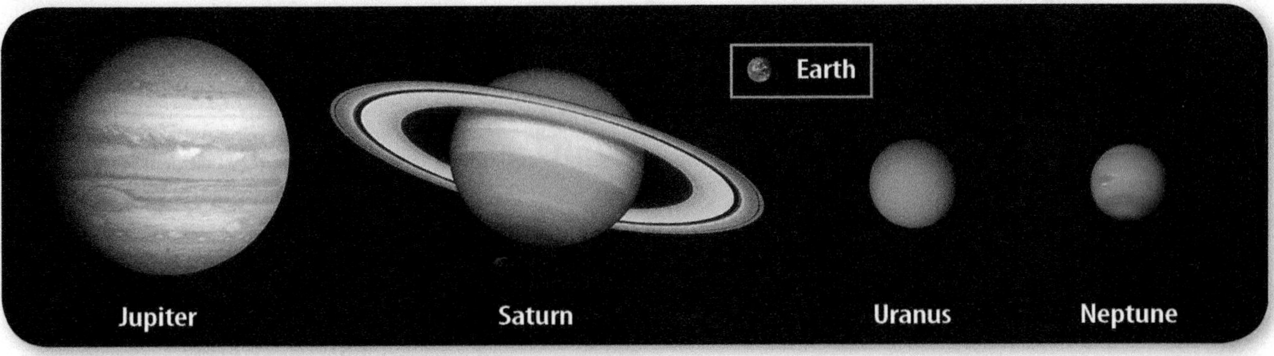

Jupiter

Figure 13 describes Jupiter, the largest planet in the solar system. Jupiter's diameter is more than 11 times larger than the diameter of Earth. Its mass is more than twice the mass of all the other planets combined. One way to understand just how big Jupiter is is to realize that more than 1,000 Earths would fit within this gaseous planet's volume.

Jupiter takes almost 12 Earth years to complete one orbit. Yet, it rotates faster than any other planet. Its period of rotation is less than 10 hours. Jupiter and all the outer planets have a ring system.

FOLDABLES®

Make a four-door book. Label each door with the name of an outer planet. Use the book to organize your notes on the outer planets.

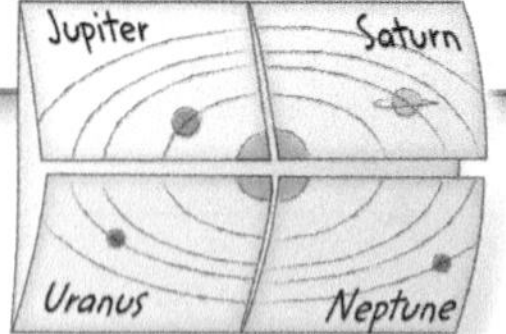

Jupiter's Atmosphere

The atmosphere on Jupiter is about 90 percent hydrogen and 10 percent helium and is about 1,000 km deep. Within the atmosphere are layers of dense, colorful clouds. Because Jupiter rotates so quickly, these clouds stretch into colorful, swirling bands. The Great Red Spot on the planet's surface is a storm of swirling gases.

Jupiter's Structure

Overall, Jupiter is about 80 percent hydrogen and 20 percent helium with small amounts of other materials. The planet is a ball of gas swirling around a thick liquid layer that conceals a solid core. About 1,000 km below the outer edge of the cloud layer, the pressure is so great that the hydrogen gas changes to liquid. This thick layer of liquid hydrogen surrounds Jupiter's core. Scientists do not know for sure what makes up the core. They suspect that the core is made of rock and iron. The core might be as large as Earth and could be 10 times more massive.

Key Concept Check Describe what makes up each of Jupiter's three distinct layers.

Figure 13  Jupiter is mainly hydrogen and helium. Throughout most of the planet, the pressure is high enough to change the hydrogen gas into a liquid.

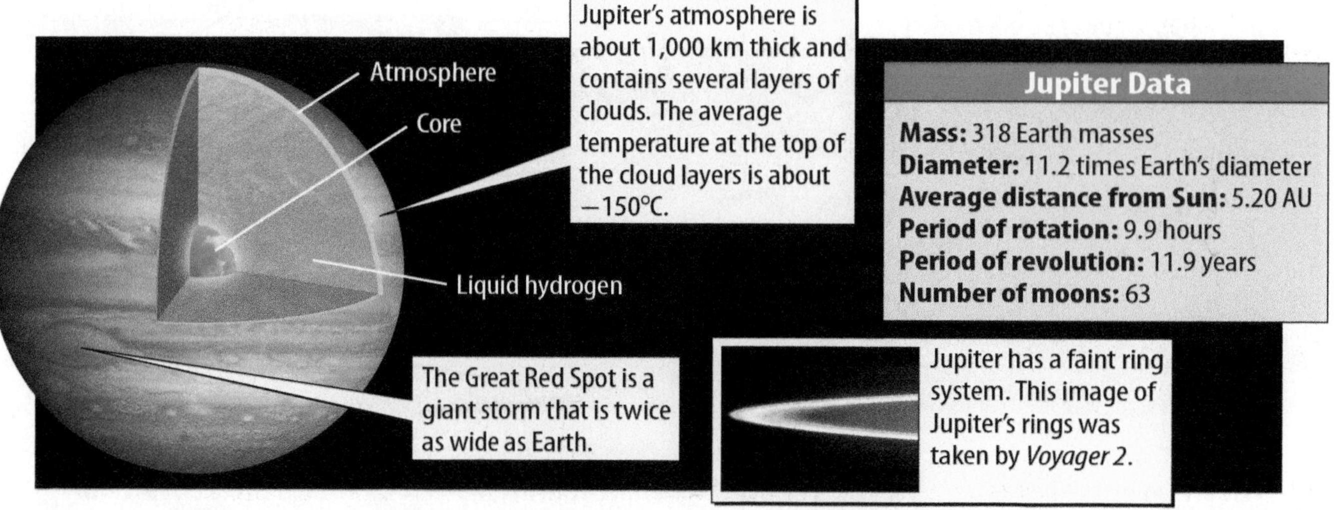

Atmosphere
Core
Liquid hydrogen
Jupiter's atmosphere is about 1,000 km thick and contains several layers of clouds. The average temperature at the top of the cloud layers is about −150°C.
Jupiter Data
Mass: 318 Earth masses
Diameter: 11.2 times Earth's diameter
Average distance from Sun: 5.20 AU
Period of rotation: 9.9 hours
Period of revolution: 11.9 years
Number of moons: 63
The Great Red Spot is a giant storm that is twice as wide as Earth.
Jupiter has a faint ring system. This image of Jupiter's rings was taken by *Voyager 2*.

The Moons of Jupiter

Jupiter has at least 63 moons, more than any other planet. Jupiter's four largest moons were first discovered by Galileo Galilei in 1610. *The four largest moons of Jupiter–Io, Europa, Ganymede, and Callisto–are known as the* **Galilean moons.** The Galilean moons all are made of rock and ice. The moons Ganymede, Callisto, and Io are larger than Earth's Moon. Collisions between Jupiter's moons and meteorites likely resulted in the particles that make up the planet's faint rings.

Saturn

Saturn is the sixth planet from the Sun. Like Jupiter, Saturn rotates rapidly and has horizontal bands of clouds. Saturn is about 90 percent hydrogen and 10 percent helium. It is the least dense planet. Its density is less than that of water.

Saturn's Structure

Saturn is made mostly of hydrogen and helium with small amounts of other materials. As shown in Figure 14, Saturn's structure is similar to Jupiter's structure–an outer gas layer, a thick layer of liquid hydrogen, and a solid core.

The ring system around Saturn is the largest and most complex in the solar system. Saturn has seven bands of rings, each containing thousands of narrower ringlets. The main ring system is over 70,000 km wide, but it is likely less than 30 m thick. The ice particles in the rings are possibly from a moon that was shattered in a collision with another icy object.

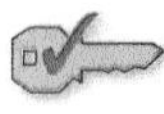

Key Concept Check Describe what makes up Saturn and its ring system.

Math Skills

Ratios

A ratio is a quotient—it is one quantity divided by another. Ratios can be used to compare distances. For example, Jupiter is 5.20 AU from the Sun, and Neptune is 30.05 AU from the Sun. Divide the larger distance by the smaller distance:

$$\frac{30.05 \text{ AU}}{5.20 \text{ AU}} = 5.78$$

Neptune is 5.78 times farther from the Sun than Jupiter.

Practice

How many times farther from the Sun is Uranus (distance = 19.20 AU) than Saturn (distance = 9.58 AU)?

Math Practice

Personal Tutor

Figure 14 Like Jupiter, Saturn is mainly hydrogen and helium. Saturn's rings are one of the most noticeable features of the solar system.

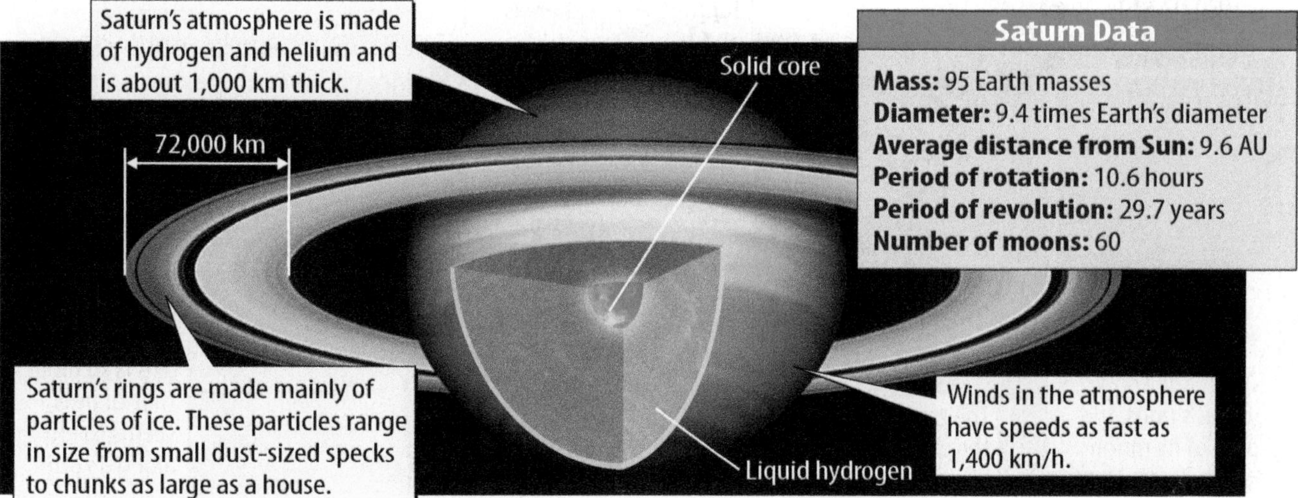

Saturn's atmosphere is made of hydrogen and helium and is about 1,000 km thick.
72,000 km
Solid core
Saturn's rings are made mainly of particles of ice. These particles range in size from small dust-sized specks to chunks as large as a house.
Liquid hydrogen
Winds in the atmosphere have speeds as fast as 1,400 km/h.

Saturn Data

Mass: 95 Earth masses
Diameter: 9.4 times Earth's diameter
Average distance from Sun: 9.6 AU
Period of rotation: 10.6 hours
Period of revolution: 29.7 years
Number of moons: 60

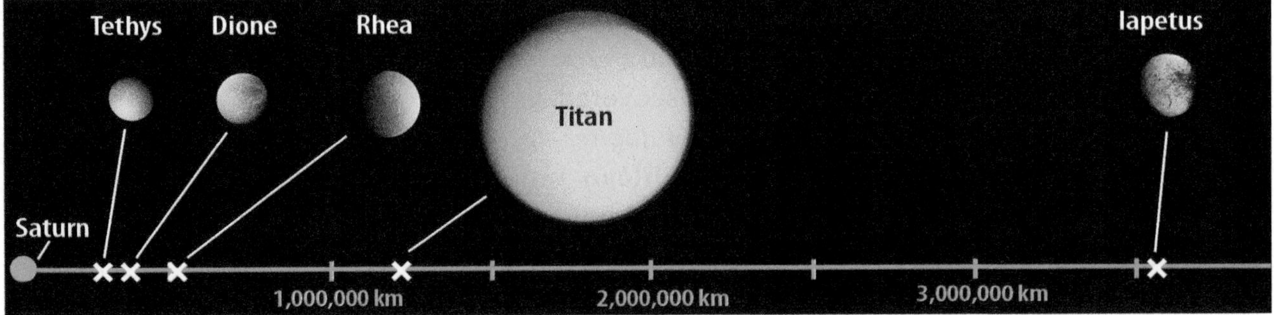
Tethys
Dione
Rhea
Titan
Iapetus
Saturn
1,000,000 km
2,000,000 km
3,000,000 km

▲ **Figure 15** The five largest moons of Saturn are shown above drawn to scale. Titan is Saturn's largest moon.

Saturn's Moons

Saturn has at least 60 moons. The five largest moons, Titan, Rhea, Dione, Iapetus, and Tethys, are shown in **Figure 15.** Most of Saturn's moons are chunks of ice less than 10 km in diameter. However, Titan is larger than the planet Mercury. Titan is the only moon in the solar system with a dense atmosphere. In 2005, the *Cassini* orbiter released the *Huygens* (HOY guns) **probe** that landed on Titan's surface.

WORD ORIGIN

probe
from Medieval Latin *proba*, means "examination"

Uranus

Uranus, shown in **Figure 16,** is the seventh planet from the Sun. It has a system of narrow, dark rings and a diameter about four times that of Earth. *Voyager 2* is the only space probe to explore Uranus. The probe flew by the planet in 1986.

Uranus has a deep atmosphere composed mostly of hydrogen and helium. The atmosphere also contains a small amount of methane. Beneath the atmosphere is a thick, slushy layer of water, ammonia, and other materials. Uranus might also have a solid, rocky core.

Key Concept Check Identify the substances that make up the atmosphere and the thick slushy layer on Uranus.

Figure 16 Uranus is mainly gas and liquid, with a small solid core. Methane gas in the atmosphere gives Uranus a bluish color. ▼

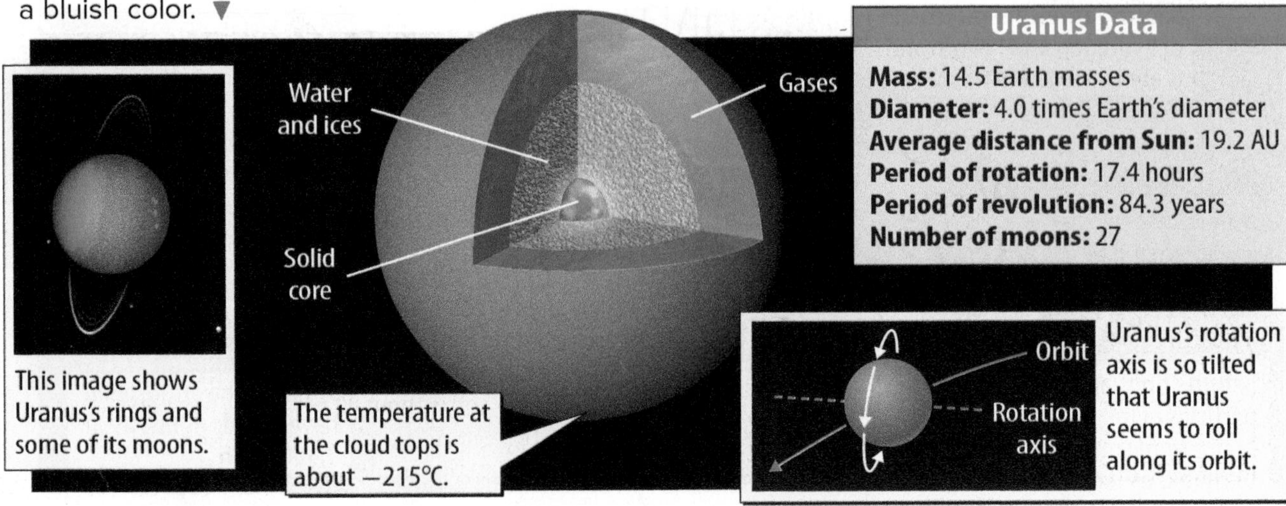
Water and ices
Gases
Solid core
This image shows Uranus's rings and some of its moons.
The temperature at the cloud tops is about −215°C.
Orbit
Rotation axis
Uranus's rotation axis is so tilted that Uranus seems to roll along its orbit.

Uranus Data
Mass: 14.5 Earth masses
Diameter: 4.0 times Earth's diameter
Average distance from Sun: 19.2 AU
Period of rotation: 17.4 hours
Period of revolution: 84.3 years
Number of moons: 27

(t)NASA/JPL/Space Science Institute; (b)NASA/ESA and Erich Karkoschka, University of Arizona; (br)NASA/JPL

Uranus's Axis and Moons

Figure 16 shows that Uranus has a tilted axis of rotation. In fact, it is so tilted that the planet moves around the Sun like a rolling ball. This sideways tilt might have been caused by a collision with an Earth-sized object.

Uranus has at least 27 moons. The two largest moons, Titania and Oberon, are considerably smaller than Earth's moon. Titania has an icy cracked surface that once might have been covered by an ocean.

Neptune

Neptune, shown in Figure 17, was discovered in 1846. Like Uranus, Neptune's atmosphere is mostly hydrogen and helium, with a trace of methane. Its interior also is similar to the interior of Uranus. Neptune's interior is partially frozen water and ammonia with a rock and iron core. It has at least 13 moons and a faint, dark ring system. Its largest moon, Triton, is made of rock with an icy outer layer. It has a surface of frozen nitrogen and geysers that erupt nitrogen gas.

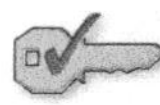

Key Concept Check How does the atmosphere and interior of Neptune compare with that of Uranus?

MiniLab — 15 minutes

How do Saturn's moons affect its rings?

In this lab, sugar models Saturn's rings. How might Saturn's moons affect its rings?

1. Read and complete a lab safety form.
2. Hold two **sharpened pencils** with their points even and then **tape** them together.
3. Insert a third pencil into the hole in a **record.** Hold the pencil so the record is in a horizontal position.
4. Have your partner sprinkle **sugar** evenly over the surface of the record. Hold the taped pencils vertically over the record so that the tips rest in the record's grooves.
5. Slowly turn the record. In your Science Journal, record what happens to the sugar.

Analyze and Conclude

1. **Compare and Contrast** What feature of Saturn's rings do the pencils model?
2. **Infer** What do you think causes the spaces between the rings of Saturn?
3. **Key Concept** What would have to be true for a moon to interact in this way with Saturn's rings?

Figure 17 The atmosphere of Neptune is similar to that of Uranus—mainly hydrogen and helium with a trace of methane. The dark circular areas on Neptune are swirling storms. In addition to the great dark spot, two other massive storms have appeared and faded over the last decade. Winds on Neptune sometimes exceed 1,000 km/h.

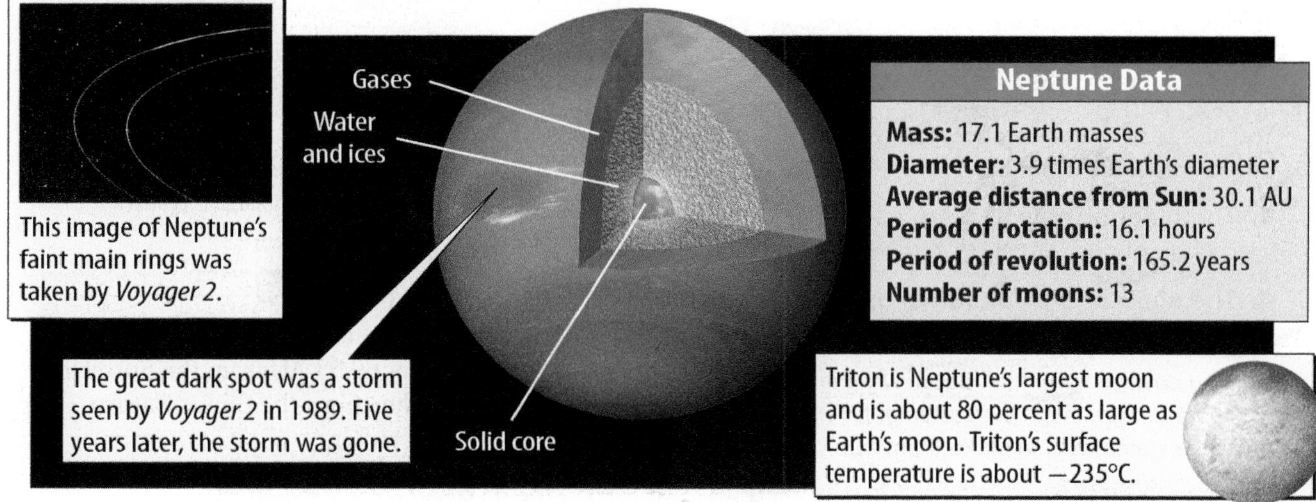

Gases
Water and ices
Solid core
This image of Neptune's faint main rings was taken by *Voyager 2*.
The great dark spot was a storm seen by *Voyager 2* in 1989. Five years later, the storm was gone.
Triton is Neptune's largest moon and is about 80 percent as large as Earth's moon. Triton's surface temperature is about −235°C.

Neptune Data

Mass: 17.1 Earth masses
Diameter: 3.9 times Earth's diameter
Average distance from Sun: 30.1 AU
Period of rotation: 16.1 hours
Period of revolution: 165.2 years
Number of moons: 13

NASA/JPL

Lesson 3 Review

Visual Summary

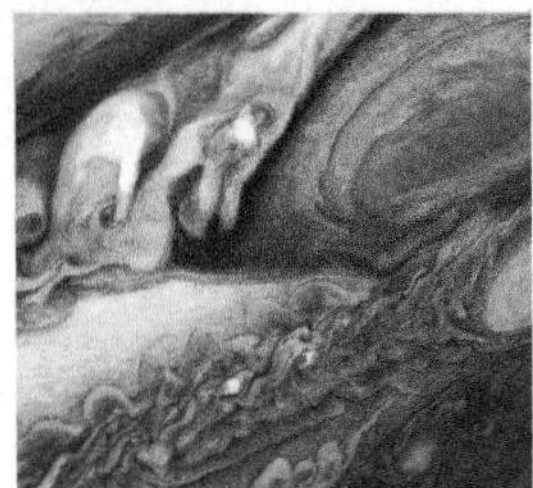

All of the outer planets are primarily made of materials that are gases on Earth. Colorful clouds of gas cover Saturn and Jupiter.

Jupiter is the largest outer planet. Its four largest moons are known as the Galilean moons.

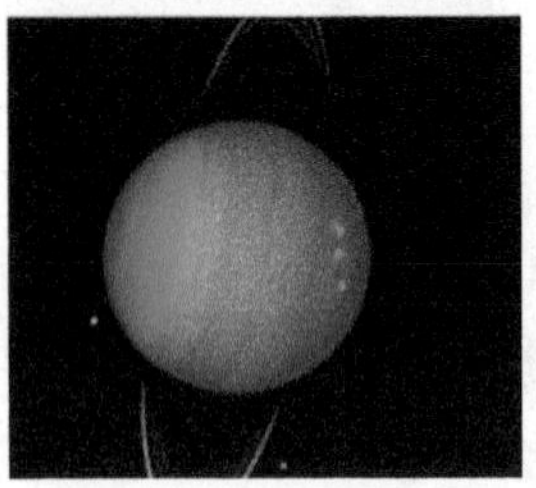

Uranus has an unusual tilt, possibly due to a collision with a large object.

Use your lesson Foldable to review the lesson. Save your Foldable for the project at the end of the chapter.

What do you think NOW?

You first read the statements below at the beginning of the chapter.

5. The outer planets also are called the gas giants.

6. The atmospheres of Saturn and Jupiter are mainly water vapor.

Did you change your mind about whether you agree or disagree with the statements? Rewrite any false statements to make them true.

Use Vocabulary

1 Identify What are the four Galilean moons of Jupiter?

Understand Key Concepts

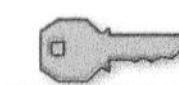

2 Contrast How are the rings of Saturn different from the rings of Jupiter?

3 Which planet's rings probably formed from a collision between an icy moon and another icy object?

A. Jupiter **C.** Saturn
B. Neptune **D.** Uranus

4 List the outer planets by increasing mass.

Interpret Graphics

5 Infer from the diagram below how Uranus's tilted axis affects its seasons.

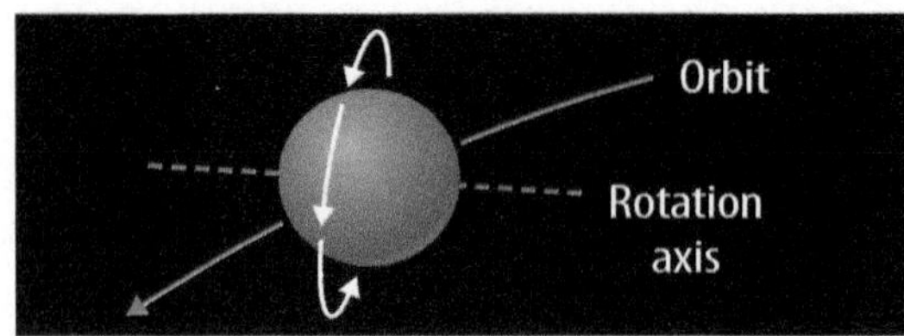

6 Organize Information Copy the organizer below and use it to list the outer planets.

Critical Thinking

7 Predict what would happen to Jupiter's atmosphere if its gravitational force suddenly decreased. Explain.

8 Evaluate Is life more likely on a dry and rocky moon or on an icy moon? Explain.

Math Skills

9 Calculate Mars is about 1.52 AU from the Sun, and Saturn is about 9.58 AU from the Sun. How many times farther from the Sun is Saturn than Mars?

AMERICAN MUSEUM ō NATURAL HISTORY

Pluto

CAREERS in SCIENCE

What in the world is it?

Since Pluto's discovery in 1930, students have learned that the solar system has nine planets. But in 2006, the number of planets was changed to eight. What happened?

Neil deGrasse Tyson is an astrophysicist at the American Museum of Natural History in New York City. He and his fellow Museum scientists were among the first to question Pluto's classification as a planet. One reason was that Pluto is smaller than six moons in our solar system, including Earth's moon. Another reason was that Pluto's orbit is more oval-shaped, or elliptical, than the orbits of other planets. Also, Pluto has the most tilted orbit of all planets—17 degrees out of the plane of the solar system. Finally, unlike other planets, Pluto is mostly ice.

Tyson also questioned the definition of a planet—an object that orbits the Sun. Then shouldn't comets be planets? In addition, he noted that when Ceres, an object orbiting the Sun between Jupiter and Mars, was discovered in 1801, it was classified as a planet. But, as astronomers discovered more objects like Ceres, it was reclassified as an asteroid. Then, during the 1990s, many space objects similar to Pluto were discovered. They orbit the Sun beyond Neptune's orbit in a region called the Kuiper belt.

These new discoveries led Tyson and others to conclude that Pluto should be reclassified. In 2006, the International Astronomical Union agreed. Pluto was reclassified as a dwarf planet—an object that is spherical in shape and orbits the Sun in a zone with other objects. Pluto lost its rank as smallest planet, but became "king of the Kuiper belt."

Pluto TIME LINE

1930
Astronomer Clyde Tombaugh discovers a ninth planet, Pluto.

1992
The first object is discovered in the Kuiper belt.

July 2005
Eris—a Pluto-sized object—is discovered in the Kuiper belt.

January 2006
NASA launches *New Horizons* spacecraft. It reached Pluto in 2015.

August 2006
Pluto is reclassified as a dwarf planet.

Neil deGrasse Tyson is director of the Hayden Planetarium at the American Museum of Natural History. ▶

This illustration shows what Pluto might look like if you were standing on one of its moons.

It's Your Turn

RESEARCH With a group, identify the different types of objects in our solar system. Consider size, composition, location, and whether the objects have moons. Propose at least two different ways to group the objects.

Lesson 4

Dwarf Planets and Other Objects

Reading Guide

Key Concepts 

ESSENTIAL QUESTIONS

- What is a dwarf planet?
- What are the characteristics of comets and asteroids?
- How does an impact crater form?

Vocabulary

meteoroid p. 252

meteor p. 252

meteorite p. 252

impact crater p. 252

 Multilingual eGlossary

6.ESS.3, SEPS.1, SEPS.2, SEPS.3, SEPS.4, SEPS.5, SEPS.7, SEPS.8, 6-8.LST.1.1, 6-8.LST.1.2, 6-8.LST.3.2, 6-8.LST.3.3, 6-8.LST.7.3

 Go to the resource tab in ConnectED to find the PBL *PBI: Planetary Bureau of Investigation.*

 Will it return?

You would probably remember a sight like this. This image of comet C/2006 P1 was taken in 2007. The comet is no longer visible from Earth. Believe it or not, many comets appear then reappear hundreds to millions of years later.

Gordon Garradd/Science Source

Launch Lab

15 minutes

How might asteroids and moons form?

In this activity, you will explore one way moons and asteroids might have formed.

1. Read and complete a lab safety form.
2. Form a small ball from **modeling clay** and roll it in **sand.**
3. Press a thin layer of modeling clay around a **marble.**
4. Tie equal lengths of **string** to each ball. Hold the strings so the balls are above a **sheet of paper.**
5. Have someone pull back the marble so that its string is parallel to the tabletop and then release it. Record the results in your Science Journal.

Think About This

1. If the collision you modeled occurred in space, what would happen to the sand?
2. **Key Concept** Infer one way scientists propose moons and asteroids formed.

Dwarf Planets

Ceres was discovered in 1801 and was called a planet until similar objects were discovered near it. Then it was called an asteroid. For decades after Pluto's discovery in 1930, it was called a planet. Then, similar objects were discovered, and Pluto lost its planet classification. What type of object is Pluto?

Pluto once was classified as a planet, but it is now classified as a dwarf planet. In 2006, the International Astronomical Union (IAU) adopted "dwarf planet" as a new category. The IAU defines a dwarf planet as an object that orbits the Sun, has enough mass and gravity to form a sphere, and has objects similar in mass orbiting near it or crossing its orbital path. Astronomers classify Pluto, Ceres, Eris, MakeMake (MAH kay MAH kay), and Haumea (how MAY uh) as dwarf planets. Figure 18 shows four dwarf planets.

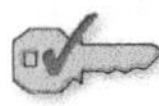

Key Concept Check Describe the characteristics of a dwarf planet.

Project-Based Learning Activity

PBI: Planetary Bureau of Investigation Go online to compare and contrast the characteristics of objects in the solar system, including Earth and the other planets, the Moon, dwarf planets, comets, asteroids, and meteoroids.

Figure 18 Four dwarf planets are shown to scale. All dwarf planets are smaller than the Moon.

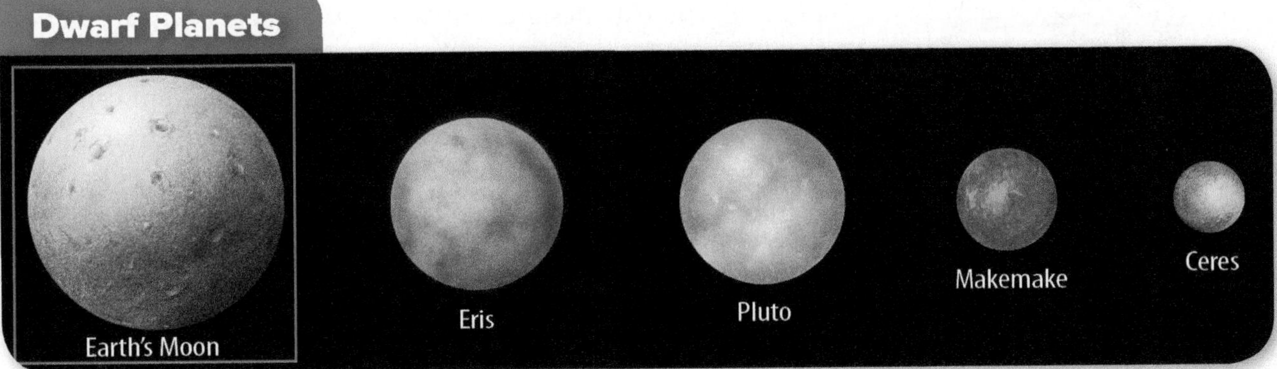

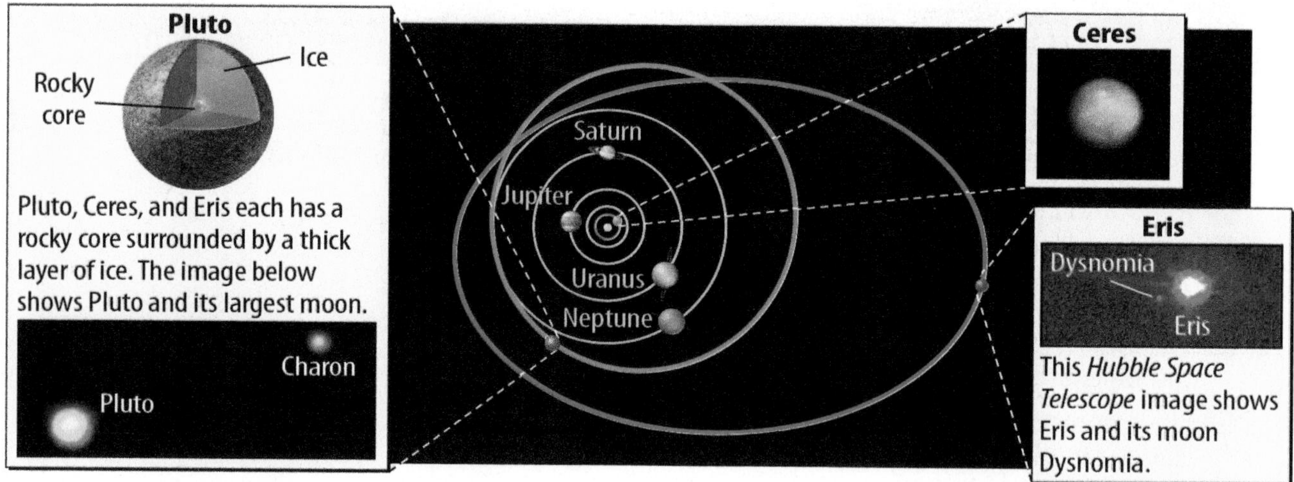
Pluto
Ice
Rocky core
Pluto, Ceres, and Eris each has a rocky core surrounded by a thick layer of ice. The image below shows Pluto and its largest moon.
Charon
Pluto
Saturn
Jupiter
Uranus
Neptune
Ceres
Eris
Dysnomia
Eris
This *Hubble Space Telescope* image shows Eris and its moon Dysnomia.

Figure 19 Because most dwarf planets are so far from Earth, astronomers do not have detailed images of them.

Visual Check Which dwarf planet orbits closest to Earth?

Ceres

Ceres, shown in **Figure 19**, orbits the Sun in the asteroid belt. With a diameter of about 950 km, Ceres is about one-fourth the size of the Moon. It is the smallest dwarf planet. Ceres might have a rocky core surrounded by a layer of water ice and a thin, dusty crust.

Pluto

Pluto is about two-thirds the size of the Moon. Pluto is so far from the Sun that its period of revolution is about 248 years. Like Ceres, Pluto has a rocky core surrounded by ice. With an average surface temperature of about −230°C, Pluto is so cold that it is covered with frozen nitrogen.

Pluto has three known moons. The largest moon, Charon, has a diameter that is about half the diameter of Pluto. Pluto also has two smaller moons, Hydra and Nix.

Eris

The largest dwarf planet, Eris, was discovered in 2003. Its orbit lasts about 557 years. Currently, Eris is three times farther from the Sun than Pluto is. The structure of Eris is probably similar to Pluto. Dysnomia (dis NOH mee uh) is the only known moon of Eris.

Makemake and Haumea

In 2008, the IAU designated two new objects as dwarf planets: Makemake and Haumea. Though smaller than Pluto, Makemake is one of the largest objects in a region of the solar system called the Kuiper (KI puhr) belt. The Kuiper belt extends from about the orbit of Neptune to about 50 AU from the Sun. Haumea is also in the Kuiper belt and is smaller than Pluto.

Reading Check Which dwarf planet is the largest? Which dwarf planet is the smallest?

FOLDABLES®

Make a layered book from two sheets of paper. Label it as shown. Use it to organize your notes on other objects in the solar system.

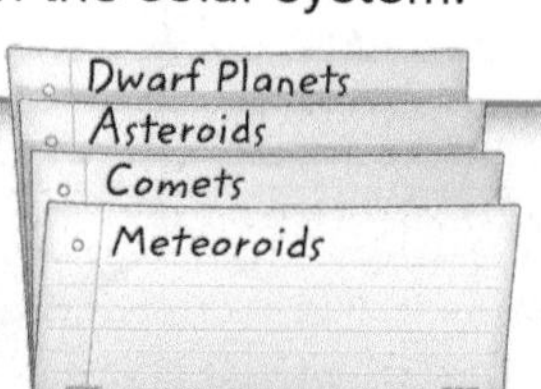
Dwarf Planets
Asteroids
Comets
Meteoroids

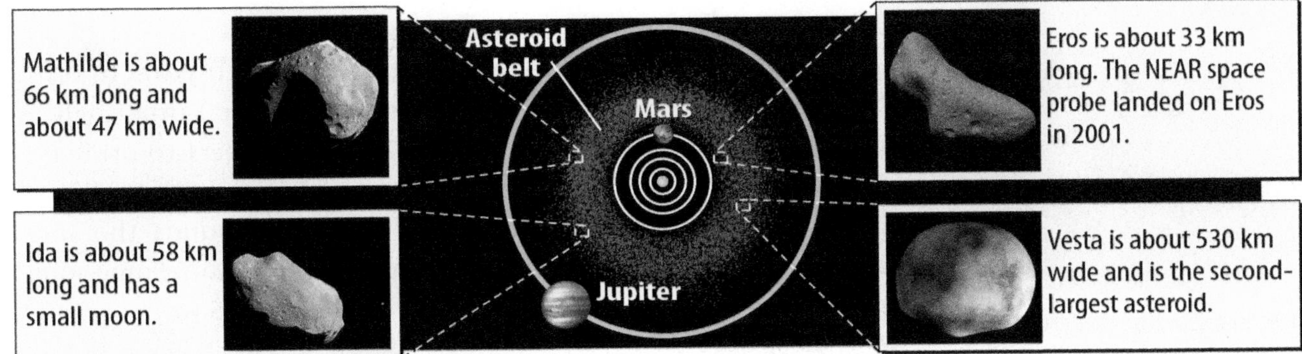

Mathilde is about 66 km long and about 47 km wide.
Asteroid belt
Mars
Jupiter
Eros is about 33 km long. The NEAR space probe landed on Eros in 2001.
Ida is about 58 km long and has a small moon.
Vesta is about 530 km wide and is the second-largest asteroid.

Figure 20 The asteroids that orbit the Sun in the asteroid belt are many sizes and shapes.

Asteroids

Recall from Lesson 1 that asteroids are pieces of rock and ice. Most asteroids orbit the Sun in the asteroid belt. The asteroid belt is between the orbits of Mars and Jupiter, as shown in **Figure 20**. Hundreds of thousands of asteroids have been discovered. The largest asteroid, Pallas, is over 500 km in diameter.

Asteroids are chunks of rock and ice that never clumped together like the rocks and ice that formed the inner planets. Some astronomers suggest that the strength of Jupiter's gravitational field might have caused the chunks to collide so violently, and they broke apart instead of sticking together. This means that asteroids are objects left over from the formation of the solar system.

 **Key Concept Check** Where do the orbits of most asteroids occur?

Comets

Recall that comets are mixtures of rock, ice, and dust. The particles in a comet are loosely held together by the gravitational attractions among the particles. As shown in **Figure 21**, comets orbit the Sun in long elliptical orbits.

The Structure of Comets

The solid, inner part of a comet is its nucleus, as shown in **Figure 21**. As a comet moves closer to the Sun, it absorbs thermal energy and can develop a bright tail. Heating changes the ice in the comet into a gas. Energy from the Sun pushes some of the gas and dust away from the nucleus and makes it glow. This produces the comet's bright tail and glowing nucleus, called a coma.

 **Key Concept Check** Describe the characteristics of a comet.

Figure 21 When energy from the Sun strikes the gas and dust in the comet's nucleus, it can create a two-part tail. The gas tail always points away from the Sun.

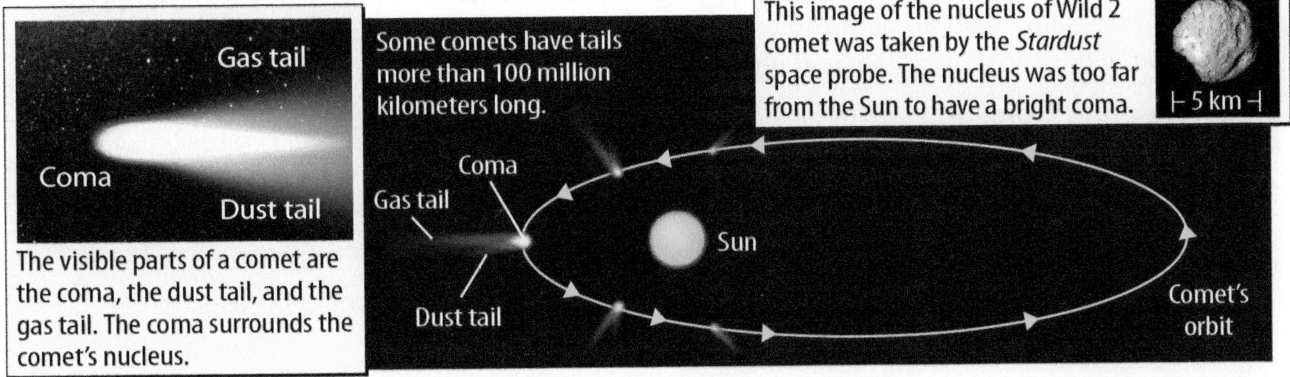

Gas tail
Coma
Dust tail
The visible parts of a comet are the coma, the dust tail, and the gas tail. The coma surrounds the comet's nucleus.
Some comets have tails more than 100 million kilometers long.
Coma
Gas tail
Dust tail
Sun
Comet's orbit
This image of the nucleus of Wild 2 comet was taken by the *Stardust* space probe. The nucleus was too far from the Sun to have a bright coma.
5 km

Figure 22 When a large meteorite strikes, it can form a giant impact crater like this 1.2-km wide crater in Arizona.

Short-Period and Long-Period Comets

A short-period comet takes less than 200 Earth years to orbit the Sun. Most short-period comets come from the Kuiper belt. A long-period comet takes more than 200 Earth years to orbit the Sun. Long-period comets come from an area at the outer edge of the solar system, called the Oort cloud. It surrounds the solar system and extends about 100,000 AU from the Sun. Some long-period comets take millions of years to orbit the Sun.

Meteoroids

WORD ORIGIN

meteor
from Greek *meteoros,* means "high up"

Every day, many millions of particles called meteoroids enter Earth's atmosphere. *A* **meteoroid** *is a small, rocky particle that moves through space.* Most meteoroids are only about as big as a grain of sand. As a meteoroid passes through Earth's atmosphere, friction makes the meteoroid and the air around it hot enough to glow. *A* **meteor** *is a meteoroid that has entered Earth's atmosphere, producing a streak of light.* Most meteoroids burn up in the atmosphere. However, some meteoroids are large enough that they reach Earth's surface before they burn up completely. When this happens, it is called a meteorite. *A* **meteorite** *is a meteoroid that strikes a planet or a moon.*

When a large meteoroite strikes a moon or planet, it often forms a bowl-shaped depression such as the one shown in Figure 22. *An* **impact crater** *is a round depression formed on the surface of a planet, moon, or other space object by the impact of a meteorite.* The limited number of impact craters on Earth is due to the processes of erosion, tectonics, and volcanism.

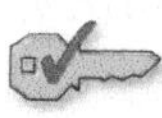

Key Concept Check What causes an impact crater to form?

MiniLab

20 minutes

How do impact craters form?

In this lab, you will model the formation of an impact crater.

1. Pour a layer of **flour** about 3 cm deep in a **cake pan.**
2. Pour a layer of **cornmeal** about 1 cm deep on top of the flour.
3. One at a time, drop different-sized **marbles** into the mixture from the same height—about 15 cm. Record your observations in your Science Journal.

Analyze and Conclude

1. **Describe** the mixture's surface after you dropped the marbles.
2. **Recognize Cause and Effect** Based on your results, explain why impact craters on moons and planets differ.
3. **Key Concept** Explain how the marbles used in the activity could be used to model meteoroids, meteors, and meteorites.

Lesson 4 Review

Visual Summary

An asteroid, such as Ida, is a chunk of rock and ice that orbits the Sun.

Comets, which are mixture of rock , ice, and dust, orbit the Sun. A comet's tail is caused by its interaction with the Sun.

When a large meteorite strikes a planet or moon, it often makes an impact crater.

Use your lesson Foldable to review the lesson. Save your Foldable for the project at the end of the chapter.

What do you think NOW?

You first read the statements below at the beginning of the chapter.

7. Asteroids and comets are mainly rock and ice.

8. A meteoroid is a meteor that strikes Earth.

Did you change your mind about whether you agree or disagree with the statements? Rewrite any false statements to make them true.

Use Vocabulary

1. **Define** *impact crater* in your own words.
2. **Distinguish** between a meteorite and a meteoroid.
3. **Use the term** *meteor* in a complete sentence.

Understand Key Concepts

4. Which produces an impact crater?
   A. comet
   B. meteor
   C. meteorite
   D. planet
5. **Reason** Are you more likely to see a meteor or a meteoroid? Explain.
6. **Differentiate** between objects located in the asteroid belt and objects located in the Kuiper belt.

Interpret Graphics

7. **Explain** why some comets have a two-part tail during portions of their orbit.

8. **Organize Information** Copy the table below and list the major characteristics of a dwarf planet.

Object	Defining Characteristic
Dwarf Planet	

Critical Thinking

9. **Compose** a paragraph describing what early sky observers might have thought when they saw a comet.
10. **Evaluate** Do you agree with the decision to reclassify Pluto as a dwarf planet? Defend your opinion.

(t)NASA/JPL/USGS; (cl)Gordon Garradd/SPL/Science Source; (bl)©Jonathan Blair/Corbis; (br) ©Rawan Hussein/Alamy Stock Photo

Lab

40 minutes

Materials

2.25 in–wide register tape (several rolls)

meterstick

masking tape

colored markers

Safety

Scaling down the Solar System

A scale model is a physical representation of something that is much smaller or much larger. Reduced-size scale models are made of very large things, such as the solar system. The scale used must reduce the actual size to a size reasonable for the model.

Question

What scale can you use to represent the distances between solar system objects?

Procedure

1. First, decide how big your solar system will be. Use the data given in the table to figure out how far apart the Sun and Neptune would be if a scale of 1 meter = 1 AU is used. Would a solar system based on that scale fit in the space you have available?
2. With your group determine the scale that results in a model that fits the available space. Larger models are usually more accurate, so choose a scale that produces the largest model that fits in the available space.
3. Once you have decided on a scale, copy the table in your Science Journal. Replace the word *(Scale)* in the third column of the table with the unit you have chosen. Then fill in the scaled distance for each planet.

Planet	Distance from the Sun (AU)	Distance from the Sun (Scale)
Mercury	0.39	
Venus	0.72	
Earth	1.00	
Mars	1.52	
Jupiter	5.20	
Saturn	9.54	
Uranus	19.18	
Neptune	30.06	

4. On register tape, mark the positions of objects in the solar system based on your chosen scale. Use a length of register tape that is slightly longer than the scaled distance between the Sun and Neptune.
5. Tape the ends of the register tape to a table or the floor. Mark a dot at one end of the paper to represent the Sun. Measure along the tape from the center of the dot to the location of Mercury. Mark a dot at this position and label it *Mercury*. Repeat this process for the remaining planets.

5

Analyze and Conclude

6. **Critique** There are many objects in the solar system. These objects have different sizes, structures, and orbits. Examine your scale model of the solar system. How accurate is the model? How could the model be changed to be more accurate?
7. **The Big Idea** Pluto is a dwarf planet located beyond Neptune. Based on the pattern of distance data for the planets shown in the table, approximately how far from the Sun would you expect to find Pluto? Explain you reasoning.
8. **Calculate** What length of register tape is needed if a scale of 30 cm = 1 AU is used for the solar system model?

Communicate Your Results

Compare your model with other groups in your class by taping them all side-by-side. Discuss any major differences in your models. Discuss the difficulties in making the scale models much smaller.

Inquiry

Extension

How can you build a scale model of the solar system that accurately shows both planetary diameters and distances? Describe how you would go about figuring this out.

Lab Tips

- A scale is the ratio between the actual size of something and a representation of it.
- The distances between the planets and the Sun are average distances because planetary orbits are not perfect circles.

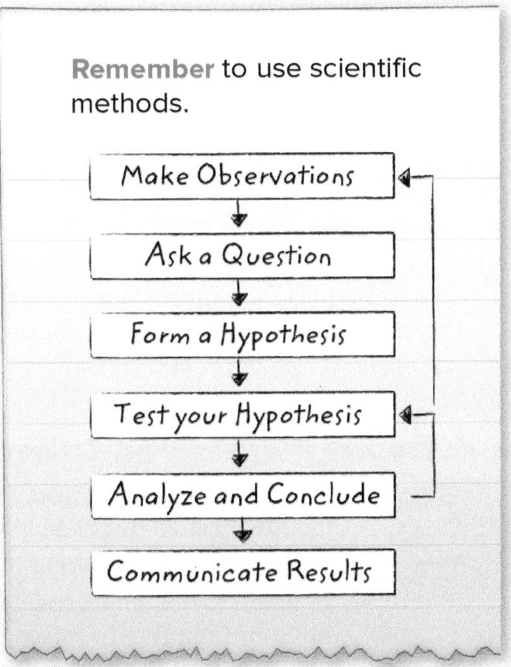

Remember to use scientific methods.
Make Observations
Ask a Question
Form a Hypothesis
Test your Hypothesis
Analyze and Conclude
Communicate Results

Hutchings Photography/Digital Light Source

Chapter 7 Study Guide

The solar system contains planets, dwarf planets, comets, asteroids, and other small solar system bodies.

Key Concepts Summary 

Lesson 1: The Structure of the Solar System

- The inner planets are made mainly of solid materials. The outer planets, which are larger than the inner planets, have thick gas and liquid layers covering a small solid core.
- Astronomers measure vast distances in space in **astronomical units;** an astronomical unit is about 150 million km.
- The speed of each planet changes as it moves along its elliptical orbit around the Sun.

Vocabulary

asteroid p. 227
comet p. 227
astronomical unit p. 228
period of revolution p. 228
period of rotation p. 228

Lesson 2: The Inner Planets

- The inner planets—Mercury, Venus, Earth, and Mars—are made of rock and metallic materials.
- The **greenhouse effect** makes Venus the hottest planet.
- Mercury has no atmosphere. The atmospheres of Venus and Mars are almost entirely carbon dioxide. Earth's atmosphere is a mixture of gases and a small amount of water vapor.

Vocabulary

terrestrial planet p. 233
greenhouse effect p. 235

Lesson 3: The Outer Planets

- The outer planets—Jupiter, Saturn, Uranus, and Neptune—are primarily made of hydrogen and helium.
- Jupiter and Saturn have thick cloud layers, but are mainly liquid hydrogen. Saturn's rings are largely particles of ice. Uranus and Neptune have thick atmospheres of hydrogen and helium.

Vocabulary

Galilean moons p. 243

Lesson 4: Dwarf Planets and Other Objects

- A dwarf planet is an object that orbits a star, has enough mass to pull itself into a spherical shape, and has objects similar in mass orbiting near it.
- An asteroid is a small rocky object that orbits the Sun. Comets are made of rock, ice, and dust and orbit the Sun in highly elliptical paths.
- The impact of a **meteorite** forms an **impact crater.**

Vocabulary

meteoroid p. 252
meteor p. 252
meteorite p. 252
impact crater p. 252

Personal Tutor

Vocabulary eGames
Vocabulary eFlashcards

Chapter Project

Assemble your lesson Foldables as shown to make a Chapter Project. Use the project to review what you have learned in this chapter.

Use Vocabulary

Match each phrase with the correct vocabulary term from the Study Guide.

1. the time it takes an object to complete one rotation on its axis
2. the average distance from Earth to the Sun
3. the time it takes an object to travel once around the Sun
4. an increase in temperature caused by energy trapped by a planet's atmosphere
5. an inner planet
6. the four largest moons of Jupiter
7. a streak of light in Earth's atmosphere made by a meteoroid

Interactive Concept Map

Link Vocabulary and Key Concepts

Copy this concept map, and then use vocabulary terms to complete the concept map.

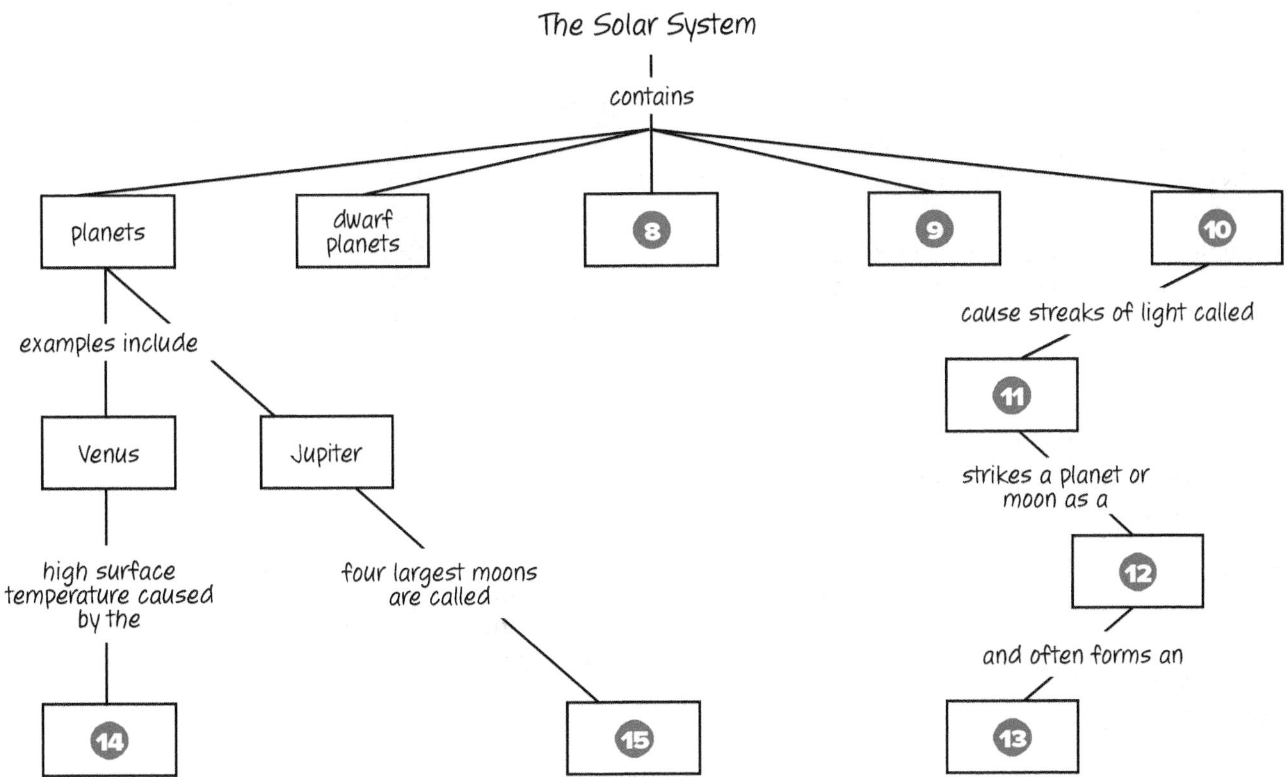

Chapter 7 Review

Understand Key Concepts

1. Which solar system object is the largest?
   A. Jupiter
   B. Neptune
   C. the Sun
   D. Saturn

2. Which best describes the asteroid belt?
   A. another name for the Oort cloud
   B. the region where comets originate
   C. large chunks of gas, dust, and ice
   D. millions of small rocky objects

3. Which describes a planet's speed as it orbits the Sun?
   A. It constantly decreases.
   B. It constantly increases.
   C. It does not change.
   D. It increases then decreases.

4. The diagram below shows a planet's orbit around the Sun. What does the blue arrow represent?
   A. the gravitational pull of the Sun
   B. the planet's orbital path
   C. the planet's path if Sun did not exist
   D. the planet's speed

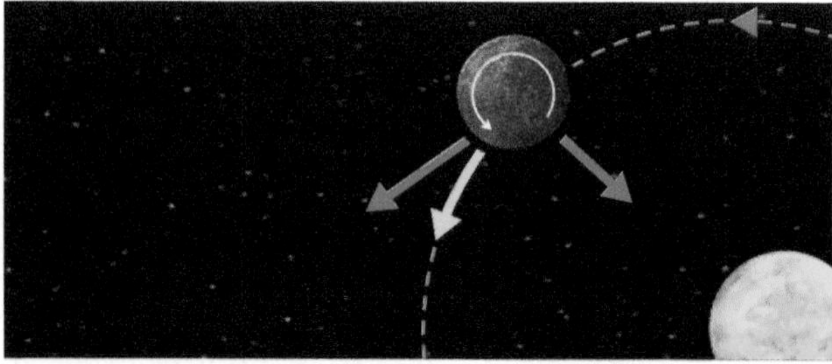

5. Which describes the greenhouse effect?
   A. effect of gravity on temperature
   B. energy emitted by the Sun
   C. energy trapped by atmosphere
   D. reflection of light from a planet

6. How are the terrestrial planets similar?
   A. similar densities
   B. similar diameters
   C. similar periods of rotation
   D. similar rocky surfaces

7. Which inner planet is the hottest?
   A. Earth
   B. Mars
   C. Mercury
   D. Venus

8. The photograph below shows how Earth appears from space. How does Earth differ from other inner planets?

   A. Its atmosphere contains large amounts of methane.
   B. Its period of revolution is much greater.
   C. Its surface is covered by large amounts of liquid water.
   D. Its surface temperature is higher.

9. Which two gases make up most of the outer planets?
   A. ammonia and helium
   B. ammonia and hydrogen
   C. hydrogen and helium
   D. methane and hydrogen

10. Which is true of the dwarf planets?
   A. more massive than nearby objects
   B. never have moons
   C. orbit near the Sun
   D. spherically shaped

11. Which is a bright streak of light in Earth's atmosphere?
   A. a comet
   B. a meteor
   C. a meteorite
   D. a meteoroid

12. Which best describes an asteroid?
   A. icy
   B. rocky
   C. round
   D. wet

NASA GSFC image by Robert Simmon and Reto Stöckli

Critical Thinking

13 **Relate** changes in speed during a planet's orbit to the shape of the orbit and the gravitational pull of the Sun.

14 **Compare** In what ways are planets and dwarf planets similar?

15 **Apply** Like Venus, Earth's atmosphere contains carbon dioxide. What might happen on Earth if the amount of carbon dioxide in the atmosphere increases? Explain.

16 **Defend** A classmate states that life will someday be found on Mars. Defend the statement and offer a reason why life might exist on Mars.

17 **Infer** whether a planet with active volcanoes would have more or fewer craters than a planet without active volcanoes. Explain.

18 **Support** Use the diagram of the asteroid belt to support the explanation of how the belt formed.

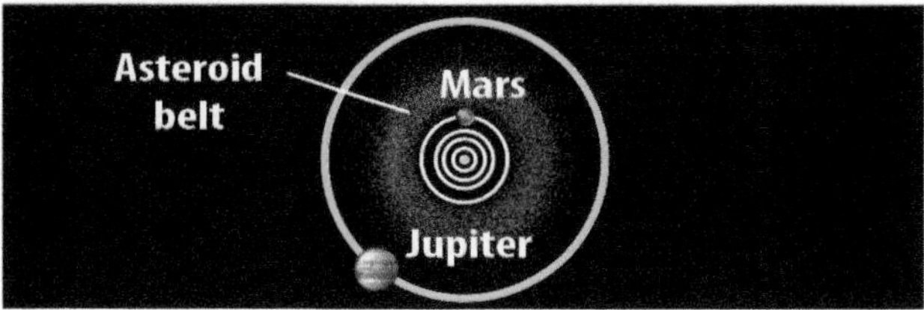

19 **Evaluate** The *Huygens* probe transmitted data about Titan for only 90 min. In your opinion, was this worth the effort of sending the probe?

20 **Explain** why Jupiter's moon Ganymede is not considered a dwarf planet, even though it is bigger than Mercury.

Writing in Science

21 **Compose** a pamphlet that describes how the International Astronomical Union classifies planets, dwarf planets, and small solar system objects.

REVIEW THE BIG IDEA

22 What kinds of objects are in the solar system? Summarize the types of space objects that make up the solar system and give at least one example of each.

23 The photo below shows part of Saturn's rings and two of its moons. Describe what Saturn and its rings are made of and explain why the other two objects are moons.

Math Skills

Use Ratios

Inner Planet Data			
Planet	Diameter (% of Earth's diameter)	Mass (% of Earth's mass)	Average Distance from Sun (AU)
Mercury	38.3	5.5	0.39
Venus	95	81.5	0.72
Earth	100	100	1.00
Mars	53.2	10.7	1.52

24 Use the table above to calculate how many times farther from the Sun Mars is compared to Mercury.

25 Calculate how much greater Venus's mass is compared to Mercury's mass.

Standardized Test Practice

Record your answers on the answer sheet provided by your teacher or on a sheet of paper.

Multiple Choice

1 Which is a terrestrial planet?

A Ceres

B Neptune

C Pluto

D Venus

2 An astronomical unit (AU) is the average distance

A between Earth and the Moon.

B from Earth to the Sun.

C to the nearest star in the galaxy.

D to the edge of the solar system.

3 Which is NOT a characteristic of ALL planets?

A exceed the total mass of nearby objects

B have a nearly spherical shape

C have one or more moons

D make an elliptical orbit around the Sun

Use the diagram below to answer question 4.

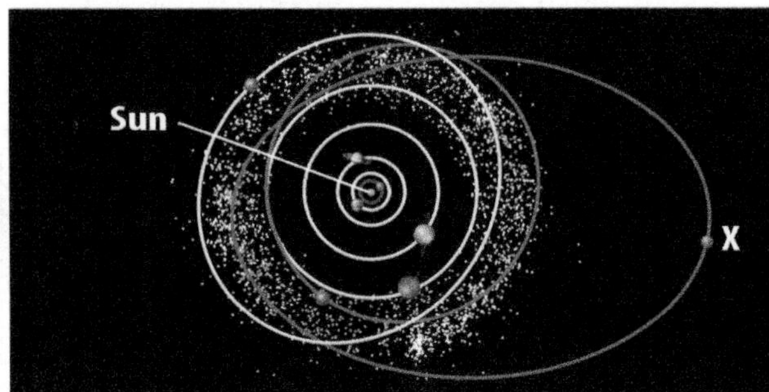

4 Which object in the solar system is marked by an *X* in the diagram?

A asteroid

B meteoroid

C dwarf planet

D outer planet

Use the diagram of Saturn below to answer questions 5 and 6.

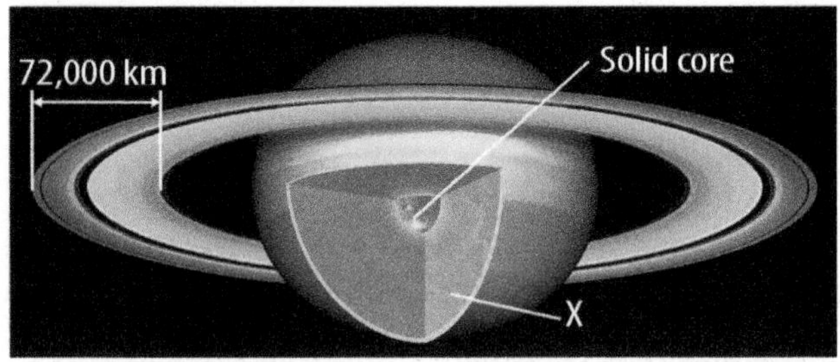

5 The thick inner layer marked *X* in the diagram above is made of which material?

A carbon dioxide

B gaseous helium

C liquid hydrogen

D molten rock

6 In the diagram, Saturn's rings are shown to be 72,000 km in width. Approximately how thick are Saturn's rings?

A 30 m

B 1,000 km

C 14,000 km

D 1 AU

7 Which are NOT found on Mercury's surface?

A high cliffs

B impact craters

C lava flows

D sand dunes

8 What is the primary cause of the extremely high temperatures on the surface of Venus?

A heat rising from the mantle

B lack of an atmosphere

C proximity to the Sun

D the greenhouse effect

Use the diagram below to answer question 9.

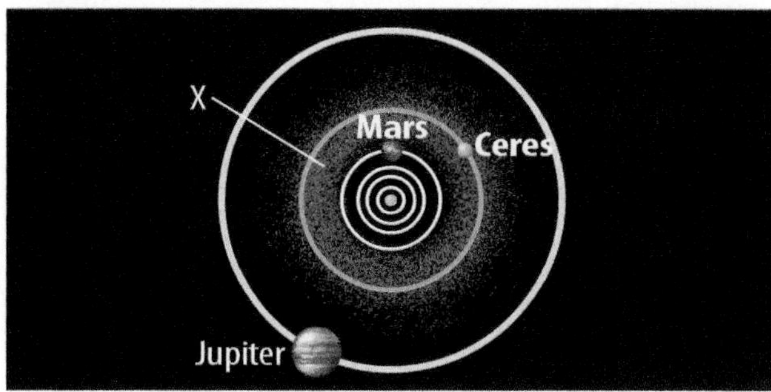

9 In the diagram above, which region of the solar system is marked by an *X*?

A the asteroid belt

B the dwarf planets

C the Kuiper belt

D the Oort cloud

10 What is a meteorite?

A a surface depression formed by collision with a rock from space

B a fragment of rock that strikes a planet or a moon

C a mixture of ice, dust, and gas with a glowing tail

D a small rocky particle that moves through space

11 What gives Mars its reddish color?

A ice caps of frozen carbon dioxide

B lava from Olympus Mons

C liquid water in gullies

D soil rich in iron oxide

Constructed Response

Use the table below to answer questions 12 and 13.

	Inner Planets	Outer Planets
Also called		
Relative size		
Main materials		
General structure		
Number of moons		

12 Copy the table and complete the first five rows to compare the features of the inner planets and outer planets.

13 In the blank row of the table, add another feature of the inner planets and outer planets. Then, describe the feature you have chosen.

14 What features of Earth make it suitable for supporting life as we know it?

15 How are planets, dwarf planets, and asteroids both similar and different?

NEED EXTRA HELP?															
If You Missed Question...	1	2	3	4	5	6	7	8	9	10	11	12	13	14	15
Go to Lesson...	2	1	1	1	3	3	2	2	1, 4	4	2	2, 3	2, 3	2	1, 4

Unit 4

INTERACTIONS OF LIFE

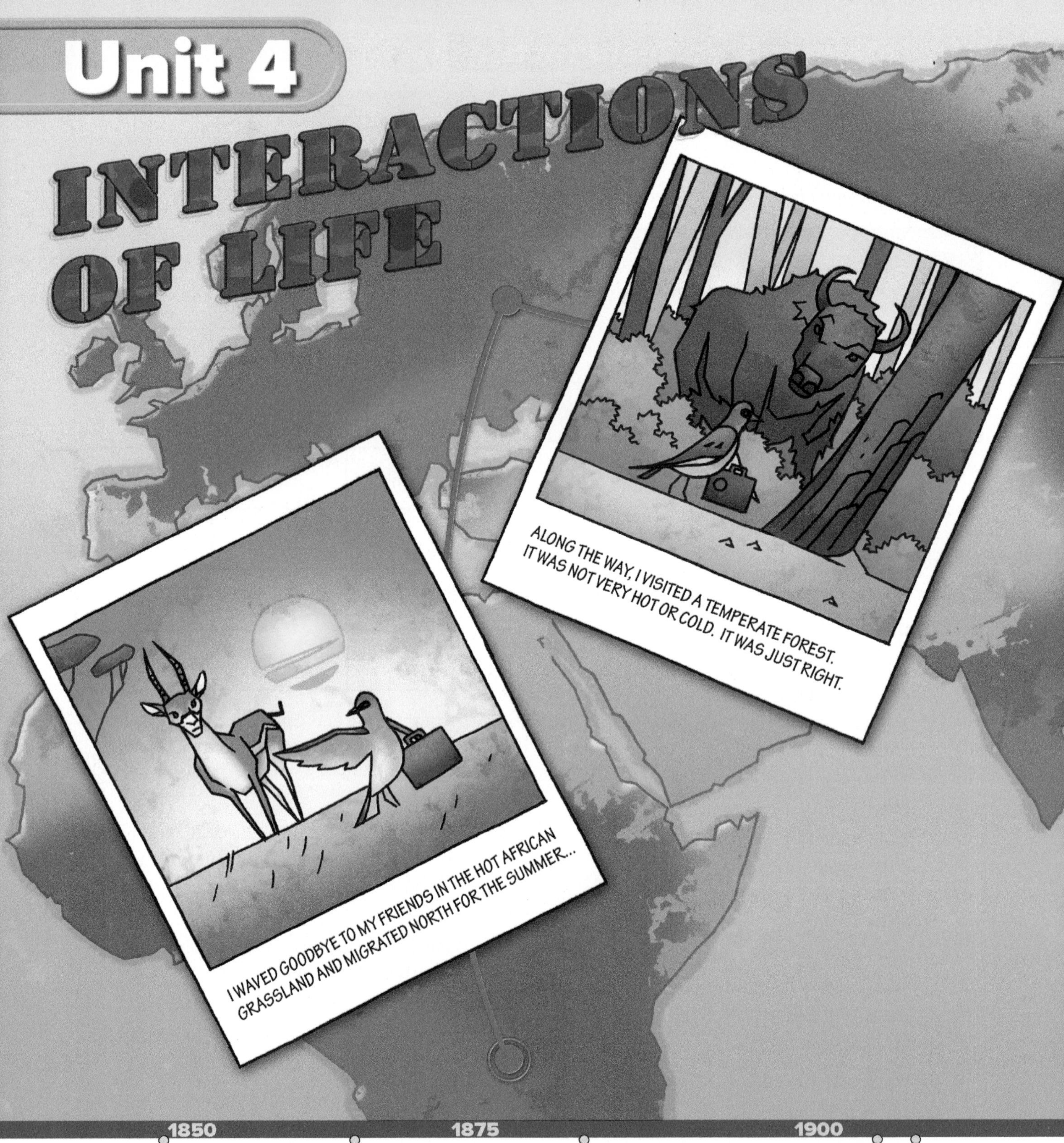

ALONG THE WAY, I VISITED A TEMPERATE FOREST. IT WAS NOT VERY HOT OR COLD. IT WAS JUST RIGHT.
I WAVED GOODBYE TO MY FRIENDS IN THE HOT AFRICAN GRASSLAND AND MIGRATED NORTH FOR THE SUMMER...

1850 | 1875 | 1900

1849
The U.S. Department of Interior is established and is responsible for the management and conservation of most federal land.

1872
The world's first national park, Yellowstone, is created.

1892
The Sierra Club is founded in San Francisco by John Muir. It goes on to be the oldest and largest grassroots environmental organization in the United States.

1915
Congress passes a bill establishing Rocky Mountain National Park in Colorado.

1920
Congress passes the Federal Water Power Act. This act creates a Federal Power Commission with authority over waterways, and the construction and use of water-power projects.

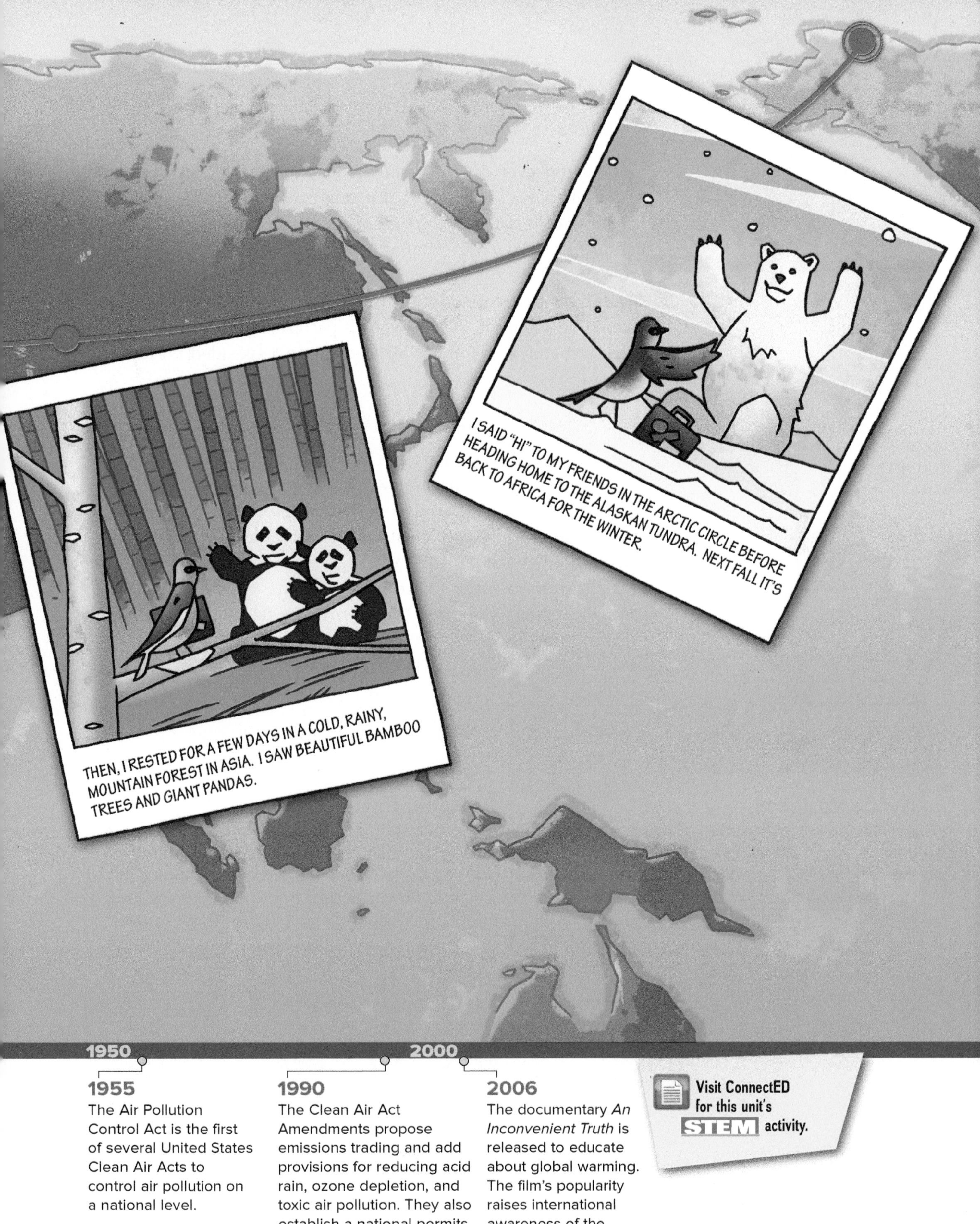

THEN, I RESTED FOR A FEW DAYS IN A COLD, RAINY, MOUNTAIN FOREST IN ASIA. I SAW BEAUTIFUL BAMBOO TREES AND GIANT PANDAS.
I SAID "HI" TO MY FRIENDS IN THE ARCTIC CIRCLE BEFORE HEADING HOME TO THE ALASKAN TUNDRA. NEXT FALL IT'S BACK TO AFRICA FOR THE WINTER.
1950
2000

1955
The Air Pollution Control Act is the first of several United States Clean Air Acts to control air pollution on a national level.

1990
The Clean Air Act Amendments propose emissions trading and add provisions for reducing acid rain, ozone depletion, and toxic air pollution. They also establish a national permits program.

2006
The documentary *An Inconvenient Truth* is released to educate about global warming. The film's popularity raises international awareness of the cause.

Visit ConnectED for this unit's **STEM** activity.

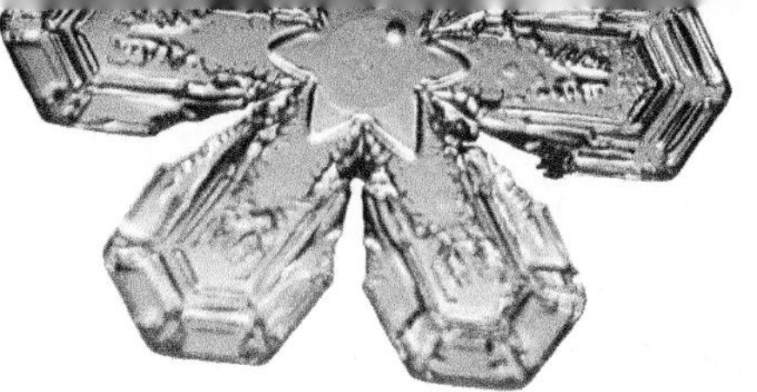

Patterns

Have you ever caught a snowflake in your hand or seen one close-up in a book or on TV? You might have heard someone say that no two snowflakes are alike. While this is true, it is also true that all snowflakes have similar patterns. A **pattern** is a consistent plan or model used as a guide for understanding or predicting things. Patterns can be created or occur naturally. The formation of snowflakes is an example of a repeating pattern. They form piece by piece, as water drops in the air freeze into a six-sided crystal.

How Scientists Use Patterns

Studying and using patterns is useful to scientists because it can help explain the natural world or predict future events. A biologist might study patterns in DNA to predict what organisms will look like. A meteorologist might study cloud formation patterns to predict the weather. When doing research, scientists also try to match patterns found in their data with patterns that occur in nature. This helps to determine whether data are accurate and helps to predict outcomes.

(cw from top)(1,2) Ted Kinsman/Science Source, (3) Esa Hiltula/Alamy, (4) ©Gary W. Carter/Corbis, (6)(7) Ted Kinsman/Science Source

Types of Patterns

Cyclic Patterns

A cycle, or repeated series of events, is a form of pattern. An organism's life cycle typically follows the pattern of birth, growth, and death. Scientists study an organism's life cycle to predict the life of its offspring.

Physical Patterns

Physical patterns have an artistic or decorative design. Physical patterns can occur naturally, such as the patterns in the colors on butterfly wings or flower petals, or they can be created intentionally, such as a design in a brick wall.

Patterns in Life Science

Why do police detectives or forensic scientists take fingerprints at a crime scene? Forensic scientists know that every fingerprint is unique. Fingerprints contain patterns that can help detectives narrow a list of suspects. The patterns on the fingerprints can then be examined more closely to identify an exact individual. This is because no two humans have the same fingerprint, just as no two zebras have the same stripe pattern.

Patterns are an important key to understanding life science. They are found across all classifications of life and are studied by scientists. Patterns help scientists understand the genetic makeup, lifestyle, and similarities of various species of plants and animals. Zoologists might study the migration patterns of animals to determine the effects climate has on different species. Botanists might study patterns in the leaves of flowering plants to classify the species of the plant and predict the characteristics of the offspring.

Mathematical Patterns

Patterns are applied in mathematics all the time. Whenever you read a number, perform a mathematical operation, or describe a shape or graph, you are using patterns.

2, 5, 8, 11, ___, ___, ___

What numbers come next in this number pattern?

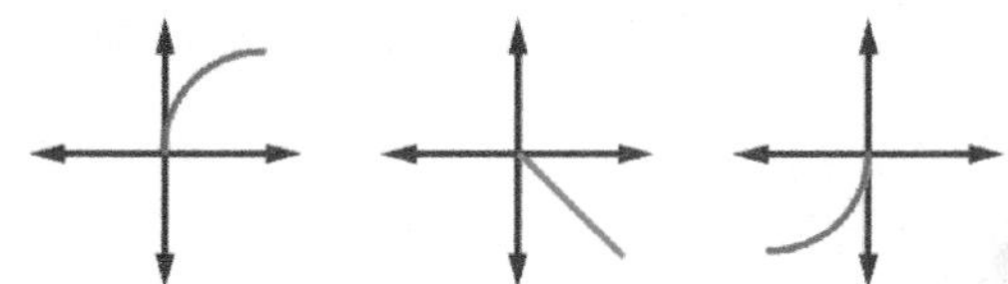

What will the next shape look like according to the pattern?

MiniLab 15 minutes

Leaf Patterns

Each species of flowering plant has leaves with unique patterns.

Leaf Venation

Pinnate
one main vein with smaller branching veins

Palmate
several main veins that branch from one point

Parallel
veins that d
branch

1. Obtain a collection of leaves.
2. Use the leaves above to identify the venation, or vein patterns, of each leaf.

Analyze and Conclude

1. **Describe** the physical pattern you see in each leaf.
2. **Choose** Besides venation, what other patterns can you use to group the leaves?
3. **Identify** What types of patterns can be used to classify other organisms?

(t) ©imagebroker/Alamy, (c) ©Frank Krahmer/zefa/Corbis, (b) Geoff du Feu/Alamy

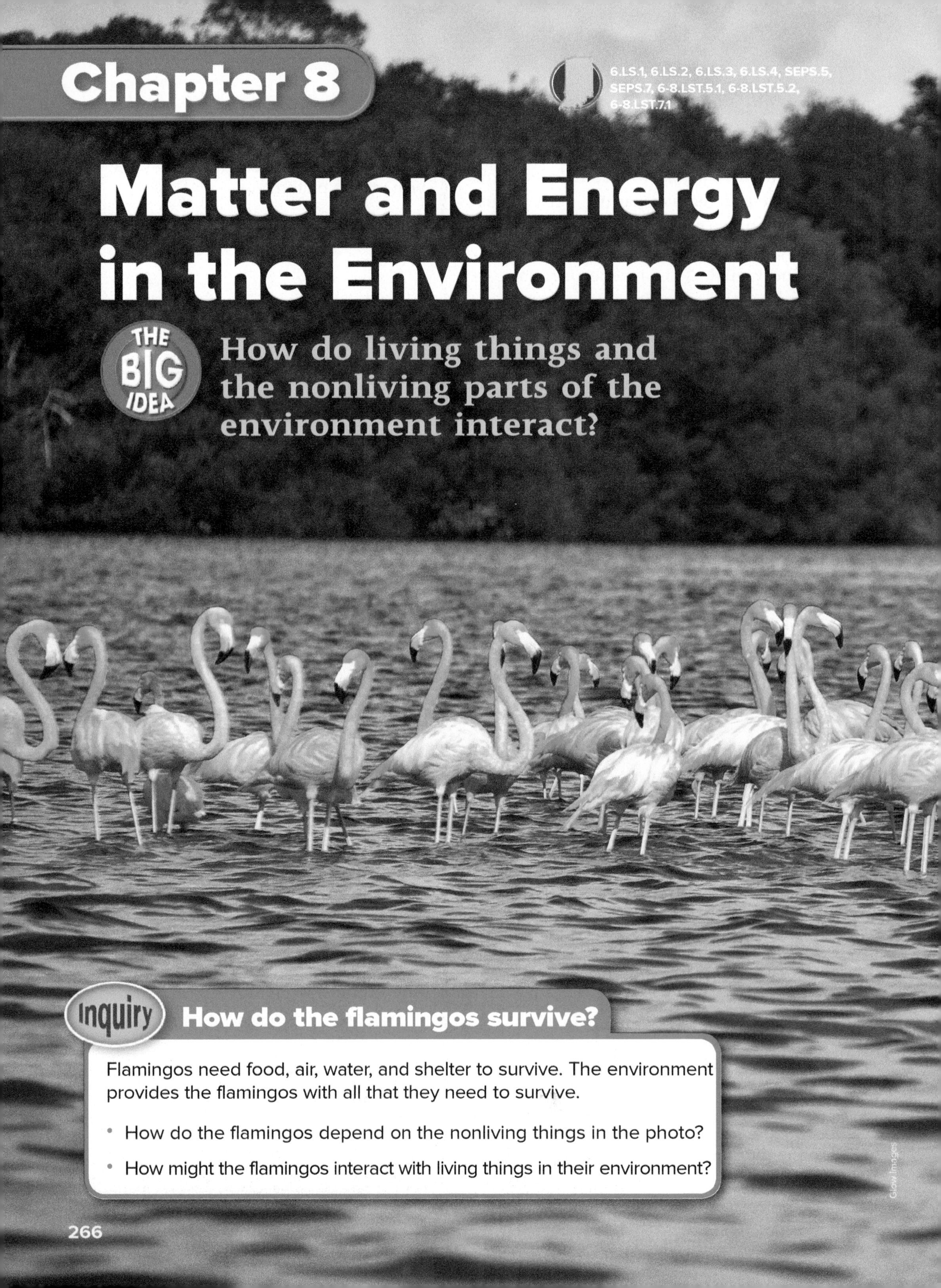

Chapter 8

6.LS.1, 6.LS.2, 6.LS.3, 6.LS.4, SEPS.5, SEPS.7, 6-8.LST.5.1, 6-8.LST.5.2, 6-8.LST.7.1

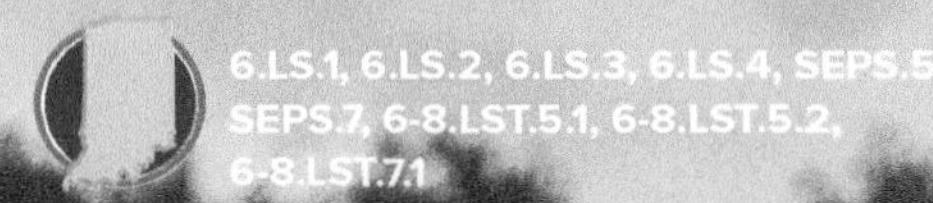

Matter and Energy in the Environment

THE BIG IDEA

How do living things and the nonliving parts of the environment interact?

Inquiry How do the flamingos survive?

Flamingos need food, air, water, and shelter to survive. The environment provides the flamingos with all that they need to survive.

- How do the flamingos depend on the nonliving things in the photo?
- How might the flamingos interact with living things in their environment?

Glow Images

Get Ready to Read

What do you think?

Before you read, decide if you agree or disagree with each of these statements. As you read this chapter, see if you change your mind about any of the statements.

1. The air you breathe is mostly oxygen.
2. Living things are made mostly of water.
3. Carbon, nitrogen, and other types of matter are used by living things over and over again.
4. Clouds are made of water vapor.
5. The Sun is the source for all energy used by living things on Earth.
6. All living things get their energy from eating other living things.

Lesson 1

Abiotic Factors

Reading Guide

Key Concept
ESSENTIAL QUESTION

- What are the nonliving parts of an environment?

Vocabulary

ecosystem p. 269
biotic factor p. 269
abiotic factor p. 269
climate p. 270
atmosphere p. 271

Multilingual eGlossary

BrainPOP®

6.LS.1, 6.LS.4, 6-8.LST.7.1

Inquiry Why So Blue?

Have you ever seen a picture of a bright blue ocean? The water looks so colorful in part because of nonliving factors such as matter in the water and the gases surrounding Earth. These nonliving things change the way you see light from the Sun, another nonliving part of the environment.

ad_foto/Getty Images

 Launch Lab

10 minutes

Is it living or nonliving?

You are surrounded by living and nonliving things, but it is sometimes difficult to tell what is alive. Some nonliving things may appear to be alive at first glance. Others are alive or were once living, but seem nonliving. In this lab, you will explore which items are alive and which are not.

1. Draw a chart with the headings *Living* and *Nonliving*.
2. Your teacher will provide you with a list of items. Decide if each item is living or nonliving.

Living	Nonliving

Think About This

1. What are some characteristics that the items in the *Living* column share?
2.  **Key Concept** How might the nonliving items be a part of your environment?

What is an ecosystem?

Have you ever watched a bee fly from flower to flower? Certain flowers and bees depend on each other. Bees help flowering plants reproduce. In return, flowers provide the nectar that bees use to make honey. Flowers also need nonliving things to survive, such as sunlight and water. For example, if plants don't get enough water, they can die. The bees might die, too, because they feed on the plants. All organisms need both living and nonliving things to survive.

An **ecosystem** *is all the living things and nonliving things in a given area.* Ecosystems vary in size. An entire forest can be an ecosystem, and so can a rotting log on the forest floor. Other examples of ecosystems include a pond, a desert, an ocean, and your neighborhood.

Biotic (bi AH tihk) **factors** *are the living things in an ecosystem.* **Abiotic** (ay bi AH tihk) **factors** *are the nonliving things in an ecosystem, such as sunlight and water.* Biotic factors and abiotic factors depend on each other. If just one factor–either abiotic or biotic–is disturbed, other parts of the ecosystem are affected. For example, severe droughts, or periods of water shortages, occurred in Australia in 2006. Many fish in rivers and lakes died. Animals that fed on the fish had to find food elsewhere. A lack of water, an abiotic factor, affected biotic factors in this ecosystem, such as the fish and the animals that fed on the fish.

Indiana FYI

How is homeostasis maintained as living things seek out their basic needs? Homeostasis is a set of stable conditions within the body of a living thing. Living things have basic needs, such as food, water, shelter, space, and air that are required for the maintenance of homeostasis. They meet those needs in their ecosystems. For example, water is an abiotic factor in ecosystems that is a basic need of living things. Water is required for living things to maintain homeostasis.

WORD ORIGIN

biotic
from Greek *biotikos,* means "fit for life"

Figure 1 Abiotic factors include sunlight, water, atmosphere, soil, temperature, and climate.

What are the nonliving parts of an ecosystem?

Some abiotic factors in an ecosystem are shown in Figure 1. Think about how these factors might affect you. You need sunlight for warmth and air to breathe. You would have no food without water and soil. These nonliving parts of the environment affect all living things.

The Sun

The source of almost all energy on Earth is the Sun. It provides warmth and light. In addition, many plants use sunlight and make food, as you'll read in Lesson 3. The Sun also affects two other abiotic factors–climate and temperature.

Reading Check How do living things use the Sun's energy?

Climate

Polar bears live in the Arctic. The Arctic has a cold, dry climate. **Climate** *describes average weather conditions in an area over time.* These weather conditions include temperature, moisture, and wind.

Climate influences where organisms can live. A desert climate, for example, is dry and often hot. A plant that needs a lot of water could not survive in a desert. In contrast, a cactus is well adapted to a dry climate because it can survive with little water.

Temperature

Is it hot or cold where you live? Temperatures on Earth vary greatly. Temperature is another abiotic factor that influences where organisms can survive. Some organisms, such as tropical birds, thrive in hot conditions. Others, such as polar bears, are well adapted to the cold. Tropical birds don't live in cold ecosystems, and polar bears don't live in warm ecosystems.

Water

All life on Earth requires water. In fact, most organisms are made mostly of water. All organisms need water for important life processes, such as growing and reproducing. Every ecosystem must contain some water to support life.

Gases in Atmosphere

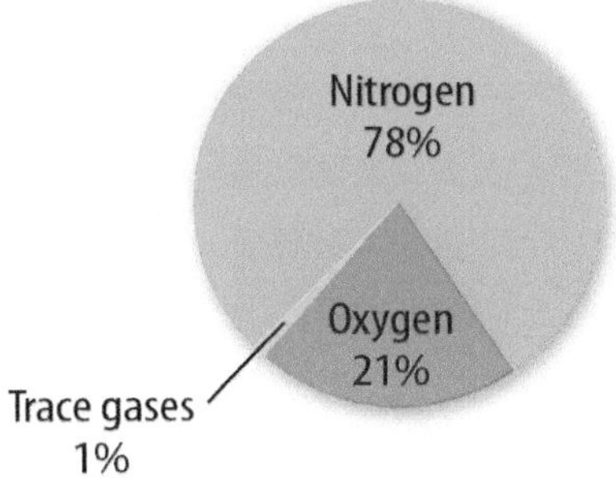

Climate

Precipitation (cm): 0, 5, 10, 15, 20, 25, 30
Temperature (°C): 0, 5, 10, 15, 20, 25, 30
Temperature
Precipitation
Month: Jan, Mar, May, Jul, Sep, Nov

Visual Check How do the elephants interact with the abiotic factors in their ecosystem?

Atmosphere

Every time you take a breath you are interacting with another abiotic factor that is necessary for life—the atmosphere. *The* **atmosphere** (AT muh sfir) *is the layer of gases that surrounds Earth.* The atmosphere is mostly nitrogen and oxygen with trace amounts of other gases, also shown in Figure 1. Besides providing living things with oxygen, the atmosphere also protects them from certain harmful rays from the Sun.

Soil

Bits of rocks, water, air, minerals, and the remains of once-living things make up soil. When you think about soil, you might picture a farmer growing crops. Soil provides water and nutrients for the plants we eat. However, it is also a home for many organisms, such as insects, bacteria, and fungi.

Factors such as water, soil texture, and the amount of available nutrients affect the types of organisms that can live in soil. Bacteria break down dead plants and animals, returning nutrients to the soil. Earthworms and insects make small tunnels in the soil, allowing air and water to move through it. Even very dry soil, like that in the desert, is home to living things.

 **Key Concept Check** List the nonliving things in ecosystems.

FOLDABLES®

Fold and cut a sheet of paper to make a six-door book. Label it as shown. Use it to organize information about the abiotic parts of an ecosystem.

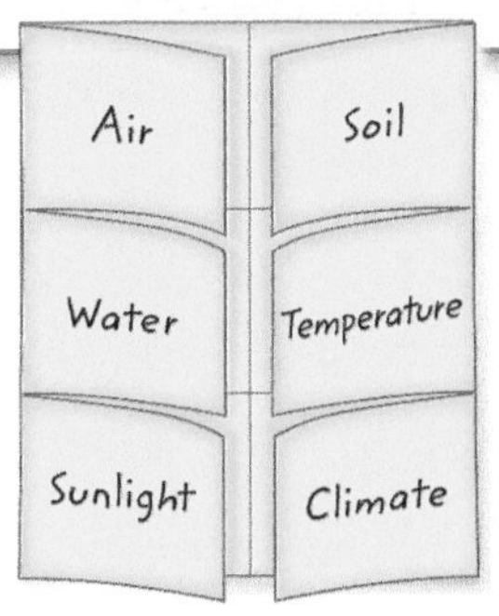

Lesson 1 Review

Visual Summary

Ecosystems include all the biotic and abiotic factors in an area.

Biotic factors are the living things in ecosystems.

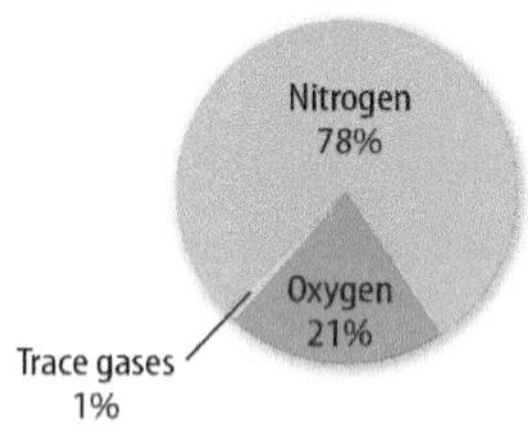

Abiotic factors are the nonliving things in ecosystems, including water, sunlight, temperature, climate, air, and soil.

FOLDABLES®

Use your lesson Foldable to review the lesson. Save your Foldable for the project at the end of the chapter.

What do you think NOW?

You first read the statements below at the beginning of the chapter.

1. The air you breathe is mostly oxygen.

2. Living things are made mostly of water.

Did you change your mind about whether you agree or disagree with the statements? Rewrite any false statements to make them true.

Use Vocabulary

1. **Distinguish** between biotic and abiotic factors.
2. **Define** *ecosystem* in your own words.
3. **Use the term** *climate* in a complete sentence.

Understand Key Concepts

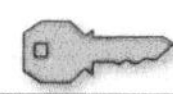

4. What role do bacteria play in soil ecosystems?
   - **A.** They add air to soil.
   - **B.** They break down rocks.
   - **C.** They return nutrients to soil.
   - **D.** They tunnel through soil.
5. **Explain** How would a forest ecosystem change if no sunlight were available to it?

Interpret Graphics

6. **Analyze** The graph below shows climate data for an area. How would you describe this climate?

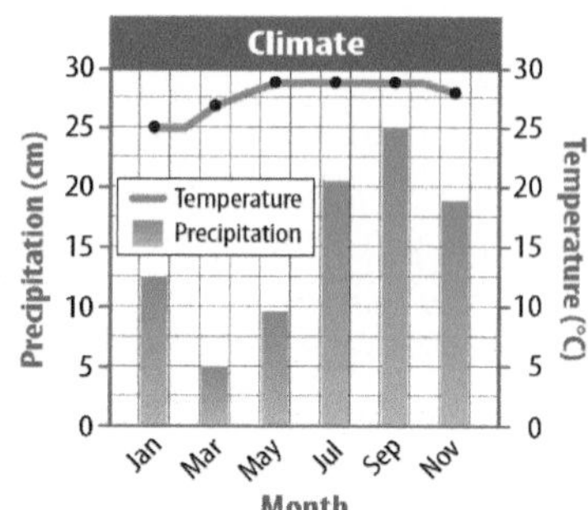

7. **Organize** Copy the graphic organizer below and fill in each oval with an abiotic factor.

Critical Thinking

8. **Predict** Imagine that the soil in an area is carried away by wind and water, leaving only rocks behind. How would this affect the living things in that area?

(t)Glow Images; (b)Zoonar RF/Getty Images

SCIENCE & SOCIETY

Terraforming Mars

Life on Another Planet

◀ **Mars is cold and dry, with no sign of life on its dusty, red surface.**

Terraforming is the process of transforming an environment that cannot support life into one that can. Making Mars like Earth would take more than just growing plants and adding water. You would need to consider how every abiotic factor needed to support life would be included in the new environment.

First, consider Mars's temperature. Although Mars gets plenty of sunlight, it is farther from the Sun than Earth is. Air temperatures go no higher than 0°C on a midsummer Martian day. Don't even think about trying to survive a winter night on Mars, as temperatures fall below –89°C.

How could you change the temperature on Mars? Releasing greenhouse gases such as chlorofluorocarbons (CFCs) into the atmosphere can cause the planet to get warmer. Raising the average temperature by only 4°C would melt the polar ice caps, releasing frozen CO_2, another greenhouse gas. This also would cause bodies of water to form. As temperatures rise, liquid water trapped in the soil would turn into a gas, providing the planet with water vapor, an important abiotic factor.

With water and warmer temperatures, plant life could be introduced. While turning light energy into food, plants would introduce another abiotic factor—oxygen. With all the needed abiotic factors accounted for, NASA scientists think that in a few centuries Mars could support life similar to that on Earth.

Life as it is on Earth does not exist on Mars. However, when you compare all the planets in our solar system, Mars is the most like Earth.

It's Your Turn

DEBATE Why would people want to move to Mars? Would this be the right choice? Research these questions and then debate the issues.

Lesson 2

Reading Guide

Key Concept
ESSENTIAL QUESTION

- How does matter move in ecosystems?

Vocabulary

evaporation p. 276

condensation p. 276

precipitation p. 276

nitrogen fixation p. 278

Multilingual eGlossary

BrainPOP®

Cycles of Matter

Inquiry Where does the water go?

All water, including the water in this waterfall, can move throughout an ecosystem in a cycle. It can also change forms. What other forms do you think water takes as it moves through an ecosystem?

IIC/ Axiom/Gatty Images

Launch Lab

15 minutes

How can you model raindrops? 

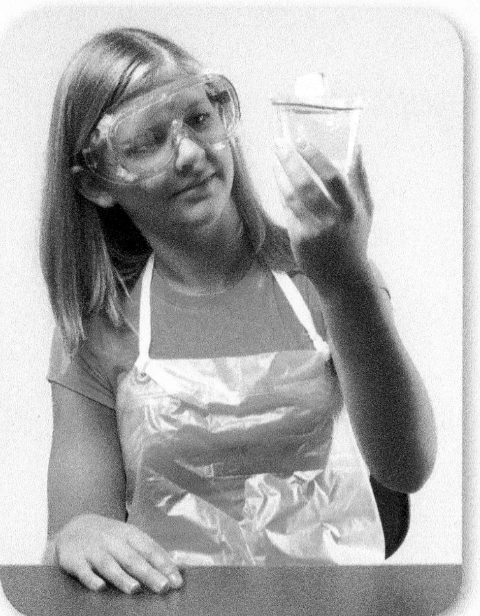

Like all matter on Earth, water is recycled. It constantly moves between Earth and its atmosphere. You could be drinking the same water that a *Tyrannosaurus rex* drank 65 million years ago!

1. Read and complete a lab safety form.
2. Half-fill a **plastic cup** with warm water.
3. Cover the cup with **plastic wrap.** Secure the plastic with a **rubber band.**
4. Place an **ice cube** on the plastic wrap. Observe the cup for several minutes. Record your observations in your Science Journal.

Think About This

1. What did you observe on the underside of the plastic wrap? Why do you think this happened?
2. How does this activity model the formation of raindrops?
3.  **Key Concept** Do you think other matter moves through the environment? Explain your answer.

How does matter move in ecosystems?

The water that you used to wash your hands this morning might have once traveled through the roots of a tree in Africa or even have been part of an Antarctic glacier. How can this be? Water moves continuously through ecosystems. It is used over and over again. The same is true of carbon, oxygen, nitrogen, and other types of matter. This idea is called the law of conservation of mass. Elements that move through one matter cycle may also play a role in another, such as oxygen's role in the water cycle.

SCIENCE USE V. COMMON USE

element

Science Use one of a class of substances that cannot be separated into simpler substances by chemical means

Common Use a part or piece

The Water Cycle

Look at a globe or a map. Notice that water surrounds the landmasses. Water covers about 70 percent of Earth's surface.

Most of Earth's water—about 97 percent—is in oceans. Water is also in rivers and streams, lakes, and underground reservoirs. In addition, water is in the atmosphere, glaciers, and living things.

Water continually cycles from Earth to its atmosphere and back again. This movement of water is called the water cycle. It involves three processes: evaporation, condensation, and precipitation.

The Water Cycle

Personal Tutor

Figure 2 During the water cycle, the processes of evaporation, condensation, and precipitation move water from Earth's surface into the atmosphere and back again.

Evaporation

The Sun supplies the energy for the water cycle, as shown in **Figure 2**. As the Sun heats Earth's surface waters, evaporation occurs. **Evaporation** (ih va puh RAY shun), *is the process during which liquid water changes into a gas called water vapor.* This water vapor rises into the atmosphere. Temperature, humidity, and wind affect how quickly water evaporates.

Water is also released from living things. Transpiration is the release of water vapor from the leaves and stems of plants. Recall that cellular respiration is a process that occurs in many cells. A by-product of cellular respiration is water. This water leaves cells and enters the environment and atmosphere as water vapor.

Condensation

The higher in the atmosphere you are, the cooler the temperature is. As water vapor rises, it cools and condensation occurs. **Condensation** (kahn den SAY shun), *is the process during which water vapor changes into liquid water.* Clouds form because of condensation.

Clouds are made of millions of tiny water droplets or crystals of ice. These form when water vapor condenses on particles of dust and other substances in the atmosphere.

Precipitation

Water that falls from clouds to Earth's surface is called **precipitation** (prih sih puh TAY shun). It enters bodies of water or soaks into soil. Precipitation can be rain, snow, sleet, or hail. It forms as water droplets or ice crystals join together in clouds. Eventually, these droplets or crystals become so large and heavy that they fall to Earth. Over time, living things use this precipitation, and the water cycle continues.

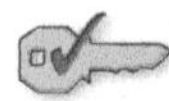

Key Concept Check What forms does water take as it moves through ecosystems?

MiniLab **20 minutes**

Is your soil rich in nitrogen? 

Plants get the nitrogen they need to grow from soil. Test the soil near your home to see how much nitrogen it contains. Will the soil support plant growth?

1. Read and complete a lab safety form.
2. Collect a sample of **soil** from around your home.
3. Carefully follow the directions on a **soil nitrogen test kit** and test your soil.
4. Use the color chart to determine the quantity of nitrogen in your soil sample.
5. Compare your results with those of your classmates.

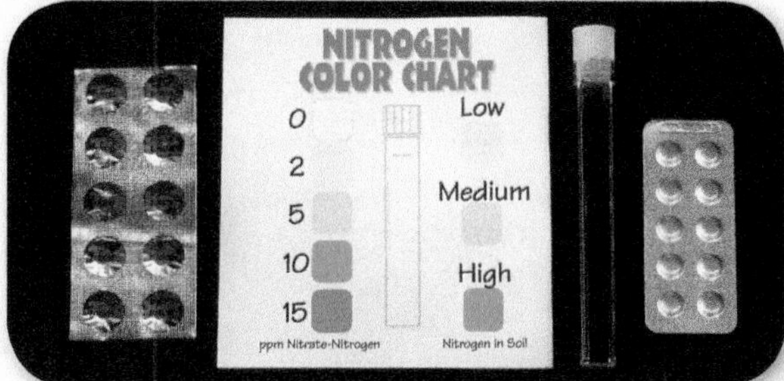

Analyze and Conclude

1. **Determine** if your soil sample has enough nitrogen to support most plant growth.
2. **Hypothesize** why the amount of nitrogen in your soil sample differed from those of your classmates.
3. **Key Concept** Deduce how nitrogen got into your soil sample.

The Nitrogen Cycle

Just as water is necessary for life on Earth, so is the element nitrogen. It is an essential part of proteins, which all organisms need to stay alive. Nitrogen is also an important part of DNA, the molecule that contains genetic information. Nitrogen, like water, cycles between Earth and its atmosphere and back again as shown in **Figure 3**.

 **Reading Check** What do living things use nitrogen for?

Figure 3 Different forms of nitrogen are in the atmosphere, soil, and organisms.

 **Animation**

Bacteria in soil convert nitrogen compounds into nitrogen gas, which is released into the air.

Nitrogen gas in atmosphere

Lightning changes nitrogen gas in the atmosphere to nitrogen compounds. The nitrogen compounds fall to the ground when it rains.

Animals eat plants.

Nitrogen-fixing bacteria on plant roots convert unusable nitrogen in soil to usable nitrogen compounds.

Decaying organic matter and animal waste return nitrogen compounds to the soil.

Plants take in and use nitrogen compounds from the soil.

Nitrogen compounds in soil

From the Environment to Organisms

Recall that the atmosphere is mostly nitrogen. However, this nitrogen is in a form that plants and animals cannot use. How do organisms get nitrogen into their bodies? The nitrogen must first be changed into a different form with the help of certain bacteria that live in soil and water. These bacteria take in nitrogen from the atmosphere and change it into nitrogen compounds that other living things can use. *The process that changes atmospheric nitrogen into nitrogen compounds that are usable by living things is called* **nitrogen fixation** (NI truh jun • fihk SAY shun). Nitrogen fixation is shown in Figure 4.

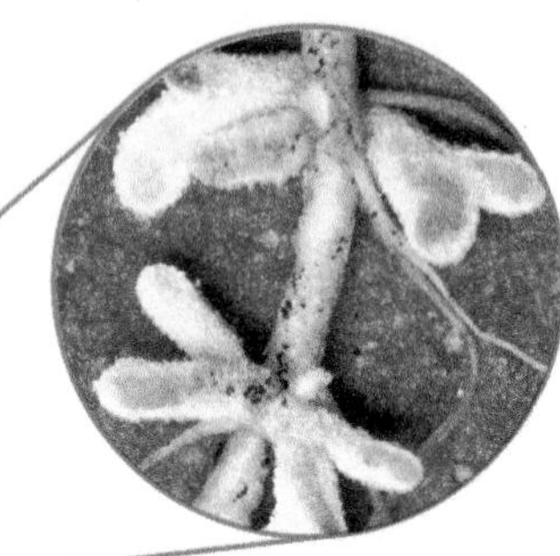

Figure 4 Certain bacteria convert nitrogen in soil and water into a form usable by plants.

Plants and some other organisms take in this changed nitrogen from the soil and water. Then, animals take in nitrogen when they eat the plants or other organisms.

Reading Check What is nitrogen fixation?

From Organisms to the Environment

Some types of bacteria can break down the tissues of dead organisms. When organisms die, these bacteria help return the nitrogen in the tissues of dead organisms to the environment. This process is shown in Figure 5.

Nitrogen also returns to the environment in the waste products of organisms. Farmers often spread animal wastes, called manure, on their fields during the growing season. The manure provides nitrogen to plants for better growth.

Figure 5 Bacteria break down the remains of dead plants and animals.

The Oxygen Cycle

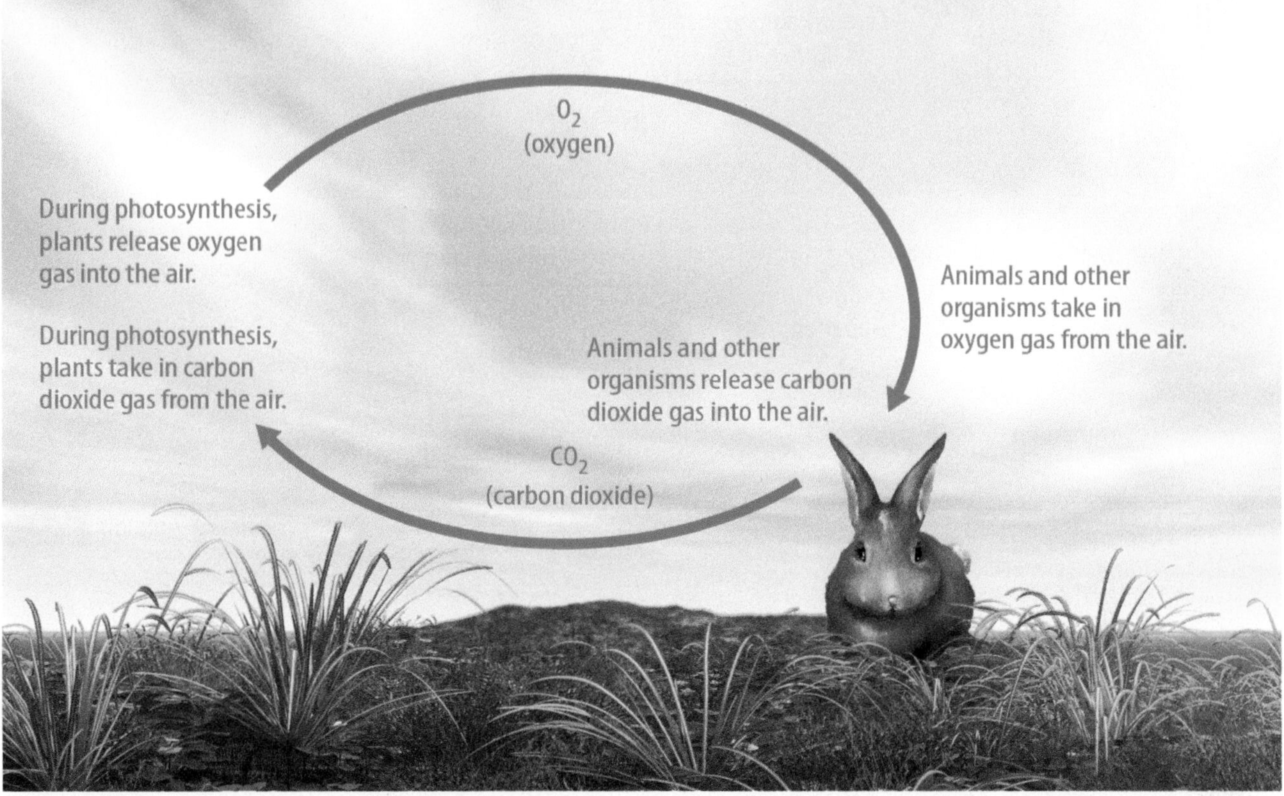
O_2
(oxygen)
During photosynthesis, plants release oxygen gas into the air.
During photosynthesis, plants take in carbon dioxide gas from the air.
Animals and other organisms take in oxygen gas from the air.
Animals and other organisms release carbon dioxide gas into the air.
CO_2
(carbon dioxide)

Figure 6 Most oxygen in the air comes from plants and algae.

Visual Check
Describe your part in the oxygen cycle.

The Oxygen Cycle

Almost all living things need oxygen for cellular processes that release energy. Oxygen is also part of many substances that are important to life, such as carbon dioxide and water. Oxygen cycles through ecosystems, as shown in **Figure 6.**

Earth's early atmosphere probably did not contain oxygen gas. Oxygen might have entered the atmosphere when certain **bacteria** evolved that could carry out the process of photosynthesis and make their own food. A by-product of photosynthesis is oxygen gas. Over time, other photosynthetic organisms evolved and the amount of oxygen in Earth's atmosphere increased. Today, photosynthesis is the primary source of oxygen in Earth's atmosphere. Some scientists estimate that unicellular organisms in water, called phytoplankton, release more than 50 percent of the oxygen in Earth's atmosphere.

Many living things, including humans, take in the oxygen and release carbon dioxide. The interaction of the carbon and oxygen cycles is one example of a relationship between different types of matter in ecosystems. As the matter cycles through an ecosystem, both the carbon and the oxygen take different forms and play a role in the other element's cycle.

REVIEW VOCABULARY

bacteria
a group of microscopic unicellular organisms without a membrane-bound nucleus

The Carbon Cycle

Animation

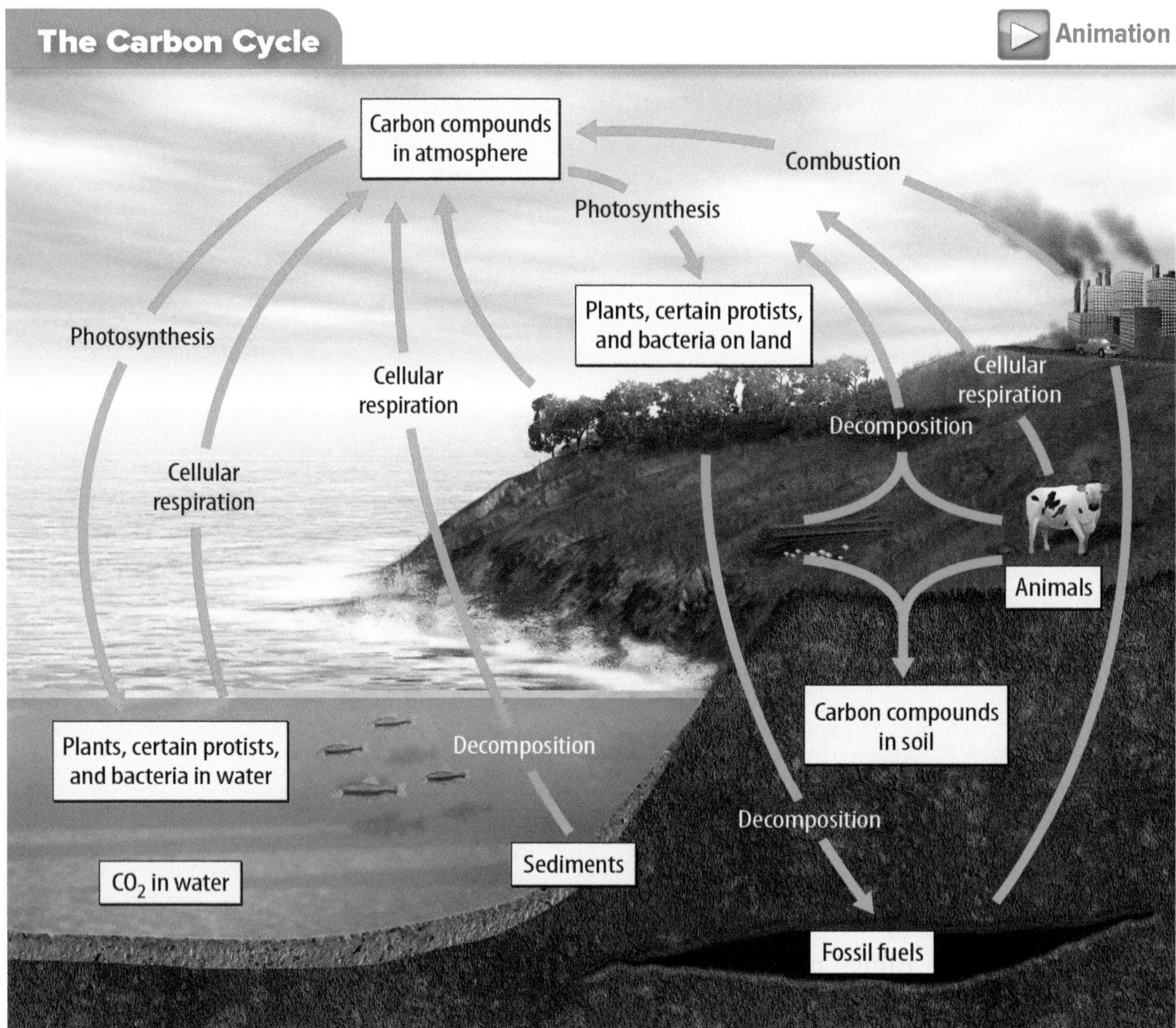

Figure 7 In the carbon cycle, all organisms return carbon to the environment.

The Carbon Cycle

All organisms contain carbon. It is part of proteins, sugars, fats, and DNA. Some organisms, including humans, get carbon from food. Other organisms, such as plants, get carbon from the atmosphere or bodies of water. Like other types of matter, carbon cycles through ecosystems, as shown in Figure 7.

Carbon in Soil

Like nitrogen, carbon can enter the environment when organisms die and decompose. This returns carbon compounds to the soil and releases carbon dioxide (CO_2) into the atmosphere for use by other organisms. Carbon is also found in fossil fuels, which formed when decomposing organisms were exposed to pressure, high temperatures, and bacteria over hundreds of millions of years.

FOLDABLES®

Make a half book from a sheet of paper. Select a cycle of matter and use your book to organize information about the biotic and abiotic parts of that cycle.

Cycles in Nature

Carbon in Air

Recall that carbon is found in the atmosphere as carbon dioxide. Plants and other photosynthetic organisms take in carbon dioxide and water and produce energy-rich sugars. These sugars are a source of carbon and energy for organisms that eat photosynthetic organisms. When the sugar is broken down by cells and its energy is **released,** carbon dioxide is released as a by-product. This carbon dioxide gas enters the atmosphere, where it can be used again.

ACADEMIC VOCABULARY
release
(verb) to set free or let go

The Greenhouse Effect

Carbon dioxide is one of the gases in the atmosphere that absorbs thermal energy from the Sun and keeps Earth warm. This process is called the greenhouse effect. The Sun produces solar radiation, as shown in **Figure 8.** Some of this energy is reflected back into space, and some passes through Earth's atmosphere. Greenhouse gases in Earth's atmosphere absorb thermal energy that reflects off Earth's surface. The more greenhouse gases released, the greater the gas layer becomes and the more thermal energy is absorbed. These gases are one factor that keeps Earth from becoming too hot or too cold.

Reading Check What is the greenhouse effect?

While the greenhouse effect is essential for life, a steady increase in greenhouse gases can harm ecosystems. For example, carbon is stored in fossil fuels such as coal, oil, and natural gas. When people burn fossil fuels to heat homes, for transportation, or to provide electricity, carbon dioxide gas is released into the atmosphere. The amount of carbon dioxide in the air has increased due to both natural and human activities.

Figure 8 Some thermal energy remains close to the Earth due to greenhouse gases.

Visual Check What might happen if heat were not absorbed by greenhouse gases?

Animation

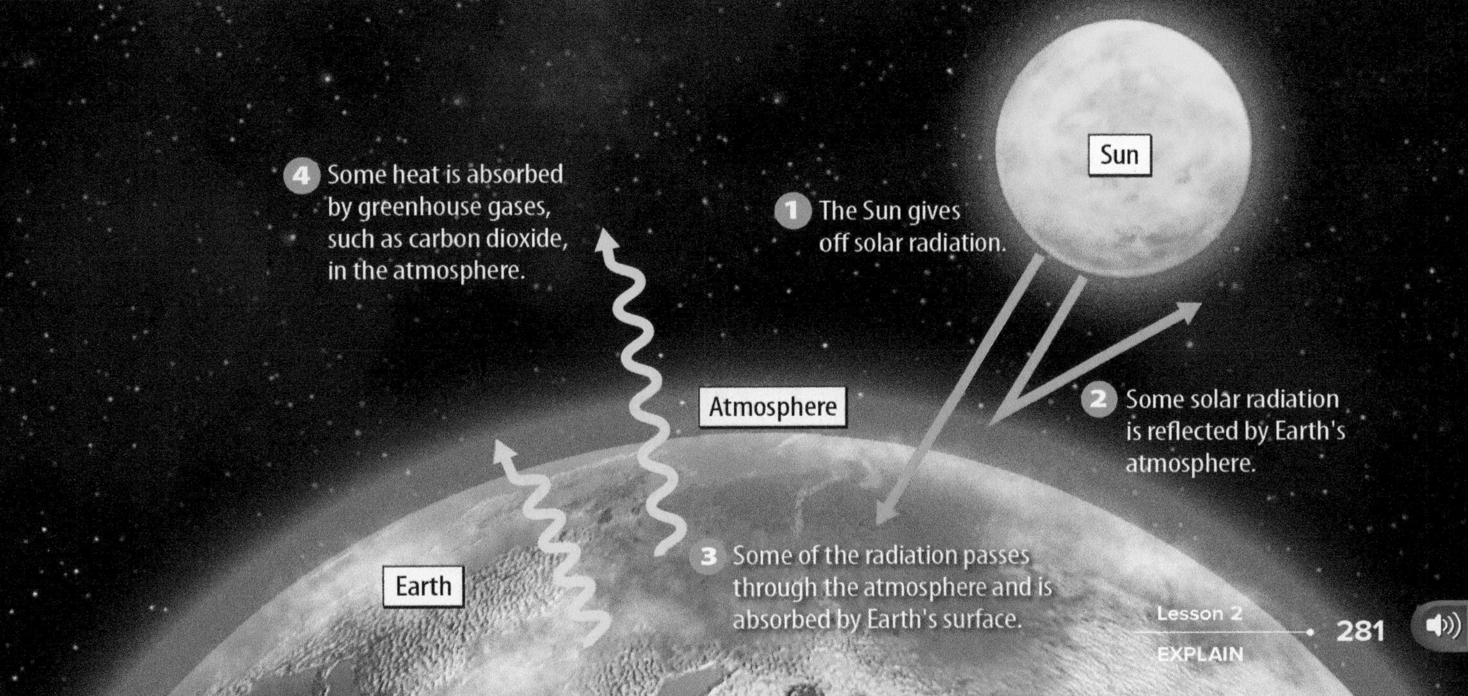

Sun
1 The Sun gives off solar radiation.
2 Some solar radiation is reflected by Earth's atmosphere.
3 Some of the radiation passes through the atmosphere and is absorbed by Earth's surface.
4 Some heat is absorbed by greenhouse gases, such as carbon dioxide, in the atmosphere.
Atmosphere
Earth

Lesson 2 Review

Visual Summary

Matter such as water, oxygen, nitrogen, and carbon cycles through ecosystems.

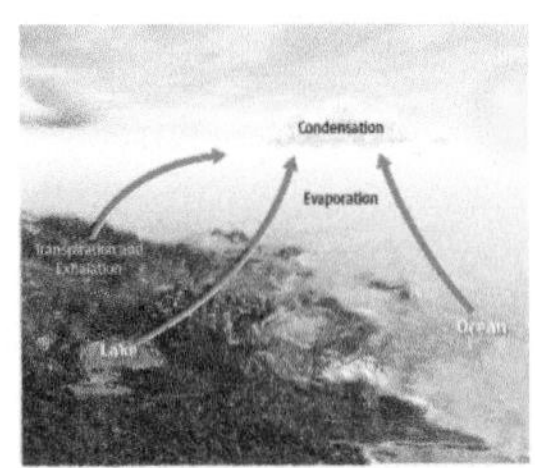

The three stages of the water cycle are evaporation, condensation, and precipitation.

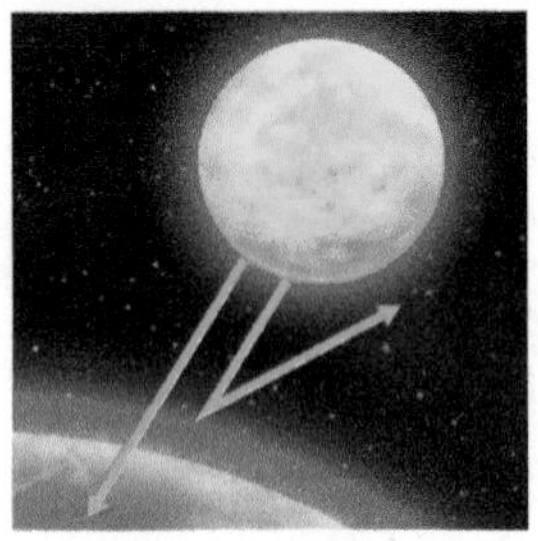

The greenhouse effect helps keep the Earth from getting too hot or too cold.

FOLDABLES®

Use your lesson Foldable to review the lesson. Save your Foldable for the project at the end of the chapter.

What do you think NOW?

You first read the statements below at the beginning of the chapter.

3. Carbon, nitrogen, and other types of matter are used by living things over and over again.

4. Clouds are made of water vapor.

Did you change your mind about whether you agree or disagree with the statements? Rewrite any false statements to make them true.

Use Vocabulary

1. **Distinguish** between evaporation and condensation.
2. **Define** *nitrogen fixation* in your own words.
3. Water that falls from clouds to Earth's surface is called ________.

Understand Key Concepts 

4. What is the driving force behind the water cycle?
   A. gravity
   B. plants
   C. sunlight
   D. wind
5. **Infer** Farmers add nitrogen to their fields every year to help their crops grow. Why must farmers continually add nitrogen when this element recycles naturally?

Interpret Graphics

6. **Sequence** Draw a graphic organizer like the one below and sequence the steps in the water cycle.

7. **Summarize** how the greenhouse effect moderates temperatures on Earth.

Critical Thinking

8. **Explain** how oxygen cycles through the ecosystem in which you live.
9. **Consider** How might ecosystems be affected if levels of atmospheric CO_2 continue to rise?

Melbourne Etc/Alamy

 Use Variables 30 minutes

How do scientists use variables?

Materials

rubber ball

styrene ball

meterstick

Safety

If you wanted to find out what made one ball bounce higher than another, you might design an experiment that uses variables. You could test whether balls made of one material bounce higher than those made of another. By changing only one variable, the experiment tests only the effect of that factor.

Learn It

When experimenting, scientists often **use variables.** A variable is anything that can be changed. For example, a scientist might want to study the effect that different amounts of water have on a plant's growth. The amount of water is the variable in the experiment. Other factors, such as soil type and amount of sunlight, stay the same.

Try It

1. Read and complete a lab safety form.
2. Examine both the rubber ball and the styrene ball. Predict which ball will bounce higher. Record your prediction in your Science Journal.
3. With your partner, hold the rubber ball 35 cm above the table and drop it. Record how high it bounces. Drop the ball a total of three times, recording the height it bounces each time. Calculate the average height that the rubber ball bounced.
4. Repeat step 3 with the styrene ball.

Apply It

5. Compare the average height of each ball's bounce and determine which bounced higher. Did your data support your prediction?
6. Identify two other variables you could test in this experiment. Would you test them together or separately? Explain.
7. **Key Concept** What variables might affect a study of the water cycle in your neighborhood?

3

	Rubber Ball	Styrene Ball
Trial 1		
Trial 2		
Trial 3		
Average bounce		

Hutchings Photography/Digital Light Source

Lesson 3

Reading Guide

Key Concepts
ESSENTIAL QUESTIONS

- How does energy move in ecosystems?
- How is the movement of energy in an ecosystem modeled?

Vocabulary

photosynthesis p. 286
chemosynthesis p. 286
food chain p. 288
food web p. 289
energy pyramid p. 290

Multilingual eGlossary

BrainPOP®

6.LS.1, 6.LS.2, 6.LS.3, SEPS.5, SEPS.7, 6-8.LST.5.1, 6-8.LST.5.2, 6-8.LST.7.1

Go to the resource tab in ConnectED to find the PBLs *Web of Life* and *Sun Block*.

Energy in Ecosystems

Inquiry Time for a snack?

All organisms need energy, and many get it from eating other organisms. Can you guess how each of the living things in this picture gets the energy it needs?

Art Wolfe/Getty Images

Launch Lab

10 minutes

How does energy change form?

Every day, sunlight travels hundreds of millions of kilometers and brings warmth and light to Earth. Energy from the Sun is necessary for nearly all life on Earth. Without it, most life could not exist.

1. Read and complete a lab safety form.
2. Obtain **UV-sensitive beads** from your teacher. Write a description of them in your Science Journal.
3. Place half the beads in a sunny place. Place the other half in a dark place.
4. Wait a few minutes, and then observe both sets of beads. Record your observations in your Science Journal.

Think About This

1. Compare and contrast the two sets of beads after the few minutes. How are they different? How are they the same?
2. Hypothesize why the beads looked different.
3. **Key Concept** How do you think living things use energy?

How does energy move in ecosystems?

When you see a picture of an ecosystem, it often looks quiet and peaceful. However, ecosystems are actually full of movement. Birds squawk and beat their wings, plants sway in the breeze, and insects buzz.

Each movement made by a living thing requires energy. All of life's functions, including growth and reproduction, require energy. The main source of energy for most life on Earth is the Sun. Unlike other resources, such as water and carbon, energy does not cycle through ecosystems. Instead, energy flows in one direction, as shown in Figure 9. In most cases, energy flow begins with the Sun, and moves from one organism to another. Many organisms get energy by eating other organisms. Sometimes organisms change energy into different forms as it moves through an ecosystem. Not all the energy an organism gets is used for life processes. Some is released to the environment as thermal energy. You might have read that energy cannot be created or destroyed, but it can change form. This idea is called the law of conservation of energy.

Key Concept Check How do the movements of matter and energy differ?

Cycle and Flow

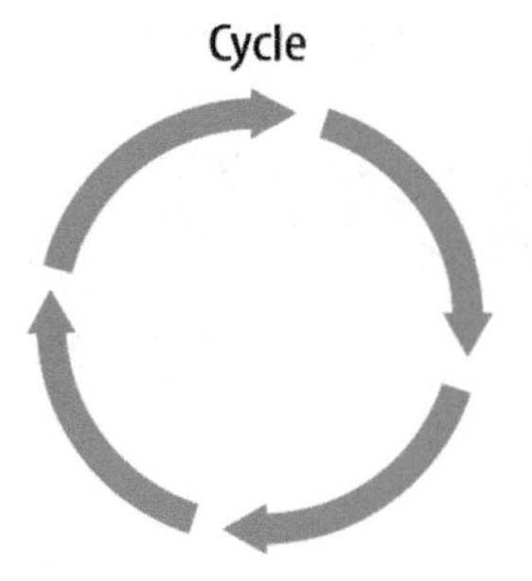

Flow

Figure 9 Matter moves in a cycle pattern, and energy moves in a flow pattern.

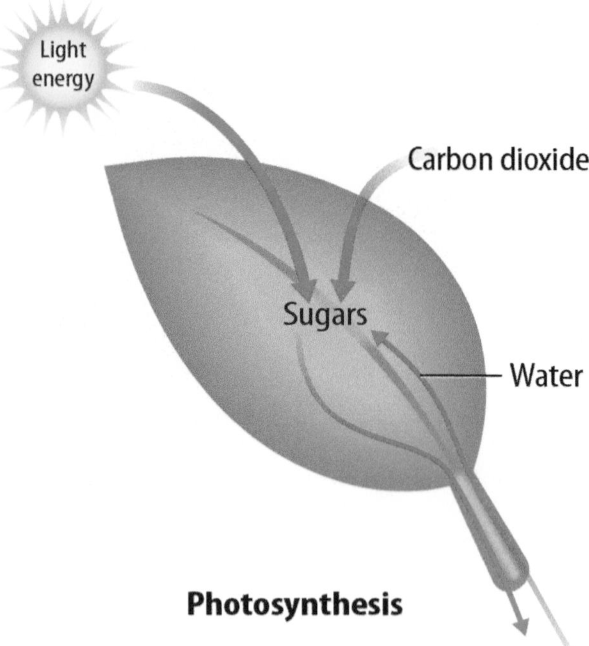

▲ **Figure 10** Most producers make their food through the process of photosynthesis.

WORD ORIGIN

photosynthesis
from Greek photo, meaning "light"; and synthese, meaning "synthesis"

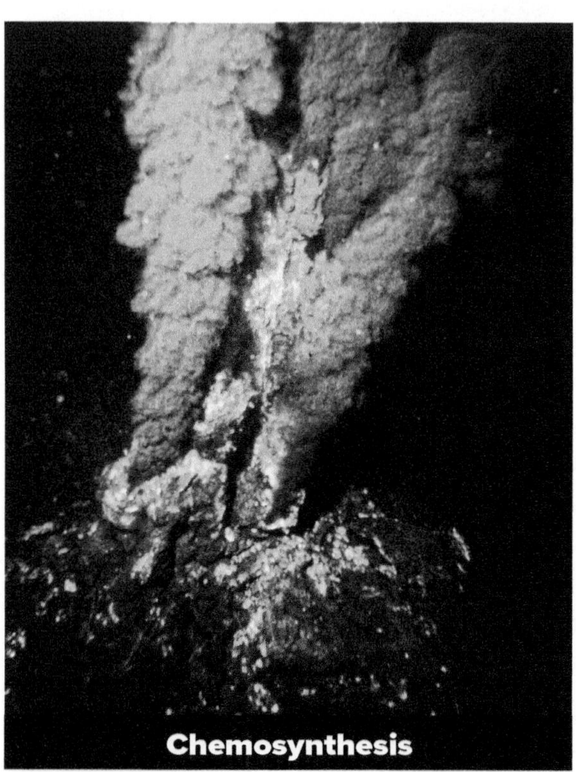

▲ **Figure 11** The producers at a hydrothermal vent make their food using chemosynthesis.

Producers

People who make things or products are often called producers. In a similar way, living things that make their own food are called producers. Producers make their food from materials found in their environments. Most producers are photosynthetic (foh toh sihn THEH tihk). They use the process of photosynthesis (foh toh SIHN thuh sus), which is described below. Grasses, trees, and other plants, algae and some other protists, and certain bacteria are photosynthetic. Other producers, including some bacteria, are chemosynthetic (kee moh sihn THEH tihk). They make their food using chemosynthesis (kee moh SIHN thuh sus).

Photosynthesis Recall that in the carbon cycle, carbon in the atmosphere cycles through producers such as plants, into other organisms, and then back into the atmosphere. This and other matter cycles involve photosynthesis, as shown in **Figure 10**. **Photosynthesis** *is a series of chemical reactions that convert light energy, water, and carbon dioxide into the food-energy molecule glucose and give off oxygen.*

Chemosynthesis As you read earlier, some producers make food using chemosynthesis. **Chemosynthesis** *is the process during which producers use chemical energy in matter rather than light energy and make food.* One place where chemosynthesis can occur is on the deep ocean floor. There, inorganic compounds that contain hydrogen and sulfur, along with thermal energy from Earth's interior, flow out from cracks in the ocean floor. These cracks are called hydrothermal vents. These vents, such as the one shown in **Figure 11**, are home to chemosynthetic bacteria. These bacteria use the chemical energy contained in inorganic compounds in the hot water and produce food.

 **Reading Check** What materials do producers use to make food during chemosynthesis?

Figure 12 Organisms can be classified by the type of food that they eat.

Consumers

Some consumers are shown in Figure 12. Consumers do not produce their own energy-rich food, as producers do. Instead, they get the energy they need to survive by consuming other organisms.

Consumers can be classified by the type of food that they eat. Herbivores feed on only producers. For example, a deer is an herbivore because it eats only plants. Carnivores eat other animals. They are usually predators, such as lions and wolves. Omnivores eat both producers and other consumers. A bird that eats berries and insects is an omnivore.

Another group of consumers is detritivores (dih TRI tuh vorz). They get their energy by eating the remains of other organisms. Some detritivores, such as insects, eat dead organisms. Other detritivores, such as bacteria and mushrooms, feed on dead organisms and help decompose them. For this reason, these organisms often are called decomposers. During decomposition, decomposers produce carbon dioxide that enters the atmosphere. Some of the decayed matter enters the soil. In this way, detritivores help recycle nutrients through ecosystems. They also help keep ecosystems clean. Without decomposers, dead organisms would pile up in an ecosystem.

MiniLab — 15 minutes

How can you classify organisms?

Most organisms get their energy from the Sun or by consuming other organisms. In this lab, you will use photographs to classify organisms based on their feeding relationships.

1. Search through a **magazine** for photographs of ecosystems. Select a photograph that shows several different organisms.
2. In your Science Journal, identify the organisms. Include a description of their environment.
3. Describe how the organisms are interacting with one another and with their environment.

Analyze and Conclude

1. **Classify** the organisms as producers or consumers. Use details from the photograph to support your classification scheme.
2. **Key Concept** How do the producers in your photo obtain energy? How do the consumers get their energy?

FOLDABLES®

Make a pyramid book from a sheet of paper. Use each side to organize information about one of the ways energy flows in an ecosystem. You can add additional information on the inside of your pyramid book.

Food Web
Food Chain

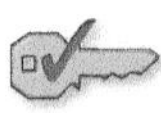

Project-Based Learning Activity

Sun Block Go online to research the role of sunlight and photosynthesis in food webs.

Modeling Energy in Ecosystems

Unlike matter, energy does not cycle through ecosystems because it does not return to the Sun. Instead, energy flows through ecosystems. Organisms use some energy for life processes. In addition, organisms store some energy in their bodies as chemical energy. When consumers eat these organisms, this chemical energy moves into the bodies of consumers. However, with each transfer of energy from organism to organism, some energy changes to thermal energy. The bodies of consumers emit excess thermal energy, which then enters the environment. Scientists use models to study this flow of energy through an ecosystem. They use different models depending on how many organisms they are studying.

Food Chains

A **food chain** *is a model that shows how energy flows in an ecosystem through feeding relationships.* In a food chain, arrows show the transfer of energy. A typical food chain is shown in Figure 13. Notice that there are not many links in this food chain. That is because the amount of available energy decreases every time it is transferred from one organism to another.

Key Concept Check How does a food chain model energy flow?

Figure 13 This food chain shows how the energy in animals' food was once energy from the sun. Photosynthesis is the process by which the sun's energy is converted to energy-rich food.

Food Chain
1 The Sun emits energy.
2 Plants make energy-rich food using sunlight.
3 The mouse obtains energy by eating the plant.
4 The snake obtains energy by eating the mouse.
5 The hawk obtains energy by eating the snake.

Food Webs

Imagine you have a jigsaw puzzle of a tropical rain forest. Each piece of the puzzle shows only one small part of the forest. A food chain is like one piece of an ecosystem jigsaw puzzle. It is helpful when studying certain parts of an ecosystem, but it does not show the whole picture.

In the food chain on the previous page, the mouse might also eat the seeds of several producers, such as corn, berries, or grass. The snake might eat other organisms such as frogs, crickets, lizards, or earthworms too. The hawk hunts mice, squirrels, rabbits, and fish, as well as snakes. *Scientists use a model of energy transfer called a* **food web** *to show how food chains in a community are interconnected,* as shown in **Figure 14.** You can think of a food web as many overlapping food chains. Like in a food chain, arrows show how energy flows in a food web. Some organisms in the food web might be part of more than one food chain in that web.

Key Concept Check What models show the transfer of energy in an ecosystem?

Personal Tutor

Figure 14 A food web shows the complex feeding relationships among organisms in an ecosystem. Photosynthesis is the process by which the diatoms convert the sun's energy to energy-rich food.

Project-Based Learning Activity

Web of Life Go online to create a model that shows how the energy in animals' food was once energy from the sun.

Math Skills

Use Percentages

The first trophic level—producers—obtains energy from the Sun. They use 90 percent of the energy for their own life processes. Only 10 percent of the energy remains for the second trophic level—herbivores. Assume that each trophic level uses 90 percent of the energy it receives. Use the following steps to calculate how much energy remains for the next trophic level.

First trophic level gets 100 units of energy.

First trophic level uses 90 percent = 90 units

Energy remaining for second trophic level = 10 units

Second trophic level uses 90 percent = 9 units

Energy remaining for third trophic level = 1 unit

Practice

If the first trophic level receives 10,000 units of energy from the Sun, how much energy is available for the second trophic level?

 Math Practice

 Personal Tutor

Energy Pyramids

Food chains and food webs show how energy moves in an ecosystem. However, they do not show how the amount of energy in an ecosystem changes. *Scientists use a model called an* **energy pyramid** *to show the amount of energy available in each step of a food chain,* as shown in Figure 15. The steps of an energy pyramid are also called trophic (TROH fihk) levels.

Producers that carry out photosynthesis make up the trophic level at the bottom of the pyramid. Consumers that eat producers, such as squirrels, make up the next trophic level. Consumers such as hawks that eat other consumers make up the highest trophic level. Notice that less energy is available for consumers at each higher trophic level. As you read earlier, organisms use some of the energy they get from food for life processes. During life processes, some energy is changed to thermal energy and is transferred to the environment. Only about 10 percent of the energy available at one trophic level transfers on to the next trophic level.

Figure 15 An energy pyramid shows the amount of energy available at each trophic level.

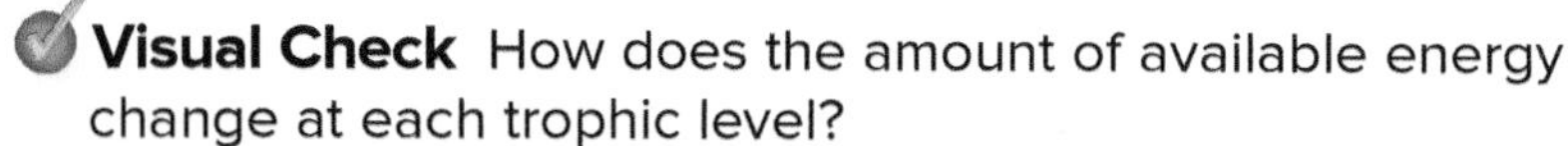

Visual Check How does the amount of available energy change at each trophic level?

 Animation

Trophic level 3
(1 percent of energy available)

Trophic level 2
(10 percent of energy available)

Trophic level 1
(100 percent of energy available)

Available energy decreases.

Lesson 3 Review

Visual Summary

Energy flows in ecosystems from producers to consumers.

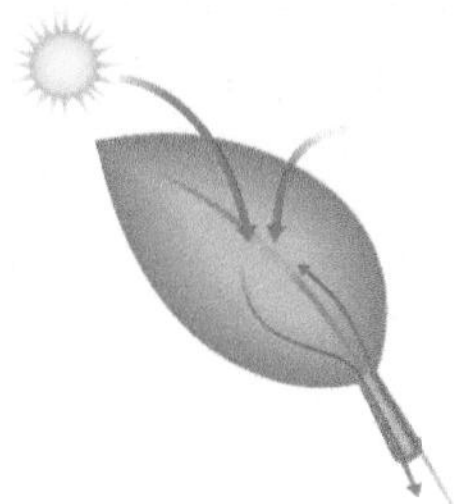

Producers make their own food through the processes of photosynthesis or chemosynthesis.

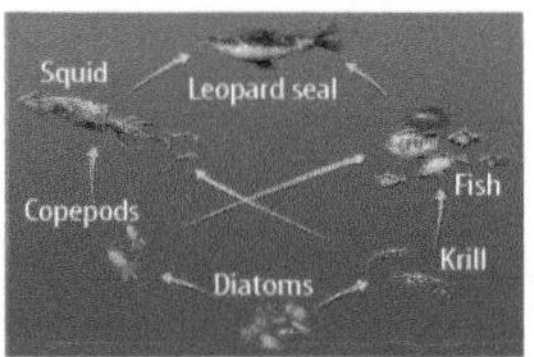

Food chains and food webs model how energy moves in ecosystems.

FOLDABLES®

Use your lesson Foldable to review the lesson. Save your Foldable for the project at the end of the chapter.

What do you think NOW?

You first read the statements below at the beginning of the chapter.

5. The Sun is the source for all energy used by living things on Earth.

6. All living things get their energy from eating other living things.

Did you change your mind about whether you agree or disagree with the statements? Rewrite any false statements to make them true.

Use Vocabulary

1. Scientists use a(n) __________ to show how energy moves in an ecosystem.
2. **Distinguish** between photosynthesis and chemosynthesis.

Understand Key Concepts 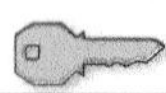

3. Which organism is a producer?
   A. cow
   B. dog
   C. grass
   D. human
4. **Construct** a food chain with four links.

Interpret Graphics

5. **Assess** Which trophic level has the most energy available to living things?

Ecosystem

Trophic level 3

Trophic level 2

Trophic level 1

Critical Thinking

6. **Recommend** A friend wants to show how energy moves in ecosystems. Which model would you recommend? Explain.

Math Skills

 Math Practice

7. The plants in level 1 of a food pyramid obtain 30,000 units of energy from the Sun. How much energy is available for the organisms in level 2? Level 3?

Lab

3 class periods

Design an Ecosystem

Materials

5–10-gallon aquarium

assorted ecosystem materials

Safety

You have read about the connections between biotic and abiotic factors of an ecosystem and how they depend on each other. An ecosystem requires abiotic factors to meet the basic needs of the organisms that inhabit it. In addition, the organisms of the ecosystem serve different roles. Some organisms are producers, some are consumers, and some are decomposers. In this lab, you will create an ecosystem with abiotic and biotic factors that function together. Then you will investigate and describe how homeostasis is maintained as living things meet their basic needs in the ecosystem you assembled.

Ask a Question

What biotic and abiotic factors can you assemble to create a functioning ecosystem?

Make Observations

1. Read and complete a lab safety form.
2. In your Science Journal, make three columns with the following headings: *Organism*, *Abiotic Needs*, and *Biotic Needs*.
3. Visit a pet store or go online to research the types of organisms that can live in your glass aquarium. As you research, list the organisms in your Science Journal. Along with the types of organisms, list the specific biotic and abiotic needs of each organism.
4. Using your research, design an ecosystem that you can build in your aquarium. The ecosystem can be aquatic or terrestrial. Your plan must provide for the basic needs of all organisms in your ecosystem so they can maintain homeostasis.
5. Have your teacher approve your design before you create your ecosystem.

7

Form a Hypothesis

6. After receiving approval for your ecosystem design, formulate a hypothesis about what your ecosystem requires to function successfully.

Test Your Hypothesis

7 With your teacher's help, obtain the resources and organisms you need to construct your ecosystem. Work with your teacher to put your ecosystem together and add the living organisms. Take care to research the needs of each organism you use. You might consult a biologist or a specialist at a pet store to make sure the needs of all your organisms will be met.

8 Observe your ecosystem over several days. Record your observations. Provide details on the ways that the parts of your ecosystem interact and connect with each other.

Analyze and Conclude

9 **Analyze** Describe the parts and interactions of your ecosystem. How well does your ecosystem sustain itself? What things, if any, must you add to the ecosystem to maintain it? Were the living things in the ecosystem able to maintain homeostasis as they sought out their basic needs?

10 **Classify** Write a list of the organisms in your ecosystem. Classify each organism as a producer, a consumer, or a decomposer.

11 The Big Idea Create a food-web diagram of your ecosystem. Diagram the connections that occur between the organisms. Describe how nutrients and resources cycle through the ecosystem. Explain how matter and energy are transformed.

Communicate Your Results

Prepare a scientific report on your ecosystem. Include descriptions of the niches occupied by the organisms, explanations of relationships between organisms, and data on population changes.

Extension

A successful ecosystem recycles all the things needed for survival. What additions or changes could you make to your ecosystem so that nothing would need to be added or removed for it to sustain itself? Write a brief plan.

Lab Tips

- ☑ Ask for help from several different sources for obtaining and working with the organisms in your ecosystem.
- ☑ Remember that your organisms will need an appropriate environment in which to live. Find a suitable location, with proper light and temperature, in which to keep your aquarium.

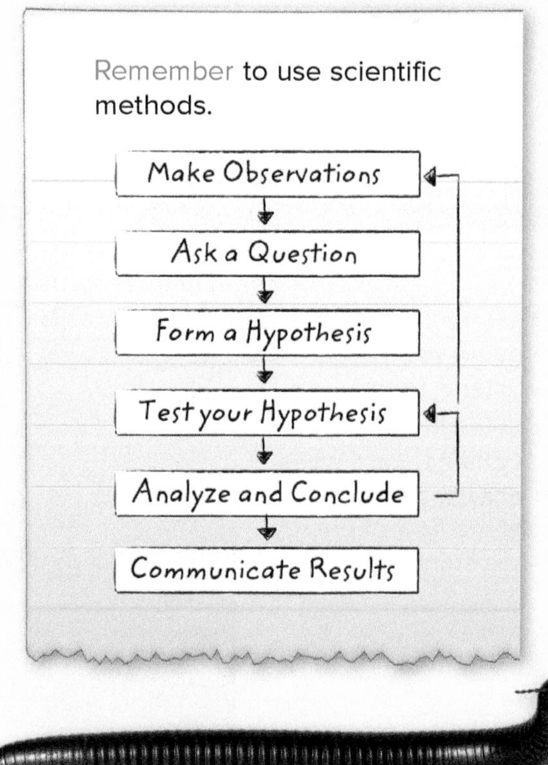

Chapter 8 Study Guide

Living things interact with and depend on each other and on the nonliving things in an ecosystem.

Key Concepts Summary 

Lesson 1: Abiotic Factors

- The **abiotic factors** in an environment include sunlight, temperature, climate, air, water, and soil.

Vocabulary

ecosystem p. 269
biotic factor p. 269
abiotic factor p. 269
climate p. 270
atmosphere p. 271

Lesson 2: Cycles of Matter

- Matter such as oxygen, nitrogen, water, carbon, and minerals moves in cycles in the ecosystem.

Vocabulary

evaporation p. 276
condensation p. 274
precipitation p. 274
nitrogen fixation p. 278

Lesson 3: Energy in Ecosystems

- Energy flows through ecosystems from producers to consumers.
- **Food chains, food webs,** and **energy pyramids** model the flow of energy in ecosystems.

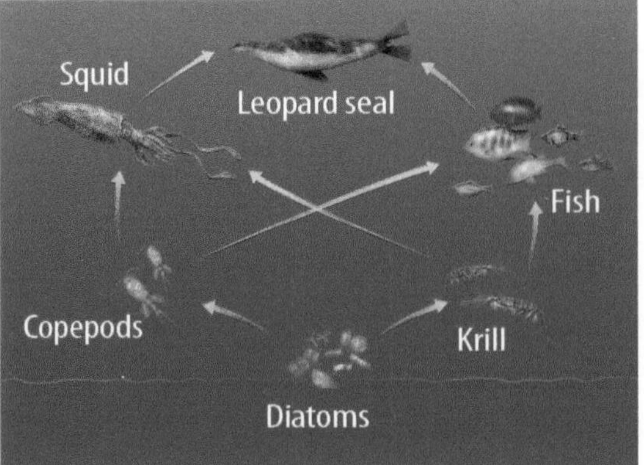

Vocabulary

photosynthesis p. 286
chemosynthesis p. 286
food chain p. 258
food web p. 289
energy pyramid p. 290

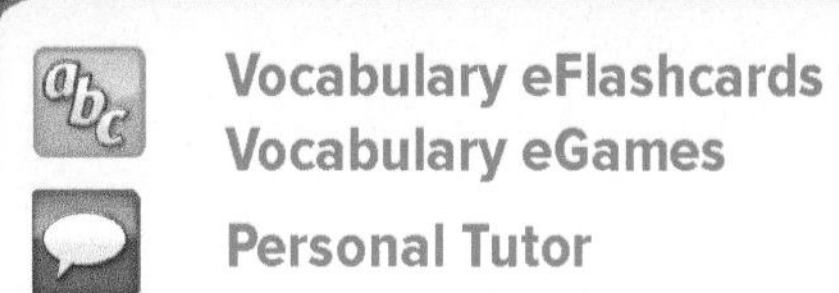

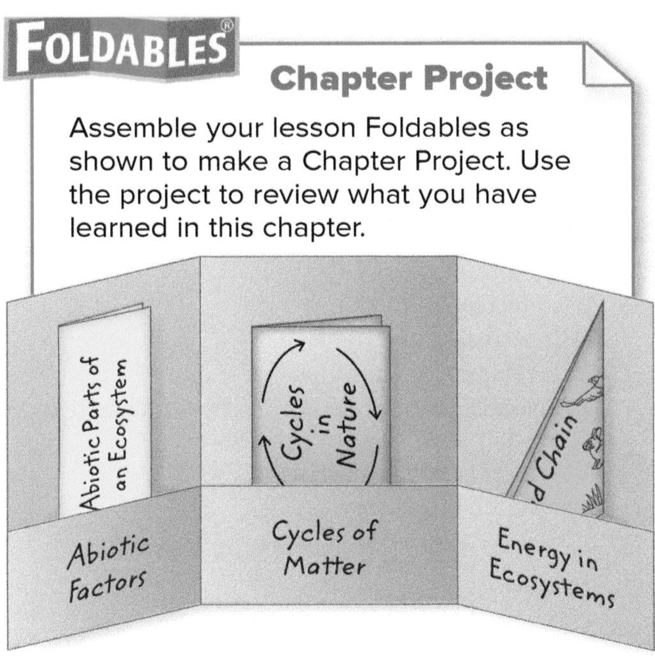

FOLDABLES
Chapter Project
Assemble your lesson Foldables as shown to make a Chapter Project. Use the project to review what you have learned in this chapter.
Abiotic Parts of an Ecosystem
Cycles in Nature
d Chain
Abiotic Factors
Cycles of Matter
Energy in Ecosystems

Use Vocabulary

1. Distinguish between climate and atmosphere.
2. The atmosphere is made mainly of the gases ________ and ________.
3. Living organisms in an ecosystem are called ________, while the nonliving things are called ________.
4. The process of converting nitrogen in the air into a form that can be used by living organisms is called ________ ________.
5. Use the word precipitation in a complete sentence.
6. Define condensation in your own words.
7. How does a food chain differ from a food web?
8. The process of ________ uses energy from the Sun.
9. Define chemosynthesis in your own words.

Link Vocabulary and Key Concepts

Copy this concept map, and then use vocabulary terms from the previous page and other terms from the chapter to complete the concept map.

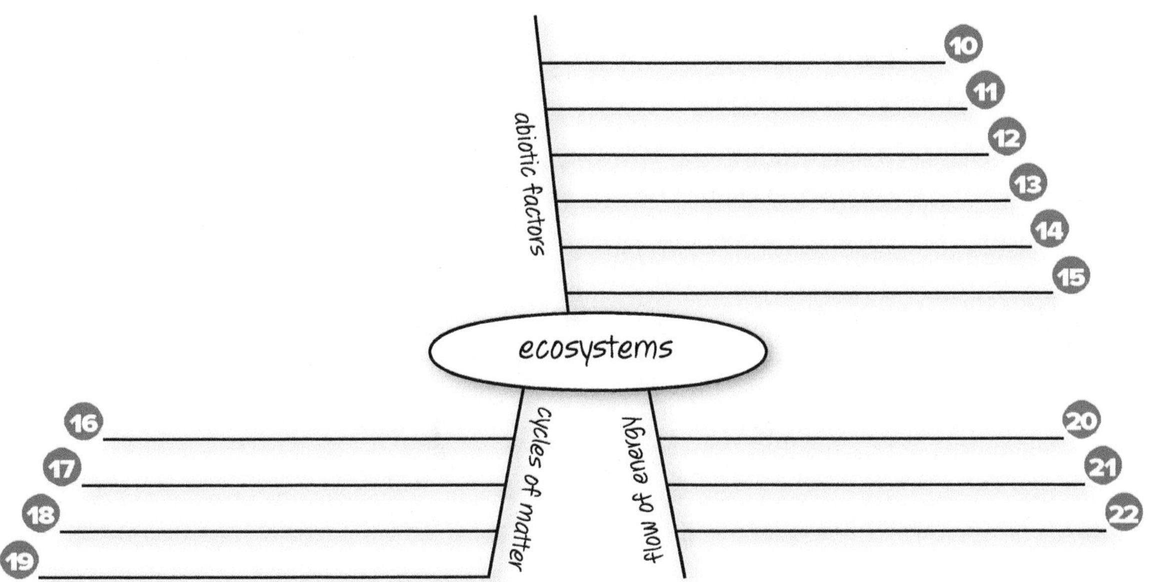

Chapter 8 Review

Understand Key Concepts 

1. What is the source of most energy on Earth?
   A. air
   B. soil
   C. the Sun
   D. water

2. Which is a biotic factor in an ecosystem?
   A. a plant living near a stream
   B. the amount of rainfall
   C. the angle of the Sun
   D. the types of minerals present in soil

3. Study the energy pyramid shown here.

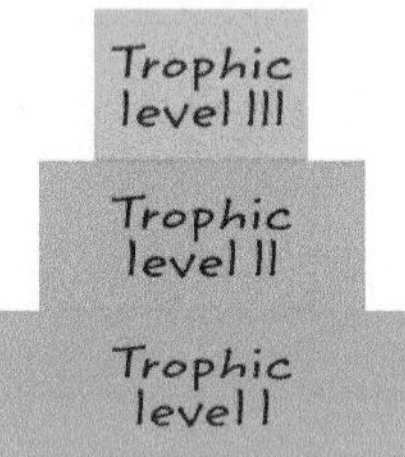

   Which organism might you expect to find at trophic level I?
   A. fox
   B. frog
   C. grass
   D. grasshopper

4. Which includes both an abiotic and a biotic factor?
   A. a chicken laying an egg
   B. a deer drinking from a stream
   C. a rock rolling down a hill
   D. a squirrel eating an acorn

5. Which process helps keep temperatures on Earth from becoming too hot or too cold?
   A. condensation
   B. global warming
   C. greenhouse effect
   D. nitrogen fixation

6. During the carbon cycle, ________ take in carbon dioxide from the atmosphere.
   A. animals
   B. consumers
   C. decomposers
   D. plants

7. Which is true of the amount of matter in ecosystems?
   A. It decreases over time.
   B. It increases over time.
   C. It remains constant.
   D. Scientists cannot determine how it changes.

8. Which process is occurring at the location indicated by the arrow?

   A. condensation
   B. nitrogen fixation
   C. precipitation
   D. transpiration

9. Which best represents a food chain?
   A. Sun → rabbit → fox → grass
   B. Sun → grass → rabbit → fox
   C. fox → grass → rabbit → Sun
   D. grass → rabbit → fox → Sun

10. A person who ate a salad made of lettuce, tomatoes, cheese, and ham is a(n)
   A. carnivore.
   B. detritivore.
   C. herbivore.
   D. omnivore.

Critical Thinking

11 **Compare and contrast** the oxygen cycle and the nitrogen cycle.

12 **Create** a plan for making an aquatic ecosystem in a jar. Include both abiotic and biotic factors.

13 **Recommend** a strategy for decreasing the amount of carbon dioxide in the atmosphere.

14 **Role-Play** Working in a group, perform a skit about organisms living near a hydrothermal vent. Be sure to include information about how the organisms obtain energy.

15 **Describe** the role of photosynthesis in the flow of energy in food chains, food webs, and energy pyramids.

16 Study the food web below. **Classify** each organism according to what it eats.

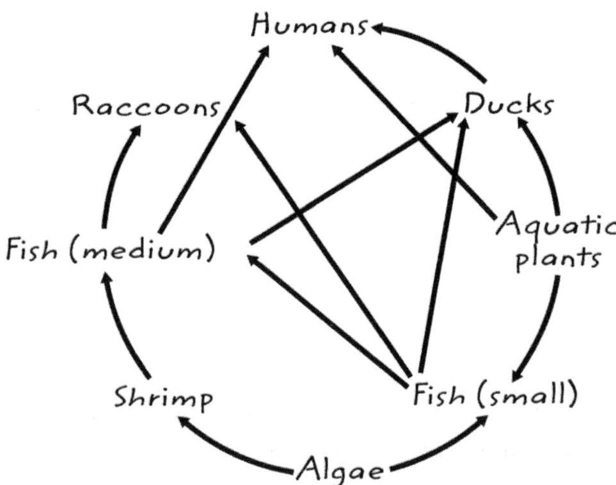

17 **Create** the following diagrams to show how the energy in animals' food was once energy from the sun: food chain, food web, energy pyramid.

Writing in Science

18 **Write** an argument for or against the following statement. *The energy humans use in cars originally came from the Sun.*

REVIEW THE BIG IDEA

19 Describe an interaction between a living thing and a nonliving thing in an ecosystem.

20 How might the flamingos interact with nonliving things in their environment?

Math Skills

Use Percentages

21 A group of plankton, algae, and other ocean plants absorb 150,000 units of energy.

a. How much energy is available for the third trophic level?

b. How much energy would remain for a fourth trophic level?

22 Some organisms, such as humans, are omnivores. They eat both producers and consumers. How much more energy would an omnivore get from eating the same mass of food at the first trophic level than at the second trophic level?

Standardized Test Practice

Record your answers on the answer sheet provided by your teacher or on a sheet of paper.

Multiple Choice

1 In which process do producers use chemical energy and make food?

A chemosynthesis

B fermentation

C glycolysis

D photosynthesis

Use the image below to answer question 2.

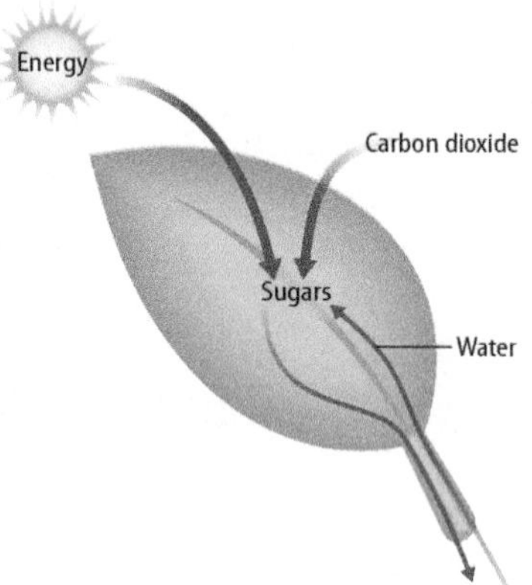

2 What process is shown above?

A chemosynthesis

B decomposition

C nitrogen fixation

D photosynthesis

3 What organisms help break down dead leaves in an ecosystem?

A carnivores

B detritivores

C herbivores

D omnivores

4 Which process converts atmospheric nitrogen to a form organisms can use?

A absorption

B fixation

C retention

D stabilization

Use the diagram below to answer question 5.

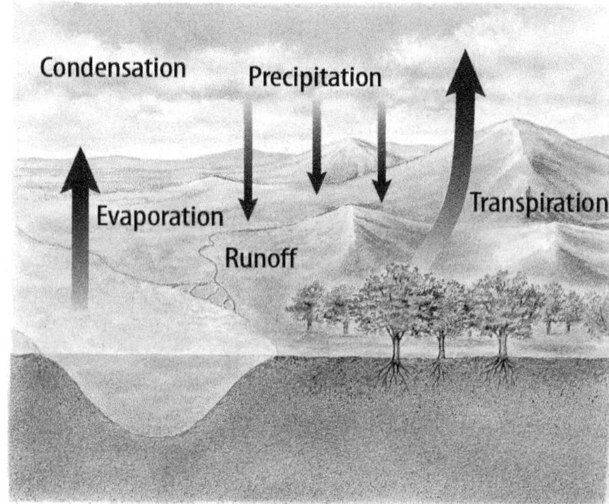

5 Which step of the water cycle shown above occurs in plants?

A condensation

B evaporation

C precipitation

D transpiration

6 Which is true of energy in ecosystems?

A It never changes form.

B It is both created and destroyed.

C It flows in one direction.

D It follows a cycle pattern.

7 Which organism would most likely appear at the top of an energy pyramid?

A grass

B hawk

C mouse

D snake

Use the diagram below to answer questions 8 and 9.

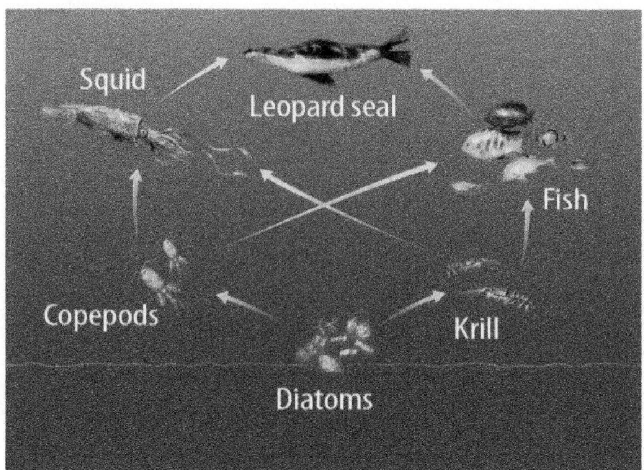

8 How does energy move in the food web pictured above?

A from leopard seal to squid

B from diatoms to krill

C from fish to krill

D from squid to diatoms

9 Which is an example of a food chain shown above?

A diatoms → krill → leopard seal

B fish → krill → squid

C diatoms → krill → fish

D squid → fish → leopard seal

10 During which process is oxygen gas released into the atmosphere?

A chemosynthesis

B decomposition

C photosynthesis

D transpiration

Constructed Response

11 Most ecosystems contain six nonliving factors: atmosphere, climate, soil, temperature, sunlight, and water. Briefly explain how each factor affects the life of a large predator, such as a jaguar, in a jungle ecosystem.

Use the diagram below to answer questions 12 and 13.

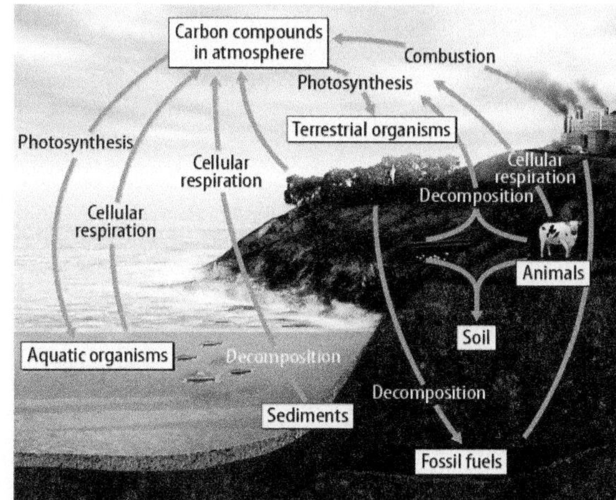

12 Using the image of the carbon cycle shown above, identify three locations of carbon other than the atmosphere. What form does the carbon take in each example?

13 Describe a biological process of the carbon cycle that removes carbon from the atmosphere and a biological process that adds carbon dioxide to the atmosphere.

NEED EXTRA HELP?													
If You Missed Question...	1	2	3	4	5	6	7	8	9	10	11	12	13
Go to Lesson...	3	2	3	2	2	3	3	3	3	2	1	2	2

Chapter 9

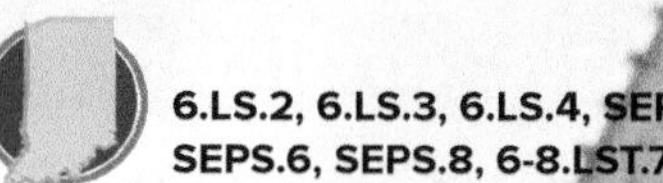

Populations and Communities

THE BIG IDEA How do populations and communities interact and change?

Inquiry Too Many Pigeons?

This group of pigeons does not depend only on the environment for food. Tourists visiting the area also feed the pigeons. Because so much food is available, more pigeons than normal live in this part of the city.

- Do you think this large number of pigeons affects other organisms in the area?
- How do you think groups of pigeons and other organisms interact and change?

Get Ready to Read

What do you think?

Before you read, decide if you agree or disagree with each of these statements. As you read this chapter, see if you change your mind about any of the statements.

1. Some life exists in the ice caps of the North Pole and the South Pole.
2. A community includes all organisms of one species that live in the same area.
3. Some populations decrease in numbers because of low birthrates.
4. An extinct species has only a few surviving individuals.
5. No more than two species can live in the same habitat.
6. A cow is a producer because it produces food for other organisms.

McGraw Hill Education **connectED**

Your one-stop online resource

connectED.mcgraw-hill.com

- LS LearnSmart®
- Chapter Resources Files, Reading Essentials, Get Ready to Read, Quick Vocabulary
- Animations, Videos, Interactive Tables
- Self-checks, Quizzes, Tests
- PBL Project-Based Learning Activities
- Lab Manuals, Safety Videos, Virtual Labs & Other Tools
- Vocabulary, Multilingual eGlossary, Vocab eGames, Vocab eFlashcards
- Personal Tutors

Lesson 1

Reading Guide

Key Concepts 
ESSENTIAL QUESTIONS

- What defines a population?
- What factors affect the size of a population?

Vocabulary

biosphere p. 303
community p. 304
population p. 304
competition p. 305
limiting factor p. 305
population density p. 306
biotic potential p. 306
carrying capacity p. 307

Multilingual eGlossary

6.LS.4, 6-8.LST.7.1

Populations

Go to the resource tab in ConnectED to find the PBL *Snake Invaders.*

Inquiry Looking for Something?

Meerkats live in family groups. They help protect each other by watching for danger from eagles, lions, and other hunters of the Kalahari Desert. What other ways might the meerkats interact?

Launch Lab

15 minutes

How many times do you interact?

Every day, you interact with other people in different ways, including talking, writing, or shaking hands. Some interactions involve just one other person, and others happen between many people. Like humans, other organisms interact with each other in their environment.

1. Make a list in your Science Journal of all the ways you have interacted with other people today.
2. Use a **highlighter** to mark the interactions that occurred between you and one other person.
3. Use a **highlighter** of another color to mark interactions that occurred among three or more people.

Think About This

1. Were your interactions mainly with one person or with three or more people?
2. **Key Concept** How might your interactions change if the group of people were bigger?

The Biosphere and Ecological Systems

Imagine flying halfway around the world to Africa. When your plane flies over Africa, you might see mountains, rivers, grasslands, and forests. As you get closer to land, you might see a herd of elephants at a watering hole. You also might see a group of meerkats, like the ones on the previous page.

Now imagine hiking through an African forest. You might see monkeys, frogs, insects, spiders, and flowers. Maybe you catch sight of crocodiles sunning themselves by a river or birds perching on trees.

You are exploring Earth's **biosphere** (BI uh sfir)–*the parts of Earth and the surrounding atmosphere where there is life.* The biosphere includes all the land of the continents and islands. It also includes all of Earth's oceans, lakes, and streams, as well as the ice caps at the North Pole and the South Pole.

Parts of the biosphere with large amounts of plants or algae often contain many other organisms as well. The biosphere's distribution of chlorophyll, a green pigment in plants and algae, is shown in Figure 1.

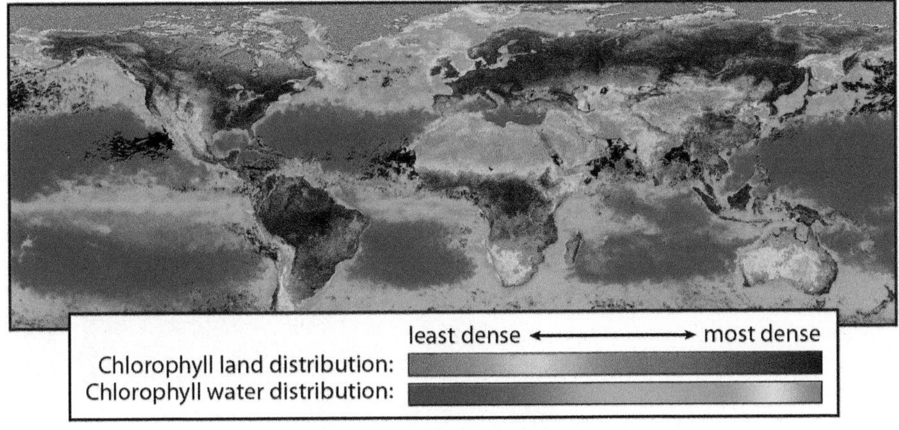

Figure 1 The colors in this satellite image represent the densities of chlorophyll, a green pigment found in plants and algae.

Visual Check Why might the North Pole have very little green?

What is a population?

The Kalahari Desert in Africa is a part of the Earth's biosphere. A wildlife refuge in the Kalahari Desert is home to several groups of meerkats. Meerkats are small mammals that live in family groups and help each other care for their young.

Meerkats rely on interactions among themselves to survive. They sleep in underground burrows at night and hunt for food during the day. They take turns standing upright to watch for danger and call out warnings to others.

Meerkats are part of an ecosystem, as shown in Figure 2. An ecosystem is a group of organisms that lives in an area at one time, as well as the climate, soil, water, and other nonliving parts of the environment. The Kalahari Desert is an ecosystem. The study of all ecosystems on Earth is ecology.

Many species besides meerkats live in the Kalahari Desert. They include scorpions, spiders, insects, snakes, and birds such as eagles and owls. Also, large animals like zebras, giraffes, and lions live there. Plants that grow in the Kalahari Desert include shrubs, grasses, small trees, and melon vines. Together, all these plants, animals, and other organisms form a community. *A* **community** *is all the populations of different species that live together in the same area at the same time.*

All the meerkats in this refuge form a population. *A* **population** *is all the organisms of the same species that live in the same area at the same time.* A species is a group of organisms that have similar traits and are able to produce fertile offspring.

Key Concept Check What defines a population?

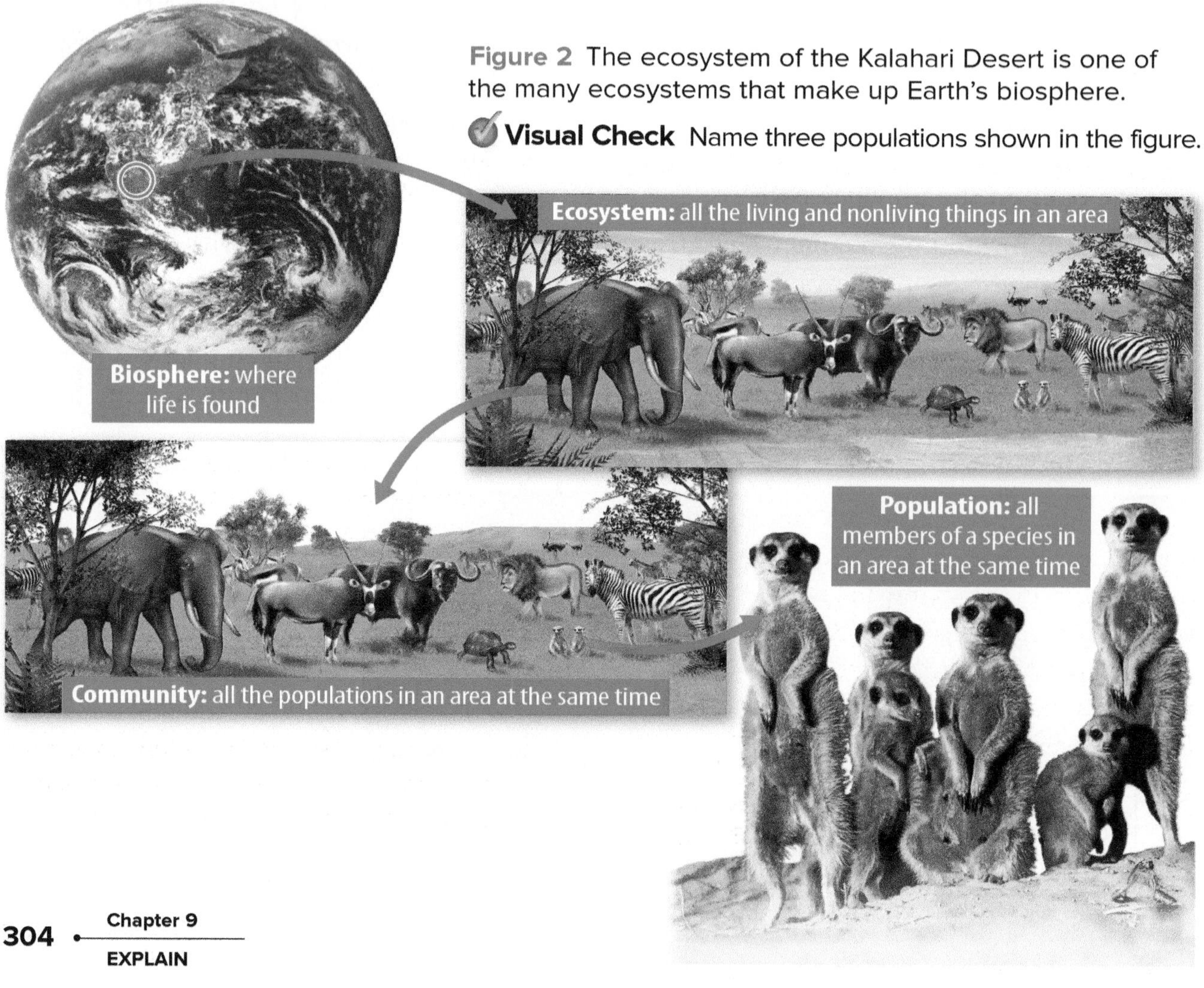

Figure 2 The ecosystem of the Kalahari Desert is one of the many ecosystems that make up Earth's biosphere.

Visual Check Name three populations shown in the figure.

Biosphere: where life is found

Ecosystem: all the living and nonliving things in an area

Community: all the populations in an area at the same time

Population: all members of a species in an area at the same time

Competition

At times, not enough food is available for every organism in a community. Members of a population, including those in the Kalahari Desert, must compete with other populations and each other for enough food to survive. **Competition** *is the demand for resources, such as food, water, and shelter, in short supply in a community.* When there are not enough resources available to survive, there is more competition in a community.

Population Sizes

If the amount of available food decreases, what do you think happens to a population of meerkats? Some meerkats might move away to find food elsewhere. Female meerkats cannot raise as many young. The population becomes smaller. If there is plenty of food, however, the size of the population grows larger as more meerkats survive to adulthood and live longer. Changes in a given habitat can be beneficial or harmful to populations.

Limiting Factors

Environmental factors, such as available water, food, shelter, sunlight, and temperature, are possible limiting factors for a population. A **limiting factor** *is anything that restricts the size of a population.* Available sunlight is a limiting factor for most organisms. If there is not enough sunlight, green plants cannot make food by photosynthesis. Organisms that eat plants are affected if little food is available.

Temperature is a limiting factor for some organisms. When the temperature drops below freezing, many organisms die because it is too cold to carry out their life functions. Disease, predators–animals that eat other animals–and natural disasters such as fires or floods are limiting factors as well.

Key Concept Check What factors affect the size of a population?

Hutchings Photography/Digital Light Source

MiniLab 15 minutes

What are limiting factors?

Certain factors, called limiting factors, can affect the size of a population.

1. Read and complete a lab safety form.
2. Your teacher will divide your class into groups.
3. Using a **meterstick** and **masking tape,** mark a 1-m square on the floor. Place a piece of paper in the middle of the square.
4. All members of your group will stand entirely within the square. While one member keeps time with a **stopwatch,** members of the group will write the alphabet on the sheet of paper one at a time.

5. In your Science Journal, calculate the average time it took each person to write the alphabet.

Analyze and Conclude

1. **Describe** how the space limitations affected each member's ability to complete the task.
2. **Key Concept** What functions must an organism perform that can be limited by the amount of available space?

Figure 3 A sedated lynx is fitted with a radio collar and then returned to the wild.

Measuring Population Size

Sometimes it is difficult to determine the size of a population. How would you count scampering meerkats or wild lynx? One method used to count and monitor animal populations is the capture-mark-and-release method. The lynx in Figure 3 is a member of a population in Poland that is monitored using this method. Biologists using this method sedate animals and fit them with radio collars before releasing them back into the wild. By counting how many observed lynx are wearing collars, scientists can estimate the size of the lynx population. Biologists also use the collars to track the lynx's movements and monitor their activities.

Suppose you want to know how closely together Cumberland azaleas (uh ZAYL yuhz), a type of flower, grow in the Great Smoky Mountains National Park. **Population density** *is the size of a population compared to the amount of space available.* One way of estimating population density is by sample count. Rather than counting every azalea shrub, you count only those in a representative area, such as 1 km^2. By multiplying the number of square kilometers in the park by the number of azaleas in 1 km^2, you find the estimated population density of azalea shrubs in the entire park.

Reading Check Describe two ways you can estimate population size.

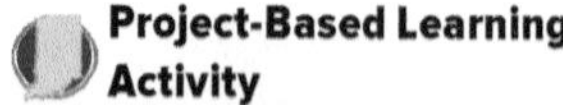

Project-Based Learning Activity

Snake Invaders Go online to research invasive species and discuss their impact on ecosystems.

FOLDABLES®

Make a horizontal half book and label it as shown. Use it to organize your notes on the relationship between population size and carrying capacity in an ecosystem.

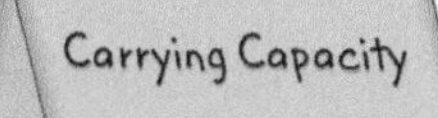

Biotic Potential

Imagine that a population of raccoons has plenty of food, water, and den space. In addition, there is no disease or danger from other animals. The only limit to the size of this population is the number of offspring the raccoons can produce. **Biotic potential** *is the potential growth of a population if it could grow in perfect conditions with no limiting factors.* No population on Earth ever reaches its biotic potential because no ecosystem has an unlimited supply of natural resources.

Carrying Capacity

What would happen if a population of meerkats reached its biotic potential? It would stop growing when it reached the limit of available resources that the ecosystem could provide, such as food, water, or shelter. *The largest number of individuals of one species that an environment can support is the* **carrying capacity.** A population grows until it reaches the carrying capacity of an environment, as shown in Figure 4. Disease, space, predators, and food are some of the factors that limit the carrying capacity of an ecosystem. However, the carrying capacity of an environment is not constant. It increases and decreases as the amount of available resources increases and decreases. At times, a population can temporarily exceed the carrying capacity of an environment.

Reading Check What is carrying capacity?

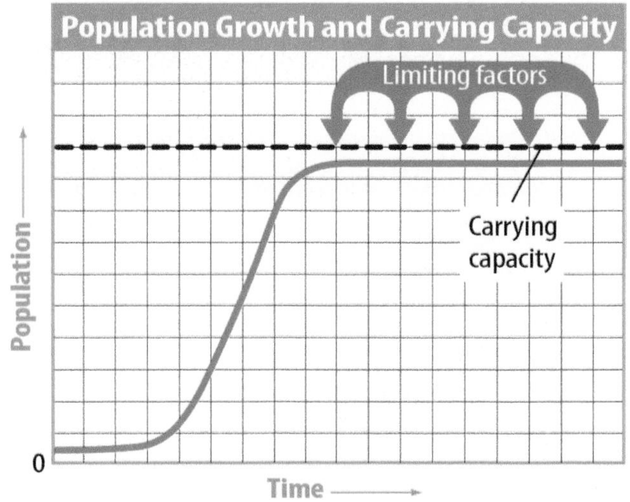

▲ **Figure 4** Carrying capacity is determined in part by limiting factors.

Visual Check What affects population size in the graph above?

Overpopulation

When the size of a population becomes larger than the carrying capacity of its ecosystem, overpopulation occurs. Overpopulation can cause problems for organisms. For example, meerkats eat spiders. An overpopulation of meerkats causes the size of the spider population in that community to decrease. Populations of birds and other animals that eat spiders also decrease when the number of spiders decreases.

Elephants in Africa's wild game parks are another example of overpopulation. Elephants searching for food caused the tree damage shown in Figure 5. They push over trees to feed on the uppermost leaves. Other species of animals that use the same trees for food and shelter must compete with the elephants. The loss of trees and plants can also damage soil. Trees and plants might not grow in that area again for a long time.

Reading Check How can overpopulation affect a community?

▲ **Figure 5** An overpopulation of elephants can cause damage to trees and other plants as the herd searches for food in the community.

Lesson 1 Review

Online Quiz

Visual Summary

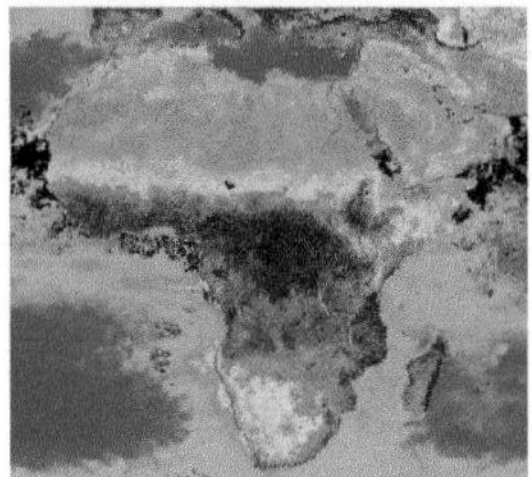

The population density of organisms, including green plants and algae, varies throughout the world.

A community is all the populations of different species that live together in the same area at the same time.

The number of individuals in a population varies as the amount of available resources varies.

FOLDABLES®

Use your lesson Foldable to review the lesson. Save your Foldable for the project at the end of the chapter.

What do you think NOW?

You first read the statements below at the beginning of the chapter.

1. Some life exists in the ice caps of the North Pole and the South Pole.

2. A community includes all organisms of one species that live in the same area.

Did you change your mind about whether you agree or disagree with the statements? Rewrite any false statements to make them true.

Use Vocabulary

1. **Define** *population.*
2. **Distinguish** between carrying capacity and biotic potential.
3. Food, water, living space, and disease are examples of ________.

Understand Key Concepts

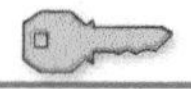

4. **Explain** how competition could limit the size of a bird population.
5. One example of competition among members of a meerkat population is
   - **A.** fighting over mates.
   - **B.** warning others of danger.
   - **C.** huddling together to stay warm.
   - **D.** teaching young to search for food.

Interpret Graphics

6. **Sequence** Draw a graphic organizer like the one below to show the sequence of steps in one type of population study.

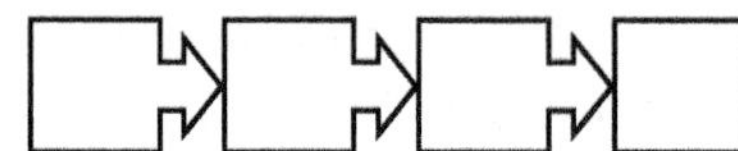

7. **Explain** the changes in population size at each point marked on the graph below.

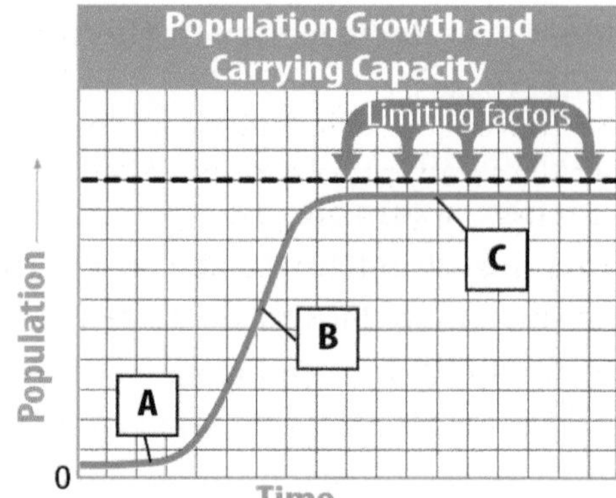

Critical Thinking

8. **Explain** Is the problem of elephants destroying trees in southern Africa overpopulation, competition, or both?

Purple Loosestrife: An Invasive Plant Species

GREEN SCIENCE

Stamping Out the Purple Plague

AMERICAN MUSEUM OF NATURAL HISTORY

Wetlands, such as swamps and marshes, are important ecosystems. These soggy areas control flooding, affect the flow of rivers, and filter pollution from water. They also are home to a diversity of wildlife, such as birds, fish, mammals, and plants. But not every species in a wetland is native to the habitat. In North America, one invasive species in particular has caused trouble for many wetland ecosystems.

In the early 1800s, European ships brought a hardy plant to America's shores—purple loosestrife. Settlers used it as a medicinal herb to treat digestive problems, such as diarrhea and ulcers. Before long, the tall plant with reddish-purple flowers was growing in wetlands across the United States.

The fast-growing plant is devastating for wetlands. Its thick roots crowd out native plants that provide food, shelter, and nesting sites for many animal species. Loosestrife also can disrupt the flow of water to rivers and canals and clog irrigation systems. The effect of loosestrife on biodiversity and local communities is so harmful that the plants have become known as the purple plague.

Scientists have tried many ways of controlling purple loosestrife, including plant-eating animals, bacteria, and herbicides. Cutting down the plants doesn't work because new plants sprout from even tiny pieces of root left in the soil. The best solution to date has been the introduction of organisms that eat purple loosestrife. Scientists have identified five species of beetles that eat purple loosestrife in its native range in Europe. These beetles do not harm other North American plants, so they have been released into the wetlands. Since 1996, the insects have successfully controlled the spread of purple loosestrife in many regions.

Scientists release leaf-eating beetles such as this one into a wetland invaded by purple loosestrife. ▼

▲ A sea of purple loosestrife overruns a wetland. It spreads quickly because one plant can produce up to three million seeds a year. The hardy seeds are scattered long distances by wind, water, animals, and even people.

It's Your Turn

RESEARCH AND REPORT Choose another invasive species. Describe how it was introduced into an ecosystem, its impact on the environment, and the steps taken to control it. Present your findings to the class.

Lesson 2

Reading Guide

Key Concepts
ESSENTIAL QUESTIONS

- How do populations change?
- Why do human populations change?

Vocabulary

birthrate p. 311
death rate p. 311
extinct species p. 313
endangered species p. 313
threatened species p. 313
migration p. 314

Multilingual eGlossary

BrainPOP®

6.LS.4, SEPS.3

Changing Populations

Go to the resource tab in ConnectED to find the PBL *The Fox and the Hare.*

Inquiry Same Mother?

Have you ever seen newly hatched baby spiders? Baby spiders can have hundreds or even thousands of brothers and sisters. What keeps the spider population from growing out of control?

Dr. Jeremy Burgess/Science Source

Launch Lab

15 minutes

What events can change a population?

Investigate and use data to explain how changes in a given habitat can be beneficial or detrimental to native populations of plants and animals.

1. Read and complete a lab safety form.
2. Record in your Science Journal the number of **counting objects** you have been given. Each object represents an organism, and all the objects together represent a native population of plants or animals.
3. Turn over one of the **event cards** you were given and follow the instructions on the card. Determine the event's impact on your population.
4. Repeat step 3 for four more "seasons," or turns.

Think About This

1. Compare the size of your population with other groups. Do you all have the same number of organisms at the end of five seasons?
2.  **Key Concept** Use data to explain how the different events affected the population.

How Populations Change

Have you ever seen a cluster of spider eggs? Some female spiders lay hundreds or even thousands of eggs in their lifetime. What happens to a population of spiders when a large group of eggs hatches all at once? The population suddenly becomes larger. It doesn't stay that way for long, though. Many spiders die or become food, like the one being eaten in Figure 6, before they grow enough to reproduce. The size of the spider population increases when the eggs hatch but decreases as the spiders die.

A population change can be measured by the population's birthrate and death rate. *A population's* **birthrate** *is the number of offspring produced over a given time period. The* **death rate** *is the number of individuals that die over the same time period.* If the birthrate is higher than the death rate, the population increases. If the death rate is higher than the birthrate, the population decreases.

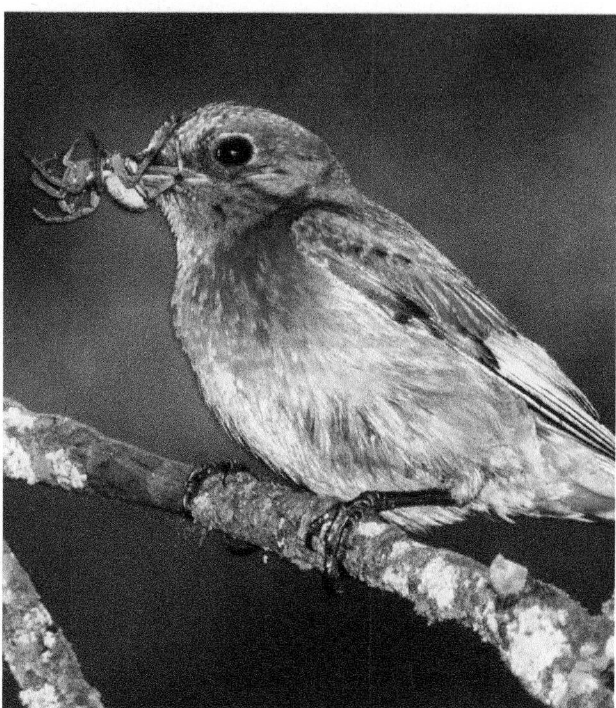

Figure 6 Spiders have a high birthrate, but they usually have a high death rate too. Many spiders die or are eaten before they can reproduce.

(t)Hutchings Photography/Digital Light Source; (b)Jupiterimages/Getty Images

Exponential Growth

When a population is in ideal conditions with unlimited resources, it grows in a pattern called **exponential** growth. During exponential growth, the larger a population gets, the faster it grows. *E. coli* bacteria are microscopic organisms that undergo exponential growth. This population doubles in size every half hour, as shown in **Figure 7**. It takes only 10 hours for the *E. coli* population to grow from one organism to more than 1 million. Exponential growth cannot continue for long. Eventually, limiting factors stop population growth.

SCIENCE USE V. COMMON USE

exponential

Science Use a mathematical expression that contains a constant raised to a power, such as 2^3 or x^2

Common Use in great amounts

Exponential Population Growth

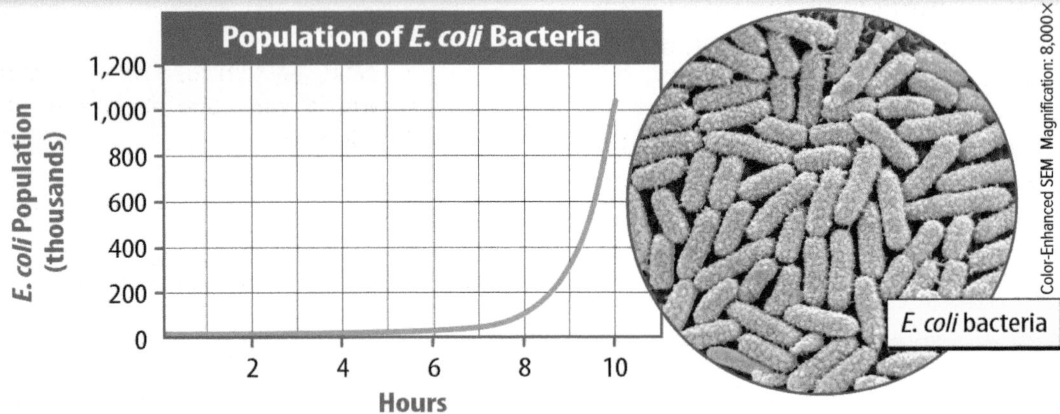

Figure 7 When grown in the laboratory, this population of *E. coli* bacteria is given everything it needs to briefly achieve exponential growth.

Population Size Decrease

Population size can increase, but it also can decrease. For example, a population of field mice might decrease in size in the winter because there is less food. Some mice might not be able to find enough food and will starve. More mice will die than will be born, so the population size decreases. When food is plentiful, the population size usually increases.

Natural disasters such as floods, fires, or volcanic eruptions also affect population size. For example, if a hurricane rips away part of a coral reef, the populations of coral and other organisms that live on the reef also decrease in size.

Disease is another cause of population decrease. In the mid-1900s, Dutch elm disease spread throughout the United States and destroyed many thousands of elm trees. Because of the disease, the size of population of elm trees decreased.

Predation—the hunting of organisms for food—also reduces population size. For example, a farmer might bring cats into a barn to reduce the size of a mouse population.

Reading Check What are four reasons that a population might decrease in size?

WORD ORIGIN

extinct

from Latin *extinctus,* means "extinguish"

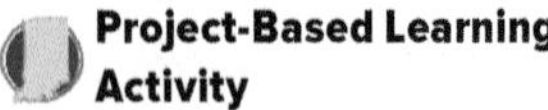

Project-Based Learning Activity

The Fox and the Hare Go online to investigate and use data to explain how changes in a habitat affects populations.

Extinction If populations continue to decrease in numbers, they disappear. *An* **extinct species** *is a species that has died out and no individuals are left.* Extinctions can be caused by predation, natural disasters, or damage to the environment.

Some extinctions in Earth's history were large events that involved many species. Most scientists think the extinction of the dinosaurs about 65 million years ago was caused by a meteorite crashing into Earth. The impact would have sent tons of dust into the atmosphere, blocking sunlight. Without sunlight, plants could not grow. Animals, such as dinosaurs, that ate plants probably starved.

Most extinctions involve fewer species. For example, New Zealand was once home to a large, flightless bird called the giant moa, as shown in Figure 8. Humans first settled these islands about 700 years ago. They hunted the moa for food. As the size of the human population increased, the size of the moa population decreased. Within 200 years, all the giant moas had been killed and the species became extinct.

Endangered Species The mountain gorillas shown in Figure 8 are an example of a species that is endangered. *An* **endangered species** *is a species whose population is at risk of extinction.*

Threatened Species California sea otters almost became extinct in the early 1900s due to overhunting. In 1977, California sea otters were classified as a **threatened species**–*a species at risk, but not yet endangered.* Laws were passed to protect the otters and by 2007 there were about 3,000 sea otters. Worldwide, there are more than 23,000 species that are classified as endangered or threatened.

Reading Check What is the difference between an endangered species and a threatened species?

Figure 8 Organisms are classified as extinct, endangered, or threatened.

Extinct The giant moa, a large bird that was nearly four meters tall, was hunted to extinction.

Endangered Just over 700 mountain gorillas remain in the wild in Africa.

Threatened California sea otters are at risk of becoming endangered because there are so few of them remaining in the wild.

MiniLab

20 minutes

How does migration affect population size?

Your class will model a population of birds that migrates during the fall and the spring.

1. Read and complete a lab safety form.
2. Begin at the summer station. Record in your Science Journal the size of the bird population represented by your class. When your teacher signals, move to the fall station.
3. Pick a piece of **paper** out of the **jar.** If the paper has a minus sign, drop out of the game. If it has a plus sign, bring a classmate into the game.
4. Record the size of the remaining population at the fall station.
5. Migrate to the winter station and repeat steps 3 and 4. Move two more times and repeat for spring and summer.

Analyze and Conclude

1. **Draw Conclusions** What might happen if the birds did not migrate each year?
2. **Key Concept** How did the population change throughout the year?

Migration

Figure 9 During the winter, humpback whales mate and give birth in warm ocean waters near the Bahamas. In the summer, they migrate north to food-rich waters along the coast of New England.

Movement

Populations also change when organisms move from place to place. When an animal population becomes overcrowded, some individuals might move to find more food or living space. For example, zebras might overgraze an area and move to areas that are not so heavily grazed.

Plant populations can also move from place to place. Have you ever blown on a dandelion puff full of seeds? Each tiny dandelion seed has a feathery part that enables it to be carried by the wind. Wind often carries seeds far from their parent plants. Animals also help spread plant seeds. For example, some squirrels and woodpeckers collect acorns. They carry the acorns away and store them for a future food source. The animal forgets some acorns, and they sprout and grow into new trees far from their parent trees.

Migration Sometimes an entire population moves from one place to another and later returns to its original location. **Migration** *is the instinctive seasonal movement of a population of organisms from one place to another.* Ducks, geese, and monarch butterflies are examples of organisms that migrate annually. Some fish, frogs, insects, and mammals–including the whales described in Figure 9–migrate to find food and shelter.

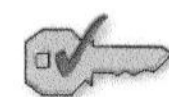 **Key Concept Check** List three ways populations change.

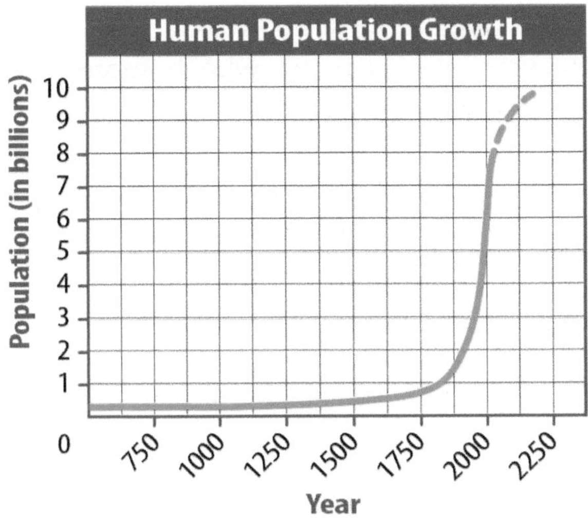

◄ **Figure 10** The human population has grown faster in the past 150 years than at any time in Earth's history.

Visual Check How does this population curve compare with the graph of the *E. coli* population in **Figure 7?**

Human Population Changes

Human population size is affected by the same three factors that determine the sizes of all populations–birthrate, death rate, and movement. But, unlike other species, humans have developed ways to increase the carrying capacity of their environment. Improved crop yields, domesticated farm animals, and timely methods of transporting foods and other resources enable people to survive in all types of environments.

ACADEMIC VOCABULARY

estimate
(verb) to determine roughly the size, nature, or extent of something

Scientists **estimate** that there were about 300 million humans on Earth a thousand years ago. Today there are more than 7 billion humans on Earth, as shown in **Figure 10.** By 2050 there could be over 9 billion. No one knows when the human population will reach Earth's carrying capacity. However, some scientists estimate Earth's carrying capacity is about 11 billion.

As the human population grows, people need to build more houses and roads and clear more land for crops. This means less living space, food, and other resources for other species. In addition, people use more energy to heat and cool homes; to fuel cars, airplanes, and other forms of transportation; and to produce electricity. This energy use contributes to pollution that affects other populations.

One example of the consequences of human population growth is the destruction of tropical forests. Each year, humans clear thousands of acres of tropical forest to make room for crops and livestock, as shown in **Figure 11.** Clearing tropical forests is harmful because these forests contain a large variety of species that are not in other ecosystems.

Reading Check Explain how human population growth affects other species.

Figure 11 Tropical forests are cleared for crops and livestock. The habitats of many organisms are destroyed, resulting in many species becoming endangered or extinct. ▼

Math Skills 

Use Graphs

Graphs are used to make large amounts of information easy to interpret. Line graphs show how data changes over a period of time. A circle graph, or pie graph, shows how portions of a set of data compare with the whole set. The circle represents 100 percent and each segment represents one part making up the whole. For example, Figure 14 shows all the moves made by people in the United States during 2013-2014. Approximately 73 percent of all moves were within the same county.

Practice

Based on Figure 14,

1. What percentage of the moves were from one state to another?
2. What percentage of the moves were within the same state?

 Math Practice

 Personal Tutor

Population Size Increase

Do you know anyone who is more than 100 years old? In 2010, more than 53,000 people living in the United States were at least 100 years old. People are living longer today than in previous generations, and more children reach adulthood. Recall that when the birthrate of a population is higher than its death rate, the population grows. There are several factors that keep the human birthrate higher than its death rate. Some of these factors are discussed below.

Food For some, finding food might be as easy as making a trip to the grocery store, but not everyone can get food as easily. Advances in agriculture have made it possible to produce food for billions of people.

Resources Fossil fuels, cloth, metals, foods, and many other materials are easily transported around the world by planes, trains, trucks, or boats. Today, people have access to more resources because of better transportation methods.

Sanitation As recently as 100 years ago, diseases such as typhoid, cholera, and diphtheria were major causes of death. These diseases spread through unclean water supplies and untreated sewage. Modern water treatment technologies have reduced the occurrence of many diseases. Less expensive and more effective cleaning products are now available to help prevent the spread of disease-causing organisms. As a result, deaths from these illnesses are less common in many countries.

Medical Care Modern medical care is keeping people alive and healthy longer than ever before. As shown in Figure 12, scientists have developed vaccines, antibiotics, and other medicines that prevent and treat disease. As a result, fewer people get sick, and human death rates have decreased. Medical technologies and new medicines help people survive heart attacks, cancer, and other major illnesses.

Figure 12 Before vaccinations, many children died in infancy. The use of vaccines has significantly reduced death rates.

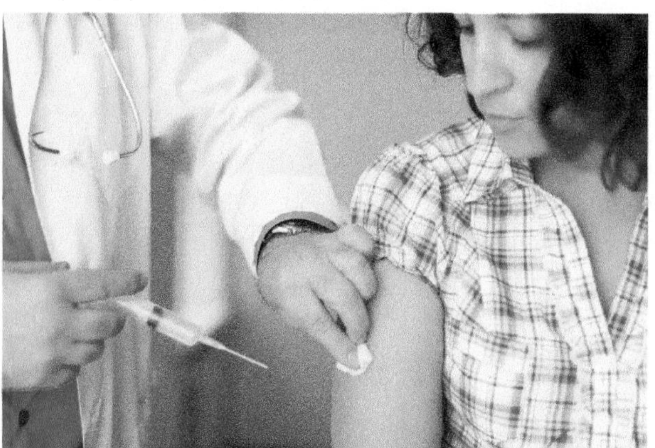

Decreases in Human Population Size

Human populations in some parts of the world are decreasing in size. Diseases such as AIDS and malaria cause high death rates in some countries. Severe drought has resulted in major crop failures and lack of food. Floods, earthquakes, and other natural disasters can cause the deaths of hundreds or even thousands of people at a time. Damage from disasters, such as the damage shown in **Figure 13**, can keep people from living in the area for a long time. All of these factors cause decreases in human population sizes in some areas.

▲ **Figure 13** Natural disasters such as a tsunami can cause severe damage to people's homes, as well as drastically reduce the population size.

 **Reading Check** What are three events that can decrease human population size?

Population Movement

Have you ever moved to a different city, state, or country? The size of a human population changes as people move from place to place. The graph in **Figure 14** shows the percentages of each kind of move people make. Like other organisms, populations of humans might move when more resources become available in a different place.

Did your parents, grandparents, or great grandparents come to the United States from another country? Immigration takes place when organisms move into an area. Most of the U.S. population is descended from people who immigrated from Europe, Africa, Asia, and Central and South America.

 **Key Concept Check** What makes human populations increase or decrease in size?

FOLDABLES®

Make a horizontal two-tab book and label it as shown. Use it to summarize why human populations change in size.

Human Population Increase | Human Population Decrease

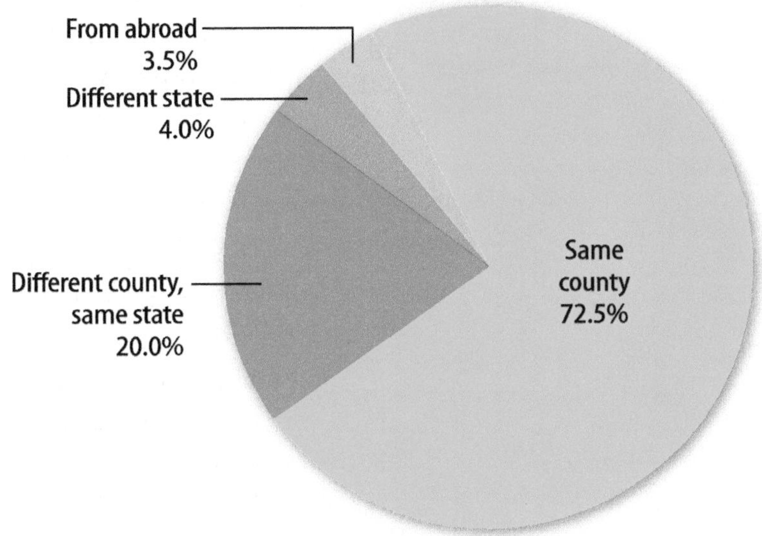

◄ **Figure 14** Populations can move between counties and states or even from another country.

Visual Check Which type of move did the largest percentage of the population make?

Lesson 2 Review

Visual Summary

The birthrate and the death rate of any population affects its population size.

The giant moa is classified as an extinct species because there are no surviving members.

A population that is at risk but not yet endangered is a threatened species.

FOLDABLES®

Use your lesson Foldable to review the lesson. Save your Foldable for the project at the end of the chapter.

What do you think 

You first read the statements below at the beginning of the chapter.

3. Some populations decrease in numbers because of low birthrates.

4. An extinct species has only a few surviving individuals.

Did you change your mind about whether you agree or disagree with the statements? Rewrite any false statements to make them true.

Use Vocabulary

1. **Define** *endangered species* in your own words.
2. **Distinguish** between birthrate and death rate.
3. The instinctive movement of a population from one place to another is ________.

Understand Key Concepts 

4. Rabbits move into a new field where there is plenty of room to dig new burrows. This is an example of
   A. overpopulation.
   B. immigration.
   C. carrying capacity.
   D. competition.

Interpret Graphics

5. **Summarize** Copy and fill in the graphic organizer below to identify the three major factors that affect population size.

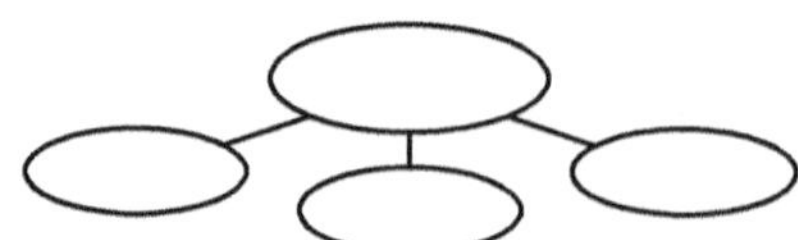

Critical Thinking

6. **Predict** what could happen to the size of the human population if a cure for all cancers were discovered.
7. **Recommend** an action humans could take to help prevent the extinction of tropical organisms.

Math Skills

Use the graph in the Skill Practice on the next page to answer these questions.

8. What does each unit on the y-axis represent?
9. What does the lowest point on the blue line represent?

(t)Jupiterimages/Getty Images; (c)Mary Evans Picture Library/Alamy; (b)Tory Kallman/Getty Images

How do populations change in size?

Birthrate and death rate change the size of a population. In the 1700s the death rate of sea otters in central California was extremely high because many people hunted them. By the 1930s only about 50 sea otters remained. Today, the Marine Mammal Protection Act protects sea otters from being hunted. Every spring, scientists survey the central California Coast to determine the numbers of adult and young sea otters (called pups) in the population. The numbers on the graph indicate population sizes at the end of a breeding season.

Learn It

Most scientists collect some type of data when testing a hypothesis. Once data are collected, scientists look for patterns or trends in the data and draw conclusions. This process is called **interpreting data.**

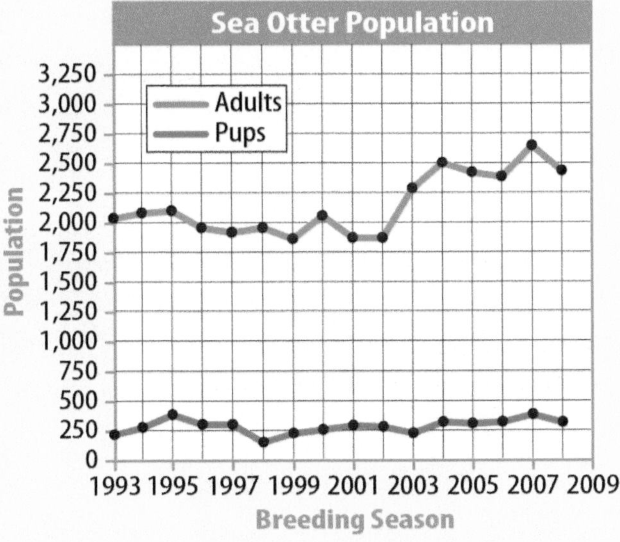

Try It

1. The above graph shows changes in adult and pup sea otter populations over many years. Assume that the number of pups seen during the survey represents all the pups that were born and survived in one year—the birthrate. For example, in the 1997 breeding season, the birthrate was 300.

2. In your Science Journal, make a table showing the population size and the birthrate for the 2001 breeding season. Repeat for 2002, 2003, and 2004.

3. In each breeding season, the population increases by the number of pups born and decreases by the number of sea otters that die. Use the following equation to find the death rate for 2002.

   Death rate in 2002 = population size in 2001 + birthrate in 2002 – population size in 2002

Apply It

4. Calculate the death rate in 2004 and compare it to the death rate in 2002.

5. What environmental factors might account for the difference in the death rate between 2002 and 2004?

6. How do you think the population size changed in 2009 and 2010?

7. **Key Concept** Determine how the birthrate compared to the death rate in 2002 and 2004. Explain how these rates affected the population sizes in 2002 and 2004.

Lesson 3

Communities

Reading Guide

Key Concepts

ESSENTIAL QUESTIONS

- What defines a community?
- How do the populations in a community interact?

Vocabulary

habitat p. 321
niche p. 321
producer p. 322
consumer p. 322
symbiosis p. 325
mutualism p. 325
commensalism p. 326
parasitism p. 326

Multilingual eGlossary

6.LS.2, 6.LS.3, SEPS.2, SEPS.6, SEPS.8

PBL Go to the resource tab in ConnectED to find the PBL *The Hungry Games: Eat or Be Eaten.*

Inquiry Time for Lunch?

This Hoopoe (HOO poo) has captured its next meal. Some of the energy needed by this bird for its life processes will come from the energy stored in the body of the beetle. Where did the beetle get its energy?

Jnrocek/iStock/360/Getty Images

Launch Lab

15 minutes

What are the roles in your school community?

Within a community, different organisms have different roles. Trees produce their own food from the environment. Then, they become food for other organisms. Mushrooms break down dead organisms and make the nutrients useful to other living things. Think about the members of your school community such as the students, teachers, and custodians. What roles do they have?

1. Draw a table with two columns in your Science Journal. Label one column *Community Member* and the other column *Role in the Community.*
2. Fill in the table with examples from your school.

Community Member	Role in the Community
Principal	Manages school staff including students and teachers

Think About This

1. Are there any community members who have more than one role?
2. What is your role in the school community?
3. **Key Concept** Explain how it is beneficial for members of a community to have different roles.

Communities, Habitats, and Niches

High in a rain forest tree, a two-toed sloth munches leaves. Ants crawl on a branch, carrying away a dead beetle. Two birds build a nest. A flowering vine twists around the tree trunk. These organisms are part of a rain forest community. You read in Lesson 1 that a community is made up of all the species that live in the same ecosystem at the same time.

The place within an ecosystem where an organism lives is its **habitat.** A habitat, like the one in Figure 15, provides all the resources an organism needs, including food and shelter. A habitat also has the right temperature, water, and other conditions the organism needs to survive.

The rain forest tree described above is a habitat for sloths, insects, birds, vines, and many other species. Each species uses the habitat in a different way. *A* **niche** (NICH) *is what a species does in its habitat to survive.* For example, butterflies feed on flower nectar. Sloths eat leaves. Ants eat insects or plants. These species have different niches in the same environment. Each organism shown in Figure 15 has its own niche on the tree. The plants anchor themselves to the tree and can capture more sunlight. Termites use the tree for food.

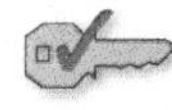

Key Concept Check What is a community?

WORD ORIGIN

habitat
from Latin *habitus,* means "to live, dwell"

Figure 15 This tree trunk is a habitat for ferns.

Jacques Jangoux/Science Source

MiniLab 20 minutes

How can you model a food web?

Populations interact through feeding relationships. A food web shows overlapping feeding relationships in a community.

1. Read and complete a lab safety form.
2. On a sheet of **paper,** make a list of at least 10 different organisms within a community of your choice. Include a variety of producers and consumers.
3. Use **scissors** to cut out the name of each organism on your list.
4. **Glue** the names onto a piece of **construction paper.**

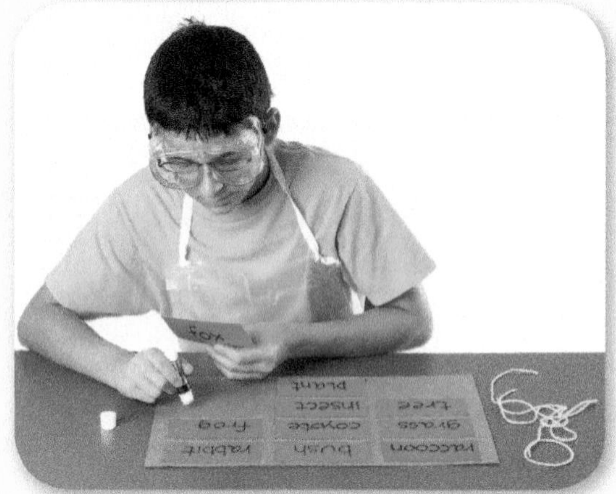

5. Use **yarn** and glue to connect organisms that have feeding relationships. For example, a piece of yarn would connect a rabbit and grass.

Analyze and Conclude

1. **Use Models** Add the label *Sun* to your model. Which organisms would be connected to the Sun?
2. **Infer** Imagine that you removed three organisms from your food web. How would this affect the community?
3. **Key Concept** Which organisms in your model interact through feeding relationships?

Energy in Communities

Sloths are the slowest mammals on Earth. They hardly make a sound, and they sleep 15 to 20 hours a day. Squirrel monkeys, however, chatter as they swing through treetops hunting for fruit, insects, and eggs. Sloths might appear to use no energy at all. However, sloths, squirrel monkeys, and all other organisms need energy to live. All living things use energy and carry out life processes such as growth and reproduction.

Energy Roles

How an organism obtains energy is an important part of its niche. Almost all the energy available to life on Earth originally came from the Sun. However, some organisms, such as those that live near deep-sea vents, are exceptions. They obtain energy from chemicals such as hydrogen sulfide.

Producers *are organisms that get energy from the environment, such as sunlight, and make their own food.* For example, most plants are producers that get their energy from sunlight. They use the process of photosynthesis and make sugar molecules that they use for food. Producers near deep-sea vents use hydrogen sulfide and carbon dioxide and make sugar molecules.

Consumers *are organisms that get energy by eating other organisms.* Consumers are also classified by the type of organisms they eat. Herbivores get their energy by eating plants. Cows and sheep are herbivores. Carnivores get their energy by eating other consumers. Harpy eagles, lions, and wolves are carnivores. Omnivores, such as most humans, get their energy by eating producers and consumers. Detritivores (dee TRI tuh vorz) get their energy by eating dead organisms or parts of dead organisms. Some bacteria and some fungi are detritivores.

Reading Check Identify a producer, an herbivore, a carnivore, and an omnivore.

Hutchings Photography/Digital Light Source

Energy Flow

A food chain is a way of showing how energy moves through a community. In a rain forest community, energy flows from the Sun to a rain forest tree, a producer. The tree uses the energy and grows, producing leaves and other plant structures. Energy moves to consumers, such as the sloth that eats the leaves of the tree, and then to the eagle that eats the sloth. When the eagle dies, detritivores, such as bacteria, feed on its body. That food chain can be written like this:

Sun ⟶ leaves ⟶ sloth ⟶ eagle ⟶ bacteria

A food chain shows only part of the energy flow in a community. A food web, like the one in Figure 16, shows many food chains within a community and how they overlap.

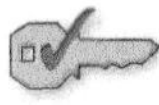

Key Concept Check Identify a food chain in a community near your home. List the producers and consumers in your food chain.

Figure 16 Organisms in a rain forest community get their energy in different ways.

Visual Check List the members of two different food chains shown in the figure.

Personal Tutor

Food Web

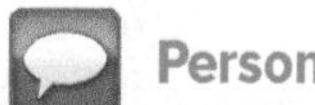

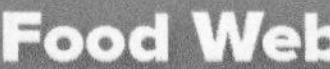

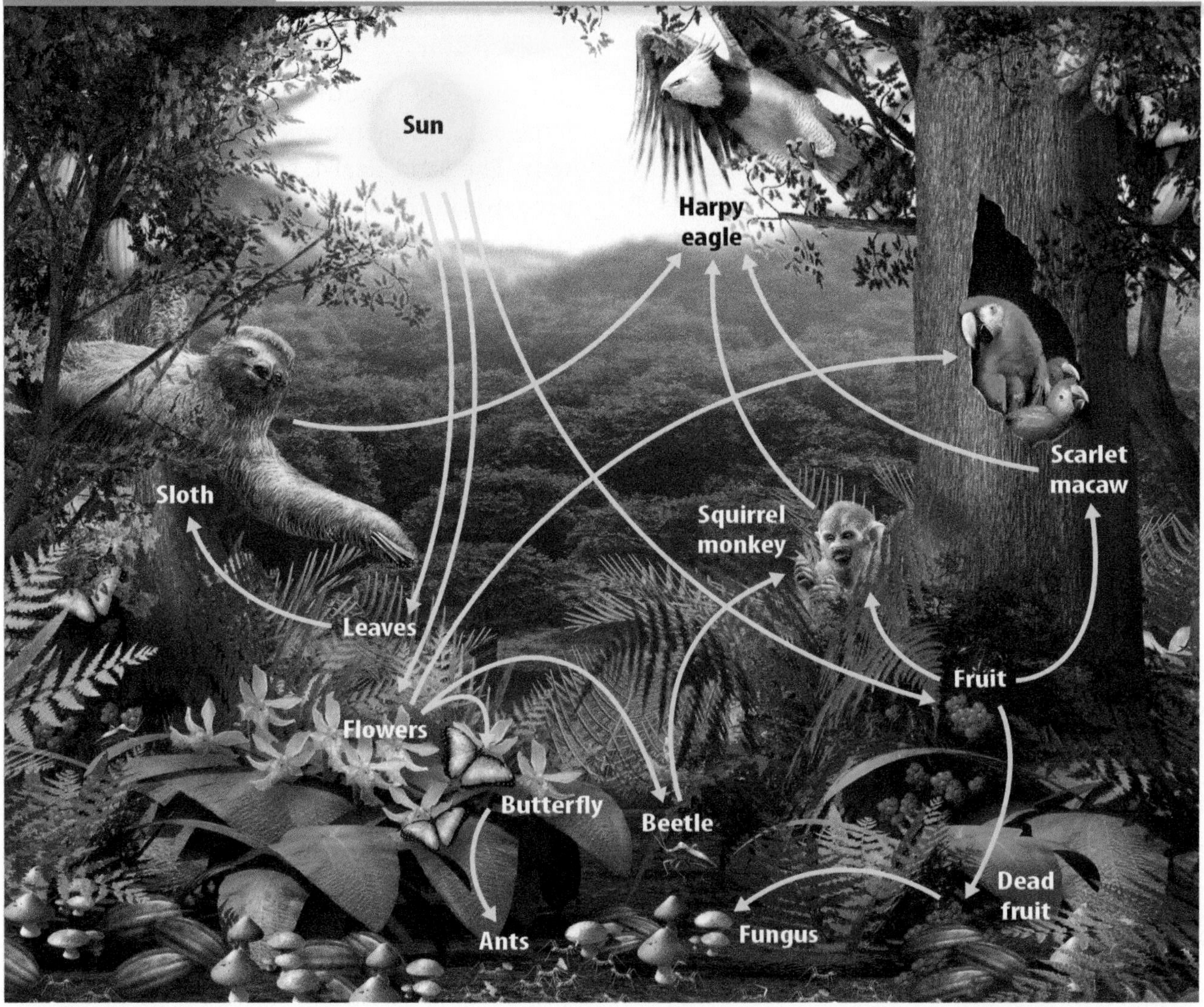

Relationships in Communities

The populations that make up a community interact with each other in a variety of ways. Some species have feeding relationships–they either eat or are eaten by another species. Some species interact with another species to get the food or shelter they need.

Predator-Prey Relationships

Hungry squirrel monkeys quarrel over a piece of fruit. They don't notice the harpy eagle above them. Suddenly, the eagle swoops down and grabs one of the monkeys in its talons. Harpy eagles and monkeys have a predator-prey relationship. The eagle, like other **predators,** hunts other animals for food. The hunted animals, such as the squirrel monkey or the lizard shown at the beginning of this lesson, are called prey.

As you read in Lesson 1, predators help prevent prey populations from growing too large for the carrying capacity of the ecosystem. The sand lizard, shown in Figure 17, is a predator in most of Europe. Like all predators, they often capture weak or injured individuals of a prey population. When the weak members of a population are removed, there are more resources available for the remaining members. This helps keep the prey population healthy.

Reading Check Why are predators important to a prey population?

FOLDABLES®

Make a vertical three-tab book and label it as shown. Use it to organize information about the types of relationships that can exist among organisms within a community.

REVIEW VOCABULARY

predator
an organism that survives by hunting another

Applying Practices

What can analyzing data reveal about predator-prey populations? Go online to analyze data to describe predator-prey relationships.

Project-Based Learning Activity

The Hungry Games: Eat or be Eaten Use data to help predict and describe interactions between predators and prey.

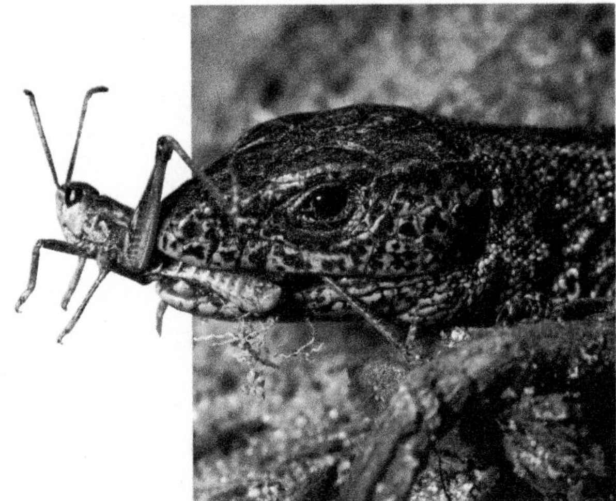

Figure 17 Sand lizards eat slugs, spiders, insects, fruits, and flowers.

Visual Check Which type of consumers are sand lizards?

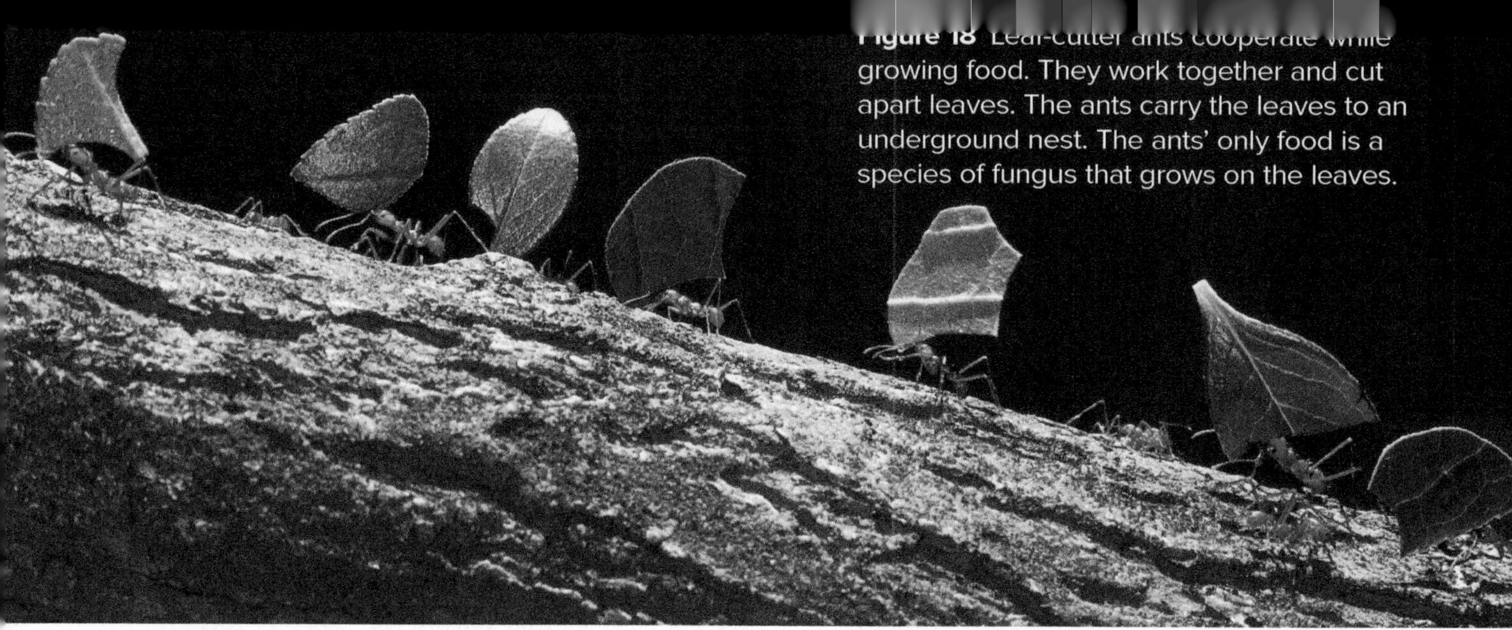

Figure 18 Leaf-cutter ants cooperate while growing food. They work together and cut apart leaves. The ants carry the leaves to an underground nest. The ants' only food is a species of fungus that grows on the leaves.

Cooperative Relationships

The members of some populations work together in cooperative relationships for their survival, like the leaf-cutter ants shown in Figure 18. As you read in Lesson 1, meerkats cooperate with each other and raise young and watch for predators. Squirrel monkeys benefit in a similar way by living in groups. They cooperate as they hunt for food and watch for danger.

Symbiotic Relationships

Some species have such close relationships that they are almost always found living together. *A close, long-term relationship between two species that usually involves an exchange of food or energy is called* **symbiosis** (sihm bee OH sus). There are three types of symbiosis–mutualism, commensalism, and parasitism.

Mutualism Boxer crabs and sea anemones share a mutualistic partnership, as shown in Figure 19. *A symbiotic relationship in which both partners benefit is called* **mutualism.** Boxer crabs and sea anemones live in tropical coral reef communities. The crabs carry sea anemones in their claws. The sea anemones have stinging cells that help the crabs fight off predators. The sea anemones eat leftovers from the crabs' meals.

◀ Figure 19 Boxer crabs and sea anemones have a mutualistic relationship because both partners benefit from the relationship.

Applying Practices

How can you model a symbiotic relationship? Go online to model and describe symbiotic relationships between organisms.

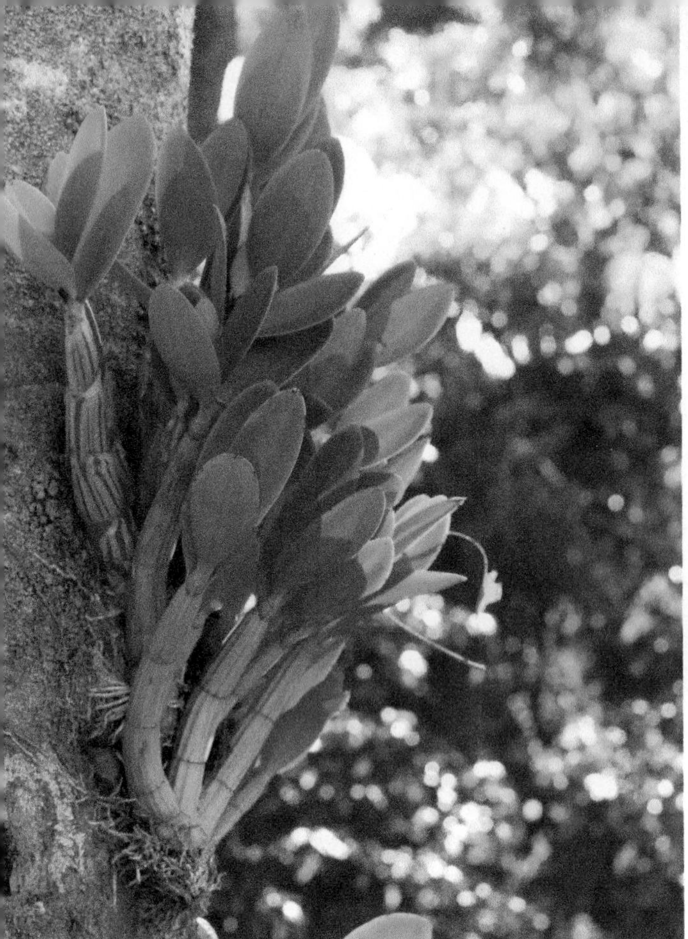

▲ Figure 20 Epiphytes and trees share a commensal relationship.

Figure 21 Hunting wasps are examples of parasites. The larvae use the paralyzed spider as food while they mature. ▼

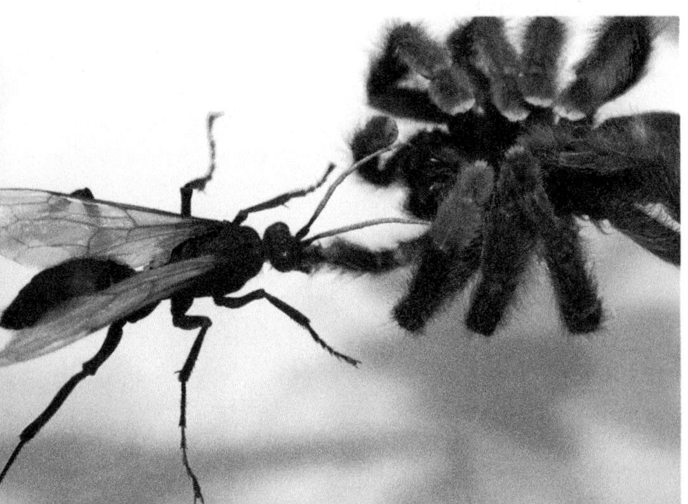

Commensalism *A symbiotic relationship that benefits one species but does not harm or benefit the other is* **commensalism.** Plants called epiphytes (EH puh fites), shown in Figure 20, grow on the trunks of trees and other objects. The roots of an epiphyte anchor it to the object. The plant's nutrients are absorbed from the air. Epiphytes benefit from attaching to tree trunks by getting more living space and sunlight. The trees are neither helped nor harmed by the plants. Orchids are another example of epiphytes that have commensal relationships with trees.

Parasitism *A symbiotic relationship that benefits one species and harms the other is* **parasitism.** The species that benefits is the parasite. The species that is harmed is the host. Heartworms, tapeworms, fleas, and lice are parasites that feed on a host organism, such as a human or a dog. The parasites benefit by getting food. The host usually is not killed, but it can be weakened. For example, heartworms in a dog can cause the heart to work harder. Eventually, the heart can fail, killing the host. Other common parasites include the fungi that cause ringworm and toenail fungus. The fungi that cause these ailments feed on keratin (KER ah tihn), a protein in skin and nails.

The larvae of the hunting wasp is another example of a parasite. The female wasp, shown in Figure 21, stings a spider to paralyze it. Then she lays eggs in its body. When the eggs hatch into larvae, they eat the paralyzed spider's body. Another example of parasitism is the strangler fig. The seeds of the strangler fig sprout on the branches of a host tree. The young strangler fig sends roots into the tree and down into the ground below. The host tree provides the fig with nutrients and a trunk for support. Strangler figs grow fast and they can kill a host tree.

 **Key Concept Check** List five ways species in a community interact.

Lesson 3 Review

Visual Summary

Each organism in a community has its own habitat and niche within the ecosystem.

Within a community, each organism must obtain energy for life processes. Some organisms are producers and some are consumers.

Some organisms have cooperative relationships and some have symbiotic relationships. The hunting wasp and spider have a symbiotic relationship.

FOLDABLES®

Use your lesson Foldable to review the lesson. Save your Foldable for the project at the end of the chapter.

What do you think NOW?

You first read the statements below at the beginning of the chapter.

5. No more than two species can live in the same habitat.

6. A cow is a producer because it produces food for other organisms.

Did you change your mind about whether you agree or disagree with the statements? Rewrite any false statements to make them true.

Use Vocabulary

1. **Define** *symbiosis.*
2. **Distinguish** between producers and consumers.

Understand Key Concepts 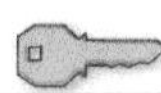

3. **Explain** how energy from the Sun flows through a rain forest community.
4. **Compare and contrast** predator-prey relationships and cooperative relationships.
5. A shrimp removes and eats the parasites from the gills of a fish. The fish stays healthier because the parasites are removed. This relationship is

   A. commensalism.
   B. competition.
   C. mutualism.
   D. parasitism.

Interpret Graphics

6. **Organize Information** Copy and fill in the table below with details about the three different types of symbiosis.

7. **Identify** the type of diagram shown below and explain what it means.

Critical Thinking

8. **Predict** what could happen to a population of ants if anteaters, a predator of the ants, disappeared.
9. **Decide** which type of symbiosis this is: Bacteria live in the skin under the eyes of deep-sea fish. The bacteria give off light that helps the fish find food. The bacteria get food from the fish.

Lab

40 minutes

Materials

symbiosis cards

How can you model a symbiotic relationship?

As you read earlier, organisms in communities can have many different types of relationships. Symbiotic relationships occur when two organisms live in direct contact and form a relationship. Symbiotic relationships include mutualism, commensalism, and parasitism. Although communities around the world have symbiotic relationships, coral reef communities often include all three types of symbiosis. Many of the organisms in these communities, such as clownfish, sea anemones, and even microscopic copepods, have some type of symbiotic relationship. In this lab, you will research and model one type of symbiosis in a coral reef community.

Question

How do you model a symbiotic relationship and determine its type?

Procedure

1. Read and complete a lab safety form.
2. Get a card from your teacher with the name of an organism that has a symbiotic relationship. Find your partner(s) in the symbiotic relationship.
3. With your partner, brainstorm what type of symbiotic relationship your organism and your partner's organism might have. List and explain your choice(s) in your Science Journal.

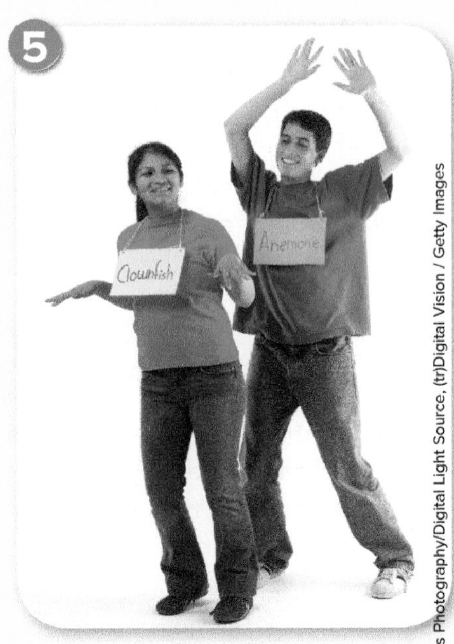

(l,br)Hutchings Photography/Digital Light Source, (tr)Digital Vision / Getty Images

4. Using your library and reference books, research your organism with your partner.
5. Develop a visual presentation, such as a skit, a slide presentation, or a series of posters with your partner showing how your symbiotic relationship works and how your organisms interact with other members of the community.
6. Show your presentation to the class.

Analyze and Conclude

7. **Identify** What type of symbiotic relationship did your organism have? What was your organism's role in the relationship?
8. **Compare** How would your organism interact in the community if its partner were not present?
9. **Contrast** What other organisms in a coral reef community have the same type of symbiotic relationship as your organism? If none, explain why.
10. **The Big Idea** How did your organism interact with other members of its population and community?

Communicate Your Results

Make a poster illustrating all the symbiotic relationships you and your classmates studied. Construct and share an explanation that predicts why these patterns of interactions develop between organisms in an ecosystem.

Inquiry Extension

All of the organisms your class studied are part of the coral reef ecosystem. Create a food web showing how the organisms obtained energy.

Lab Tips

- ☑ Think about your organism's niche in the ecosystem.
- ☑ Carefully select resources for accuracy.

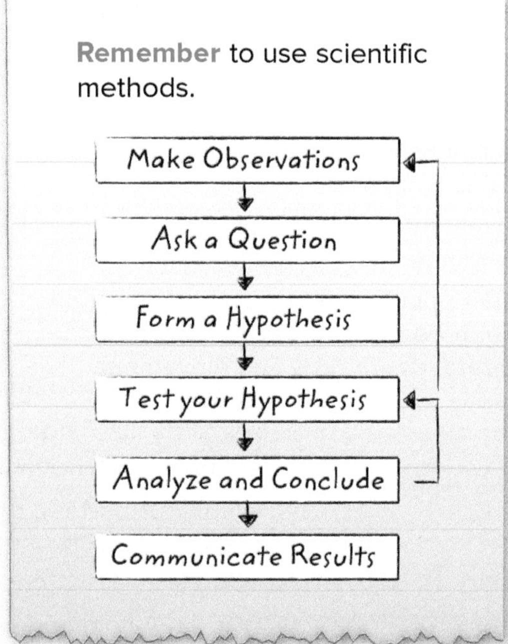

Chapter 9 Study Guide

A community contains many populations that interact in their energy roles and in their competition for resources. Populations can increase, decrease, and move, affecting the community.

Key Concepts Summary 

Lesson 1: Populations

- A **population** is all the organisms of the same species that live in the same area at the same time.
- Population sizes vary due to **limiting factors** such as environmental factors and available resources.
- Population size usually does not exceed the **carrying capacity** of the ecosystem.

Vocabulary

biosphere p. 303
community p. 304
population p. 304
competition p. 305
limiting factor p. 305
population density p. 306
biotic potential p. 306
carrying capacity p. 307

Lesson 2: Changing Populations

- Populations of living things can increase, decrease, or move.
- Populations can decrease until they are threatened, endangered, or extinct.
- Human population size is affected by the same three factors as other populations—**birthrate, death rate,** and movement.

Vocabulary

birthrate p. 311
death rate p. 311
extinct species p. 313
endangered species p. 313
threatened species p. 313
migration p. 314

Lesson 3: Communities

- A community is all the populations of different species that live together in the same area at the same time.
- The place within an ecosystem where an organism lives is its **habitat** and what an organism does in its habitat to survive is its **niche.**
- Three types of relationships within a community are predator-prey, cooperative, and symbiotic.

Vocabulary

habitat p. 321
niche p. 321
producer p. 322
consumer p. 322
symbiosis p. 325
mutualism p. 325
commensalism p. 326
parasitism p. 326

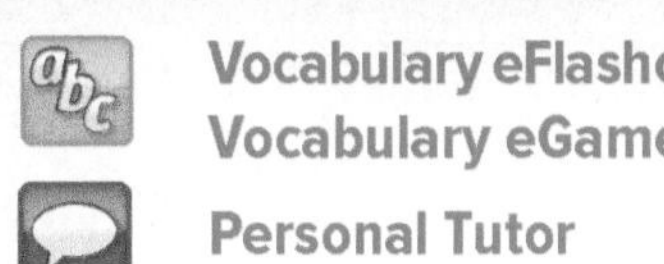

FOLDABLES®

Assemble your lesson Foldables as shown to make a Chapter Project. Use the project to review what you have learned in this chapter.

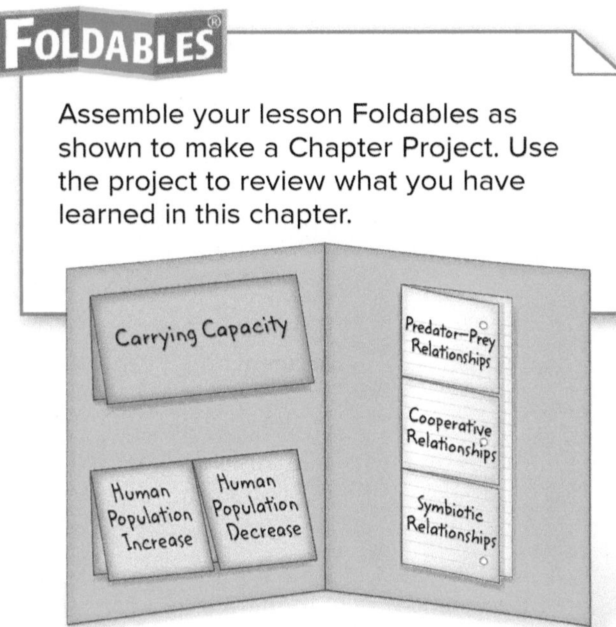

Use Vocabulary

1. The struggle in a community for the same resources is ________.
2. The part of Earth that supports life is the ________.
3. The instinctive movement of a population is ________.
4. A(n) ________ species is one at risk of becoming endangered.
5. A(n) ________ is an organism that gets energy from the environment.
6. The largest number of offspring that can be produced when there are no limiting factors is the ________.

Link Vocabulary and Key Concepts

Copy this concept map, and then use vocabulary terms from the previous page to complete the concept map.

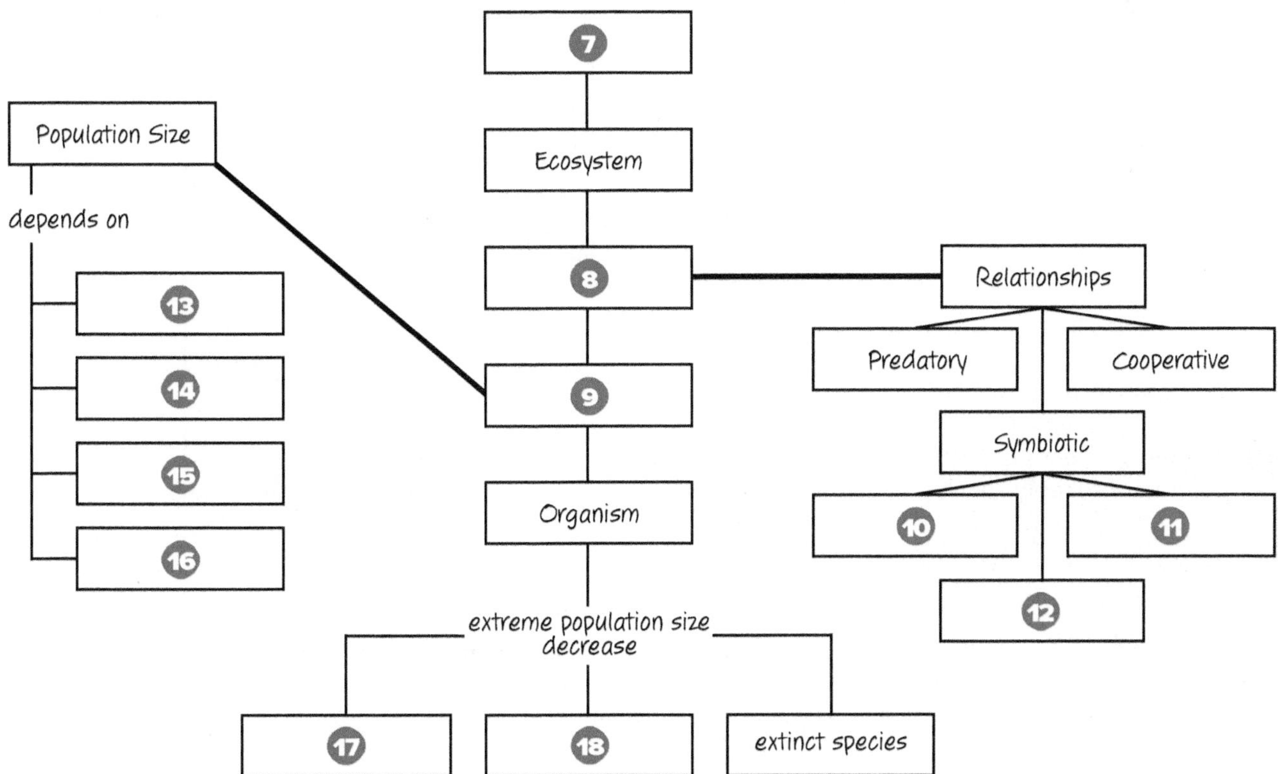

Chapter 9 Review

Understand Key Concepts 

1. What does the line indicated by the red arrow in the graph below represent?

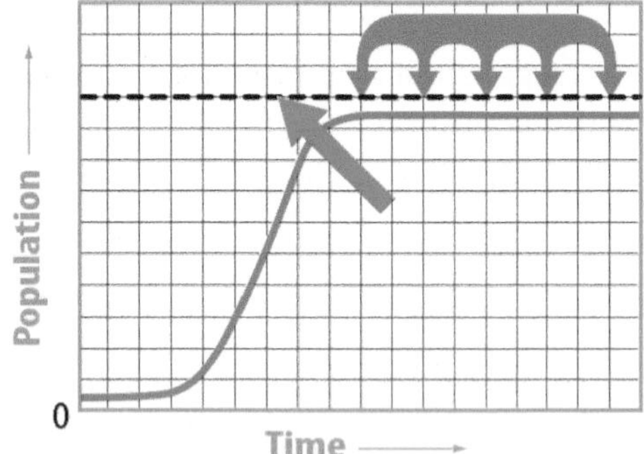

A. competition
B. biotic potential
C. carrying capacity
D. limiting factors

2. The need for organisms to rely on the same resources causes

A. competition.
B. biotic potential.
C. carrying capacity.
D. population growth.

3. The number of organisms in a specific area is

A. a community.
B. the carrying capacity.
C. the population density.
D. the population growth.

4. The number of robins that hatch in a year is the population's

A. biotic potential.
B. birthrate.
C. carrying capacity.
D. exponential growth.

5. A robin population that reaches its biotic potential probably shows

A. exponential growth.
B. low growth.
C. negative growth.
D. no growth.

6. An organism that uses sunlight to make food molecules is a(n)

A. carnivore.
B. consumer.
C. herbivore.
D. producer.

7. Which is NOT part of Earth's biosphere?

A. low atmosphere
B. surface of the Moon
C. bottom of the Pacific ocean
D. North American continent

8. Which is a limiting factor for a cottontail rabbit population on the prairie in Oklahoma?

A. a large amount of food
B. a large amount of shelter space
C. an abundance of coyotes in the area
D. an unpolluted river in the ecosystem

9. Which factor does NOT normally affect human population size?

A. birthrate
B. death rate
C. population movement
D. lack of resources

10. What type of overall population change is shown below?

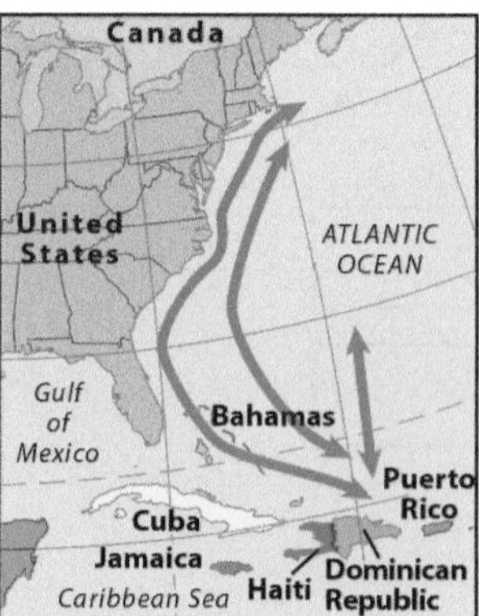

A. immigration
B. migration
C. population decrease
D. population increase

Critical Thinking

11 **Select and draw** three food chains from the food web shown.

12 **Give an Example** What problems might result from overpopulation of pigeons in a city park?

13 **Describe** What are some possible solutions that a city might use to solve a pigeon overpopulation problem?

14 **Decide** Would sample counting or capture-mark-and-release at a specified time and place be the best method for measuring each of these populations: birds, whales, bluebonnet flowers, and oak trees?

15 **Compare and contrast** the feeding habits of carnivores, omnivores, and producers.

16 **Classify** Decide whether each of these relationships is mutualism, commensalism, or parasitism.

- Butterfly pollinates flower while drinking nectar.
- Tapeworm feeds on contents of dog's intestines.
- Fish finds shelter in coral reef.

17 **Draw** a food web that describes energy flow in this community. Insects eat leaves. Spiders eat insects. Birds eat insects and spiders. Frogs eat insects. Birds eat frogs.

Writing in Science

18 **Write** a two-page story that explains how an imaginary population becomes threatened with extinction.

REVIEW THE BIG IDEA

19 Describe the following relationships between organisms: predator/prey, consumer/producer, parasite/host, and symbiosis.

20 Do you think this large number of pigeons affects other organisms in the community? Explain your answer.

Math Skills

Math Practice

Use Graphs

Use the graph to answer the questions.

21 During what range of years did the population change the least?

22 The dotted line represents a prediction. What does it predict about population growth beyond the present time?

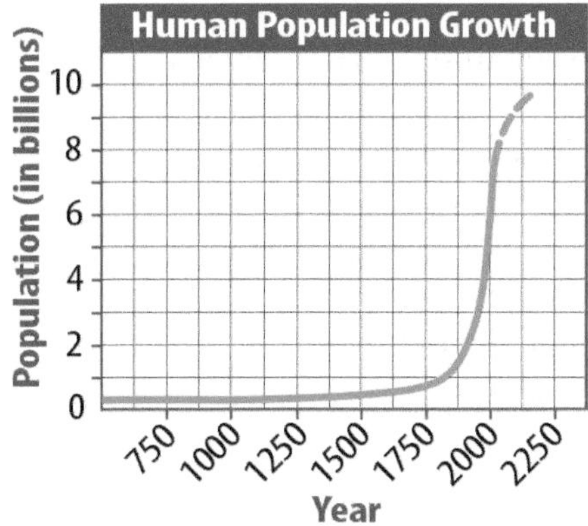

Standardized Test Practice

Record your answers on the answer sheet provided by your teacher or on a sheet of paper.

Multiple Choice

1 Which is defined as the demand for resources in short supply in a community?

A biotic potential

B competition

C density

D limiting factor

Use the diagram below to answer questions 2 and 3.

2 In the diagram above, which number represents an ecosystem?

A 1

B 2

C 3

D 4

3 According to the arrows, how are the elements of the diagram organized?

A endangered to overpopulated

B farthest to nearest

C largest to smallest

D nonliving to living

4 Which is NOT a possible result of overpopulation?

A damage to soil

B increased carrying capacity

C loss of trees and plants

D more competition

Use the diagram below to answer question 5.

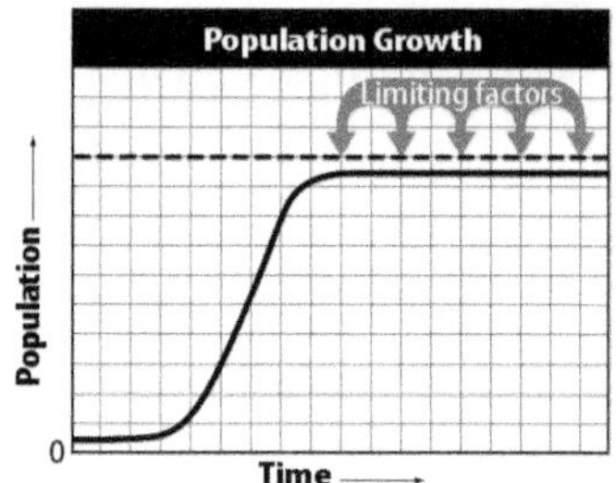

5 What does the dashed line in the diagram represent?

A biotic potential

B carrying capacity

C overpopulation

D population density

6 What does a population undergo when it has no limiting factors?

A exponential growth

B extinction

C migration

D population movement

7 What is the term for all species living in the same ecosystem at the same time?

A biosphere

B community

C habitat

D population

Online Standardized Test Practice

Use the diagram below to answer question 8.

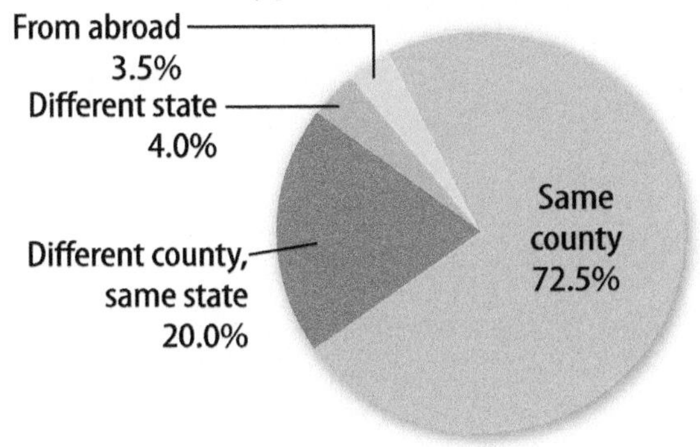

Source: U.S. Census Bureau, Migration/Geographic Mobility

8 According to the diagram, about how many of those who moved remained within the same state?

A 20 percent
B 24 percent
C 73 percent
D 93 percent

9 Which type of relationship includes mutualism and parasitism?

A competition
B cooperation
C predation
D symbiosis

10 Which is a population?

A all meerkats in a refuge
B all the types of birds in a forest
C all the types of cats in a zoo
D all the types of insects in a swamp

Constructed Response

Use the table below to answer questions 11 and 12.

Growth	Decline

11 In the table, list four factors that contribute to human population growth and four factors that lead to population decline.

12 Select one factor from each column in the table above. Which has the greatest effect on human population today? Explain your reasoning.

13 Describe a negative consequence of human population growth. How can humans minimize the effect of this change?

Use the diagram below to answer question 14.

sunlight → grasses → antelope → lion → bacteria

14 Explain how each organism in the food chain above gets energy. How might the other organisms be affected if the antelope population declines due to disease?

NEED EXTRA HELP?														
If You Missed Question...	1	2	3	4	5	6	7	8	9	10	11	12	13	14
Go to Lesson...	1	1	1	1	1	2	1	2	3	1	2	2	2	3

Chapter 10

Biomes and Ecosystems

THE BIG IDEA How do Earth's biomes and ecosystems differ?

Inquiry Modern Art?

Although it might look like a piece of art, this structure was designed to replicate several ecosystems. When Biosphere 2 was built in the 1980s near Tucson, Arizona, it included a rain forest, a desert, a grassland, a coral reef, and a wetland. Today, it is used mostly for research and education.

- How realistic do you think Biosphere 2 is?
- Is it possible to make artificial environments as complex as those in nature?
- How do Earth's biomes and ecosystems differ?

Joel McDonald/Shutterstock

Get Ready to Read

What do you think?

Before you read, decide if you agree or disagree with each of these statements. As you read this chapter, see if you change your mind about any of the statements.

1. Deserts can be cold.
2. There are no rain forests outside the tropics.
3. Estuaries do not protect coastal areas from erosion.
4. Animals form coral reefs.
5. An ecosystem never changes.
6. Nothing grows in the area where a volcano has erupted.

Lesson 1

Land Biomes

Reading Guide

Key Concepts
ESSENTIAL QUESTIONS

- How do Earth's land biomes differ?
- How do humans impact land biomes?

Vocabulary

biome p. 339
desert p. 340
grassland p. 341
temperate p. 343
taiga p. 345
tundra p. 345

Multilingual eGlossary

BrainPOP®

6-8.LST.4.3

Inquiry Plant or Animal?

Believe it or not, this is a flower. One of the largest flowers in the world, *Rafflesia* (ruh FLEE zhuh), grows naturally in the tropical rain forests of southeast Asia. What do you think would happen if you planted a seed from this plant in a desert? Would it survive?

Launch Lab

10 minutes

What is the climate in China?

Beijing, China, and New York, New York, are about the same distance from the equator but on opposite sides of Earth. How do temperature and rainfall compare for these two cities?

1. Locate Beijing and New York on a world map.
2. Copy the table to the right in your Science Journal. From the data and charts provided, find and record the average high and low temperatures in January and in June for each city.
3. Record the average rainfall in January and in June for each city.

High Temperature (°C)	January	June
Beijing		
New York		
Low Temperature (°C)	**January**	**June**
Beijing		
New York		
Rainfall (mm)	**January**	**June**
Beijing		
New York		

Think About This

1. What are the temperature and rainfall ranges for each city?
2. **Key Concept** How do you think the climates of these cities differ year-round?

Land Ecosystems and Biomes

When you go outside, you might notice people, grass, flowers, birds, and insects. You also are probably aware of nonliving things, such as air, sunlight, and water. The living or once-living parts of an environment are the biotic parts. The nonliving parts that the living parts need to survive are the abiotic parts. The biotic and abiotic parts of an environment together make up an ecosystem.

Earth's continents have many different ecosystems, from deserts to rain forests. Scientists classify similar ecosystems in large geographic areas as biomes. *A* **biome** *is a geographic area on Earth that contains ecosystems with similar biotic and abiotic features.* As shown in Figure 1, Earth has seven major land biomes. Areas classified as the same biome have similar climates and organisms.

Figure 1 Earth contains seven major biomes.

Animation

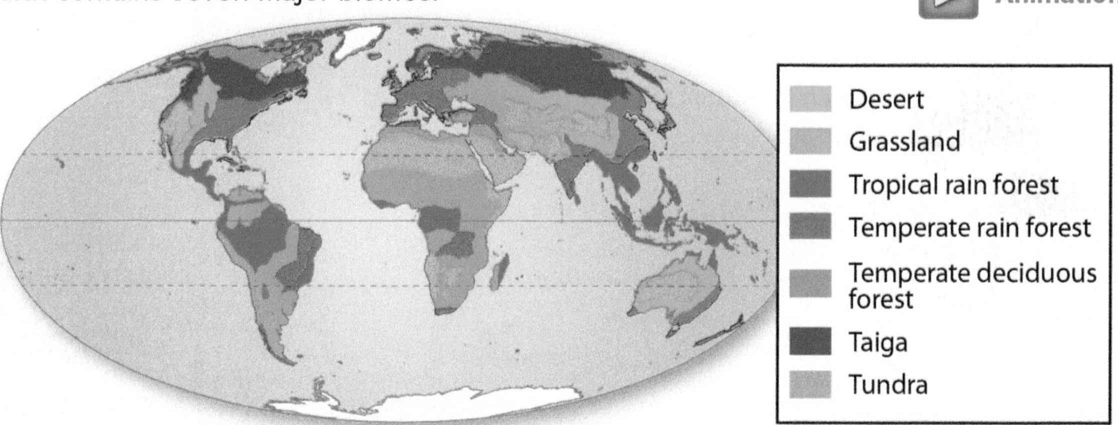

MiniLab

20 minutes

How hot is sand?

If you have ever walked barefoot on a sandy beach on a sunny day, you know how hot sand can be. But how hot is the sand below the surface?

1. Read and complete a lab safety form.
2. Position a **desk lamp** over a **container** of **sand** that is at least 7 cm deep.
3. Place one **thermometer** on the surface of the sand and bury the tip of another **thermometer** about 5 cm below the surface. Record the temperature on each thermometer in your Science Journal.
4. Turn on the lamp and record the temperatures again after 10 minutes.

Analyze and Conclude

1. **Describe** the temperatures of the sand at the surface and below the surface.
2. **Predict** what would happen to the temperature of the sand at night.
3. **Key Concept** Desert soil contains a high percentage of sand. Based on your results, predict ways in which species are adapted to living in an environment where the soil is mostly sand.

Desert Biome

Woodpecker

Deserts *are biomes that receive very little rain.* They are on nearly every continent and are Earth's driest ecosystems.

- Most deserts are hot during the day and cold at night. Others, like those in Antarctica, remain cold all of the time.
- Rainwater drains away quickly because of thin, porous soil. Large patches of ground are bare.

Biodiversity

- Animals include lizards, bats, woodpeckers, and snakes. Most animals avoid activity during the hottest parts of the day.
- Plants include spiny cactus and thorny shrubs. Shallow roots absorb water quickly. Some plants have accordion-like stems that expand and store water. Small leaves or spines reduce the loss of water.

Human Impact

- Cities, farms, and recreational areas in deserts use valuable water.
- Desert plants grow slowly. When they are damaged by people or livestock, recovery takes many years.

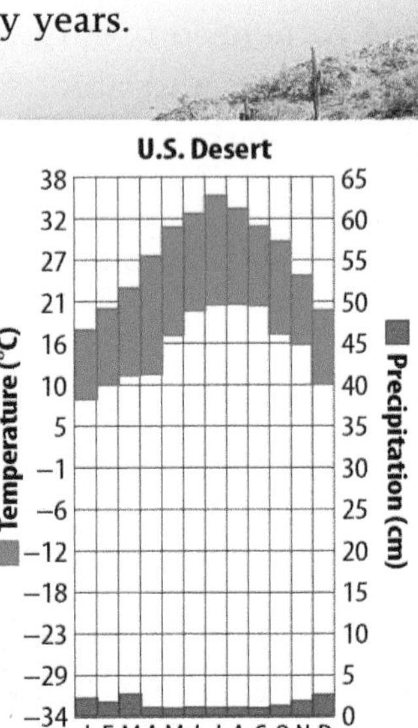

Grassland Biome

Black-footed ferret

Grassland *biomes are areas where grasses are the dominant plants.* Also called prairies, savannas, and meadows, grasslands are the world's "breadbaskets." Wheat, corn, oats, rye, barley, and other important cereal crops are grasses. They grow well in these areas.

- Grasslands have a wet and a dry season.
- Deep, fertile soil supports plant growth.
- Grass roots form a thick mass, called sod, which helps soil absorb and hold water during periods of drought.

Reading Check Why are grasslands called "breadbaskets"?

Biodiversity

- Trees grow along moist banks of streams and rivers. Wildflowers bloom during the wet season.
- In North America, large herbivores, such as bison and elk, graze here. Insects, birds, rabbits, prairie dogs, and snakes find shelter in the grasses.
- Predators in North American grasslands include hawks, ferrets, coyotes, and wolves.
- African savannas are grasslands that contain giraffes, zebras, and lions. Australian grasslands are home to kangaroos, wallabies, and wild dogs.

Human Impact

- People plow large areas of grassland to raise cereal crops. This reduces habitat for wild species.
- Because of hunting and loss of habitat, large herbivores–such as bison–are now uncommon in many grasslands.

Burrowing owl

Tropical Rain Forest Biome

Ocelot

The forests that grow near the equator are called tropical rain forests. These forests receive large amounts of rain and have dense growths of tall, leafy trees.

Toucan

- Weather is warm and wet year-round.
- The soil is shallow and easily washed away by rain.
- Less than 1 percent of the sunlight that reaches the top of forest trees also reaches the forest floor.
- Half of Earth's species live in tropical rain forests. Most live in the canopy–the uppermost part of the forest.

Reading Check Where do most organisms live in a tropical rain forest?

Tropical Rain Forest

Temperature (°C): 38, 32, 27, 21, 16, 10, 5, −1, −6, −12, −18, −23, −29, −34

Precipitation (cm): 65, 60, 55, 50, 45, 40, 35, 30, 25, 20, 15, 10, 5, 0

Month: J F M A M J J A S O N D

Biodiversity

- Few plants live on the dark forest floor.
- Vines climb the trunks of tall trees.
- Mosses, ferns, and orchids live on branches in the canopy.
- Insects make up the largest group of tropical animals. They include beetles, termites, ants, bees, and butterflies.
- Larger animals include parrots, toucans, snakes, frogs, flying squirrels, fruit bats, monkeys, jaguars, and ocelots.

Human Impact

- People have cleared more than half of Earth's tropical rain forests for lumber, farms, and ranches. Poor soil does not support rapid growth of new trees in cleared areas.
- Some organizations are working to encourage people to use less wood harvested from rain forests.

(tl)Kevin Schafer/Photolibrary/Getty Images; (tr)Gavriel Jecan/Getty Images; (bl)Brasil2/iStock/360/Getty Images; (br)©Steven P. Lynch

Temperate Rain Forest Biome

Regions of Earth between the tropics and the polar circles are **temperate** *regions.* Temperate regions have relatively mild climates with distinct seasons. Several biomes are in temperate regions, including rain forests. Temperate rain forests are moist ecosystems mostly in coastal areas. They are not as warm as tropical rain forests.

- Winters are mild and rainy.
- Summers are cool and foggy.
- Soil is rich and moist.

Biodiversity

- Forests are dominated by spruce, hemlock, cedar, fir, and redwood trees, which can grow very large and tall.
- Fungi, ferns, mosses, vines, and small flowering plants grow on the moist forest floor.
- Animals include mosquitoes, butterflies, frogs, salamanders, woodpeckers, owls, eagles, chipmunks, raccoons, deer, elk, bears, foxes, and cougars.

Human Impact

- Temperate rain forest trees are a source of lumber. Logging can destroy the habitat of forest species.
- Rich soil enables cut forests to grow back. Tree farms help provide lumber without destroying habitat.

Key Concept Check In what ways do humans affect temperate rain forests?

Elk

FOLDABLES®

Use a sheet of paper to make a horizontal two-tab book. Record what you learn about desert and temperate rain forest biomes under the tabs, and use the information to compare and contrast these biomes.

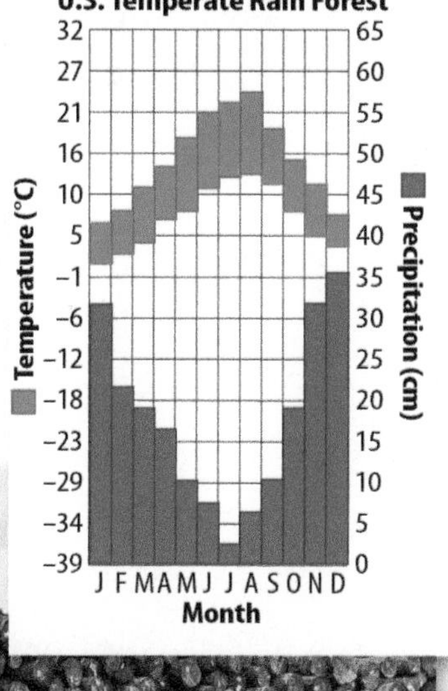

Temperate Deciduous Forest Biome

U.S. Temperate Deciduous Forest

Temperature (°C): 38, 32, 27, 21, 16, 10, 5, −1, −6, −12, −18, −23, −29, −34

Precipitation (cm): 65, 60, 55, 50, 45, 40, 35, 30, 25, 20, 15, 10, 5, 0

J F M A M J J A S O N D

Month

Temperate deciduous forests grow in temperate regions where winter and summer climates have more variation than those in temperate rain forests. These forests are the most common forest ecosystems in the United States. They contain mostly deciduous trees, which lose their leaves in the fall.

- Winter temperatures are often below freezing. Snow is common.
- Summers are hot and humid.
- Soil is rich in nutrients and supports a large amount of diverse plant growth.

Biodiversity

- Most plants, such as maples, oaks, birches, and other deciduous trees, stop growing during the winter and begin growing again in the spring.
- Animals include snakes, ants, butterflies, birds, raccoons, opossums, and foxes.
- Some animals, including chipmunks and bats, spend the winter in hibernation.
- Many birds and some butterflies, such as the monarch, migrate to warmer climates for the winter.

Human Impact

Over the past several hundred years, humans have cleared thousands of acres of Earth's deciduous forests for farms and cities. Today, much of the clearing has stopped and some forests have regrown.

Key Concept Check How are temperate deciduous rain forests different from temperate rain forests?

Red fox

Taiga Biome

A **taiga** (TI guh) *is a forest biome consisting mostly of cone-bearing evergreen trees.* The taiga biome exists only in the northern hemisphere. It occupies more space on Earth's continents than any other biome.

- Winters are long, cold, and snowy. Summers are short, warm, and moist.
- Soil is thin and acidic.

Biodiversity

- Evergreen trees, such as spruce, pine, and fir, are thin and shed snow easily.
- Animals include owls, mice, moose, bears, and other cold-adapted species.
- Abundant insects in summer attract many birds, which migrate south in winter.

Human Impact

- Tree harvesting reduces taiga habitat.

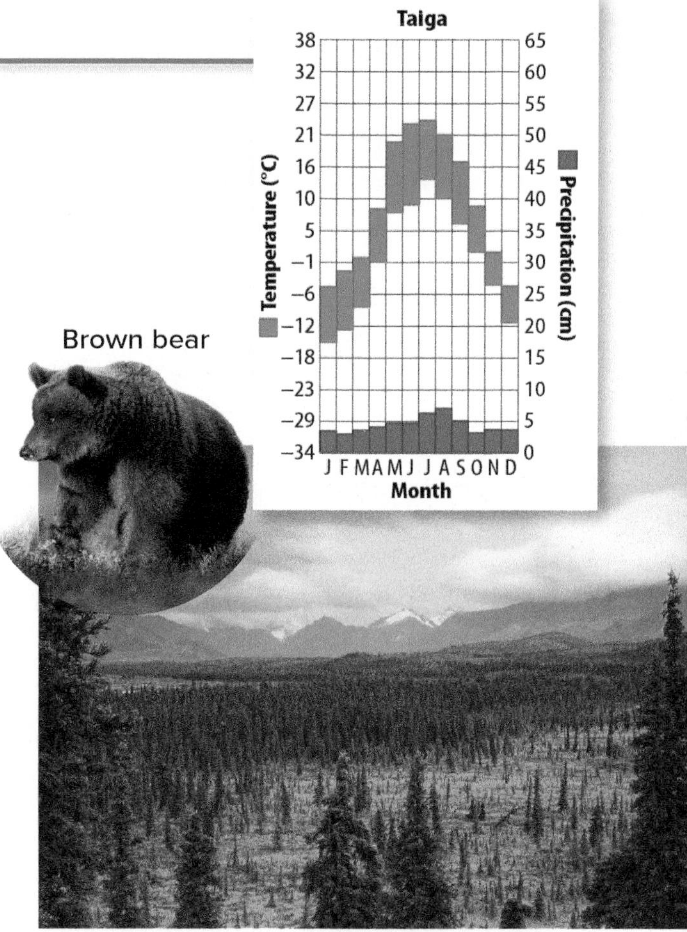

Tundra Biome

A **tundra** (TUN druh) *biome is cold, dry, and treeless.* Most tundra is south of the North Pole, but it also exists in mountainous areas at high altitudes.

- Winters are long, dark, and freezing; summers are short and cool; the growing season is only 50–60 days.
- Permafrost—a layer of permanently frozen soil—prevents deep root growth.

Biodiversity

- Plants include shallow-rooted mosses, lichens, and grasses.
- Many animals hibernate or migrate south during winter. Few animals, including lemmings, live in tundras year-round.

Human Impact

- Drilling for oil and gas can interrupt migration patterns.

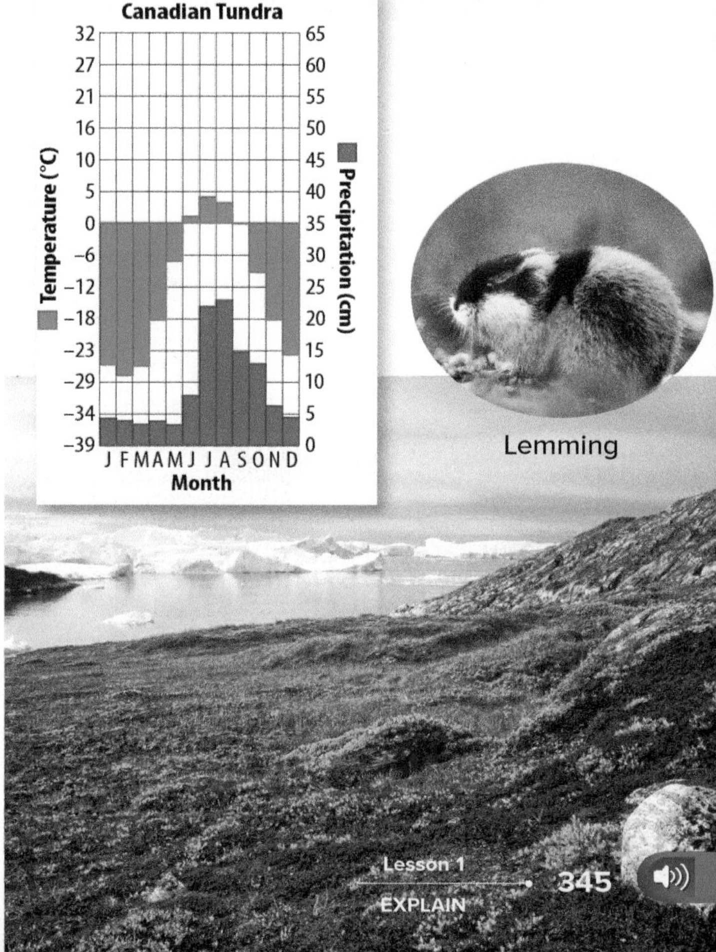

Lesson 1 Review

Visual Summary

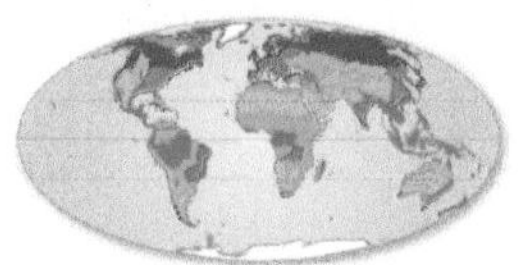

Earth has seven major land biomes, ranging from hot, dry deserts to cold, forested taigas.

Half of Earth's species live in rain forest biomes.

Temperate deciduous forests are the most common forest biome in the United States.

FOLDABLES

Use your lesson Foldable to review the lesson. Save your Foldable for the project at the end of the chapter.

What do you think 

You first read the statements below at the beginning of the chapter.

1. Deserts can be cold.

2. There are no rain forests outside the tropics.

Did you change your mind about whether you agree or disagree with the statements? Rewrite any false statements to make them true.

Use Vocabulary

1 **Define** *biome* using your own words.

2 **Distinguish** between tropical rain forests and temperate rain forests.

3 A cold, treeless biome is a(n) ________.

Understand Key Concepts 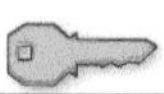

4 **Explain** why tundra soil cannot support the growth of trees.

5 **Give examples** of how plants and animals adapt to temperate deciduous ecosystems.

Interpret Graphics

6 **Determine** What is the average annual rainfall for the biome represented by the chart to the right?

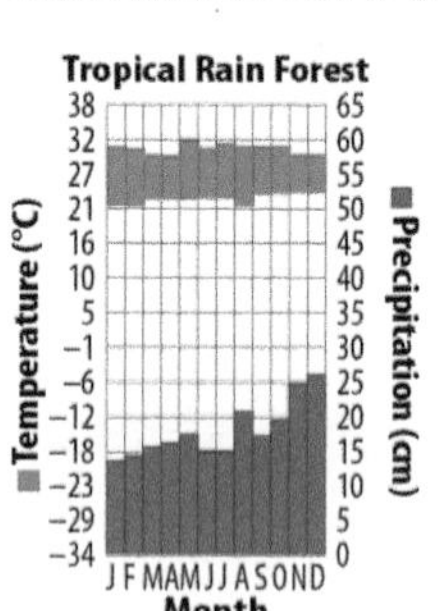

7 **Summarize Information** Copy the graphic organizer below and fill it in with animals and plants of the biome you live in.

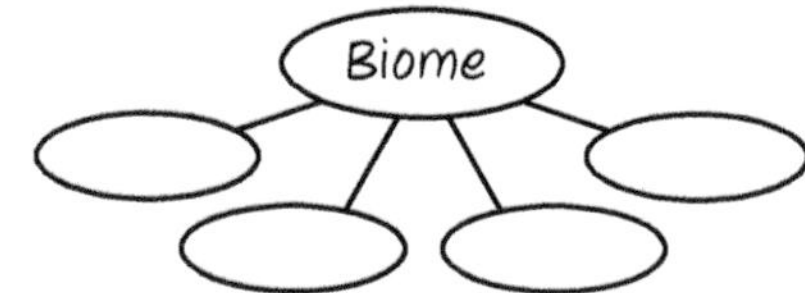

Critical Thinking

8 **Plan** an enclosed zoo exhibit for a desert ecosystem. What abiotic factors should you consider?

9 **Recommend** one or more actions people can take to reduce habitat loss in tropical and taiga forests.

Skill Practice Interpret Data

20 minutes

Which biome is it?

Materials

biome data

You have read about the major land biomes found on Earth. Within each biome are ecosystems with similar biotic and abiotic factors. In this lab, you will **interpret data** describing a particular area on Earth to identify which biome it belongs to.

Learn It

Scientists collect and present data in a variety of forms, including graphs and tables. In this activity, you will interpret data in a graph and apply the information to the ideas you learned in the lesson.

Try It

1. Examine the temperature and precipitation data in the graph given you by your teacher.
2. Create a table from these data in your Science Journal. Calculate the average temperature and precipitation during the winter and the summer.
3. Examine the image of the biome and identify some plants and animals in the image.
4. Compare your data to the information on land biomes presented in Lesson 1. Which biome is the most similar?

Apply It

5. Which land biome did your data come from? Why did you choose this biome?
6. Are the data in your graph identical to the data in the graph of the biome in Lesson 1 to which it belongs? Why or why not?
7. Describe this biome. What do you think your biome will be like six months from now?
8. **Key Concept** How might humans affect the organisms in your biome?

(t)Marvin Dembinsky Photo Associates/Alamy; (b)Andre Gallant/Getty Images

Lesson 2

Reading Guide

Key Concept 

ESSENTIAL QUESTIONS

- How do Earth's aquatic ecosystems differ?
- How do humans impact aquatic ecosystems?

Vocabulary

salinity p. 349
wetland p. 352
estuary p. 353
intertidal zone p. 355
coral reef p. 355

Multilingual eGlossary

6-8.LST.5.2

Aquatic Ecosystems

Inquiry Floating Trees?

These plants, called mangroves, are one of the few types of plants that grow in salt water. They usually live along ocean coastlines in tropical ecosystems. What other organisms do you think live near mangroves?

Launch Lab

10 minutes

What happens when rivers and oceans mix?

Freshwater and saltwater ecosystems have different characteristics. What happens in areas where freshwater rivers and streams flow into oceans?

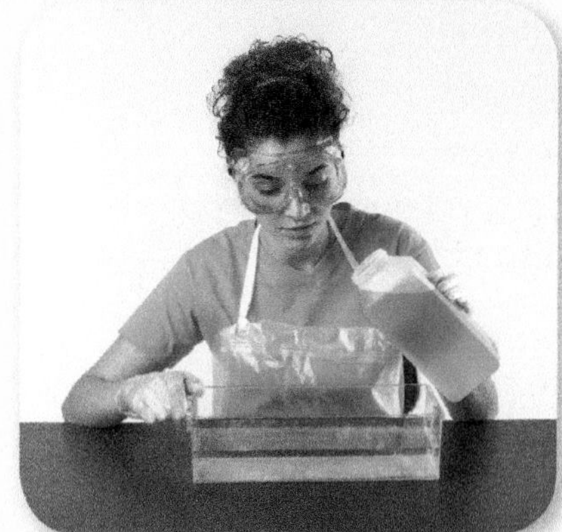

1. Read and complete a lab safety form.
2. In a **plastic tub,** add 100 g of **salt** to 2 L of water. Stir with a **long-handled spoon** until the salt dissolves.
3. In another **container,** add 5 drops of **blue food coloring** to 1 L of water. Gently pour the colored water into one corner of the plastic tub. Observe how the color of the water changes in the tub.
4. Observe the tub again in 5 minutes.

Think About This

1. What bodies of water do the containers represent?
2. What happened to the water in the tub after 5 minutes? What do you think happens to the salt content of the water?
3. **Key Concept** How do you think the biodiversity of rivers and oceans differ? What organisms do you think might live at the place where the two meet?

Aquatic Ecosystems

If you've ever spent time near an ocean, a river, or another body of water, you might know that water is full of life. There are four major types of water, or aquatic, ecosystems: freshwater, wetland, estuary, and ocean. Each type of ecosystem contains a unique variety of organisms. Whales, dolphins, and corals live only in ocean ecosystems. Catfish and trout live only in freshwater ecosystems. Many other organisms that do not live under water, such as birds and seals, also depend on aquatic ecosystems for food and shelter.

Important abiotic factors in aquatic ecosystems include temperature, sunlight, and dissolved oxygen gas. Aquatic species have adaptations that enable them to use the oxygen in water. The gills of a fish separate oxygen from water and move it into the fish's bloodstream. Mangrove plants, pictured on the previous page, take in oxygen through small pores in their leaves and roots.

Salinity (say LIH nuh tee) is another important abiotic factor in aquatic ecosystems. **Salinity** *is the amount of salt dissolved in water.* Water in saltwater ecosystems has high salinity compared to water in freshwater ecosystems, which contains little salt.

Math Skills

Use Proportions

Salinity is measured in parts per thousand (PPT). One PPT water contains 1 g salt and 1,000 g water. Use proportions to calculate salinity. What is the salinity of 100 g of water with 3.5 g of salt?

$$\frac{3.5 \text{ g salt}}{100 \text{ g seawater}} = \frac{x \text{ g salt}}{1{,}000 \text{ g seawater}}$$

$$100x = 3500$$

$$x = \frac{3500}{100} = 35 \text{ PPT}$$

Practice

A sample contains 0.1895 g of salt per 50 g of seawater. What is its salinity?

Math Practice

Personal Tutor

Great Blue Heron

Salmon

Freshwater ecosystems include streams, rivers, ponds, and lakes. Streams are usually narrow, shallow, and fast-flowing. Rivers are larger, deeper, and flow more slowly.

- Streams form from underground sources of water, such as springs or from runoff from rain and melting snow.
- Stream water is often clear. Soil particles are quickly washed downstream.
- Oxygen levels in streams are high because air mixes into the water as it splashes over rocks.
- Rivers form when streams flow together.
- Soil that washes into a river from streams or nearby land can make river water muddy. Soil also introduces nutrients, such as nitrogen, into rivers.
- Slow-moving river water has higher levels of nutrients and lower levels of dissolved oxygen than fast-moving water.

Biodiversity

- Willows, cottonwoods, and other water-loving plants grow along streams and on riverbanks.
- Species adapted to fast-moving water include trout, salmon, crayfish, and many insects.
- Species adapted to slow-moving water include snails and catfish.

Stonefly larva

Human Impact

- People take water from streams and rivers for drinking, laundry, bathing, crop irrigation, and industrial purposes.
- Hydroelectric plants use the energy in flowing water to generate electricity. Dams stop the water's flow.
- Runoff from cities, industries, and farms is a source of pollution.

(t)©Comstock/PunchStock; (tr)U.S. Fish & Wildlife Service/Frank Miles; (cl)Paul Nicklen/NGS/Getty Images; (cr)©Alan Bash/Alamy; (bcl)Jerry Moorman/iStock/360/Getty images; (b)©Medioimages/PunchStock

Freshwater: Ponds and Lakes

Ponds and lakes contain freshwater that is not flowing downhill. These bodies of water form in low areas on land.

- Ponds are shallow and warm.
- Sunlight reaches the bottom of most ponds.
- Pond water is often high in nutrients.
- Lakes are larger and deeper than ponds.
- Sunlight penetrates into the top few feet of lake water. Deeper water is dark and cold.

Biodiversity

- Plants surround ponds and lake shores.
- Surface water in ponds and lakes contains plants, algae, and microscopic organisms that use sunlight for photosynthesis.
- Organisms living in shallow water near shorelines include cattails, reeds, insects, crayfish, frogs, fish, and turtles.
- Fewer organisms live in the deeper, colder water of lakes where there is little sunlight.
- Lake fish include perch, trout, bass, and walleye.

Smallmouth bass

 **Reading Check** Why do few organisms live in the deep water of lakes?

Human Impact

- Humans fill in ponds and lakes with sediment to create land for houses and other structures.
- Runoff from farms, gardens, and roads washes pollutants into ponds and lakes, disrupting food webs.

 **Key Concept Check** How do ponds and lakes differ?

Wetlands

Common loon

Some types of aquatic ecosystems have mostly shallow water. **Wetlands** *are aquatic ecosystems that have a thin layer of water covering soil that is wet most of the time.* Wetlands contain freshwater, salt water, or both. They are among Earth's most fertile ecosystems.

- Freshwater wetlands form at the edges of lakes and ponds and in low areas on land. Saltwater wetlands form along ocean coasts.
- Nutrient levels and biodiversity are high.
- Wetlands trap sediments and purify water. Plants and microscopic organisms filter out pollution and waste materials.

Biodiversity

- Water-tolerant plants include grasses and cattails. Few trees live in saltwater wetlands. Trees in freshwater wetlands include cottonwoods, willows, and swamp oaks.
- Insects are abundant and include flies, mosquitoes, dragonflies, and butterflies.
- More than one-third of North American bird species, including ducks, geese, herons, loons, warblers, and egrets, use wetlands for nesting and feeding.
- Other animals that depend on wetlands for food and breeding grounds include alligators, turtles, frogs, snakes, salamanders, muskrats, and beavers.

Human Impact

- In the past, many people considered wetlands as unimportant environments. Water was drained away to build homes and roads and to raise crops.
- Today, many wetlands are being preserved, and drained wetlands are being restored.

Key Concept Check How do humans impact wetlands?

(t)U. S. Fish and Wildlife Service; (c)Purestock/SuperStock; (b)Steve Bly/Getty Images

Estuaries

Estuaries (ES chuh wer eez) *are regions along coastlines where streams or rivers flow into a body of salt water.* Most estuaries form along coastlines, where freshwater in rivers meets salt water in oceans. Estuary ecosystems have varying degrees of salinity.

- Salinity depends on rainfall, the amount of freshwater flowing from land, and the amount of salt water pushed in by tides.
- Estuaries help protect coastal land from flooding and erosion. Like wetlands, estuaries purify water and filter out pollution.
- Nutrient levels and biodiversity are high.

Biodiversity

- Plants that grow in salt water include mangroves, pickleweeds, and seagrasses.
- Animals include worms, snails, and many species that people use for food, including oysters, shrimp, crabs, and clams.
- Striped bass, salmon, flounder, and many other ocean fish lay their eggs in estuaries.
- Many species of birds depend on estuaries for breeding, nesting, and feeding.

Human Impact

- Large portions of estuaries have been filled with soil to make land for roads and buildings.
- Destruction of estuaries reduces habitat for estuary species and exposes the coastline to flooding and storm damage.

WORD ORIGIN

estuary
from Latin *aestuarium,* means "a tidal marsh or opening."

FOLDABLES®

Make a horizontal two-tab book and label it as shown. Use it to compare how biodiversity and human impact differ in wetlands and estuaries.

Harvest mouse

Ocean: Open Oceans

Sunlit zone

200 m

Twilight zone

Continental shelf

1,000 m

Dark zone

3,800 m

Seafloor

Jellyfish

Most of Earth's surface is covered by ocean water with high salinity. The oceans contain different types of ecosystems. If you took a boat trip several kilometers out to sea, you would be in the open ocean–one type of ocean ecosystem. The open ocean extends from the steep edges of continental shelves to the deepest parts of the ocean. The amount of light in the water depends on depth.

- Photosynthesis can take place only in the uppermost, or sunlit, zone. Very little sunlight reaches the twilight zone. None reaches the deepest water, known as the dark zone.
- Decaying matter and nutrients float down from the sunlit zone, through the twilight and dark zones, to the seafloor.

Biodiversity

- Microscopic algae and other producers in the sunlit zone form the base of most ocean food chains. Other organisms living in the sunlit zone are jellyfish, tuna, mackerel, and dolphins.
- Many species of fish stay in the twilight zone during the day and swim to the sunlit zone at night to feed.
- Sea cucumbers, brittle stars, and other bottom-dwelling organisms feed on decaying matter that drifts down from above.
- Many organisms in the dark zone live near cracks in the seafloor where lava erupts and new seafloor forms.

Reading Check Which organisms are at the base of most ocean food chains?

Human Impact

- Overfishing threatens many ocean fish.
- Trash discarded from ocean vessels or washed into oceans from land is a source of pollution. Animals such as seals become tangled in plastic or mistake it for food.

Fur seal

(t)Purestock/SuperStock; (c)Gregory Ochocki/Science Source; (b)Doug Allan/Getty Images

Ocean: Coastal Oceans

Sea stars

Coastal oceans include several types of ecosystems, including continental shelves and intertidal zones. *The* **intertidal zone** *is the ocean shore between the lowest low tide and the highest high tide.*

- Sunlight reaches the bottom of shallow coastal ecosystems.
- Nutrients washed in from rivers and streams contribute to high biodiversity.

Biodiversity

- The coastal ocean is home to mussels, fish, crabs, sea stars, dolphins, and whales.
- Intertidal species have adaptations for surviving exposure to air during low tides and to heavy waves during high tides.

Human Impact

- Oil spills and other pollution harm coastal organisms.

Ocean: Coral Reefs

Another ocean ecosystem with high biodiversity is the coral reef. *A* **coral reef** *is an underwater structure made from outside skeletons of tiny, soft-bodied animals called coral.*

- Most coral reefs form in shallow tropical oceans.
- Coral reefs protect coastlines from storm damage and erosion.

Biodiversity

- Coral reefs provide food and shelter for many animals, including parrotfish, groupers, angelfish, eels, shrimp, crabs, scallops, clams, worms, and snails.

Human Impact

- Pollution, overfishing, and harvesting of coral threaten coral reefs.

MiniLab

15 minutes

How do ocean ecosystems differ?

Ocean ecosystems include open oceans, coastal oceans, and coral reefs—each one a unique environment with distinctive organisms.

1. Read and complete a lab safety form.
2. In a **large plastic tub,** use **rocks** and **sand** to make a structure representing an open ocean, a coastal ocean, or a coral reef.

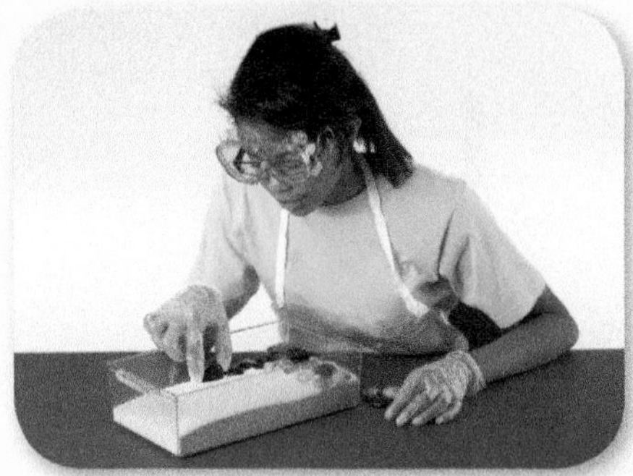

3. Fill the tub with **water.**
4. Make waves by gently moving your hand back and forth in the water.

Analyze and Conclude

1. **Observe** What happened to your structure when you made waves? How might a hurricane affect the organisms that live in the ecosystem you modeled?
2. **Key Concept** Compare your results with results of those who modeled other ecosystems. Suggest what adaptations species might have in each ecosystem.

Grouper

Lesson 2 Review

Visual Summary

Freshwater ecosystems include ponds and lakes.

Wetlands can be saltwater ecosystems or freshwater ecosystems.

Coral reefs and coastal ecosystems have high levels of biodiversity.

FOLDABLES®

Use your lesson Foldable to review the lesson. Save your Foldable for the project at the end of the chapter.

Use Vocabulary

1. **Define** the term *salinity*.
2. **Distinguish** between a wetland and an estuary.
3. An ocean ecosystem formed from the skeletons of animals is a(n) ________.

Understand Key Concepts

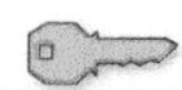

4. Which ecosystem contains both salt water and freshwater?
   A. estuary
   B. lake
   C. pond
   D. stream
5. **Describe** what might happen to a coastal area if its estuary were filled in to build houses.

Interpret Graphics

6. **Describe** Copy the drawing to the right and label the light zones. Describe characteristics of each zone.

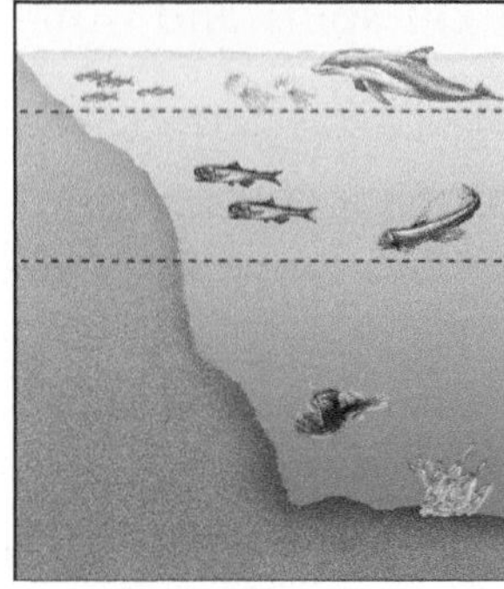

Critical Thinking

7. **Recommend** actions people might take to prevent pollutants from entering coastal ecosystems.

Math Skills

8. The salinity of the Baltic Sea is about 10 PPT. What weight of salt is present in 2,000 g of its seawater?

What do you think NOW?

You first read the statements below at the beginning of the chapter.

3. Estuaries do not protect coastal areas from erosion.

4. Animals form coral reefs.

Did you change your mind about whether you agree or disagree with the statements? Rewrite any false statements to make them true.

Saving an Underwater Wilderness

How do scientists help protect coral reefs?

Pollution and human activities, such as mining and tourism, have damaged many ecosystems, including coral reefs. Scientists and conservation groups are working together to help protect and restore coral reefs and areas that surround them. One way is to create marine reserves where no fishing or collection of organisms is allowed.

A team of scientists, including marine ecologists Dr. Dan Brumbaugh and Kate Holmes from the American Museum of Natural History, are investigating how well reserves are working. These scientists compare how many fish of one species live both inside and outside reserves. Their results indicate that more species of fish and greater numbers of each species live inside reserves than outside—one sign that reefs in the area are improving.

A researcher takes a water sample from a marine reserve. ▼

Reef ecosystems do not have to be part of a reserve in order to improve, however. Scientists can work with local governments to find ways to limit damage to reef ecosystems. One way is to prevent overfishing by limiting the number of fish caught. Other ways include eliminating the use of destructive fishing practices that can harm reefs and reducing runoff from farms and factories.

By creating marine reserves, regulating fishing practices, and reducing runoff, humans can help reefs that were once in danger become healthy again.

Kate Holmes examines a coral reef. ▶

It's Your Turn

WRITE Write a persuasive essay describing why coral reefs are important habitats.

AMERICAN MUSEUM OF NATURAL HISTORY

Lesson 3

Reading Guide

Key Concepts
ESSENTIAL QUESTIONS

- How do land ecosystems change over time?
- How do aquatic ecosystems change over time?

Vocabulary

ecological succession p. 359
climax community p. 359
pioneer species p. 360
eutrophication p. 362

Multilingual eGlossary

Science Video
What's Science Got to do With It?

6.LS.4, 6-8.LST.2.1, 6-8.LST.7.3

How Ecosystems Change

Inquiry How did this happen?

This object was once part of a mining system used to move copper and iron ore. Today, so many forest plants have grown around it that it is barely recognizable. How do you think this happened? What do you think this object will look like after 500 more years?

Launch Lab

15 minutes

How do communities change?

An ecosystem can change over time. Change usually happens so gradually that you might not notice differences from day to day.

1. Your teacher has given you **two pictures of ecosystem communities.** One is labeled *A* and the other is labeled *B*.

2. Imagine community A changed and became like community B. On a blank piece of **paper**, draw what you think community A might look like midway in its change to becoming like community B.

Think About This

1. What changes did you imagine? How long do you think it would take for community A to become like community B?
2. **Key Concept** Summarize the changes you think would happen as the community changed from A to B.

How Land Ecosystems Change

Have you ever seen weeds growing up through cracks in a concrete sidewalk? If they were not removed, the weeds would keep growing. The crack would widen, making room for more weeds. Over time, the sidewalk would break apart. Shrubs and vines would move in. Their leaves and branches would grow large enough to cover the concrete. Eventually, trees could start growing there.

This process is an example of **ecological succession**–*the process of one ecological community gradually changing into another.* Ecological succession occurs in a series of steps. These steps can usually be predicted. For example, small plants usually grow first. Larger plants, such as trees, usually grow last.

The final stage of ecological succession in a land ecosystem is a **climax community**–*a stable community that no longer goes through major ecological changes.* Climax communities differ depending on the type of biome they are in. In a tropical forest biome, a climax community would be a mature tropical forest. In a grassland biome, a climax community would be a mature grassland. Climax communities are usually stable over hundreds of years. As plants in a climax community die, new plants of the same species grow and take their places. The community will continue to contain the same kinds of plants as long as the climate remains the same.

Key Concept Check What is a climax community?

FOLDABLES®

Fold a sheet of paper into fourths. Use two sections on one side of the paper to describe and illustrate what land might look like before secondary succession and the other side to describe and illustrate the land after secondary succession is complete.

REVIEW VOCABULARY

community
all the organisms that live in one area at the same time

SCIENCE USE V. COMMON USE

pioneer

Science Use the first species that colonize new or undisturbed land

Common Use the first human settlers in an area

Primary Succession

What do you think happens to a lava-filled landscape when a volcanic eruption is over? As shown in Figure 2, volcanic lava eventually becomes new soil that supports plant growth. Ecological succession in new areas of land with little or no soil, such as on a lava flow, a sand dune, or exposed rock, is primary succession. *The first species that colonize new or undisturbed land are* **pioneer species.** The lichens and mosses in Figure 2 are pioneer species.

Figure 2 Following a volcanic eruption, a landscape undergoes primary succession.

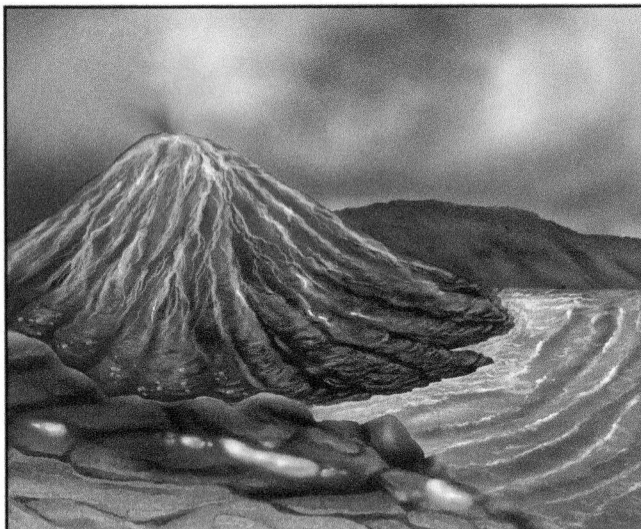

During a volcanic eruption, molten lava flows over the ground and into the water. After the eruption is over, the lava cools and hardens into bare rock.

Lichen spores carried on the wind settle on the rock. Lichens release acid that helps break down the rock and create soil. Lichens add nutrients to the soil as they die and decay.

Airborne spores from mosses and ferns settle onto the thin soil and add to the soil when they die. The soil gradually becomes thick enough to hold water. Insects and other small organisms move into the area.

After many years the soil is deep and has enough nutrients for grasses, wildflowers, shrubs, and trees. The new ecosystem provides habitats for many animals. Eventually, a climax community develops.

Secondary Succession

In areas where existing ecosystems have been disturbed or destroyed, secondary succession can occur. One example is forestland in New England that early colonists cleared hundreds of years ago. Some of the cleared land was not planted with crops. This land gradually grew back to a climax forest community of beech and maple trees, as illustrated in **Figure 3.**

 **Reading Check** Where does secondary succession occur?

Figure 3 When disturbed land grows back, secondary succession occurs.

Settlers in New England cleared many acres of forests to create cropland. In places where people stopped planting crops, the forest began to grow back.

Seeds of grasses, wildflowers, and other plants quickly began to sprout and grow. Young shrubs and trees also started growing. These plants provided habitats for insects and other small animals, such as mice.

White pines and poplars were the first trees in the area to grow to their full height. They provided shade and protection to slower growing trees, such as beech and maple.

Eventually, a climax community of beech and maple trees developed. As older trees die, new beech and maple seedlings grow and replace them.

Aquatic Succession

Personal Tutor

Aquatic succession begins with a body of water such as a pond.
Over time, sediments and decaying organisms build up and create soil. This soil fills the bottom of the pond or lake.
Eventually the pond or lake fills completely with soil and a land ecosystem develops.

Figure 4 The water in a pond is slowly replaced by soil. Eventually, land plants take over and the pond disappears.

How Freshwater Ecosystems Change

Like land ecosystems, freshwater ecosystems change over time in a natural, predictable process. This process is called aquatic succession.

Aquatic Succession

Aquatic succession is illustrated in Figure 4. Sediments carried by rainwater and streams accumulate on the bottoms of ponds, lakes, and wetlands. The decomposed remains of dead organisms add to the buildup of soil. As time passes, more and more soil accumulates. Eventually, so much soil has collected that the water disappears and the area becomes land.

Key Concept Check What happens to a pond, a lake, or a wetland over time?

Eutrophication

As decaying organisms fall to the bottom of a pond, a lake, or a wetland, they add nutrients to the water. **Eutrophication** (yoo troh fuh KAY shun) *is the process of a body of water becoming nutrient-rich.*

WORD ORIGIN

eutrophication
from Greek *eutrophos*, means "nourishing"

Eutrophication is a natural part of aquatic succession. However, humans also contribute to eutrophication. The fertilizers that farmers use on crops and the waste from farm animals can be very high in nutrients. So can other forms of pollution. When fertilizers and pollution run off into a pond or lake, nutrient concentrations increase. High nutrient levels support large populations of algae and other microscopic organisms. These organisms use most of the dissolved oxygen in the water and less oxygen is available for fish and other pond or lake organisms. As a result, many of these organisms die. Their bodies decay and add to the buildup of soil, speeding up succession.

Lesson 3 Review

Visual Summary

Ecosystems change in predictable ways through ecological succession.

The final stage of ecological succession in a land ecosystem is a climax community.

The final stage of aquatic succession is a land ecosystem.

FOLDABLES®

Use your lesson Foldable to review the lesson. Save your Foldable for the project at the end of the chapter.

What do you think 

You first read the statements below at the beginning of the chapter.

5. An ecosystem never changes.

6. Nothing grows in the area where a volcano has erupted.

Did you change your mind about whether you agree or disagree with the statements? Rewrite any false statements to make them true.

Use Vocabulary

1. **Define** *pioneer species* in your own words.
2. The process of one ecological community changing into another is ______.
3. **Compare and contrast** succession and eutrophication in freshwater ecosystems.

Understand Key Concepts 

4. **Draw** a picture of what your school might look like in 500 years if it were abandoned.
5. Which process occurs after a forest fire?
   - **A.** eutrophication
   - **B.** photosynthesis
   - **C.** primary succession
   - **D.** secondary succession

Interpret Graphics

6. **Determine** What kind of succession—primary or secondary—might occur in the environment pictured to the right? Explain.

7. **Summarize Information** Copy the graphic organizer below and fill it with the types of succession an ecosystem can go through.

Critical Thinking

8. **Reflect** What kinds of abiotic factors might cause a grassland climax community to slowly become a forest?
9. **Recommend** actions people can take to help prevent the loss of wetland and estuary habitats.

A Biome for Radishes

Materials

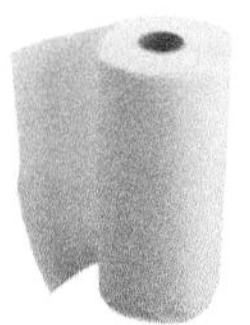

paper towels

small jar

plastic wrap

jar lid

radish seeds

desk lamp

magnifying lens

Safety

Biomes contain plant and animal species adapted to particular climate conditions. Many organisms can live only in one type of biome. Others can survive in more than one biome. A radish is a plant grown around the world. How do you think radish seeds grow in different biomes? In this lab, you will model four different biomes and ecosystems–a temperate deciduous forest, a temperate rain forest, a desert, and a pond–and determine which biome the radishes grow best in.

Ask a Question

Which biome do radishes grow best in?

Make Observations

1. Read and complete a lab safety form.
2. Fold two pieces of paper towel lengthwise. Place the paper towels on opposite sides of the top of a small jar, as shown, with one end of each towel inside the jar and one end outside. Add water until about 10 cm of the paper towels are in the water. The area inside the jar models a pond ecosystem.
3. Place a piece of plastic wrap loosely over the end of one of the paper towels hanging over the jar's edge. Do not completely cover the paper towel. This paper towel models a temperate rain forest ecosystem. The paper towel without plastic wrap models a temperate deciduous forest.
4. Place the jar lid upside-down on the top of the jar. The area in the lid models a desert.

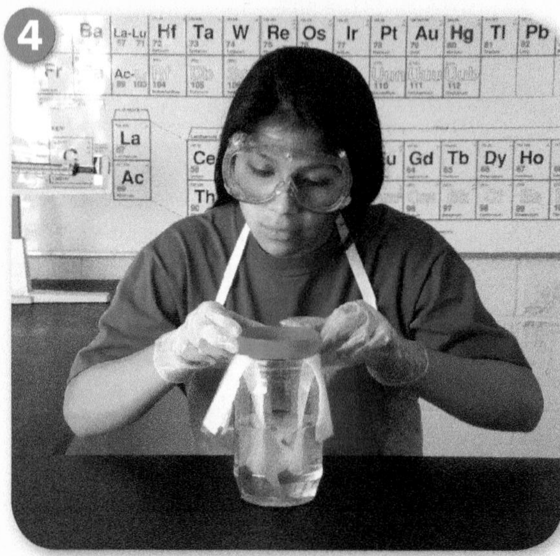

Form a Hypothesis

5. Observe the four biomes and ecosystems you have modeled. Based on your observations and your knowledge of the abiotic factors a plant requires, hypothesize which biome or ecosystem you think radish seeds will grow best in.

By permission of TOPS Learning Systems, www.topscience.org.

Test Your Hypothesis

6. Place three radish seeds in each biome: pond, temperate forest, temperate rain forest, and desert. Gently press the seeds to the paper towel until they stick.
7. Place your jar near a window or under a desk lamp that can be turned on during the day.
8. In your Science Journal, record your observations of the seeds and the paper towel.
9. After five days, use a magnifying lens to observe the seeds and the paper towels again. Record your observations.

Analyze and Conclude

10. **Compare and Contrast** How did the appearance of the seeds change after five days in each model biome?
11. **Critique** Evaluate your hypothesis. Did the seeds grow the way you expected? In which biome did the seeds grow the most?
12. **The Big Idea** In the biome with the most growth, what characteristics do you think made the seeds grow best?

Communicate Your Results

Working in a group of three or four, create a table showing results for each biome. Present the table to the class.

Inquiry Extension

In this lab, you determined which biome produced the most growth of radish seeds. Seeds of different species might sprout in several different biomes. However, not all sprouted seeds grow to adulthood. Design a lab to test what conditions are necessary for radishes to grow to adulthood.

Lab Tips

- Do not eat the radish seeds.
- If your seeds fall off the paper towel strips, do not replace them.

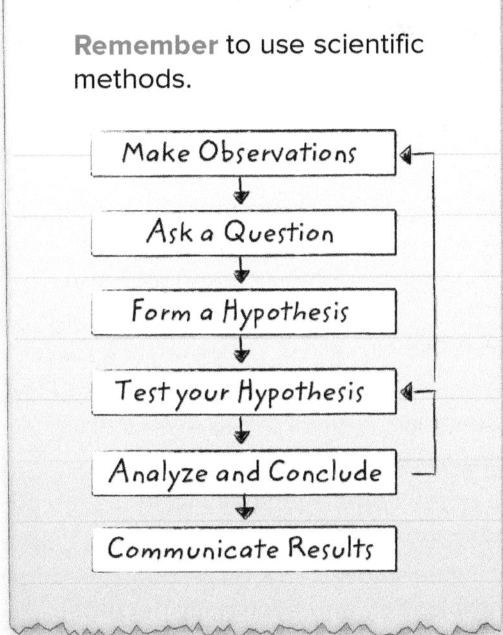

Chapter 10 Study Guide

Each of Earth's land biomes and aquatic ecosystems is characterized by distinct environments and organisms. Biomes and ecosystems change by natural processes of ecological succession and by human activities.

Key Concepts Summary

Lesson 1: Land Biomes

- Each land **biome** has a distinct climate and contains animals and plants well adapted to the environment. Biomes include **deserts, grasslands,** tropical rain forests, **temperate** rain forests, deciduous forests, **taigas,** and **tundras.**
- Humans affect land biomes through agriculture, construction, and other activities.

Vocabulary

biome p. 339
desert p. 340
grassland p. 341
temperate p. 343
taiga p. 345
tundra p. 345

Lesson 2: Aquatic Ecosystems

- Earth's aquatic ecosystems include freshwater and saltwater ecosystems. **Wetlands** can contain either salt water or freshwater. The **salinity** of **estuaries** varies.
- Human activities such as construction and fishing can affect aquatic ecosystems.

Vocabulary

salinity p. 349
wetland p. 352
estuary p. 353
intertidal zone p. 355
coral reef p. 355

Lesson 3: How Ecosystems Change

- Land and aquatic ecosystems change over time in predictable processes of **ecological succession.**
- Land ecosystems eventually form **climax communities.**
- Freshwater ecosystems undergo **eutrophication** and eventually become land ecosystems.

Vocabulary

ecological succession p. 359
climax community p. 359
pioneer species p. 360
eutrophication p. 362

(t)erperl/Alamy; (c)Christopher Hope-Fitch/Moment Open/Getty Images

Vocabulary eFlashcards
Vocabulary eGames

Personal Tutor

FOLDABLES®

Chapter Project

Assemble your lesson Foldables as shown to make a Chapter Project. Use the project to review what you have learned in this chapter.

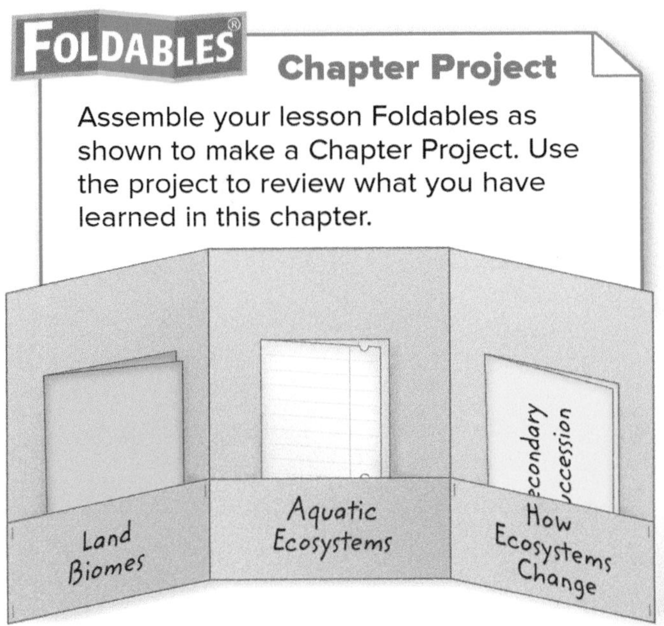

Use Vocabulary

Choose the vocabulary word that fits each description.

1. group of ecosystems with similar climate
2. area between the tropics and the polar circles
3. land biome with a layer of permafrost
4. the amount of salt dissolved in water
5. area where a river empties into an ocean
6. coastal zone between the highest high tide and the lowest low tide
7. process of one ecological community gradually changing into another
8. a stable community that no longer goes through major changes
9. the first species to grow on new or disturbed land

Interactive Concept Map

Link Vocabulary and Key Concepts

Copy this concept map, and then use vocabulary terms from the previous page and other terms from this chapter to complete the concept map.

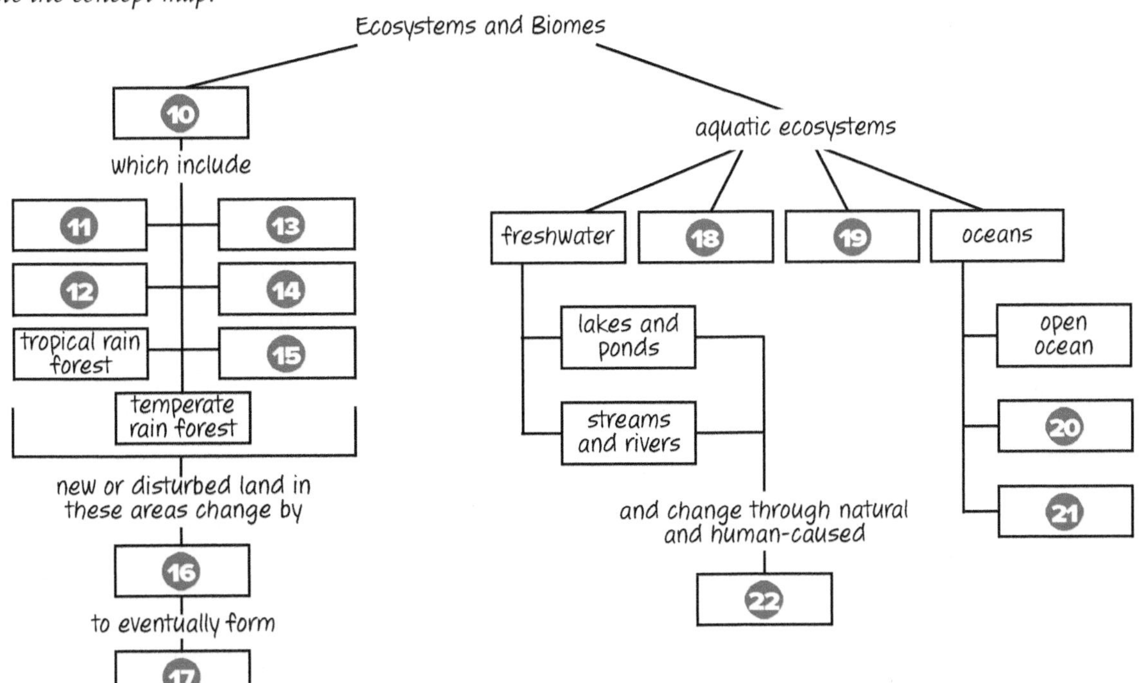

Chapter 10 Review

Understand Key Concepts

1 Where would you find plants with stems that can store large amounts of water?

A. desert
B. grassland
C. taiga
D. tundra

2 What does the pink area on the map below represent?

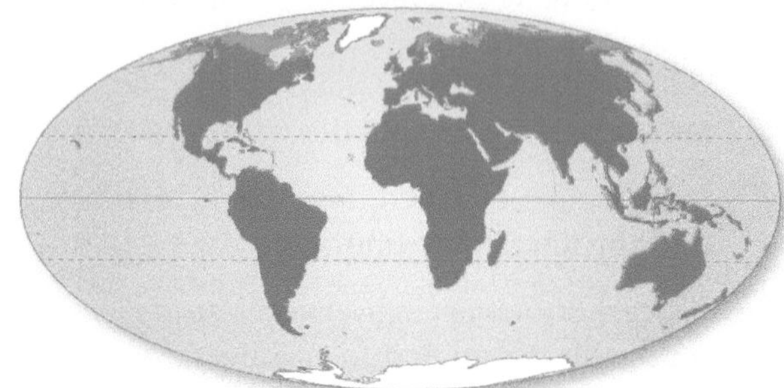

A. taiga
B. tundra
C. temperate deciduous forest
D. temperate rain forest

3 Where would you find trees that have no leaves during the winter?

A. estuary
B. tundra
C. temperate deciduous forest
D. temperate rain forest

4 Which biomes have rich, fertile soil?

A. grassland and taiga
B. grassland and tundra
C. grassland and tropical rain forest
D. grassland and temperate deciduous forest

5 Which is NOT a freshwater ecosystem?

A. oceans
B. ponds
C. rivers
D. streams

6 Where would you find species adapted to withstand strong wave action?

A. estuaries
B. wetlands
C. intertidal zone
D. twilight zone

7 Which ecosystem has flowing water?

A. estuary
B. lake
C. stream
D. wetland

8 Which ecosystems help protect coastal areas from flood damage?

A. estuaries
B. ponds
C. rivers
D. streams

9 Which organism below would be the first to grow in an area that has been buried in lava?

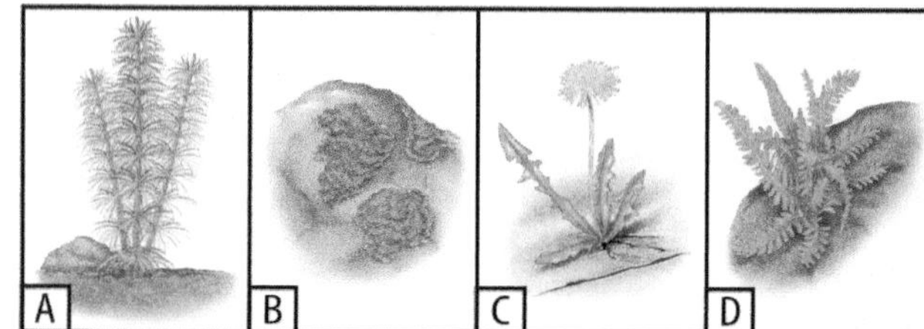

A. A
B. B
C. C
D. D

10 What is a forest called that has had the same species of trees for 200 years?

A. climax community
B. pioneer species
C. primary succession
D. secondary succession

11 What is eutrophication?

A. decreasing nutrients
B. decreasing salinity
C. increasing nutrients
D. increasing salinity

Critical Thinking

12 **Compare** mammals that live in tundra biomes with those that live in desert biomes. What adaptations does each group have that help them survive?

13 **Analyze** You are invited to go on a trip to South America. Before you leave, you read a travel guide that says the country you will be visiting has hot summers, cold winters, and many wheat farms. What biome will you be visiting? Explain your reasoning.

14 **Contrast** How are ecosystems in the deep water of lakes and oceans different?

15 **Analyze** Which type of ocean ecosystem is likely to have the highest levels of dissolved oxygen? Why?

16 **Hypothesize** Why are the first plants that appear in primary succession small?

17 **Interpret Graphics** The following climate data were recorded for a forest ecosystem. To which biome does this ecosystem likely belong?

Climate Data	June	July	August
Average temperature (°C)	16.0	16.5	17.0
Average rainfall (cm)	3.0	2.0	2.0

Writing in Science

18 **Write** a paragraph explaining the succession process that might occur in a small pond on a cow pasture. Include a main idea, supporting details, and concluding sentence.

REVIEW THE BIG IDEA

19 Earth contains a wide variety of organisms that live in different conditions. How do Earth's biomes and ecosystems differ?

20 The photo below shows Biosphere 2, built in Arizona as an artificial Earth. Imagine that you have been asked to build a biome of your choice for Biosphere 3. What biotic and abiotic features should you consider?

Math Skills

Math Practice

Use Proportions

21 At its highest salinity, the water in Utah's Great Salt Lake contained about 14.5 g of salt in 50 g of lake water. What was the salinity of the lake?

22 The seawater in Puget Sound off the coast of Oregon has a salinity of about 24 PPT. What weight of salt is there in 1,000 g of seawater?

Standardized Test Practice

Record your answers on the answer sheet provided by your teacher or on a sheet of paper.

Multiple Choice

1 Which aquatic ecosystem contains a mixture of freshwater and salt water?

- **A** coral reef
- **B** estuary
- **C** pond
- **D** river

Use the diagram below to answer question 2.

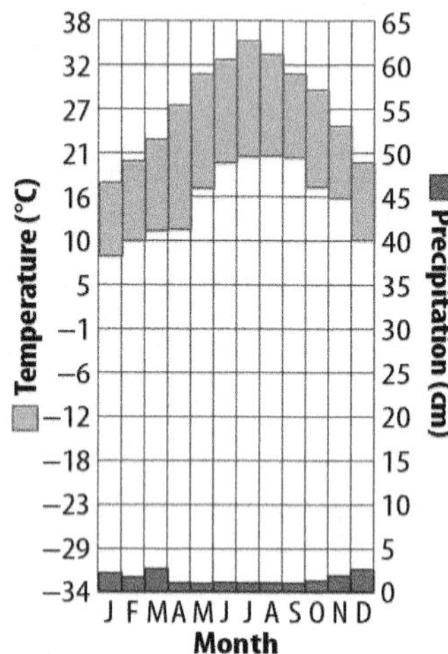

2 The diagram above most likely illustrates the climate of which biome?

- **A** desert
- **B** grassland
- **C** tropical rain forest
- **D** tundra

3 Which occurs during the first stage of ecological succession?

- **A** eutrophication
- **B** settlement
- **C** development of climax community
- **D** growth of pioneer species

4 Which biome has lost more than half its trees to logging activity?

- **A** grassland
- **B** taiga
- **C** temperate deciduous forest
- **D** tropical rain forest

Use the diagram below to answer question 5.

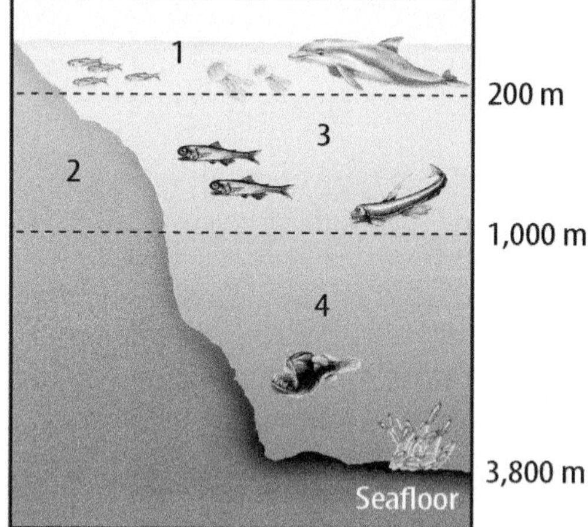

5 In the diagram above, where might you find microscopic photosynthetic organisms?

- **A** 1
- **B** 2
- **C** 3
- **D** 4

6 During aquatic succession, freshwater ponds

- **A** become saltwater ponds.
- **B** fill with soil.
- **C** gain organisms.
- **D** increase in depth.

Use the diagram below to answer question 7.

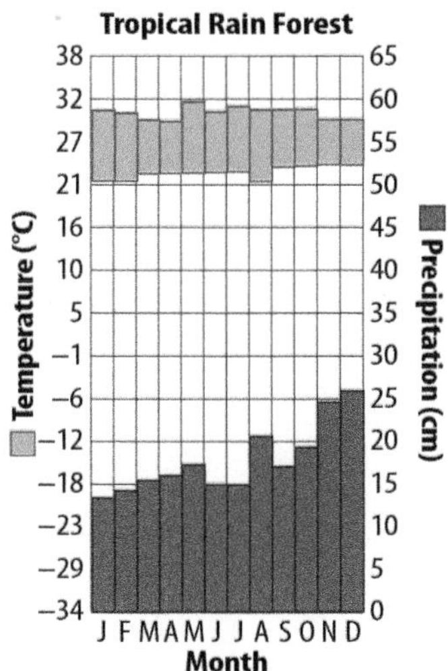

7 Based on the diagram above, which is true of the tropical rain forest biome?

- **A** Precipitation increases as temperatures rise.
- **B** Rainfall is greatest mid-year.
- **C** Temperatures rise at year-end.
- **D** Temperatures vary less than rainfall amounts.

8 Which aquatic biome typically has many varieties of nesting ducks, geese, herons, and egrets?

- **A** coral reefs
- **B** intertidal zones
- **C** lakes
- **D** wetlands

Constructed Response

Use the table below to answer questions 9 and 10.

Land Biome	Climate and Plant Life	Location
Desert		
Grassland		
Taiga		
Temperate deciduous forest		
Temperate rain forest		
Tropical rain forest		
Tundra		

9 Briefly describe the characteristics of Earth's seven land biomes. List one example of each biome, including its location.

10 How does human activity affect each land biome?

Use the table below to answer question 11.

Aquatic Ecosystem	Aquatic Animal
Coastal ocean	
Coral reefs	
Estuaries	
Lakes and ponds	
Open ocean	

11 Complete the table above with the name of an aquatic animal that lives in each of Earth's aquatic ecosystems.

NEED EXTRA HELP?											
If You Missed Question...	1	2	3	4	5	6	7	8	9	10	11
Go to Lesson...	2	1	2	3	2	2	2	2	1	1	2

Student Resources

For Students and Parents/Guardians

These resources are designed to help you achieve success in science. You will find useful information on laboratory safety, math skills, and science skills. In addition, science reference materials are found in the Reference Handbook. You'll find the information you need to learn and sharpen your skills in these resources.

Table of Contents

Scientific Methods

Scientists use an orderly approach called the scientific method to solve problems. This includes organizing and recording data so others can understand them. Scientists use many variations in this method when they solve problems.

Identify a Question

The first step in a scientific investigation or experiment is to identify a question to be answered or a problem to be solved. For example, you might ask which gasoline is the most efficient.

Gather and Organize Information

After you have identified your question, begin gathering and organizing information. There are many ways to gather information, such as researching in a library, interviewing those knowledgeable about the subject, and testing and working in the laboratory and field. Fieldwork is investigations and observations done outside of a laboratory.

Researching Information Before moving in a new direction, it is important to gather the information that already is known about the subject. Start by asking yourself questions to determine exactly what you need to know. Then you will look for the information in various reference sources, like the student is doing in **Figure 1.** Some sources may include textbooks, encyclopedias, government documents, professional journals, science magazines, and the Internet. Always list the sources of your information.

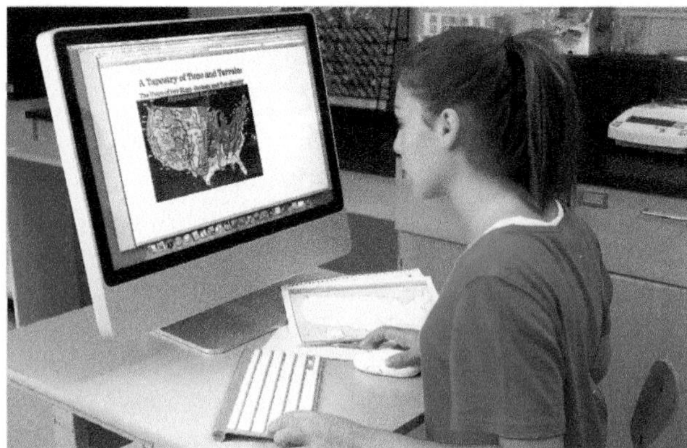

Figure 1 The Internet can be a valuable research tool.

Evaluate Sources of Information Not all sources of information are reliable. You should evaluate all of your sources of information, and use only those you know to be dependable. For example, if you are researching ways to make homes more energy efficient, a site written by the U.S. Department of Energy would be more reliable than a site written by a company that is trying to sell a new type of weatherproofing material. Also, remember that research always is changing. Consult the most current resources available to you. For example, a 1985 resource about saving energy would not reflect the most recent findings.

Sometimes scientists use data that they did not collect themselves, or conclusions drawn by other researchers. This data must be evaluated carefully. Ask questions about how the data were obtained, if the investigation was carried out properly, and if it has been duplicated exactly with the same results. Would you reach the same conclusion from the data? Only when you have confidence in the data can you believe it is true and feel comfortable using it.

Interpret Scientific Illustrations As you research a topic in science, you will see drawings, diagrams, and photographs to help you understand what you read. Some illustrations are included to help you understand an idea that you can't see easily by yourself, like the tiny particles in an atom in **Figure 2.** A drawing helps many people to remember details more easily and provides examples that clarify difficult concepts or give additional information about the topic you are studying. Most illustrations have labels or a caption to identify or to provide more information.

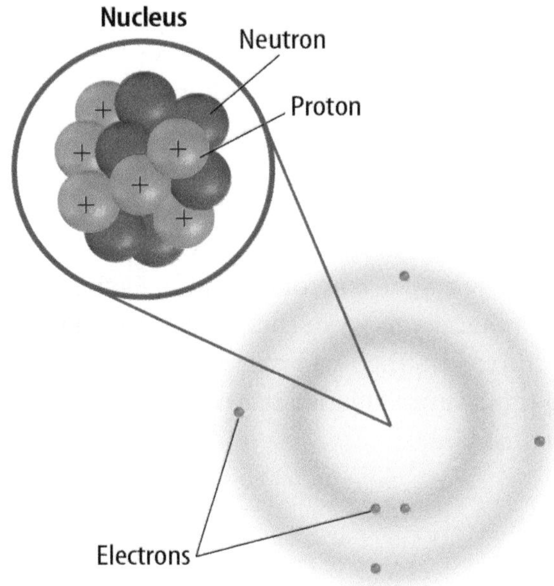

Figure 2 This drawing shows an atom of carbon with its six protons, six neutrons, and six electrons.

Concept Maps One way to organize data is to draw a diagram that shows relationships among ideas (or concepts). A concept map can help make the meanings of ideas and terms more clear, and help you understand and remember what you are studying. Concept maps are useful for breaking large concepts down into smaller parts, making learning easier.

Network Tree A type of concept map that not only shows a relationship, but how the concepts are related is a network tree, shown in **Figure 3.** In a network tree, the words are written in the ovals, while the description of the type of relationship is written across the connecting lines.

When constructing a network tree, write down the topic and all major topics on separate pieces of paper or notecards. Then arrange them in order from general to specific. Branch the related concepts from the major concept and describe the relationship on the connecting line. Continue to more specific concepts until finished.

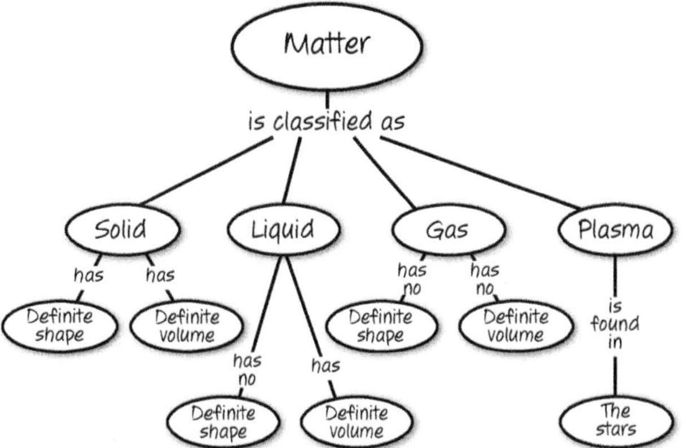

Figure 3 A network tree shows how concepts or objects are related.

Events Chain Another type of concept map is an events chain. Sometimes called a flow chart, it models the order or sequence of items. An events chain can be used to describe a sequence of events, the steps in a procedure, or the stages of a process.

When making an events chain, first find the one event that starts the chain. This event is called the initiating event. Then, find the next event and continue until the outcome is reached, as shown in **Figure 4** on the next page.

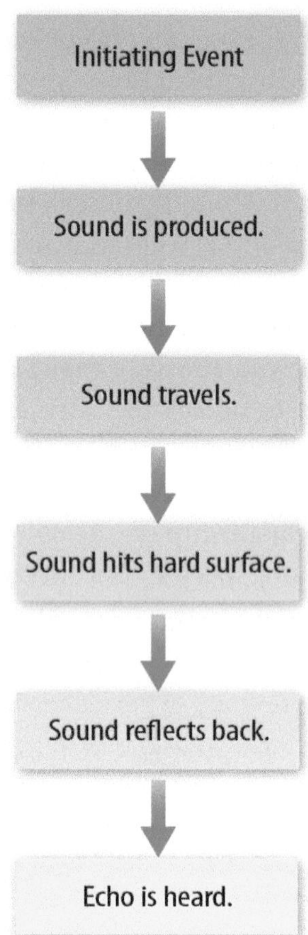

Figure 4 Events-chain concept maps show the order of steps in a process or event. This concept map shows how a sound makes an echo.

Cycle Map A specific type of events chain is a cycle map. It is used when the series of events do not produce a final outcome, but instead relate back to the beginning event, such as in **Figure 5.** Therefore, the cycle repeats itself.

To make a cycle map, first decide what event is the beginning event. This is also called the initiating event. Then list the next events in the order that they occur, with the last event relating back to the initiating event. Words can be written between the events that describe what happens from one event to the next. The number of events in a cycle map can vary, but usually contain three or more events.

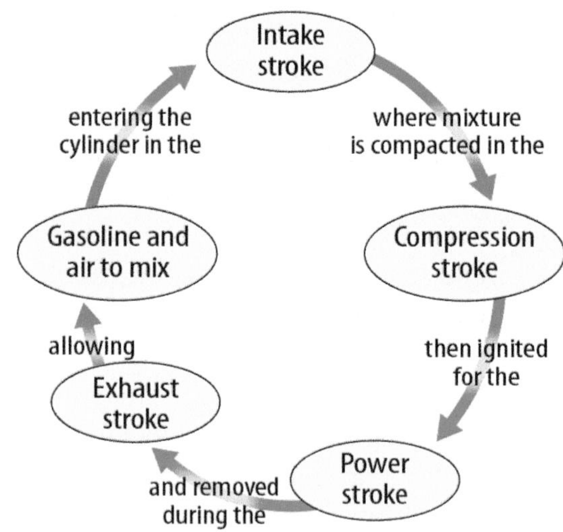

Figure 5 A cycle map shows events that occur in a cycle.

Spider Map A type of concept map that you can use for brainstorming is the spider map. When you have a central idea, you might find that you have a jumble of ideas that relate to it but are not necessarily clearly related to each other. The spider map on sound in **Figure 6** shows that if you write these ideas outside the main concept, then you can begin to separate and group unrelated terms so they become more useful.

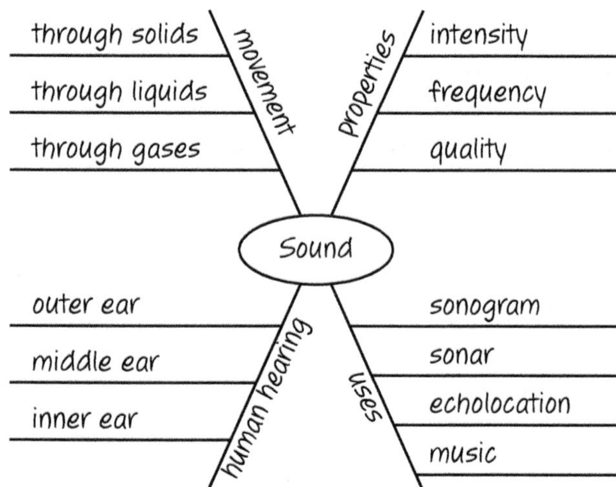

Figure 6 A spider map allows you to list ideas that relate to a central topic but not necessarily to one another.

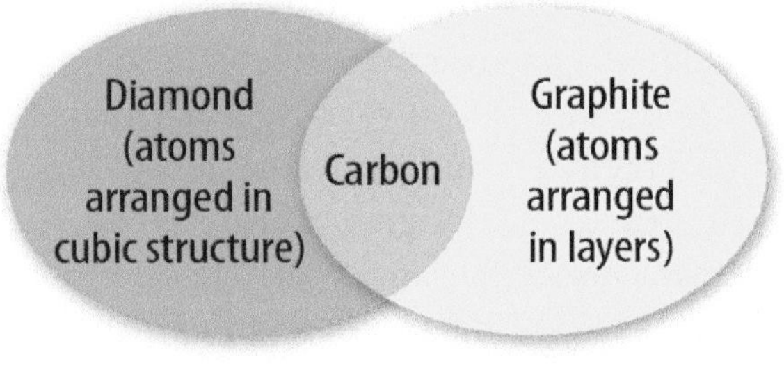

Diamond (atoms arranged in cubic structure) | Carbon | Graphite (atoms arranged in layers)

Figure 7 This Venn diagram compares and contrasts two substances made from carbon.

Venn Diagram To illustrate how two subjects compare and contrast you can use a Venn diagram. You can see the characteristics that the subjects have in common and those that they do not, shown in **Figure 7.**

To create a Venn diagram, draw two overlapping ovals that are big enough to write in. List the characteristics unique to one subject in one oval, and the characteristics of the other subject in the other oval. The characteristics in common are listed in the overlapping section.

Make and Use Tables One way to organize information so it is easier to understand is to use a table. Tables can contain numbers, words, or both.

To make a table, list the items to be compared in the first column and the characteristics to be compared in the first row. The title should clearly indicate the content of the table, and the column or row heads should be clear. Notice that in **Table 1** the units are included.

Table 1 Recyclables Collected During Week

Day of Week	Paper (kg)	Aluminum (kg)	Glass (kg)
Monday	5.0	4.0	12.0
Wednesday	4.0	1.0	10.0
Friday	2.5	2.0	10.0

Make a Model One way to help you better understand the parts of a structure, the way a process works, or to show things too large or small for viewing is to make a model. For example, an atomic model made of a plastic-ball nucleus and chenille stem electron shells can help you visualize how the parts of an atom relate to each other. Other types of models can be devised on a computer or represented by equations.

Form a Hypothesis

A possible explanation based on previous knowledge and observations is called a hypothesis. After researching gasoline types and recalling previous experiences in your family's car, you form a hypothesis—our car runs more efficiently because we use premium gasoline. To be valid, a hypothesis has to be something you can test by using an investigation.

Predict When you apply a hypothesis to a specific situation, you predict something about that situation. A prediction makes a statement in advance, based on prior observation, experience, or scientific reasoning. People use predictions to make everyday decisions. Scientists test predictions by performing investigations. Based on previous observations and experiences, you might form a prediction that cars are more efficient with premium gasoline. The prediction can be tested in an investigation.

Design an Experiment A scientist needs to make many decisions before beginning an investigation. Some of these include: how to carry out the investigation, what steps to follow, how to record the data, and how the investigation will answer the question. It also is important to address any safety concerns.

Test the Hypothesis

Now that you have formed your hypothesis, you need to test it. Using an investigation, you will make observations and collect data, or information. This data might either support or not support your hypothesis. Scientists collect and organize data as numbers and descriptions.

Follow a Procedure In order to know what materials to use, as well as how and in what order to use them, you must follow a procedure. **Figure 8** shows a procedure you might follow to test your hypothesis.

Procedure

Step 1	Use regular gasoline for two weeks.
Step 2	Record the number of kilometers between fill-ups and the amount of gasoline used.
Step 3	Switch to premium gasoline for two weeks.
Step 4	Record the number of kilometers between fill-ups and the amount of gasoline used.

Figure 8 A procedure tells you what to do step-by-step.

Identify and Manipulate Variables and Controls In any experiment, it is important to keep everything the same except for the item you are testing. The one factor you change is called the independent variable. The change that results is the dependent variable. Make sure you have only one independent variable, to assure yourself of the cause of the changes you observe in the dependent variable. For example, in your gasoline experiment the type of fuel is the independent variable. The dependent variable is the efficiency.

Many experiments also have a control—an individual instance or experimental subject for which the independent variable is not changed. You can then compare the test results to the control results. To design a control you must have two cars of the same type. The control car uses regular gasoline for four weeks. After you are done with the test, you can compare the experimental results to the control results.

Collect Data

Whether you are carrying out an investigation or a short observational experiment, you will collect data, as shown in **Figure 9.** Scientists collect data as numbers and descriptions and organize them in specific ways.

Observe Scientists observe items and events, then record what they see. When they use only words to describe an observation, it is called qualitative data. Scientists' observations also can describe how much there is of something. These observations use numbers, as well as words, in the description and are called quantitative data. For example, if a sample of the element gold is described as being "shiny and very dense" the data are qualitative. Quantitative data on this sample of gold might include "a mass of 30 g and a density of 19.3 g/cm^3."

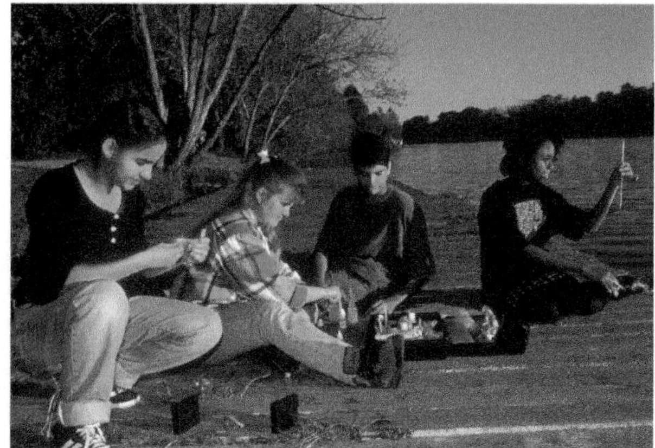

Figure 9 Collecting data is one way to gather information directly.

Figure 10 Record data neatly and clearly so it is easy to understand.

When you make observations, you should examine the entire object or situation first, and then look carefully for details. It is important to record observations accurately and completely. Always record your notes immediately as you make them, so you do not miss details or make a mistake when recording results from memory. Never put unidentified observations on scraps of paper. Instead they should be recorded in a notebook, like the one in **Figure 10.** Write your data neatly so you can easily read it later. At each point in the experiment, record your observations and label them. That way, you will not have to determine what the figures mean when you look at your notes later. Set up any tables that you will need to use ahead of time, so you can record any observations right away. Remember to avoid bias when collecting data by not including personal thoughts when you record observations. Record only what you observe.

Estimate Scientific work also involves estimating. To estimate is to make a judgment about the size or the number of something without measuring or counting. This is important when the number or size of an object or population is too large or too difficult to accurately count or measure.

Sample Scientists may use a sample or a portion of the total number as a type of estimation. To sample is to take a small, representative portion of the objects or organisms of a population for research. By making careful observations or manipulating variables within that portion of the group, information is discovered and conclusions are drawn that might apply to the whole population. A poorly chosen sample can be unrepresentative of the whole. If you were trying to determine the rainfall in an area, it would not be best to take a rainfall sample from under a tree.

Measure You use measurements every day. Scientists also take measurements when collecting data. When taking measurements, it is important to know how to use measuring tools properly. Accuracy also is important.

Length The SI unit for length is the meter (m). Smaller measurements might be measured in centimeters or millimeters.

Length is measured using a metric ruler or meterstick. When using a metric ruler, line up the 0-cm mark with the end of the object being measured and read the number of the unit where the object ends. Look at the metric ruler shown in **Figure 11.** The centimeter lines are the long, numbered lines, and the shorter lines are millimeter lines. In this instance, the length would be 4.50 cm.

Figure 11 This metric ruler has centimeter and millimeter divisions.

Mass The SI unit for mass is the kilogram (kg). Scientists can measure mass using units formed by adding metric prefixes to the unit gram (g), such as milligram (mg). To measure mass, you might use a triple-beam balance similar to the one shown in **Figure 12.** The balance has a pan on one side and a set of beams on the other side. Each beam has a rider that slides on the beam.

When using a triple-beam balance, place an object on the pan. Slide the largest rider along its beam until the pointer drops below zero. Then move it back one notch. Repeat the process for each rider proceeding from the larger to smaller until the pointer swings an equal distance above and below the zero point. Sum the masses on each beam to find the mass of the object. Move all riders back to zero when finished.

Instead of putting materials directly on the balance, scientists often take a tare of a container. A tare is the mass of a container into which objects or substances are placed for measuring their masses. To find the mass of objects or substances, find the mass of a clean container. Remove the container from the pan, and place the object or substances in the container. Find the mass of the container with the materials in it. Subtract the mass of the empty container from the mass of the filled container to find the mass of the materials you are using.

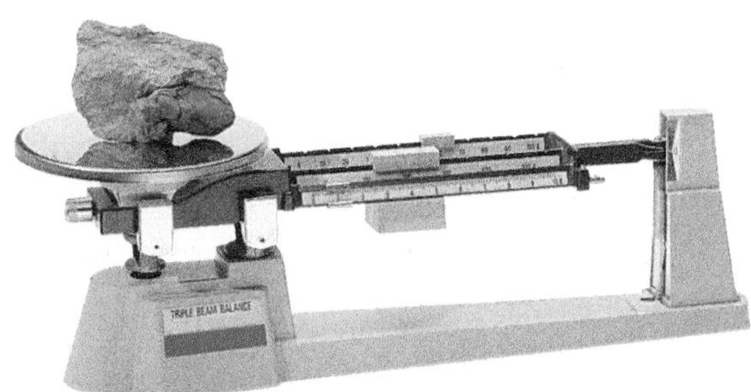

Figure 12 A triple-beam balance is used to determine the mass of an object.

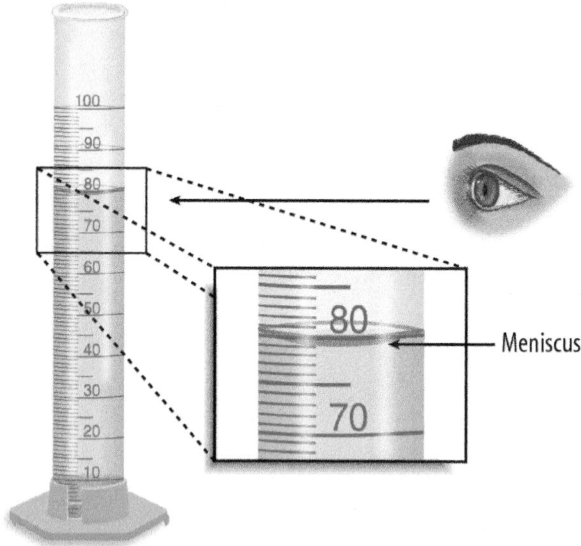

Figure 13 Graduated cylinders measure liquid volume.

Liquid Volume The SI unit for measuring liquids is the liter (l). When a smaller unit is needed, scientists might use a milliliter. Because a milliliter takes up the volume of a cube measuring 1 cm on each side it also can be called a cubic centimeter ($cm^3 = cm \times cm \times cm$).

You can use beakers and graduated cylinders to measure liquid volume. A graduated cylinder, shown in **Figure 13,** is marked from bottom to top in milliliters. In lab, you might use a 10-mL graduated cylinder or a 100-mL graduated cylinder. When measuring liquids, notice that the liquid has a curved surface. Look at the surface at eye level, and measure the bottom of the curve. This is called the meniscus. The graduated cylinder in **Figure 13** contains 79.0 mL, or 79.0 cm^3, of a liquid.

Temperature Scientists often measure temperature using the Celsius scale. Pure water has a freezing point of 0°C and boiling point of 100°C. The unit of measurement is degrees Celsius. Two other scales often used are the Fahrenheit and Kelvin scales.

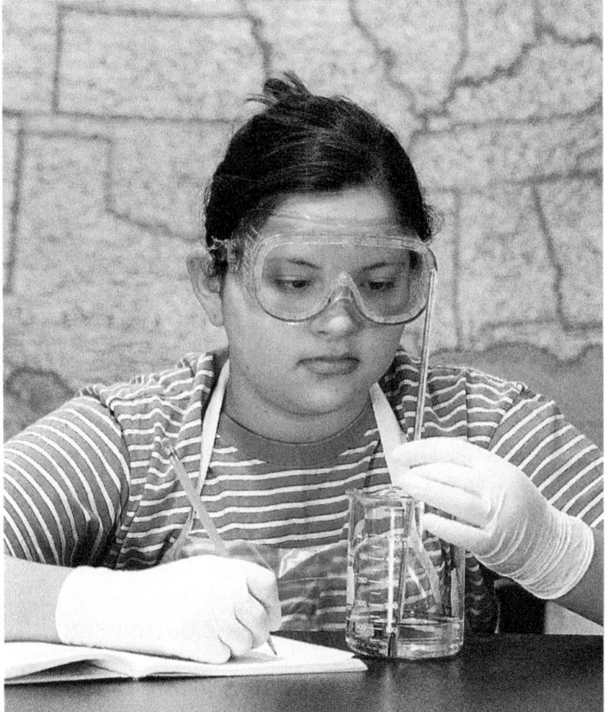

Figure 14 A thermometer measures the temperature of an object.

Scientists use a thermometer to measure temperature. Most thermometers in a laboratory are glass tubes with a bulb at the bottom end containing a liquid such as colored alcohol. The liquid rises or falls with a change in temperature. To read a glass thermometer like the thermometer in **Figure 14,** rotate it slowly until a red line appears. Read the temperature where the red line ends.

Form Operational Definitions An operational definition defines an object by how it functions, works, or behaves. For example, when you are playing hide and seek and a tree is home base, you have created an operational definition for a tree.

Objects can have more than one operational definition. For example, a ruler can be defined as a tool that measures the length of an object (how it is used). It can also be a tool with a series of marks used as a standard when measuring (how it works).

Analyze the Data

To determine the meaning of your observations and investigation results, you will need to look for patterns in the data. Then you must think critically to determine what the data mean. Scientists use several approaches when they analyze the data they have collected and recorded. Each approach is useful for identifying specific patterns.

Interpret Data The word *interpret* means "to explain the meaning of something." When analyzing data from an experiment, try to find out what the data show. Identify the control group and the test group to see whether changes in the independent variable have had an effect. Look for differences in the dependent variable between the control and test groups.

Classify Sorting objects or events into groups based on common features is called classifying. When classifying, first observe the objects or events to be classified. Then select one feature that is shared by some members in the group, but not by all. Place those members that share that feature in a subgroup. You can classify members into smaller and smaller subgroups based on characteristics. Remember that when you classify, you are grouping objects or events for a purpose. Keep your purpose in mind as you select the features to form groups and subgroups.

Compare and Contrast Observations can be analyzed by noting the similarities and differences between two or more objects or events that you observe. When you look at objects or events to see how they are similar, you are comparing them. Contrasting is looking for differences in objects or events.

Recognize Cause and Effect A cause is a reason for an action or condition. The effect is that action or condition. When two events happen together, it is not necessarily true that one event caused the other. Scientists must design a controlled investigation to recognize the exact cause and effect.

Draw Conclusions

When scientists have analyzed the data they collected, they proceed to draw conclusions about the data. These conclusions are sometimes stated in words similar to the hypothesis that you formed earlier. They may confirm a hypothesis, or lead you to a new hypothesis.

Infer Scientists often make inferences based on their observations. An inference is an attempt to explain observations or to indicate a cause. An inference is not a fact, but a logical conclusion that needs further investigation. For example, you may infer that a fire has caused smoke. Until you investigate, however, you do not know for sure.

Apply When you draw a conclusion, you must apply those conclusions to determine whether the data supports the hypothesis. If your data do not support your hypothesis, it does not mean that the hypothesis is wrong. It means only that the result of the investigation did not support the hypothesis. Maybe the experiment needs to be redesigned, or some of the initial observations on which the hypothesis was based were incomplete or biased. Perhaps more observation or research is needed to refine your hypothesis. A successful investigation does not always come out the way you originally predicted.

Avoid Bias Sometimes a scientific investigation involves making judgments. When you make a judgment, you form an opinion. It is important to be honest and not to allow any expectations of results to bias your judgments. This is important throughout the entire investigation, from researching to collecting data to drawing conclusions.

Communicate

The communication of ideas is an important part of the work of scientists. A discovery that is not reported will not advance the scientific community's understanding or knowledge. Communication among scientists also is important as a way of improving their investigations.

Scientists communicate in many ways, from writing articles in journals and magazines that explain their investigations and experiments, to announcing important discoveries on television and radio. Scientists also share ideas with colleagues on the Internet or present them as lectures, like the student is doing in **Figure 15.**

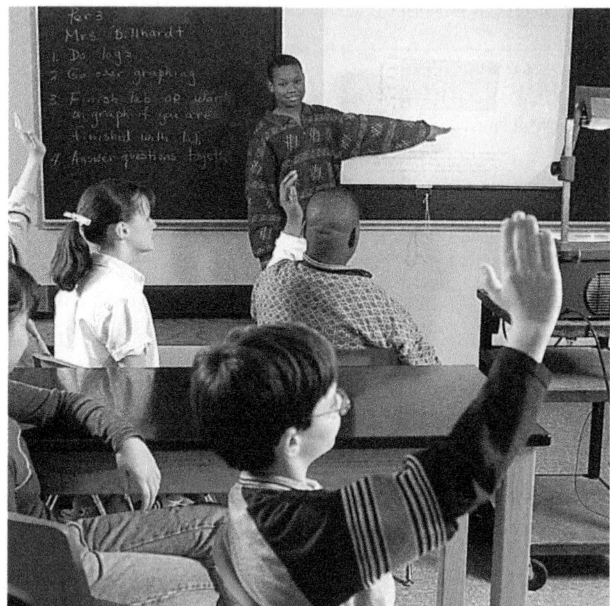

Figure 15 A student communicates to his peers about his investigation.

These safety symbols are used in laboratory and field investigations in this book to indicate possible hazards. Learn the meaning of each symbol and refer to this page often. *Remember to wash your hands thoroughly after completing lab procedures.*

PROTECTIVE EQUIPMENT

Do not begin any lab without the proper protection equipment.

GOGGLES 	Proper eye protection must be worn when performing or observing science activities that involve items or conditions as listed below.
APRON 	Wear an approved apron when using substances that could stain, wet, or destroy cloth.
SOAP 	Wash hands with soap and water before removing goggles and after all lab activities.
GLOVES 	Wear gloves when working with biological materials, chemicals, animals, or materials that can stain or irritate hands.

LABORATORY HAZARDS

Symbols	Potential Hazards	Precaution	Response
DISPOSAL	contamination of classroom or environment due to improper disposal of materials such as chemicals and live specimens	• DO NOT dispose of hazardous materials in the sink or trash can. • Dispose of wastes as directed by your teacher.	• If hazardous materials are disposed of improperly, notify your teacher immediately.
EXTREME TEMPERATURE	skin burns due to extremely hot or cold materials such as hot glass, liquids, or metals; liquid nitrogen; dry ice	• Use proper protective equipment, such as hot mitts and/or tongs, when handling objects with extreme temperatures.	• If injury occurs, notify your teacher immediately.
SHARP OBJECTS	punctures or cuts from sharp objects such as razor blades, pins, scalpels, and broken glass	• Handle glassware carefully to avoid breakage. • Walk with sharp objects pointed downward, away from you and others.	• If broken glass or injury occurs, notify your teacher immediately.
ELECTRICAL	electric shock or skin burn due to improper grounding, short circuits, liquid spills, or exposed wires	• Check condition of wires and apparatus for fraying or uninsulated wires, and broken or cracked equipment. • Use only GFCI-protected outlets	• DO NOT attempt to fix electrical problems. Notify your teacher immediately.
CHEMICAL	skin irritation or burns, breathing difficulty, and/or poisoning due to touching, swallowing, or inhalation of chemicals such as acids, bases, bleach, metal compounds, iodine, poinsettias, pollen, ammonia, acetone, nail polish remover, heated chemicals, mothballs, and any other chemicals labeled or known to be dangerous	• Wear proper protective equipment such as goggles, apron, and gloves when using chemicals. • Ensure proper room ventilation or use a fume hood when using materials that produce fumes. • NEVER smell fumes directly. • NEVER taste or eat any material in the laboratory.	• If contact occurs, immediately flush affected area with water and notify your teacher. • If a spill occurs, leave the area immediately and notify your teacher.
FLAMMABLE	unexpected fire due to liquids or gases that ignite easily such as rubbing alcohol	• Avoid open flames, sparks, or heat when flammable liquids are present.	• If a fire occurs, leave the area immediately and notify your teacher.
OPEN FLAME	burns or fire due to open flame from matches, Bunsen burners, or burning materials	• Tie back loose hair and clothing. • Keep flame away from all materials. • Follow teacher instructions when lighting and extinguishing flames. • Use proper protection, such as hot mitts or tongs, when handling hot objects.	• If a fire occurs, leave the area immediately and notify your teacher.
ANIMAL SAFETY	injury to or from laboratory animals	• Wear proper protective equipment such as gloves, apron, and goggles when working with animals. • Wash hands after handling animals.	• If injury occurs, notify your teacher immediately.
BIOLOGICAL	infection or adverse reaction due to contact with organisms such as bacteria, fungi, and biological materials such as blood, animal or plant materials	• Wear proper protective equipment such as gloves, goggles, and apron when working with biological materials. • Avoid skin contact with an organism or any part of the organism. • Wash hands after handling organisms.	• If contact occurs, wash the affected area and notify your teacher immediately.
FUME	breathing difficulties from inhalation of fumes from substances such as ammonia, acetone, nail polish remover, heated chemicals, and mothballs	• Wear goggles, apron, and gloves. • Ensure proper room ventilation or use a fume hood when using substances that produce fumes. • NEVER smell fumes directly.	• If a spill occurs, leave area and notify your teacher immediately.
IRRITANT	irritation of skin, mucous membranes, or respiratory tract due to materials such as acids, bases, bleach, pollen, mothballs, steel wool, and potassium permanganate	• Wear goggles, apron, and gloves. • Wear a dust mask to protect against fine particles.	• If skin contact occurs, immediately flush the affected area with water and notify your teacher.
RADIOACTIVE	excessive exposure from alpha, beta, and gamma particles	• Remove gloves and wash hands with soap and water before removing remainder of protective equipment.	• If cracks or holes are found in the container, notify your teacher immediately.

Safety in the Science Laboratory

Introduction to Science Safety

The science laboratory is a safe place to work if you follow standard safety procedures. Being responsible for your own safety helps to make the entire laboratory a safer place for everyone. When performing any lab, read and apply the caution statements and safety symbol listed at the beginning of the lab.

General Safety Rules

1. Complete the *Lab Safety Form* or other safety contract BEFORE starting any science lab.
2. Study the procedure. Ask your teacher any questions. Be sure you understand safety symbols shown on the page.
3. Notify your teacher about allergies or other health conditions that can affect your participation in a lab.
4. Learn and follow use and safety procedures for your equipment. If unsure, ask your teacher.
5. Never eat, drink, chew gum, apply cosmetics, or do any personal grooming in the lab. Never use lab glassware as food or drink containers. Keep your hands away from your face and mouth.
6. Know the location and proper use of the safety shower, eye wash, fire blanket, and fire alarm.

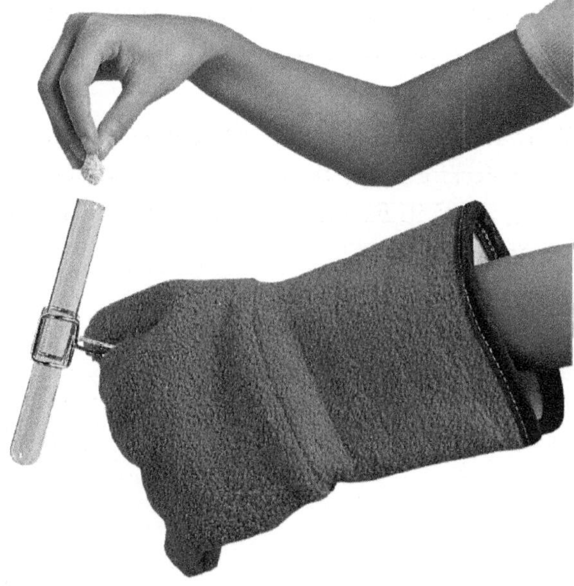

Prevent Accidents

1. Use the safety equipment provided to you. Goggles and a safety apron should be worn during investigations.
2. Do NOT use hair spray, mousse, or other flammable hair products. Tie back long hair and tie down loose clothing.
3. Do NOT wear sandals or other open-toed shoes in the lab.
4. Remove jewelry on hands and wrists. Loose jewelry, such as chains and long necklaces, should be removed to prevent them from getting caught in equipment.
5. Do not taste any substances or draw any material into a tube with your mouth.
6. Proper behavior is expected in the lab. Practical jokes and fooling around can lead to accidents and injury.
7. Keep your work area uncluttered.

Laboratory Work

1. Collect and carry all equipment and materials to your work area before beginning a lab.
2. Remain in your own work area unless given permission by your teacher to leave it.

3. Always slant test tubes away from yourself and others when heating them, adding substances to them, or rinsing them.
4. If instructed to smell a substance in a container, hold the container a short distance away and fan vapors toward your nose.
5. Do NOT substitute other chemicals/substances for those in the materials list unless instructed to do so by your teacher.
6. Do NOT take any materials or chemicals outside of the laboratory.
7. Stay out of storage areas unless instructed to be there and supervised by your teacher.

Laboratory Cleanup

1. Turn off all burners, water, and gas, and disconnect all electrical devices.
2. Clean all pieces of equipment and return all materials to their proper places.
3. Dispose of chemicals and other materials as directed by your teacher. Place broken glass and solid substances in the proper containers. Never discard materials in the sink.
4. Clean your work area.
5. Wash your hands with soap and water thoroughly BEFORE removing your goggles.

Emergencies

1. Report any fire, electrical shock, glassware breakage, spill, or injury, no matter how small, to your teacher immediately. Follow his or her instructions.
2. If your clothing should catch fire, STOP, DROP, and ROLL. If possible, smother it with the fire blanket or get under a safety shower. NEVER RUN.
3. If a fire should occur, turn off all gas and leave the room according to established procedures.
4. In most instances, your teacher will clean up spills. Do NOT attempt to clean up spills unless you are given permission and instructions to do so.
5. If chemicals come into contact with your eyes or skin, notify your teacher immediately. Use the eyewash, or flush your skin or eyes with large quantities of water.
6. The fire extinguisher and first-aid kit should only be used by your teacher unless it is an extreme emergency and you have been given permission.
7. If someone is injured or becomes ill, only a professional medical provider or someone certified in first aid should perform first-aid procedures.

Math Review

Use Fractions

A fraction compares a part to a whole. In the fraction $\frac{2}{3}$, the 2 represents the part and is the numerator. The 3 represents the whole and is the denominator.

Reduce Fractions To reduce a fraction, you must find the largest factor that is common to both the numerator and the denominator, the greatest common factor (GCF). Divide both numbers by the GCF. The fraction has then been reduced, or it is in its simplest form.

Example

Twelve of the 20 chemicals in the science lab are in powder form. What fraction of the chemicals used in the lab are in powder form?

Step 1 Write the fraction.

$\frac{\text{part}}{\text{whole}} = \frac{12}{20}$

Step 2 To find the GCF of the numerator and denominator, list all of the factors of each number.

Factors of 12: 1, 2, 3, 4, 6, 12 (the numbers that divide evenly into 12)

Factors of 20: 1, 2, 4, 5, 10, 20 (the numbers that divide evenly into 20)

Step 3 List the common factors.

1, 2, 4

Step 4 Choose the greatest factor in the list. The GCF of 12 and 20 is 4.

Step 5 Divide the numerator and denominator by the GCF.

$\frac{12 \div 4}{20 \div 4} = \frac{3}{5}$

In the lab, $\frac{3}{5}$ of the chemicals are in powder form.

Practice Problem At an amusement park, 66 of 90 rides have a height restriction. What fraction of the rides, in its simplest form, has a height restriction?

Add and Subtract Fractions with Like Denominators To add or subtract fractions with the same denominator, add or subtract the numerators and write the sum or difference over the denominator. After finding the sum or difference, find the simplest form for your fraction.

Example 1

In the forest outside your house, $\frac{1}{8}$ of the animals are rabbits, $\frac{3}{8}$ are squirrels, and the remainder are birds and insects. How many are mammals?

Step 1 Add the numerators.

$\frac{1}{8} + \frac{3}{8} = \frac{(1 + 3)}{8} = \frac{4}{8}$

Step 2 Find the GCF.

$\frac{4}{8}$ (GCF, 4)

Step 3 Divide the numerator and denominator by the GCF.

$\frac{4 \div 4}{8 \div 4} = \frac{1}{2}$

$\frac{1}{2}$ of the animals are mammals.

Example 2

If $\frac{7}{16}$ of the Earth is covered by freshwater, and $\frac{1}{16}$ of that is in glaciers, how much freshwater is not frozen?

Step 1 Subtract the numerators.

$\frac{7}{16} - \frac{1}{16} = \frac{(7 - 1)}{16} = \frac{6}{16}$

Step 2 Find the GCF.

$\frac{6}{16}$ (GCF, 2)

Step 3 Divide the numerator and denominator by the GCF.

$\frac{6 \div 2}{16 \div 2} = \frac{3}{8}$

$\frac{3}{8}$ of the freshwater is not frozen.

Practice Problem A bicycle rider is riding at a rate of 15 km/h for $\frac{4}{9}$ of his ride, 10 km/h for $\frac{2}{9}$ of his ride, and 8 km/h for the remainder of the ride. How much of his ride is he riding at a rate greater than 8 km/h?

Add and Subtract Fractions with Unlike Denominators To add or subtract fractions with unlike denominators, first find the least common denominator (LCD). This is the smallest number that is a common multiple of both denominators. Rename each fraction with the LCD, and then add or subtract. Find the simplest form if necessary.

Example 1

A chemist makes a paste that is $\frac{1}{2}$ table salt (NaCl), $\frac{1}{3}$ sugar ($C_6H_{12}O_6$), and the remainder is water (H_2O). How much of the paste is a solid?

Step 1 Find the LCD of the fractions.

$\frac{1}{2} + \frac{1}{3}$ (LCD, 6)

Step 2 Rename each numerator and each denominator with the LCD.

Step 3 Add the numerators.

$\frac{3}{6} + \frac{2}{6} = \frac{(3+2)}{6} = \frac{5}{6}$

$\frac{5}{6}$ of the paste is a solid.

Example 2

The average precipitation in Grand Junction, CO, is $\frac{7}{10}$ inch in November, and $\frac{3}{5}$ inch in December. What is the total average precipitation?

Step 1 Find the LCD of the fractions.

$\frac{7}{10} + \frac{3}{5}$ (LCD, 10)

Step 2 Rename each numerator and each denominator with the LCD.

Step 3 Add the numerators.

$\frac{7}{10} + \frac{6}{10} = \frac{(7+6)}{10} = \frac{13}{10}$

$\frac{13}{10}$ inches total precipitation, or $1\frac{3}{10}$ inches.

Practice Problem On an electric bill, about $\frac{1}{8}$ of the energy is from solar energy and about $\frac{1}{10}$ is from wind power. How much of the total bill is from solar energy and wind power combined?

Example 3

In your body, $\frac{7}{10}$ of your muscle contractions are involuntary (cardiac and smooth muscle tissue). Smooth muscle makes $\frac{3}{15}$ of your muscle contractions. How many of your muscle contractions are made by cardiac muscle?

Step 1 Find the LCD of the fractions.

$\frac{7}{10} - \frac{3}{15}$ (LCD, 30)

Step 2 Rename each numerator and each denominator with the LCD.

$\frac{7 \times 3}{10 \times 3} = \frac{21}{30}$

$\frac{3 \times 2}{15 \times 2} = \frac{6}{30}$

Step 3 Subtract the numerators.

$\frac{21}{30} - \frac{6}{30} = \frac{(21-6)}{30} = \frac{15}{30}$

Step 4 Find the GCF.

$\frac{15}{30}$ (GCF, 15)

$\frac{1}{2}$

$\frac{1}{2}$ of all muscle contractions are cardiac muscle.

Example 4

Tony wants to make cookies that call for $\frac{3}{4}$ of a cup of flour, but he only has $\frac{1}{3}$ of a cup. How much more flour does he need?

Step 1 Find the LCD of the fractions.

$\frac{3}{4} - \frac{1}{3}$ (LCD, 12)

Step 2 Rename each numerator and each denominator with the LCD.

$\frac{3 \times 3}{4 \times 3} = \frac{9}{12}$

$\frac{1 \times 4}{3 \times 4} = \frac{4}{12}$

Step 3 Subtract the numerators.

$\frac{9}{12} - \frac{4}{12} = \frac{(9-4)}{12} = \frac{5}{12}$

$\frac{5}{12}$ of a cup of flour

Practice Problem Using the information provided to you in Example 3 above, determine how many muscle contractions are voluntary (skeletal muscle).

Multiply Fractions

To multiply with fractions, multiply the numerators and multiply the denominators. Find the simplest form if necessary.

Example

Multiply $\frac{3}{5}$ by $\frac{1}{3}$.

Step 1 Multiply the numerators and denominators.

$\frac{3}{5} \times \frac{1}{3} = \frac{(3 \times 1)}{(5 \times 3)} \frac{3}{15}$

Step 2 Find the GCF.

$\frac{3}{15}$ (GCF, 3)

Step 3 Divide the numerator and denominator by the GCF.

$\frac{3 \div 3}{15 \div 3} = \frac{1}{5}$

$\frac{3}{5}$ multiplied by $\frac{1}{3}$ is $\frac{1}{5}$.

Practice Problem Multiply $\frac{3}{14}$ by $\frac{5}{16}$.

Find a Reciprocal

Two numbers whose product is 1 are called multiplicative inverses, or reciprocals.

Example

Find the reciprocal of $\frac{3}{8}$.

Step 1 Inverse the fraction by putting the denominator on top and the numerator on the bottom.

$\frac{8}{3}$

The reciprocal of $\frac{3}{8}$ is $\frac{8}{3}$.

Practice Problem Find the reciprocal of $\frac{4}{9}$.

Divide Fractions

To divide one fraction by another fraction, multiply the dividend by the reciprocal of the divisor. Find the simplest form if necessary.

Example 1

Divide $\frac{1}{9}$ by $\frac{1}{3}$.

Step 1 Find the reciprocal of the divisor.

The reciprocal of $\frac{1}{3}$ is $\frac{3}{1}$.

Step 2 Multiply the dividend by the reciprocal of the divisor.

$\frac{\frac{1}{9}}{\frac{1}{3}} = \frac{1}{9} \times \frac{3}{1} = \frac{(1 \times 3)}{(9 \times 1)} = \frac{3}{9}$

Step 3 Find the GCF.

$\frac{3}{9}$ (GCF, 3)

Step 4 Divide the numerator and denominator by the GCF.

$\frac{3 \div 3}{9 \div 3} = \frac{1}{3}$

$\frac{1}{9}$ divided by $\frac{1}{3}$ is $\frac{1}{3}$.

Example 2

Divide $\frac{3}{5}$ by $\frac{1}{4}$.

Step 1 Find the reciprocal of the divisor.

The reciprocal of $\frac{1}{4}$ is $\frac{4}{1}$.

Step 2 Multiply the dividend by the reciprocal of the divisor.

$\frac{\frac{3}{5}}{\frac{1}{4}} = \frac{3}{5} \times \frac{4}{1} = \frac{(3 \times 4)}{(5 \times 1)} = \frac{12}{5}$

$\frac{3}{5}$ divided by $\frac{1}{4}$ is $\frac{12}{5}$ or $2\frac{2}{5}$.

Practice Problem Divide $\frac{3}{11}$ by $\frac{7}{10}$.

Use Ratios

When you compare two numbers by division, you are using a ratio. Ratios can be written 3 to 5, 3:5, or $\frac{3}{5}$. Ratios, like fractions, also can be written in simplest form.

Ratios can represent one type of probability, called odds. This is a ratio that compares the number of ways a certain outcome occurs to the number of possible outcomes. For example, if you flip a coin 100 times, what are the odds that it will come up heads? There are two possible outcomes, heads or tails, so the odds of coming up heads are 50:100. Another way to say this is that 50 out of 100 times the coin will come up heads. In its simplest form, the ratio is 1:2.

Example 1

A chemical solution contains 40 g of salt and 64 g of baking soda. What is the ratio of salt to baking soda as a fraction in simplest form?

Step 1 Write the ratio as a fraction.

$$\frac{\text{salt}}{\text{baking soda}} = \frac{40}{64}$$

Step 2 Express the fraction in simplest form. The GCF of 40 and 64 is 8.

$$\frac{40}{64} = \frac{40 \div 8}{64 \div 8} = \frac{5}{8}$$

The ratio of salt to baking soda in the chemical solution is 5:8.

Example 2

Sean rolls a 6-sided die 6 times. What are the odds that the side with a 3 will show?

Step 1 Write the ratio as a fraction.

$$\frac{\text{number of sides with a 3}}{\text{number of possible sides}} = \frac{1}{6}$$

Step 2 Multiply by the number of attempts.

$\frac{1}{6} \times 6$ attempts $= \frac{6}{6}$ attempts $= 1$ attempt

1 attempt out of 6 will show a 3.

Practice Problem Two metal rods measure 100 cm and 144 cm in length. What is the ratio of their lengths in simplest form?

Use Decimals

A fraction with a denominator that is a power of ten can be written as a decimal. For example, 0.27 means $\frac{27}{100}$. The decimal point separates the ones place from the tenths place.

Any fraction can be written as a decimal using division. For example, the fraction $\frac{5}{8}$ can be written as a decimal by dividing 5 by 8. Written as a decimal, it is 0.625.

Add or Subtract Decimals When adding and subtracting decimals, line up the decimal points before carrying out the operation.

Example 1

Find the sum of 47.68 and 7.80.

Step 1 Line up the decimal places when you write the numbers.

```
 47.68
+ 7.80
```

Step 2 Add the decimals.

```
  1 1
 47.68
+ 7.80
 55.48
```

The sum of 47.68 and 7.80 is 55.48.

Example 2

Find the difference of 42.17 and 15.85.

Step 1 Line up the decimal places when you write the number.

```
 42.17
-15.85
```

Step 2 Subtract the decimals.

```
 3 11
 42.17
-15.85
 26.32
```

The difference of 42.17 and 15.85 is 26.32.

Practice Problem Find the sum of 1.245 and 3.842.

Multiply Decimals To multiply decimals, multiply the numbers like numbers without decimal points. Count the decimal places in each factor. The product will have the same number of decimal places as the sum of the decimal places in the factors.

Example

Multiply 2.4 by 5.9.

Step 1 Multiply the factors like two whole numbers.

$24 \times 59 = 1416$

Step 2 Find the sum of the number of decimal places in the factors. Each factor has one decimal place, for a sum of two decimal places.

Step 3 The product will have two decimal places.

14.16

The product of 2.4 and 5.9 is 14.16.

Practice Problem Multiply 4.6 by 2.2.

Divide Decimals When dividing decimals, change the divisor to a whole number. To do this, multiply both the divisor and the dividend by the same power of ten. Then place the decimal point in the quotient directly above the decimal point in the dividend. Then divide as you do with whole numbers.

Example

Divide 8.84 by 3.4.

Step 1 Multiply both factors by 10.

$3.4 \times 10 = 34$, $8.84 \times 10 = 88.4$

Step 2 Divide 88.4 by 34.

```
     2.6
 34)88.4
   -68
    204
   -204
      0
```

8.84 divided by 3.4 is 2.6.

Practice Problem Divide 75.6 by 3.6.

Use Proportions

An equation that shows that two ratios are equivalent is a proportion. The ratios $\frac{2}{4}$ and $\frac{5}{10}$ are equivalent, so they can be written as $\frac{2}{4} = \frac{5}{10}$. This equation is a proportion.

When two ratios form a proportion, the cross products are equal. To find the cross products in the proportion $\frac{2}{4} = \frac{5}{10}$, multiply the 2 and the 10, and the 4 and the 5. Therefore $2 \times 10 = 4 \times 5$, or $20 = 20$.

Because you know that both ratios are equal, you can use cross products to find a missing term in a proportion. This is known as solving the proportion.

Example

The heights of a tree and a pole are proportional to the lengths of their shadows. The tree casts a shadow of 24 m when a 6-m pole casts a shadow of 4 m. What is the height of the tree?

Step 1 Write a proportion.

$$\frac{\text{height of tree}}{\text{height of pole}} = \frac{\text{length of tree's shadow}}{\text{length of pole's shadow}}$$

Step 2 Substitute the known values into the proportion. Let h represent the unknown value, the height of the tree.

$\frac{h}{6} \times \frac{24}{4}$

Step 3 Find the cross products.

$h \times 4 = 6 \times 24$

Step 4 Simplify the equation.

$4h = 144$

Step 5 Divide each side by 4.

$\frac{4h}{4} = \frac{144}{4}$

$h = 36$

The height of the tree is 36 m.

Practice Problem The ratios of the weights of two objects on the Moon and on Earth are in proportion. A rock weighing 3 N on the Moon weighs 18 N on Earth. How much would a rock that weighs 5 N on the Moon weigh on Earth?

Use Percentages

The word *percent* means "out of one hundred." It is a ratio that compares a number to 100. Suppose you read that 77 percent of Earth's surface is covered by water. That is the same as reading that the fraction of Earth's surface covered by water is $\frac{77}{100}$. To express a fraction as a percent, first find the equivalent decimal for the fraction. Then, multiply the decimal by 100 and add the percent symbol.

Example 1

Express $\frac{13}{20}$ as a percent.

Step 1 Find the equivalent decimal for the fraction.

$$\begin{array}{r} 0.65 \\ 20\overline{)13.00} \\ \underline{12\,0} \\ 1\,00 \\ \underline{1\,00} \\ 0 \end{array}$$

Step 2 Rewrite the fraction $\frac{13}{20}$ as 0.65.

Step 3 Multiply 0.65 by 100 and add the % symbol.

$0.65 \times 100 = 65 = 65\%$

So, $\frac{13}{20} = 65\%$.

This also can be solved as a proportion.

Example 2

Express $\frac{13}{20}$ as a percent.

Step 1 Write a proportion.

$\frac{13}{20} = \frac{x}{100}$

Step 2 Find the cross products.

$1300 = 20x$

Step 3 Divide each side by 20.

$\frac{1300}{20} = \frac{20x}{20}$

$65 = x = 65\%$

So, $\frac{13}{20} = 65\%$

Practice Problem In one year, 73 of 365 days were rainy in one city. What percent of the days in that city were rainy?

Solve One-Step Equations

A statement that two expressions are equal is an equation. For example, $A = B$ is an equation that states that A is equal to B.

An equation is solved when a variable is replaced with a value that makes both sides of the equation equal. To make both sides equal the inverse operation is used. Addition and subtraction are inverses, and multiplication and division are inverses.

Example 1

Solve the equation $x - 10 = 35$.

Step 1 Find the solution by adding 10 to each side of the equation.

$$x - 10 = 35$$
$$x - 10 + 10 = 35 + 10$$
$$x = 45$$

Step 2 Check the solution.

$$x - 10 = 35$$
$$45 - 10 = 35$$
$$35 = 35$$

Both sides of the equation are equal, so $x = 45$.

Example 2

In the formula $a = bc$, find the value of c if $a = 20$ and $b = 2$.

Step 1 Rearrange the formula so the unknown value is by itself on one side of the equation by dividing both sides by b.

$$a = bc$$
$$\frac{a}{b} = \frac{bc}{b}$$
$$\frac{a}{b} = c$$

Step 2 Replace the variables a and b with the values that are given.

$$\frac{a}{b} = c$$
$$\frac{20}{2} = c$$
$$10 = c$$

Step 3 Check the solution.

$$a = bc$$
$$20 = 2 \times 10$$
$$20 = 20$$

Both sides of the equation are equal, so $c = 10$ is the solution when $a = 20$ and $b = 2$.

Practice Problem In the formula $h = gd$, find the value of d if $g = 12.3$ and $h = 17.4$.

Use Statistics

The branch of mathematics that deals with collecting, analyzing, and presenting data is statistics. In statistics, there are three common ways to summarize data with a single number—the mean, the median, and the mode.

The **mean** of a set of data is the arithmetic average. It is found by adding the numbers in the data set and dividing by the number of items in the set.

The **median** is the middle number in a set of data when the data are arranged in numerical order. If there were an even number of data points, the median would be the mean of the two middle numbers.

The **mode** of a set of data is the number or item that appears most often.

Another number that often is used to describe a set of data is the range. The **range** is the difference between the largest number and the smallest number in a set of data.

Example

The speeds (in m/s) for a race car during five different time trials are 39, 37, 44, 36, and 44.

To find the mean:

Step 1 Find the sum of the numbers.

$39 + 37 + 44 + 36 + 44 = 200$

Step 2 Divide the sum by the number of items, which is 5.

$200 \div 5 = 40$

The mean is 40 m/s.

To find the median:

Step 1 Arrange the measures from least to greatest.

36, 37, 39, 44, 44

Step 2 Determine the middle measure.

36, 37, 39, 44, 44

The median is 39 m/s.

To find the mode:

Step 1 Group the numbers that are the same together.

44, 44, 36, 37, 39

Step 2 Determine the number that occurs most in the set.

44, 44, 36, 37, 39

The mode is 44 m/s.

To find the range:

Step 1 Arrange the measures from greatest to least.

44, 44, 39, 37, 36

Step 2 Determine the greatest and least measures in the set.

44, 44, 39, 37, 36

Step 3 Find the difference between the greatest and least measures.

$44 - 36 = 8$

The range is 8 m/s.

Practice Problem Find the mean, median, mode, and range for the data set 8, 4, 12, 8, 11, 14, 16.

A **frequency table** shows how many times each piece of data occurs, usually in a survey. **Table 1** below shows the results of a student survey on favorite color.

Table 1 Student Color Choice

Color	Tally	Frequency
red	IIII	4
blue	卌	5
black	II	2
green	III	3
purple	卌 II	7
yellow	卌 I	6

Based on the frequency table data, which color is the favorite?

Use Geometry

The branch of mathematics that deals with the measurement, properties, and relationships of points, lines, angles, surfaces, and solids is called geometry.

Perimeter The **perimeter** (P) is the distance around a geometric figure. To find the perimeter of a rectangle, add the length and width and multiply that sum by two, or $2(l + w)$. To find perimeters of irregular figures, add the length of all the sides.

Example 1

Find the perimeter of a rectangle that is 3 m long and 5 m wide.

Step 1 You know that the perimeter is 2 times the sum of the width and length.

$P = 2(3 \text{ m} + 5 \text{ m})$

Step 2 Find the sum of the width and length.

$P = 2(8 \text{ m})$

Step 3 Multiply by 2.

$P = 16 \text{ m}$

The perimeter is 16 m.

Example 2

Find the perimeter of a shape with sides measuring 2 cm, 5 cm, 6 cm, 3 cm.

Step 1 You know that the perimeter is the sum of all the sides.

$P = 2 + 5 + 6 + 3$

Step 2 Find the sum of the sides.

$P = 2 + 5 + 6 + 3$

$P = 16$

The perimeter is 16 cm.

Practice Problem Find the perimeter of a rectangle with a length of 18 m and a width of 7 m.

Practice Problem Find the perimeter of a triangle measuring 1.6 cm by 2.4 cm by 2.4 cm.

Area of a Rectangle The **area** (A) is the number of square units needed to cover a surface. To find the area of a rectangle, multiply the length times the width, or $l \times w$. When finding area, the units also are multiplied. Area is given in square units.

Example

Find the area of a rectangle with a length of 1 cm and a width of 10 cm.

Step 1 You know that the area is the length multiplied by the width.

$A = (1 \text{ cm} \times 10 \text{ cm})$

Step 2 Multiply the length by the width. Also multiply the units.

$A = 10 \text{ cm}^2$

The area is 10 cm^2.

Practice Problem Find the area of a square whose sides measure 4 m.

Area of a Triangle To find the area of a triangle, use the formula:

$A = \frac{1}{2}(\text{base} \times \text{height})$

The base of a triangle can be any of its sides. The height is the perpendicular distance from a base to the opposite endpoint, or vertex.

Example

Find the area of a triangle with a base of 18 m and a height of 7 m.

Step 1 You know that the area is $\frac{1}{2}$ the base times the height.

$A = \frac{1}{2}(18 \text{ m} \times 7 \text{ m})$

Step 2 Multiply $\frac{1}{2}$ by the product of 18 × 7. Multiply the units.

$A = \frac{1}{2}(126 \text{ m}^2)$

$A = 63 \text{ m}^2$

The area is 63 m^2.

Practice Problem Find the area of a triangle with a base of 27 cm and a height of 17 cm.

Circumference of a Circle The **diameter** (d) of a circle is the distance across the circle through its center, and the **radius** (r) is the distance from the center to any point on the circle. The radius is half of the diameter. The distance around the circle is called the **circumference** (C). The formula for finding the circumference is:

$C = 2\pi r$ or $C = \pi d$

The circumference divided by the diameter is always equal to 3.1415926... This nonterminating and nonrepeating number is represented by the Greek letter π (pi). An approximation often used for π is 3.14.

Example 1

Find the circumference of a circle with a radius of 3 m.

Step 1 You know the formula for the circumference is 2 times the radius times π.

$C = 2\pi(3)$

Step 2 Multiply 2 times the radius.

$C = 6\pi$

Step 3 Multiply by π.

$C \approx 19$ m

The circumference is about 19 m.

Example 2

Find the circumference of a circle with a diameter of 24.0 cm.

Step 1 You know the formula for the circumference is the diameter times π.

$C = \pi(24.0)$

Step 2 Multiply the diameter by π.

$C \approx 75.4$ cm

The circumference is about 75.4 cm.

Practice Problem Find the circumference of a circle with a radius of 19 cm.

Area of a Circle The formula for the area of a circle is: $A = \pi r^2$

Example 1

Find the area of a circle with a radius of 4.0 cm.

Step 1 $A = \pi(4.0)^2$

Step 2 Find the square of the radius.

$A = 16\pi$

Step 3 Multiply the square of the radius by π.

$A \approx 50\ \text{cm}^2$

The area of the circle is about 50 cm^2.

Example 2

Find the area of a circle with a radius of 225 m.

Step 1 $A = \pi(225)^2$

Step 2 Find the square of the radius.

$A = 50625\pi$

Step 3 Multiply the square of the radius by π.

$A \approx 159043.1$

The area of the circle is about 159043.1 m^2.

Example 3

Find the area of a circle whose diameter is 20.0 mm.

Step 1 Remember that the radius is half of the diameter.

$A = \pi\left(\frac{20.0}{2}\right)^2$

Step 2 Find the radius.

$A = \pi(10.0)^2$

Step 3 Find the square of the radius.

$A = 100\pi$

Step 4 Multiply the square of the radius by π.

$A \approx 314\ \text{mm}^2$

The area of the circle is about 314 mm^2.

Practice Problem Find the area of a circle with a radius of 16 m.

SCIENCE SKILL HANDBOOK
MATH SKILL HANDBOOK
FOLDABLES HANDBOOK
REFERENCE HANDBOOK
GLOSSARY/GLOSARIO
INDEX

Volume The measure of space occupied by a solid is the **volume** (V). To find the volume of a rectangular solid, multiply the length times width times height, or $V = l \times w \times h$. It is measured in cubic units, such as cubic centimeters (cm^3).

Example

Find the volume of a rectangular solid with a length of 2.0 m, a width of 4.0 m, and a height of 3.0 m.

Step 1 You know the formula for volume is the length times the width times the height.

$V = 2.0 \text{ m} \times 4.0 \text{ m} \times 3.0 \text{ m}$

Step 2 Multiply the length times the width times the height.

$V = 24 \text{ m}^3$

The volume is 24 m^3.

Practice Problem Find the volume of a rectangular solid that is 8 m long, 4 m wide, and 4 m high.

To find the volume of other solids, multiply the area of the base times the height.

Example 1

Find the volume of a solid that has a triangular base with a length of 8.0 m and a height of 7.0 m. The height of the entire solid is 15.0 m.

Step 1 You know that the base is a triangle, and the area of a triangle is $\frac{1}{2}$ the base times the height, and the volume is the area of the base times the height.

$V = \left[\frac{1}{2}(b \times h)\right] \times 15$

Step 2 Find the area of the base.

$V = \left[\frac{1}{2}(8 \times 7)\right] \times 15$

$V = \left(\frac{1}{2} \times 56\right) \times 15$

Step 3 Multiply the area of the base by the height of the solid.

$V = 28 \times 15$

$V = 420 \text{ m}^3$

The volume is 420 m^3.

Example 2

Find the volume of a cylinder that has a base with a radius of 12.0 cm, and a height of 21.0 cm.

Step 1 You know that the base is a circle, and the area of a circle is the square of the radius times π, and the volume is the area of the base times the height.

$V = (\pi r^2) \times 21$

$V = (\pi 12^2) \times 21$

Step 2 Find the area of the base.

$V = 144\pi \times 21$

$V = 452 \times 21$

Step 3 Multiply the area of the base by the height of the solid.

$V \approx 9{,}500 \text{ cm}^3$

The volume is about 9,500 cm^3.

Example 3

Find the volume of a cylinder that has a diameter of 15 mm and a height of 4.8 mm.

Step 1 You know that the base is a circle with an area equal to the square of the radius times π. The radius is one-half the diameter. The volume is the area of the base times the height.

$V = (\pi r^2) \times 4.8$

$V = \left[\pi\left(\frac{1}{2} \times 15\right)^2\right] \times 4.8$

$V = (\pi 7.5^2) \times 4.8$

Step 2 Find the area of the base.

$V = 56.25\pi \times 4.8$

$V \approx 176.71 \times 4.8$

Step 3 Multiply the area of the base by the height of the solid.

$V \approx 848.2$

The volume is about 848.2 mm^3.

Practice Problem Find the volume of a cylinder with a diameter of 7 cm in the base and a height of 16 cm.

Science Applications

Measure in SI

The metric system of measurement was developed in 1795. A modern form of the metric system, called the International System (SI), was adopted in 1960 and provides the standard measurements that all scientists around the world can understand.

The SI system is convenient because unit sizes vary by powers of 10. Prefixes are used to name units. Look at **Table 2** for some common SI prefixes and their meanings.

Table 2 Common SI Prefixes

Prefix	Symbol	Meaning	
kilo–	k	1,000	thousandth
hecto–	h	100	hundred
deka–	da	10	ten
deci–	d	0.1	tenth
centi–	c	0.01	hundreth
milli–	m	0.001	thousandth

Example

How many grams equal one kilogram?

Step 1 Find the prefix *kilo–* in **Table 2.**

Step 2 Using **Table 2,** determine the meaning of *kilo–*. According to the table, it means 1,000. When the prefix *kilo–* is added to a unit, it means that there are 1,000 of the units in a "kilounit."

Step 3 Apply the prefix to the units in the question. The units in the question are grams. There are 1,000 grams in a kilogram.

Practice Problem Is a milligram larger or smaller than a gram? How many of the smaller units equal one larger unit? What fraction of the larger unit does one smaller unit represent?

Dimensional Analysis

Convert SI Units In science, quantities such as length, mass, and time sometimes are measured using different units. A process called dimensional analysis can be used to change one unit of measure to another. This process involves multiplying your starting quantity and units by one or more conversion factors. A conversion factor is a ratio equal to one and can be made from any two equal quantities with different units. If 1,000 mL equal 1 L then two ratios can be made.

$$\frac{1{,}000\ \text{mL}}{1\ \text{L}} = \frac{1\ \text{L}}{1{,}000\ \text{mL}} = 1$$

One can convert between units in the SI system by using the equivalents in **Table 2** to make conversion factors.

Example

How many cm are in 4 m?

Step 1 Write conversion factors for the units given. From **Table 2,** you know that 100 cm = 1 m. The conversion factors are

$$\frac{100\ \text{cm}}{1\ \text{m}} \text{ and } \frac{1\ \text{m}}{100\ \text{cm}}$$

Step 2 Decide which conversion factor to use. Select the factor that has the units you are converting from (m) in the denominator and the units you are converting to (cm) in the numerator.

$$\frac{100\ \text{cm}}{1\ \text{m}}$$

Step 3 Multiply the starting quantity and units by the conversion factor. Cancel the starting units with the units in the denominator. There are 400 cm in 4 m.

$$4\ \cancel{\text{m}} = \frac{100\ \text{cm}}{1\ \cancel{\text{m}}} = 400\ \text{cm}$$

Practice Problem How many milligrams are in one kilogram? (Hint: You will need to use two conversion factors from **Table 2.**)

Table 3 Unit System Equivalents

Type of Measurement	Equivalent
Length	1 in = 2.54 cm 1 yd = 0.91 m 1 mi = 1.61 km
Mass and weight*	1 oz = 28.35 g 1 lb = 0.45 kg 1 ton (short) = 0.91 tonnes (metric tons) 1 lb = 4.45 N
Volume	1 in^3 = 16.39 cm^3 1 qt = 0.95 L 1 gal = 3.78 L
Area	1 in^2 = 6.45 cm^2 1 yd^2 = 0.83 m^2 1 mi^2 = 2.59 km^2 1 acre = 0.40 hectares
Temperature	$°C = \frac{(°F - 32)}{1.8}$ K = °C + 273

*Weight is measured in standard Earth gravity.

Convert Between Unit Systems **Table 3** gives a list of equivalents that can be used to convert between English and SI units.

Example

If a meterstick has a length of 100 cm, how long is the meterstick in inches?

Step 1 Write the conversion factors for the units given. From **Table 3,** 1 in = 2.54 cm.

$$\frac{1 \text{ in}}{2.54 \text{ cm}} \text{ and } \frac{2.54 \text{ cm}}{1 \text{ in}}$$

Step 2 Determine which conversion factor to use. You are converting from cm to in. Use the conversion factor with cm on the bottom.

$$\frac{1 \text{ in}}{2.54 \text{ cm}}$$

Step 3 Multiply the starting quantity and units by the conversion factor. Cancel the starting units with the units in the denominator. Round your answer to the nearest tenth.

$$100 \cancel{\text{cm}} \times \frac{1 \text{ in}}{2.54 \cancel{\text{cm}}} = 39.37 \text{ in}$$

The meterstick is about 39.4 in long.

Practice Problem 1 A book has a mass of 5 lb. What is the mass of the book in kg?

Practice Problem 2 Use the equivalent for in and cm (1 in = 2.54 cm) to show how 1 in3 ≈ 16.39 cm3.

SCIENCE SKILL HANDBOOK | MATH SKILL HANDBOOK | FOLDABLES HANDBOOK | REFERENCE HANDBOOK | GLOSSARY/GLOSARIO | INDEX

Precision and Significant Digits

When you make a measurement, the value you record depends on the precision of the measuring instrument. This precision is represented by the number of significant digits recorded in the measurement. When counting the number of significant digits, all digits are counted except zeros at the end of a number with no decimal point such as 2,050, and zeros at the beginning of a decimal such as 0.03020. When adding or subtracting numbers with different precision, round the answer to the smallest number of decimal places of any number in the sum or difference. When multiplying or dividing, the answer is rounded to the smallest number of significant digits of any number being multiplied or divided.

Example

The lengths 5.28 and 5.2 are measured in meters. Find the sum of these lengths and record your answer using the correct number of significant digits.

Step 1 Find the sum.

5.28 m 2 digits after the decimal

+ 5.2 m 1 digit after the decimal

10.48 m

Step 2 Round to one digit after the decimal because the least number of digits after the decimal of the numbers being added is 1.

The sum is 10.5 m.

Practice Problem 1 How many significant digits are in the measurement 7,071,301 m? How many significant digits are in the measurement 0.003010 g?

Practice Problem 2 Multiply 5.28 and 5.2 using the rule for multiplying and dividing. Record the answer using the correct number of significant digits.

Scientific Notation

Many times numbers used in science are very small or very large. Because these numbers are difficult to work with, scientists use scientific notation. To write numbers in scientific notation, move the decimal point until only one non-zero digit remains on the left. Then count the number of places you moved the decimal point and use that number as a power of ten. For example, the average distance from the Sun to Mars is 227,800,000,000 m. In scientific notation, this distance is 2.278×10^{11} m. Because you moved the decimal point to the left, the number is a positive power of ten.

The mass of an electron is about 0.000 000 000 000 000 000 000 000 000 000 911 kg. Expressed in scientific notation, this mass is 9.11×10^{-31} kg. Because the decimal point was moved to the right, the number is a negative power of ten.

Example

Earth is 149,600,000 km from the Sun. Express this in scientific notation.

Step 1 Move the decimal point until one non-zero digit remains on the left.

1.496 000 00

Step 2 Count the number of decimal places you have moved. In this case, eight.

Step 2 Show that number as a power of ten, 10^8.

Earth is 1.496×10^8 km from the Sun.

Practice Problem 1 How many significant digits are in 149,600,000 km? How many significant digits are in 1.496×10^8 km?

Practice Problem 2 Parts used in a high performance car must be measured to 7×10^{-6} m. Express this number as a decimal.

Practice Problem 3 A CD is spinning at 539 revolutions per minute. Express this number in scientific notation.

SCIENCE SKILL HANDBOOK
MATH SKILL HANDBOOK
FOLDABLES HANDBOOK
REFERENCE HANDBOOK
GLOSSARY/GLOSARIO
INDEX

Make and Use Graphs

Data in tables can be displayed in a graph—a visual representation of data. Common graph types include line graphs, bar graphs, and circle graphs.

Line Graph A line graph shows a relationship between two variables that change continuously. The independent variable is changed and is plotted on the x-axis. The dependent variable is observed, and is plotted on the y-axis.

Example

Draw a line graph of the data below from a cyclist in a long-distance race.

Table 4 Bicycle Race Data

Time (h)	Distance (km)
0	0
1	8
2	16
3	24
4	32
5	40

Step 1 Determine the x-axis and y-axis variables. Time varies independently of distance and is plotted on the x-axis. Distance is dependent on time and is plotted on the y-axis.

Step 2 Determine the scale of each axis. The x-axis data ranges from 0 to 5. The y-axis data ranges from 0 to 50.

Step 3 Using graph paper, draw and label the axes. Include units in the labels.

Step 4 Draw a point at the intersection of the time value on the x-axis and corresponding distance value on the y-axis. Connect the points and label the graph with a title, as shown in **Figure 8.**

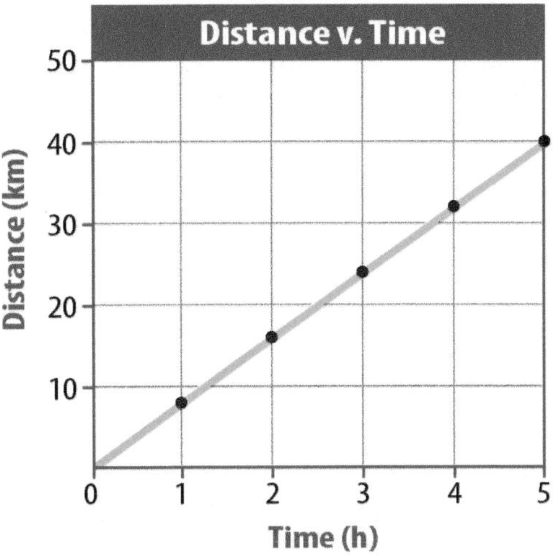

Figure 8 This line graph shows the relationship between distance and time during a bicycle ride.

Practice Problem A puppy's shoulder height is measured during the first year of her life. The following measurements were collected: (3 mo, 52 cm), (6 mo, 72 cm), (9 mo, 83 cm), (12 mo, 86 cm). Graph this data.

Find a Slope The slope of a straight line is the ratio of the vertical change, rise, to the horizontal change, run.

$$\text{Slope} = \frac{\text{vertical change (rise)}}{\text{horizontal change (run)}} = \frac{\text{change in } y}{\text{change in } x}$$

Example

Find the slope of the graph in **Figure 8**.

Step 1 You know that the slope is the change in y divided by the change in x.

$$\text{Slope} = \frac{\text{change in } y}{\text{change in } x}$$

Step 2 Determine the data points you will be using. For a straight line, choose the two sets of points that are the farthest apart.

$$\text{Slope} = \frac{(40 - 0)\text{ km}}{(5 - 0)\text{ h}}$$

Step 3 Find the change in y and x.

$$\text{Slope} = \frac{40\text{ km}}{5\text{ h}}$$

Step 4 Divide the change in y by the change in x.

$$\text{Slope} = \frac{8\text{ km}}{\text{h}}$$

The slope of the graph is 8 km/h.

SCIENCE SKILL HANDBOOK
MATH SKILL HANDBOOK
FOLDABLES HANDBOOK
REFERENCE HANDBOOK
GLOSSARY/GLOSARIO
INDEX

Bar Graph To compare data that does not change continuously you might choose a bar graph. A bar graph uses bars to show the relationships between variables. The *x*-axis variable is divided into parts. The parts can be numbers such as years, or a category such as a type of animal. The *y*-axis is a number and increases continuously along the axis.

Example

A recycling center collects 4.0 kg of aluminum on Monday, 1.0 kg on Wednesday, and 2.0 kg on Friday. Create a bar graph of this data.

Step 1 Select the *x*-axis and *y*-axis variables. The measured numbers (the masses of aluminum) should be placed on the *y*-axis. The variable divided into parts (collection days) is placed on the *x*-axis.

Step 2 Create a graph grid like you would for a line graph. Include labels and units.

Step 3 For each measured number, draw a vertical bar above the *x*-axis value up to the *y*-axis value. For the first data point, draw a vertical bar above Monday up to 4.0 kg.

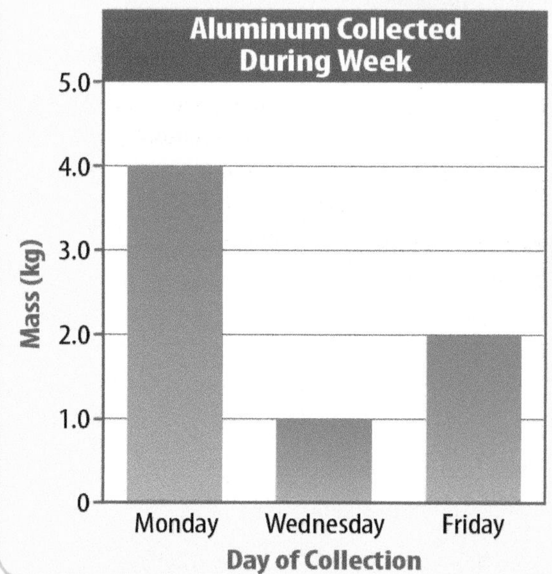

Practice Problem Draw a bar graph of the gases in air: 78% nitrogen, 21% oxygen, 1% other gases.

Circle Graph To display data as parts of a whole, you might use a circle graph. A circle graph is a circle divided into sections that represent the relative size of each piece of data. The entire circle represents 100%, half represents 50%, and so on.

Example

Air is made up of 78% nitrogen, 21% oxygen, and 1% other gases. Display the composition of air in a circle graph.

Step 1 Multiply each percent by 360° and divide by 100 to find the angle of each section in the circle.

$$78\% \times \frac{360°}{100} = 280.8°$$

$$21\% \times \frac{360°}{100} = 75.6°$$

$$1\% \times \frac{360°}{100} = 3.6°$$

Step 2 Use a compass to draw a circle and to mark the center of the circle. Draw a straight line from the center to the edge of the circle.

Step 3 Use a protractor and the angles you calculated to divide the circle into parts. Place the center of the protractor over the center of the circle and line the base of the protractor over the straight line.

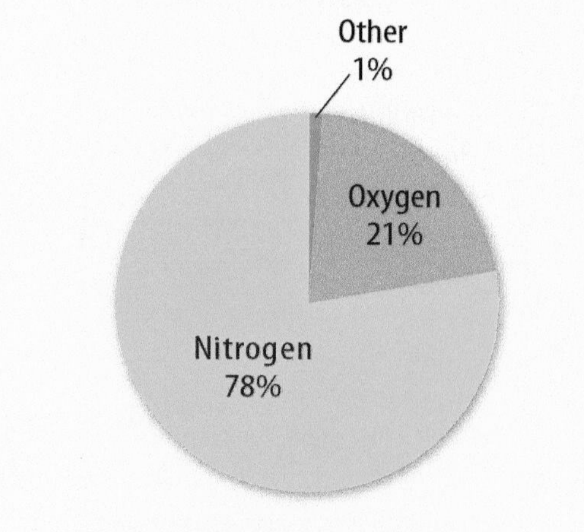

Practice Problem Draw a circle graph to represent the amount of aluminum collected during the week shown in the bar graph to the left.

Student Study Guides & Instructions

By Dinah Zike

1. You will find suggestions for Study Guides, also known as Foldables or books, in each chapter lesson and as a final project. Look at the end of the chapter to determine the project format and glue the Foldables in place as you progress through the chapter lessons.

2. Creating the Foldables or books is simple and easy to do by using copy paper, art paper, and internet printouts. Photocopies of maps, diagrams, or your own illustrations may also be used for some of the Foldables. Notebook paper is the most common source of material for study guides and 83% of all Foldables are created from it. When folded to make books, notebook paper Foldables easily fit into 11" × 17" or 12" × 18" chapter projects with space left over. Foldables made using photocopy paper are slightly larger and they fit into Projects, but snugly. Use the least amount of glue, tape, and staples needed to assemble the Foldables.

3. Seven of the Foldables can be made using either small or large paper. When 11" × 17" or 12" × 18" paper is used, these become projects for housing smaller Foldables. Project format boxes are located within the instructions to remind you of this option.

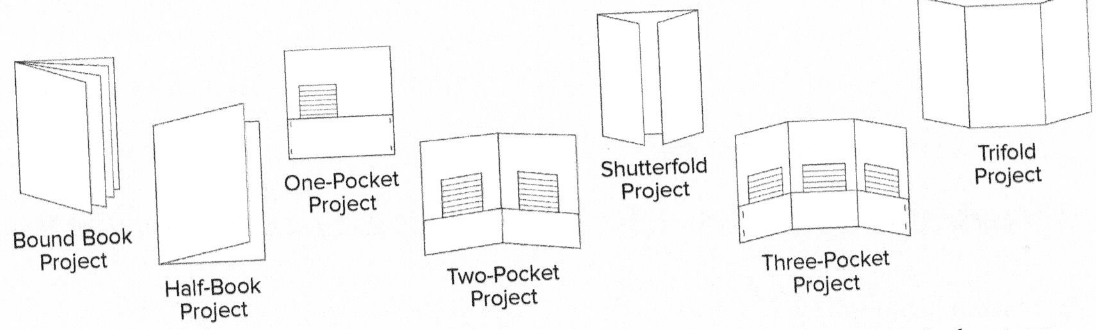

4. Use one-gallon self-locking plastic bags to store your projects. Place strips of two-inch clear tape along the left, long side of the bag and punch holes through the taped edge. Cut the bottom corners off the bag so it will not hold air. Store this Project Portfolio inside a three-hole binder. To store a large collection of project bags, use a giant laundry-soap box. Holes can be punched in some of the Foldable Projects so they can be stored in a three-hole binder without using a plastic bag. Punch holes in the pocket books before gluing or stapling the pocket.

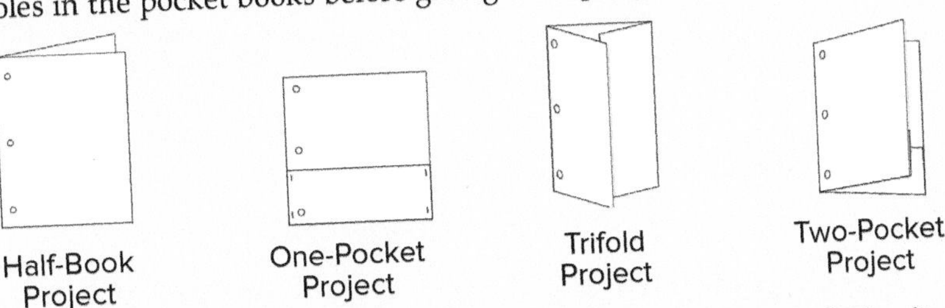

5. Maximize the use of the projects by collecting additional information and placing it on the back of the project and other unused spaces of the large Foldables.

Half-Book Foldable® By Dinah Zike

Step 1 Fold a sheet of notebook or copy paper in half.

Label the exterior tab and use the inside space to write information.

PROJECT FORMAT
Use 11" × 17" or 12" × 18" paper on the horizontal axis to make a large project book.

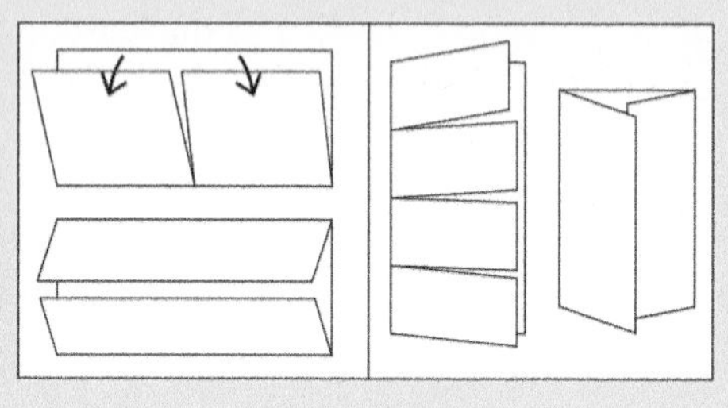

Variations

Paper can be folded horizontally, like a *hamburger* or vertically, like a *hot dog.*

A 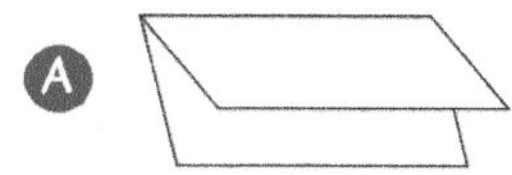

B 

C Half-books can be folded so that one side is ½ inch longer than the other side. A title or question can be written on the extended tab.

Worksheet Foldable or Folded Book® By Dinah Zike

Step 1 Make a half-book (see above) using work sheets, internet printouts, diagrams, or maps.

Step 2 Fold it in half again.

Variations

A This folded sheet as a small book with two pages can be used for comparing and contrasting, cause and effect, or other skills.

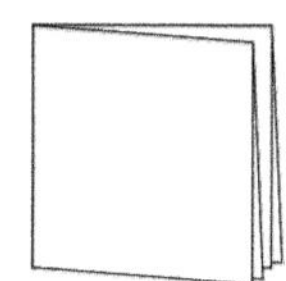

B When the sheet of paper is open, the four sections can be used separately or used collectively to show sequences or steps.

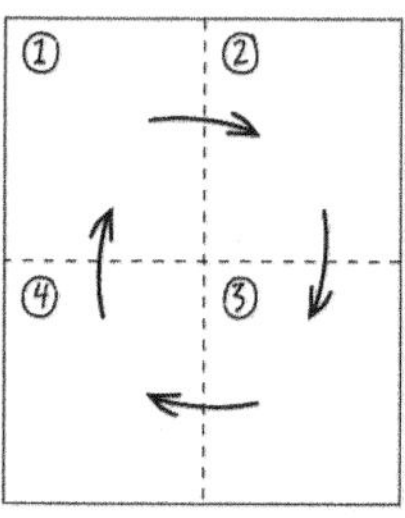

Two-Tab and Concept-Map Foldable® By Dinah Zike

Step 1 Fold a sheet of notebook or copy paper in half vertically or horizontally.

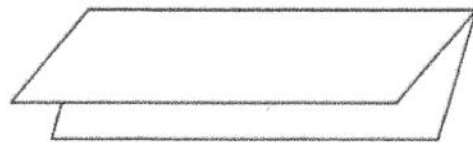

Step 2 Fold it in half again, as shown.

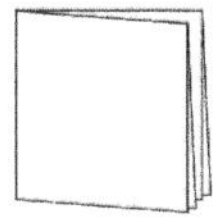

Step 3 Unfold once and cut along the fold line or valley of the top flap to make two flaps.

Variations

A Concept maps can be made by leaving a ½ inch tab at the top when folding the paper in half. Use arrows and labels to relate topics to the primary concept.

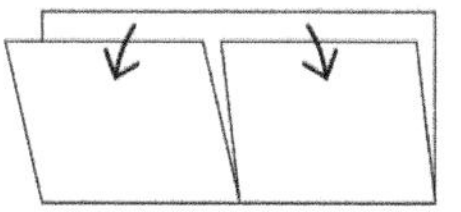

B Use two sheets of paper to make multiple page tab books. Glue or staple books together at the top fold.

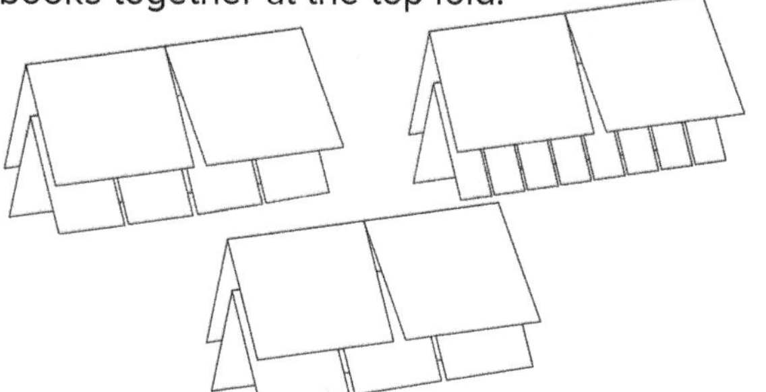

Three-Quarter Foldable® By Dinah Zike

Step 1 Make a two-tab book (see above) and cut the left tab off at the top of the fold line.

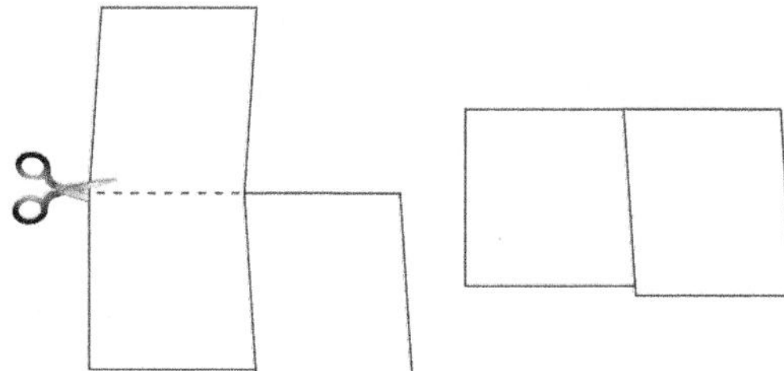

Variations

A Use this book to draw a diagram or a map on the exposed left tab. Write questions about the illustration on the top right tab and provide complete answers on the space under the tab.

B Compose a self-test using multiple choice answers for your questions. Include the correct answer with three wrong responses. The correct answers can be written on the back of the book or upside down on the bottom of the inside page.

Three-Tab Foldable® By Dinah Zike

Step 1 Fold a sheet of paper in half horizontally.

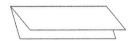

Step 2 Fold into thirds.

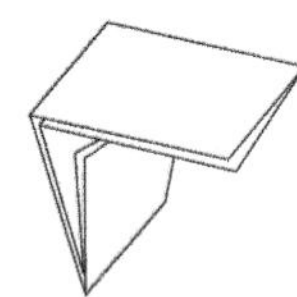

Step 3 Unfold and cut along the folds of the top flap to make three sections.

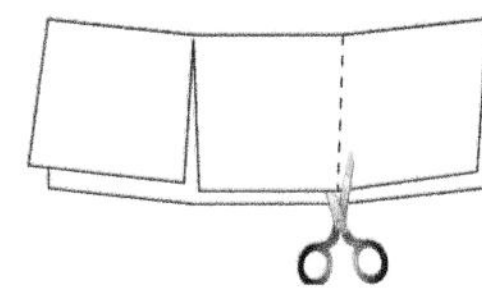

Variations

A Before cutting the three tabs draw a Venn diagram across the front of the book.

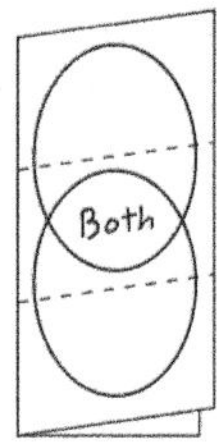

B Make a space to use for titles or concept maps by leaving a ½ inch tab at the top when folding the paper in half.

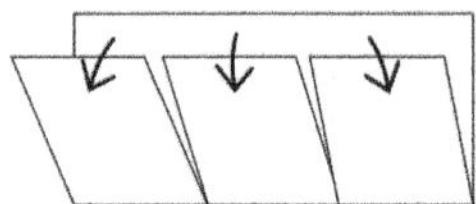

Four-Tab Foldable® By Dinah Zike

Step 1 Fold a sheet of paper in half horizontally.

Step 2 Fold in half and then fold each half as shown below.

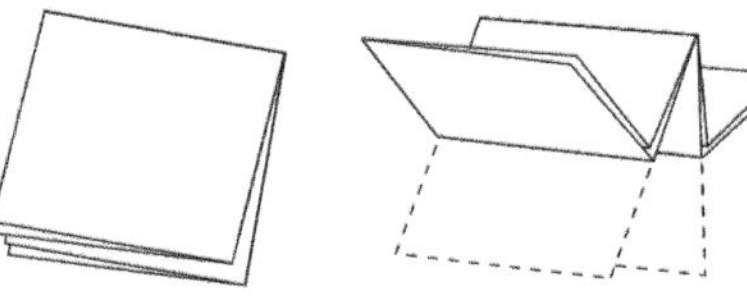

Step 3 Unfold and cut along the fold lines of the top flap to make four tabs.

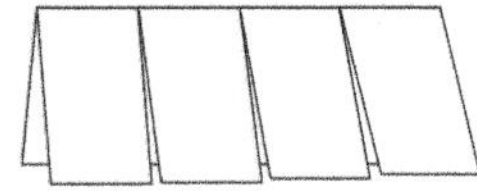

Variations

A Make a space to use for titles or concept maps by leaving a ½ inch tab at the top when folding the paper in half.

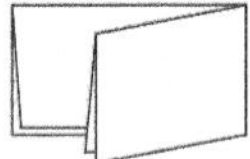

B Use the book on the vertical axis, with or without an extended tab.

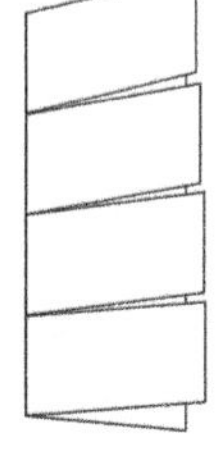

Folding Fifths for a Foldable® By Dinah Zike

Step 1 Fold a sheet of paper in half horizontally.

Step 2 Fold again so one-third of the paper is exposed and two-thirds are covered.

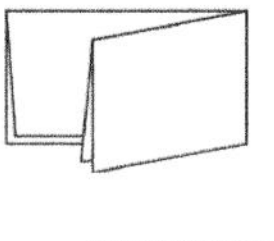

Step 3 Fold the two-thirds section in half.

Step 4 Fold the one-third section, a single thickness, backward to make a fold line.

Variations

A Unfold and cut along the fold lines to make five tabs.

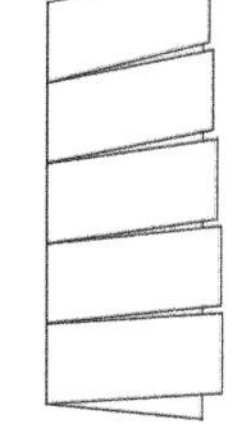

B Make a five-tab book with a ½ inch tab at the top (see two-tab instructions).

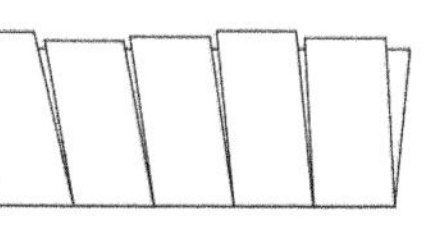

C Use 11" × 17" or 12" × 18" paper and fold into fifths for a five-column and/or row table or chart.

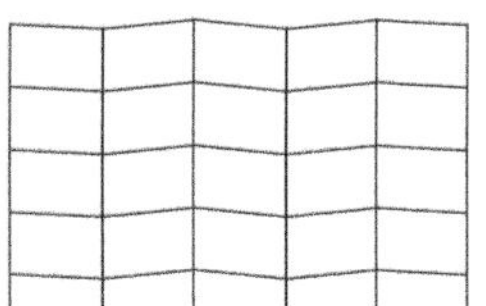

Folded Table or Chart, and Trifold Foldable® By Dinah Zike

Step 1 Fold a sheet of paper in the required number of vertical columns for the table or chart.

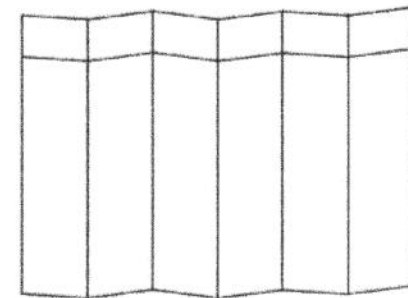

Step 2 Fold the horizontal rows needed for the table or chart.

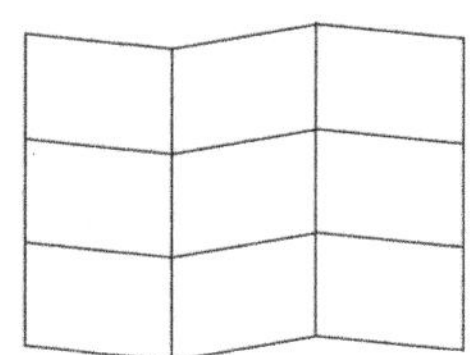

PROJECT FORMAT
Use 11" × 17" or 12" × 18" paper and fold it to make a large trifold project book or larger tables and charts.

Variations

A Make a trifold by folding the paper into thirds vertically or horizontally.

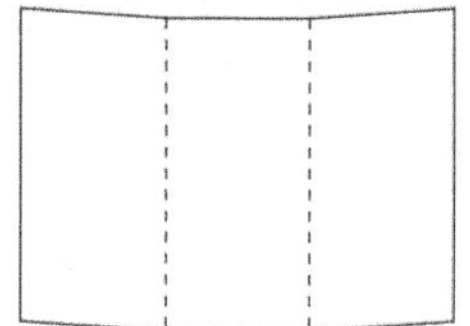

B Make a trifold book. Unfold it and draw a Venn diagram on the inside.

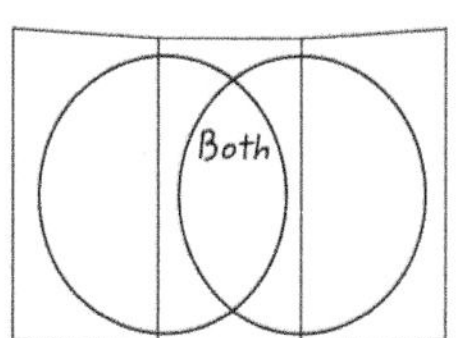

SCIENCE SKILL HANDBOOK
MATH SKILL HANDBOOK
FOLDABLES HANDBOOK
REFERENCE HANDBOOK
GLOSSARY/ GLOSARIO
INDEX

Two or Three-Pockets Foldable® By Dinah Zike

Step 1 Fold up the long side of a horizontal sheet of paper about 5 cm.

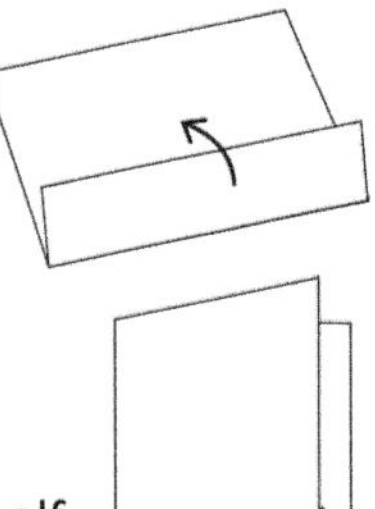

Step 2 Fold the paper in half.

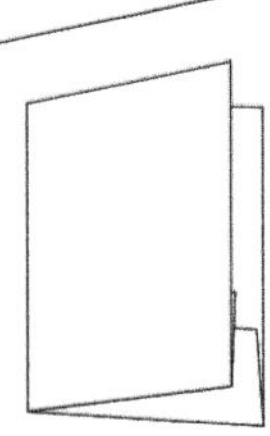

Step 3 Open the paper and glue or staple the outer edges to make two compartments.

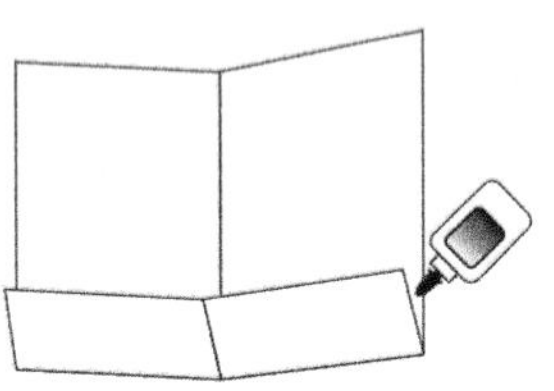

Variations

A Make a multi-page booklet by gluing several pocket books together.

B Make a three-pocket book by using a trifold (see previous instructions).

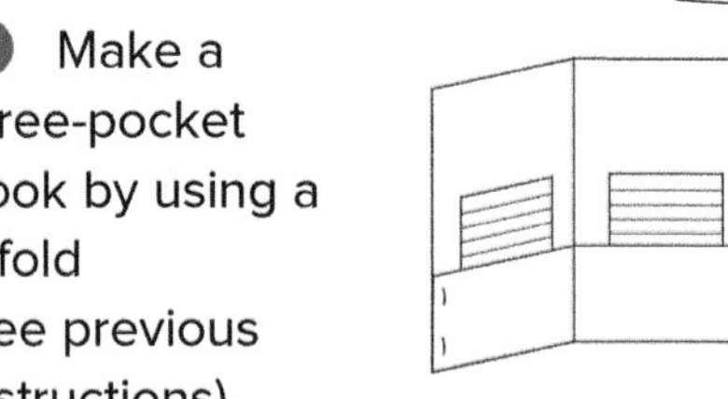

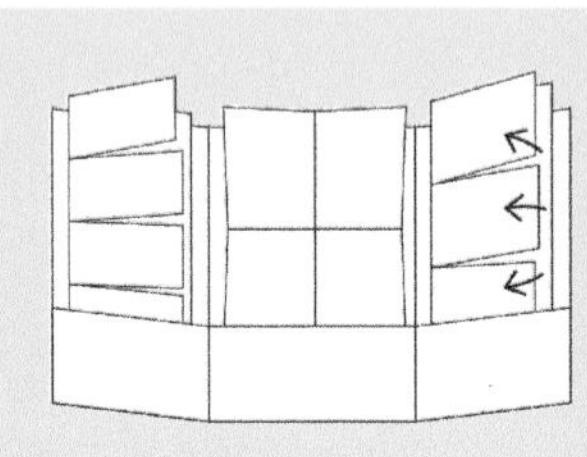

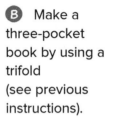

PROJECT FORMAT
Use 11" × 17" or 12" × 18" paper and fold it horizontally to make a large multi-pocket project.

Matchbook Foldable® By Dinah Zike

Step 1 Fold a sheet of paper almost in half and make the back edge about 1–2 cm longer than the front edge.

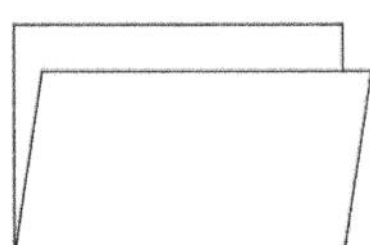

Step 2 Find the midpoint of the shorter flap.

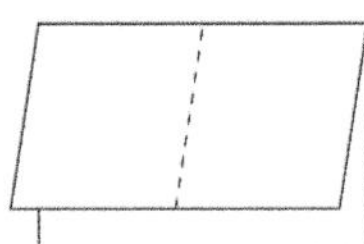

Step 3 Open the paper and cut the short side along the midpoint making two tabs.

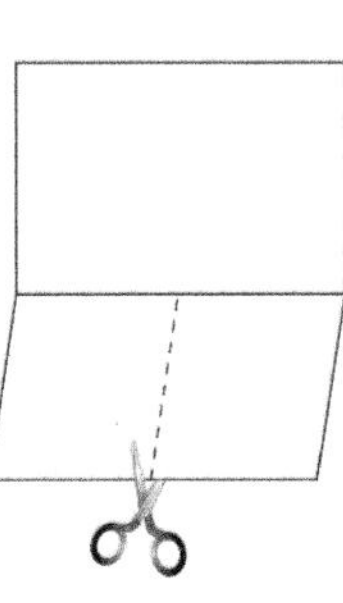

Step 4 Close the book and fold the tab over the short side.

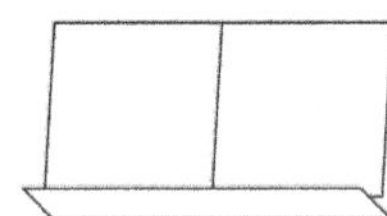

Variations

A Make a single-tab matchbook by skipping Steps 2 and 3.

B Make two smaller matchbooks by cutting the single-tab matchbook in half.

Shutterfold Foldable® By Dinah Zike

Step 1 Begin as if you were folding a vertical sheet of paper in half, but instead of creasing the paper, pinch it to show the midpoint.

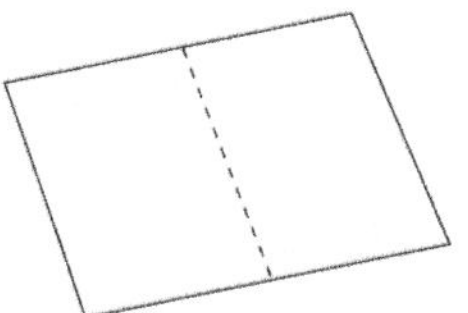

PROJECT FORMAT
Use 11" × 17" or 12" × 18" paper and fold it to make a large shutterfold project.

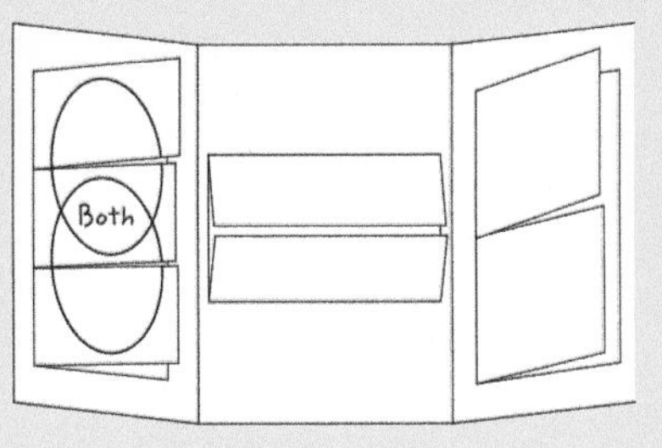

Step 2 Fold the top and bottom to the middle and crease the folds.

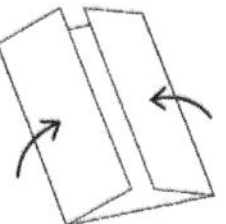

Variations

A Use the shutterfold on the horizontal axis.

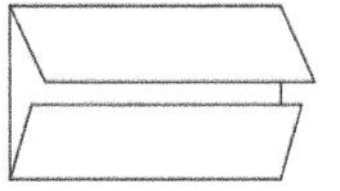

B Create a center tab by leaving .5–2 cm between the flaps in Step 2.

Four-Door Foldable® By Dinah Zike

Step 1 Make a shutterfold (see above).

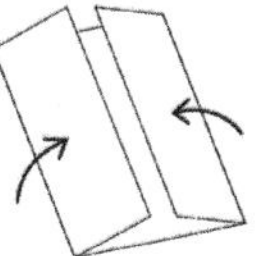

Step 2 Fold the sheet of paper in half.

Step 3 Open the last fold and cut along the inside fold lines to make four tabs.

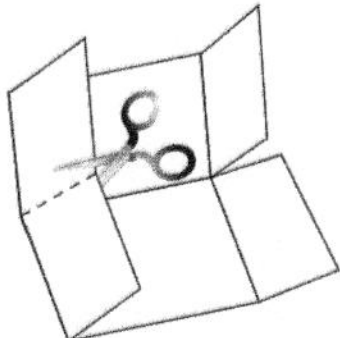

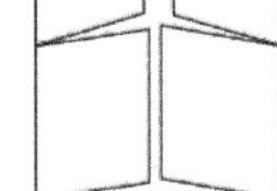

Variations

A Use the four-door book on the opposite axis.

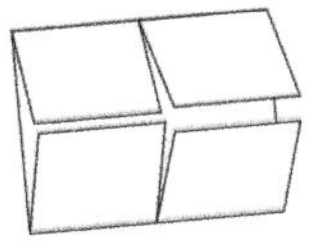

B Create a center tab by leaving .5–2 cm between the flaps in Step 1.

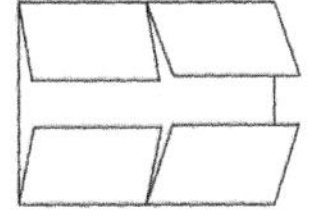

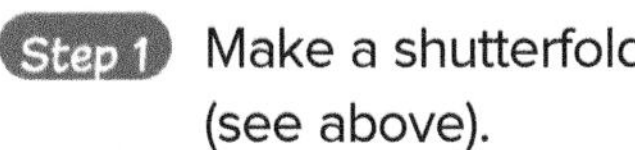

Bound Book Foldable® By Dinah Zike

Step 1 Fold three sheets of paper in half. Place the papers in a stack, leaving about .5 cm between each top fold. Mark all three sheets about 3 cm from the outer edges.

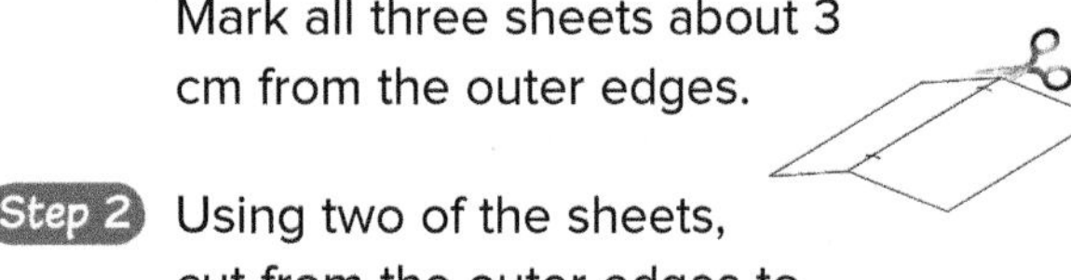

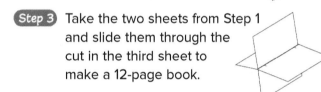

Step 2 Using two of the sheets, cut from the outer edges to the marked spots on each side. On the other sheet, cut between the marked spots.

Step 3 Take the two sheets from Step 1 and slide them through the cut in the third sheet to make a 12-page book.

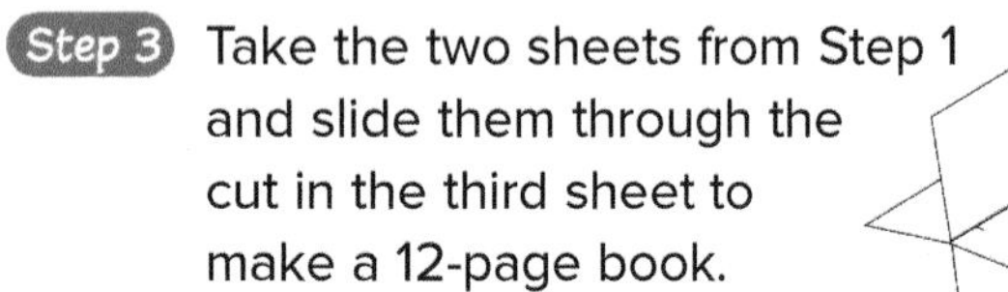

Step 4 Fold the bound pages in half to form a book.

Variation

A Use two sheets of paper to make an eight-page book, or increase the number of pages by using more than three sheets.

PROJECT FORMAT

Use two or more sheets of 11" × 17" or 12" × 18" paper and fold it to make a large bound book project.

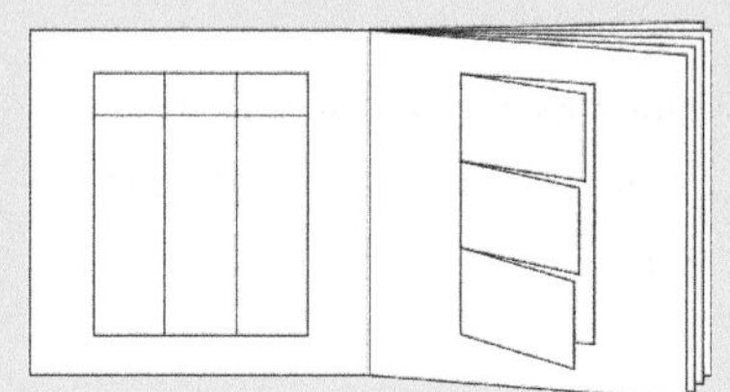

Accordion Foldable® By Dinah Zike

Step 1 Fold the selected paper in half vertically, like a *hamburger*.

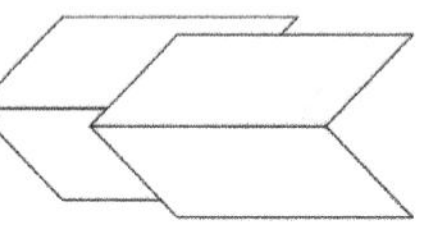

Step 2 Cut each sheet of folded paper in half along the fold lines.

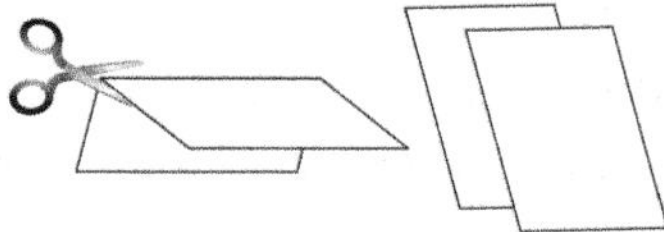

Step 3 Fold each half-sheet almost in half, leaving a 2 cm tab at the top.

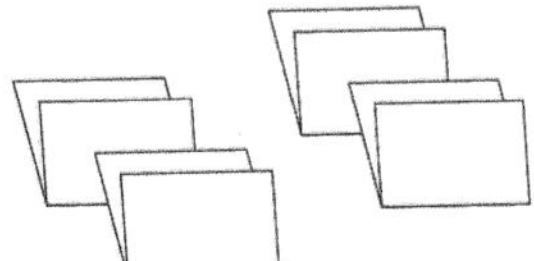

Step 4 Fold the top tab over the short side, then fold it in the opposite direction.

Variations

A Glue the straight edge of one paper inside the tab of another sheet. Leave a tab at the end of the book to add more pages.

B Tape the straight edge of one paper to the tab of another sheet, or just tape the straight edges of nonfolded paper end to end to make an accordion.

C Use whole sheets of paper to make a large accordion.

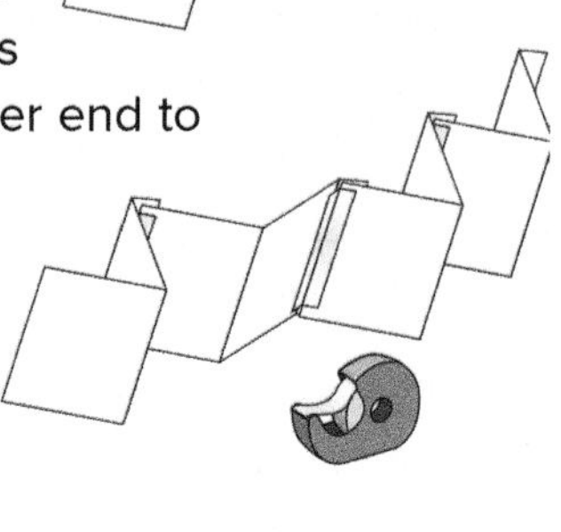

Layered Foldable® By Dinah Zike

Step 1 Stack two sheets of paper about 1–2 cm apart. Keep the right and left edges even.

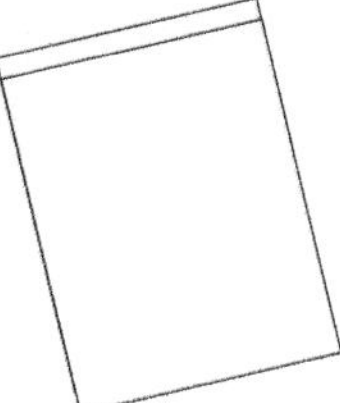

Step 2 Fold up the bottom edges to form four tabs. Crease the fold to hold the tabs in place.

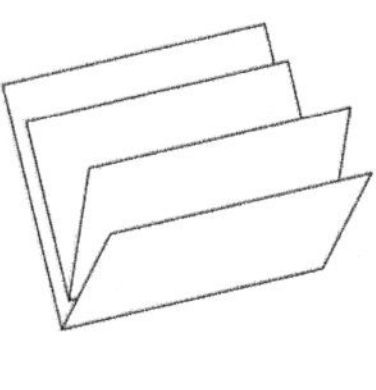

Step 3 Staple along the folded edge, or open and glue the papers together at the fold line.

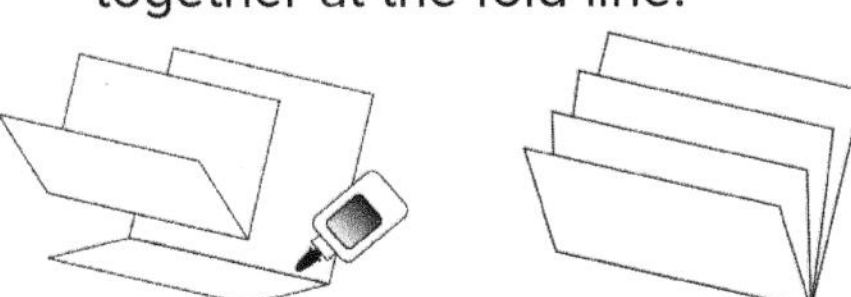

Variations

A Rotate the book so the fold is at the top or to the side.

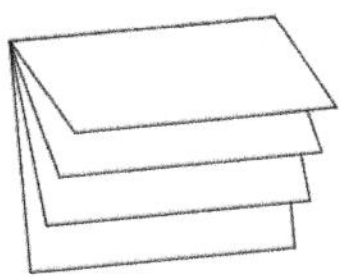

B Extend the book by using more than two sheets of paper.

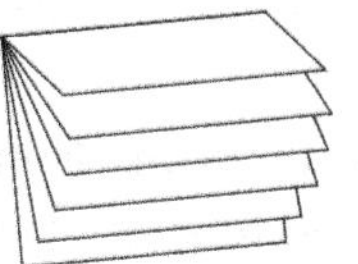

Envelope Foldable® By Dinah Zike

Step 1 Fold a sheet of paper into a *taco*. Cut off the tab at the top.

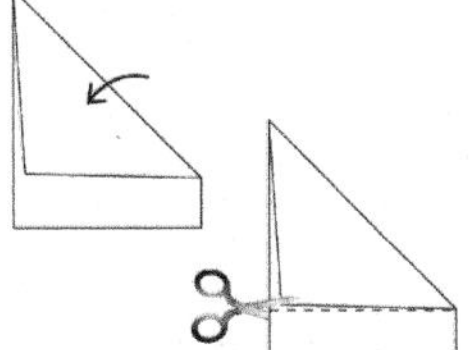

Step 2 Open the *taco* and fold it the opposite way making another *taco* and an X-fold pattern on the sheet of paper.

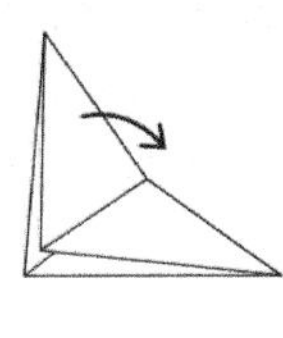

Step 3 Cut a map, illustration, or diagram to fit the inside of the envelope.

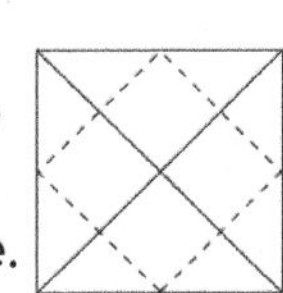

Step 4 Use the outside tabs for labels and inside tabs for writing information.

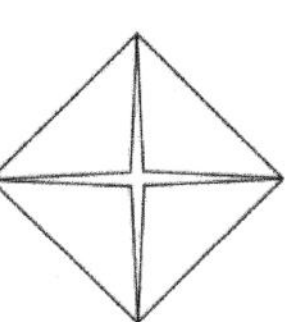

Variations

A Use 11" × 17" or 12" × 18" paper to make a large envelope.

B Cut off the points of the four tabs to make a window in the middle of the book.

Sentence Strip Foldable® By Dinah Zike

Step 1 Fold two sheets of paper in half vertically, like a *hamburger*.

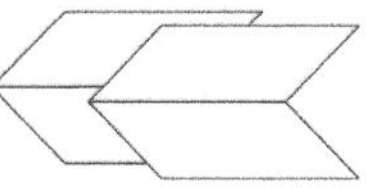

Step 2 Unfold and cut along fold lines making four half sheets.

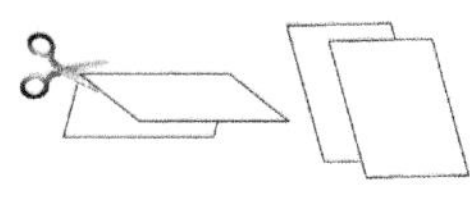

Step 3 Fold each half sheet in half horizontally, like a *hot dog*.

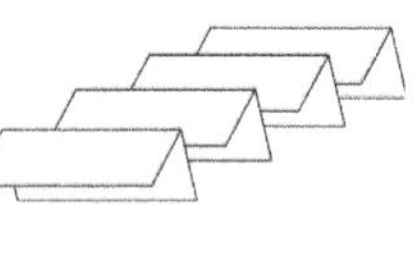

Step 4 Stack folded horizontal sheets evenly and staple together on the left side.

Step 5 Open the top flap of the first sentence strip and make a cut about 2 cm from the stapled edge to the fold line. This forms a flap that can be raised and lowered. Repeat this step for each sentence strip.

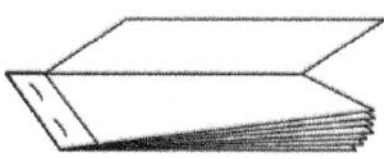

Variations

A Expand this book by using more than two sheets of paper.

B Use whole sheets of paper to make large books.

Pyramid Foldable® By Dinah Zike

Step 1 Fold a sheet of paper into a *taco*. Crease the fold line, but do not cut it off.

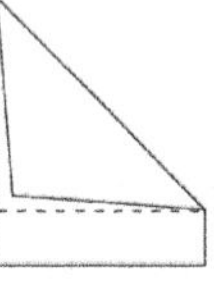

Step 2 Open the folded sheet and refold it like a *taco* in the opposite direction to create an X-fold pattern.

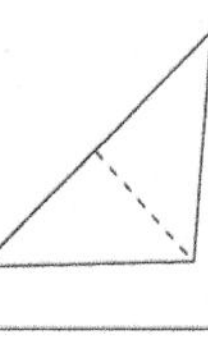

Step 3 Cut one fold line as shown, stopping at the center of the X-fold to make a flap.

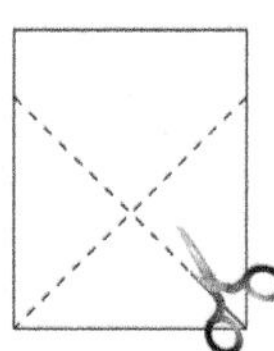

Step 4 Outline the fold lines of the X-fold. Label the three front sections and use the inside spaces for notes. Use the tab for the title.

Step 5 Glue the tab into a project book or notebook. Use the space under the pyramid for other information.

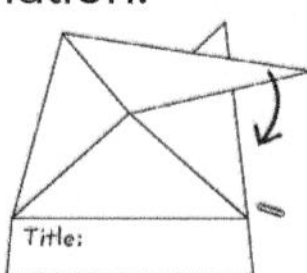

Step 6 To display the pyramid, fold the flap under and secure with a paper clip, if needed.

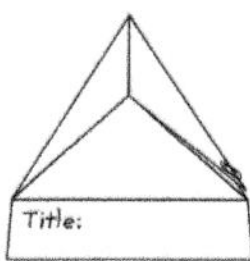

Single-Pocket or One-Pocket Foldable® By Dinah Zike

Step 1 Using a large piece of paper on a vertical axis, fold the bottom edge of the paper upwards, about 5 cm.

Step 2 Glue or staple the outer edges to make a large pocket.

PROJECT FORMAT

Use 11" × 17" or 12" × 18" paper and fold it vertically or horizontally to make a large pocket project.

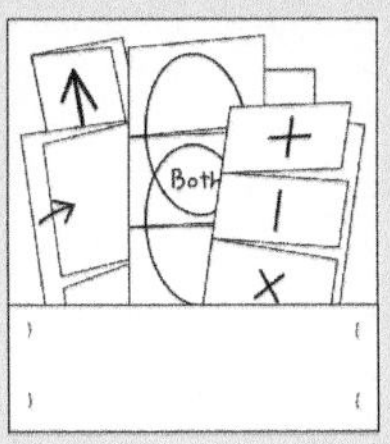

Variations

A Make the one-pocket project using the paper on the horizontal axis.

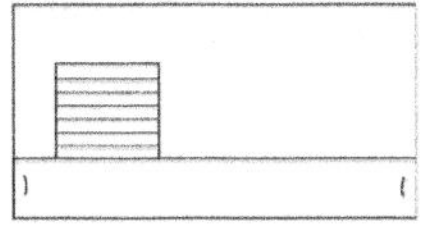

B To store materials securely inside, fold the top of the paper almost to the center, leaving about 2–4 cm between the paper edges. Slip the Foldables through the opening and under the top and bottom pockets.

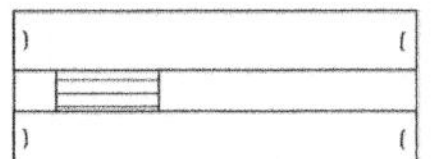

Multi-Tab Foldable® By Dinah Zike

Step 1 Fold a sheet of notebook paper in half like a *hot dog*.

Step 2 Open the paper and on one side cut every third line. This makes ten tabs on wide ruled notebook paper and twelve tabs on college ruled.

Step 3 Label the tabs on the front side and use the inside space for definitions or other information.

Variation

A Make a tab for a title by folding the paper so the holes remain uncovered. This allows the notebook Foldable to be stored in a three-hole binder.

SCIENCE SKILL HANDBOOK
MATH SKILL HANDBOOK
FOLDABLES HANDBOOK
REFERENCE HANDBOOK
GLOSSARY/GLOSARIO
INDEX

PERIODIC TABLE OF THE ELEMENTS

Element — Hydrogen
Atomic number — 1
Symbol — H
Atomic mass — 1.01
State of matter

Gas
Liquid
Solid
Synthetic

A column in the periodic table is called a **group.**

A row in the periodic table is called a **period.**

Period	1	2	3	4	5	6	7	8	9
1	Hydrogen 1 H 1.01								
2	Lithium 3 Li 6.94	Beryllium 4 Be 9.01							
3	Sodium 11 Na 22.99	Magnesium 12 Mg 24.31							
4	Potassium 19 K 39.10	Calcium 20 Ca 40.08	Scandium 21 Sc 44.96	Titanium 22 Ti 47.87	Vanadium 23 V 50.94	Chromium 24 Cr 52.00	Manganese 25 Mn 54.94	Iron 26 Fe 55.85	Cobalt 27 Co 58.93
5	Rubidium 37 Rb 85.47	Strontium 38 Sr 87.62	Yttrium 39 Y 88.91	Zirconium 40 Zr 91.22	Niobium 41 Nb 92.91	Molybdenum 42 Mo 95.96	Technetium 43 Tc (98)	Ruthenium 44 Ru 101.07	Rhodium 45 Rh 102.91
6	Cesium 55 Cs 132.91	Barium 56 Ba 137.33	Lanthanum 57 La 138.91	Hafnium 72 Hf 178.49	Tantalum 73 Ta 180.95	Tungsten 74 W 183.84	Rhenium 75 Re 186.21	Osmium 76 Os 190.23	Iridium 77 Ir 192.22
7	Francium 87 Fr (223)	Radium 88 Ra (226)	Actinium 89 Ac (227)	Rutherfordium 104 Rf (267)	Dubnium 105 Db (268)	Seaborgium 106 Sg (271)	Bohrium 107 Bh (272)	Hassium 108 Hs (270)	Meitnerium 109 Mt (276)

The number in parentheses is the mass number of the longest lived isotope for that element.

Lanthanide series	Cerium 58 Ce 140.12	Praseodymium 59 Pr 140.91	Neodymium 60 Nd 144.24	Promethium 61 Pm (145)	Samarium 62 Sm 150.36	Europium 63 Eu 151.96
Actinide series	Thorium 90 Th 232.04	Protactinium 91 Pa 231.04	Uranium 92 U 238.03	Neptunium 93 Np (237)	Plutonium 94 Pu (244)	Americium 95 Am (243)

Metal
Metalloid
Nonmetal
Recently discovered

10	11	12	13	14	15	16	17	18
								Helium 2 He 4.00
			Boron 5 B 10.81	Carbon 6 C 12.01	Nitrogen 7 N 14.01	Oxygen 8 O 16.00	Fluorine 9 F 19.00	Neon 10 Ne 20.18
			Aluminum 13 Al 26.98	Silicon 14 Si 28.09	Phosphorus 15 P 30.97	Sulfur 16 S 32.07	Chlorine 17 Cl 35.45	Argon 18 Ar 39.95
Nickel 28 Ni 58.69	Copper 29 Cu 63.55	Zinc 30 Zn 65.38	Gallium 31 Ga 69.72	Germanium 32 Ge 72.64	Arsenic 33 As 74.92	Selenium 34 Se 78.96	Bromine 35 Br 79.90	Krypton 36 Kr 83.80
Palladium 46 Pd 106.42	Silver 47 Ag 107.87	Cadmium 48 Cd 112.41	Indium 49 In 114.82	Tin 50 Sn 118.71	Antimony 51 Sb 121.76	Tellurium 52 Te 127.60	Iodine 53 I 126.90	Xenon 54 Xe 131.29
Platinum 78 Pt 195.08	Gold 79 Au 196.97	Mercury 80 Hg 200.59	Thallium 81 Tl 204.38	Lead 82 Pb 207.20	Bismuth 83 Bi 208.98	Polonium 84 Po (209)	Astatine 85 At (210)	Radon 86 Rn (222)
Darmstadtium 110 Ds (281)	Roentgenium 111 Rg (280)	Copernicium 112 Cn (285)	Ununtrium * 113 Uut (284)	Flerovium * 114 Fl (289)	Ununpentium * 115 Uup (288)	Livermorium * 116 Lv (293)	Ununseptium * 117 Uus (294)	Ununoctium * 118 Uuo (294)

* The names and symbols for elements 113, 115, 117, and 118 are temporary. Final names will be approved by IUPAC (International Union of Pure and Applied Chemistry)

Gadolinium 64 Gd 157.25	Terbium 65 Tb 158.93	Dysprosium 66 Dy 162.50	Holmium 67 Ho 164.93	Erbium 68 Er 167.26	Thulium 69 Tm 168.93	Ytterbium 70 Yb 173.05	Lutetium 71 Lu 174.97
Curium 96 Cm (247)	Berkelium 97 Bk (247)	Californium 98 Cf (251)	Einsteinium 99 Es (252)	Fermium 100 Fm (257)	Mendelevium 101 Md (258)	Nobelium 102 No (259)	Lawrencium 103 Lr (262)

Topographic Map Symbols

Topographic Map Symbols			
	Primary highway, hard surface		Index contour
	Secondary highway, hard surface		Supplementary contour
	Light-duty road, hard or improved surface		Intermediate contour
	Unimproved road		Depression contours
	Railroad: single track		
	Railroad: multiple track		Boundaries: national
	Railroads in juxtaposition		State
			County, parish, municipal
	Buildings		Civil township, precinct, town, barrio
cem	Schools, church, and cemetery		Incorporated city, village, town, hamlet
	Buildings (barn, warehouse, etc.)		Reservation, national or state
	Wells other than water (labeled as to type)		Small park, cemetery, airport, etc.
	Tanks: oil, water, etc. (labeled only if water)		Land grant
	Located or landmark object; windmill		Township or range line, U.S. land survey
	Open pit, mine, or quarry; prospect		Township or range line, approximate location
	Marsh (swamp)		
	Wooded marsh		Perennial streams
	Woods or brushwood		Elevated aqueduct
	Vineyard		Water well and spring
	Land subject to controlled inundation		Small rapids
	Submerged marsh		Large rapids
	Mangrove		Intermittent lake
	Orchard		Intermittent stream
	Scrub		Aqueduct tunnel
	Urban area		Glacier
			Small falls
x7369	Spot elevation		Large falls
670	Water elevation		Dry lake bed

Rocks

Rocks		
Rock Type	**Rock Name**	**Characteristics**
Igneous (intrusive)	Granite	Large mineral grains of quartz, feldspar, hornblende, and mica. Usually light in color.
	Diorite	Large mineral grains of feldspar, hornblende, and mica. Less quartz than granite. Intermediate in color.
	Gabbro	Large mineral grains of feldspar, augite, and olivine. No quartz. Dark in color.
Igneous (extrusive)	Rhyolite	Small mineral grains of quartz, feldspar, hornblende, and mica, or no visible grains. Light in color.
	Andesite	Small mineral grains of feldspar, hornblende, and mica or no visible grains. Intermediate in color.
	Basalt	Small mineral grains of feldspar, augite, and possibly olivine or no visible grains. No quartz. Dark in color.
	Obsidian	Glassy texture. No visible grains. Volcanic glass. Fracture looks like broken glass.
	Pumice	Frothy texture. Floats in water. Usually light in color.
Sedimentary (clastic)	Conglomerate	Coarse grained. Gravel or pebble-size grains.
	Sandstone	Sand-sized grains 1/16 to 2 mm.
	Siltstone	Grains are smaller than sand but larger than clay.
	Shale	Smallest grains. Often dark in color. Usually platy.
Sedimentary (chemical or biochemical)	Limestone	Major mineral is calcite. Usually forms in oceans and lakes. Often contains fossils.
	Coal	Forms in swampy areas. Compacted layers of organic material, mainly plant remains.
Sedimentary (chemical)	Rock Salt	Commonly forms by the evaporation of seawater.
Metamorphic (foliated)	Gneiss	Banding due to alternate layers of different minerals, of different colors. Parent rock often is granite.
	Schist	Parallel arrangement of sheetlike minerals, mainly micas. Forms from different parent rocks.
	Phyllite	Shiny or silky appearance. May look wrinkled. Common parent rocks are shale and slate.
	Slate	Harder, denser, and shinier than shale. Common parent rock is shale.
Metamorphic (nonfoliated)	Marble	Calcite or dolomite. Common parent rock is limestone.
	Soapstone	Mainly of talc. Soft with greasy feel.
	Quartzite	Hard with interlocking quartz crystals. Common parent rock is sandstone.

Minerals

Mineral (formula)	Color	Streak	Hardness Pattern	Breakage Properties	Uses and Other
Graphite (C)	black to gray	black to gray	1–1.5	basal cleavage (scales)	pencil lead, lubricants for locks, rods to control some small nuclear reactions, battery poles
Galena (PbS)	gray	gray to black	2.5	cubic cleavage perfect	source of lead, used for pipes, shields for X rays, fishing equipment sinkers
Hematite (Fe_2O_3)	black or reddish-brown	reddish-brown	5.5–6.5	irregular fracture	source of iron; converted to pig iron, made into steel
Magnetite (Fe_3O_4)	black	black	6	conchoidal fracture	source of iron, attracts a magnet
Pyrite (FeS_2)	light, brassy, yellow	greenish-black	6–6.5	uneven fracture	fool's gold
Talc ($Mg_3\ Si_4O_{10}(OH)_2$)	white, greenish	white	1	cleavage in one direction	used for talcum powder, sculptures, paper, and tabletops
Gypsum ($CaSO_4{\cdot}2H_2O$)	colorless, gray, white, brown	white	2	basal cleavage	used in plaster of paris and dry wall for building construction
Sphalerite (ZnS)	brown, reddish-brown, greenish	light to dark brown	3.5–4	cleavage in six directions	main ore of zinc; used in paints, dyes, and medicine
Muscovite ($KAl_3Si_3O_{10}(OH)_2$)	white, light gray, yellow, rose, green	colorless	2–2.5	basal cleavage	occurs in large, flexible plates; used as an insulator in electrical equipment, lubricant
Biotite ($K(Mg,Fe)_3(AlSi_3O_{10})(OH)_2$)	black to dark brown	colorless	2.5–3	basal cleavage	occurs in large, flexible plates
Halite (NaCl)	colorless, red, white, blue	colorless	2.5	cubic cleavage	salt; soluble in water; a preservative

SCIENCE SKILL HANDBOOK MATH SKILL HANDBOOK FOLDABLES HANDBOOK REFERENCE HANDBOOK GLOSSARY/GLOSARIO INDEX

Minerals

Minerals					
Mineral (formula)	**Color**	**Streak**	**Hardness**	**Breakage Pattern**	**Uses and Other Properties**
Calcite ($CaCO_3$)	colorless, white, pale blue	colorless, white	3	cleavage in three directions	fizzes when HCl is added; used in cements and other building materials
Dolomite ($CaMg(CO_3)_2$)	colorless, white, pink, green, gray, black	white	3.5–4	cleavage in three directions	concrete and cement; used as an ornamental building stone
Fluorite (CaF_2)	colorless, white, blue, green, red, yellow, purple	colorless	4	cleavage in four directions	used in the manufacture of optical equipment; glows under ultraviolet light
Hornblende ($(CaNa)_{2-3}(Mg,Al,Fe)_5$-$(Al,Si)_2Si_6O_{22}(OH)_2$)	green to black	gray to white	5–6	cleavage in two directions	will transmit light on thin edges; 6-sided cross section
Feldspar ($(KAlSi_3O_8)$ $(NaAlSi_3O_8)$, $(CaAl_2Si_2O_8)$)	colorless, white to gray, green	colorless	6	two cleavage planes meet at 90° angle	used in the manufacture of ceramics
Augite ($((Ca,Na)(Mg,Fe,Al)(Al,Si)_2O_6)$)	black	colorless	6	cleavage in two directions	square or 8-sided cross section
Olivine ($((Mg,Fe)_2SiO_4)$)	olive, green	none	6.5–7	conchoidal fracture	gemstones, refractory sand
Quartz (SiO_2)	colorless, various colors	none	7	conchoidal fracture	used in glass manufacture, electronic equipment, radios, computers, watches, gemstones

SCIENCE SKILL HANDBOOK
MATH SKILL HANDBOOK
FOLDABLES HANDBOOK
REFERENCE HANDBOOK
GLOSSARY/GLOSARIO
INDEX

Weather Map Symbols

Sample Station Model

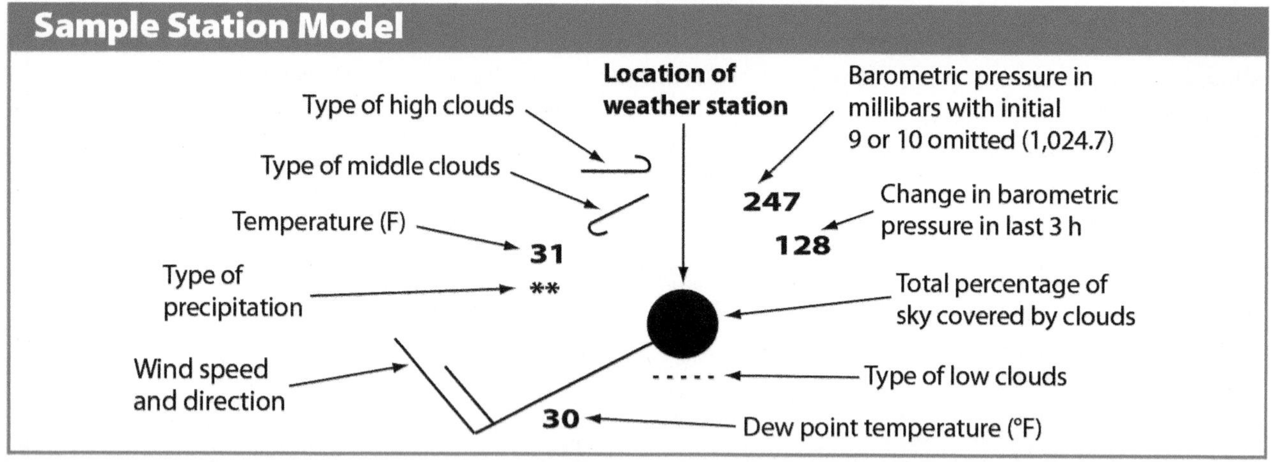

Sample Plotted Report at Each Station

Precipitation	Wind Speed and Direction	Sky Coverage	Some Types of High Clouds
Fog	0 calm	No cover	Scattered cirrus
Snow	1–2 knots	1/10 or less	Dense cirrus in patches
Rain	3–7 knots	2/10 to 3/10	Veil of cirrus covering entire sky
Thunderstorm	8–12 knots	4/10	Cirrus not covering entire sky
Drizzle	13–17 knots	–	
Showers	18–22 knots	6/10	
	23–27 knots	7/10	
	48–52 knots	Overcast with openings	
	1 knot = 1.852 km/h	Completely overcast	

Some Types of Middle Clouds	Some Types of Low Clouds	Fronts and Pressure Systems	
Thin altostratus layer	Cumulus of fair weather	(H) or High (L) or Low	Center of high- or low-pressure system
Thick altostratus layer	Stratocumulus		Cold front
Thin altostratus in patches	Fractocumulus of bad weather		Warm front
Thin altostratus in bands	Stratus of fair weather		Occluded front
			Stationary front

Glossary/Glosario

Multilingual eGlossary

A science multilingual glossary is available on ConnectEd. The glossary includes the following languages:

Arabic	Hmong	Tagalog
Bengali	Korean	Urdu
Chinese	Portuguese	Vietnamese
English	Russian	
Haitian Creole	Spanish	

Cómo usar el glosario en español:

1. Busca el término en inglés que desees encontrar.
2. El término en español, junto con la definición, se encuentran en la columna de la derecha.

Pronunciation Key

Use the following key to help you sound out words in the glossary:

a	**b**ack (BAK)	**ew**	f**oo**d (FEWD)
ay	d**ay** (DAY)	**yoo**	p**ure** (PYOOR)
ah	f**a**ther (FAH thur)	**yew**	f**ew** (FYEW)
ow	fl**ow**er (FLOW ur)	**uh**	comm**a** (CAH muh)
ar	c**ar** (CAR)	**u (+ con)**	r**u**b (RUB)
e	l**e**ss (LES)	**sh**	**sh**elf (SHELF)
ee	l**ea**f (LEEF)	**ch**	na**t**ure (NAY chur)
ih	tr**i**p (TRIHP)	**g**	**g**ift (GIHFT)
i (i + con + e)	**i**dea (i DEE uh)	**j**	**g**em (JEM)
oh	g**o** (GOH)	**ing**	s**ing** (SING)
aw	s**o**ft (SAWFT)	**zh**	vi**s**ion (VIH zhun)
or	**or**bit (OR buht)	**k**	**c**ake (KAYK)
oy	c**oi**n (COYN)	**s**	**s**eed, **c**ent (SEED, SENT)
oo	f**oo**t (FOOT)	**z**	**z**one, rai**s**e (ZOHN, RAYZ)

English — A — Español

abiotic factor/astronomical unit

factor abiótico/unidad astronómica

abiotic factor (ay bi AH tihk • FAK tuhr): a nonliving thing in an ecosystem. (p. 269)

absorption: the transfer of energy from a wave to the medium through which it travels. (p. 94)

acceleration: a measure of the change in velocity during a period of time. (p. 27)

amplitude: the maximum distance a wave varies from its rest position. (p. 85)

asteroid: a small, rocky object that orbits the Sun. (p. 227)

astrobiology: the study of the origin, development, distribution, and future of life on Earth and in the universe. (p. 175)

astronomical unit (AU): the average distance from Earth to the Sun—about 150 million km. (p. 228)

factor abiótico: componente no vivo de un ecosistema. (pág. 269)

absorción: transferencia de energía desde una onda hacia el medio a través del cual viaja. (pág. 94)

aceleración: medida del cambio de velocidad durante un período de tiempo. (pág. 27)

amplitud: distancia máxima que varía una onda desde su posición de reposo. (pág. 85)

asteroide: un objeto de piedra que está en órbita alrededor del sol. (pág. 227)

astrobiología: estudio del origen, desarrollo, distribución y futuro de la vida en la Tierra y en el universo. (pág. 175)

unidad astronómica (UA): distancia media entre la Tierra y el Sol , aproximadamente 150 millones de km. (pág. 228)

atmosphere (AT muh sfir): a thin layer of gases surrounding Earth. (p. 271)

average speed: the total distance traveled divided by the total time taken to travel that distance. (p. 19)

atmósfera: capa delgada de gases que rodean la Tierra. (pág. 271)

rapidez promedio: distancia total recorrida dividida por el tiempo usado para recorrerla. (pág. 19)

biome: a geographic area on Earth that contains ecosystems with similar biotic and abiotic features. (p. 339)

biosphere (BI uh sfihr): the parts of Earth and the surrounding atmosphere where there is life. (p. 303)

biotic factor (bi AH tihk • FAK tuhr): a living or once-living thing in an ecosystem. (p. 269)

biotic potential: the potential growth of a population if it could grow in perfect conditions with no limiting factors. (p. 306)

birthrate: the number of offspring produced by a population over a given time period. (p. 311)

bioma: área geográfica en la Tierra que contiene ecosistemas con características bióticas y abióticas similares. (pág. 339)

biosfera: partes de la Tierra y de la atmósfera que la rodea donde hay vida. (pág. 303)

factor biótico: vida cosa o anteriormente vida cosa en un ecosistema. (pág. 269)

potencial biótico: crecimiento potencial de una población si esta puede crecer en condiciones perfectas sin factores limitantes. (pág. 306)

tasa de nacimientos: número de crías que tiene una población durante un período de tiempo dado. (pág. 311)

C

carrying capacity: the largest number of individuals of one species that an ecosystem can support over time. (p. 307)

chemosynthesis (kee moh sihn THUH sus): the process during which producers use chemical energy in matter rather than light energy to make food. (p. 286)

climate: the long-term average weather conditions that occur in a particular region. (p. 270)

climax community: a stable community that no longer goes through major ecological changes. (p. 359)

comet: a small, rocky and icy object that orbits the Sun. (p. 227)

commensalism: a symbiotic relationship that benefits one species but does not harm or benefit the other. (p. 326)

community: all the populations living in an ecosystem at the same time. (p. 304)

competition: the demand for resources, such as food, water, and shelter, in short supply in a community. (p. 305)

capacidad de carga: número mayor de individuos de una especie que un medioambiente puede mantener. (pág. 307)

quimiosíntesis: proceso durante el cual los productores usan la energía química en la materia en vez de la energía lumínica, para elaborar alimento. (pág. 286)

clima: promedio a largo plazo de las condiciones del tiempo atmosférico de una región en particular. (pág. 270)

comunidad clímax: comunidad estable que ya no sufrirá mayores cambios ecológicos. (pág. 359)

cometa: un objeto de piedra e hielo que está en órbita alrededor del sol. (pág. 227)

comensalismo: relación simbiótica que beneficia a una especie pero no causa daño ni beneficia a la otra. (pág. 326)

comunidad: todas las poblaciones que viven en un ecosistema, al mismo tiempo. (pág. 304)

competición: demanda de recursos, tales como alimento, agua y refugio, cuyo suministro es escaso en una comunidad. (pág. 305)

compression: region of a longitudinal wave where the particles of the medium are closest together. (p. 78)
condensation (kahn den SAY shun): the process during which water vapor changes into liquid water. (p. 276)
constant speed: the rate of change of position in which the same distance is traveled each second. (p. 18)
constants: the factors in an experiment that remain the same. (p. NOS 27)
consumer: an organism that cannot make its own food and gets energy by eating other organisms. (p. 322)
control group: the part of a controlled experiment that contains the same factors as the experimental group, but the independent variable is not changed. (p. NOS 27)
coral reef: an underwater structure made from outside skeletons of tiny, soft-bodied animals called coral. (p. 355)
cornea (KOR nee uh): a convex lens made of transparent tissue located on the outside of the eye. (p. 132)
crest: the highest point on a transverse wave. (p. 77)
critical thinking: comparing what you already know about something to new information and deciding whether or not you agree with the new information. (p. NOS 10)
critical thinking: comparing what you already know with information you are given in order to decide whether you agree with it. (p. NOS 10)

compresión: región de una onda longitudinal donde las partículas del medio están más cerca. (pág. 78)
condensación: proceso durante el cual el vapor de agua cambia en agua líquida. (pág. 276)
velocidad constante: velocidad a la que se cambia de posición, en la cual se recorre la misma distancia por segundo. (pág. 18)
constantes: factores que no cambian en un experimento. (pág. NOS 27)
consumidor: organismo que no puede hacer sus propios alimentos y obtiene energía comiendo otros organismos. (pág. 322)
grupo de control: parte de un experimento controlado que contiene los mismos factores que el grupo experimental, pero la variable independiente no se cambia. (pág. NOS 27)
arrecife de coral: estructura bajo el agua formada por exoesqueletos de animales diminutos y de cuerpo blando. (pág. 355)
córnea: lente convexo hecho de tejido transparente, ubicado en la parte externa del ojo. (pág. 132)
cresta: punto más alto en una onda transversal. (pág. 77)
pensamiento crítico: el comparar de lo que ya se sabe de un asunto con información nueva y el decidir si está de acuerdo con la información nueva. (pág. NOS 10)
pensamiento crítico: comparación que se hace cuando se sabe algo acerca de información nueva, y se decide si se está o no de acuerdo con ella. (pág. NOS 10)

D

death rate: the number of individuals in a population that die over a given time period. (p. 311)
dependent variable: the factor a scientist observes or measures during an experiment. (p. NOS 27)
dependent variable: the factor a scientist observes or measures during an experiment. (p. NOS 27)
description: a spoken or written summary of an observation. (p. NOS 12)

tasa de mortalidad: número de individuos que mueren en una población en un período de tiempo dado. (pág. 311)
variable dependiente: factor que el científico observa o mide durante un experimento. (pág. NOS 27)
variable dependiente: factor que el científico observa o mide durante un experimento. (pág. NOS 27)
descripción: resumen oral o escrito de una observación. (pág. NOS 12)

description: a spoken or written summary of an observation. (p. NOS 18)
descripción: resumen oral o escrito de una observación de. (pág. NOS 18)

desert: a biome that receives very little rain. (p. 340)
desierto: bioma que recibe muy poca lluvia. (pág. 340)

diffraction: the change in direction of a wave when it travels by the edge of an object or through an opening. (p. 96)
difracción: cambio en la dirección de una onda cuando ésta viaja por el borde de un objeto o a través de una abertura. (pág. 96)

displacement: the difference between the initial, or starting, position and the final position of an object that has moved. (p. 13)
desplazamiento: diferencia entre la posición inicial, o salida, y la final de un objeto que se ha movido. (pág. 13)

E

echo: a reflected sound wave. (p. 117)
eco: onda sonora reflejada. (pág. 117)

ecological succession: the process of one ecological community gradually changing into another. (p. 359)
sucesión ecológica: proceso en el que una comunidad ecológica cambia gradualmente en otra. (pág. 359)

ecosystem: all the living things and nonliving things in a given area. (p. 269)
ecosistema: todos los seres vivos y los componentes no vivos de un área dada. (pág. 269)

electric energy: energy carried by an electric current. (p. 49)
energía eléctrica: energía transportada por una corriente eléctrica. (pág. 49)

electromagnetic (ih lek troh mag NEH tik) spectrum: the entire range of electromagnetic waves with different frequencies and wavelengths. (p. 154)
espectro electromagnético: de toda la gama de ondas electromagnéticas con diferentes frecuencias y longitudes de onda. (pág. 154)

electromagnetic wave: a transverse wave that can travel through empty space and through matter. (p. 81)
onda electromagnética: onda transversal que puede viajar a través del espacio vacío y de la materia. (pág. 81)

endangered species: a species whose population is at risk of extinction. (p. 313)
especie en peligro: especie cuya población se encuentra en riesgo de extinción. (pág. 313)

energy pyramid: a model that shows the amount of energy available in each link of a food chain (p. 290)
pirámide energética: modelo que explica la cantidad de energía disponible en cada vínculo de una cadena alimentaria. (pág. 290)

energy: the ability to cause change. (p. 45)
energía: capacidad de ocasionar cambio. (pág. 45)

equinox: when Earth's rotation axis is tilted neither toward nor away from the Sun. (p. 195)
equinoccio: al eje de rotación de la Tierra está inclinado ni hacia fuera ni desde el sol. (pág. 195)

estuary (ES chuh wer ee): a coastal area where freshwater from rivers and streams mixes with salt water from seas or oceans. (p. 353)
estuario: zona costera donde el agua dulce de los ríos y arroyos se mezcla con el agua salada de los mares y los océanos. (pág. 353)

eutrophication (yoo troh fuh KAY shun): the process of a body of water becoming nutrient-rich. (p. 362)
eutrofización: proceso por el cual un cuerpo de agua se vuelve rico en nutrientes. (pág. 362)

evaporation (ih va puh RAY shun): the process of a liquid changing to a gas at the surface of the liquid. (p. 276)
evaporación: proceso de cambio de un líquido a un gas en la superficie del líquido. (pág. 276)

experimental group: the part of the controlled experiment used to study relationships among variables. (p. NOS 27)
grupo experimental: parte del experimento controlado que se usa para estudiar las relaciones entre las variables. (pág. NOS 27)

SCIENCE SKILL HANDBOOK
MATH SKILL HANDBOOK
FOLDABLES HANDBOOK
REFERENCE HANDBOOK
GLOSSARY/GLOSARIO
INDEX

SCIENCE SKILL HANDBOOK
MATH SKILL HANDBOOK
FOLDABLES HANDBOOK
REFERENCE HANDBOOK
GLOSSARY/GLOSARIO
INDEX

explanation: an interpretation of observations. (p. NOS 12)

explicación: interpretación de las observaciones. (pág. NOS 12)

explanation: an interpretation of observations. (p. NOS 18)

explicación: interpretación de las observaciones. (pág. NOS 18)

extinct species: a species that has died out and no individuals are left. (p. 313)

especie extinta: especie que ha dejado de existir y no quedan individuos de ella. (pág. 313)

extraterrestrial (ek struh tuh RES tree ul) life: life that originates outside Earth. (p. 175)

vida extraterrestre: vida que se origina fuera de la Tierra. (pág. 175)

F

food chain: a model that shows how energy flows in an ecosystem through feeding relationships. (p. 288)

cadena alimentaria: modelo que explica cómo la energía fluye en un ecosistema a través de relaciones alimentarias. (pág. 288)

food web: a model of energy transfer that can show how the food chains in a community are interconnected (p. 289)

red alimentaria: modelo de transferencia de energía que explica cómo las cadenas alimentarias están interconectadas en una comunidad. (pág. 289)

frequency: the number of wavelengths that pass by a point each second. (p. 88)

frecuencia: número de longitudes de onda que pasan por un punto cada segundo. (pág. 88)

friction: a contact force that resists the sliding motion of two surfaces that are touching. (p. 55)

fricción: fuerza que resiste el movimiento de dos superficies que están en contacto. (pág. 55)

G

Galilean moons: the four largest of Jupiter's 63 moons discovered by Galileo. (p. 243)

lunas de Galileo: las cuatro lunas más grandes de las 63 lunas de Júpiter, descubiertas por Galileo. (pág. 243)

grassland: a biome where grasses are the dominant plants. (p. 341)

pradera: bioma donde los pastos son las plantas dominantes. (pág. 341)

greenhouse effect: the natural process that occurs when certain gases in the atmosphere absorb and reradiate thermal energy from the Sun. (p. 235)

efecto invernadero: proceso natural que ocurre cuando ciertos gases en la atmósfera absorben y vuelven a irradiar la energía térmica del Sol. (pág. 235)

H

habitat: the place within an ecosystem where an organism lives; provides the biotic and abiotic factors an organism needs to survive and reproduce. (p. 321)

hábitat: lugar en un ecosistema donde vive un organismo; proporciona los factores bióticos y abióticos de un organismo necesita para sobrevivir y reproducirse. (pág. 321)

hypothesis: a possible explanation for an observation that can be tested by scientific investigations. (p. NOS 4)

hipótesis: explicación posible para una observación que puede ponerse a prueba en investigaciones científicas. (pág. NOS 4)

hypothesis: a possible explanation for an observation that can be tested by scientific investigations. (p. NOS 6)

hipótesis: explicación posible de una observación que se puede probar por medio de investigaciones científicas. (pág. NOS 6)

I

impact crater: a round depression formed on the surface of a planet, moon, or other space object by the impact of a meteorite. (p. 252)

independent variable: the factor that is changed by the investigator to observe how it affects a dependent variable. (p. NOS 27)

independent variable: the factor that is changed by the investigator to observe how it affects a dependent variable. (p. NOS 27)

inference: a logical explanation of an observation that is drawn from prior knowledge or experience. (p. NOS 6)

inference: a logical explanation of an observation that is drawn from prior knowledge or experience. (p. NOS 6)

instantaneous speed: an object's speed at a specific instant in time. (p. 18)

interference: occurs when waves overlap and combine to form a new wave. (p. 97)

International System of Units (SI): the internationally accepted system of measurement. (p. NOS 10)

International System of Units (SI): the internationally accepted system of measurement. (p. NOS 18)

intertidal zone: the ocean shore between the lowest low tide and the highest high tide. (p. 355)

iris: the colored part of the eye. (p. 133)

cráter de impacto: depresión redonda formada en la superficie de un planeta, luna u otro objeto espacial debido al impacto de un meteorito. (pág. 252)

variable independiente: factor que el investigador cambia para observar cómo afecta la variable dependiente. (pág. NOS 27)

variable independiente: factor que el investigador cambia para observar cómo afecta la variable dependiente. (pág. NOS 27)

inferencia: explicación lógica de una observación que se obtiene a partir de conocimiento previo o experiencia. (pág. NOS 6)

inferencia: explicación lógica de una observación que se extrae de un conocimiento previo o experiencia. (pág. NOS 6)

velocidad instantánea: velocidad de un objeto en un instante específico en el tiempo. (pág. 18)

interferencia: ocurre cuando las ondas coinciden y combinan para forma una onda nueva. (pág. 97)

Sistema Internacional de Unidades (SI): sistema de medidas aceptado internacionalmente. (pág. NOS 10)

Sistema Internacional de Unidades (SI): sistema de medidas aceptado internacionalmente. (pág. NOS 18)

zona intermareal: playa en medio de la marea baja más baja y la marea alta más alta. (pág. 355)

iris: parte coloreada del ojo. (pág. 133)

K

kinetic (kuh NEH tik) energy: energy due to motion. (p. 46)

energía cinética: energía debida al movimiento. (pág. 46)

L

law of conservation of energy: law that states that energy can be transformed from one form to another, but it cannot be created or destroyed. (p. 54)

law of reflection: law that states that when a wave is reflected from a surface, the angle of reflection is equal to the angle of incidence. (p. 95)

ley de la conservación de la energía: ley que plantea que la energía puede transformarse de una forma a otra, pero no puede crearse ni destruirse. (pág. 54)

ley de la reflexión: ley que establece que cuando una onda se refleja desde una superficie, el ángulo de reflexión es igual al ángulo de incidencia. (pág. 95)

lens: a transparent object with at least one curved side that causes light to change direction. (p. 131)
lens: a transparent object with at least one curved side that causes light to change direction.
light ray: represents a narrow beam of light that travels in a straight line. (p. 123)
light source: something that emits light. (p. 123)
limiting factor: a factor that can limit the growth of a population. (p. 305)
longitudinal (lahn juh TEWD nul) wave: a wave in which the disturbance is parallel to the direction the wave travels. (p. 78)
lunar eclipse: an occurrence during which the Moon moves into Earth's shadow. (p. 210)

lunar: term that refers to anything related to the Moon. (p. 165)

lente: objeto transparente que tiene, al menos, un lado curvo que hace que la luz cambie de dirección. (pág. 131)
lente: un objeto transparente con al menos un lado curvo que hace que la luz para cambiar de dirección.
rayo de luz: haz de luz angosto que viaja en línea recta. (pág. 123)
fuente lumínica: algo que emite luz. (pág. 123)
factor limitante: factor que puede limitar el crecimiento de una población. (pág. 305)
onda longitudinal: onda en la que la perturbación es paralela a la dirección en que viaja la onda. (pág. 78)
eclipse lunar: ocurrencia durante la cual la Luna se mueve hacia la zona de sombra de la Tierra. (pág. 210)
lunar: término que hace referencia a todo lo relacionado con la luna. (pág. 165)

M

maria (MAR ee uh): the large, dark, flat areas on the Moon. (p. 200)
mechanical energy: sum of the potential energy and the kinetic energy in a system. (p. 49)
mechanical wave: a wave that can travel only through matter. (p. 77)
medium: a material in which a wave travels. (p. 77)
meteor: a meteoroid that has entered Earth's atmosphere and produces a streak of light. (p. 252)
meteorite: a meteoroid that strikes a planet or a moon. (p. 252)
meteoroid: a small rocky particle that moves through space. (p. 252)
migration: the instinctive, seasonal movement of a population of organisms from one place to another. (pp. 314)
mirror: any reflecting surface that forms an image by regular reflection. (p. 130)
motion: the process of changing position. (p. 13)
mutualism: a symbiotic relationship in which both organisms benefit. (p. 325)

mares: áreas extensas, oscuras y planas en la Luna. (pág. 200)
energía mecánica: suma de la energía potencial y la energía cinética en un sistema. (pág. 49)
onda mecánica: onda que puede viajar sólo a través de la materia. (pág. 77)
medio: material en el cual viaja una onda. (pág. 77)
meteoro: un meteorito que ha entrado en la atmósfera de la Tierra y produce un rayo de luz. (pág. 252)
meteorito: meteoroide que impacta un planeta o una luna. (pág. 252)
meteoroide: partícula rocosa pequeña que se mueve por el espacio. (pág. 252)
migración: movimiento instintivo de temporada de una población de organismos de un lugar a otro. (pág. 314)
espejo: cualquier superficie reflectora que forma una imagen por reflexión común. (pág. 130)
movimiento: proceso de cambiar de posición. (pág. 13)
mutualismo: relación simbiótica en la cual los dos organismos se benefician. (pág. 325)

N

niche (NICH): the way a species interacts with abiotic and biotic factors to obtain food, find shelter, and fulfill other needs. (p. 321)

nicho: forma de una especie interacciona con los factores abióticos y bióticos para obtener comida, encontrar refugio, y satisfacer otras necesidades. (pág. 321)

nitrogen fixation (NI truh jun • fihk SAY shun): the process that changes atmospheric nitrogen into nitrogen compounds that are usable by living things. (p. 278)

fijación del nitrógeno: proceso que cambia el nitrógeno atmosférico en componentes de nitrógeno útiles para los seres vivos. (pág. 278)

nuclear energy: energy stored in and released from the nucleus of an atom. (p. 49)

energía nuclear: energía almacenada en y liberada por el núcleo de un átomo. (pág. 49)

O

observation: the act of using one or more of your senses to gather information and take note of what occurs. (p. NOS 6)

observación: acción de usar uno o más sentidos para reunir información y tomar notar de lo que ocurre. (pág. NOS 6)

observation: the act of using one or more of your senses to gather information and take note of what occurs. (p. NOS 6)

observación: acción de mirar algo y tomar nota de lo que ocurre. (pág. NOS 6)

opaque: a material through which light does not pass. (p. 124)

opaco: material por el que no pasa la luz. (pág. 124)

orbit: the path an object follows as it moves around another object. (p. 190)

órbita: trayectoria que un objeto sigue a medida que se mueve alrededor de otro objeto. (pág. 190)

P

parasitism: a symbiotic relationship in which one organism benefits and the other is harmed. (p. 326)

parasitismo: relación simbiótica en la cual se perjudica organismo se beneficia y el otro. (pág. 326)

penumbra: the lighter part of a shadow where light is partially blocked. (p. 207)

penumbra: parte más clara de una sombra donde la luz se bloquea parcialmente. (pág. 207)

percent error: the expression of error as a percentage of the accepted value. (p. NOS 15)

error porcentual: expresión del error como porcentaje del valor aceptado. (pág. NOS 15)

period of revolution: the time it takes an object to travel once around the Sun. (p. 228)

período de revolución: tiempo que gasta un objeto en dar una vuelta alrededor del Sol. (pág. 228)

period of rotation: the time it takes an object to complete one rotation. (p. 228)

período de rotación: tiempo que gasta un objeto para completar una rotación. (pág. 228)

phase: the portion of the Moon or a planet reflecting light as seen from Earth. (p. 202)

fase: parte de la Luna o de un planeta que refleja la luz que se ve desde la Tierra. (pág. 202)

photosynthesis (foh toh SIHN thuh sus): a series of chemical reactions that convert light energy, water, and carbon dioxide into the food-energy molecule glucose and give off oxygen. (p. 286)

fotosíntesis: serie de reacciones químicas que convierte la energía lumínica, el agua y el dióxido de carbono en glucosa, una molécula de energía alimentaria, y libera oxígeno. (pág. 286)

pioneer species: the first species that colonizes new or undisturbed land. (p. 360)

especie pionera: primera especie que coloniza tierra nueva o tierra virgen. (pág. 360)

pitch: the perception of how high or low a sound is; related to the frequency of a sound wave. (p. 115)

population density: the size of a population compared to the amount of space available. (p. 306)

population: all the organisms of the same species that live in the same area at the same time. (p. 304)

position: an object's distance and direction from a reference point. (p. 9)

potential (puh TEN chul) energy: stored energy due to the interactions between objects or particles. (p. 46)

precipitation (prih sih puh TAY shun): water, in liquid or solid form, that falls from the atmosphere (p. 276)

prediction: a statement of what will happen next in a sequence of events. (p. NOS 6)

prediction: a statement of what will happen next in a sequence of events. (p. NOS 6)

producer: an organism that uses an outside energy source, such as the Sun, and produces its own food (p. 322)

Project Apollo: a series of space missions designed to send people to the Moon. (p. 166)

pupil: an opening into the interior of the eye at the center of the iris. (p. 133)

tono: percepción de qué tan alto o bajo es el sonido; relacionado con la frecuencia de la onda sonora. (pág. 115)

densidad poblacional: tamaño de una población comparado con la cantidad de espacio disponible. (pág. 306)

población: todos los organismos de la misma especie que viven en la misma área al mismo tiempo. (pág. 304)

posición: distancia y dirección de un objeto según un punto de referencia. (pág. 9)

energía potencia: energía almacenada debido a las interacciones entre objetos o partículas. (pág. 46)

precipitación: agua, en forma líquida o sólida, que cae de la atmósfera. (pág. 276)

predicción: afirmación de lo que ocurrirá después en una secuencia de eventos. (pág. NOS 6)

predicción: afirmación de lo que ocurrirá a continuación en una secuencia de eventos. (pág. NOS 6)

productor: organismo que usa una fuente de energía externa, como el Sol, y fabricar su propio alimento. (pág. 322)

Proyecto Apolo: serie de misiones espaciales diseñadas para enviar personas a la Luna. (pág. 166)

pupila: abertura en el interior del ojo y en el centro del iris. (pág. 133)

Q

qualitative data: the use of words to describe what is observed in an experiment. (p. NOS 27)

quantitative data: the use of numbers to describe what is observed in an experiment. (p. NOS 27)

datos cualitativos: uso de palabras para describir lo que se observa en un experimento. (pág. NOS 27)

datos cuantitativos: uso de números para describir lo que se observa en un experimento. (pág. NOS 27)

R

radiant energy: energy carried by an electromagnetic wave. (p. 49)

radio telescope: a telescope that collects radio waves and some microwaves using an antenna that looks like a TV satellite dish. (p. 157)

rarefaction (rayr uh FAK shun): the region of a longitudinal wave where the particles of the medium are farthest apart. (p. 78)

energía radiante: energía que transporta una onda electromagnética. (pág. 49)

radiotelescopio: telescopio que recoge ondas de radio y algunas microondas por medio de una antena parecida a una antena parabólica de TV. (pág. 157)

rarefacción: región de una onda longitudinal donde las partículas del medio están más alejadas. (pág. 78)

SCIENCE SKILL HANDBOOK
MATH SKILL HANDBOOK
FOLDABLES HANDBOOK
REFERENCE HANDBOOK
GLOSSARY/GLOSARIO
INDEX

reference point: the starting point you use to describe the motion or the position of an object. (p. 9)

reflecting telescope: a telescope that uses a mirror to gather and focus light from distant objects. (p. 156)

reflection: the bouncing of a wave off a surface. (p. 94)

refracting telescope: a telescope that uses lenses to gather and focus light from distant objects. (p. 156)

refraction: the change in direction of a wave as it changes speed in moving from one medium to another. (p. 96)

retina (RET nuh): an area at the back of the eye that includes special light-sensitive cells—rod cells and cone cells. (p. 134)

revolution: the orbit of one object around another object. (p. 190)

rocket: a vehicle propelled by the exhaust made from burning fuel. (p. 163)

rotation axis: the line on which an object rotates. (p. 191)

rotation: the spin of an object around its axis. (p. 191)

punto de referencia: punto que se escoge para describir la ubicación, o posición, de un objeto. (pág. 9)

telescopio reflector: telescopio que usa un espejo para recoger y enfocar la luz de los objetos distantes. (pág. 156)

reflexión: rebote de una onda desde una superficie. (pág. 94)

telescopio refractor: telescopio que usa un lente para recoger y enfocar la luz de los objetos distantes. (pág. 156)

refracción: cambio en la dirección de una onda a medida que cambia de velocidad al moverse de un medio a otro. (pág. 96)

retina: área en la parte posterior del ojo que incluye especiales sensibles a la luz—bastones y conos. (pág. 134)

revolución: movimiento de un objeto alrededor de otro objeto. (pág. 190)

cohete: vehículo propulsado por gases de escape producidos por la ignición de combustible. (pág. 163)

eje de rotación: línea sobre la cual un objeto rota. (pág. 191)

rotación: el giro de un objeto alrededor de su eje. (pág. 191)

S

salinity (say LIH nuh tee): a measure of the mass of dissolved salts in a mass of water. (p. 349)

satellite: any small object that orbits a larger object other than a star. (p. 164)

science: the investigation and exploration of natural events and of the new information that results from those investigations. (p. NOS 4)

science: the investigation and exploration of natural events and of the new information that results from those investigations. (p. NOS 4)

scientific law: a rule that describes a pattern in nature. (p. NOS 9)

scientific law: a rule that describes a pattern in nature. (p. NOS 9)

scientific notation: a method of writing or displaying very small or very large values in a short form. (p. NOS 15)

salinidad: medida de la masa de sales disueltas en una masa de agua. (pág. 349)

satélite: cualquier objeto pequeño que orbita un objeto más grande diferente de una estrella. (pág. 164)

ciencia: la investigación y exploración de los eventos naturales y de la información nueva que es el resultado de estas investigaciones. (pág. NOS 4)

ciencia: investigación y exploración de eventos naturales y la información nueva que resulta de dichas investigaciones. (pág. NOS 4)

ley científica: regla que describe un patrón en la naturaleza. (pág. NOS 9)

ley científica: regla que describe un patrón dado en la naturaleza. (pág. NOS 9)

notación científica: método para escribir o expresar números muy pequeños o muy grandes en una forma corta. (pág. NOS 15)

scientific theory: an explanation of observations or events that is based on knowledge gained from many observations and investigations. (p. NOS 9)

teoría científica: explicación de las observaciones y los eventos basada en conocimiento obtenido en muchas observaciones e investigaciones. (pág. NOS 9)

scientific theory: an explanation of observations or events that is based on knowledge gained from many observations and investigations. (p. NOS 9)

teoría científica: explicación de observaciones o eventos con base en conocimiento obtenido de muchas observaciones e investigaciones. (pág. NOS 9)

significant digits: the number of digits in a measurement that that are known with a certain degree of reliability. (p. NOS 20)

cifras significativas: número de dígitos que se conoce con cierto grado de fiabilidad en una medida. (pág. NOS 20)

solar eclipse: an occurrence during which the Moon's shadow appears on Earth's surface. (p. 208)

eclipse solar: acontecimiento durante el cual la sombra de la Luna aparece sobre la superficie de la Tierra. (pág. 208)

solstice: when Earth's rotation axis is tilted directly toward or away from the Sun. (p. 195)

solsticio: al eje de rotación de la Tierra se inclina directamente hacia o desde el sol. (pág. 195)

sound energy: energy carried by sound waves. (p. 49)

energía sonora: energía que transportan las ondas sonoras. (pág. 49)

sound wave: a longitudinal wave that can travel only through matter. (p. 111)

onda sonora: onda longitudinal que sólo viaja a través de la materia. (pág. 111)

space probe: an uncrewed spacecraft sent from Earth to explore objects in space. (p. 165)

sonda espacial: nave espacial sin tripulación enviada desde la Tierra para explorar objetos en el espacio. (pág. 165)

space shuttles: reusable spacecraft that transport people and materials to and from space. (p. 166)

transbordador espacial: nave espacial reutilizable que transporta personas y materiales hacia y desde el espacio. (pág. 166)

speed: the distance an object moves divided by the time it takes to move that distance. (p. 17)

rapidez: distancia que un objeto recorre dividida por el tiempo que éste tarda en recorrer dicha distancia. (pág. 17)

symbiosis (sihm bee OH sus): a close, long-term relationship between two species that usually involves an exchange of food or energy. (p. 325)

simbiosis: relación intrínseca a largo plazo entre dos especies que generalmente involucra intercambio de alimento o energía. (pág. 325)

T

taiga (TI guh): a forest biome consisting mostly of cone-bearing evergreen trees. (p. 345)

taiga: bioma de bosque constituido en su mayoría por coníferas perennes. (pág. 345)

technology: the practical use of scientific knowledge, especially for industrial or commercial use. (p. NOS 9)

tecnología: uso práctico del conocimiento científico, especialmente para empleo industrial o comercial. (pág. NOS 9)

technology: the practical use of scientific knowledge, especially for industrial or commercial use. (p. NOS 8)

tecnología: uso práctico del conocimiento científico, especialmente para uso industrial o comercial. (pág. NOS 8)

temperate: the term describing any region of Earth between the tropics and the polar circles. (p. 343)

temperatura: término que describe cualquier región de la Tierra entre los trópicos y los círculos polares. (pág. 343)

terrestrial planets: Mercury, Venus, Earth, and Mars—the planets closest to the Sun that are made of rock and metallic minerals and have solid outer layers. (p. 233)

planetas terrestres: Mercurio, Venus, Tierra, y Marte—los planetas que están más cercanos al Sol y que están compuestos por roca, materiales metálicos y tienen capas externas sólidas. (pág. 233)

thermal energy: the sum of the kinetic energy and the potential energy of the particles that make up an object. (p. 49)

energía térmica: suma de la energía cinética y potencial de las partículas que componen un objeto. (pág. 49)

threatened species: a species at risk, but not yet endangered. (p. 313)

especie amenazada: especie en riesgo, pero que todavía no está en peligro. (pág. 313)

tide: the periodic rise and fall of the ocean's surface caused by the gravitational force between Earth and the Moon, and between Earth and the Sun. (p. 211)

marea: ascenso y descenso periódico de la superficie del océano causados por la fuerza gravitacional entre la Tierra y la Luna, y entre la Tierra y el Sol. (pág. 211)

translucent: a material that allows most of the light that strikes it to pass through, but through which objects appear blurry. (p. 124)

translúcido: material que permite el paso de la mayor cantidad de luz que lo toca, pero a través del cual los objetos se ven borrosos. (pág. 124)

transmission: the passage of light through an object. (p. 94)

transmisión: paso de la luz a través de un objeto. (pág. 94)

transparent: a material that allows almost all of the light striking it to pass through, and through which objects can be seen clearly. (p. 124)

transparente: material que permite el paso de la mayor cantidad de luz que lo toca, y a través del cual los objetos pueden verse con nitidez. (pág. 124)

transverse wave: a wave in which the disturbance is perpendicular to the direction the wave travels. (p. 77)

onda transversal: onda en la que la perturbación es perpendicular a la dirección en que viaja la onda. (pág. 77)

trough: the lowest point on a transverse wave. (p. 77)

seno: punto más bajo en una onda transversal. (pág. 77)

tundra (TUN druh): a biome that is cold, dry, and treeless. (p. 345)

tundra: bioma frío, seco y sin árboles. (pág. 345)

U

umbra: the central, darker part of a shadow where light is totally blocked. (p. 207)

umbra: parte central más oscura de una sombra donde la luz está completamente bloqueada. (pág. 207)

V

variable: any factor that can have more than one value. (p. NOS 27)

variable: cualquier factor que tenga más de un valor. (pág. NOS 27)

variable: any factor that can have more than one value. (p. NOS 27)

variable: cualquier factor que tenga más de un valor. (pág. NOS 27)

velocity: the speed and the direction of a moving object. (p. 23)

velocidad: rapidez y dirección de un objeto en movimiento. (pág. 23)

waning phases: phases of the Moon during which less of the Moon's near side is lit each night. (p. 202)

wave: a disturbance that transfers energy from one place to another without transferring matter. (p. 75)

wavelength: the distance between one point on a wave and the nearest point just like it. (p. 87)

waxing phases: phases of the Moon during which more of the Moon's near side is lit each night. (p. 202)

wetland: an aquatic ecosystem that has a thin layer of water covering soil that is wet most of the time. (p. 352)

work: the amount of energy used as a force that moves an object over a distance. (p. 48)

fases menguantes: fases de la Luna durante las cuales el lado cercano de la Luna está menos iluminado cada noche. (pág. 202)

onda: perturbación que transfiere energía de un lugar a otro sin transferir materia. (pág. 75)

longitud de onda: distancia entre un punto de una onda y el punto más cercano similar al primero. (pág. 87)

fases crecientes: fases de la Luna durante las cuales el lado cercano de la Luna está más iluminado cada noche. (pág. 202)

Humedal: ecosistema acuático que tiene una capa delgada de suelo cubierto de agua que permanece húmedo la mayor parte del tiempo. (pág. 352)

trabajo: cantidad de energía usada como fuerza que mueve un objeto a cierta distancia. (pág. 48)

Index

Italic numbers = illustration/photo **Bold numbers = vocabulary term**
lab = indicates entry is used in a lab on this page

A

B